W9-CTB-222

Social Studies for Children in a Democracy

Sixth Edition

Social Studies for Children in a Democracy

Recent Trends & Developments

JOHN U. MICHAELIS

University of California, Berkeley

Prentice-Hall, Inc., Englewood Cliffs, New Jersey

Library of Congress Cataloging in Publication Data

MICHAELIS, JOHN UDELL, date
Social studies for children in a democracy.

Includes bibliographies and index.
1. Social sciences—Study and teaching (Elementary)
I. Title.
LB1584.M43 1976 372.8'3'044 75-42067
ISBN 0-13-818872-6

Printed in the United States of America

10 9 8 7 6 5 4 3 2 1

PRENTICE-HALL INTERNATIONAL, INC., *London*
PRENTICE-HALL OF AUSTRALIA PTY. LIMITED, *Sydney*
PRENTICE-HALL OF CANADA, LTD., *Toronto*
PRENTICE-HALL OF INDIA PRIVATE LIMITED, *New Delhi*
PRENTICE-HALL OF JAPAN, INC., *Tokyo*
PRENTICE-HALL OF SOUTHEAST ASIA (PTE.), *Singapore*

To

Elizabeth Ann Michaelis

John Barry Michaelis

Susan Ann Michaelis

Contents

Preface

A persistent problem in the improvement of instruction is the integration of new developments with the best of the ideas gleaned from past experience. This problem has been critical in recent years because of the many new project materials, developments in environmental, ethnic, and other studies, and the continuing flood of new instructional media. Along with these have come new developments related to values and valuing, intercultural education, law-related instruction, equality for women, career education, concept development, thinking and inquiry processes, competency-based instruction, evaluation, and accountability. Teachers have been faced with an enormous selection task in creating viable programs of instruction.

This new edition has been revised primarily to aid teachers in this task. Special efforts have been made to identify guidelines and teaching strategies that are most useful in improving social studies instruction. New programs, instructional media, and the developments noted above have been screened to identify elements most useful to teachers. These elements have been brought together with a critical selection of ideas of proven value in a synthesis that can be used to improve instruction.

Each chapter is organized to facilitate study. Focusing questions give an overview of the chapter and serve as study guides. Guidelines, teaching strategies, examples of applications, charts, checklists, and photographs are included to provide practical approaches to instruction.

Questions and activities at the end of chapters facilitate discussion, evaluation, extension, and application of ideas in the text. Instructors and students in competency-based programs will find the focusing questions and activities at the end of chapters to be helpful in pre- and postassessment as well as in developing basic competencies.

The following clusters of competencies may be developed as the various chapters are used:

Describing and defining goals, objectives, trends, guidelines for improving learning, principles and patterns of organization, characteristics of exemplary programs, models of units of instruction (Chapters 1–3)

Identifying, describing, and applying developmental growth characteristics, ways to meet individual differences, concepts, concept clusters and generalizations from the social sciences, thinking and inquiry processes, values and valuing processes (Chapters 4–7)

Locating, selecting, and using instructional media and developing skills involved in using reading materials, maps and globes, and other resources (Chapters 11–14)

Planning and conducting ongoing evaluation of cognitive and affective outcomes of instruction (Chapter 15)

Special acknowledgment is made to the following individuals who contributed ideas, charts, and photographs, or suggested changes: Ruth H. Grossman, Val Arnsdorf, Haig Rushdoonny, Lewis C. Vinson, Pat Harvey, John Green, Robert Griffin, Emma Wiley, David Fish, Fred Wilson, Donald Bye, Mrs. Benjamin F. Benson, Thomas A. Sinks, Leonard F. Dalton, Sandra Crosby, Fred Harris, Gerald Hunter, Gerald Olson, Eileen McNab, Douglas Superka, Douglas MacDonald, David Wright, and Herb Wong. Special acknowledgment is also made to the many instructors of social studies courses and their students for practical suggestions that have been incorporated in this edition.

JOHN U. MICHAELIS

1

Focusing Questions

How is the social studies program defined?
What are its foundations?
What contributions should social studies make to basic educational goals?
What are the goals and objectives of social studies?
How should instructional objectives be stated?
What are the dominant major trends?
What guidelines to the improvement of learning can be used throughout the program?

The Social Studies Program: An Overview

Now more than ever, the social studies program has a vital place in the curriculum of American schools, for surely the events of the past few years have sharpened the need to evaluate and improve the operation of the democratic process in all our institutions. As the country enters its third century, the challenges and responsibilities facing those involved in social studies instruction have never been greater.

This book has been written to bring together the most promising and useful trends and developments in the teaching of social studies. Chapter 1 sets the stage by providing a definition of social studies, indicating the foundations on which the program is based, identifying goals and objectives, suggesting guidelines for composing instructional objectives, reviewing recent trends, and proposing guidelines for the improvement of social learning.

A DEFINITION

The social studies program includes those aspects of human relationships and social values, conditions, and changes believed to be of greatest importance for the general education of students. Human interaction is explored in depth in the study of relationships among people, between people and institutions, between people and the earth, and between people and value systems. Social, economic, and political aspects of our changing cultural background are investigated in a variety of settings—the school, the family, and the community, the state, the region, and the nation. Other cultures, ancient and modern, are also studied. The purposes of individuals and groups are considered along with the processes used to achieve them, the problems that have emerged and the various solutions devised, the material and nonmaterial products of cultures, and prospects for the future. The entire program is grounded in the social, psychological, disciplinary, and philosophical foundations of curriculum planning. Chart 1–1 shows in graphic form some of the major interrelationships.

There are also cognitive and affective elements directly related to the personal and social dimensions of human interaction and to social learning. The cognitive or intellectual elements are the concepts, main ideas, thinking processes, and skills that are developed and used in the exploration of human relationships. The affective or emotional elements are the values, attitudes, feelings, and interests that are key ingredients in learning about human affairs. Cognitive and affective elements are intertwined with the personal and social dimensions of students' involvement in the social studies program. The personal dimension includes the conceptions, values, and learning styles that students bring to each unit of study and enrich and extend as they progress through the program. The social dimension includes interaction among students, participation in community and other activities, and the discovery of processes of interaction during units of study.

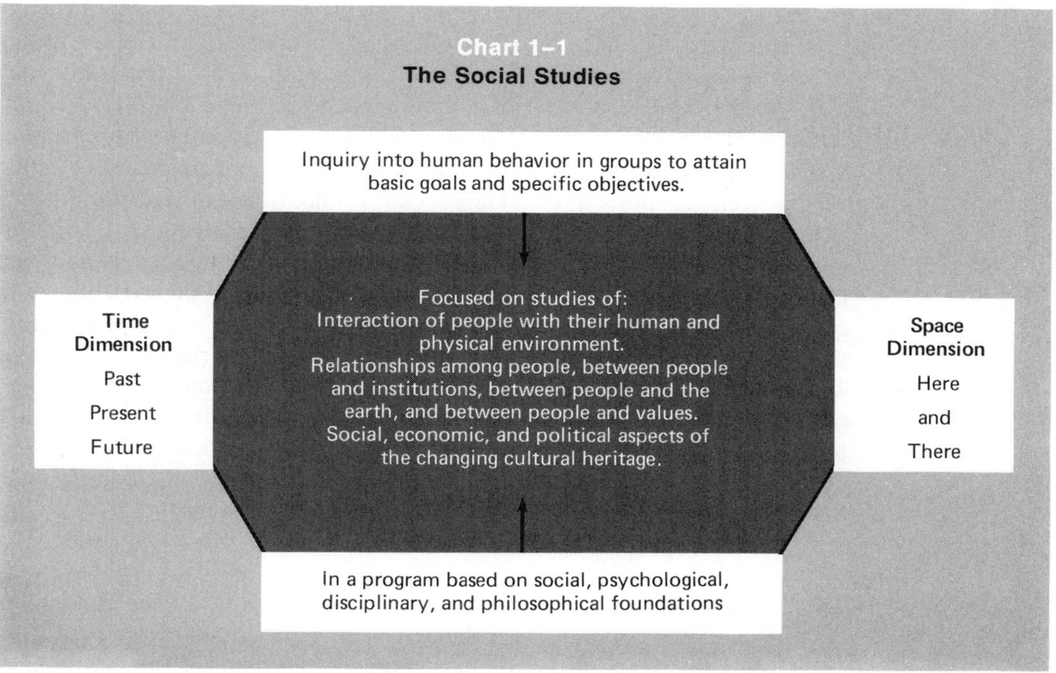
Chart 1–1
The Social Studies
Inquiry into human behavior in groups to attain basic goals and specific objectives.
Time Dimension
Past
Present
Future
Focused on studies of:
Interaction of people with their human and physical environment.
Relationships among people, between people and institutions, between people and the earth, and between people and values.
Social, economic, and political aspects of the changing cultural heritage.
Space Dimension
Here
and
There
In a program based on social, psychological, disciplinary, and philosophical foundations

Educators in some school systems refer to social studies as social science education, as history and the social sciences, as history, geography, and the social sciences, or as citizenship education. At the present time, however, the term *social studies* is commonly used throughout the country by people in general and by school personnel. History, geography, and the social sciences are given attention along with material drawn from the humanities and from the experiences of students. Citizenship education is a key component of social studies. In a curricular sense, social studies serves as an encompassing title similar to the language arts, science education, and humanities education. Each denotes a broad area of the curriculum that has specific objectives yet contributes to the attainment of the fundamental goals of education.

Social studies should not be confused with the following terms, which are much broader in meaning: Social competence—one's ability to engage in group enterprises, both in and out of school; social learning—all the experiences that help one to become oriented in society; or social education—all school activities designed to promote social learning and to improve social competence. Social competence may be developed in or out of school, in the social studies program, and in other areas of the curriculum. Social learning takes place in situations in which students interact with others—at home, at school, in the community. Social education takes place in the family, in the school, and in other institutions. Children's social concepts, skills, and values grow and develop as a result of many experiences, including those provided in social studies programs.

But social studies go far beyond students' own experiences. Aspects of social living and social learning at home and in the community may make contributions to learning in the social studies, but they do not replace instruction. Social studies make up a developmental program of instruction grounded in curriculum development and designed to attain certain central objectives. The social foundations of curriculum development provide societal values, beliefs, trends, changes, traditions, and demands—including legal requirements—that must be considered in program planning. The psychological foundations provide views of child development and learning and of cognitive and affective development, and their implications for instructional and curriculum planning. The disciplinary foundations provide conceptual and process components drawn from the social sciences and such humanities as art, music, and literature. The philosophical foundations provide the values, goals, objectives, approach, and views of the individual, society, and knowledge held by those involved in the program.

GOALS AND OBJECTIVES

The goals and objectives of all areas of the curriculum should be related to the basic goals of education, as shown in Chart 1–2. When this is done, we can identify the unique con-

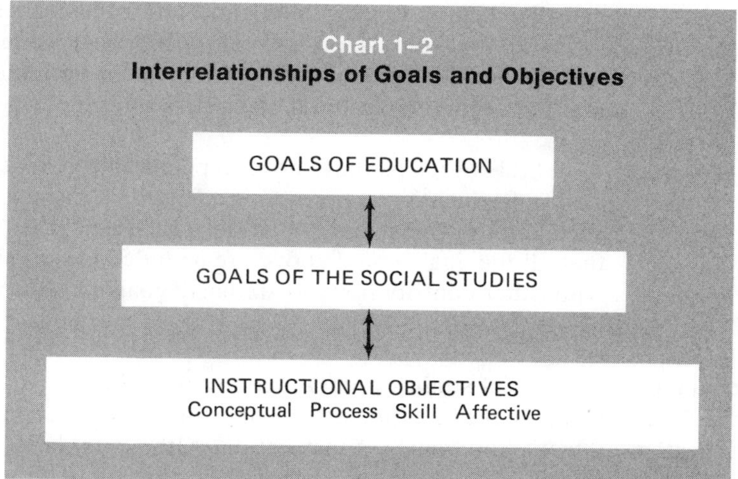

tributions of each area of the curriculum and maintain a sense of direction.[1] Let us first consider the goals of the social studies program and then note its contributions to the goals of education.

Goals of the Social Studies Program

Goals are indicative of general directions and desired outcomes of the social studies program for grades K to 12. They serve as broad guides to planning, development, and evaluation of curriculum and instruction. Recent goal statements include attention to conceptual, process, skill, and affective outcomes, as shown in the following summary.[2]

> To enable students to function effectively as citizens in accord with such values as respect for each individual, equality, justice, and the general welfare
>
> To develop understanding of human interactions and relationships based on data, concepts, and generalizations drawn from the social sciences
>
> To develop thinking, decision-making, inquiring, and valuing processes
>
> To develop and practice individual and group work-study skills appropriate to social studies
>
> To develop the attitudes and skills involved in learning how to learn

[1]John U. Michaelis, Ruth H. Grossman, and Lloyd F. Scott, *New Designs for Elementary Curriculum and Instruction* (New York: McGraw-Hill, 1975), Chapter IV.
[2]For example, see *Social Sciences Education Framework for California Public Schools* (Sacramento, Calif.: State Department of Education, 1974).

To help students understand and reflect on society's values and to develop and clarify personal values

To enable students to participate in activities in society as individuals and as members of groups

Goals such as these need to be put into perspective with the overall goals of education. One way to do this is to indicate the contributions social studies may make to widely accepted goals of education. Notice that all the goals noted above are included in the following section, along with other contributions to six basic goals of education.

Contributions to the Goals of Education

The social studies program contributes directly to the goals of education through the attainment of some of the conceptual, process, skill, and affective outcomes of instruction. Although there is no real agreement on the ultimate goals of education, at the present time the emphasis is on developing thinking and decision-making ability, self-realization, human relationships, civic responsibility, economic competence, and learning how to learn.

Thinking and decision-making ability. The social studies program contributes to the development of two skills essential in a democratic society—thinking and decision making—through learning experiences that involve problem solving, critical and creative thinking, and development of interpretive, analytical, and evaluative abilities. Students construct and test hypotheses, analyze issues and problems, and synthesize ideas in creative ways. Decision-making processes are developed as students clarify values, analyze and evaluate proposals, consider alternatives, and weigh the consequences of different courses of action. Thinking and decision making are enriched and extended as concepts and values are applied to concrete events and situations of immediate concern to them and to individuals and groups in their community. Open-mindedness, objectivity, respect for the views of others, and related attitudes are also part of critical thinking and decision making.

Self-realization. The social studies program contributes to self-realization through experiences that foster growth of each individual's potentialities, self-concept, and personal set of values. The special needs of gifted, average, and less able students may be met by varied approaches to topics, issues, and problems. Reading, listening, group work, and other skills are put to use and refined, making it possible for children to become increasingly self-directive as they move through the program. Creativeness, self-esteem, and competence are developed in independent and in group work. Concepts and intergroup understandings related to school, family, and community activities are developed, helping each child to increase his personal effectiveness in living and working with others.

How might this experience contribute to the goal of improving human relationships? What specific concepts and values are involved? (Berkeley, California)

Human relationships. Of basic importance is the development of concepts essential to effective human relationships, such as interdependence, cooperation, and an awareness of the effects of different cultural backgrounds on ways of valuing, believing, and acting. International, intercultural, and ethnic understandings and appreciations are developed by considering the needs, problems, and points of view of others. Interpersonal skills are developed as children participate in activities, engage in role playing, play simulation games, and analyze intergroup problems and conflicts. Ethnic studies reveal the need for change in human relationships and the ways in which interaction has limited or enhanced equality of opportunity. The study of different ways of living and of the contributions of individuals and groups of various backgrounds fosters tolerance and respect for others.

Civic responsibility. Always given central attention in the social studies program, civic responsibility has assumed new importance in recent years. The acceptance and discharge of responsibilities by students themselves at home, in school, and in the community are prime considerations, as well as concepts related to the functions of government, the legal rights of individuals and groups, the accountability and integrity of public officials, and the responsibilities individuals and groups must assume to ensure the proper functioning of the social system. School and community service projects provide opportunities to participate in civic activities. Understanding of American values, problems, and ways of living may be developed in studies of the community, the state, and the nation. The values, needs, and problems of others are considered in units on various cultures as a part of global education. As issues and problems are investigated, students sharpen decision making, critical thinking, reading, and other skills.

Economic competence. The social studies program contributes to this goal by providing information and experiences that develop concepts, skills, and attitudes related to people's use of limited resources to meet their needs and wants. Illustrative concepts are specialization to increase production; operation of supply and demand in the market; use of land, labor, and capital to produce goods and services; contributions of different workers; and wise use of resources. Skills and attitudes essential to good workmanship are highlighted as children learn about the work of others and carry out their own responsibilities. Decision making, career awareness, consumer or personal economics, and a recognition of the opportunities American society affords are also emphasized.

Learning how to learn. Related to all the broad goals noted above and emphasized in new materials is learning how to learn. Effective thinking is characterized by the ability to learn on one's own, to find new solutions to problems, and to employ processes of inquiry independently. Self-realization, human relationships, economic efficiency, and civic responsibility call for competence in exploring and handling problems and issues independently and in cooperation with others. The accelerating explosion of knowledge characteristic of our time has given new importance to the idea of lifelong learning as both a personal and a social responsibility. Learning how to learn is therefore receiving high priority in instruction programs. Models and processes of inquiry, skills for independent study, techniques for using a variety of instructional media, and self-evaluation as a means of continuing self-improvement are among the current emphases related to this basic goal. Social studies, along with other areas of curriculum, contribute directly to making the idea of lifelong learning a reality.

Objectives in New Programs

Four interrelated sets of objectives are used in instructional planning, and both cognitive and affective elements are a part of the objectives in each category. Conceptual objectives make use of concepts, themes, and generalizations. Process objectives encompass methods and processes of thinking, inquiring, and decision making along with such attitudes as open-mindedness and objectivity. Skill objectives include reading, listening, working in groups, and using instructional media. Affective objectives include the attitudes, values, interests, and valuing processes to be developed in the program of instruction.

Conceptual objectives. To develop an understanding of data, concepts, themes, and generalizations, including the ability to identify, describe, or demonstrate, students learn role, interaction, and other concepts used as tools of inquiry; the use of resources to meet basic needs for food, shelter, and clothing; the contributions of individuals and groups to the changing cultural heritage; the influences of cultural and environmental factors on human behavior; environmental and energy problems and changes needed to improve the quality of life; the functions of the family, education, government, and other institutions; decision-making processes and the influence of individuals and groups; and democratic value concepts like individual worth, the general welfare, and civil liberties.

Process objectives. To develop competence in using methods and processes of thinking, inquiring, and decision making, students learn to make plans for and carry out problem solving and critical and creative thinking; collect and process data by reading, interviewing, and other methods; and use such inquiry processes as recalling and observing, interpreting, defining, comparing, classifying and generalizing, analyzing and synthesizing, inferring, hypothesizing and predicting, and evaluating. They also learn to derive generalizations in the analytic mode, study one setting in depth in the integrative mode, and appraise alternatives in the decision-making mode. They are taught to distinguish facts from opinions, what is from what ought to be, warranted from unwarranted conclusions, narrow from broad generalizations, and to consider multiple causes of events and evidence that is contrary to personal or popularly held views.

Skill objectives. To develop competence in using basic skills in social studies, students learn to use a variety of data sources including primary and secondary materials, textbooks, library materials, current periodicals, community resources, and audiovisual materials; locate, gather, appraise, summarize, and report information; and read material critically, listen critically, and study independently. They are taught to interpret and make maps, graphs, tables, time lines, and to use other graphic materials; to organize material from several sources and present it in pictorial, oral, written, and graphic form; and to work in groups, participating in decision making, carrying out plans, adhering to group standards, and evaluating individual and group efforts.

Affective objectives. Students learn to identify, describe, and demonstrate in individual behavior and group activities the attitudes, values, and feelings of individuals who are open-minded, responsible, cooperative, and creative, and who show concern for others; who have self-respect and show respect for others regardless of their race, creed, sex, status, national origin, and culture; who are sensitive to the influences of moral, ethical, and spiritual values; who demand honesty and integrity in government, due process of law, and lawful procedures for making changes; who value the contributions of ethnic groups to our cultural heritage; and who recognize the importance of participation in civic activities and world affairs.

Stating Instructional Objectives

Broad objectives and goals are translated into instructional objectives by stating them in performance or behavioral terms. Performance objectives are helpful in planning, individualizing, and evaluating instruction and are widely used in accountability programs. They should indicate a sampling or a product of behavior, such as a map, that will be evidence of students' having attained the objective, as well as conditions, performance level, and object of study, as shown in the following examples:

Conceptual objective: Students will state [behavior] at least two [performance level] features of the four zones in a city [object] as presented in the text [conditions].

Process objective: Given data on the first cities as presented in the text [conditions], students will state [behavior] at least one [performance level] hypothesis about the origin of cities [object].

Skill objective: Using a pencil, crayons, and an outline map [conditions], each student will make [behavior] a map showing four [performance level] zones in our city [object].

Affective objective: Students will describe [behavior] the two [performance level] values underlying the plan for urban renewal [object] presented by the resource visitor [conditions].

In some school systems teachers present detailed performance objectives for accountability systems in which the following elements are included: behavior, object of study, who should attain the objective, performance level, conditions, and time of attainment. Here is an example:

> By April 30 [time], 80 percent of the students [who] will state [behavior] from memory [conditions] at least four [performance level] civil liberties guaranteed by the Constitution [object].

Both open and closed objectives are used in the social studies program. Open objectives are used when varied responses from students are desired; for example, students will state at least two reasons why they believe that concern for others should be shown to all groups in the community. Closed objectives are used when similar responses from students are desired; for example, using the legend as a guide, students will point to the symbols for towns and cities.

Notice that action terms are used in these examples to focus teacher observation on a sampling of behavior related to the object of study. These verbs are often used to indicate observable behavior: tell, state, describe, list, make, point, demonstrate, whereas verbs such as make, construct, and prepare indicate a product of behavior. A fairly complete list of action verbs follows:

Recognize, identify, indicate, locate, match, select, find
Describe, tell, explain, express, suggest, present
Write, list, name, label, define, state, summarize
Arrange, group, classify, put in order, collect

Apply, use, complete, answer questions, follow directions
Distinguish, differentiate, break into parts (analyze), point out
Demonstrate, show, act out, pretend, role play, pantomime
Make, construct, prepare, design, draw, produce, combine

Verbs that do not indicate observable behavior or a product include understand, know, appreciate, believe, develop insight into, enjoy, and the like. The following examples illustrate the difficulties generated by using such terms and show how they may be changed to provide greater clarity.

To *know* the zones of a city. [How will the student demonstrate a knowledge of the zones? The objective will be clearer if *describe, locate on a map,* or *list* is substituted for *know*.]

To *understand* that cities provide basic services. [How should the student reveal understanding? It would be better to use *describe, recognize*, or another action verb in place of *understand*.]

To *appreciate* the reasons why people live in cities. [It would be more meaningful to use *identify, describe*, or *list three or four interesting features of city life* so that the student's expression of affective dimensions of learning could be observed.]

Goals containing statements of covert behavior may be translated into instructional objectives that indicate observable or overt behavior, as shown in these examples:

To demonstrate understanding of the many contributions of black Americans to our way of life, students will prepare a report that includes at least five contributions since 1950, list three contributions in science as shown in the film, or write at least one contribution for each of ten black Americans presented on a list.

To demonstrate appreciation of the importance of values and attitudes in people's behavior, students will state how a personal activity in school was guided by respect for others, describe at least two events that show the importance of open-mindedness, describe at least two events in which disregard for equality of opportunity resulted in discrimination.

A similar procedure may be used to write objectives for inquiry processes such as inferring, generalizing, and synthesizing, as shown in the following examples:

After seeing the film "Trails Westward," students will infer [covert behavior] traits of behavior needed by scouts by stating [overt behavior] two or more traits and giving reasons for each trait.

Students will develop the ability to generalize [covert behavior] by stating [overt behavior] in their own words how price is related to supply and demand.

Students will develop the ability to synthesize [covert behavior] by making [overt behavior] a map that shows the main travel routes westward.

Taxonomies of Cognitive and Affective Objectives

Several sources of behavioral objectives are available for reference.[3] The examples that follow are based on categories in the taxonomies of objectives by Bloom and Krathwohl; they are used as guides to the writing of objectives. The cognitive objectives are arranged by level of complexity and include conceptual, skill, and process objectives. The affective objectives are arranged by degree of internatization and include values, attitudes, and interests. The categories in each domain are presented below with a sample objective in abbreviated form for each category.

COGNITIVE DOMAIN

Knowledge: Of terms, facts, trends, concepts, generalizations (*To describe goods and services produced at home*)

Comprehension: Translation of material into another form; interpretation by relating parts, making qualifications, recognizing essential elements (*To distinguish facts from opinions*)

Application: Of concepts, generalizations, criteria, models (*To use concepts of fair play and equal rights in discussion*)

Analysis: Of elements, relationships, principles of organization (*To identify instances in which equal rights were and were not accorded to minority groups*)

[3]See references by Bloom, Krathwohl, Flanagan, SCORE, and the Instructional Objectives Exchange at the end of the chapter.

Synthesis: Of ideas in an original communication, a plan, a generalization, a hypothesis (*To make a mural that shows the recycling of materials*)

Evaluation: Making judgments in terms of internal evidence and external criteria (*To state a judgment based on defined criteria*)

AFFECTIVE DOMAIN

Receiving: Awareness, willingness to receive, attention (*To recognize incidents involving fair play*)

Responding: Compliance, willingness to respond, satisfaction in responding (*To discuss fair play and state ways of extending it*)

Valuing: Acceptance, preference, commitment (*To describe and defend freedom of speech*)

Organization: Conceptualization of a value, organization of a value system (*To defend assumptions underlying freedom of speech*)

Characterization: Generalized set, internalized value system (attained by mature adults) (*To make judgments on the basis of principles inherent in a consistent philosophy of life*)

All the categories in the cognitive domain are relevant to social studies instruction in the elementary school. Knowledge, comprehension, and application are prerequisites to analysis, synthesis, and evaluation. If students do not understand and cannot apply key learnings, they cannot attain the more complex levels of analysis, synthesis, and evaluation. On the other hand, instruction should move from mere knowledge and comprehension to higher levels of cognition. Beginning in the early grades children should have opportunities to bring ideas together in a chart or plan (synthesis), to evaluate how well they are working, and to engage in other activities related to the more complex objectives. Analysis, synthesis, and evaluation are not reserved for secondary school and college.

The first three categories in the affective domain are most relevant to social studies instruction. The teacher must develop children's awareness of values and attitudes as they are expressed in social studies materials as well as in daily activities. The responding and valuing levels call for a variety of experiences in cross-cultural studies as well as depth studies of people and events in communities, states, and regions of the United States. Such values and attitudes as respect for the views of others, freedom of speech, fair play, and equal rights for all take on dimensions of meaning and feeling in unit after unit, year after year, and both in and out of school. A prime function of social studies instruction is to ground such values in events and situations that make sense to students and enable them to develop deeper dimensions of meaning and feeling as they progress through school. The two top levels of the affective domain are lifelong tasks that few adults fully master.

MAJOR TRENDS IN SOCIAL STUDIES

A concise summary of dominant trends is given in this section as background for new developments presented in later chapters. Such a perspective is helpful in relating various elements of the social studies program and in interpreting recent changes, for those concerned with improving social studies make the greatest progress when they are alert to the directions in which thinking and practice are moving.

Openness Within a Planned Curriculum

One basic trend is to provide openness to meet the changing needs of students and society within a planned program of instruction and to avoid a rigidly organized curriculum that does not permit the incorporation of new units, materials, and strategies attuned to individual and social concerns. A program must be designed to include core units, materials, and strategies essential to the attainment of key objectives. By providing for openness within a planned curriculum, it is possible to incorporate current affairs, ethnic studies, new materials on environmental studies, and other developments directly related to social changes and the needs of students. The best features of the open classroom and open education are incorporated in a planned curriculum by teachers who guide learning toward instructional objectives.

Values and Valuing Processes

Increased attention to values and valuing processes is bringing a better balance between the cognitive and affective dimensions of instruction. New programs include attention to the values, attitudes, and valuing processes needed to handle value-laden issues. Strategies for clarifying values and feelings in events under study and in situations vital to students have been developed (see Chapter 7), and attention is now being given to the development of an understanding and appreciation of religion in the lives of people in our country and in other lands.[4] The impact of religious values on life styles, the use of values in decision making, and the influence of social, economic, and political values on human behavior are brought to higher levels of understanding as students progress through the program. The historical, cultural, and social con-

[4] *Moral and Civic Education and Teaching About Religion* (Sacramento, Calif.: State Department of Education, 1973).

What contributions did these Americans make? What other contributions have black Americans made to United States' history? (Richmond, California)

ditions that have contributed to the diversity of religious and other values are included in units for middle and high schools.

Major Societal Changes Special efforts are being made to keep the curriculum up to date by providing instruction on current trends and changes. Particular attention is being given to a certain group of long-term changes, which are a useful frame of reference for unit planning, putting current affairs in perspective, and making predictions about the future. One such change is the worldwide spread of movements for freedom and equality. In the United States, individuals and groups are now working to extend freedom and equality to minority groups and to women. All over the world, new nations are struggling to achieve economic and political freedom. This trend has been accompanied by a push to widen the decision-making process to include more than an individual or a small power group. The demand for involvement and participation by individuals and groups is increasing and has manifested itself in, for example, the community programs that have come to be part of the urban pattern of life. Freedom, equality, and participation movements coexist with a trend toward increasing interdependence within and among nations that will become even greater as steps are taken to solve problems such as hunger, poverty, and the use of energy on a global scale. And the dream of world peace has in this century led to the formation of international organizations and agencies designed to develop cooperative approaches to dealing with international problems.

From education of the elite to education of the masses to the current emphasis on improving the quality of education and on lifelong learning, increasing attention is being given to the development of each individual's capacities in a variety of formal and open approaches to teaching and learning. This trend has been aided and accelerated by a knowledge explosion that has opened new horizons in all aspects of living and shows no sign of abating. The technological change that began with the Industrial Revolution continues to provide us with new and ever more complex tools for producing the food, clothing, and shelter needed to sustain life in new and imaginative forms. Transportation has become faster and faster, and the electronic inventions that permit instant sharing of ideas around the world may provide a variety of new educational techniques in the future.

But along with these advances have come problems. Concern about the rights of consumers, the quality of products and services, the waste of energy and resources, and rising costs have accentuated the need for consumer protection. Population growth and shifts have created food shortages, and urban, environmental, and other problems that are currently under intensive study and will require concerted action in the years to come. The shift from rural to urban centers and the development of urban sprawl and the megalopolis have created needs for housing and services that will tax the efforts of both governmental and private agencies for the foreseeable future. Industrialization and a rising standard of living for more and more people have accelerated the use of resources and energy, polluted the environment, and made immediate action and future planning mandatory.

As efforts are made to consider the long-range impact of various new developments, we have turned from an emphasis on the past and the problems of the present to a consideration of the future. Attempts to resolve and manage conflict are changing our institutions—the family, the church, the school, the government—even as we interact with them.

How has transportation changed? What will it be like in the future? (Social Studies Workshop, University of California, Berkeley)

Perhaps this latter change is the greatest challenge in education: how to keep up with change and yet maintain a coherent program within an institution that is itself part of a larger society in flux.

Conceptual Structure

As in other areas of the curriculum, the trend in social studies is to clarify the conceptual structure of the instructional program. Key concepts and generalizations from the social sciences are used to structure content within units and to plan sequences of instruction. For example, the following concept clusters and related generalizations may be used as organizers in various units and brought to higher levels of development as students put them to use in a variety of settings.

Resources (water, soil, plants, animals, minerals):
Families use resources to meet needs for food, shelter, and clothing.
Communities use resources to produce goods.
States plan for both use and conservation of resources.
Nations differ in the kind and quality of resources available for production.
Wise use and conservation of resources are worldwide problems.

Culture Change (invention, discovery, diffusion, adaptation):
Families today have many things that were not available in earlier times.
Many ideas and things in our community have been borrowed from others.
Ideas developed in one area are spread to others.
Nations adapt inventions and discoveries made by others.
Changes occur in countries as people invent, borrow, and adapt ideas.

Conceptual development such as this results from guided learning experiences in which students observe, interpret, classify, and generalize. Careful attention must be given to vocabulary and concept development, the grouping of data around key concepts, and the wording of generalizations. The specific teaching strategies for guiding conceptual learning presented in later chapters should be used with a clear understanding of the meaning and role of words, facts, concepts, concept clusters, themes, and generalizations.

Words are arbitrary associations—the names given to objects, events, qualities, or processes, such as *lake*, *election*, *red*, or *transportation*. Such terms are taught through meaningful association and practice so that children can use them accurately and quickly. The most helpful sources of information on vocabulary development are the lists in units of instruction, courses of study, manuals for instructional materials, and textbooks. Such lists include the actual terms children will use as they study various topics.

Facts are specific items of information about an object, activity, or condition. Facts are the data or information used to develop concepts and generalizations; they should not be confused with general statements. For example, "Los Angeles has serious traffic problems" and "Tokyo has serious traffic problems" are facts about specific situations, whereas the statement "Large cities have serious traffic problems" is a generalization.

Concepts are abstractions that apply to a class or group of objects or activities that have certain qualities in common. Thus *lake* as a concept refers to a general class of objects and not to a particular object. In social studies students learn the names of various items, discriminate similarities and differences among them, and abstract common elements within a given class or group of items. This process of discriminating and abstracting common elements leads to concept attainment and to the use of such terms as *lake*, *election*, and *transportation* to refer to a general class or group of items rather than to a particular item.

Concept clusters are sets of related concepts subsumed under a major concept. They are widely used in basic disciplines and throughout social studies. For example, geographers inevitably cluster the concepts *plains*, *hills*, *plateaus*, and *mountains* around the key concept *major landforms*. Other examples of key concepts and related clusters are these: *factors of production*—land, labor, capital, management; *cultural change*—invention, discovery, diffusion, adaptation; and *processes of social interaction*—cooperation, competition, conflict, assimilation, accommodation. Students discover and use clusters as specific concepts are developed and brought together. The teacher's task is to guide students so that they group related concepts into clusters and use them to locate and organize data, pose questions, and formulate generalizations.

Generalizations are statements of broad applicability that indicate the relationships between concepts. Generalizations are stated as main ideas, major understandings, principles, laws, rules, and conclusions. Students develop and extend generalizations as they engage in problem-solving experiences, discover the relationships between concepts, and express those relationships in general statements. As new problems or situations are met and similar relationships between concepts are discovered, students develop a greater understanding of generalizations and can state them with greater precision and clarity.

Themes are two or more concepts in a phrase that highlights a topic, issue, problem, or trend. Such themes as growth of the community, the westward movement, contributions of ethnic groups, equality for women, honesty in government, justice under law, and conservation of energy are emphasized in individual units of instruction. Broader themes such as local environment studies, families around the world, American people and regions, and major culture regions are used to designate the focus of instruction in various grades.

Thinking and Inquiry Processes

Using guidelines drawn from the psychological foundations, of education, the social studies program emphasizes the development of thinking ability. Effective thinking is basic to effective learning in school—and throughout life. Defining problems and breaking them down into manageable parts; finding, analyzing, and appraising information; and making, testing, and revising conclusions are skills that enable one to improve and accelerate learning. Students learn concepts and generalizations more effectively when they react thoughtfully to what they learn, discover key ideas, distinguish fact from opinion, relate information to basic questions, consider differing points of view, note similarities and differences, evaluate ideas, and check conclusions.

The current emphasis on inquiry is based on the assumption that thinking is improved and maximum learning takes place when students are actively involved in learning. Students should be investigators who use textbooks, films, maps, and other media as sources of data to answer questions, test hypotheses, check conclusions, and extend or limit generalizations. Their search should be guided by questions and hypotheses they understand, some of which they have formulated themselves. Some new programs go beyond general inquiry approaches to develop specific inquiry processes. First-level processes for the intake and initial processing of data are recalling, observing, classifying, defining, comparing/contrasting, and interpreting. Higher-level processes are generalizing, inferring, hypothesizing, predicting, analyzing, synthesizing, and evaluating. These processes are of vital importance in problem solving and in individual and group inquiry. When combined with key concepts, they can be used to lift thinking to high levels in all units of instruction. Examples of how this can be done are presented in the following section and in greater detail in Chapters 3 and 6 and in the Appendix, which includes a unit on environmental problems.

Inquiry-Conceptual Programs

Some programs using what is called a conceptual approach, are organized around concepts and main ideas; others, via what is called an inquiry approach, are organized to emphasize modes and processes of inquiry; still others, via what is called a topical approach, are traditionally organized around themes and topics. A promising new development is to link all three together in an inquiry-conceptual approach to the study of significant settings or topics. Chart 1–3 indicates how inquiry, conceptual, and topical approaches can be combined to investigate various settings.

Processes are the cognitive or thinking operations used to study a topic; concepts are the tools of inquiry that improve observing, interpreting, analyzing, and the application of processes. The settings or topics of study provide the context in which concepts and processes are put to use as problem solving procedures. The most common technique in an inquiry-conceptual program is to combine concepts and processes in questions designed to guide study. The following examples show the

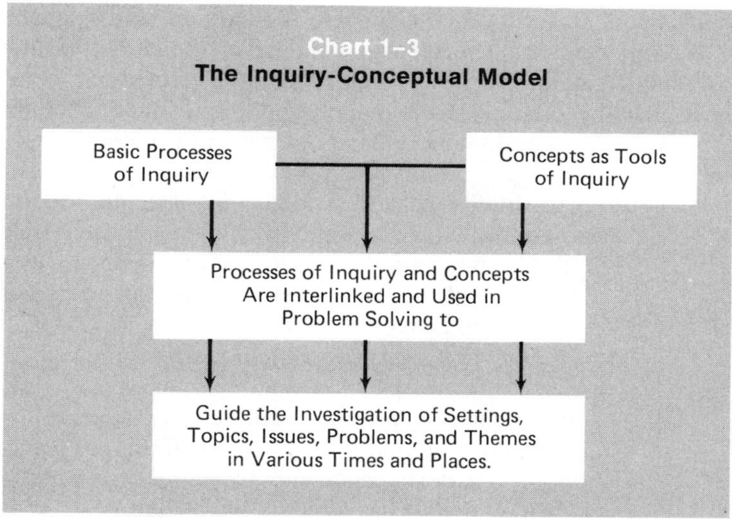

concepts in italics and the inquiry process in brackets after each question (see other examples in Chapter 3 and in the Appendix).

UNIT ON THE BAKERY

What do these pictures show? [observing] What are the people *producing*? [interpreting]
How many different *bakery products* can you find? [observing]
How might we group the different *products*? [classifying] Which ones do we use the most? [analyzing] Which ones are most healthful? [evaluating]

UNIT ON CANADA

What is a *province*? [defining] How it is like a *state*? [comparing]
How many *provinces* can you find on this map? [observing] Which ones are *Atlantic provinces*? [interpreting] Why are they called Atlantic provinces? [inferring] How might the other provinces be grouped? [classifying]
What are *territories*? [defining] How are they different from *provinces*? [contrasting] How much *land area* do they occupy? [interpreting]
What do you think we will find to be the major *production activities* in the *Atlantic provinces*? In other groups of *provinces*? [hypothesizing]

Citizenship, Decision Making, Legal Rights and Responsibilities

Education for citizenship is provided with special emphasis on participation and involvement, and on the legal and political knowledge needed to cope with current problems. For example, students at all levels may become involved in action programs and field studies related to neighborhood and community improvement projects, environmental problems, or school-community relations, as noted in Chapter 13. Legal rights and responsibilities are considered in case studies that deal with rules and regulations, constitutional provisions of free speech, free press, other civil liberties, and legal issues of significance to students. Decision making processes are developed and put to use as students assess proposals for improving the neighborhood, renewing urban centers, curbing pollution, improving opportunities for minority groups and for women, and tackle other problems that call for weighing alternatives, considering consequences, clarifying standards of appraisal, and setting priorities. Clarification of values and valuing processes are receiving greater attention so that decision making activities will include attention to affective as well as cognitive elements (see Charts 1–4 and 1–5).

Key concepts such as rights, responsibilities, rules, laws, civil rights, justice, freedom, privacy, property, and diversity are developed, along with main ideas such as "each individual has civic rights and responsibilities"; "laws include rules and regulations that guide behavior believed to be essential to the well-being of society"; "due process under law is needed to ensure justice for everyone"; "freedom of speech, press, and thought provide the information needed for effective decision making and action on issues and problems."

Consumer and Career Education

Consumer education is included in social studies units at various levels and tied to such economic concepts as market, supply, demand, price, value, money, banking, and credit. Key objectives are to enable students to clarify values, to make decisions based on values, to assess alternatives, to carry out rights and responsibilities as consumers, and to

Chart 1–4
Decision Making

What is the issue or problem?
What values are most important in this situation?
What alternative decisions might be made?
What are the possible consequences of each decision?
Which decision is best in terms of consequences and values?

Chart 1–5
Case Studies

Determine the facts (evidence) in the case.
State the legal issue that must be resolved.
Organize the facts for and against (pro and con).
Make a decision after weighing the pros and cons.
State reasons for the decision—how justice will be served.

play an active role in our economic system. Learning activities range from operating a classroom store, discussing ways to spend one's allowance, saving for special needs, and comparing prices in different stores to evaluating advertisements, analyzing impulse buying in supermarkets, doing comparative shopping studies, figuring the cost of credit buying, using data from *Consumer Reports* to make comparisons, and playing simulation games focused on consumer decision making.

The emphasis in career education is on the development of career awareness. Direct attention is given to the roles of workers in the community in the early grades and to workers in a variety of occupations far removed from the local scene in later grades. One current effort is to portray women and members of various ethnic groups in a variety of careers to avoid the stereotyping that has been characteristic of instructional materials in the past. Classroom instruction is enriched by the use of resource visitors and study trips that extend awareness of career opportunities and responsibilities.

Ethnic Studies, Equality for Women

A variety of units and materials have been developed to provide instruction on ethnic and minority groups—black history, black studies, Chicano studies, Afro-American studies, Asian American studies, native American studies. Units and materials on United States history have been revised to include the activities of these groups, and efforts are being made to combat racism and prejudice, root out stereotypes, and correct erroneous ideas in existing materials. Educators from minority groups have prepared materials designed to develop a wholesome self-concept, a sense of pride, and a feeling of group identity on the part of minority students, and to develop insight into the contributions, culture, and struggle for equality and justice of various ethnic and minority groups on the part of all students. The trend is toward the inclusion of ethnic studies as an integral part of the social studies curriculum.

Similar steps have been taken to improve the treatment of women in units and instructional materials. Special attention has been given to the elimination of stereotypes related to the roles of women, to clarification of inequalities in social, economic, and political opportunities, and to the use of language that is not demeaning and chauvinistic. A primary goal has been to make such values as freedom, equality, and justice equally applicable to all individuals regardless of sex.

Intercultural and International Education

There has also been a surge of interest in improving studies that cut across groups, cultures, and nations. A useful two-level model has been proposed by Bohannon in a report on intercultural and international education.[5] One level includes the microcultures (subcultures) that

[5] Paul Bohannon, *A Rationale for Intercultural Education, A Preliminary Review of the Intercultural Dimension in Intercultural/International Education* (Boulder, Colo.: Social Science Education Consortium, 1973).

abound in society—yours, mine, those of ethnic and minority groups. The second level is the macroculture or larger culture within which microcultures exist—ours and those of other democracies, the varieties of communism, the varieties of socialism. Microcultures provide intimacy and security, whereas the macroculture takes care of large-scale social, economic, and political affairs and is the locus of power in a society. Problems and conflicts arise when microcultures such as ethnic or minority groups are denied participation in the macroculture, when there is fear of selected microcultures, and when there is a lack of communication between them. Difficulties also arise when melting pot approaches are used to obliterate cultural differences, when the strengths of pluralism are overlooked, when the values and customs of minority groups are denigrated, and when the changes needed to accord equality and justice to all groups are not made.

A promising practice for developing intercultural and international understanding is to explore *why* one group's way of living differs from another's. By asking *why* as well as *what* and *how* questions, teachers can guide students to discover underlying reasons for behavior in cultures that differ from their own. And direct contributions may be made to the development of these main ideas: (1) Values of individuals and groups are basic forces in human behavior. (2) Differences between individuals and groups need to be understood in terms of the values and customs on which they are based. (3) All people learn beliefs, values, and customs from the family and other institutions in their culture. (4) There is a growing interdependence of peoples throughout the world.

Attitude change is a key factor in improving intercultural and intergroup relations. A variety of strategies such as role playing, participation in activities with others, and value clarification may be used, as shown in Chapter 7. Of critical importance is evaluation by the students themselves in which they reflect on biases, prejudices, and stereotypes and discover fallacies and the damage to oneself and to others that results from negative attitudes. Provision for culture studies and for participation in community and other activities should be accompanied by opportunities for value clarification in which self-evaluation by students is given high priority.

Various strategies are used to develop intercultural and international understanding. One of the most effective is to provide units of instruction that enable children to study selected cultures in depth; that is, to consider historical, geographic, economic, political, anthropological, and sociological information along with problems, needs, changes, arts, crafts, music, and literature. Special efforts should be made to view ways of living with an open mind and to consider local beliefs and customs from the point of view of the people under study. Changes may be viewed in terms of the concept cluster *cultural change* (invention, discovery, diffusion, adaptation) as children discover the creative ideas of the people themselves and the ideas they have borrowed from others and adapted to their needs. Other useful strategies include exchange of letters or other materials through pen-pal activities, participation in civic activities of various groups, attending festivals, viewing and discussing selected television programs, studying current affairs, studying the United Nations and its agencies, learning about other cultures through foreign language instruction, planning assemblies and school programs, seeing exhibits, engaging in arts and crafts activities, learning songs and rhythms, and providing direct contacts with individuals or groups.

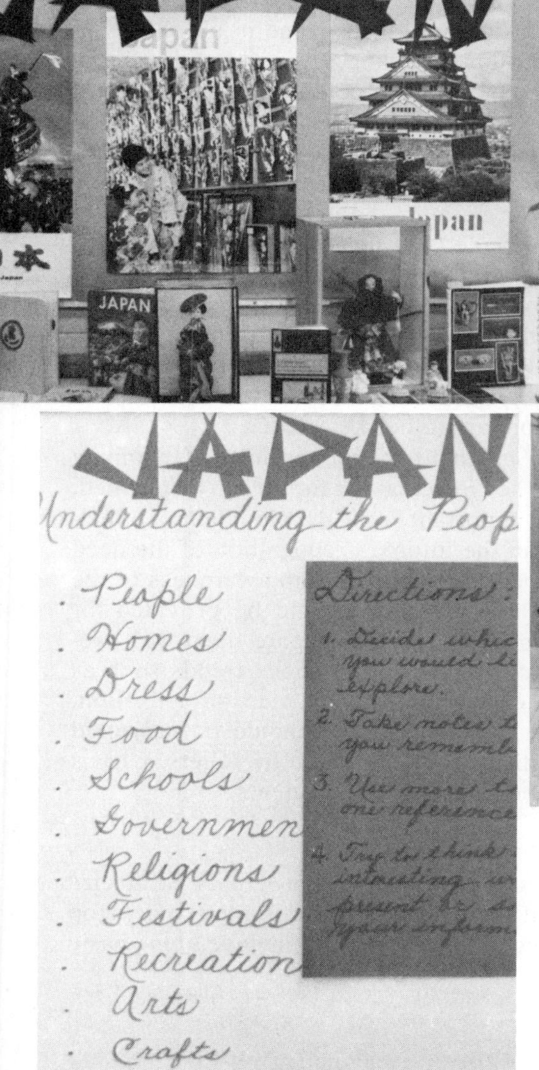

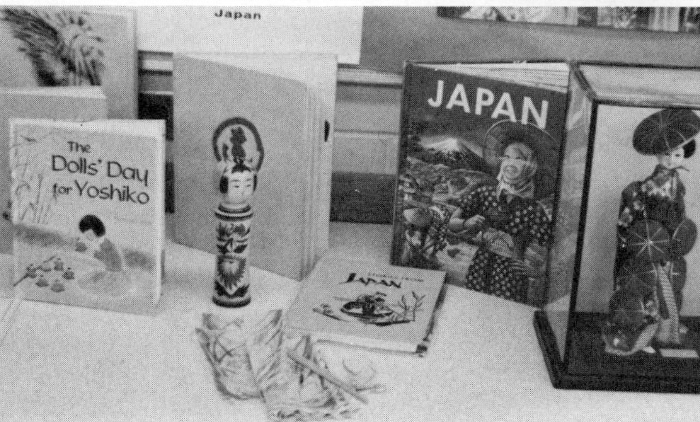

What intercultural understandings can be developed by studying ways of life in other lands? (Tucson, Arizona)

Action projects that involve children in Junior Red Cross, CARE, and UNICEF activities may be used to take learning beyond the verbal level. The abundance of free or inexpensive materials available from the sources listed at the end of Chapter 11 may be used to supplement classroom materials. All these are most helpful when related to or made a part of basic units of instruction in which children have opportunities to develop cultural understanding in depth.

Education for the Future

We know that the world of the future will be marked by even more impermanence and a faster tempo of change in attitudes, values, and human relationships as well as in technology, economic and political affairs, and social institutions. Because of accelerating change in all phases of life, we need to inquire into the reasons for change, to develop the ability to cope with and to direct change, and to develop an orientation toward and an acceptance of change so that "future shock" can be controlled and guided into productive channels.[6]

A consideration of the future may be provided as part of basic units of instruction in social studies. For example, homes, schools, and communities of the future should be included in primary units along with the study of those in the present and past. Units on the state, region, and country should include future developments in transportation, industry, conservation, and other basic social functions with appropriate comparisons to the present and the past. And studies of other lands and regions around the world should include projections and predictions related to population, conservation, education, and other key topics.

Special attention should be given to the importance of planning now for a desirable future—to the key idea that the future can be planned, that it need not just happen. Also important is the development of a feeling for the importance of people in the future, a recognition of the need for continuing concern about the environment, and an awareness of the limitations of predictions. Many opportunities should be provided for students to make predictions themselves and to compare them with predictions made by others. In this connection basic social trends such as technological change, extension of freedom and justice, urbanization, interdependence, and changes in the environment should be projected into the future and compared with predictions made by others. Charts 1–6 to 1–11 illustrate activities and questions for students.

Teaching Strategies

A variety of teaching strategies may be found in new programs. Strategies for guiding cognitive development range from those designed to develop concepts and generalizations to those that are helpful in developing basic

[6] Alvin Toffler, ed., *Learning for Tomorrow: The Role for the Future in Education* (New York: Random House, 1974).

Chart 1–6
Your Own Future

What about your future?
Health, height, weight?
Appearance, personality?
Work, recreation?
Family, Group membership?
Likes, dislikes?
Concerns?
Other items?

Chart 1–7
Ways to Influence Change

Know what we and others value
Consider causes and effects
Consider alternative proposals
Consider consequences of actions
Join with others to take action
Make plans for the future now
Can you add other ways?

Chart 1–8
Considering Alternatives

What if:
Cities get larger and larger?
Domed cities are built?
No more gasoline is available?
Pollution problems are solved?
Mass transit replaces cars?
Each individual is respected?

Chart 1–9
The Year 2000

What will be most important?

education	recreation
conservation	health
the environment	wealth
jobs for everyone	leisure
family life	housing
community life	justice

Chart 1–10
Projecting Basic Trends

What is the future for these?
Freedom and equality for all
Changes in the family and other institutions
Scientific developments and new inventions
Careers for women and men

Chart 1–11
The 21st Century

What do you predict?
Population of our community? state? nation?
Population of the world?
Types of energy to use?
Modes of transportation?
Modes of communication?

skills and inquiry processes. Strategies related to affective objectives include techniques for clarifying values, developing attitudes, handling interpersonal conflicts, and dealing with value-laden issues.

Both discovery-learning and directed-learning strategies are used in the social studies program. Problems arise when inquiry approaches are interpreted to mean that the student must discover everything. What is needed is sufficient discovery learning to enable students to obtain a feeling for the excitement and lure of discovery, insight into productive ways of solving problems, and meaningful verbal learning in which direct instruction is provided to develop concepts, build related vocabulary, and develop skills that produce a wider range of discoveries and open new horizons. To be limited to one's own discoveries would generally narrow the range of learning and future discovery. The teacher's role therefore runs a gamut from co-inquirer to director of instruction, depending upon student needs and capabilities. A balance must be struck between independent and group inquiry (in which students apply and extend key learnings) and directed instruction (in which key ideas, attitudes, skills, and other needs are the focus of teaching). Related teaching strategies are presented in the chapters that follow.

Instructional Technology

New developments in instructional technology range across nearly all phases of instruction. Open space schools provide easy access to media centers stocked with instructional materials and to a variety of teaching and learning centers useful for individual, small-group, and large-group activities. Multimedia materials kits, televised instruction, collections of documents and other materials for ethnic and environmental studies, and a host of materials to supplement instruction are available. Computer-assisted and computer-managed instruction, materials on various levels of difficulty, self-instructional materials, and programed materials have been developed to individualize instruction. Other developments include more use of transparencies and single-concept film loops, shortstrips for young children, games and simulations, tryouts of dial-access retrieval systems to facilitate utilization of materials, microteaching and team teaching, and growth of instructional materials centers.

New instructional materials developed in social studies projects illustrate several trends and developments.[7] For example, Our Working World and Economic Man emphasize economic reasoning and include such concepts as goods, services, producer, consumer, and specialization. Casebooks from the Committee on Civic Education and the Law in American Society Foundation include concepts and case study methods from law. The People: Culture, Time, Place program combines such concepts as role, resources, and environment with processes such as classifying, synthesizing, and evaluating and applies them in settings and cultures around the world, using the inquiry-conceptual model described earlier. A completely packaged multimedia approach is exemplified in Man: A Course of Study program, which is focused on three questions: What is human about human beings? How did they get that way? How can they be made more so? The World Studies Inquiry program provides for interpreting, analyzing, and evaluating stories,

[7]For detailed review, see the *Social Studies Curriculum Materials Data Book* and the Henrie book in the References at the end of this chapter.

cases, and vignettes presented in booklets on Asia, Africa, Latin America, and Europe, drawing concepts from the social sciences and the humanities. Multimedia kits such as Family of Man and MATCH include realia, photographs, and other materials selected or designed to give reality and authenticity to learning.

Many of the new developments in instructional technology have been aimed at dealing with individual differences. Special materials have been prepared for disadvantaged students, minority students, and less able students. Strategies and techniques for meeting individual differences are now included in teaching guides and units of instruction, and the creation of instructional materials centers in many school systems has given teachers the materials they need to individualize instruction. There is a detailed presentation of the most useful strategies and techniques in Chapter 4.

Team teaching is used in some schools. A team made up of teachers with special preparation in the social sciences, science and arithmetic, language arts, and fine arts may be assigned to work with eighty to a hundred children. Under the direction of the team leader, both large- and small-group activities are planned, and teachers take responsibility for instruction in their special areas of competence. Relationships among areas of the curriculum, grouping of children for instruction, ways to meet special needs of individuals, and other phases of the program are planned and carried out by the team. The point is to try to achieve greater depth of learning in each subject and to avoid the pitfalls of extreme departmentalization.

Evaluation

Four distinct trends in evaluation are evident. First, diagnostic, formative, and summative evaluation of reading-study skills, map-reading skills, inquiry processes, and critical thinking and problem-solving abilities are getting more attention. Formal devices such as tests and informal devices such as checklists and rating scales are being used to evaluate skills in social studies. Second, ways of appraising grasp of concepts, relationships, and generalizations are receiving high priority, and teacher-made tests and appraisals of students' understanding as revealed in discussion and other means of expression are being used along with criterion- and norm-referenced tests. Third, the social studies program as an area of the curriculum is being evaluated in terms of carefully formulated statements on the characteristics of an effective social studies program. Fourth, evaluation is a major component of the accountability systems that have mushroomed in schools throughout the country in recent years. These and related developments in evaluation are discussed in Chapter 15.

GUIDELINES TO THE IMPROVEMENT OF LEARNING

From studies of learning and teaching have come guidelines that are helpful in improving learning in social studies. One current trend is for teachers to use a brief statement of selected principles in planning units and in improving classroom instruction at all levels. In this way, the principles become guidelines that provide consistent approaches to learning and teaching from level to level. Each of the following principles is elaborated briefly to illustrate specific implications for social studies.

Clarification of objectives promotes learning. Teachers must understand the central objectives of social studies so that their contributions to the overall goals of education are clear. The next step is to state performance objectives for units of instruction and daily plans. As instruction progresses in the classroom, the teacher should set clear objectives for reading various selections, seeing films, making things, taking study trips, and utilizing other resources. Time is wasted and little or no learning results when children do things without knowing *why*, without having specific goals to guide them. Specific objectives can be made clear to students through group planning, discussion, and evaluation, and by direct comments, questions, and suggestions from the teacher.

A clearly planned program of instruction improves learning. Definition of objectives, assignment of topics by grades, gradation of concepts and skills, and provision of related instructional materials are overall aspects of planning in social studies. Each teacher must plan daily lessons and units of instruction in terms of students' capabilities and prior social studies experiences. If planning is done within the overall framework of social studies during the year and from year to year, learning can be continuous, gaps in learning can be avoided, and the objectives of the social studies program can be kept in focus.

Direct attention to inquiry processes promotes learning. Out of new developments in social studies projects and new instructional materials have come strategies that can be used to develop processes that are at the core of thinking and learning. The belief that students will develop basic cognitive or inquiry processes on their own is being abandoned in favor of a program of guided instruction. The desired outcome is the development of processes that are useful in the social studies and in lifelong learning.

Attention to learning styles of children promotes learning. Many learning styles may be found in a given classroom: there are reflective and systematic students who need time to organize ideas and impulsive risk takers who plunge ahead in discussion and other activities; anxious students who are uncomfortable with ambiguity and those who ponder conflicting data and try to make sense out of them; conforming students who accept authoritative beliefs and those who question them; problem solvers who consider the whole problem and those who focus on details or parts; and analyzers who break topics and problems into parts and those who describe them more generally. Effective teachers recognize a variety of learning styles and help students to develop and use the thinking and valuing processes that they can handle with increasing skill.

Attention to affective as well as cognitive elements improves learning. How students feel about a topic, the attitudes they have toward groups under study, and other affective dimensions of learning need attention in each unit of instruction. The strategies for dealing with feelings and values presented in Chapter 7 should be used to promote wholesome affective development.

The meeting of individual differences promotes learning. A variety of strategies and techniques should be used to provide for the needs of average, able, less able, disadvantaged, handicapped—indeed, all children. To do less is to limit learning. Because of the vital importance of individualizing instruction, most of Chapter 4 is devoted to reviewing the latest developments.

Critical use of varied activities and materials promotes learning. Key ideas are remembered longer, appreciations are deeper, and interest in social studies is higher when varied avenues to learning are used. If activities and materials are selected in terms of instructional objectives and individual student capabilities, interest, effort, and reflective learning are bound to be stimulated. Significant information related to clearly defined problems can be secured from reading materials, audiovisual resources, and community resources. Many different skills can be put to use as ideas are gathered, organized, summarized, and expressed through language activities, creative activities, and the making of maps, charts, booklets, and other items.

Active teacher guidance promotes learning. The clarification of objectives, use of problem-solving techniques, provision of varied activities and materials, and meeting of individual differences call for more, not less, teacher guidance. Excessive permissiveness leads to confusion and misunderstanding. In order to guide learning toward stated objectives, the teacher must introduce materials as they are needed, raise questions and point out difficulties as they arise, direct discussion, formulate work standards, provide directions for new activities, and guide planning and evaluation.

Systematic evaluation of student progress promotes learning. Teachers should gather data through observation, discussion, appraisal of students' work, testing, and review of previous records. Each individual's progress should be studied, with special attention paid to clues for use in planning and directing learning. Student self-evaluation should be encouraged in order to stimulate individual learning and self-understanding.

Helping the student to develop a wholesome self-concept promotes learning. A student's self-concept is especially important in social studies because it conditions attitudes toward others, perception of others, and participation in group activities. Through successful participation in various activities in social studies, a student can be helped to develop more self-understanding, which in turn contributes to a wholesome self-concept and acceptance of others. It is especially important that all students develop pride in their ethnic backgrounds, earn recognition from members of the class, become aware of and accept their strengths and weaknesses, and develop greater skill in evaluating their own behavior.

A democratic atmosphere promotes learning. Mutual respect, concern for others, open-mindedness, responsibilities, self-discipline, respect for constituted authority, recognition of individual differences, critical thinking, adherence to high standards of self-conduct and self-appraisal, individual integrity, teamwork, fair play—these are the elements that teachers must stress if they are to develop an atmosphere that will promote maximum learning for everyone.

QUESTIONS, ACTIVITIES, EVALUATION

1. Obtain a local curriculum guide and check it for the following:
   a. How are the social studies defined? How does the definition differ from the one given in this chapter? What foundations are mentioned as being basic?
   b. What goals are identified? What contributions to the goals of education are noted? What cognitive and affective objectives are noted? What performance or behavioral objectives are noted?
   c. What position is taken on citizenship education? ethnic studies? equality for women? intercultural and international education? legal rights and responsibilities?
   d. Which of the major trends presented in this chapter can you find? Which are not included? How might the lack of attention to certain trends be accounted for?
   e. Is a statement of guidelines to the improvement of learning included? If so, how is it similar to the one presented in this chapter? Are additional characteristics listed?
2. Write in your own words a definition of social studies that you might use with parents. Discuss it with other students or teachers and obtain any suggestions they have for improving it. Discuss it with nonprofessionals and find out if it is clear to them.
3. Which of the objectives of social studies do you believe to be most meaningful in your situation? Discuss your selection with others and see if they agree.

4. Write a set of performance objectives for a lesson of your choice, using the guidelines presented in this chapter. Do at least one objective for each of the four categories: conceptual, inquiry, skill, and affective.
5. Which of the trends presented in this chapter do you believe to be most significant in improving children's learning in social studies? What might you do as a teacher to implement them in your situation?

REFERENCES

BANKS, JAMES A., ed., *Teaching Ethnic Studies* (43rd Yearbook). Washington, D. C.: National Council for the Social Studies, 1973. Guidelines and strategies.

BLOOM, BENJAMIN S., ed., *Taxonomy of Educational Objectives: Cognitive Domain.* New York: McKay, 1956. Objectives arranged by levels of complexity.

BURNS, RICHARD W., *New Approaches to Behavioral Objectives.* Dubuque, Iowa: Wm. C. Brown, 1972. How to write objectives and restate goals as objectives.

"The Consumer: Another Forgotten American?" *Social Education,* October 1974. Issue on consumer education; approaches, integration into social studies, resources, bibliography.

FRASER, DOROTHY M., ed., *Social Studies Curriculum Development* (39th Yearbook). Washington, D.C.: National Council for the Social Studies, 1969. Trends in organization of social studies.

EHMAN, LEE, HOWARD MEHLINGER, and JOHN PATRICK, *Toward Effective Instruction In Secondary Social Studies.* Boston: Houghton Mifflin, 1974. See especially the chapter on goals and objectives.

FLANAGAN, JOHN C., WILLIAM M. SHANNER, and ROBERT F. MAGER, *Social Studies Behavioral Objectives.* Palo Alto: Westinghouse Learning Press, 1971. Examples of instructional objectives.

GROSS, NORMAN, ed., *Directory of Law-related Educational Activities* (2nd ed.). Chicago: American Bar Association, 1974. Current projects in various states.

GROSSMAN, RUTH H., and JOHN U. MICHAELIS, *Schools, Families, Neighborhoods; Working, Playing, Learning; People, Places, Products.* Menlo Park, Calif.: Addison-Wesley, 1976. Teacher's editions contain examples of inquiry-conceptual questions.

HENRIE, SAMUEL N., ed., *Alert: A Sourcebook of Elementary Curricula Programs and Projects.* Washington, D.C.: U.S. Government Printing Office, 1972. Review of projects in social studies, ethnic studies, environmental studies.

Instructional Objectives Exchange, *Social Science.* Los Angeles: P.O. Box 24095, 1974. Booklets of objectives and related test items on this and other topics.

JAROLIMEK, JOHN, and HUBER M. WALSH, eds., *Readings for Social Studies in Elementary Education* (3rd ed.). New York: Macmillan, 1974. Readings on objectives and trends.

JOYCE, BRUCE R., *New Strategies for Social Education* (2ND ed.). Chicago: Science Research Associates, 1972. Chapter on intellectual, social, and personal dimensions.

KRATHWOHL, DAVID R., BENJAMIN S. BLOOM, and BERTRAM B. MASIA, *Taxonomy of Educational Objectives: Affective Domain*. New York: McKay, 1964. Objectives arranged by degree of internalization.

MCASHAN, H. H., *The Goals Approach to Performance Objectives*. Philadelphia: Saunders, 1974. How to state goals and objectives; examples of competency modules; accountability guidelines.

MICHAELIS, JOHN U., and EVERETT KEACH, eds., *Teaching Strategies for Elementary Social Studies*. Itasca, Ill.: Peacock, 1972. Readings on objectives and new trends.

REMY, RICHARD C. et al. *International Learning and International Education in a Global Age*. Washington, D.C.: National Council for the Social Studies, 1975. Sections on learning about the world, alternative views of the world, and designing world studies programs.

Public Education Religion Studies: Questions and Answers. Dayton, O.: Public Education Religion Studies Center, 1974. Guidebook for teachers and administrators.

SCORE, School Curriculum Objective-Referenced Evaluation. Iowa City, Iowa: Westinghouse Learning Corporation, 1974. Instructional objectives and related test items.

Social Studies Curriculum Materials Data Book. Boulder, Colo.: Social Science Education Consortium, 1973. Reviews of project materials, media, games; annual supplements on new media.

WEBSTER, STATEN W., *The Education of Black Americans*. New York: Intext, 1974. Guidelines and points of view.

WESLEY, EDGAR B., and STANLEY P. WRONSKI, *Teaching Secondary Social Studies in a World Society*. Lexington, Mass.: Heath, 1973. Chapters on society, analyzing contemporary society, curriculum decisions, objectives, world perspectives.

Guides to Current Materials

The following sources should be checked for current materials in the social studies and other areas:

Current Index to Journals in Education. Guide to articles.

Education Index. Guide to articles and other publications.

Resources in Education (until 1975, *Research in Education*). Guide to articles, research, units, teaching guides and other materials available in microfiche and reproduced form from ERIC Document

Reproduction Service, P.O. Box 190, Arlington, Va. 22210. ERIC microfiche available in many college and school district professional libraries.

Periodicals

Use the following to keep abreast of new developments and materials:

Social Education and *The Social Studies Professional* (journal and newsletter of the National Council for the Social Studies)

Journal of Geography and *Perspective* (journal and newsletter of the National Council for Geographic Education)

SSEC Newsletter (Social Science Education Consortium)

The ERIC Chess Board and *Looking At* (newsletter and occasional bulletin from ERIC Clearinghouse for Social Studies)

The Social Studies (journal, McKinley Publishing Co.)

Progress in Economic Education and *Checklist* (Joint Council on Economic Education)

Focusing Questions

What patterns and strands are used to organize the K to 12 program?

What themes, units, and topics are frequently included at various levels?

How are concepts and generalizations put to use in overall organization and in the design of units?

What basic guidelines are used to plan the curriculum?

How are key elements brought together in daily planning?

How can the characteristics of new programs be summarized?

Organizing the Program of Instruction

An understanding of the organization of the social studies program is helpful to teachers in several ways. Goals and objectives can be kept in focus and implications from the foundations of social studies can be related to instruction at all levels. Planning for a group can be more effective when clear suggestions are available regarding units or topics at each level. Needless repetition can be avoided, gaps in learning prevented, and a more balanced program assured. More appropriate instructional media can be reviewed, selected, and arranged for use. Continuity of learning can be maintained as each teacher builds on what has gone before. Both depth and breadth of learning can be given attention as instruction is planned for topics and units at each level. Key concepts and generalizations can be kept in focus as students progress through the program. Evaluation can be planned and carried out in terms of areas of emphasis at each level.

This chapter includes attention to trends in organization, topics and units in the curriculum, organization of new programs, organization around concepts and generalizations, types of studies, guidelines for program development, and characteristics of new programs.

PATTERNS AND STRANDS OF ORGANIZATION

Patterns of organization may be viewed on a continuum ranging from unified or interdisciplinary approaches, in which disciplines are indistinguishable, to separate-subject approaches, in which history, geography, or other disciplines are singled out for emphasis. Interdisciplinary approaches are usually found in such units as schools, families, and neighborhoods around the world, our community, and communities around the world; they also may be found in courses in secondary schools that deal with contemporary problems such as urbanization, international relations, or other topics that require the use of material drawn from several disciplines. The separate-subject approach is predominant in high schools in such courses as United States history, world history, economics, and American government. In between the interdisciplinary and separate-subject approaches are multidisciplinary approaches that bring the perspectives of different disciplines to bear on topics and problems in such units as our state, the New England states, changing Japan, Latin America, and the Middle East. In multidisciplinary approaches the geographic, historical, economic, political, and sociocultural features of the area under study are considered and relationships among them highlighted. But each discipline is clearly visible, and the content is not brought together into an amalgam that renders the disciplines indistinguishable.

The trend is clearly toward interdisciplinary approaches with appropriate use of other approaches depending on the focus of study. For example, interdisciplinary approaches are used when relationships are emphasized and topics, issues, and problems call for the use of a mix of concepts, as in the study of families, communities, and world cultures. On the other hand, when the focus is on economic, political, geographic, or historical factors, there is good reason to use the concepts and processes that are directly relevant.

Four strands, found in well-designed programs (see Chart 2-1), provide for cumulative and spiral learning. The conceptual strand includes the concepts and main ideas used to structure units. The thinking processes strand includes classifying, generalizing, and other processes. The skill strand includes reading skills, map and globe skills, time and chronology skills, and other skills needed to gather and organize data from a variety of media. The values strand includes the values and valuing processes needed to deal with value-laden topics and issues. Additional information on current trends and developments is presented in the next section in the context of topics and units at each level of instruction.

AN OVERVIEW OF DOMINANT TOPICS AND UNITS

What main themes or areas of emphasis are frequently included in different grades? What specific topics and units are included? What are the current trends at various levels? Answers to these questions are helpful as background information for reviewing and interpreting courses of study. State and local control of educational policies has produced many differences among schools throughout the country. In fact, greater

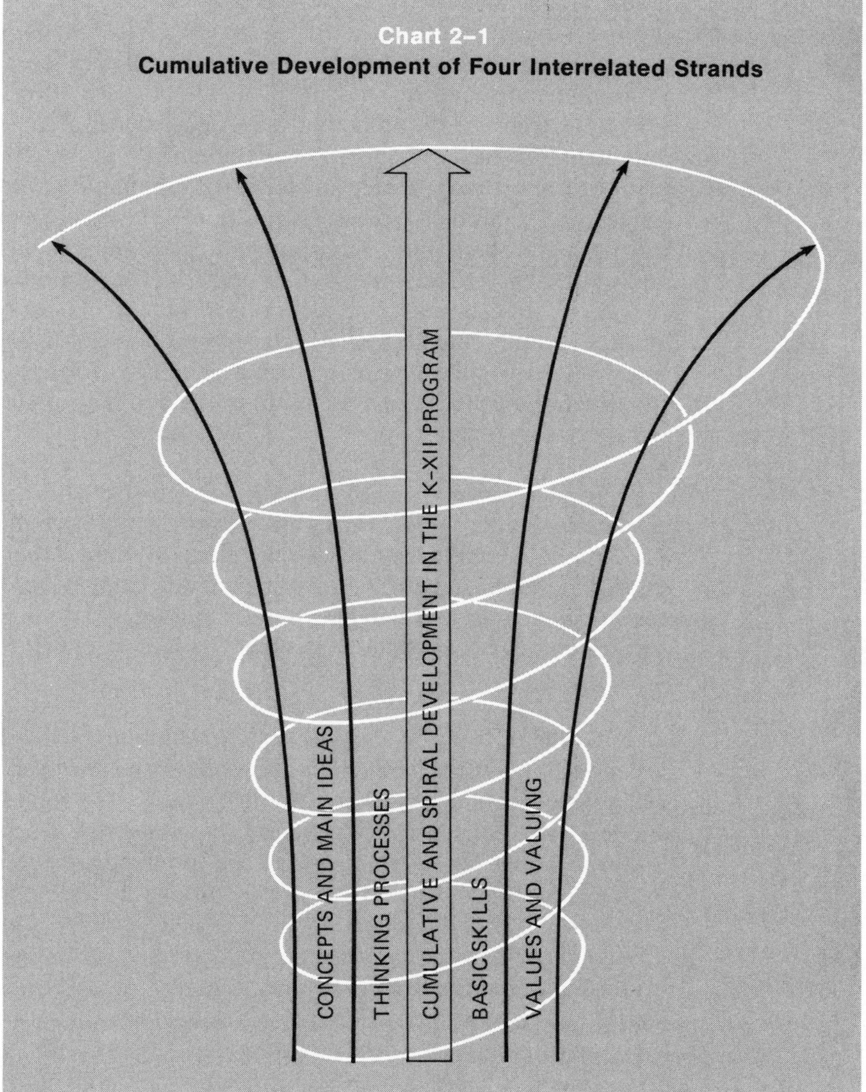

diversity may be noted in social studies than in other areas of the curriculum. Nevertheless, certain similarities in content exist at various levels of instruction. The greatest similarities may be found in the early grades, which include such units as family life, the school, our community and communities around the world. Differences are more noticeable in grades 4, 6, and 7. Even at these levels, one can find similar topics and units, but they are placed in different grades. For example, some schools provide for the study of western hemisphere countries in grade 6 and eastern hemisphere countries in grade 7; in other schools, the reverse may be true.

Several recurring topics are given attention within regular units or in special units and lessons at all levels of instruction. Current affairs, holidays, commemorations, and contributions of great men and women are included in all programs. Career education, with the emphasis on career awareness, is related to studies of community workers in the early grades and to studies of the role and contributions of workers in units on the state and the nation. Environmental education is part of regular units and is emphasized in special units such as the urban environment, conservation of resources, and pollution problems. Future education is included in both regular and special units. The following grade-by-grade overview shows the dominant theme or themes for each grade, followed by illustrative topics, units in each grade, and a brief statement of recent trends.

Kindergarten. Local Environment Studies: Short-term experiences and units are provided on home, school, neighborhood, store, service station, how we learn, the airport, trucks, and other aspects of the immediate environment. Current trends are to provide deeper studies of the home, school and neighborhood, children and families in other lands, our global earth, and how people change the neighborhood and the community.

Grade 1. Family, School, and Community Life: Illustrative units are the family; our school and other schools; the family at work; neighbors at work; community workers; the fire station; the supermarket; families, schools, and neighborhoods around the world; the dairy farm; farm life; and how we learn. Current trends are to introduce economic, anthropological, and other concepts from the various disciplines, such as division of labor, extended family, and role; to teach map and globe skills in greater depth; to provide comparative studies of families and schools at home and abroad; to compare rural and city life; to consider homes of the future; and begin to develop career awareness.

Grade 2. Community Studies: Units and topics include community workers; public services; how we get our food, shelter, and clothing; transportation; communication; our community and other communities; living in different communities; and workers around the world. Current trends are to provide for comparative studies of communities; to extend map and globe concepts; to study and compare changes in communities; to include some historical material on the community; to investigate food, shelter, and clothing in other lands; to emphasize specialization and division of labor within and among communities; to consider future developments; and to develop career awareness.

How can native American and other ethnic studies contribute to a well-rounded curriculum? (Social Studies Workshop, University of California, Berkeley)

How are these furnishings in early American homes like ones we use today? How are they different? What other changes can we find? (Boston, Massachusetts)

Grade 3. Metropolitan Communities, City Life, Cities Around the World: Illustrative units and topics are neighboring communities, different kinds of communities, transportation, communication, urban problems, living in metropolitan communities, communities around the world, pioneer communities, native Americans, development of our community, comparative studies of our community and other communities, and future communities. Among the trends at this level are increased attention to interdependence among communities; urban problems, planning, and renewal; past, present, and future changes in cities and metropolitan areas; how the community is governed; and careers in the community.

Grade 4. Our State, Regions around the World, Regions of the United States, Great People in American History: Units and topics that illustrate the diversity at this level are our state in early times, our state today, living in different world regions, our global world, conservation, area study of India, changing Japan, and how Americans obtain goods and services. Significant trends at this level are to provide cross-cultural comparative studies; to study historical, geographic, and economic aspects of the home state in greater depth; to give more attention to state government; to study the contributions of individuals from all groups to the development of the state and nation; to explore future prospects and proposals for change; to give attention to environmental problems; and to explore careers and roles of workers at the state level.

Grade 5. Living in Early and Modern America, Regional Studies of the United States, Canada, and Latin America: Illustrative units and topics are discovery and exploration of America, colonial life, pioneer life, westward movement, contributions of leaders, regions of the United States, relationships with Canada, living in the Americas, and our neighbors to the north and south. Current trends are to stress relationships among countries in the Americas; to study urbanization in different regions; to explore the impact of scientific and technological developments in the past and present; to give more attention to the contributions and history of minority groups; to include environmental studies; to include law-based instruction on rights and responsibilities; to include new programs such as Man, A Course of Study; to provide a more balanced treatment of the past, present and future; and to extend career awareness to the national level.

Grade 6. World Cultures, Western or Eastern Hemisphere: Illustrative units and topics stressing the western hemisphere are early cultures of South America; the ABC countries, Argentina, Brazil, Chile; living in Mexico; countries of Central America; historical and cultural beginnings in the Western world; and economic and social problems. Units and topics focusing on the eastern hemisphere are backgrounds of American history, Western Europe, Central Europe, Mediterranean lands, Eastern Europe, the USSR, the Middle East, North Africa, Africa south of the Sahara, India, and China. Schools that focus on global geography provide for a selection of units on culture regions and countries around the world.

Trends at this level are to program grades 6 and 7 so that students may study both Eastern and Western culture regions; to highlight interdependence among countries; to explore the problems of developing nations; to consider the work of international agencies; to study the impact of culture on ways of living; to analyze social, economic, and political systems in greater depth; and to explore current problems and possible future developments.

Grade 7. World Cultures, Eastern or Western Hemisphere Studies, Study of Our State, United States History: The history and geography of eastern hemisphere areas, especially Europe, are predominant, with emphasis on such units and topics as Old World backgrounds, early man, early civilizations, Greece and Rome, the Middle Ages, and Western European nations. Schools that focus on countries in the western hemisphere tend to stress geography and include units and topics similar to those listed above for grade 6. World geography is offered in some schools, and in several places our state is studied in grade 7 instead of in grade 4. Much of the work in grade 7 is planned to provide background for units on United States history in grade 8.

Current trends are to include studies of the cultures of Asia, Africa, and Latin America; to interrelate state and national history; to include ethnic studies; to explore the problems of new nations; and to study historical, geographic, social, economic, and political aspects of development in greater depth.

Grade 8. United States History; The Constitution; Federal, State, and Local Government: Specific topics and units include exploration and discovery; colonization; the thirteen colonies; the winning of independence; the Constitution; building a government; emergence of American patterns of living; the Civil War and Reconstruction; growth of industry and agriculture; enrichment of American life; contributions of leaders; contributions of minority groups; preserving and extending human rights; becoming a world power; relations with other nations; government at the local, state, and national levels; and geography of the United States. The typical practice is to emphasize the study of early American history up to the Reconstruction era with about one-third of the time on later American history; the reverse is generally true in grade 11 in which United States history is studied intensively.

Current trends are to provide fewer units and to study them in depth; to provide primary source materials for analysis and interpretation by students; to give more attention to minorities in the history of the United States; to emphasize the interrelationships of federal, state, and local government; to provide case studies on selected aspects of government; to relate historical trends to current problems and future developments; and to clarify the legal rights and responsibilities of all citizens.

STAND YOUR GROUND
DONT FIRE UNLESS FIRED UPON
BUT IF THEY MEAN TO HAVE A WAR
LET IT BEGIN HERE
CAPTAIN PARKER

PLYMOUTH ROCK
LANDING PLACE OF THE
PILGRIMS
1620

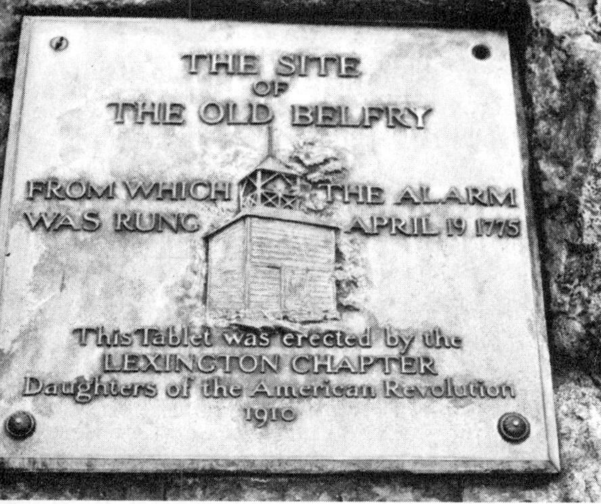

THE SITE
OF
THE OLD BELFRY
FROM WHICH THE ALARM
WAS RUNG APRIL 19 1775
This Tablet was erected by the
LEXINGTON CHAPTER
Daughters of the American Revolution
1910

What concepts and values should we emphasize in early American studies? In Bicentennial commemorations? How might they be made meaningful to students today? (Boston, Massachusetts)

Grades 9–12. Government, World Geography, World History, United States History, United States Government, Economics, Current Problems: Government is required in many schools in grade 9 with special attention to the legal rights and responsibilities of youth and adults. World geography and world history are electives in most secondary schools in grades 9 and 10. United States history is a standard requirement in grade 11, and many schools require a course in government and current problems in grade 12. Larger high schools offer electives in such courses as sociology, anthropology, state history, black history, Chicano studies, economics, international relations, European history, Afro-American studies, Asian studies, and psychology.

Current trends are to provide courses on comparative economic and political systems, to increase the amount of time given to Asian civilizations in world history, to require work in economics, to offer a two-year block in United States history rather than the separate offerings in grades 8 and 11, to provide mini-courses of six to nine weeks' duration, and to view elective courses as capstone offerings that bring together concepts and modes of inquiry included at various points earlier in the program.

This brief overview shows that most programs begin with the student's immediate environment and move outward to larger and more distant areas. The trend is to introduce comparative studies of other families, communities, and cultures early in the program. Although major attention still is given to history, geography, and political science in current social studies programs, more content is being drawn from anthropology, psychology, economics, sociology, and law. That study of the United States is not neglected may be shown by pointing to the study of the local community in primary grades; state history and geography in middle or upper grades; United States history in grades 4 or 5, 7, 8, and 11; and relationships between the United States and other countries at different levels. New countries and new problems receive attention at various levels.

THE ORGANIZATION OF NEW PROGRAMS

The features of new programs can be determined only by examining them in detail. For example, continuity from level to level, the planning of blocks of instruction, the emphasis given to United States history at different levels, and the scope and breadth of instruction need to be considered in the context of a particular plan or framework. Readers are urged to review the program in the area in which they live. The following examples illustrate themes and units in a county and a city school system.

Baltimore County

The primary program includes studies of people around the world in a variety of activities in families, neighborhoods, communities, and cities within the theme of a changing world.[1] Grades 4 and 5 include groups and their government and United States regional studies, followed by world culture studies in grades 6 and 7. Depth studies of America's past and contemporary America are provided in grades 8 and 9, followed by international perspectives, the American experience, and a variety of electives in the last three grades.

Kindergarten. Getting to know myself and people in the environment
Grade 1. A Changing World: Families, family ways, earning and using income, shelter, clothing, food
Grade 2. A Changing World: Community patterns, individuals and groups, government at work, recreation, producing goods and services, distributing and marketing goods
Grade 3. A Changing World: Urban life; cities; where and why cities grow; case studies of New York, Washington, London, Tokyo; ancient cities; urban problems and promises
Grade 4. Groups and Their Government: Group process; early American group—the Pilgrims; the Amish—an American subculture; regulating groups: order through law; colonial settlements; a new government—Revolutionary period; a national government—the Constitution; change: impact of individuals and groups; a racial minority; improving our environment
Grade 5. Regional Studies of the United States: Mid-Atlantic, with focus on Maryland, Midwest, Southwest
Grade 6. World Cultures: India—villages, cities, arts; Latin America—early, colonial, contemporary
Grade 7. World Cultures: Africa, Japan, Southeast Asia, Middle East, Europe, Soviet Union
Grade 8. America's Past: Beginning, revolution, settling the frontier, conflict, industrialization, a sober America (1920–1939), international responsibility, time of change: toward a new America
Grade 9. Contemporary America: American political, economic, and social behavior
Grade 10. International Perspectives: Culture: a way of life; patterns of response; contemporary China; historical and contemporary change; networks of global relationships; conflict and the international political system; economic change and development; the future
Grade 11. The American Experience: Expanding the democratic ideal, minority experiences, responses to social and technological change, changing perceptions of the United States in the world
Grade 12. Electives: Area study of selected regions, dynamics of behavior, exploring the past, social justice, physical environment, urban studies, political behavior, twentieth-century world, Western heritage

[1] *The Curriculum Handbook* (Towson, Md.: Board of Education of Baltimore County, 1973).

New York City The New York City program begins in prekindergarten and extends through grade 12.[2] Unnecessary repetition of content has been eliminated, there is flexibility in themes and case studies, and teachers are advised to adapt to neighborhood needs. Themes and topics are:

Prekindergarten. Orientation to the World We Live In: Developing individuality and self-respect, relating to people, responsibilities, future rewards, people and places nearby and far away, special days

Kindergarten. Home and School Environment: Together in the classroom and school and its environment, how the family meets its needs, needs met by people far away, adapting to change, special days

Grade 1. Living and Working in the Community: People live in groups, workers supply needs, government services, communities are interdependent, community changes, special days

Grade 2. City Communities Around the World: New York City and suburbs, other U.S. cities, world cities, communication and transportation bring people closer together, special days and customs

Grade 3. Cultures Around the World: Comparative studies of how people live in tropical rainforests, deserts, grasslands, northern forests, and mountain regions; man's inventiveness; good citizenship

Grade 4. American People and Leaders, and How the United States Began and Grew: How people discovered and explored America, settled and developed the colonies, established the United States, developed our nation (to 1900), and have been developing a great society (since 1900)

Grade 5. Our World—Geographic and Economic Studies: How people of the United States and Canada use their geography, how Latin Americans use technology, new economic relationships in Europe, how the people of Asia or Africa (select one) use their geography

Grade 6. Our World—Early Civilizations: How we learn about the past, how man developed, Western civilization, (two of the following) how civilization developed in India, China, pre-Colombian America, Africa

Grade 7. American History: Why people moved to the New World (1492–1775), permanent settlements (1607–1775), how the thirteen colonies became a nation (1660–1789), changing political climate (1783–1890), response to twentieth-century needs (1890 to the present)

Grade 8. Urban Growth: New York metropolitan area, urbanization in New York State, urbanization at home and abroad, changing federalism in urban America

Grades 9–12. World Studies: Eastern civilization in 9, Western civilization in 10, a two-year sequence; American studies in 11, economics in 12a, one elective course in 12b.

[2] *Course of Study*, New York City Schools, 1973–74.

ORGANIZING PROGRAMS AND UNITS AROUND CONCEPTS AND GENERALIZATIONS

Programs such as those outlined above are organized around concepts, themes, and generalizations drawn from the social sciences. In fact, there is widespread agreement that conceptual strands or threads should be the focuses for planning the K through 12 program. Continuity from level to level is facilitated by planning for the spiral development of concepts, concept clusters, generalizations, processes of inquiry, and related values, attitudes, and skills. An example of how concepts in cultural change and related generalizations may be developed at different levels of instruction is shown in Chart 2–2.

Note that cultural change is not shown as a single concept because it consists of a cluster of concepts. If attention is not given to the related concepts, important dimensions of cultural change will be neglected. Instruction at each level is designed to provide for the use of concepts at increasingly higher levels of abstraction and complexity, and for the development of related generalizations that encompass broader domains of content. At each level, instruction should include adequate samplings of concrete and familiar material so that cumulative development of each concept is nurtured without gaps or breaks in the student's changing cognitive structures.

Planning for Spiral Development

The general procedure in planning for the spiral development of concepts and generalizations is to identify applications that can be made to units and topics at each level of instruction. Several examples are given below.

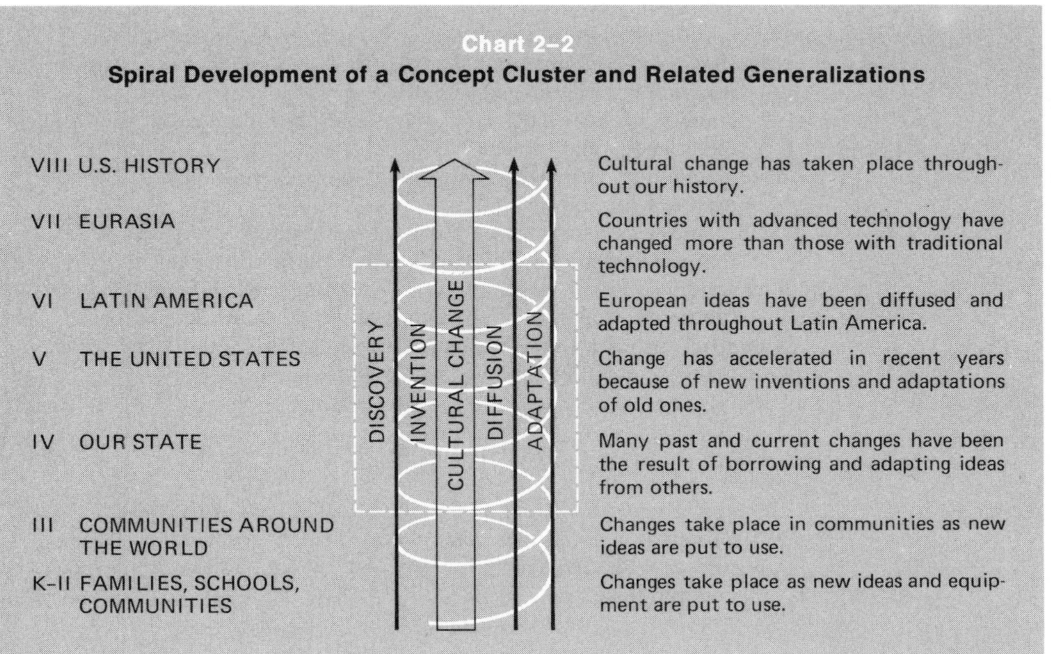
Chart 2–2
Spiral Development of a Concept Cluster and Related Generalizations
VIII U.S. HISTORY
Cultural change has taken place throughout our history.
VII EURASIA
Countries with advanced technology have changed more than those with traditional technology.
VI LATIN AMERICA
European ideas have been diffused and adapted throughout Latin America.
V THE UNITED STATES
Change has accelerated in recent years because of new inventions and adaptations of old ones.
IV OUR STATE
Many past and current changes have been the result of borrowing and adapting ideas from others.
III COMMUNITIES AROUND THE WORLD
Changes take place in communities as new ideas are put to use.
K-II FAMILIES, SCHOOLS, COMMUNITIES
Changes take place as new ideas and equipment are put to use.
DISCOVERY
INVENTION
CULTURAL CHANGE
DIFFUSION
ADAPTATION

The first shows applications of the concept *interdependence* to units in blocks of grades; the second shows applications of main ideas related to a generalization based on the concept *specialization*; and the third illustrates the practical questions that can be used to guide students toward the development of a generalization based on *social control*.

INTERDEPENDENCE

K and 1: Interdependence among members of the family, neighbors, school workers, community workers, producers and consumers, buyers and sellers

2 and 3: Interdependence among families in communities, among neighborhoods in communities, between communities, between farms and markets, factory workers and transportation workers

4 and 5: Interdependence among communities and areas within the state, between industries and government, between states, between regions of the United States, between the United States and other countries

6 and 7: Interdependence among countries in the Americas, in Europe, and throughout the world

SPECIALIZATION

Specialization has led to interdependence among individuals, communities, regions, and nations.

Members of the family have special jobs. Each member depends on others for some things.

Community workers have special jobs and depend on each other for many goods and services.

Our community produces some things but depends on other communities for many goods.

States and regions in our country use resources to produce goods that are exchanged with goods produced in other places.

Our country imports and exports a variety of goods. We depend on other countries for some goods, and they in turn depend on us.

Countries around the world have specialized in producing some goods that can be sold to other countries.

SOCIAL CONTROL

Societies require a system of social control in order to survive.

What rules do families have? Why must members of families stick to rules? What happens if they don't? What responsibilities do children have?

What rules do we have in our class? In our school? What might happen if we had no rules? How can the rules be changed? Why must rules be changed at times?
How do safety regulations help to protect us in the community? food regulations? others? What responsibilities do fire fighters have? police? other public workers? What are our responsibilities?
How do state laws help to protect us? food inspection? highway traffic laws? business regulations? others? What responsibilities do officials have? What responsibilities do we and others have?
What responsibilities are taken by the federal government for internal control? law enforcement? lawmaking? individual rights? others? How are local, state, and federal means of control interrelated? How does our government participate in controlling international problems?

Interdisciplinary Concepts

Because so many topics and problems in the social studies cut across and draw upon many different disciplines, there is a trend toward the use of interdisciplinary concepts. These concepts are helpful as organizers and tools of inquiry in many different social studies units. The following examples are from the *Social Sciences Education Framework for California Public Schools*:[3] citizenship, justice, freedom, morality, truth, multiple causation, authority/power, social control, interdependence, culture, diversity, change, conflict, needs, property, scarcity, resources.

A concise set of powerful and broadly applicable interdisciplinary concepts has been proposed by Engle and Longstreet:[4] conflict, power, valuing, interaction, change, adjustment. Taba[5] used the following key concepts as organizers to give continuity to instruction planned in a hierarchical order from grade to grade: causality, conflict, cooperation, cultural change, differences, interdependence, modification, power, societal control, tradition, values.

Using Organizing Elements in Units of Instruction

Main ideas derived from concepts and generalizations are used to structure units in many programs. The process is one of choosing the components of a main idea that can be applied in a given unit. Chart 2–3 includes main ideas that have been derived from a set of core concepts and related generalizations drawn from several disciplines. Notice that each main idea is indicative of the kind of content that should be provided in the unit.

[3] Sacramento, Department of Education, 1974.
[4] Shirley Engle and Wilma S. Longstreet, *A Design for Social Education in the Open Curriculum* (New York: Harper & Row, 1972).
[5] Hilda Taba et al., *Teacher's Handbook for Elementary Social Studies*, 2nd ed. (Reading, Mass.: Addison-Wesley, 1971).

Chart 2–3
Main Ideas in a Unit on Food Production

Core Concepts and Generalizations		Main Ideas To Be Developed
Basic needs. People work to satisfy needs for food, clothing, and shelter.	→	Every community provides food.
Group action. The work of society is carried on through groups.	→	Many groups work to produce and distribute food.
Culture. Individual behavior is influenced by the culture.	→	People eat different foods to obtain the nourishment they need.
Interdependence. People depend on others.	→	The food store provides a community service.
Standards. People act in accordance with laws and regulations.	→	Laws and regulations apply to the production and distribution of food.
Technology. The level of technology is related to production.	→	Transportation, refrigeration, and processing plants make possible a wide variety of foods.
Contributions. Others have contributed to our cultural heritage.	→	Some foods have been brought from other lands.
Change. Change is characteristic of the social and physical environment.	→	Ways of producing food have changed.

A variety of derived main ideas may be found in new units of instruction. One helpful practice is to state main ideas in terms that are fairly close to the kind of generalization the students themselves will formulate after a series of learning experiences. Examples of main ideas are given in Charts 2–4 to 2–15. Other examples are given in the following chapters.

Chart 2–4
Home and Family

Families differ in size and composition.
Everyone at home has work to do.
Changes take place in homes and families.
Money may be earned by one or more members of the family.
Some members of the family produce goods and services.

Chart 2–5
Living on Farms

Our country has many different kinds of farms.
Different kinds of work are done as seasons change.
Water, soil, and weather are important to the farmer.
New machines have changed the work of farmers.
People depend on farmers and farmers depend on other workers.

Chart 2–6
Living in Our Community

People work at many different jobs to provide goods and services.
People depend on one another for food, clothes, and other goods.
Many goods that we need are made in other communities.
Many changes have taken place since our community was founded.

Chart 2–7
Life in Tribal Villages

People make most of the things they need.
Members of the family work to get food, shelter, and clothing.
People depend on their own skills and their environment more than we do.
Customs and traditions are very important in people's lives.

Chart 2–8
Communities in Other Lands

Weather, climate, and landforms vary from place to place.
People work for food, shelter, and clothing.
Changes take place as new ideas are put to use.
Some communities are like ours in some ways, but different in others.

Chart 2–9
Growth of Our State

Industries have been set up to use capital, resources, and the labor supply.
Some ways of living brought by early settlers are still evident.
Many people have contributed to the growth of our state.
Changes have taken place faster in recent years.

Chart 2–10
In Early America

Many settlers came in search of a better life.
The reasons for coming to America differed among settlers from different countries.
Ways of living in the colonies were related to beliefs, past experiences, and new problems.
The idea of self-government was expressed in many ways.

Chart 2–11
Contributions of Black Americans

Many contributions have been made in response to critical problems.
Contributions have been made to science, medicine, and the social sciences.
Contributions have been made to law, education, and other professions.
Contributions have been made to art, music, literature, and sports.

Chart 2–12
Some Main Ideas about Japan

The shift from a traditional to a modern society was made rapidly.
New ideas have been combined with old to improve ways of living.
Trade with other countries is essential for many reasons.
Economic activities are related to resources, population, know-how, and geographic conditions.

Chart 2–13
Living in Mexico

The distribution of landforms and climates is distinctive.
The diffusion of Spanish traditions has been great.
The population is more dense in the highlands than in the lowlands because the climate is more favorable.
Agriculture is the major industry, but manufacturing is increasing.

Chart 2–14
Living in South America

The countries of South America attained freedom from European nations after a long struggle.
Countries in the Americas are interdependent in many ways.
Economic development projects are designed to improve conditions of living.
A single major industry exists in many nations.

Chart 2–15
Growth of Democracy

Democratic concepts of government began to emerge early in Anglo-America.
The Constitution provided the basic framework of government.
Principles of democracy were extended as frontiers were opened.
Many individuals and groups have contributed to the growth of democracy.

PROVIDING FOR THREE TYPES OF STUDIES

A new development is to plan the overall K to 12 program so that students have opportunities to carry out three different types of inquiry or study.[6] Each of us uses all three intuitively in daily activities, and all three are used in the social sciences. For years we have been using them in social studies without being aware of differences among them. As Chart 2–16 shows, the three types or modes of inquiry are (1) the analytic multisetting mode to develop generalizations; (2) the integrative single-setting mode to study particular people, places, and events; and (3) the decision-making mode to evaluate proposals and actions.

[6] Statewide Social Sciences Study Committee, *K–12 Social Sciences Education Framework* (Sacramento, Calif.: State Department of Education, 1968); and *Retrieval: Area III Social Sciences, A Handbook for Teachers* (Sacramento, Calif.: County Superintendent of Schools, 1972).

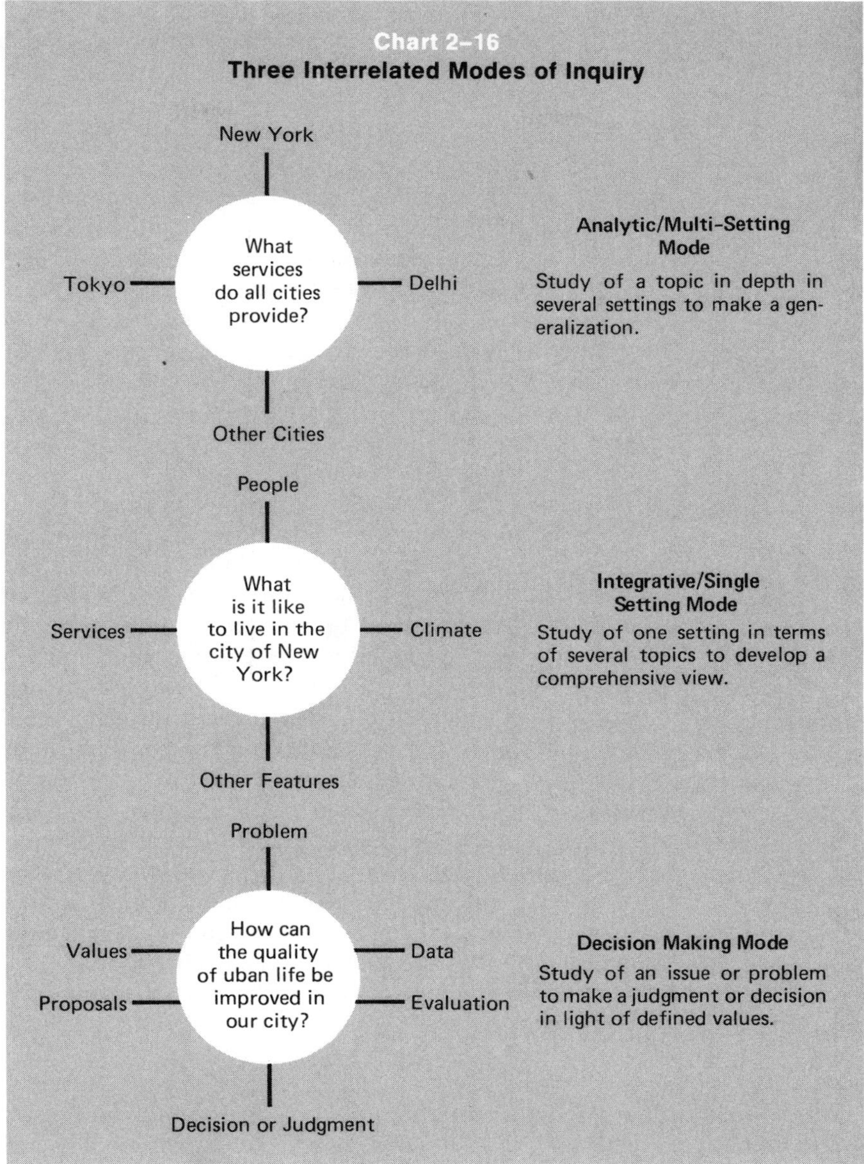
Chart 2–16
Three Interrelated Modes of Inquiry
New York
What services do all cities provide?
Tokyo
Delhi
Other Cities
Analytic/Multi-Setting Mode
Study of a topic in depth in several settings to make a generalization.
People
What is it like to live in the city of New York?
Services
Climate
Other Features
Integrative/Single Setting Mode
Study of one setting in terms of several topics to develop a comprehensive view.
Problem
How can the quality of uban life be improved in our city?
Values
Proposals
Data
Evaluation
Decision or Judgment
Decision Making Mode
Study of an issue or problem to make a judgment or decision in light of defined values.

The analytic mode develops main ideas or generalizations by studying a topic such as the role of mothers or food production in depth in several different settings; it is on the scientific side of the social studies program. The integrative mode brings together the unique and particular aspects of events, individuals, cities, countries, and other selected settings; it is on the humanities side of the social studies. The decision-making mode is used to make decisions or judgments related to environmental, urban, economic, political, and other issues and problems; it is on the evaluative, action side of the social studies.

We use these three modes every day in thinking about vacations, shopping practices, and other activities. For example, say we wish to arrive at a generalization about the cost of a week's vacation. We must analyze several vacations, not a single one, to make a reasonable generalization. On the other hand, if we wish to tell others about a particular vacation, we must focus on several elements, not just cost, so we intuitively use the integrative mode. For example, we might tell others the important details of the best (or worst) vacation we ever had. Here the emphasis is on bringing together the special features of the event so that others will grasp its particularity. We use the decision-making mode when we are confronted with proposals, alternatives, or choices and must make a judgment. For example, if we are to make a decision on where to go on a vacation, we assess the alternatives in terms of costs, past experience, and the values most important to us.

In the social sciences these three modes are used in a refined and systematic way. For example, people in various disciplines study topics such as the following to develop basic generalizations: social classes (sociology), the impact of technology on culture (anthropology), distribution of cities (geography), production (economics), the legislative process (political science), the nature of revolutions (history). Examples of integrative studies are these: a minority group (sociology), a tribal group (anthropology), a region (geography), a particular factory (economics), the government of a particular country (political science), the growth of a country (history). Illustrative decision-making studies are urban planning (sociology and geography), community development (anthropology), appraisal of tax proposals (economics), studies of governmental reform (political science), and assessment of individual and group actions (history). A new trend in social studies is to provide a balanced program that includes each type of study. The following sections contain examples of each type and a review of related processes and outcomes.

Analytic Multisetting Studies

The objective of these studies is to help students increase their ability to generalize as they analyze a topic in order to develop main ideas. For example, if main ideas are to be developed about the primary roles of family members, the division of work, common urban problems, or other topics, first the focus of study is clarified, and then several different families, community workers, or urban centers are studied in depth. The emphasis is on the process of generalizing, and other processes are used to gather and evaluate the data needed to make a solid generalization. A question such as "What is the main role of mayors?" may be used to guide study. Observing is then focused specifically on the role of mayors,

What data should be brought together to show what is special about Tokyo? What topics should be included in an integrative study? (International Society for Study of Education, Tokyo)

data are classified and interpreted, and a generalization is developed and checked against the data.

Students should learn that an adequate number of cases or situations must be studied to make a good generalization. They should also learn that it is sometimes wise to put limits on generalizations—for example, a generalization about the main role of mayors may be limited to "the mayor of our town." Then as the role of mayors in other places is studied, students can extend their generalization accordingly. This kind of learning will help students to avoid generalizing from a single instance or a few cases, or generalizing beyond the reasonable limits of the data they have collected. Furthermore, it will help them to identify faulty generalizations made by others.

Integrative Single-Setting Studies One objective of these studies is to help students develop the ability to synthesize data on a person, region, culture, or historical period. Instead of focusing on one topic in several settings, the student brings together information on a variety of aspects of the single setting selected for study. For example, a variety of topics need to be studied in such units as our school; our community; our state; living in Mexico, Nigeria, the Middle East; and the history of our country. Special features are included along with basic elements to give a feeling for the distinctiveness of the setting under study, but now the emphasis is on the process of synthesizing, and other processes are used to aid in bringing together relevant findings. For example, observing is focused on several topics, interpreting includes attention to values and feelings as well as data, generalizing is limited to the culture or area under study, and analyzing is used to clarify the elements or parts to be synthesized.

A key learning for students is that every person, city, region, country, culture, or historical event has distinctive characteristics that set it apart from others. There is only one Abraham Lincoln, one New York, one New England, and one Brazil; no other school, community, or state is just like our own; the American Revolution differs from other revolutions; and no two countries have identical histories (though some similarities in development may be identified). To investigate a particular setting thoroughly, therefore, it is necessary to do a comprehensive study that integrates key elements. A second key learning is that generalizations made in one situation may not hold up in others. To find out if they do, it is necessary to do an adequate number of analytic multisetting studies. A third key learning is that some concepts have special meanings and that terms such as the Loop in Chicago, the French Quarter in New Orleans, carpetbaggers and muckrakers in American history, the caste system in India, and the meaning of democracy in China must often be defined in specific contexts. Finally, students should develop an appreciation of art, music, literature, and other material from the humanities in order to acquire well-rounded views of cultures, areas, and historical periods.

Decision-Making Studies

A central objective of these studies is to develop competence in making decisions, weighing alternatives, assessing policies, evaluating proposals, and anticipating consequences of various actions. A variety of issues and problems may be considered in various units. Here are some examples: Which proposals for curbing air pollution should be adopted? What steps should be taken to provide an adequate water supply? Which housing development plans fill the needs of low-income groups best? How can the quality of life in large cities be improved? Which proposals for aiding Latin American countries should be supported? The emphasis is on the process of evaluating, as students clarify values and formulate standards for making judgments. Other processes are used to gather and interpret data to determine how standards are met, and what the consequences of different proposals or actions may be. Data from other studies may also be used; for instance, studies of ways of curbing air pollution can be used in considering local, state, and federal proposals.

Key learnings for students are (1) that the issue or problem must be clearly defined, and (2) that related values must also be clarified. When students have different notions about an issue and use different values to appraise it, they make little progress until they learn to interpret and analyze situations in which individuals arrived at different conclusions or decisions because of differing views of the problem and differing values. After clarifying the issue and related values, students proceed to evaluate proposals, project consequences, and make a judgment, as noted in the section on evaluation in Chapter 6.

Relationships to Other Subjects The social studies program is related to other areas of the curriculum in a variety of ways. In the early grades, many teachers use study trips, filmstrips, and other social studies resources to develop children's language power and readiness for reading. Science, health, and social studies can be interrelated in studies of family life, the farm, how we get our food, how weather affects what we do, communication, and transportation. In middle and upper grades such interrelationships are found in units on conservation, the environment, transportation and communication, weather and climate, living in regions around the world, our state, and our country. At all levels, appropriate material from art, literature, and music can enrich learning.

The trend is to include material pertinent to the questions and problems under study. Only rarely today is social studies used as an all-inclusive core of learning to which all other subjects are related; usually related subjects are drawn upon to improve problem solving and thinking in social studies. Reading and other language skills are put to use and strengthened, and special problems of reading social studies material are given attention. Related ideas from the realms of science, health, and mathematics are included and reinforced as appropriate, but a forced relating of content is avoided because the inevitable result is confusion and an imbalance among basic areas of the curriculum.

A SUMMARY OF GUIDELINES

Guidelines widely used in planning and organizing the social studies program are given below. Selected guidelines proposed by a special committee of the National Council for the Social Studies[7] have been included, along with others of critical importance at the school and district level.

1. The K–12 program should be based on a clearly formulated point of view. Attention should be given to goals and objectives, implications drawn from the foundations, and a rationale for the pattern of organization. Of special importance to teachers are guidelines for unit planning, adapting the program to local conditions, meeting individual differences, using teaching strategies, and evaluating outcomes.

[7]"Social Studies Curriculum Guidelines," *Social Education*, 35 (December 1971), 853–69.

2. Teachers should have a central role in planning the social studies program, with the assistance of resource experts. Teachers' experience, values, and insights into learning and teaching should be brought to bear on all aspects of planning. Assistance should be provided as needed by other school personnel, experts on the foundations of education, social studies specialists, and curriculum directors. The professional growth of teachers and other school personnel should be a primary outcome of participation in curriculum committees, grade-level meetings, cooperative unit planning, selection of materials, workshops, and other in-service activities.

3. The organization of the program should provide for flexibility and revision as needed. Flexibility enables teachers to adapt the program to local conditions and to the educational needs of children. New developments in the social sciences, in societal conditions, and in child development and learning should be reflected in the program. Studies should be made to determine the value of new proposals, and the program should be continually revised to keep it up to date.

4. The scope of the program should include fundamental strands that link the program from level to level. In essence, the scope of the program should be comprehensive—it should include analytic, integrative, and decision-making studies in both Western and non-Western settings; the real social world and concerns of students; the study of one's own and other cultural, racial, religious, and ethnic groups; local, national, and world affairs; and past, present, and future time dimensions. It should be balanced in terms of conceptual, process, skill, and affective learning, and study of the immediate environment and the larger world. It should relate to daily living—there should be opportunities to deal with educationally significant problems, events, and activities as they arise. And it should facilitate the development of relationships—the teacher should be free to draw on content from whatever disciplines are needed to achieve the objects of the social studies program.

5. The sequence of the program should be planned using both logical and psychological considerations. The theme for each grade should indicate the broad area of study to be emphasized and be an extension of preceding experiences. Units of instruction should be selected critically for each grade in light of the theme, the capabilities of children, and the objectives of the social studies program. Recurring topics and units should be planned to go beyond earlier emphases and avoid needless repetition and duplication. At each level, provision should be made for intensive study of new content organized around key concepts and generalizations from the social sciences. Provision should also be made at each level for the strengthening of skills involved in thinking, valuing, and decision-making processes, independent study, group work, and use of instructional media. And areas of study at each level must be feasible in terms of teachers' backgrounds and available instructional materials.

6. Newly developed curriculum materials should be analyzed critically in terms of local educational needs.[8] Special attention should be given to the rationale and objectives, including assumptions, point of view, basic goals, and instructional objectives; to cognitive (data, concepts, themes, generalizations, thinking processes) and affective content (values, attitudes, appreciations, valuing processes); and to the guidelines to learning and teaching, the cognitive and affective teaching strategies. Grade level and type of student—able, typical, less able—for whom the materials are intended and extent to which individual differences can be met are important points to be checked, along with the feasibility of local use in terms of teacher preparation, in-service requirements, community acceptance, and the time, effort, and expense required to use the materials. Their effects on the balance and continuity of the curriculum in general and of the social studies program in particular also need evaluation. One of the best ways to evaluate is to use the materials experimentally in the classroom to gauge student response and teacher ability to use them effectively.

7. The content of the program should be selected critically, for it should meet such basic criteria as these: Can it be used to develop key concepts, main ideas, processes, skills, attitudes, and values? Is it related to truly significant human problems, the real social world, the concerns of students? Is it valid, reliable, and up to date? Is it adaptable to students' capabilities and backgrounds? Are instructional materials readily available?

8. Care should be taken to meet legal requirements. The strong popular interest in education has resulted in many state requirements. For example, most states have specific provisions regarding instruction in United States history, geography, civics, the Constitution, observance of special days, display of the flag, state history and government, loyalty, and patriotism. In addition to legal requirements, state and local boards of education also impose regulations that extend and implement state laws.

Every teacher should assume responsibility for carrying out the intent and purpose of existing requirements. Existing provisions may be found by checking the school code, summaries published by the state department of education, the course of study, or the school register of enrollment and attendance. If any provisions appear to be detrimental to the development of an effective program of instruction, they should be called to the attention of the local authorities who can take steps to bring about the appropriate changes.

9. Statewide curriculum guides should provide a framework for local planning. They should be designed to give direction to the planning,

[8] See the Morrissett and Stephens reference at the end of this chapter for a detailed materials analysis system. Check the *Social Studies Curriculum Materials Data Book* and supplements to it for reviews of new materials.

organizing, and development of social studies programs in local school systems; to suggest implications for social studies instruction derived from studies of changes taking place in society and from the latest studies in child development and learning; to indicate goals and objectives and the characteristics of an effective social studies program; and to give clear descriptions of basic principles of instruction, newer trends and practices, and legal requirements. They should also indicate areas of emphasis and units of work in broad outlines that can be adapted and modified to meet local conditions; provide guidelines for the selection of instructional media, teaching strategies, evaluation of learning, appraisal of the social studies program, and accountability; and include suggestions for staff development and for in-service and pre-service education.

10. The course of study for the local school system should go beyond the state framework to include detailed suggestions for teachers to use in planning, guiding, and evaluating social studies instruction. Among the topics commonly included in courses of study are the following:

1. Point of view or rationale underlying the program
2. The local setting and adaptations to community needs and conditions
3. Goals and objectives of the social studies program
4. Organization of the instructional program
   a. Principles of organization
   b. Definition of scope to show strands running through the program
   c. Sequence of themes and units of instruction for each level
   d. Recurring topics such as current affairs, special days and weeks
5. Basic principles and procedures of instruction
   a. Planning and developing units of instruction
   b. Teaching strategies for conceptual, process, skill, and affective objectives
   c. Procedures for meeting individual differences
   d. Techniques for utilizing instructional media
6. Essential instructional media and their place in the program
   a. Textbooks and other reading materials
   b. Maps, globes, films, and other audio-visual materials
   c. Community resources
7. Evaluation of outcomes of instruction
   a. Guiding principles for use at all levels
   b. Techniques for use at different levels

11. Unit plans—guides for teaching units of instruction—should be provided for teacher reference. Unit plans are an extension of the local course of study; they are the teacher's instructional guide for developing the units assigned to each grade. Specific objectives are included along with the learning experiences, related instructional

materials, and evaluation procedures that may be used to guide and evaluate learning. Because of its importance, the entire next chapter is devoted to unit planning.

12. Daily planning should be carried out to provide instruction that meets the needs of students and leads to the attainment of specific objectives. In many ways the daily planning of lessons is a critical and culminating phase of curriculum organization. It is through lesson plans that the curriculum is brought to life in the classroom. Many different formats are used, but most include attention to objectives, teaching strategies, materials, and evaluation activities. One new development is to use the inquiry-conceptual model for making plans that link processes and concepts together. The following example for early grades (1–3) illustrates one way in which this may be done. Notice that major understandings and instructional objectives are stated first, and then teaching strategies.

WHERE IS OUR COUNTRY?

Major Understandings

Location of the United States. We live on a certain part of the earth. The name of our part of the earth is the United States.

Objectives

The students should develop the ability to:

Recognize the name "United States of America," and state that it is the name of our country

Point to the location of the United States, including Alaska and Hawaii, on a pictorial map of the United States and on the classroom globe

State the colors used to show land and water in textbook picture maps and on the classroom globe

Teaching Strategy

Inquiry Processes	Questions and Activities	Data, Concepts, Generalizations
	Introduction:	
Observing	Look at the large picture map on the bottom of page 5. What does this picture map show? Where would you have to be to make a picture like this?	Map: Pictorial map that shows United States borders and Hawaii.

(cont.)

Inquiry Processes	Questions and Activities	Data, Concepts, Generalizations
Interpreting	What does the blue color show? What colors show land? Point to a part that shows water; that shows land.	Color symbols: Blue is used for water, various naturalistic colors for land.
	Development:	
Observing	Something special is marked on this drawing of the earth. What is it?	Line symbols: Lines are used on globes to show the borders between countries.
Interpreting	Point to the two white lines that go across part of the land. What is shown between the two white lines? What is the name of our country? Point to this part of our country.	Boundary lines: The area between the white lines is the largest part of the United States.
Observing, interpreting	Other places on the earth are part of our country too. What can you see on this picture that marks off another part of our country? Point to that part. What is that part called?	Line symbol: The white line in the north area marks off the state of Alaska.
Observing, interpreting	Look at the part that shows an ocean. What do you see there that shows another part of our country? What is that part called?	Line symbol: Arrows are used to point out specific, small areas. The state of Hawaii is shown in the Pacific Ocean.
	Conclusion:	
Synthesizing	Our country, the United States, is shown in different places. Who can point to all of them to show us our whole country?	Location: States and communities in the United States can be located on the globe.
Classifying	Which part of our country is the largest? Which part has water all around it? Which part is closer to the North Pole? Which parts are away from the largest part of our country?	Parts of the United States: Hawaii is surrounded by water; Alaska is to the north. Both of these states are away from the largest part of our country.

CHARACTERISTICS OF NEW PROGRAMS A promising practice in curriculum planning, workshops, and conferences on the social studies is the consideration given to statements of the characteristics of an effective social studies program. Such statements have been found to be helpful in overall planning, in evaluating social studies programs, in providing guidance to curriculum workers, and in interpreting the program to nonprofessionals. In a way, a statement of the characteristics of an effective program can be viewed as a summary of major trends, for it reflects dominant points of view on basic aspects of the program. The following checklist is intended to serve this purpose and to be used to appraise basic features of the social studies program.

Checklist 2–1

BASIC FEATURES

Definition

The social studies program is defined to include inquiry into ______ group behavior ______ human interaction ______ human relationships ______ social, economic, and political activities in a variety of cultures ______ the cultural heritage in the past, present, and future.

Foundations

The program is based on four foundations. ______ social ______ psychological ______ disciplinary ______ philosophical.

Goals and Objectives

Goals are stated and contributions to goals of education are indicated: ______ thinking and decision making ______ self-realization ______ human relationships ______ civic responsibility ______ economic competence ______ learning how to learn

Objectives are stated in performance or behavioral terms: ______ conceptual objectives ______ skill objectives ______ process objectives ______ affective objectives.

Organization of the Program

A K–12 program is provided with units and topics at each level of instruction. Four basic strands run throughout the program: ______ concepts and generalizations ______ social studies skills ______ thinking and inquiry processes ______ values and valuing processes.

There is openness to include concerns of students and new developments:

______ ethnic studies ______ career education ______ future education ______ intercultural and international education ______ environmental studies ______ other new developments.

_____ Attention is given to the real social world, contemporary affairs, significant holidays, and special events.

_____ Scope and sequence are defined to ensure breadth, depth, and continuity of learning.

_____ Relationships to other areas of the curriculum are indicated.

_____ A curriculum guide and units of instruction are provided and teachers are encouraged to use them creatively to meet students' needs.

Teaching Strategies

A variety of teaching strategies are used: _____ cognitive _____ discovery-learning _____ individual inquiry _____ affective _____ directed learning _____ group inquiry.

Instructional Technology

Criteria are used to select materials and learning activities that may be used to _____ achieve goals and objectives _____ spark creative teaching _____ individualize instruction _____ meet local needs and conditions.

_____ A variety of printed, audiovisual, and community resources are provided.

_____ Use of the school and community as a learning laboratory is recommended.

Evaluation, Revision, Accountability

Guidelines and procedures are given for _____ evaluating learning _____ revising the program _____ evaluating the program _____ an accountability system.

Instructional Personnel

_____ Teachers have the depth and breadth of preparation to provide instruction in the areas of study included in the program.

_____ Supervisory assistance is provided to help teachers meet instructional problems.

_____ In-service education is provided to improve instruction in the social studies.

QUESTIONS, ACTIVITIES, EVALUATION

1. Appraise the selected programs presented in this chapter. How might they be improved to meet conditions in your area? Which parts of each program do you prefer?
2. Plan what you believe to be an ideal social studies program for grades K–12. Indicate the theme and topics or units for each grade. Discuss your proposed program with others, getting their views on its strengths and weaknesses.
3. Examine a course of study being used in a nearby school system and

review it critically to answer the following questions:

a. What themes, topics, and units are recommended for each grade? Are any optional units suggested? Is there openness to incorporate new developments?
b. Note any suggested topics or units that are not included in the overview presented in this chapter. Do you think they should be included? Give reasons for your position.
c. What suggestions are made for the spiral development of key ideas and concepts?
d. What suggestions are made for incorporating key ideas in units?
e. What legal requirements are noted? What suggestions are made for the observance of holidays and special events?
f. Which of the characteristics of new programs can you identify?

REFERENCES

BANKS, JAMES A., ed., *Teaching Ethnic Studies* (43rd Yearbook). Washinton, D.C.: National Council for the Social Studies, 1973. Guidelines for curricular emphases.

Curriculum Materials Washington, D.C.: Association for Supervision and Curriculum Development, annual. New curriculum guides and units.

ENGLE, SHIRLEY, and WILMA S. LONGSTREET, *A Design for Social Education in the Open Curriculum.* New York: Harper & Row, 1972. Design around core concepts.

FRAENKEL, JACK R., *Helping Students Think and Value: Strategies for Teaching the Social Studies.* Englewood Cliffs, N.J.: Prentice-Hall, 1973. Chapter on organization of subject matter.

FRASER, DOROTHY M., ed., *Social Studies Curriculum Development: Prospects and Problems* (39th Yearbook). Washington, D.C.: National Council for the Social Studies, 1969. Guidelines for organizing the curriculum.

HANNA, LAVONE A., GLADYS L. POTTER, and ROBERT W. REYNOLDS, *Dynamic Elementary Social Studies* (3rd ed.). New York: Holt, Rinehart and Winston, 1973. Chapter on the structure of the program.

JAROLIMEK, JOHN, and HUBERT M. WALSH, eds., *Readings for Social Studies in Elementary Education.* New York: Macmillan, 1974. Articles on organization.

LEE, JOHN R., *Teaching Social Studies in the Elementary School.* New York: Free Press, 1974. Chapter on programs and courses.

MICHAELIS, JOHN U., and EVERETT T. KEACH, JR., *Teaching Strategies for Elementary Social Studies.* Itasca, Ill.: Peacock, 1972. Articles on designing the curriculum.

PRESTON, RALPH C., and WAYNE L. HERMAN, JR., *Teaching Social Studies in the Elementary School.* New York: Holt, Rinehart and Winston, 1974. Chapter on curriculum.

TABA, HILDA, MARY DURKIN, JACK R. FRAENKEL, and ANTHONY H. MCNAUGHTON, *Teacher's Handbook for Elementary Social Studies* (2nd ed.). Reading, Mass.: Addison-Wesley, 1971. Guidelines for building programs around main ideas.

THOMAS, R. MURRAY, and DALE L. BRUBAKER, *Teaching Elementary Social Studies: Readings.* Belmont, Calif.: Wadsworth, 1972. Articles on organization.

Social Sciences Education Framework For California Public Schools. Sacramento, Calif.: Department of Education, 1974. Concepts for organizing the program.

3

Focusing Questions

What criteria are used to select, plan, and develop units?

What models are used to organize units of instruction?

What steps are needed to build a background of knowledge and identify instructional materials?

What learning activities and means of evaluation are included?

Planning Units of Instruction

A unit of instruction is a plan to achieve specific objectives through the use of content and learning activities related to a designated topic or problem. Content and learning activities are selected and sequenced to attain stated objectives and meet individual differences. Techniques of evaluation, books and other instructional media for children, and background materials for teacher reference are also included. There is a difference between teaching units and resource units. A teaching unit provides instruction for a particular class; it contains the questions, activities, and materials to be used with the group. A resource unit is a rich source of questions, activities, and materials from which a teacher selects and adapts those to be used. Examples of teaching units are presented in this chapter; an example of a resource unit is given in the Appendix.

MAJOR TRENDS

In planning units of instruction, several new trends are evident. There has been a shift away from units with general teaching suggestions to units with practical learning activities and means of evaluation. Objectives are more clearly stated in performance terms to guide teaching and evaluation and to facilitate accountability. There is less emphasis on individual teacher preparation of units, and many school systems provide units that are easily adapted to meet the needs of students in a given classroom. Multimedia approaches are used to enrich learning and meet individual differences. Various models are used to develop units around main ideas, concepts and processes, specific objectives, and competency-based modules.

Criteria One continuing trend is to use criteria for selecting, planning, adapting, and developing units. Some of the major general criteria are these: (1) Each unit should help to achieve the objectives of the social studies program. The emphasis may vary from unit to unit, but attention should be on conceptual, process, skill, and affective objectives. (2) Continuity of learning should be maintained within each unit and from unit to unit. One should be able to relate each unit to students' past experiences, to build on these experiences, and to lead to broader and deeper experiences. (3) Each unit should be suitable in terms of students' maturation levels, interests, instructional needs, and individual differences. A variety of learning activities and instructional materials should be provided so that each student can engage in productive individual and group work.

The following criteria apply to more specific concerns: (1) Each unit should provide for student involvement in activities that clarify democratic values and behavior. Provision should be made for individual and group work in which there is planning, discussion, action, sharing and evaluation, coupled with opportunities to make decisions, choices, and judgments in light of clear standards and values. (2) Each unit should provide opportunities for creative expression. Students' creativeness may be given outlets through individual and group work, planning, organization and expression of ideas, discovery of relationships, interpretation and application of ideas to new situations, evaluation, and other activities calling for original responses. Varied modes of expression should be employed such as art, music, role playing, dramatic representation, construction, and oral and written language. (3) Each unit should be practical from the standpoint of available time and instructional resources. Adequate time is essential to develop depth and breadth of understanding; appropriate reading, audiovisual, and other resources should be available. (4) Each unit should contain suggested means of evaluation both for teachers and for pupil self-evaluation.

Main Sections of Units In order to select, plan, adapt, and develop units that meet these criteria, teachers should be acquainted with the various sections of unit plans. Although unit plans vary considerably, the following sections are ordinarily included.

The title describes the area of study, expressed as a theme, problem, or topic, such as families around the world, legal rights and responsibilities, colonial life, changing China. Background information is sometimes included to highlight content, issues, or new developments to bring teachers accurate and up-to-date information. It is followed by a statement of objectives that gives the main ideas, major understandings, and specific instructional objectives to be achieved, and that sometimes includes contributions to overall social studies objectives. How to begin the unit and open up questions and problems that will motivate learning and provide a base for subsequent activities is given in an initiation or approach section that precedes the listing of content, learning activities, and instructional materials. These include a suggested sequence, questions and activities, and instructional media to use to attain objectives; *opening* activities to initiate thinking, *developmental* activities to develop main ideas and attain specific objectives, and *concluding* activities to summarize and synthesize learning and state main ideas.

Sometimes a group of culminating activities is included to synthesize several main ideas or objectives of a major unit in the form of a mural, scrapbook, exhibit, program, or other activity. Evaluation techniques for appraising learning in terms of objectives by means of charts, checklists, tests, and other devices follow; this section may include preassessment as well as assessment during the unit, and postassessment to facilitate learning and accountability. There is usually a bibliography of materials for students, background references for teachers, community resources, and audiovisual materials.

FIVE MODELS

The following excerpts from selected units illustrate different models in current use, ranging from units designed around main ideas to those based on specific competences. The suggested activities in each example involve several instructional sessions except for the independent study module, which students usually complete in one session.

A Model Based on Main Ideas

The first step is to identify the main ideas to be developed. This may be done by generating main ideas from concepts such as interdependence, environment, and culture; referring to a master list of generalizations like those noted in Chapters 2 and 5; or generating main ideas based on the materials students will be using. The first two methods must always be checked against materials for students to make sure that supporting data and concepts will be used in instruction.

Although the main idea is stated first in unit plans, teachers are not expected to pass it on directly to students. Rather, the main idea should be developed through a series of learning experiences. A helpful procedure is to prepare a focusing question to guide inquiry and discovery on the part of students so that the main idea is developed inductively—moving from data and concepts to main ideas.

The following example prepared by the author illustrates planning around main ideas. The main ideas in a unit on changing Japan and related focusing questions are presented first to show the scope of the unit. This is followed by a teaching plan for one main idea. Notice that needed instructional materials are presented first to aid teachers in selecting or requesting them. Instructional objectives are given in performance terms to guide teaching and ongoing evaluation during the unit. Related content is presented with learning experiences for teacher reference. The learning experiences begin with an opener to initiate thinking, move to development to provide for learning related to the main idea, and end with conclusion to provide for expression of the main idea—a basic feature of the main idea unit model. Inquiry questions related to the main idea and focusing question are included at appropriate points to lift thinking and guide inquiry.

CHANGING JAPAN

Identification of Main Ideas

The following were formulated after reviewing concepts, concept clusters, and generalizations (such as those presented in Chapters 2 and 5), and the instructional materials to be used in the unit.

1. Japan is a mountainous island nation with diversity in its natural environment. [Focusing question: What are the main features of Japan's natural environment?]
2. The history of Japan is distinctive in many ways, yet it has been greatly influenced by other peoples. [Focusing question: How have contacts with other people influenced Japan?]
3. Japan has made rapid progress in providing health services, education, and democratic government. [Focusing question: What has Japan done to meet health needs, provide schools, and improve government?]
4. Japan is an industrial nation with a variety of economic activities. [Focusing question: How can Japan be an industrial nation with such limited natural resources?]
5. The Japanese have a distinctive culture that is related in many ways to the modes of living of other peoples. [Focusing question: How is Japan's culture related to other cultures?]
6. The Japanese have developed crafts and art forms to a high level of creativity. [Focusing question: What are the distinctive features of arts and crafts in Japan?]
7. The Japanese engage in a variety of native and adopted recreational activities. [Focusing question: What recreational activities are popular in Japan?]

Initiation

Arrange a display that includes news articles, pictures, and objects placed around a large map of Japan. Provide time for group discussion of the materials on display. Use open questions during discussion that will bring out children's background of understanding: What have you heard or read about Japan recently? What have you seen on television?

Each of the main ideas above serves as a basis for organizing instructional objectives, materials, and learning experiences. The following example for the sixth main idea shows the pattern of organization.

Main Idea: The Japanese Have Developed Crafts and Art Forms to a High Level of Creativity

Instructional objectives: During this phase of the unit, the student will state the meaning of lacquerware and cloisonné and describe their main features; describe pottery making and use Japanese designs in making a clay object; state how cloisonné and lacquerware are made and the materials used; state a main idea about creative features of Japanese art and crafts.

Instructional materials: Reading—Minugh and Cory, *Japan*, pp. 144, 148–49; Pitts, *Japan*, pp. 129–31, 134–35; Johnes, *Japanese Art*, pp. 23–40. Visual—films such as *Handcrafts of Japan* and *Ceramic Art of Japan* (Japanese Consulate).

Focusing question: What are the distinctive features of arts and crafts in Japan?

Notes and Concepts

Note: Use the following concept cluster, which includes both hand- and factory-made crafts, to find out about crafts in Japan and your own area: handcrafts, ceramics, cloisonné, lacquer, porcelain woodcarving, doll making, bamboo work.

A. Japanese craftsmen make useful and beautiful things by hand.
   1. Craftsmen still make many art objects; ceramics, lacquerware, porcelain, cloisonné, dolls.
   2. Factory production is more prevalent.
   3. Ceramics is one of Japan's oldest crafts:
      a. Clay prepared by kneading
      b. Clay shaped; freehand; coil or potter's wheel
      c. Object dried and fired

Learning Experiences

Opener

1. Arrange a display of crafts pictures and objects from Japan and at least two other cultures. Guide children to identify the major crafts shown. Define crafts. Which ones do you thing are Japanese? Why? Why are crafts an important part of a culture? How are they used?

Development

1. Show film *Handcrafts of Japan.* Discuss the different kinds of crafts and have the children classify them. Are all crafts handcrafts? Have children compare crafts produced in Japan and in their own area.
2. Find out how the Japanese make pottery. Read Minugh and Cory, pp. 149–50, and Pitts, pp. 134–35.
3. Take a study trip to a local potter to gather information on

Notes and Concepts *(cont.)*

d. Design applied
e. Fired in kiln
f. Porcelain, finest chinaware, nonpourous clay used, fired at high temperature, translucent

4. Cloisonné ware is made of metal; includes bowls, vases, small boxes:
   a. Designs formed on objects with silver, gold, or brass wires
   b. Wires heated
   c. Shiny paint applied between wires
   d. Objects baked and polished
5. Lacquerware made of cypress wood, used for trays, bowls, dishes, furniture:
   a. Lacquer tapped from trees:
      (1) Sap mixed with iron powder, other minerals
      (2) Colors: black, red, or green
   b. Cloth stretched over object

Learning Experiences *(cont.)*

processes that are used.

4. Discuss pictures in Johnes, pp. 23–40.
5. Make a pottery bowl, using Japanese designs.
6. Show film *Ceramic Art of Japan* and have children identify the processes used to produce ceramics.
7. How is cloisonné ware made? See Minugh and Cory, p. 148. What objects may be decorated with enamel?
8. How is lacquerware made? See Minugh and Cory, p. 144, and Pitts, pp. 129–31. What kinds of things are made of lacquer? Do we make lacquerware and cloisonné? Why or why not? Why are these wares expensive? Discuss time, patience, and skill involved.

Conclusion

1. Discuss features of arts and crafts most appealing to children.
2. Elicit main ideas by asking, "In general, what can we say about Japanese art?"
3. Discuss how arts and crafts enrich daily life.

Culminating activities: Discuss with the class possible objects and demonstrations that might be included in a culminating activity at the end of the unit. Consider displays of art objects, pictures, art books, and other items related to this part of the unit.

Evaluation: Teacher observation should be the primary means of evaluation during this phase of the unit, with a focus on the attainment of the instructional objectives given above.

The Inquiry-Conceptual Model This approach to unit planning includes generalizations directly related to unit content, performance objectives, inquiry-conceptual questions and activities, and techniques of evaluation. Thinking or inquiry processes are suggested and sequenced to guide learning to progressively

A current trend is to provide kits that contain instructional media for basic units. Find out if kits are available in your area. (MATCH Box Project, Children's Museum, Boston, Massachusetts)

higher levels in the cognitive and affective domains. Detailed descriptions, sample questions, and teaching strategies for each process are given in Chapter 6. The three examples that follow on various aspects of the environment are presented as teaching units. They may be followed by teaching units adapted from the resource unit in the Appendix. Activities have been included to show ways to make a smooth transition from unit to unit.

THE ENVIRONMENT

Major Understandings

Our environment includes all our surroundings—living things, cities, farms, land, water, air, everything on earth. The natural environment includes living and nonliving things. The cultural environment includes things made by people.

Objective

To define environment by describing living and nonliving things in the natural environment and things made by people in the cultural environment.

Inquiry Questions and Activities

Opener:
What does the word *environment* mean to you? [recalling]
How many things can you think of that are part of the environment? [recalling]

Development:
As we look around us, what are some things we see that are part of the environment? [observing] If we were to travel across the land, what would we see? [recalling, inferring] If we were to fly across the earth, what would we see? [recalling, inferring] Can you think of others to add to our list? [recalling]
Which items on our list are living things? which are nonliving? [classifying] Look at the pictures on the bulletin board. Which ones show living things? nonliving things? Why can we group them this way? [classifying]
Look carefully at the pictures of living things. [observing] Three major kinds are shown (people, animals, plants). What are they? [interpreting]
Why is each kind of living thing important in a study of our environment? [analyzing] Why are sunlight, air, water, and soil important? [analyzing]
So far we have given primary attention to living and nonliving things in the natural environment. What does *natural environment* mean? [defining] Check the definition in the glossary.
Now let's consider things made by people. Which of the items listed on the chalkboard are made by people? [recalling] What are some other things in our environment made by people? [recalling]
Watch this filmstrip on cities to see how many other things we can find that are made by people. [observing] We will add new ones to our list.
Look at our list of things made by people. [observing] How might we group them? [classifying] What other ways might we group them? [classifying]
Things made by people are included in the cultural environment. What does *cultural environment* mean? [defining] Check the glossary.
Who can state the main difference between the natural and the cultural environment? [contrasting]

Conclusion:
In general, what can we say is included in the environment? [generalizing] What is included in the natural environment? the cultural environment? [classifying]

Make a cinquain on the environment, as follows: [synthesizing]
Use one word to name the subject. ___
Use two words to describe it. ___ ___
Use three words for what it is doing. ___ ___ ___
Use four words to tell how you feel about it. ___ ___ ___ ___
Use the last word as a synonym for the first word. ___

Clarify values by having students make a list of "ten things I really like." After each item have them write any effects that production, use, and disposing of the item may have on the environment. Have students trade papers, if they wish, and try to add other effects on the environment. [evaluating]

Evaluation

Complete the following:

Major Things in the Natural and Cultural Environments

Natural Environment		Cultural Environment: Things Made by People
Living Things	Nonliving Things	

Directions. Listed below are items in the natural and cultural environments. Write an *N* next to those in the natural environment; write a *C* next to those in the cultural environment.

__ bottles	__ rocks	__ cans	__ concrete
__ wool	__ sheep	__ metal wheels	__ steel
__ iron ore	__ plants	__ people	__ animals
__ tree farm	__ forest	__ air	__ soil

Complete this sentence:
Our environment includes ______________________________.

Self-evaluation:
Provide for self-evaluation by having each student choose a concept such as environment, resources, or pollution. Each student should keep a record of everything that is done to learn about the concept. Self-evaluative questions are: How can I improve? In what other ways can I learn about the concept? How can meaning be enriched and extended? Provide for sharing of ways to improve.

(Note: The following activity may be used to make a transition to the next unit and thus serve to bring immediate past learning to bear on a new problem.)
Which aspects of the environment change the most? How might we find out about changes in the environment of our community? [hypothesizing]

CHANGES IN THE COMMUNITY ENVIRONMENT

Generalizations

The environment of our community has changed in the past, is changing now and will continue to change in the future. Changes in the environment may be judged to be desirable or undesirable by different people.

Objectives

To describe major changes in the environment of our community. To describe desirable and undesirable changes, and state at least two reasons for selecting them.

Inquiry Questions and Activities

Opener:
What are some changes in our community that have taken place since you started going to school? [recalling] I'll list them on the chalkboard.

Development:
Look at the changes we have listed. [observing] Which ones are changes in the natural environment? [analyzing, classifying] Which ones are changes in the cultural environment? [analyzing, classifying]
Why do you suppose we have listed more changes in the cultural environment? [inferring] Why might we be more aware of them? [inferring]
How might we group the main changes in the cultural environment? Under buildings, streets, parks? other? [classifying]
What changes do you think are desirable? why? Which ones are undesirable? why? [evaluating]

Why did the changes take place? What were the main causes of them or the main reasons for them? [analyzing]
Where have the most changes occurred? Let's mark the changes on the map of our community. Which changes are in the residential area? Which are in these areas: business, industrial, open space? [interpreting, analyzing]
What changes do you think will occur next? why? In what part of the community will they take place? why? [predicting]
How do the things that you do affect the environment? [analyzing] How do the things that others do affect the environment? [analyzing]
For one week keep a list of everything you do and things you observe others doing that change the environment in any way. Be on the lookout for things that change the quality of air and water and other aspects of the natural environment as well as construction, roadwork, and other changes in the cultural environment. [observing] Organize your findings as follows: [synthesizing]

Our Changing Community

Changes	How the Changes Are Taking Place	Causes of the Changes

Use role playing to portray how different individuals in a community might react to a proposal that will greatly alter the environment, such as building a mall downtown, building a mass transit system, construction of a new waste disposal plant, or others of concern to students. Include the roles of ecologist, leader of an active environmental group, city planner, consumer, business person, and other representatives of interested groups. [analyzing, synthesizing]

Conclusion:
Who can summarize the main changes in the cultural environment? [generalizing]
Who can summarize the main changes in the natural environment? [generalizing]
What were the main causes of (reasons for) each change? [analyzing]
What should we include on a mural map that shows major changes in the environment of our community? What pictures and drawings might we use? [synthesizing]

Clarify values by having the following simulation: [synthesizing, evaluating] Students list the things they use each day such as food, clothing, water, electricity, paper, bicycles, skates, and other items. Because of a crisis, the use of items must be cut in half and bicycles and other items must be shared. Each student must decide what to cut. Discuss the cuts and reasons for them.

Have students simulate the creation of a perfect place to live—Ecology Paradise Island. Provide for brainstorming in large-group discussion to stimulate creative thinking. Divide the class into small groups to work out plans, make maps, design laws, consider needs of wildlife, and work out other arrangements students themselves consider important. Provide for sharing and discussion when groups are ready. [synthesizing, evaluating]

Evaluation

Use the list of changes in the environment kept by each student to assess awareness of changes and ability to identify them. Also use items such as the following:

Directions: Listed below are the major zones of our community. How much change has taken place in each zone? Mark as follows: 1—much change, 2—some change, 3—little change, 4—no change.

__ residential __ commercial __ industrial __ open space

Directions: Do the following on the outline map of our community that is on your desk: Make an X to show where major changes have occurred in each zone. Use a green X to show a desirable change. Use a red X to show an undesirable change.

Directions: Write the main change that has taken place in facilities for each of the following:

transportation____________________
parks____________________
housing____________________
industry____________________
education____________________
business____________________
health____________________

(*Note: The following may be used to make a transition to the next unit.*) What natural resources would be needed in the perfect place to live? [hypothesizing] Let's explore this question in depth by considering different types of natural resources and how they are used.

NATURAL RESOURCES

Generalizations

People everywhere depend on natural resources and use them to meet basic needs. Some resources are renewable. Others are nonrenewable.

Objectives

To identify and describe natural resources and state how they are used to meet basic needs. To identify natural resources in the immediate area and in other areas. To distinguish between renewable and nonrenewable resources.

Inquiry Questions and Activities

Opener:
What are natural resources? [defining] How many different kinds can you think of? [recalling]
How many different ways do you use natural resources? [recalling]
How many different ways do others use natural resources? [recalling]

Development:
How do workers in the community use natural resources? What is the origin of the resources? Complete the following: [classifying]

Activities of Workers	*Resources Used*	*Origin of Resources*
Tailor making clothes	______	______
Electrician using a wire	______	______
Bricklayer making a fireplace	______	______
Butcher cutting meat	______	______
Carpenter building a house	______	______
Plumber sawing metal pipe	______	______

Let's begin a retrieval chart on the uses of natural resources. We will list them on the chart (Chart 3–1) on the bulletin board. [classifying]
What kind of fuel is used to heat our homes? [recalling] Let's make a survey to find out: Where does the fuel come from? Who controls the supply? Why have shortages developed? [observing, interpreting, inferring]

Chart 3–1
Uses of Natural Resources

Air	Water	Soil	Plants	Animals	Minerals

What is meant by renewable resources? nonrenewable resources? [defining]
What natural resources are renewable? nonrenewable? Which ones are in danger of depletion, according to our reading for today? [recalling, observing, interpreting]
What natural resources are in and around our community? Which ones are in danger of depletion? Which are renewable? [observing, interpreting]
What natural resources do we have in our state? Our region? Which are in danger of depletion? Which are renewable? [observing, interpreting]
What natural resources do we have in our country? Which are in danger of depletion? Which are renewable? [observing, interpreting]
What natural resources do we get from other countries? Are they in danger of depletion? Are they renewable? [observing, interpreting]
What is the extent of natural resources in our country? What additional information can we find to include in Chart 3–2? [observing, classifying]
To which of the agencies listed in our reading might we write to obtain materials on natural resources? [observing, evaluating]
What are the major water resources in our area? In our state? In our country? [observing, interpreting, generalizing]
Why is air such an important resource? What special problems exist in conserving air? [recalling, interpreting]
What are the major mineral resources in our country? What minerals do we get from other areas? Why is the rate of use of minerals so high in our country? in other industrialized countries? [observing, interpreting, inferring]

Conclusion:
Make a summary of natural resources that are used to meet needs for each of the following: [classifying] food, shelter, clothing, transportation

Chart 3–2
What Additional Ideas Can You Find on Natural Resource Areas in Our Country and State?

Questions	Rural Areas	Forest Areas	Mineral Lands	Water, Waterways
How big is the area?	90 percent of our country	One-third of our country's land surface	Around three million acres surface mined	60,000 miles of shoreline
What is found in the area?	Wildlife, farmland,	Timberland, tree farms,	Coal mines, iron ore,	Estuaries, beaches,
How do we use the area?	Camping, hiking,	Timber, recreation,	Strip mining, quarries,	Boating, swimming,
What is in our own state?	Mt. Tamalpais, Sierra,	Northern California,	Mother Lode country,	Sacramento River,

Look carefully at the chart on natural resources in our country and state. Make two lists headed as follows: [classifying] (1) Renewable Resources, (2) Nonrenewable Resources.

We have been asked to plan a program in which we will present key ideas and findings on natural resources to another class. What should we include? How should we organize key ideas and findings? In what form should we present them? [synthesizing]

Evaluation

Examine the students' summaries of ways in which resources are used to meet needs to identify needs for further instruction. Do the same for the lists of renewable and nonrenewable resources. Observe students as they make plans for presenting key ideas and findings to others to identify those who have achieved the stated objectives and those who have not. Assess affective dimensions of learning by items such as the following:

Directions. Write 1 next to the item below that you think is most important. Write 2 beside the next most important item, 3 beside the next most important, and so on.

__ Doing everything I can as an individual to conserve resources

__ Getting the government to pass stricter laws on use of resources

How are soil resources used? What steps are being taken to conserve them? (Social Studies Workshop, University of California, Berkeley)

__ Joining a group set up to conserve endangered species
__ Writing letters to urge government officials to take action
__ Setting up a community action program to conserve resources
__ Increasing taxes on the use of scarce resources
__ Regulating industries so that the use of scarce resources is decreased

Model for Performance-based Competency Modules

Competency modules usually contain these features: introduction or rationale, instructions for students, objectives or competences, learning strategies and materials, pre- and postassessment and related reteaching (recycling).[1] The following example shows the central features of part of a module on map skills.

DEVELOPMENT OF MAP SKILLS

COURSE TITLE: SOCIAL STUDIES FOR GRADE 5
TITLE OF MODULE: MAP SKILLS FOR GRADE 5
CODE: MODULE 4, PART A, MAP SKILLS, 5

Introduction, Part A

Maps are used to portray selected areas of the earth on a flat surface. We encounter maps in newspapers, magazines, textbooks, atlases, and other printed materials. They are shown on TV news programs and travelogs. We use maps on trips and at various times to locate places and find distance, direction, and other information.

This module is designed to develop basic map skills. Part A is designed to develop skills for interpreting the legend and scale. Later sections deal with other skills as outlined in *Social Studies for Children In A Democracy*, Chapter 14.

Instructions

Begin by using the preassessment items. Students who complete the preassessment successfully may do part B of this module or other work. Students doing this part should proceed from objective to objective after the desired level of competence is achieved. Reteaching (recycling) may be provided as needed to develop each competence.

Specific Competences

The competences in this part of the module are part of the total map skills program for grade 5. They are stated in terms of these objectives for the student: To interpret the legend of a given map by writing the symbols for trails and objects on a map of routes to the West. To demonstrate use of the scale by measuring and writing distances between designated places along the shortest trail.

Preassessment

The following items are to be used to determine which students will proceed with this part of the map skills module:

Using crayons, write the symbols in color of the following

[1]See McAshan in the References for several examples.

trails shown on the legend of the map, page 206, of our textbook:

Old Spanish ______ Oregon ______ Pony Express ______

Using a pencil, draw the symbol for the following:

settlement ______ ranch ______ trail campsite ______

Use the scale to estimate the distance between these places along the shortest trail:

Fort Laramie to Salt Lake City ______

Denver to San Francisco ______

Objectives, Learning Activities, and Materials

To interpret the legend by writing the symbols for trails and places shown on a map:

Find the legend of the map on page 206 of your textbooks.

Find the symbol for the Old Spanish Trail. Next locate the Old Spanish Trail on the map. What is the name of the place where it begins? Where does it end?

Find the symbol for the Santa Fe Trail. Locate it on the map and note where it begins and ends. Do the same for the other trails listed in the legend.

Look at the legend and find the symbols for places shown on the map. What is the symbol for a settlement? Find two settlements along the Mormon Trail.

What is the symbol for a fort? Locate two forts.

What do the other symbols represent? Locate each of them on the map.

To use the scale as a means of determining distance between places along the shortest trail:

Find the scale of miles at the bottom of the legend. Measure it with a ruler. How many miles to the inch?

Find Denver and San Francisco on the map. Use your ruler to measure the inches between them. How many miles between them?

Do the same for the following: Denver to Independence, St. Joseph to Portland, St. Joseph to San Francisco.

Postassessment

Using crayons, make the symbol for the following trails:

Santa Fe ____ California ____ Butterfield Overland ____

Using a pencil, draw the symbol for the following:

fort ______ mission ______ Indian village ______

Use the scale to estimate distances between these places along the shortest trail:

Springfield to El Paso ______

Fort Bridger to Portland ______

A Model for Independent Study Modules

The example below illustrates plans designed for students to use on their own in designated learning centers. Students are given a specific objective, a statement of needed materials, and procedures to follow. Self-evaluation procedures are built into each plan.

MANSA MUSA AND THE GRANDEUR OF AFRICA

Objective

You are to answer correctly six questions about the great Mali empire ruled by Mansa Musa in Africa around 600 years ago.

Materials

You will need a pencil, paper, a copy of the booklet *Africa*, and the world map on the bulletin board by the learning center.

Learning Center Instructions

1. Look at the picture map that shows Mansa Musa holding a gold nugget, page 100 in the booklet *Africa*.
2. Mansa Musa was a ruler of Mali. It was a great empire, 1000 miles from one end to the other. There were poets, artists, scholars, and architects. During its golden age, Mali had a level of civilization that was higher than many others during the 1300s.
3. Look at the map of the Mali Empire on page 102. Find the location of Mali today on the wall map.
4. Read the story about the trader from England who visits Mansa Musa in his palace, pages 99–101. How do you think a person from England will react to what he sees? How do you think Mansa Musa will react to what the trader tells him about England?

5. After you have read the story, answer the questions on Activity Sheet 1.
6. Read the story again and correct your answers.

Activity Sheet 1: Working on Your Own

Directions: After you have read the story, answer the questions below. Find the best answer and make an X on the line next to the answer you choose.

1. In what year did Sadin, the trader from England, come to the palace of Mansa Musa?
   __ 1300 __ 1327 __ 1350 __ 1377
2. As Mansa Musa entered the courtyard, he was followed by
   __ 100 slaves __ 200 slaves __ 300 slaves __ 400 slaves
3. Sadin was invited to sit by Mansa Musa on
   __ the throne __ cushions __ chairs __ a bench
4. Never before had Sadin seen a man of such
   __ strength __ size __ dignity __ aloofness
5. Mansa Musa traveled to Mecca because
   __ he wanted gold __ he wanted to be safe
   __ he was an explorer __ he was religious
6. To Mansa Musa, England seemed to be a
   __ backward country __ a great empire __ a safe country
   __ a large country
7. Your rating of Mansa Musa's empire is
   __ one of the greatest __ great __ just fair __ not so great
8. Your rating of England as described by the trader is
   __ one of the greatest places __ great __ just fair __ not so great
9. Your interest in this story was
   __ very high __ high __ fair __ low

An Objective-Referenced Model to Facilitate Accountability

The example below is the last section of a unit designed to facilitate accountability.[2] The course objective is the last of ten terminal objectives for an ethnic studies unit. The instructional objectives spell out details of the course objective in performance terms and are to be adapted by the teacher. Notice that objectives, activities, and means of evaluation are numbered to show one-to-one correspondences. For example, objective 10.1 is met by activity 10.1 and evaluated by means of evaluation 10.1. Accountability is handled by using the means of evaluation for both pre- and postassessment and recording students' progress on accountability forms.

[2] San Diego City Schools, *People of Our Community: A Social Studies Unit in Intergroup Relations*, 1973.

THE PEOPLE OF OUR COMMUNITY

Course Objective 10.0

The learner will increase the ability to accept the differences in people in a positive way, relating the difference itself to scientific explanations rather than evaluating people on obvious superficial characteristics.

Sample Instructional Objectives

(Based on audiovisual and unit set materials available to all teachers, and the entire Color of Man kit)

10.1. Learner *draws conclusions* (orally or graphically) about the existence of prejudice in the community in spite of people's contributions.

10.2. Learner *proposes solutions* (orally or graphically) to intergroup problems that have been identified during this unit.

10.3. Learner *discourages* (orally) name-calling, ethnic jokes, or negative stereotyping.

10.4. Learner *projects* (orally) positive attitudes for groups to which he belongs, directed to groups he is not a member of.

10.5. Learner *discusses* (orally) changes in his own attitude as a result of learnings he has gained in this unit.

10.6. Learner *commits himself* (orally or graphically) to actions which demonstrate a positive concern for the rights and dignity of all people.

Unit Materials

Film: *King of the Hill*
Soundstrip: Ss 177 Acceptance of Differences and Recognition of Responsibilities

Suggested Activities and Behaviors

10.1. Learner brings in newspaper articles which report examples of intergroup problems and contributions of community people. The entire news period is devoted to this type of reporting and discussion.

10.4. Learner makes a list of good things about a group to which he belongs. All lists are exchanged. (The class must discover that everyone thinks his group is best in order to understand this fallacy.)

10.2. Learners form teams to take news stories and make a bulletin board out of them along with proposed solutions. Discussions of the solutions follows.

10.3. Learners role-play situations where they refuse to listen to ethnic jokes, stereotyping, going along with the crowd, etc.

10.5. Learner writes a haiku verse telling what he learned in this unit. He also discusses his learnings with family members at home.

10.6. Learner sits on a committee to draft human relations reminders for the class. He then follows the reminders in his daily actions.

Suggested Means of Evaluation

10.1. Learner states two or more conclusions he has come to about the existence of prejudice in our community. These conclusions must be based on physical evidence.

10.2. Learner proposes two or more solutions to intergroup problems identified during this unit. Solutions need not be strictly original.

10.3. Learner simply refuses to listen to, or laugh at, ethnic jokes, name calling, or stereotyping by peers or others.

10.4. Learner describes two or more positive feelings he has about his own group and tells how he could project those feelings to different groups.

10.5. Learner states two or more changes in his attitudes toward others as a result of learnings presented in this unit.

10.6. Learner states orally and behaviorally that his actions toward others will demonstrate The Golden Rule.

These examples are illustrative of current developments in unit planning and teaching. Other examples may be found in the sources of units and in the references at the end of this chapter. Let us turn next to a consideration of guidelines for planning that are essential to the development and use of all types of units.

GUIDELINES FOR PLANNING

Selecting a Unit

The most widely used selection procedure is to refer to the course of study, note the units proposed for each grade, and select a unit that matches the backgrounds and capabilities of students in a given class. This procedure avoids repetition, promotes the use of appropriate instructional materials for each unit, and prevents the selection of insignificant units. Basic or required units are usually listed in the course of study, and one or more optional units may be suggested. The criteria given in the first part of this chapter should be applied in selecting optional units.

Special attention should be given to the educational backgrounds and growth characteristics of those for whom the unit is intended. Among the most helpful specific items of information about children in the class are the units studied in previous grades, level of reading ability, oral and written language skills, independent study and group work skills, special talents and interests, home study and library skills, cultural background, socioeconomic level, home background, and the like. A teacher can make a profile of the members of a class by reviewing cumulative records, observing children in class, and conferring with former teachers. When planning is done before school opens, teachers should plan resource units in terms of the growth characteristics cited in Chapter 4. The resource unit can then be converted to a teaching unit after information on students is obtained.

Building a Background and Identifying Instructional Materials

An essential step in preparing to teach a unit is to build up a background of knowledge and to identify instructional materials. Texts, pamphlets, and other resources available for children and background materials for the teacher should be reviewed. Most teachers find it best to review basic materials first, and other resources as time permits. Audiovisual materials should be previewed and notes made regarding their use in the unit. If time permits, community resources should be checked, trips taken to those places in the community that may be used for study trips, and interviews held with potential resource visitors. Pictures, photographs, maps, sketches, charts, and diagrams should be collected and filed with notations regarding their use in the unit. Related art activities, demonstrations, and experiments should be tried out. Collections should be made of pictures, stories, songs, records, poems, simulation games, and realia such as utensils, instruments, and clothing. If realia are unavailable, the teacher should try to get pictures of them and arrange for students to see them in a museum.

The materials listed in units and in the school's media catalog should be reviewed first, using a checklist like that shown here (Checklist 3–1).

Checklist 3–1

CHECKLIST OF INSTRUCTIONAL MEDIA

Reading Materials

__ Textbooks that focus on geography, history, or civics, or those that contain all the social sciences
__ Unit booklets on a variety of topics ranging from family life and neighborhood workers to other lands and famous people
__ Reference materials, including almanacs, anthologies, atlases, dictionaries, directories, encyclopedias, gazetteers, government bulletins, scrapbooks, yearbooks, and data banks
__ Fugitive materials, including bulletins, clippings, folders, leaflets, simulation games, pamphlets, and free or inexpensive materials
__ Current materials, including children's weekly news publications, children's magazines, daily newspapers, and adult magazines
__ Literary materials, including biography, fiction, folklore, short stories, and travel books
__ Source materials, including ballots, diaries, directions, logs, maps, minutes of meetings, recipes, and timetables
__ Programed materials, including geographic, historical, and other content arranged in a step-by-step sequence
__ Self-help materials, including charts, checklists, directions, outlines, study guides, teacher-prepared practice materials, and workbooks
__ Display materials, including titles, captions, signs, and labels
__ Teacher-prepared materials, including charts, rewritten material, scrapbooks

Audiovisual Materials

Realia and Representations of Realia:

__ models
__ objects
__ samples
__ exhibits
__ textiles
__ costumes
__ instruments
__ collections
__ products
__ miniatures
__ ornaments
__ utensils
__ tools
__ facsimiles
__ museums
__ dioramas
__ panoramas
__ mockups
__ marionettes
__ puppets
__ dolls
__ other: ______________________________

Sound and Film Resources:

__ films
__ radio and television
__ videotapes
__ cassettes
__ film loops
__ recordings
__ sound filmstrips

Pictures and Pictorial Representations:

__ photographs
__ pictures
__ drawings
__ sketches
__ slides
__ postcards
__ prints
__ etchings
__ albums
__ scrapbooks
__ montages
__ murals
__ filmstrips
__ silent films
__ opaque projections

__ transparencies __ microfilms __ storyboards
__ other: ______

Symbolic and Graphic Representations:

__ maps	__ cartoons	__ chalkboard
__ globes	__ posters	__ bulletin board
__ atlases	__ diagrams	__ flannel board
__ charts	__ graphs	__ time lines

__ other: ______

Projectors and Viewers:

__ slide	__ film	__ opaque
__ stereoscope	__ overhead	__ film loop

Players and Recorders:

__ record	__ tape	__ cassette

Supplies and Materials for Production:

__ lettering devices	__ slide making	__ bookbinding
__ map outlines	__ chart making	__ map making
__ transparencies	__ picture mounting	__ model making

__ other: ______

Community Resources

__ Study (or field) trips (industries, museums, etc.): ______

__ Resource visitors (panel or individuals): ______

__ Television (travel programs, historical plays): ______

__ Published materials (newspapers, libraries, chamber of commerce bulletins): ______

__ Persons to interview (travelers, police): ______

__ Welfare and service organizations (Red Cross, service clubs): ______

__ Service projects (safety programs, cleanup): ______

__ Possible field studies (housing, pollution): ______

__ Visual resources (pictures, realia): ______

__ Local current events (campaigns, drives): ______

__ Resources within the school (collections of materials, teachers who have traveled): ______

__ Community recreational resources (parks, marinas): ______

__ Other: ______

The Initiation The initiation of a unit should be designed to stimulate thinking, learning, and planning; it should open up truly meaningful ways to begin the study of a unit. Problems and questions that grow out of the initiation should be discussed and defined so that thinking-learning processes will be directed along profitable lines. Each student should be an active participant from the very beginning so that maximum individual learning and growth will take place.

Many different approaches or combinations of approaches, some of which are described below, can be used, but whatever the particular method chosen, a good initiation (1) stimulates interest and arouses questions and problems in each child's mind; (2) provides opportunities for pupils to become directly involved in planning and discussing learning opportunities; (3) starts the unit on significant questions, problems, or the development of a main idea; (4) does not create confusion by stimulating interest in too many problems at one time, or in problems and questions beyond the capabilities of those in the group; (5) focuses attention on the central topic to be studied and serves to set the scope of the study.

Ongoing study. One of the most effective approaches is that in which a unit grows out of the preceding unit as an ongoing study. For example a study of the wholesale market may be an outgrowth of the study of the farm and lead to a study of the supermarket. Other examples are a study of the community growing out of a study of neighboring communities, a study of transportation leading to a study of communication, and a study of colonial life leading to a study of pioneer life and the westward movement. The essence of this approach is the clarification of relationships between final activities in one unit and beginning activities in the next so that a smooth, uninterrupted transition is made. These relationships may be made by raising questions and problems that stimulate children to think of next steps and by providing learning experiences that grow out of concluding activities, as illustrated in the examples earlier in this chapter.

Teacher suggestion. In some instances, direct teacher suggestion is used to initiate a unit—for example, basic units that are required, optional units that are appropriate for the class, or units on current affairs that are truly significant. To be effective, this approach should be planned to get involvement and participation on the part of the students. Challenging questions may be raised, problems posed, related past experiences shared, or an attractive display arranged and discussed, a film shown to open up questions, or reasons for undertaking the unit discussed.

Events. A unit may be initiated as the result of a significant event in the community, state, nation, or other lands. For example, an election,

How might such a display be used to initiate a unit? (Alameda County, California)

a new invention, a new transportation speed record, or other event may be used as a springboard to more intensive study. The problem is one of timing, which can be met only in part by planning certain units to coincide with elections or other scheduled events. Because of this difficulty, most teachers make other plans to initiate units but do make use of events whenever possible.

Pretest. A pretest may be used to initiate a unit if it is designed to open up questions and problems and is followed by discussion that is well directed by the teacher. Backgrounds of understanding can be assessed quickly, and areas in need of further study can be identified. Many students will profit from further stimulation, such as discussing pictures that highlight topics to be studied or seeing a film or filmstrip that opens up questions and problems. Generally, a pretest should be used with other procedures to initiate a unit.

Books. Books that are new to the group are sometimes used to initiate a unit. Displays of textbooks and library books may be discussed, selected pictures may be shown, and passages may be read to the group. Special comments may be made on the interesting information and ideas presented in supplementary materials. Books of interest to individuals in the group may also be discussed. One difficulty with this approach is that of developing a common background for planning and discussion. It can be met in part by having a variety of books and by discussing a wide sampling of the material and pictures contained in them. Generally, this approach works best if the books are supplemented by other materials.

Audiovisual materials. A film, filmstrip, set of slides, radio program, television program, recording, map, or display of pictures may be used to initiate a unit. For example, one teacher used a film that gave an overview of village life in India to stimulate a discussion of related problems; another used a carefully selected set of slides to open up problems of living in Africa; still another guided discussion of a set of pictures on the farm. Pitfalls to be avoided are failure to secure the film at the right time, presenting so many ideas that the group cannot isolate immediate problems to attack, failure to stimulate thinking on the part of all students, and passive reception by the group instead of active participation. These difficulties can be avoided by careful preplanning and by formulating questions and comments to guide students' use of the resource and to direct followup discussion.

Community resources. A study trip or a resource visitor may be used to initiate a unit. If careful plans are made, a common experience that focuses on selected problems and stimulates thinking on the part of each child can be provided. Generally speaking, community resources are effective when the class plans for their use in relation to specific questions and problems under study. They are most effective as an approach to a new unit when used as an ongoing activity growing out of the preceding unit. For example, in concluding a study of life on the farm, one group made plans to visit a wholesale market in order to find out how farm produce was processed and distributed. The visit to the market initiated the unit on the wholesale market in a smooth manner, and with no interruption in the overall emphasis for the year, which was on how we secure food, shelter, and clothing.

Arranged environment. The arrangement of materials to initiate a unit is one of the most widely used approaches. The classroom is attractively decorated with pictures, realia, maps, books, pamphlets, and other materials related to the first problems to be considered. Students are given an opportunity to examine the materials and to raise questions about them, and so are able to participate actively in the initiation. A film, story, or recording may also be used. During discussion, questions and problems are clarified, and perhaps listed on the chalkboard or on a chart. The teacher may raise further questions to make sure that important points are not overlooked and to guide thinking in profitable directions. Even when an ongoing study is the main approach, arranging materials that focus attention on the next unit is helpful.

A brief description of an arranged environment, and the response to it, may serve to clarify its use in the initiation of a unit. The example is taken from a unit on the westward movement. The classroom was arranged as follows:

1. Pictures of scenes in an early pioneer town on the Missouri River were posted on the bulletin board. They included a general store, a wagon being loaded, a blacksmith shop, a general street scene, a covered wagon being built, and a wagon leaving the city for the West.
2. Another section of the bulletin board had pictures related to the Oregon Trail, including a caravan fording a river, life in a camp, a herd of buffalo, three Indian scouts watching a wagon train, wagons crossing the plains, and pioneers building cabins.
3. Another section of the bulletin board showed several pictures of Plains Indians, including the hunting of buffalo, an attack on a wagon train, and Indian scouts.
4. On a table in a corner of the room were several articles that children could handle. These included a model of a covered wagon, pioneer dolls (a man, a woman, a child), a powder horn, a flintlock rifle, candle molds, a water pouch, shot pouches, buffalo horns, a bull whip, arrows, bows, a corn grinder, and flint used in making arrows.
5. In another section of the room was a large map of the United States, showing various mountain barriers, rivers, and trails.
6. In the library corner, attractively displayed, were several books about Indians, pioneers, covered wagons, cities in the early West, and traveling in pioneer days.

As the students eagerly examined the different items in the arranged environment, the teacher noted their comments, questions, needs, interests, desires, and problems. Typical comments and questions included the following:

What kind of gun is this? How did they work it?
Look at these wagons. Would they hold very much?
I'll bet it was hard to ride in these wagons. They're different from cars, aren't they?
I wonder if it's hard to make a covered wagon.
How did they carry their food and water in these wagons?
Look at the clothes they wore!
Oh! I see how they got across rivers with the covered wagon.
See how this town is different from ours?

The teacher noted these and other questions and problems raised by the group. These were clues for the development of significant experiences in the unit. After the children had examined the materials, teacher and class engaged in a lively discussion of the many interesting materials and activities related to the westward movement. Through group planning, subsequent interests and problems were identified, and specific plans were made for working on them. Thus, the unit was begun in an exciting and challenging manner.

Evaluating approaches. Which type of initiation is best? No one approach can meet the needs of every situation. Sometimes a film may be available, an event may occur, or a field trip may be possible, while other resources may not be available at the moment. In other situations, a discussion of common experiences during the summer may lead to a rich study of some aspect of community living, transportation, or conservation. A teacher must be alert to these possibilities and use them creatively. In general, however, the arranged environment and the initiation growing out of another unit as an ongoing activity are the two most effective approaches. In each unit that is planned, a sound procedure is to consider the previous experiences of the group so that each unit can be an ongoing activity, and to arrange an environment that can be used to get off to a good start. Then the teacher is prepared to guide the initiation so that it creates keen interest in the unit, provokes significant questions, provides for pupil participation, employs a variety of materials, leads to group planning, and points the class in profitable directions.

SELECTING OPENING, DEVELOPMENTAL, AND CONCLUDING ACTIVITIES

Whatever model of unit organization is used, special attention must be given to the selection and use of a variety of learning activities. The best results are obtained if learning activities are viewed in terms of problem-solving processes to be put to use in dynamic programs of instruction. Because most unit models include openers, developmental activities, and concluding activities, this section has been organized to show how activities may be selected and used in connection with different phases of problem solving.

Initiating or opening activities, for example, are useful for clarifying and defining questions and problems and for recalling information, observing materials, and hypothesizing; developmental activities, for group planning of next steps and for finding, interpreting, and classifying information. Concluding activities may be directed toward further processing of information, including generalizing and synthesizing, and for evaluating processes and outcomes. As different kinds of learning experiences in the form of the activities for each phase are presented, the appropriate type of problem-solving technique is used. Depending on the circumstances, one or another technique may be given greater emphasis. For example, as opening activities are provided, primary attention may sometimes be given to the recall of related information in order to assess backgrounds of understanding. This may be followed by locating, selecting, and organizing information needed to answer questions or to solve problems. In other instances, attention might be given first to setting hypotheses, and then to planning ways to test them, collecting data, and forming tentative conclusions. Questions and hypotheses may be further clarified during developmental activities, even though they received attention during initiating or opening activities.

The lists of activities that follow will help to clarify relationships to problem solving and may be used as a checklist in unit planning.

Activities

Opening activities. Openers, or initiating activities, are provided to open up questions or problems, to find out what children know about the topic, to recall relevant information, to relate present learning to past learning, and to set the stage for activities that are to follow. Among the activities used in this introductory phase are the following:

- Pose an open-ended question for the group to discuss.
- Ask students to report what they or others have done in a given situation.
- Have them say what they would do if they were in a particular situation.
- Arrange pictures, books, and objects to stimulate discussion and to elicit comments and questions from the group.
- Have students draw pictures, tell about earlier experiences, report on places they have visited, examine and discuss pictures, or recall ideas related to questions raised by the teacher in order to reveal their background of understanding.
- Show a film, filmstrip, pictures, maps, or objects, followed by a discussion.
- Start a chart, scrapbook, time line, map, or bulletin board display that children are to complete.
- List questions, problems, or things to do on a chart or on the chalkboard.
- Have the group read an introductory section of their textbooks, review scrapbooks and materials prepared by others, or examine maps to identify questions and problems for study.
- Have students attempt to complete an unfinished story, write a statement or paragraph related to a topic, or complete an unfinished sentence.

Developmental activities. A variety of learning activities may be used in this phase of a unit. Each learning experience should grow out of preceding ones to provide a smooth problem-solving sequence. The following developmental activities are useful for group planning of next steps:

- Displaying books and other materials to stimulate thinking and planning

Asking questions to focus thinking on the main ideas to be developed, problems to be solved, or questions to be answered

Reviewing the ideas and materials related to problems under study

Listing questions and problems to guide study as they are proposed in group discussion

Considering possible sources of information such as reading materials, films and other audiovisual materials, and community resources

Listing needs for materials, steps to take to solve problems, and individual responsibilities

Collecting available books, pictures, maps, and other materials

Finding out about related radio and television programs

Planning an imaginary trip to the place to be studied

Locating places to be studied on a map and sharing known information

Defining terms, phrases, concepts, work standards, and procedures to be followed

Deciding on ways of working as individuals and as members of small groups

Considering individual, small-group, and whole-class activities

Formulating rules and standards to guide both individual and group work

These activities may be used for finding, interpreting, appraising, and classifying information:

Sharing information on references that have been located by students or by the teacher

Using contents, indexes, study guides, and reading lists

Building a card file on topics that may be found in textbooks, library materials, periodicals, pamphlets, yearbooks, almanacs

Setting up individual and small-group projects to gather needed information

Deciding on the form for organizing information as it is gathered

Reading textbooks, references, periodicals, pamphlets, charts, graphs, diagrams, encyclopedias, yearbooks, almanacs, other pertinent materials

Listening to reports, stories read by the teacher or other pupils, radio programs, recordings, resource visitors

Writing letters to request information or materials related to topics under study

Seeing films, filmstrips, slides, stereographs, pictures, exhibits, displays, television programs, dioramas, panoramas, demonstrations
Studying maps, the globe, and atlases
Utilizing community resources through study trips, interviewing experts, doing field studies, participating in service projects, finding documentary materials
Observing demonstrations, experiments, individuals at work, seasonal changes, community activities
Collecting news articles, pictures, maps, graphs, objects
Examining collections, models, specimens, textiles, instruments, costumes, utensils
Learning songs, games, rhythmic expression, folk dances, musical accompaniments, and how to play instruments related to the area of study
Tabulating information obtained from interviews, reading, field studies, experiments.
Taking notes, outlining material, adding to scrapbooks, notebooks, and classroom charts
Recording information on tapes, charts, graphs, maps, diagrams
Keeping a log or diary of experiments, activities, events, seasonal changes
Appraising information by checking one source against another, finding proof for statements, asking experts, reviewing materials
Contrasting and comparing ideas, events, activities, processes, ways of living

These activities can be used for further processing of information:

Discussing reasons underlying likenesses and differences in ways of living, customs, traditions, beliefs
Conducting class panel discussions, debates, forums, and round-table discussions
Classifying information under appropriate headings
Preparing and sharing outlines, summaries, reports, reviews, notebooks, scrapbooks
Writing descriptive statements, classroom newspaper articles, stories, and playlets
Making charts, maps, time lines, diagrams, tables
Arranging displays, bulletin boards, pictures in sequence, exhibits, files of related material
Drawing or painting pictures, murals, cartoons, posters
Modeling objects out of clay, papier-mâché, or other materials

- Engaging in industrial and fine arts experiences such as processing raw materials, bookmaking, weaving, stenciling, lettering, labeling
- Making costumes and scenery for use in a skit or play
- Role playing, having a mock trial, playing simulation games
- Constructing objects, models, looms, movie box rolls, puppets, marionettes, other items
- Creating original rhymes, stories, poems, songs, musical accompaniments, rhythms, dances, plays, skits, simulation games
- Interpreting moods and feelings through dramatic play, rhythmic expression, singing, playing instruments, folk dancing, playing folk games

Concluding activities. Closely related to and usually flowing out of developmental activities, concluding activities help children to pull together related information into generalizations, and to synthesize and evaluate learning. The following are some possible activities:

- Group discussion and evaluation of individual and committee reports prepared by the children
- Writing and sharing summaries, digests, reviews, interpretations, and reports centered on main ideas, questions, or problems
- Completing unfinished statements or stories
- Engaging in debates, round-table discussions, and panel discussions
- Selecting and discussing pictures, maps, charts, and other items that highlight the main idea
- Planning and putting on a skit, quiz program, puppet show, choral reading program
- Planning demonstrations and presentations that focus on the main idea, problem, or question
- Using a film or a study trip as a basis for discussing relationships between activities, content, and the main idea or problem in the unit
- Completing charts, maps, notebooks, scrapbooks, murals, or other items that organize information around the main idea
- Formulating generalizations based on summarized information
- Discussing similarities between and differences from the main idea under consideration and main ideas formulated during preceding activities or units
- Evaluating depth and breadth of understanding through tests, checklists, discussion, self-evaluation, and other procedures

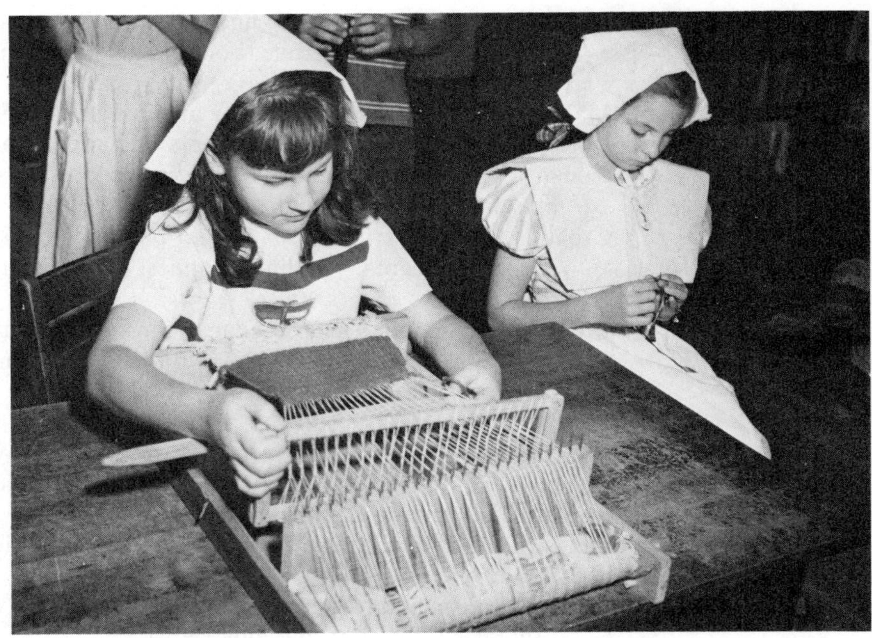

How can authentic costumes and other realia be used to increase depth of understanding and appreciation? How might those shown in this picture be used in concluding activities? (Los Angeles, California)

Culmination of a unit. Culminating activities are used to summarize and organize the high points, main ideas, or major outcomes of a unit of instruction. To be stressed are relationships among main ideas or problems, appraisal of larger outcomes, review of major topics, synthesis of information around basic concepts, and sharing of key learnings. In some units that have a series of concluding activities related to each main idea or problem, little or no time may be given to the culmination of the unit. In other units, the culmination consists of a directed discussion of relationships to the next unit, and thus serves as an ongoing activity from unit to unit. In still other units, various possibilities are suggested for culminating the unit.

In all instances, a teacher should consider such questions as the following to determine whether to have a culminating activity: Will a culminating activity help to clarify relationships among main ideas or problems? Will it contribute to students' ability to organize and share information built around basic concepts and generalizations? Will it provide for a review of fundamental learnings and contribute to evaluation of objectives set for the unit? Will it provide additional learning opportunities for each individual? If the answers to these questions indicate that a culminating activity *will* have real educational value for the group, then one should be used. A culmination used merely to "put on a show," however, will have little instructional value in terms of the objectives of the unit.

Listed below are examples of culminating activities that have been successfully used in different units. Notice that many of them are similar to the concluding activities presented in the preceding section. The main difference is in their breadth or scope. Culminating activities are more inclusive and draw together key learnings from the entire unit rather than from one major part of it.

Displaying pictures, maps, charts, objects, and other materials in arrangements that highlight main ideas or problems that have been investigated

Having students report main points related to each main idea or problem with emphasis on interrelationships

Presenting summary reports related to pictures arranged in sequence, or related to scenes depicted in a mural

Presenting a program or pageant in which songs, rhythms, folk dances, commentary, pictures, and other materials are used to highlight main ideas

Dramatizing major events, episodes, or activities studied during the unit

Having a round-table or panel discussion in which key points related to each main idea or problem are discussed

Having a quiz program in which the questions used relate to different main ideas or problems

Planning and taking a study trip to see a group at work; for example, city council meeting, state legislature

Putting on a mock meeting; for example, a New England town meeting, a city council meeting, a meeting of the UN

Evaluation

Information obtained through evaluation should be used to improve daily planning, individual and group work, the selection of appropriate materials, the extension of concepts, the correction of errors, and the meeting of individual children's needs. The entire process of evaluation should be seen as an inseparable part of the learning experiences provided in the unit.

A variety of evaluative devices should be used. Some devices are prepared as the unit progresses—for example, charts on work standards, informal rating devices for use in observation by the teacher, and checklists for use in self-evaluation. Many devices may be prepared ahead of time even though some changes may have to be made in the light of changes in the unit. The following list is illustrative of devices or procedures that may be used (examples are presented in Chapter 15):

Objective tests
Essay tests
Teacher observation
Group discussion
Individual self-checking
Checking by a partner
Checking of written work
Anecdotal records on selected individuals
Reviewing files of each student's work
Teacher analysis of tape recordings
Student analysis of tape recordings
Keeping individual and group logs or diaries
Attitude and interest inventories
Rating scales and checklists

Keeping a log to evaluate the unit. An item that needs special comment is the keeping of a log. Teachers who have kept a log report that it is a great help in evaluating the unit and gathering ideas to use in revising the unit. A satisfactory log is a simple, brief running account of the unit that includes notes on strengths and weaknesses of instructional materials, changes to be made in learning experiences, and other ways in which the unit should be modified. Items may be jotted down during or at the end of the day, and kept in a folder. After the culmination of the unit, notes related to all main ideas or problems should be brought together and used as a basis for revising the unit.

SUMMARY OF UNIT PLANNING

Although the order may vary, the following steps are essential in planning units of instruction:

1. The unit is selected after reviewing the course of study and studying the capabilities and growth characteristics of those for whom it is intended.
2. A rich background of experience is developed by the teacher through reading and annotating references, interviewing, visiting, trying out processes and experiments, making collections, previewing audiovisual materials, and reviewing units prepared by others.
3. An outline is made of objectives, main ideas or problems, related content, and related learning activities and instructional materials.
4. The initiation or approach is planned.
5. Each main idea or problem is placed in sequence.
6. Related instructional objectives and learning experiences are listed under each main idea or problem.
7. Ways of evaluating outcomes are noted.
8. Lists of materials are prepared for both the children and the teacher.
9. Necessary materials are prepared or obtained and organized in a box or file.
10. A simple plan is made for keeping a log of the unit.

Checklist 3–2 contains a summary of specific points in planning and reviewing units. The items included may be readily adapted to fit different patterns of unit organization.

Checklist 3–2

CHECKLIST FOR UNITS OF INSTRUCTION

Title: ______ Descriptive of a major area of study ______ Focused on a topic problem, or theme

Background Information: ______ Indicative of content to be emphasized ______ Related to main ideas, problems, or questions ______ Accurate and up to date

Objectives: ______ Related to objectives of social studies ______ Directly related to the unit topic ______ Conceptual Thinking processes ______ Skill ______ Affective

Initiation: ______ Focused on main idea or problem to be studied first ______ Outgrowth of the preceding unit ______ An arranged environment ______ Teacher suggestion ______ Current happening ______ Community or audiovisual resources ______ Other ______

Main Ideas, Problems, or Questions: ______ Main ideas identified as organizing centers for content and learning experiences ______ Or, problems identified ______ Or, questions identified ______ Arranged in a sequence

Learning Experiences: ______ Critically selected ______ Related to main ideas, problems, or questions ______ Related instructional materials noted ______ Arranged in a sequence as follows:

Openers: ______ To introduce each main idea, problem, or question ______ Different types suggested such as ______ recalling related earlier experiences ______ examining and discussing related pictures and objects ______ other ______________

Developmental Activities: ______ related to each main idea, problem, or question ______ Outgrowth of opening activities ______ Arranged in a problem-solving sequence ______ Varied activities suggested such as ______ reading ______ independent study ______ group work ______ creative writing ______ reporting ______ dramatization ______ rhythmic expression ______ art ______ music ______ construction ______ Other ______________

Concluding Activities: ______ Related to each main idea, problem, or question ______ Designed to lead to the development of generalizations ______ Different types suggested such as ______ completing charts ______ sharing reports ______ dramatization ______ quiz program ______ class newspaper ______ completing notebooks ______ other ______________

Culmination: ______ Needed to round out and summarize key learnings stressed throughout the entire unit ______ Provision for participation of each child ______ Contributory to evaluation of objectives set for the unit ______ Different possibilities suggested such as ______ leads to the next unit ______ program ______ pageant ______ other ______________

Instructional Materials: _____ Critically selected _____ Related to each main idea, problem, or question _____ Different types suggested such as _____ books _____ periodicals _____ maps and globes _____ community resources _____ audiovisual materials _____ art _____ music _____ construction _____ demonstration _____ other _______________

Evaluation: _____ Related to objectives _____ Made a part of experiences related to each main idea, problem, or question _____ Different techniques suggested such as _____ tests _____ charts _____ checklists _____ discussion _____ observation _____ other _______________

Bibliography: _____ Materials for children listed _____ Background materials for teachers listed

WHERE TO OBTAIN UNITS OF INSTRUCTION

A large number of preplanned units of instruction are available and may be obtained from local, county, and state courses of study; libraries and curriculum laboratories in local, county, and state school libraries; and libraries of colleges and universities. Other sources include magazines such as *Teacher, Instructor,* and *Junior Scholastic* (for a detailed list, check the *Education Index* and *Resources in Education* under the subheading "Units"), and publications of commercial organizations such as Compton's Picture Encyclopedia, 1000 North Dearborn St., Chicago, Ill.; the World Book Encyclopedia, Merchandise Mart, Chicago, Ill. (for other examples, check the sources of information on free or inexpensive materials listed in Chapter 11). Some other good sources are *Contra Costa County Units, Taba Curriculum Project,* Reading Mass., Addison-Wesley, 1969, and John U. Michaelis, *Teaching Units Based on the Social Sciences,* Chicago, Rand McNally, 1966. These are three paperback volumes, one each for grades K–2, 3–4, and 5–6. Be sure to check the unit outlines in teacher's manuals accompanying social studies textbooks and the professional textbooks for teachers (see the references at the end of this chapter).

QUESTIONS, ACTIVITIES, EVALUATION

1. Obtain a unit of instruction from one of the sources noted above and do the following:
   - **a.** Note the contents of each major section. Does the unit include the same general sections noted in this chapter?
   - **b.** Evaluate the unit in terms of the criteria presented in the first part of this chapter.

c. Summarize the opening, developmental, and concluding activities that you believe to be most helpful.
d. Note techniques of evaluation that are suggested.
e. Note references that may be useful in your own future planning.

2. Plan a short teaching unit similar to one of those presented in this chapter. Select a topic of your choice, a topic in the local course of study, or adapt a section of the unit in the Appendix. Review as many related instructional resources as time permits. Add to the unit as ideas are obtained from subsequent chapters.
3. Prepare a kit or box of materials that can be used with the unit you are planning. Include pictures, maps, free or inexpensive materials, songs, directions for arts and crafts, and other resources.
4. Arrange to visit a classroom in which a unit of instruction of interest to you is in progress. Try to visit several times in order to observe the initiation, subsequent activities, and the culmination. Discuss questions that you would ask the teacher in charge.

REFERENCES

Note: For examples of objectives, see references at the end of Chapter 1 by Bloom, Flanagan et al., Instructional Objectives Exchange, and Krathwohl et al. See references at the end of Chapter 11 for additional guides to various media, materials, and strategies.

ALMY, MILLIE, *The Early Childhood Educator at Work.* New York: McGraw-Hill, 1975. Chapter on teaching young children.

BANKS, JAMES, *Strategies for Teaching Ethnic Studies.* Boston: Allyn and Bacon, 1975. Sections on materials and procedures.

Curriculum Materials. Washington, D.C.: Association for Supervision and Curriculum Development, annual. Listing of units for various school systems.

GENGLER, CHARLES, ed., *The Heritage of America's Youth.* Salem: Oregon Association for Supervision and Curriculum Development, 1975. Sourcebook of readings, songs, and poems on our American heritage.

HANNA, LAVONE A., GLADYS L. POTTER, and ROBERT W. REYNOLDS, *Dynamic Elementary Social Studies* (3rd ed.). New York: Holt, Rinehart, and Winston, 1973. Chapter on unit planning.

Index and Curriculum Briefs. Ann Arbor, Mich.: Xerox University Microfilms, 1974. Guide to selected units in social studies and other areas.

JONES, RALPH H., ed., *Social Studies for Young Americans.* Dubuque, Iowa: Kendall/Hunt, 1970. Articles on unit teaching.

MCASHAN, H. H., *The Goals Approach to Performance Objectives.* Philadelphia: Saunders, 1974. Chapter on performance-based competence modules.

MICHAELIS, JOHN U., RUTH H. GROSSMAN, and LLOYD SCOTT, *New Designs for Elementary Curriculum and Instruction.* New York: McGraw-Hill, 1975. Sections on objectives, unit planning, teaching strategies, and evaluation.

———, and EVERETT T. KEACH, JR., eds., *Teaching Strategies for Elementary Social Studies.* Itasca, Ill.: Peacock, 1972. Section on sample lessons and units.

MURPHY, PATRICIA D., *Consumer Education Curriculum Modules.* Washington, D.C.: U.S. Government Printing Office, 1974. Competences, objectives, activities, and materials; adaptable to varying ability levels.

QUIGLEY, CHARLES N., *Law in a Free Society.* Santa Monica, Calif.: 606 Wilshire Blvd., 90401. Teaching units based on concepts of authority, justice, privacy, responsibility, participation, diversity, property, and freedom.

STANLEY, JUSTIN A., *Bibliography of Law-Related Curriculum Materials: Annotated.* Chicago: American Bar Association, 1974. List of currently available materials by topics and levels.

TABA, HILDA, MARY C. DURKIN, JACK R. FRAENKEL, and ANTHONY H. MCNAUGHTON, *A Teacher's Handbook To Elementary Social Studies.* Reading, Mass.: Addison-Wesley, 1971. Planning units around main ideas; main and organizing ideas in Appendix.

WISNIEWSKI, RICHARD, ed., *Teaching About Life in the City* (42nd Yearbook). Washington, D.C.: National Council for the Social Studies, 1972. Approaches to urban studies.

Focusing Questions

How can knowledge of developmental characteristics be used in planning instruction?

What strategies and techniques can be used to provide for individual differences?

How can reading in the social studies be individualized?

How can the special needs of the disadvantaged, the less able, and the gifted be met?

Relating Instruction to Growth Characteristics & Individual Differences

Guidelines drawn from studies of child development and learning are a basic part of the psychological foundations of social studies. Developmental characteristics serve as a background for overall planning, for studying a particular group, and for considering ways to meet individual needs and so provide optimum conditions for learning.

DEVELOPMENTAL CHARACTERISTICS

Child development is marked by stages and growth characteristics from which implications for social studies instruction can be drawn. The characteristics presented in this section, however, should be viewed as *descriptions,* not as *prescriptions* of what children can and cannot do. The intent is to illustrate how knowledge of child development is put to use in planning social studies programs, and to indicate ways to use such knowledge to plan instruction.

Primary Level

When children first enter school, they exhibit a variety of characteristics developed through experiences at home and in the neighborhood. Most have acquired such physical skills as running, jumping, and using simple tools like scissors. Language and mental development have reached a point where most children have a speaking vocabulary of over 2,500 words and a larger listening vocabulary. They play make-believe, have begun to identify with others in group play, and are moving from an exclusive interest in self to concern with what others are doing. They need to make the transition from home to school and to find security and affection in the classroom.

In school, young children need to engage in physical activity, to move around, explore the school environment, handle objects and materials, and make things. They must also learn to read, listen to stories, show things they have made or brought from home, and take part in individual and group activities. Their hands seem to get into everything, and they spend what seems like limitless energy in physical activity, dramatic play, rhythms, talking, experimenting with materials, and making things; yet they tire easily and need frequent periods of rest. Eye-hand coordination is not well developed, large muscles are better developed than small muscles, and far-sightedness is usual.

The intellectual development of children beginning school is characterized by great curiosity, inquisitiveness, and a short attention span. Young children's interests tend to focus on immediate ends, the here and now, and on matters related to their own problems. They ask many questions. *What* questions are most frequent; the number of *why* and *how* questions increases later as they gain insight into casual relationships. Their concepts of time, space, and distance are limited, and they have many misconceptions regarding home and community life, property rights, and when and how events took place. Fact and fancy may be mixed, imagination is evident in speaking and other activities, and spontaneity of expression is characteristic.

Piaget's studies[1] indicate that children from the ages of around two to seven are in a preoperational stage; they do not carry on such internalized mental operations as joining objects in a class, putting items in a series, or reversing or retracing various processes. Rather, they manipulate objects, move them around, arrange them in various ways, and base conclusions on superficial impressions. The transition from preoperational to operational thinking requires that the child actively participate in constructing a view of the world. Almy's findings[2] suggest that progress is more a matter of advance and retreat than the forward-moving sequence some people infer from Piaget's theory. Almy recommends that provision be made for more individualization of instruction, more interaction among children, more cognitive exchanges between adults and children, more searching explanations, more small-group work, and more time for children to sort out personal knowledge from knowledge shared with others.

[1] Millie Almy, *Young Children's Thinking* (New York: Teachers College Press, Columbia University, 1966).

[2] Millie Almy et al., *Logical Thinking in Second Grade* (New York: Teachers College Press, Columbia University, 1970), pp. 169–73.

Why is direct observation useful in developing concepts during the stage of concrete operations? (Bethlehem School District, Pennsylvania)

As children progress to grade 3, their individual differences increase, attention spans lengthen, eye-hand coordination improves, far-sightedness decreases, their ability to carry out tasks over longer periods of time improves, and more detail is evident in their construction and artwork. Growth in reading ability and experiences with television extend intellectual horizons and make possible the study of topics beyond the immediate environment. Other growth trends include clearer differentiation between reality and fantasy, extension of interests beyond the community, and less dependence on adults.

Moral development is in the first of the three levels described by Kohlberg.[3] Each level has two stages. Children from around four to ten years of age are at the preconventional level; they respond to rules and labels involving good or bad and right or wrong, and they show respect for physical power. Children in stage one obey to avoid punishment, relate physical consequences to goodness and badness, and defer to superior power. Children who are in stage two of the preconventional level conform to get rewards and have favors returned—"If you help me I'll help you." They tend to make a pragmatic and physical interpretation of fairness and equal sharing. Attitudes are developing toward authority, officials, and other aspects of political culture as well as toward children and adults in groups and social classes different from the child's. Verbal expression of negative attitudes (prejudices) may be evident, and some

[3] Kohlberg, Lawrence. "The Cognitive-Developmental Approach to Moral Education," *Phi Delta Kappan,* 61: 660–670, June 1975.

children openly express dislike for members of certain groups in ways they have learned at home.

In recent years, the characteristics of disadvantaged children have received special attention. It has been found that their language is simpler in syntax, and that they use fewer descriptive terms and modifiers than do middle class children. Few books and magazines are found in their homes, the naming of objects and activities is not emphasized, and they are less able to use language to handle problems. Their perceptions of social situations, authority figures, the school, and other institutions is conditioned by an environment that provides fewer opportunities to develop positive attitudes. Even children whose parents are migrant workers have not developed time and space concepts from their travel experiences. They need planned instruction in order to develop language power and to nurture the attitudes and values that will enable them to function effectively in school and community situations.

Implications. Beginners need help and guidance in making the transition from home to school. Teachers must show them affection, encouragement, and understanding, and give them specific directions for what to do, where to work, when to play, when to rest, and how to get and use materials and return them to their places. Overstimulation can be avoided by careful selection and planning of activities interspersed with periods of rest and relaxation. Short work and discussion periods of ten to fifteen minutes should be followed by rhythms, dramatic expression, games, or other physical activities. Blocks, clay work, large illustrative materials, books with large type, simple construction, easel painting, experience charts, story telling, reading by the teacher, rhythms, singing, playing simple instruments, dramatic representation, sharing periods, and observation of activities and seasonal changes in the neighborhood are some of the materials and activities that can be used to promote learning in social studies.

The transition from self-centered activities is facilitated by providing parallel activities in which two children work side by side, partnership activities in which two children build with blocks or make something, small-group activities in which several children use the playhouse or other centers of interest, and whole-class activities in which the entire group shares ideas, sings, makes plans, or discusses problems. Work areas should be small, involving two or three children at first and increasing to five or six as children are more able to use materials and work with others. Concern for others, cooperation, and responsibility are emphasized by teacher comments such as: "Now it is Ben's turn," "That is a good way to help," "Paul is finishing his work," "We share materials," and "That's a good way to use our brushes."

In grades 2 and 3, growth in reading ability, attention span, language facility, and thinking processes makes possible longer work periods and more intensive units of instruction. Broader aspects of community living, contributions of community workers, community services, modes of transportation and communication, and ways of getting food, shelter, and clothing may be studied in greater depth. Relationships between the child's community and other communities and comparisons of ways of living in communities in other lands may be undertaken to extend concepts and generalizations and to tap interests created by television, other mass media, and contacts with adults.

Intermediate Level

The transition from grade 3 to 4 is not a sharp break in a child's development. Each child has a growth pattern: individual differences continue to increase, and there is much overlapping of growth characteristics between grades. Children make rapid progress in concept attainment, tend to form more cohesive sets of values, and take a more clear-cut sex role. Physical growth in grades 4 to 6 continues to be steady, with a lag just before puberty. Some girls enter the puberty cycle, and girls are generally more advanced than boys.

Social development is marked by emerging peer values, sex cleavage, formation of groups, and increased interest in cooperative activities. Children wish to become self-directive, more independent, more self-assertive. Acceptance by their peers becomes more important, and rejection by them may create feelings of insecurity and anxiety. Rejection by adults or ridicule and sarcasm that lead to feelings of rejection also create feelings of insecurity. They need to maintain security with adults and at the same time gain a place among their peers. Middle class children are more responsive to long-range goals, more willing to comply with regulations, more respectful, less fearful of authority, and less prone to fighting than are children from lower socioeconomic classes.

Piaget's studies of intellectual development[4] indicate that from around the ages of seven to eleven children are in a stage of concrete operations; they can think in terms of concepts and symbols related to objects and actions they have experienced. Children can carry out such internalized operations as classifying objects, putting events in a series, and anticipating consequences without having objects before them, and these operations can be reversed.

Intellectual growth is marked by active curiosity, wider interests, more realistic creative expression of thoughts and feelings, refinements of reading ability, improvement of independent study skills, growth in problem-solving ability, and greater insight into causal relationships. Level of aspiration increases and is reflected in more effective self-evaluation, and in criticism of maps, murals, reports, and other materials prepared by pupils. A rapid growth in knowledge of social studies concepts occurs in grades 4 through 8. Time, distance, space, and map

[4]J. H. Flavell, *The Developmental Psychology of Jean Piaget* (Princeton, N.J.: Van Nostrand, 1963).

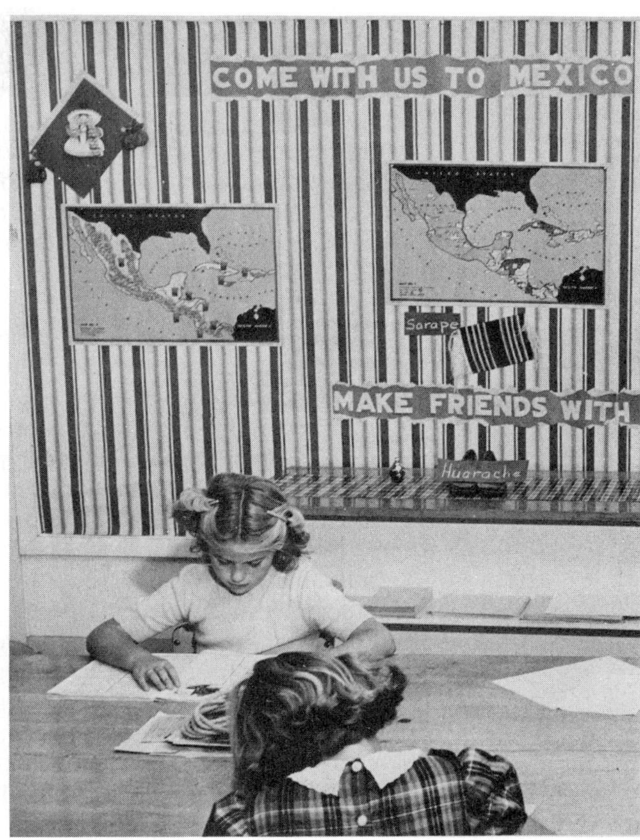

The ability to develop cross-cultural understandings may be brought to higher levels in the middle grades. What understandings might be emphasized in a study of Mexico? (San Diego City Schools, California)

concepts develop in relationship to the extent to which they are stressed in the social studies program. Chronology and historical time are difficult for children to grasp, and such concepts as latitude and longitude must be intensively taught if they are to be truly learned and put to use.

Moral development may be at the conventional level, which emerges from the age of around ten to fourteen.[5] There is maintenance and support of rules and expectations of one's family, group, and nation. Many children are in the stage characterized by a "good boy" and "nice girl" orientation. Behavior may be judged by intention—"He means well." There is conformity to avoid disapproval and dislike by individuals who are respected by one's peer group.

Social attitudes are sharpening, and some children show negative attitudes; stereotypes about other groups appear. Children from authoritarian homes tend to be more prejudiced than children from homes with a democratic atmosphere. Children show a growing sense of right and wrong and a willingness to use persuasion and reason in attaining their goals. A more critical sense of justice is expressed in fair play, teamwork,

[5] Kohlberg, *op. cit.*

being a good sport, and helping others. This sense of fair play contributes much to the success with which teachers can develop wholesome attitudes and appreciations.

Implications. A child's transition from primary to intermediate grades must be smooth. Increasing individual differences should be taken into account by including a variety of activities and materials in each unit of instruction, flexible grouping, individualized assignments, variation in time requirements, and variation in what is expected of individual children.

Teachers should give direct attention to cross-cultural understandings, geographic relationships, and historical time concepts. Comparing ways of living at home and in other lands, discovering and presenting relationships on maps, blocking out major time periods on charts and time lines, reading to discover relationships and to make comparisons, and classifying ideas under key concepts and generalizations are helpful procedures. The heavy load of terms and concepts in reading materials requires direct instruction in vocabulary development.

Individual study and group work skills can be used extensively. Teachers should have clear purposes for individual and group work, and should provide direct instruction on related skills. Classifying, interpreting, and other processes can be brought to high levels of development. Committees should be organized to gather information on topics related to questions and problems defined by the group. The use of children's weekly newspapers, clippings, magazines, newspapers, and radio and television programs should be carefully planned to extend the development of key concepts, generalizations, attitudes, and appreciations.

Thinking processes can be developed through problem solving, with emphasis not only on the *what, when, where,* and *who,* but also on the *how* and *why*. Key concepts and generalizations can be used to guide inquiry and organize data. Valuing processes can be developed by employing appropriate clarification strategies, as outlined in Chapter 7.

Creative expression should be encouraged through related language activities, artwork, construction, musical activities, weaving, making dioramas, and dramatic representation. The art, music, literature, and folk dances of early America can be used to help children identify more closely with the hopes, feelings, and aspirations of the colonists and pioneers, and similar experiences should be provided as other lands and peoples are studied.

Upper Level

The in-between age, the awkward transition from childhood to adulthood, the uneasy shift to more mature forms of behavior—this is adolescence. Many children in grades 7 and 8 are already in its beginning stages and suffering the uncertainties, the vacillation between independence and dependence, the desire for freedom from adult controls yet the need for

Creative expression reaches a high level in the middle grades. How might musical activities be used in the social studies? What other activities might be used? (School District 281, Minneapolis, Minnesota; photo by Tom Tripet)

adult guidance. They will act adult one minute and be childish the next; they want to do the right thing without revealing that they are not sure just what the right thing is. Yet some seventh- and eighth-graders (boys more frequently than girls) still exhibit characteristics of intermediate-grade children. Their physical growth rates are slower than those of girls, and they have not yet developed the physical and social characteristics that typify those entering the adolescent period. Because of differences in rate of maturation, home background, and the impact of the educational program, individual differences among pupils are great in grades 7 and 8. Reading abilities range from primary to high school level, mental abilities show great variation, and a given child may have high linguistic ability yet relatively low quantitative ability.

Certain general characteristics emerge in the upper grades. Greater identification with age mates leads children to differentiate more sharply between their own world and that of adults. Social development is marked by increasing ability to cooperate, a strong desire for group approval, and more critical selection of friends. Concern about self is great, and peer values serve as guides to behavior in many situations. Speech is patterned after that of the gang or clique. Self-criticism in terms of peer values, a desire for freedom from adult domination, and eagerness to make one's own decisions are evident. Their interests are broadening. The impact of the mass media in certain ways expands these interests, in other ways channels them. They have greater understanding of contemporary affairs at home and in other countries; at the same time, they are deeply involved in their own styles of language, modes of dress, popular music, and other aspects of the mass culture of youth. Hero worship is typical, and the behavior of "ideal types" is copied.

Piaget's studies[6] indicate that children move from the stage of concrete operations to that of formal operations around the age of eleven. In this stage they can carry on hypothetical reasoning, analyze, synthesize, and carry out other cognitive operations without being limited to their own firsthand experiences. They can handle abstractions with increasing facility and can manage a variety of logical operations if they receive appropriate instruction. Moral development is at the conventional level. There is an orientation toward conformity, fixed rules, and avoidance of censure by peers and authorities.[7]

Implications. The development of the ability to do abstract thinking, develop generalizations, and use reading-study skills opens new horizons of inquiry. Social, political, historical, economic, and geographic aspects of living in the United States, other lands, and early cultures can be studied in greater depth. Greater use can be made of multiple textbooks, library resources, and individual study projects. Practical application of democratic values and processes should be made to community living and to

[6] J. H. Flavell, op. cit.
[7] Kohlberg, op. cit.

The skills children possess at this level can be used to analyze models and other materials in depth. (Bethlehem School District, Pennsylvania)

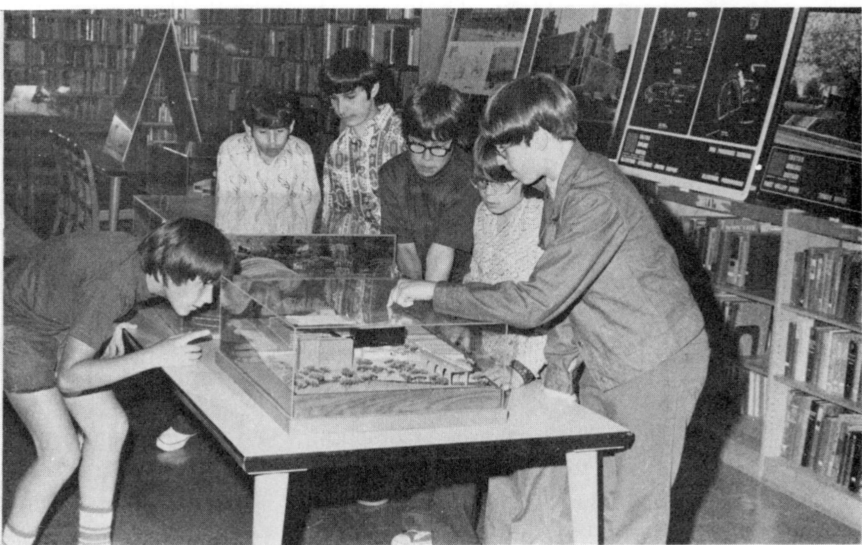

problems of government at the local, state, and national levels. As the contributions of ethnic groups are studied, individual responsibilities of citizenship and conceptions of equality and justice should be clarified and intensified.

Teachers must "understand" and meet individual differences without causing embarrassment. Sarcasm, ridicule, and talking down to pupils should be avoided. Pupils at this age want to be treated as adults, but they still need much help in handling problems arising from their schoolwork and the personal and social problems characteristic of this period of development.

Teachers should guide students' study of reading materials and other resources in order to help them detect conflicting points of view, clarify issues, and improve their ability to secure reliable sources of information. Substantial progress can be made in the analysis of propaganda and persuasion materials. Criteria for judging materials, points of view, and proposed solutions to problems are useful in improving critical thinking skills; these may be related to pupils' activities and to significant topics in the social studies program through group discussion and planning. Thinking and valuing processes may be brought to higher levels of development by using the teaching strategies outlined in Chapters 6 and 7.

PLANNING TO MEET INDIVIDUAL DIFFERENCES

Probably no factor is more important in meeting individual differences than the teacher's point of view. Teachers who truly value differences and recognize the uniqueness of each child are the ones who plan most effectively to meet individual differences. They care deeply about all children—the average as well as the gifted, disadvantaged, and less able—and they recognize that individualized instruction is a right as well as a need of all children. Without a deep concern for each child there is usually insufficient drive to do the hard work necessary to individualize instruction.

Basic Strategies and Techniques

Teachers who individualize instruction effectively are also flexibile, open to new ideas, and willing to put each child's educational welfare above arbitrary grade standards. They believe that each child's maximum growth is more important than minimum standards for the group, that some children can go far beyond grade standards, whereas others can make substantial progress only if instruction is geared to their needs. They are approachable, they welcome questions and other indications of a need for help, and they accept each child for what he or she is and can do. Instead of blaming other teachers, parents, or home and neighborhood conditions, they try to provide effective instruction for each child. Instead of being defensive when instructional problems arise, they try to find solutions to them.

Why are people important? What is special abou each individual? (Baton Rouge, Louisiana)

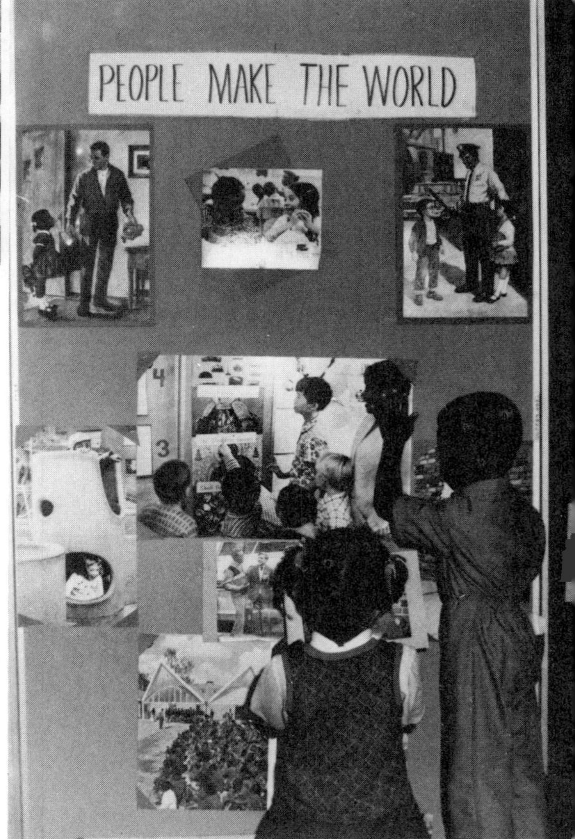

Making a diagnosis. Knowing each child—background, achievements, interests, level of mental maturity, language power, and related abilities—is essential if the teacher is to make adequate provisions for individual differences. In addition to checking cumulative records and available test data, the teacher should also informally diagnose needs during actual classroom activities. For example, as children engage in group planning, discussion, and evaluation, it is possible to identify interests, difficulties, language skills, and levels of understanding about selected topics. As children observe and interpret pictures, maps, graphs, and other resources, it is possible to identify those who need special help and those who have attained adequate levels of development. As students prepare reports, make murals, dramatize activities, and engage in other expressive experiences, it is possible to detect interests, needs for further study, and misconceptions.

Caution should be exercised in interpreting data obtained from tests. It is well known that intelligence tests do not give an accurate assessment of the ability of students from disadvantaged homes and neighborhoods, that they are not "culturally fair." Because tests and inventories designed to measure personality, attitudes, and social adjustment are less reliable than achievement and intelligence tests, their data should be interpreted in the light of continuing direct study of children as they work in the classroom.

Teachers should be careful to avoid the pitfall of self-fulfilling prophecies. For example, a child may be classified as less able, disadvantaged, or otherwise handicapped and thereafter presumed to have all the characteristics of that classification. As a consequence, instruction is shaped to fit the classification rather than the individual. Expectations may be set too low, with no challenge to move to higher levels of development or attainment. For example, a minority child in a disadvantaged neighborhood was placed in a fourth-grade classroom because the school psychologist and the teacher had used intelligence and achievement test data to establish what seemed to them to be reasonable expectations. But the teacher soon discovered that the child could reach higher levels in reading and other activities because of the ways he responded to questions, selected materials in the library corner, and participated in group discussion. Had the teacher not been alert, the student could have continued indefinitely at a low level of learning.

Varying instructional guidance and supervision. Probably no strategy for meeting individual differences can be modified and adapted on the spot more than that of varying the amount and kind of instructional assistance given by the teacher. For example, one child may need help in settling down to work, another may need help in completing an outline, and a group working on a map may be puzzled about the location of particular items. By moving about the room and observing children at work, a teacher can give guidance at the point of need. Because each child is a unique person, guidance should be personalized to fit emotional as well as intellectual needs. A smile, an encouraging comment, or an understanding nod may be just right for one child, whereas another may need a thought-provoking question, a specific suggestion, or direct assistance on a problem.

In general, children in primary grades need more supervision and direction than children in higher grades, but there are students at all levels who need special instruction while the rest of the class works on other activities. Once special needs are identified, children can be grouped at times for special instruction in vocabulary development; reading to get main ideas and supporting details; locating information; using the contents, index, and glossary in social studies books; interpreting and making maps; interpreting and making graphs, tables, and time lines; and interpreting time concepts and chronology.

The teacher's role should vary from that of instructor to that of colleague. At times a child may need and should receive a direct answer to a question on such matters as how to find a booklet, how to complete an outline, or where to locate particular items on a map. At other times the teacher may counter with a question: Have you checked the study guide? Will the outline form on the chart be useful? Do you think the atlas will be a good source? If a student needs to move ahead, then direct assistance may be given, but if the objective is to improve inquiry skills and to help students become more self-directive, then a question or comment may be adequate.

Varying levels of conceptualization. There are great differences in the levels at which children state main ideas, make interpretations of pictures and reading selections, draw inferences, and state hypotheses. For example, a less able student may interpret a picture of a harbor scene by describing the main activities, whereas a more able student may go beyond description to point out the primary function of a harbor. The aim is the progressive lifting of each student's thinking to higher levels. For example, the questions in Charts 4–1 and 4–2 begin at basic observing or recalling levels and move to interpreting, classifying, or other higher level processes.

One individualizing technique is to provide questions on different levels and to accept differing levels of achievement on the part of students. For example, some students might need to begin with the first question in Chart 4–1, Interpreting the Map of Mexico, and then answer every succeeding question in order to build their understanding to the levels represented by the last two questions; more able students might begin with the last two questions. In Chart 4–2, less able students might work with the first two questions and present findings to the class, after which all students might consider the findings as they discuss the next four questions. More able students might work on the last question and present their findings to the class for further discussion and analysis. Another adaptation for able students would be to extend Chart 4–1 to include a question such as "How is location of the three most populous cities related to terrain and transportation facilities?" Chart 4–2 could be adapted for less able students by reducing the number of industries to be studied to one or two.

The same principle can be used in adjusting expectations related to using concepts and making generalizations. For example, varied responses should be expected and accepted from students as they bring facts together and state main ideas. This can be illustrated by comparing the following generalizations, which vary in complexity and generality: (1) People in the home have different jobs. (2) Work is divided in the home and neighborhood. (3) Division of labor helps to get more work done. By accepting generalizations that fit the facts the student has collected, the teacher is making an important adjustment to each child's ability.

Varying learning activities. As noted in the chapter on unit planning, a variety of learning experiences should be provided to meet individual differences as well as to develop skills in using different types of materials. In providing for individual differences, two basic principles should be followed. First, students should have opportunities to engage in activties that they can handle with success. Out of them they should draw ideas related to questions under study so that they can share them in group planning, discussion, and evaluation. The use of students' ideas in group activities is needed to extend learning, provide for interaction, stimulate interest in further learning, and give all students a feeling that they are contributing to group goals.

The second principle is to plan and guide instruction so that every student engages in a variety of learning activities. All too frequently some students do a single activity over and over because they are good at it. For

Chart 4–1
Interpreting the map of Mexico

What does each symbol in the key stand for?
Where is the capital? What is its name?
Where are other large cities located?
Where are the main roads?
What relationships can you find between the location of cities and roads?
How are the locations of cities, roads, and mountains interrelated?

Chart 4–2
Stating Main Ideas about Mexican Industries

What data did you find on each industry?
Which facts seem to go together?
What is common or general about them?
Have the common facts and ideas been grouped together?
What can we say in general about each industry?
Do our general statements fit the facts? Are changes needed?
What is the order of importance of the industries? Why?

example, students who are talented in art may miss important learnings because they spend too much time painting and drawing. This principle should be kept in mind as you read the following section.

Providing opportunities to choose. One of the great advantages of unit instruction is that it provides students with many opportunities to choose worthwhile instructional materials. In a well-arranged classroom environment, students can select the reading materials and other resources they can handle. Teachers who are truly concerned about developing initiative and the skills involved in learning how to learn provide many such opportunities and guide students' self-evaluation of the choices made so that they grow in self-direction.

In order to optimize the educational values of students' choices, the social studies program can use principles and techniques employed in individualized reading programs. The classroom environment should include a variety of books, pictures filed by topics, tapes and records in the listening corner, slides and filmstrips in the viewing center, and maps and atlases for reference. Silent or quiet work time should be provided so that individuals and small groups can gather data related to questions and hypotheses. Some may be using textbooks, booklets, and material brought from the library while others are using materials in the different work centers. Students should be told what materials are available in each work center and how to use them, as Charts 4–3 through 4–6 illustrate, and individuals and small groups can receive additional guidance as they work

Chart 4–3
Choosing and Using Materials

Choose materials you want to use.
Use one item at a time.
Identify ideas to share.
Return the item to its place.
Choose another item. Return it when you are finished.

Chart 4–4
Did you choose well?

What ideas did you find?
Which ideas were most interesting? Most useful?
Which ideas should be shared?
Did any problems arise in using materials?
If so, what can be done to solve them?

Chart 4–5
Listening Corner

Have you listened to these?
Story of what two children did about pollution at home
Report on kinds of waste pollution
Report on steps taken to halt waste pollution in our city
Story of what one group did to help prevent waste pollution

Chart 4–6
Using Materials in the Reading Center

Top shelf: materials for the Transportation Committee
Middle shelf: materials for the Urban Renewal Committee
Bottom shelf: materials for the Pollution Committee
On the table: city map for the Mapping Committee

in centers. Records of materials used should be kept for guidance and evaluation.

Allowing for variations in time. Probably no two people ever need or take the same amount of time to complete a given activity. Certainly this is true of students as they read, get ideas from maps, prepare reports, and engage in other activities. Varying amounts of time are also needed in building readiness for the use of reading and other materials, for assimilating new concepts, and for accommodating new ideas within one's cognitive structure. Effective individualization therefore requires planning for variations in the time that may be needed to introduce a topic, collect and organize data, and express ideas in oral or written form.

Teaching children how to individualize. A new development is to provide instruction that enables children to individualize for themselves. When this is combined with steps taken by the teacher to individualize, each child's chances of getting tailored instruction are greatly improved. The guiding principle is to teach students specific ways in which they can vary materials, activities, time, individual work, group work, and standards to fit their own needs. In short, children should discover what heretofore has been kept secret by some teachers. If the goal of learning how to learn is to be achieved, children themselves must be able to identify and apply guidelines and techniques of individualization appropriate to their level of development. Charts 4–7 through 4–12 illustrate ways in which this can be done.

Chart 4–7
Because We Are Different

We vary the time on some activities.
We work together on some projects and in groups on others.
We have individual projects each of us can do.
We find materials we can use.
We give help on some things and get help on others.

Chart 4–8
Can You Find

Reading materials from which you can get ideas on questions under study?
Maps, charts, diagrams, and other aids in books and references from which you can get ideas?
Pictures and clippings in newspapers and magazines that you can use in sharing and reporting?
Other sources of ideas?

Chart 4–9
What Ideas Can You Find

On questions and problems we are studying?
For use in group planning?
For use in discussion?
For use in committees?
For use in oral or written reports?
For other uses?

Chart 4–10
Use Free Time

To work on individual projects
To listen to tapes and records related to our unit
To view slides and filmstrips related to our unit
To find ideas in the picture file
To find materials in the reading center

Chart 4–11
Do You Know How To

Use the materials in the listening center?
Find materials in the library corner?
Get ideas from pictures, maps, and charts in books too hard to read?
Find books you can use in the school library and the local library?

Chart 4–12
Help Yourself To Learn

By raising questions when you are not sure of something
By asking for help when you need it
By finding and using different materials
By getting clear directions for activities and home study
By interviewing and observing

Preplanned programs. Some schools are using preplanned programs designed to meet individual differences.[8] These programs are organized into teaching-learning units or as contracts for students to fulfill at their own rates. The units are designed for use on a self-service or self-instructional basis. The teacher's role is to choose the units that children undertake, then to diagnose and prescribe learning, assisting students as needs arise during work on the units. Some programs have been computerized to relieve the teacher of such routine details as determining the correctness of students' work and identifying next steps in learning. There is a variety of materials, ranging from books and selected readings to tapes and material projected via television.

The teacher's role in social studies instruction should in no way be diminished by the use of preplanned programs. The importance of group interaction and group problem solving in attaining key objectives makes it mandatory that self-instruction systems be used to meet specific individual needs, not as a substitute for small- or large-group activities. In all programs there should be a balance between independent and group inquiry. Preplanned programs should be viewed as an additional aid to the meeting of the individual differences, and the teacher should guide and adapt their use in the classroom along with other viable strategies and techniques.

Summary of ways to meet individual differences. The main strategies and techniques for meeting individual differences are summarized in Checklist 4–1. It is arranged so that teachers can quickly identify procedures they might use.

Planning for Differences in Reading Ability

A wide range of reading abilities may be found in any class. It is not unusual to find a five- to seven-year range of achievement in a class of middle-grade children. The following reading achievement levels for a fifth-grade class are illustrative: between second- and fourth-grade level of achievement—five children; between fourth- and sixth-grade achieve-

[8] For examples and a critique, see Vera Ohanian, "Educational Technology: A Critique," *Elementary School Journal*, 71 (January 1971), 183–97.

Checklist 4–1

CHECKLIST OF VARIATIONS AND ADJUSTMENTS TO MEET INDIVIDUAL DIFFERENCES

Diagnosis

Has information been collected on individual differences?

______ interests	______ capabilities	______ language skills
______ problems	______ reading level	______ achievement

______ other: ______________________________

Individual Study

What variations and adjustments can be made in individual research activities?

______ topics to investigate	______ depth and breadth	______ type of report
______ sources of data	______ people to interview	______ use of library
______ assistance from others	______ use of free time	______ form of presentation

______ other: ______________________________

Individual Tutorial

______ by the teacher	______ by another pupil	______ by programed material
______ by a parent	______ by a teacher aide	______ by computer

______ other: ______________________________

Subgroups

What subgroups might be formed within the class?

______ interest groups	______ groups needing special instruction
______ reading groups	______ groups to make maps, murals, and the like
______ committees	______ groups of two or three for team learning
______ work centers	______ groups for interviewing, finding materials, and the like

______ other: ______________________________

Methods and Activities

______ individual	______ small group	______ whole group
______ discovery lessons	______ expository lessons	______ home study
______ different questions for subgroups	______ different explanations for subgroups	______ varied directions for subgroups
______ different standards for individuals	______ varied assignments for individuals or groups	______ varied assessment of outcomes

______ other: ______________________________

Materials

What variations or adjustments can be made in instructional materials?

______ reading materials on various levels	______ audiovisual materials for group and individual use	______ community resources for group and individual use
______ rewritten material	______ library resources	______ work centers
______ study guides	______ practice materials	______ taped material
______ reading lists	______ use of material in kits	______ picture sets

______ other: ____

Time

What variations in time should be made for individuals and groups?

______ building readiness for use of materials	______ introducing a topic or problem	______ carrying out basic activities
______ assimilation of new ideas	______ accommoda-tion of new ideas	______ expressing one's own ideas
______ making maps and other items	______ preparing oral and written reports	______ home study and use of community resources

______ other: ____

Standards and Evaluation

What variations and adjustments should be made in expectations and assessment of outcomes?

______ quantitative	______ qualitative	______ vocabulary
______ concepts	______ information	______ main ideas
______ use of inquiry processes	______ use of map reading and other skills	______ expression of feelings
______ self-evaluation	______ evaluative charts	______ testing

______ other: ____

ment—twenty-two children; between sixth- and eighth-grade achievement—four children and above eighth-grade achievement—two children. Should a single textbook be used in such a class? No. Should the pace of the class be set by the middle group, the low group, or the high group? None of these. Differentiated planning is necessary so that each child can learn as much as possible. This does not mean that no group activity is possible, but it does mean that a variety of reading materials and activities should be provided. In order to have the right mixture, the teacher should gather background information on each child, locate and select the appropriate materials, and plan small-group and whole-class activities.

Gathering information on each child's reading abilities. A teacher may obtain information from standardized tests, from tests of his or her own devising, from tests and exercises in workbooks, and by observing children as they read selected paragraphs. This last source of information—observation—is especially helpful in getting clues to a child's ability to read social studies materials. Tests and exercises in workbooks that accompany social studies textbooks are helpful in getting specific information on such abilities as finding main ideas, noting details, using maps, and reading charts, graphs, and tables. Analysis of reading and study-skills tests provides clues to children's specific needs and problems.

After information is gathered, it should be summarized on a class sheet or on an individual card for each child and should include the items shown below.

Child's name ____________ Age ______ Grade ______ Mental age ______ Reading group ______ Scores on reading tests ______ Scores on study skills test ______ Reading level for individual reading ______ Reading level for group instruction ______ Ability to use: contents ______ indexes ______ glossaries ______ Ability to read: maps ______ graphs ______ tables ______ charts ______ diagrams ______
Ability to use: encyclopedias ______ atlases ______ dictionaries ______ card catalogs ______
Comments (special notes on reading difficulties, interests, and the like)
____
____
____
____

Locating and selecting appropriate reading materials. One of the best sources of information is the list of materials in resource units for each grade. This usually includes materials that are available in the local school system. In some school systems, kits of materials on varying readability levels have been assembled for different units and may be requisitioned by the teacher. In others, materials may be requisitioned by the teacher from the instructional materials center. Another good source is the list of additional reading materials included in basic social studies textbooks and accompanying teacher's manuals. Poems, stories, biographies, and other related materials may be included.

The room library, school library, and neighborhood or community library are excellent sources. Cooperation among teachers in sharing books contained in room libraries is helpful. For example, when such units as our community, our state, life in early America, or other lands are being studied, one can be sure that reading materials on various grade levels may be found in different classrooms.

Guides to children's books and free or inexpensive materials should be used to build up a basic collection of reading materials related to different units of instruction (see the References at the end of this chapter). Some may be placed in the classroom library, and more general materials may be placed in the school library. Free or inexpensive materials may be placed in the classroom resource file so that children can have direct access to them.

Providing for small-group and whole-class reading activities. Small-group instruction is helpful in developing needed reading skills, building vocabulary, interpreting material, providing practice, meeting needs that several children have in common, and providing for depth studies of selected topics and problems. Groups may be organized on the basis of (1) achievement level, in which those who read on approximately the same level are grouped together and materials on the appropriate level are provided for them; (2) special needs, in which students are given instruction in using the index, interpreting material, or other basic skills; (3) assigned topics, in which students are given a topic or problem to investigate in depth; (4) common interest, in which those who have chosen a topic or problem read materials related to it; and (5) partner or group-leader study, in which one child assists a partner, or two or three children, in reading selected materials.

Reading materials must be selected to meet the needs of those in each group. In achievement and special needs groups, materials are selected in accordance with level of reading ability and reading difficulties. In assigned topic and common interest grouping, materials on varying levels of readability are provided in accordance with the differing reading abilities of those in the groups. In partner and group-leader study groupings, materials on which the less able need assistance are provided.

Activities that include the whole class are provided when skills, concepts, and problems of common concern are given attention. The following examples are illustrative: providing an introduction to questions and problems at the beginning of a unit; identifying questions for further study; interpreting pictures, maps, diagrams, and other graphic aids; reviewing selected passages to highlight key concepts; oral reading of selected paragraphs by the teacher; audience reading of selected sections by pupils; reviewing key ideas presented in tables, charts, or graphs; providing instruction in the use of the glossary, index, or other parts of a book; using the index to find selected topics; and using maps and reference tables. Such activities may be followed by individual and small-

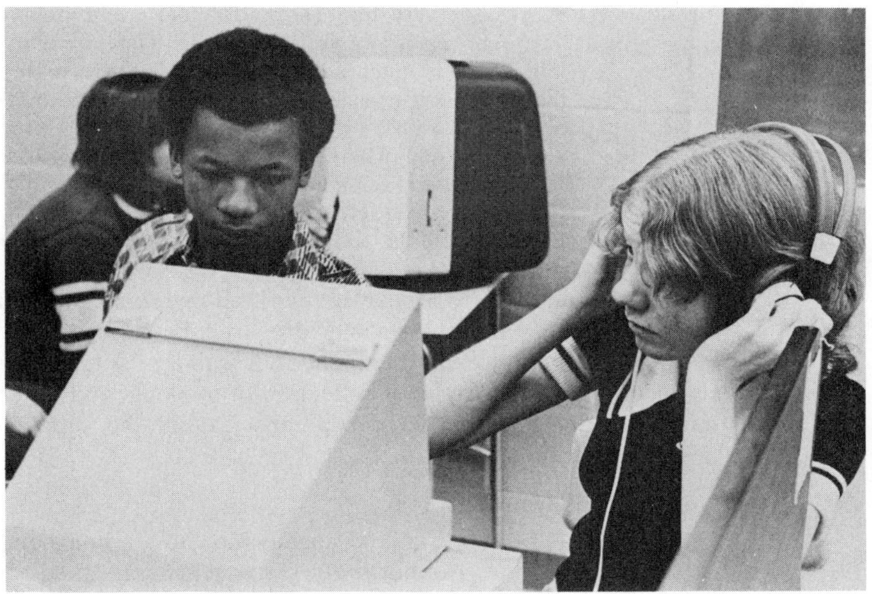

How might a listening and viewing center be used to meet individual differences? (Chichester School District, Pennsylvania)

group work in which the concepts and skills developed in whole-class activities are applied and refined.

Preparing Rewritten Material One of the most helpful procedures is to prepare or adapt such materials as articles and selections from textbooks to the students' level. A good approach is to imagine that you are writing a letter or an exciting account to a child, and to keep in mind that every idea must be expressed as simply and as clearly as possible. Vocabulary, phrasing, and sentences should be similar to those used by children. New terms should be defined as they are used, or clarified in context. Sentences and paragraphs should be short, as they are in children's periodicals. Pictures clipped from magazines may be added to clarify ideas. A collection of rewritten materials built up over a period of time greatly extends the opportunities to individualize reading in the social studies. The following example is illustrative:[9]

PEDRO MAKES HIS HOUSE

Pedro lives in a house made of bricks. In Mexico, these bricks are made of clay. This clay is called adobe. Pedro's father will put hay or straw with the clay. It makes adobe stick together. He then makes the adobe into bricks.

[9] Prepared by Mrs. Jerome F. Harrington, Oakland Public Schools, California.

The bricks are very big. They are about twenty-four inches long. They are about twelve inches wide. They are about six inches tall. There is much adobe in Mexico. There is so much adobe that many houses in Mexico are made of adobe brick.

Adobe houses can have a roof of palm leaves. They sometimes have a roof of wood. Many times they have a roof of tile. Tile is red. Have you ever seen a house with a tile roof? Pedro's father made his roof of wood. He used the wood he saw near the house. He made the roof flat and put adobe in the cracks. Can you tell why?

In addition to preparing rewritten material, some teachers adapt and edit reports and scrapbooks prepared by students in former classes. Those illustrated and couched in children's language are especially useful. By building up a collection of booklets and other items prepared by students, a teacher can greatly extend the supply of materials for different units of study.

THE DISADVANTAGED

For the disadvantaged in our society, equality of opportunity is an American ideal that has not been fulfilled. Children who come from disadvantaged homes and neighborhoods have special needs, characteristics, and capabilities that need to be identified and provided for through individualized programs of instruction that will enable them to develop their potential to the fullest. To do less is to deny them the educational opportunity without which they cannot hope to participate in any real sense in the life of this country.

Needs and Characteristics

Studies indicate[10] that disadvantaged students have several needs and characteristics in common (though there are of course differences among individual cases). Their language development is marked by the use of special expressions, limited use of adverbs and adjectives, and a group dialect that makes communication with speakers of standard English difficult. Many disadvantaged need help in overcoming self-concepts marked by feelings of insecurity, self-doubt, and low self-esteem. Such skills as observing, reading, listening, and writing may not have been emphasized in the home.

Disadvantaged students should not be confused with so-called less able or slow-learning students. They may or may not be less able, because a wide range of capabilities exists in all social groups; but what appears to be a characteristic of low ability may in fact be the consequence of lack of instruction. Nor should the disadvantaged be viewed as a single group: they may be blacks or whites from the rural South or Appalachia, Puerto Ricans, Mexicans, immigrants from eastern or southern Europe, or other students who have been denied the conditions necessary for self-fulfillment.

[10] For a detailed discussion, see the references at the end of the chapter by Bloom et al, Frost and Hawkes, and Webster.

Special Instructional Emphases

Active involvement. Direct participation in question-raising, planning, discussion, role-playing, construction, evaluation, and other activities is essential. Special provision needs to be made for reading materials, map work, writing activities, and individual study so that students are involved in work geared to their level of achievement. Rewritten material, reading charts made after a study trip, stories dictated by children and reproduced by the teacher, commercial materials on a high interest level but low reading level, maps uncluttered with detail, and construction of paper and wooden models related to topics under study are illustrative of materials and activities that can produce active involvement. Extensive use may be made of community resources as primary data sources—resource visitors, people to interview, study trips, exhibits, museums, news media. Audiovisual materials may be used to build and extend concepts and to involve children in discussions that will build language power. Specific procedures for using these materials are presented in Chapter 13.

Clear objectives and directions. Specific performance objectives are helpful in getting active involvement, providing directions, gearing work to each child's level of attainment, and assessing progress. For example, the following objectives from a unit for disadvantaged children on civil rights clearly indicate tasks for students and realistic expectations for the teacher:

Each child should develop the ability to

- State the procedures to follow in requesting help from a policeman, using information presented in class by an officer from the police department
- State orally the means of such terms and phrases as free speech, the right to legal counsel, and the right to trial by jury
- Describe at least three cases that illustrate steps to take in order to preserve one's own civil rights
- Describe procedures used in the juvenile court to make sure the defendant gets a fair hearing.

With objectives such as these, it is possible to plan clear directions and questions for students to use. For example, as case studies are presented, the teacher might ask: "What are the steps to take to make sure that your own civil rights are protected?" "Can you find three steps to take that are directly related to the problems we have been discussing in class?"

Problem solving and inquiry processes. Disadvantaged children need special help in developing problem-solving skills and related inquiry processes. A cursory examination of some materials and units of study for the disadvantaged reveals a tendency on the part of some school personnel and publishers to overlook excellent opportunities to strengthen classifying, generalizing, predicting, and other thinking skills. Yet like all children, the disadvantaged need to learn how to solve problems, make choices, evaluate alternatives, and use inquiry processes. Special help should be provided as needed so that they can observe, classify, interpret, and use other processes as effectively as other students. Charts 4–13 through 4–16 illustrate specific adaptations that are helpful. The guidelines and strategies presented in later chapters should also be used with the disadvantaged; they should not be confined to rote memory work and meaningless drill but be given the same variety of learning experiences as other children.

Chart 4–13
Good Observers

Keep their eyes and ears open.
Have a question or idea in mind to guide them.
Find something to talk about when on study trips.
Get ideas from pictures, books, maps, and people.
Check their findings with others.

Chart 4–14
Leaders from Minority Groups

What did they do that is important?
Why is it important? Who was helped?
How were they helped?
Are people still helped? How does it help us today?
Who is still helping the way they did?
What can we do now to help the way they did?

Chart 4–15
Solving Problems

Know what the problem is. Ask, if it is not clear.
Remember ideas that can be used.
Tell how you feel about it.
Help make plans to solve it.
Get ideas from pictures, books, interviews, and other sources.
Put your ideas together and tell what you think.
Use the best of all ideas to solve the problem.

Chart 4–16
Determining the Best Housing Plan

What values should we use to judge them?
How are minorities helped?
How are poor people helped?
How much it will cost each family?
How good are the housing units?
How near are playgrounds and parks?
What other things are in each plan?

Language power. Language develops as a functional tool in family and neighborhood experiences. Disadvantaged children develop their language power according to the conditions and situations that confront them in daily living. They need to be able to cope with conditions and situations outside their immediate environment. In short, they need standard English as a second dialect.

Direct instruction in the social studies program can contribute greatly to their development in standard English. Such concepts as role, rules, system, division of labor, and civil rights may be developed through stories, audiovisual materials, or other resources. After several input experiences, the related vocabulary can be developed and put to use in discussion and other activities. But care should be taken to avoid giving the impression that attempts are being made to eliminate the child's home language. The issue is not standard English vs. the dialects spoken by students. Rather, the problem is to develop the communication skills each student needs in order to function in various situations. Individual benefits from learning standard English and increasing vocabulary should be clarified in terms of the interests, concerns, and needs of the students.

Diagnosis of needs should include attention to speech patterns and the use of special terms like *They are fat cats. What's that do-hickey? wuh? cuz,* and the like. Related instruction should be provided on standard English synonyms that can be used in class instruction and that disadvantaged students can use as a second language. Reading levels can be determined by having them read from charts, texts, rewrites, or other materials on different levels of difficulty. Inquiry-oriented pictorial materials available for use in social studies should be used to develop observing, classifying, and other inquiry processes, as well as to develop language power.[11]

Need for concrete experiences. Many concrete experiences through study trips, direct contact with leaders from their subculture, and expressive activities are needed to build concepts and related vocabulary. Special attention should be given to the development of observation skills so that perceptual abilities will be sharpened. Frequent comparisons should be made between daily life as they know it and ways of life in other places under study. The here and now should serve as a base to which studies of other people and historical events are related.

Self-concept. Both informal and formal means of developing a positive self-concept can be used. Informally, steps can be taken to accept each child, respect differing backgrounds, establish reasonable expectations, and provide success in school work. The teacher serves as a role model and should develop constructive relationships with each student and establish a classroom atmosphere that nurtures wholesome relationships among students. Formally, instruction on ethnic groups represented in the classroom can be provided. The roles and contributions of individuals in the community, state and national minority leaders, and background materials on African, Asian, Puerto Rican, and Mexican heritages may be highlighted. Special attention should be given to role models drawn from different cultures and ethnic groups. All groups that

[11] For example, see Ruth H. Grossman and John U. Michaelis, *Schools, Families, Neighborhoods: A Multimedia Readiness Program* (Menlo Park, Calif.: Addison-Wesley, 1972).

have contributed to and are a part of our society should be represented. Attention should also be given to detecting and assessing unfair treatment of individuals and groups in instructional materials and in the study of current affairs.

Of special importance is the student's own answer to the question "Who am I?" The social studies program includes experiences that will help each student as he or she seeks an answer. For example, many opportunities are provided for students to try different roles, pursue individual interests, engage in self-evaluation, discover how they are like and different from other children, and compare their thoughts and feelings with those of others. Of key importance is the students' discovery of their own strengths and weaknesses, values and interests, likes and dislikes, and other affective dimensions of behavior. Of critical importance is a warm and sensitive teacher who is available to students as they reach out on occasion for assistance in discovering who they are.

Two related questions are of equal importance: "Who are we?" and "Who are they?" These questions take on meaning in studies of ethnic groups, units on Africa, Latin America, and other areas, and studies of our own country. Students are members of many groups and need to know who "we" are if they are to truly understand themselves. Similarly, a focus on who "they" are opens up new conceptions of self as similarities and differences in roles and activities of others are discovered. Another benefit should be attitudes, feelings, and understandings about others that are more positive because they are based on evidence rather than on myths, stereotypes, or hearsay.

THE LESS ABLE

Less able or slower learning children have several characteristics that should be kept in mind as instruction is planned. In general, they have shorter attention spans and less ability to concentrate and to transfer learning than do average students. They need extra stimulation and encouragement to motivate learning, and praise, commendation, and immediate rewards when they complete activities. A variety of concrete firsthand experiences should precede any attempts to infer, generalize, or synthesize because of difficulties they have in working with abstractions. They need to experience success.

Less able students also need practical and immediate objectives so that interest can be sustained and feedback on achievement is not delayed. Questions and hypotheses designed to guide their study should be the type that they can handle in short periods of time, usually within a given work period, as shown in Charts 4–17 through 4–20.

Additional care and time may be needed in giving directions for activities and in providing explanations of concepts and themes encountered in instructional materials. Provision should be made for recalling and reviewing basic concepts and concept clusters essential to the devel-

Chart 4–17
Observing and Comparing Jobs of Workers

Use the pictures that show workers who build houses
Put the pictures of carpenters in one group
Put the pictures of plumbers in another group.
Do the same for electricians and roofers.
How is their work alike? How is it different?

Chart 4–18
Finding Out about Cities

What can you find in our new book on cities to show the items listed below?
transportation
housing
business
industry
urban renewal
zones in a city

Chart 4–19
Questions To Guide Study of Air Pollution

What does the rewrite tell about air pollution?
What is the main cause?
What are other causes?
What is the effect on trees?
What can be done to reduce air pollution?

Chart 4–20
Contributions of Minority Group Leaders

Select two leaders from the picture file.
Read the paragraph under each picture.
What is the leader's name?
What was his most important contribution?
How did he help us? How did he help others?

opment of an understanding of the main ideas in a given unit. At times it may be necessary to take a small group aside to give special help in interpreting a map, identifying special features presented in a flow chart, or discussing ideas presented in a film or filmstrip that are directly related to questions under study.

Experience charts based on firsthand experiences are useful in concept development and improvement of reading skills. For example, after a study trip to a dairy farm the teacher may write down main ideas the children contributed. By stating them in the children's own language and using them as reading material in subsequent activities, the teacher can reinforce learning and improve skills in reading social studies material. Similarly, rewritten material, original material prepared by the teacher, and material selected from reports prepared by students and edited by the teacher can be used to extend learning and improve competence in reading. Checklist 4–2 contains specific techniques that are helpful.

Checklist 4–2

PLANNING FOR LESS ABLE OR SLOWER LEARNING STUDENTS

_____ Variations and adjustments in reading materials made as noted in Checklist 4–1
_____ Additional explanations to clarify purposes, questions, or directions for activities
_____ Provision for review and extra practice to clinch key learnings and build a base for extended learning
_____ Emphasis on concrete and specific rather than on abstract and verbal presentations and discussions of ideas related to topics under study
_____ Extended time to complete basic map work, preparation of oral reports, and other core activities
_____ Provision of simplified study guides based on pictures, diagrams, and charts.
_____ Number of concepts and level of concept development adjusted to challenge but not frustrate each student
_____ Provision of opportunities for creative expression through art, music, dramatic activities, construction, and other activities so that the thrill of expressing oneself becomes a part of the less able child's learning in the social studies
_____ Provision to utilize special talents in drawing, painting, making models, constructing objects, making maps, and the like
_____ Identification of special contributions less able students can make in discussion and other activities such as reporting findings gleaned from pictures, maps, charts, diagrams, and easy-level reading materials
_____ Identification of students with whom they can work effectively in team learning, committee work, making murals, arranging displays, preparing group reports, planning contributions to discussion, and other group activities
_____ Appropriate reading, visual, and auditory materials arranged in learning centers
_____ Provision for making summaries of achievement at frequent intervals to provide knowledge of progress and encouragement
_____ Attention to regular feedback on progress, commendation for effort, and constructive assistance in self-evaluation in order to provide motivation
_____ Provision for home study with guided home cooperation in finding and using reading materials, pictures, clippings, current events, and other items related to topics under study

THE GIFTED

Academically talented and gifted students come from all ethnic groups and socioeconomic backgrounds. Some may have academic or intellectual potential far beyond those of their peers. Others may have special talents in artistic, literary, or other forms of expression. Still others may have a combination of intellectual, physical, and social potential that are exceptionally high. These children need a balanced program so that they can attain optimum growth in all the objectives established for the social studies program. To overemphasize knowledge outcomes at the expense of inquiry processes or group work skills is not recommended. Nor should a student with special talent in art be made to spend too much time "making murals for the group" at a cost of neglecting other vital learnings. Like all children, talented children need learning experiences that develop all their potential. Checklist 4–3 gives specific techniques for working with the gifted.

Checklist 4–3

VARIATIONS AND ADJUSTMENTS FOR GIFTED STUDENTS

______ Provision of a variety of challenging reading materials, maps, and other sources to optimize development of inquiry skills

______ Provision of a balanced program of activities to promote well-rounded development of intellectual, social, physical, and emotional growth

______ Extension of learning by means of additional opportunities to formulate hypotheses, draw inferences, state generalizations, synthesize main ideas, and contrast points of view

______ Provision of many opportunities for independent inquiry, use of library and community resources, and synthesis of data from several sources

______ Emphasis on self-direction and self-evaluation and individual growth and achievement through practice activities and group work that meet individual needs

______ Encouragement of individual initiative and planning, leadership, concern for others, sharing, teamwork, and regard for different types of contributions

______ Provision of direct instruction and guidance to develop basic skills, concepts, inquiry processes, and emotional stability and to avoid gaps or deficiences in essential learning

______ Extension of learning through wide reading of materials that take students far beyond basic and supplementary texts

______ Emphasis on positive traits and attitudes such as individualism without being overbearing, self-criticism without being overly critical of others, and respect for intellectual attainment without lack of regard for other accomplishments

______ Provision of opportunities for creative expression in individual and group work, oral and written reports, map making, construction, and other activities

______ Avoidance of activities that may be needed by other students but are boring or irrelevant to the needs and pace of learning of students, such as reteaching of selected material, reviews of concepts taught earlier in the week, drill on terms that may be useful for less able students, and other items already mastered by students

_____ Provision of home study with planned home cooperation to extend and enrich reading, construct models and other objects, use library resources, visit places, and interview experts to gather data on topics under study

QUESTIONS, ACTIVITIES, EVALUATION

1. Discuss the growth characteristics and implications suggested for different levels. Visit a class and note other characteristics that might be added to those presented in this chapter.
2. Visit an elementary classroom and note the following:
   a. Differences among children in the use of language, work habits, involvement in activities, and the like
   b. Techniques used by the teacher and activities provided to meet individual differences
   c. Work centers in the classroom and materials that might be used to meet individual differences
3. How might the basic strategies and techniques for meeting individual differences be put to use in a unit you are planning? Which are easiest to use? Which are hardest?
4. How can the problem of obtaining reading materials on varying levels of difficulty be handled in a unit you are planning? Can you find an article and rewrite it on an easy level? What resources are available in local libraries? In what ways might the use of available textbooks be adapted?
5. Select two or three of the charts presented in this chapter and adapt them for use in a unit you are planning.
6. Which of the suggestions for disadvantaged, less able, and gifted children can you put to use in a unit you are planning?
7. What is your position on each of the following problems?
   a. Studying cumulative records on children without becoming prejudiced against some of them
   b. Meeting the needs of the average child while giving special attention to other children
   c. Putting individual growth of each child ahead of minimum grade standards
   d. Avoiding the attachment of a stigma to activities and subgroups for less able or disadvantaged children

REFERENCES

BANKS, JAMES A., and W. W. JOYCE, eds., *Teaching Social Studies To Culturally Different Children.* Reading, Mass.: Addison-Wesley, 1973. Articles on problems, learning, teaching strategies.

BLOOM, BENJAMIN S., ALLISON DAVIS, and ROBERT HESS, *Compensatory Education for Cultural Deprivation.* New York: Holt, Rinehart, and Winston, 1965. Analysis of needs and differences.

BRUNK, JASON W. *Child and Adolescent Development.* New York: Wiley, 1975. Discussion of various aspects of development followed by selected readings.

CRAIG, ROBERT, WILLIAM MEHRENS, and HARVEY CLARIZIO, *Contemporary Educational Psychology: Concepts, Issues, Applications.* New York: Wiley, 1975. Applications to goals, development, learning, instruction, classroom dynamics, and evaluation.

DALLMAN, MARTHA, ROGER L. ROUCH, LYNETTE Y. C. CHANG, and JOHN J. DEBOER, *The Teaching of Reading* (4th ed.). New York: Holt, Rinehart, and Winston, 1974. Detailed guide to all phases of reading instruction.

FROST, JOE L., and GLENN R. HAWKES, eds., *The Disadvantaged Child.* Boston: Houghton Mifflin, 1970. Readings on characteristics and instructional guidelines.

GORMAN, RICHARD M., *Discovering Piaget: A Guide for Teachers.* Columbus, O.: Merrill, 1972. Practical presentation according to levels of schooling.

GOWAN, JOHN C., and E. PAUL TORRANCE, eds., *Educating the Ablest.* Itasca, Ill.: Peacock, 1971. Curriculum and instructional suggestions.

HOFFMAN, ALAN J., and THOMAS F. RYAN, *Social Studies and the Child's Expanding Self.* New York: Intext, 1973. Implications of Piaget's stages of development, conceptual teaching, illustrative activities.

KARLIN, ROBERT, *Teaching Elementary Reading.* New York: Harcourt, Brace, Jovanovich, 1975. Chapter on meeting individual differences.

MICHAELIS, JOHN U., and EVERETT KEACH, *Readings on Strategies in Elementary Social Studies.* Itasca, Ill.: Peacock, 1972. See readings on individual differences and the disadvantaged.

O'BRIEN, CARMEN, *Teaching the Language-Different Child to Read.* Columbus, O.: Merrill, 1973. Procedures and examples.

Focusing Questions

What concepts, concept clusters, themes, and generalizations can be drawn from the social sciences?

How are concepts used to prepare inquiry-conceptual questions?

What values, models, modes, and methods of inquiry may be put to use in the social studies program?

Drawing Instructional Elements from the Social Sciences

In every area of the curriculum, the program of instruction is based on material drawn from fundamental disciplines. The disciplines are sources of content for both the conceptual and the process aspects of instructional planning, but the success with which any program of instruction is implemented depends in large measure on the teacher's understanding of the disciplines themselves.

This chapter focuses on a selection of disciplines used in planning the social studies program. Emphasis is on the substantive and inquiry components of structure used to organize the curriculum. The references at the end of the chapter contain additional information that may be used to strengthen understanding of the social sciences in general and various disciplines in particular.

CORE DISCIPLINES

The social studies program draws content from geography, history, economics, political science, anthropology, sociology, psychology, and philosophy. Aspects of law are receiving increased attention, and material from art, music, and literature continues to be important in culture studies. A few points about the general nature of the disciplines of primary importance in planning should be noted. Geography, history, and anthropology are highly integrative disciplines. Geography is rooted in both the physical and social sciences, and in the schools it is used to give a well-rounded view of areas under study. History includes material from the social sciences and such humanities as art, literature, and philosophy and gives an integrated view of human events in various periods of time. Cultural anthropology deals with the whole culture of a people, their values, beliefs, social organization, economic activities, political life, esthetic and spiritual expression, technology, and artifacts. These three disciplines are used extensively to integrate or relate content: geography in a spatial context, history in a time context, and anthropology in a cultural context.

Political science and economics are more specialized and focus directly on two basic human activities. Material from these two disciplines may be embedded in units based primarily on history, geography, or anthropology, or it may be presented in separate units of instruction. The trend is clearly to give more attention to economics and political science at all levels of instruction.

Sociology and social psychology are closely related to anthropology and are sources of concepts (such as roles, groups, institutions, processes of interaction, and social control) used extensively throughout the social sciences and in social studies. These fields contribute much to the study of contemporary societies, social problems, and social change. They also provide, along with anthropology, economics, and political science, many concepts used in cultural geography and history.

Philosophy provides concepts and methods of analysis and reasoning invaluable in social studies and used throughout the social sciences. Inferring, using criteria to make judgments, finding fallacies in statements, and studying the grounds for beliefs all call for logical analysis and reasoning. In fact, much of what is done in the social studies in the name of problem solving and critical thinking is relatable to philosophic modes of study.

Several features of the disciplines from which the bulk of social studies content is drawn are shown in Chart 5–1, which includes concepts that are used as organizing centers for structuring information. Notice that for history a time gap is shown by means of a broken line to highlight the fact that past events are not observable and so must be studied nonempirically by referring to whatever records or other remains are available to the historian. Notice also that historical data may be structured around themes within periods, by areas (such as countries), and around topics (such as the Constitution). The section on geography shows how four central concepts may be used to structure the myriad of detailed information on the location of various phenomena. The other sections include selected concepts connected to show interrelationships. For example, decisions made in the economic system are central in determining production, income, consumption and so on. The study of political behavior calls for the use of several concepts such as those placed around political system. The study of culture calls for study of patterns of behavior in four areas, as noted in the anthropology section. The section on sociology illustrates the breadth of study involved in analyzing society. The section on psychology shows key concepts related to the study of the behavior of individuals and groups. Central concepts from philosophy are illustrative of key values, processes, and behaviors central to making judgments.

Identifying Structural Components

One step in good planning is to have a concise statement of the structural components of core disciplines. There is no agreement on a single structure for any given discipline, nor is a consensus likely in the near future. However, many helpful statements have been prepared for use in developing programs.[1] In these statements, both conceptual and inquiry components may be identified. The conceptual components are *concepts,* such as culture, region, values, division of labor, role; *concept clusters,* such as factors of production (land, labor, capital, knowhow); *themes,* such as the growth of industry, the westward movement; and *generalizations,* such as, culture is a primary determiner of how people use the environment. The inquiry components of structure are *values of inquiry,* such as objectivity, open-mindedness, search for truth; *models of inquiry,* including such phases as defining the problem, stating questions or hypotheses to guide study, classifying and interpreting data, and drawing conclusions; and *methods and materials of inquiry,* such as content analysis of source materials, interviews of individuals, and examination of objects.

Most programs include all of these in one form or another. Concepts and concept clusters may be identified in all materials that are based on the social sciences. Generalizations and themes are widely used in organizing content and learning experiences in units of instruction. Values, models, and methods of inquiry are used in varying degrees, depending on the extent to which inquiry is emphasized in the program.

CONCEPTUAL COMPONENTS OF STRUCTURE

What teachers need are concise summaries of the conceptual components included in materials to use as a checklist for instructional planning. Each of the summaries presented in the following pages is based on a review of the references cited at the end of this chapter and on materials available to students. Key concepts have been identified for each discipline. Examples of widely used concept clusters have been included to emphasize the point that many key concepts are multidimensional—that is, they include other concepts that must be given specific

[1]See, for example, John U. Michaelis and A. Montgomery Johnston, eds., *The Social Sciences: Foundations of the Social Studies* (Boston: Allyn and Bacon, 1965); Irving Morrisssett, ed., *Concepts and Structures in the New Social Science Curricula* (Lafayette, Ind.: Social Science Education Consortium, Purdue University, 1966); and Raymond Muessig and Vincent Rogers, *Social Science Seminar Series* (Columbus, O.: Merrill, 1965).

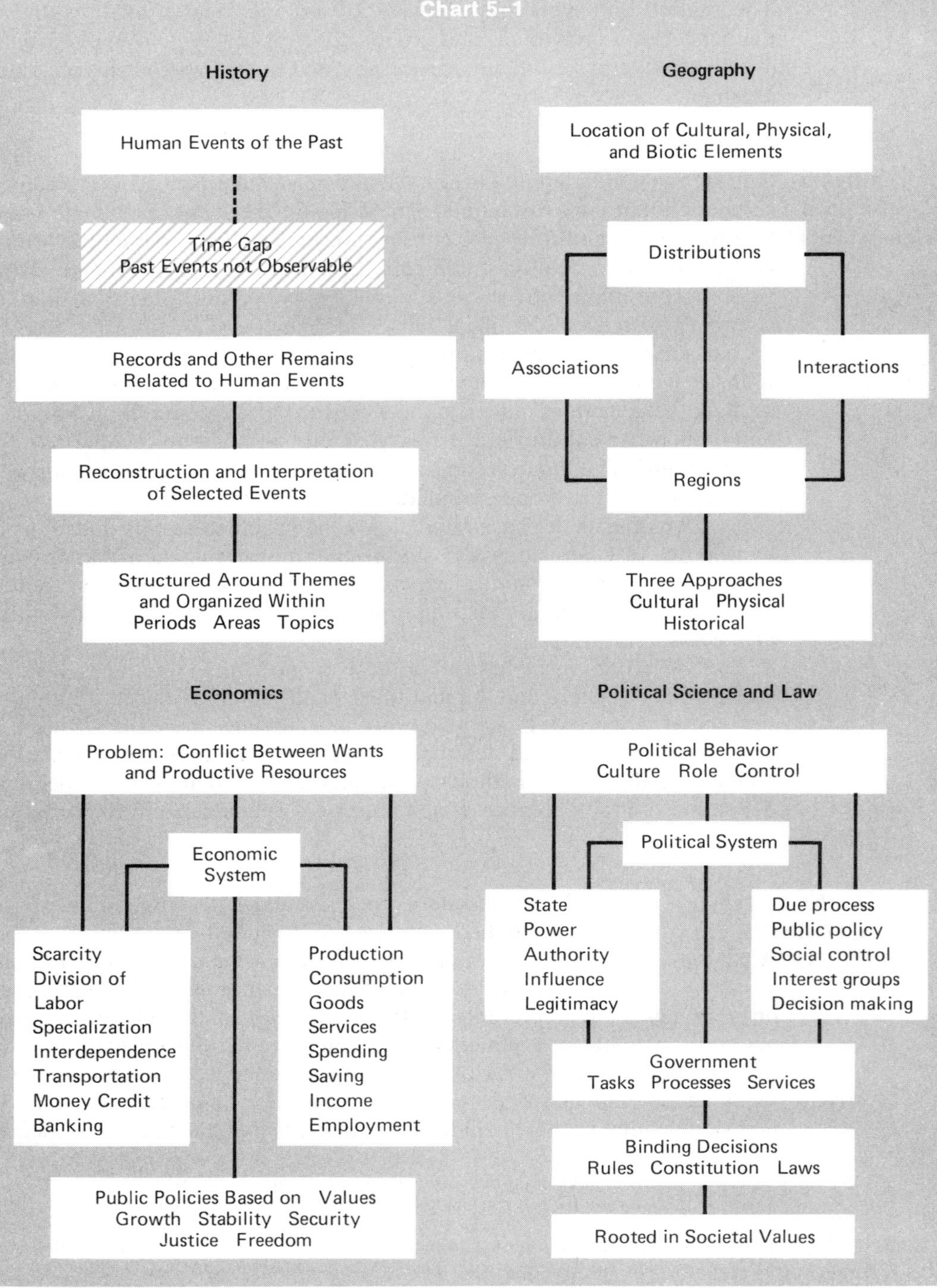
Chart 5–1
History
Human Events of the Past
Time Gap
Past Events not Observable
Records and Other Remains
Related to Human Events
Reconstruction and Interpretation
of Selected Events
Structured Around Themes
and Organized Within
Periods Areas Topics
Geography
Location of Cultural, Physical,
and Biotic Elements
Distributions
Associations
Interactions
Regions
Three Approaches
Cultural Physical
Historical
Economics
Problem: Conflict Between Wants
and Productive Resources
Economic
System
Scarcity
Division of
Labor
Specialization
Interdependence
Transportation
Money Credit
Banking
Production
Consumption
Goods
Services
Spending
Saving
Income
Employment
Public Policies Based on Values
Growth Stability Security
Justice Freedom
Political Science and Law
Political Behavior
Culture Role Control
Political System
State
Power
Authority
Influence
Legitimacy
Due process
Public policy
Social control
Interest groups
Decision making
Government
Tasks Processes Services
Binding Decisions
Rules Constitution Laws
Rooted in Societal Values

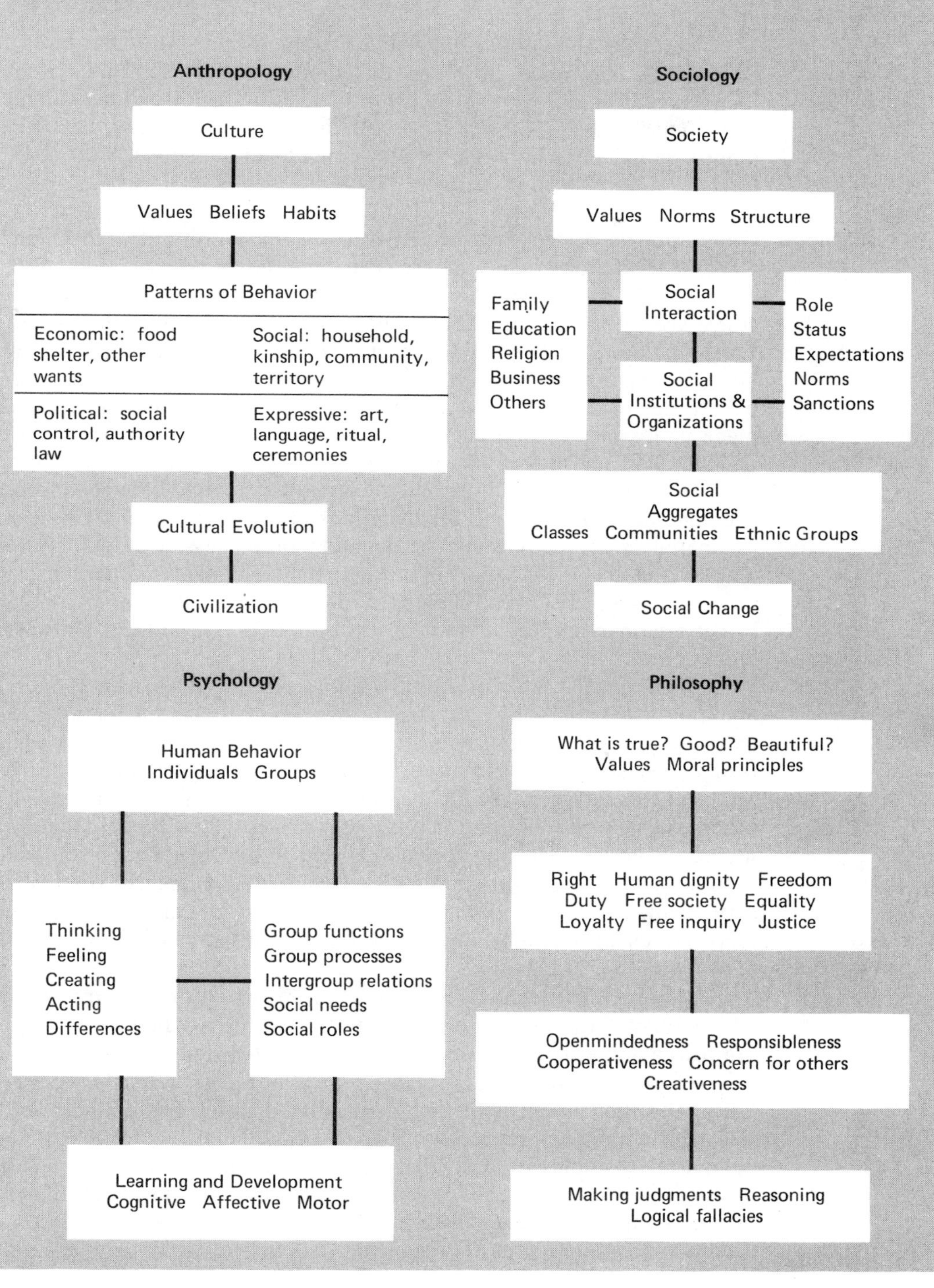

Anthropology
Culture
Values Beliefs Habits
Patterns of Behavior
Economic: food shelter, other wants
Social: household, kinship, community, territory
Political: social control, authority law
Expressive: art, language, ritual, ceremonies
Cultural Evolution
Civilization
Sociology
Society
Values Norms Structure
Family
Education
Religion
Business
Others
Social Interaction
Social Institutions & Organizations
Role
Status
Expectations
Norms
Sanctions
Social Aggregates
Classes Communities Ethnic Groups
Social Change
Psychology
Human Behavior
Individuals Groups
Thinking
Feeling
Creating
Acting
Differences
Group functions
Group processes
Intergroup relations
Social needs
Social roles
Learning and Development
Cognitive Affective Motor
Philosophy
What is true? Good? Beautiful?
Values Moral principles
Right Human dignity Freedom
Duty Free society Equality
Loyalty Free inquiry Justice
Openmindedness Responsibleness
Cooperativeness Concern for others
Creativeness
Making judgments Reasoning
Logical fallacies

attention. The examples of generalizations are illustrative of those stressed in newer materials.

Teachers should add other items to the lists as particular units are planned. Bear in mind, however, that though a list is helpful in giving a focus to central ideas, no single list of ideas from the disciplines can meet all planning needs. A sound position is to view concepts as tools of inquiry to use in formulating inquiry-conceptual questions.

Geography

Geography is drawn upon extensively in most units of instruction to clarify the characteristics of areas under study and the interaction of people with their environment. Five basic approaches to geographic study are given varying degrees of emphasis throughout the program. Earth science or physical geography is the study of landforms, water bodies, climate, and other physical features. Area or regional geography brings together the physical and cultural features that give the particular place its distinctive characteristics. Cultural geography focuses on ways of living and on human use of resources and ecology, with attention to relationships between culture and the environment, and between resource use and adaptations to and modifications of the environment. Locational or spatial approaches focus on location of places, relations between places, and the distribution or arrangement of cities, populations, and other features. Historical geography deals with changes over time and brings together selected aspects of physical, regional, cultural, and spatial approaches.

Such special fields of study within geography as urban, economic, and political geography are also drawn upon to enrich learning. For example, concepts from urban geography such as zones of a city, specialized cities, settlement patterns, and central places are included. They are used to analyze inner, middle, and outer zones of students' own and other cities; to identify and classify specialized cities as manufacturing, transport, government, or commercial cities; and to identify settlement patterns within a given region on a continuum that ranges from isolated settlement, village and town, to suburb, city, metropolitan area, and megalopolis (area stretching from north of Boston through New York to south of Washington, D.C.).

Major cities such as New York, Chicago, London, and Tokyo, which serve large areas from a central core, are studied separately as are towns and cities that serve relatively smaller areas. Special attention is given to the goods and services central cities provide, their accessibility, and their importance in the social, economic, and political activities of the people they serve. Urban sprawl may be investigated in comparative studies of cities that have mushroomed outward in a series of concentric circles, strips, and other patterns. The sphere of influence of a city may be studied in terms of the impact of its activities on its satellite cities and towns. The internal structure of a city may be studied starting with streets in the neighborhood and extending to transportation networks; how the land is used in inner, middle, and outer zones for business, industrial, residential, recreational and other purposes; the location of the central business district; relationships to the suburbs; and social variation as reflected in ethnic enclaves and ghettos and in residential areas that reflect differing income levels.

Concepts from economic and political geography are used in studies of conflcts between communities, states, and nations; changing of boundaries; the struggle for resources; and trade between areas. The importance of wise use and conservation of resources is accentuated in studies of resource use beginning with the local community and extending to studies centered in areas round the world. The importance of resources along with capital, labor, and knowhow, a key concept cluster in economics and economic geography, is helpful in analyzing and comparing selected countries and regions. Of paramount importance is the steady growth of the concept of interdependence that begins to emerge in a local context and is extended and deepened throughout the program to lead to the concept of global interdependence.

One of the most pervasive impacts of geography is in instruction on map and globe concepts and skills and map making. Because of the importance of these skills, Chapter 14 is devoted to teaching strategies that have been found to be effective. The examples given here focus on the overall concepts, concept clusters, illustrative generalizations, and inquiry-conceptual questions that may be drawn from geography as a discipline.

CONCEPTS

The environment; earth-sun relationships; location, distribution, association, interaction; region and regionalizing; cultural, physical, and biotic elements; resources; population, urbanization; culture regions; change; the globe, maps

CONCEPT CLUSTERS

The environment: spheres (hydrosphere, lithosphere, atmosphere, biosphere or life layer), human elements (people and their works), physical elements (land, water bodies, climate), biotic elements (plants, animals)

Earth-sun relationships: source of energy, rotation, revolution, inclination and parallelism of axis, circulation of atmosphere, seasons, night and day

Location: position (absolute—latitude and longitude; relative—near a known place); site (natural location such as island, continental, or maritime location); situation such as relative location expressed by such terms as strategic, central, or adjacent

Major landforms: plains, hills, plateaus, mountains

Water bodies: rivers, lakes, bays, straits, seas, oceans

Natural resources: water, soil, animal life, plant life, minerals, climate

Factors in climate: sunlight, temperature, precipitation, humidity, winds, altitude, latitude, major water bodies, mountain systems, ocean currents

Population: size, distribution, centers, density, composition, growth rate, movement, prediction, control, problems, productive potential

Settlement patterns: isolated, village, town, suburb, city, metropolis, megalopolis

Urbanization: growth of urban centers, central cities, location, functions, internal structure (residence, business, industry), interaction with other places, accessibility, changing occupancy patterns, migration, invasion, segregation, desegregation, redevelopment, urban sprawl, urban planning

Specialized cities: manufacturing, commercial, transport, port, government, other

City structure: inner, middle, outer zones; central business district; residential, industrial, suburban areas

Culture regions: Western, non-Western: European, Soviet, Middle Eastern, North African, Southwest Asian, South Asian, Southeast Asian, East Asian, African, Anglo-American, Latin American, Australian-New Zealand, Pacific

Directions: cardinal, intermediate, north and south along meridians, east and west along parallels

The globe: land and water areas; the equator; parallels, meridians; Prime Meridian, International Date Line, Tropic of Cancer, Tropic of Capricorn; high, middle, and low latitudes; hemispheres (northern, southern, eastern, western); land, water; day, night

Maps: data, scale, projection, symbols, legend

Map symbols: lines, points, colors, signs, words

GENERALIZATIONS

The location and productive activities of a community are key factors in its interaction with other places.

People everywhere identify and use resources in ways that are shaped by their culture.

Regions defined in terms of one or more common features may vary depending upon the time period and objective of inquiry.

Urbanization has necessitated the redevelopment of cities and the advantageous use of space.

Change takes place constantly on the earth's surface.

What landforms are most evident? What patterns do they make? Where are the Great Plains? (Social Studies Workshop, University of California, Berkeley)

INQUIRY–CONCEPTUAL QUESTIONS

What are natural resources? [defining]

What do you think Japan can produce with such limited natural resources? [hypothesizing]

What are the advantages and disadvantages of urbanization? [evaluating]

What kind of map should we make to bring together and show how transportation routes and cities are interrelated? [synthesizing]

Four of the spatial concepts listed above merit special comment because they may be used to structure geographic data within regions of varying size. These four concepts are helpful in any unit that deals with the spatial arrangement of surface features, and they can be used at all levels of instruction if they are couched in appropriate language. Because of their great usefulness, definitions and examples are presented below along with questions that illustrate how they may be used to guide the study of topics at various levels.

Spatial distribution. The pattern or arrangement of phenomena on the earth's surface. Examples are homes around the school, residence and business sections of a community, highways, wheat-growing areas, population, minerals, climates, mountain systems, and drainage systems in selected areas. Illustrative questions:

How are homes arranged around our school? [observing]
What is the population distribution along the East Coast? [interpreting]
How can we show the distribution of population on our map? [synthesizing]

Areal association. How distributions are related, how they tend to be found together. Examples are homes and schools, homes and shopping centers, plains and farming, cattle and corn production, and harbors and shipping. Illustrative questions:

Why are homes and schools usually found near each other? [generalizing]
What do you think we will find out about how cattle and corn production are related? [hypothesizing]
How can we explain the relation between elevation and kind of vegetation? [interpreting]

Spatial interaction. The flow, movement, or circulation of phenomena. Examples are the movement of children to and from school, people to and from stores, ideas via newspapers and other mass media, and goods and people via transportation networks. Illustrative questions:

How do we get from home to school and back? [recalling]
How can we show what is brought from other cities into our city? [synthesizing]
How are goods, people, and ideas circulated throughout our state? [generalizing]

Region. A defined area that is relatively homogeneous in one or more characteristics. Examples are neighborhoods in a community, defined areas around the community, regions of a state or the United States, regions within other countries, and culture regions of the world.

Illustrative questions:

> What is the area around our school? [recalling]
> How might our state be divided into regions? [analyzing]
> What regions can we find in our books? [observing]
> Why were they grouped that way? [inferring]

The last question is designed to develop an understanding of regionalizing as the process of using criteria to define regions. Experiences in all grades should contribute to competence in handling the concept of regionalizing as students define regions for various purposes and discover the reasons why others have defined regions in similar and different ways.

Notice in Chart 5–2 how basic concepts are used in studies of areas or regions that may vary in size from local areas to states, regions, coun-

Chart 5–2
Model for Study of an Area

Focusing Questions

What is the location of the items below? What patterns of distribution can we find?
Which of the items tend to go together? What patterns of association can we find?
What relationships are there between and among items? What patterns of interaction can we find?
How can the area be defined as a region? What characteristics or criteria should we use?

The Physical Setting

Space: area, shape, natural and political boundaries, relation to other areas
Landforms: plains, hills, plateaus, mountains, patterns made by them
Water: underground, rivers, lakes, bays, straits, coastlines, other
Climate: temperature—range, average; growing season; precipitation—average, seasonal amounts, causes
Resources: soil, water supply, vegetation, animal life, minerals

The People—Human Activities

Population: number, growth rate, shifts, settlement patterns, central cities
Economics: agriculture, industry, trade, transportation, communication, relations to other areas
Political setup: ideology, government, administrative units, relation to other areas
Culture: links to others, values, social classes, institutions, art, music, literature, changes, history
Problems and plans: economic, political, health, education, urban, ecological, other

tries or groups of countries. The key concepts distribution, association, interaction, and region serve as guides to analyzing and synthesizing data on the physical setting and the people and their activities. Notice also how concepts from several disciplines are used, particularly in the study of people and their activities. The order of study may vary in several ways: people or setting first, variable order in studying the physical setting and the people, shuttling back and forth between the setting and people. A typical order in instructional materials is to clarify the setting and then consider how people have used and changed the environment.

Some cautions. Several points should be made regarding problems related to the use of geography in the social studies program. Because so many facts are available on various cultures, cities, and regions, it is easy to fall into the trap of teaching a mass of facts about a variety of topics. It is far better to provide for study of selected areas in depth and to view facts as data to be used in solving problems, answering inquiry-conceptual questions, and testing hypotheses. Data should be organized around concepts, concept clusters, and generalizations as students investigate the use of resources, adaptations to the environment, why cities have developed in some places and not in others, values and levels of technology, and the like. A related pitfall is to emphasize superficial and romanticized studies of bizarre and exotic features of various lands and peoples. The inevitable outcomes are stereotypes and misconceptions.

A curricular issue in the middle and upper grades is the value of a depth study of selected cultures in an area vs. an overall study of cultures in the area. The issue has been resolved in some schools by giving an overview of a large region or area followed by an intensive study of one or more representative cultures or countries within the area. Care must be taken so that pupils do not generalize about all countries within the area on the basis of the study of a single country. Although certain common geographic, economic, political, and cultural characteristics are to be found among countries in the Middle East, in Africa, or in Latin America, specific differences exist that can be grasped only through the study of each country in detail. When representative countries are studied, pupils should understand that the purpose is to get a view of certain characteristics that are generally typical of the area, but that may be manifested differently in other countries. For example, aspirations to improve standards of living, provide better educational and health services, increase industrail output, and obtain stable government are characteristic of many countries in Africa, but the specific ways and means employed to attain them vary greatly from country to country.

The outmoded concept of environmental determinism has been rooted out of most new materials and should be rooted out of instruction. Geographers take the position that environmental conditions are key factors to consider in relation to ways of living, how people cope with the environment, how they adapt to it, and how they use their technology, but not as factors that *cause* ways of living. If this were so, for example, people in desert areas would all live the same way. Students can quickly discover differences in ways of living in similar environments and interpret them in terms of differences in culture. And they can discover how interaction with the environment changes as changes occur in a people's culture by studying their own community, state, and nation as well as other lands.

When referring to places relative to the equator, the phrases *middle latitudes, high latitudes,* and *low latitudes* should be used instead of *temperate, frigid,* and *torrid zones.* The latter are climatic rather than locational terms, and are not accurate descriptions of climatic conditions in the particular zones they are used to designate. However, since some writers still use the terms, children should become acquainted with them and understand the inaccuracies and limitations that exist in their usage. An example of how one group of children in the sixth grade handled this problem is shown in Chart 5–3.

Chart 5–3
Low, Middle, and High Latitudes

1. Low latitudes are between 23½ degrees north and south of the equator; this area is sometimes called the torrid zone.
2. Middle latitudes are between 23½ and 66½ degrees north, and between the same degrees south; these areas are sometimes called temperate zones.
3. High latitudes are between 66½ degrees north and the North Pole, and the same degrees south and the South Pole; these areas are sometimes called frigid zones.

History The social studies program contains much material from history. Changes in family life from colonial times to the present, growth of the community and state, United States history, and selected historical developments in other countries are usually included. The bulk of the conceptual components of history are drawn from other disciplines and used to interpret past human events. For example, role, division of labor, resources, and borrowing of ideas may be used to explain changes in family life, communities, and nations in different periods of time. Yet time, process, and organizing concepts are also widely used in historical materials. In addition, special emphasis is given to events and themes, as the following summary shows.

CONCEPTS

Time concepts: time, day, week, month, season, year, decade, generation, century, millennium, B.C., A.D., period, epoch, age, era, prehistoric, ancient, medieval, Middle Ages, modern

Process concepts: criticism, analysis, and synthesis of primary and secondary sources; reconstruction of events; interpretation; periodization

Organizing concepts: event, theme, period, place

EVENTS AND THEMES

Events and themes in local history: first settlers, homes, school, and church; beginning as a town; growth of population, transportation, communication, business, education, public services, the arts; contributions of individuals and groups; problems of growth

Events and themes in United States history: discovery and exploration, living in the colonies, gaining independence, establishing a government, living on the frontier, the westward movement, the growth of sectionalism, the Civil War, the period of reconstruction, growth of agriculture and industry, becoming a world power, the growth of cities, contributions of ethnic groups

INTERPRETATIONS AND GENERALIZATIONS

Changes in communities have been the result of the actions of many individuals and groups.

Interdependence has increased rapidly in recent times.

Social problems and instututions of today have roots in the past.

Ideas about self-government were strengthened on the frontier.

Multiple causes and consequences must be considered in studying events.

Time and space form a framework within which events can be placed.

INQUIRY–CONCEPTUAL QUESTIONS

What periods can we use to group events in the growth of our community? [classifying]

How can we show (or report on) the growth of industries in our state? [synthesizing]

What were the most serious acts of discrimination against native Americans during the settling of the West? [evaluating]

How can data gathered from visits to historical monuments be used to reconstruct human events? (Boston, Massachusetts; San Bernardino County, California)

How can study trips be used to gather data on historical events? (Plimoth Plantation, Lexington)

Economics There have probably been more advances in economics education in recent years than in any other segment of the social studies. Newer instruction materials include a clearly defined set of concepts and main ideas drawn from economics. Concepts such as division of labor are introduced in the beginning grades as children compare the production of cookies or other items on an "assembly line" where each worker does a special job with complete production of the item by individuals. The differences between producers and consumers and goods and services are discovered as children investigate roles of family members, community workers, and people in other places to find out who produces and consumes various goods and services. The opportunity cost principle is put to use as students consider such questions as "What does Billy give up if he spends his allowance for candy?" "What does a family give up when they take a trip instead of spending the money for other things?" "What does a country sacrifice when it decides to produce some things and not others?" Basic conceptual elements follow.

CONCEPTS

Conflict between wants and resources, scarcity, division of labor, specialization, interdependence, goods, services, consumers, producers, factors of production, production, consumption, exchange, distribution, market, supply, demand, prices, money, banking, credit, saving, spending, investing, trade, inputs, outputs, economic systems, economic values, opportunity cost principle

CONCEPT CLUSTERS

Basic economic problem: conflct between wants and resources, need to make choices, need for an economic system to allocate resources to alternative uses

Specialization: division of labor by occupations, technological applications, and geographic situation; resulting interdependence

Productive resources: human (workers, managers, knowhow), capital (tools, machines, factories), natural (soil, water, climate, minerals, forests)

The market: means of allocating resources; interaction of supply and demand; use of money, transportation, and communication; modification by policies related to economic values

Economic systems: market-directed or private enterprise, centrally directed or command, tradition-directed, mixed

Economic values in our system: growth, stability, security, justice, freedom

GENERALIZATIONS

Members of families, people in communities, and societies meet the basic economic problem by finding answers to these questions: What to produce? How to produce? How much to produce? How to distribute what is produced?

Division of labor increases production and leads to interdependence among individuals, communities, states, and nations.

People in a market system have more freedom of choice than do people in a command system.

Firms produce goods and services in a modified market system under policies set by government to protect consumers and producers.

In our system the government provides certain goods and services such as highways, schools, protection, and welfare services.

INQUIRY–CONCEPTUAL QUESTIONS

What are goods? What are services? [defining]

How are productive resources used in Nigeria? [analyzing]

What are the gains and losses from free trade with Japan? [evaluating]

What kind of economic system do you think is best? why? [evaluating]

Political Science and Law

Material from political science has traditionally been included in social studies under the title of civics. Now we are moving beyond civics to include dynamic aspects of the uses of power and authority in the home, school, and other institutions as well as in government. A second trend is the inclusion of material from law related to legal rights and responsi-

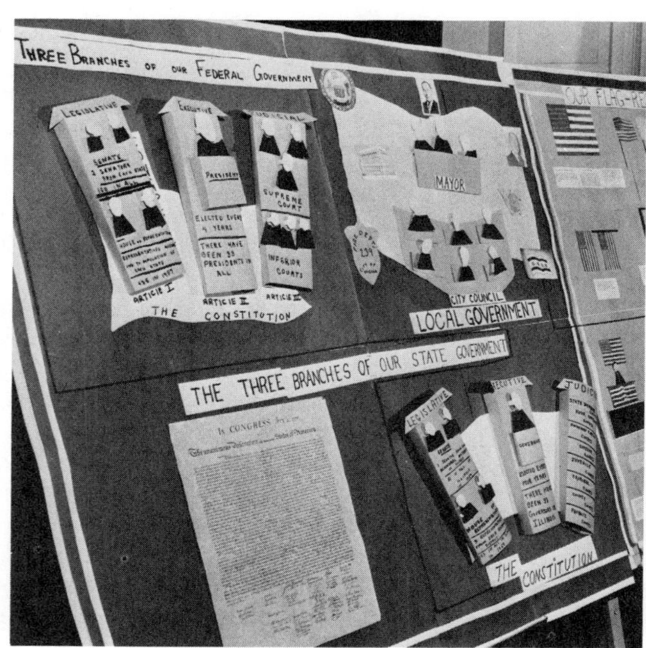

What processes of government are used at the local, state, and federal levels? (Chicago, Illinois)

bilities of individuals and groups. Because elements drawn from political science and law are so interrelated, they are treated together in this section.

Instruction may begin with attention to rule making, rule applying, and the settling of disputes in situations familiar to children. Later these concepts are extended to legislative (rule making), executive (rule applying), and judicial (rule adjudicating) processes of local, state, and national government. Attention is given in community studies to the mayor, city council, teachers, police, and other public employees; to public services such as education, protection, and recreation; to city planning and redevelopment; and to metropolitan planning to solve transportation and other cross-community problems. State and national studies include such concepts as authority, separation of powers, due process and equal protection of law, and processes of government. Historical studies include material on contributions of the Greeks and Romans to government, the Magna Carta, changes in laws in England, law and government in early America, case studies of struggles for justice, and great documents such as the Declaration of Independence and the Constitution. Studies of other lands include material on uses of power and authority by leaders, type of government in comparison to our own, roles of officials, and relations with the United States and other countries. These and other topics may be structured around the following:

CONCEPTS

State, power, authority, political system, government, constitution, rules, laws, legal system, legal processes, civil liberties, due process, equal protection, justice, freedom, responsibility, democracy

CONCEPT CLUSTERS

Tasks of government: external security, internal order, justice, public services, freedom (under democracy)

Processes: rule making (legislative), rule applying (executive), rule adjudicating (judicial)

Levels of government: local, state, national, international

Public services: police, fire, postal, education, health, welfare, sanitation, conservation, recreation, labor, business

Due process of law: protection against arrest without probable cause, unreasonable search and seizure, forced confession, self-incrimination, and double jeopardy; right to public trial, counsel, fair judge and jury, habeas corpus, knowledge of accusation, to confront and cross-examine witnesses, have witnesses for one's defense, to the assumption of innocence until proven guilty.

GENERALIZATIONS

Rules and laws provide for social stability and control, equality, and individual freedom, and limit behavior that endangers life, liberty, and property.

All societies have individuals and groups with the authority to make, carry out, and evaluate decisions related to individual and group welfare.

Due process of law is needed to provide equal opportunity, protection, and justice for all individuals and groups.

Civil liberties—freedom of thought, speech, press, worship, association, and petition—are essential to human freedom.

Conflcts arise when individuals and groups have competing goals, apply different standards of conduct, and interpret laws differently.

Laws are nonviolent means of handling conflcts.

INQUIRY–CONCEPTUAL QUESTIONS

Why do we need rules in school to limit what we do? [analyzing] Why do we need laws in the community to limit what people do? [analyzing]

What are public services? [defining] How are they like and different from private services? [comparing and contrasting]

What does equal protection mean? [defining] What should be done in our community to improve equal protection for minority groups? [evaluating]

What processes of government are common at the local, state, and national levels? [generalizing]

How can we use the Bill of Rights to decide what is just or unjust in this case? [interpreting, evaluating]

Anthropology Many concepts and key ideas from anthropology are now included in programs of instruction as a result of greater recognition of the contributions this discipline can make to the objectives of social studies, especially to attitudes, understandings, methods of inquiry, and skills related to the comparative study of cultures. The inclusive culture

How might artifacts such as these be used to make inferences about other cultures? (San Diego, California)

concept, in which values, beliefs, and patterns of learned behavior are brought together in a unified view of ways of living, is the basis for many units of instruction—for comparative studies of families, villages, and communities as well as for studies of selected areas, prehistoric peoples, and early civilizations. Specific units on Eskimos, native Americans, village life in Africa, and other peoples include anthropological material on food, shelter, clothing, utensils, social organization, arts, crafts, rituals, ceremonies, and other aspects of culture. The following summary shows the scope of anthropological sources for the social studies program.

CONCEPTS

Culture, society, values, beliefs, tradition, customs, change, social organization, role, technology, community, civilization

CONCEPT CLUSTERS

Culture: learned patterns of behavior; ways of living; arts, crafts, technology, religion, economic activities, language, other learned behaviors

Process of cultural change: invention, discovery, diffusion, adaptation

Food-getting activities: gathering, hunting, fishing, herding, gardening, agriculture

Societies: folk or preliterate, preindustrial, transitional, industrial

Families: nuclear, extended; functions—biological, affectional, economic, social

Community: territory, common culture, collective action; folk, peasant, urban

Characteristics of civilization: writing, accumulation of food and other goods for managed use, division of labor, government, arts, sciences, urbanization, trade

GENERALIZATIONS

Culture is socially transmitted in all societies, differs from society to society, and is a prime determiner of behavior.

Families around the world have common needs but vary in the ways they meet those needs.

Major differences among people are cultural, not biological.

Food-getting activities are closely related to level of technology.

The culture of modern societies has evolved from the culture of earlier societies.

INQUIRY-CONCEPTUAL QUESTIONS

What do these art objects and crafts tell us about their culture? [inferring]

What do you think we will find to be the main causes for the change from hunting and fishing to herding? [hypothesizing]

How can we group these societies? Folk? Preindustrial? Transitional? Industrial? [classifying]

In general, what conditions were necessary for the rise of civilization? [generalizing]

Sociology Concepts and key ideas from sociology are included in many units of study. Studies of the family and school, two basic social institutions, are usually provided early in the program. The positions and roles of members of the family, the teacher, and other school personnel are included. Values and expectations of children, parents, teachers, and community workers are considered in the context of children's relationships to each other and to adults. Norms and sanctions and their relation to social control are discovered in the context of children's own experiences and in units that include material on customs, regulations, rewards, punishments, and laws in communities and other places near at hand and far away. Understanding of processes of social interaction such as cooperation, competition, and conflct are also developed in the context of children's experiences and units of study. Historical and geographic studies centered on the community, state, nation, and other places typically include such concepts as role, groups, institutions, values, and social change.

Structural elements drawn from sociology are closely related to those drawn from anthropology and psychology, as shown in the following summary.

CONCEPTS

Society, values, norms, role, status, expectations, social institutions, social processes, groups, social control

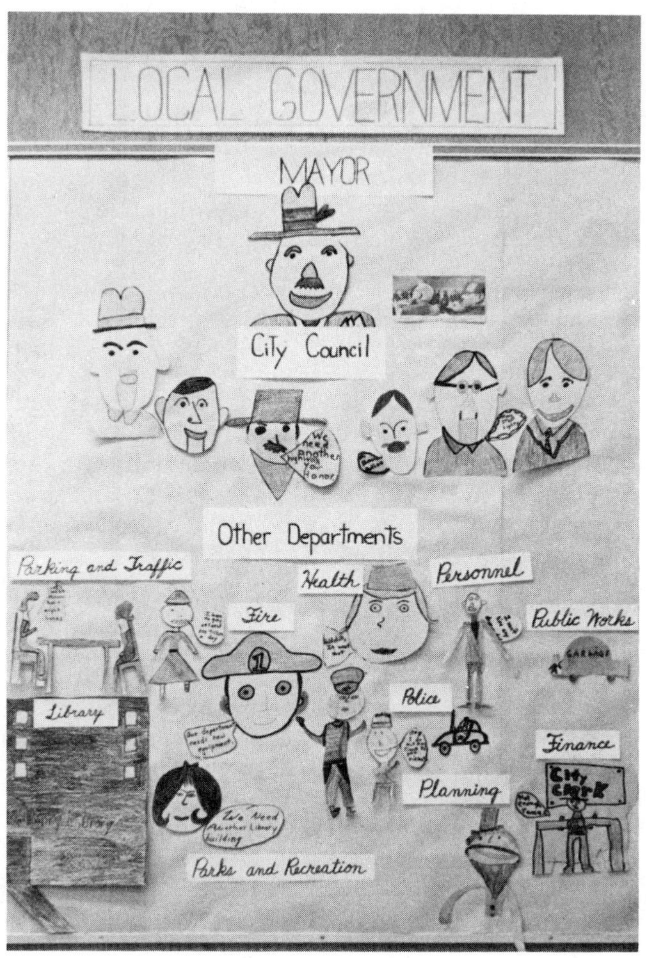

What is the role of the mayor? of other city workers? (Stanislaus County Schools, California)

CONCEPT CLUSTERS

Values: personal, social, economic, political, religious, esthetic

Social institutions: family, economic, political, educational, scientific, religious, recreational, welfare, esthetic

Processes of social interaction: cooperation, competition, conflict, assimilation, accommodation

Groups: primary, secondary, reference, in-group, out-group

Social control: dependency, rewards, sanctions, norms, laws

Minorities: foreign, religious, racial, ethnic, socioeconomic

INQUIRY-CONCEPTUAL QUESTIONS

What is an in-group? An out-group? [defining]
What are the main functions of families? [generalizing]
In a democratic country, what means of social control do you think we will find? [hypothesizing]
Which proposals for urban renewal give greatest attention to social values? [analyzing] Which one do you favor? why? [evaluating]

Psychology Concepts and key ideas from psychology are embedded in units of study at all levels of instruction. For example, the concept of individual differences is important in studies of families, schools, community workers, and people in other places. How seeing, hearing, touching, and other senses help one to observe and to learn may be included early in the program. The importance of attitudes, motives, and interests as key factors in human behavior is brought home in both contemporary and historical studies of people near at hand and far away. How to control feelings and what happens when feelings are not controlled are considered in the context of children's own experiences and in studies of others. Direct attention is given to effective ways of learning, how to remember and use what is learned, and how to improve critical thinking and problem solving.

These contributions from psychology are summarized below.

CONCEPTS

Senses, learning, remembering, group processes, attitudes, perceptions of others, personal-social needs, individual differences, intergroup relations, social roles

CONCEPT CLUSTERS

Using our senses to learn: seeing, hearing, smelling, touching, tasting, balancing
Learning and remembering: clear purposes, meaning, practice, use, review, application, grouping around main ideas, contrast, comparison, concentration, knowledge of results, ideas in own words
Perception of others: previous experience, needs, motives, attitudes, expectation, current condition of perceiver, self-concept

Group processes: goal setting, planning, doing, evaluating, decision making
Personal-social needs: acceptance, belonging, security, achievement, self-expression, interaction with others, learning, self-actualization
Individual differences: appearance, personality, role, attitudes, beliefs, family, customs, learning, abilities, habits
Social roles: leadership, followership, aggression, submission

GENERALIZATIONS

Individual differences exist among members of families, children in schools, and people in communities.
Perceptions of others vary from individual to individual and are conditioned by a variety of factors.
Both individual and group needs may be met through group action.
Learning and remembering can be improved by concentrated effort.
Individuals take different roles in different groups and situations.

INQUIRY-CONCEPTUAL QUESTIONS

How do we use our senses to learn? [generalizing]
What does this picture show about individual differences? [observing, interpreting]
What does that kind of behavior show about their values? [inferring]
What do you think will happen if the leadership is changed? [predicting]

Philosophy Better classified as a humanity than as a social science, philosophy is included as a core discipline because concepts related to values and various aspects of inquiry are emphasized in social studies. Wide agreement exists that the conceptual basis of such values as freedom, equality, responsibility, loyalty, and patriotism should be emphasized along with the positive attitudes and feelings needed to make them enduring qualities. Students should also understand the nature of logical fallacies, the meaning of the spirit of philosophical inquiry, and the processes involved in making judgments. The value-related concepts listed below are found in most social studies materials.

CONCEPTS

Values, moral and ethical principles, right, duty, freedom, equality, justice, truth, human dignity, patriotism, loyalty, free society, free inquiry, common good, individual interest, responsibility, cooperation, creativity, open-mindedness, concern for others

CONCEPT CLUSTERS

The spirit of inquiry: longing to know and understand; questioning of all things; search for data and their meaning; demand for verification; respect for logic; consideration of premises, causes, and consequences

Logical fallacies: appeal to force, argument from ignorance, appeal to pity, emphasis on false cause, snob appeal, neglect of all causes, false premises

Making judgments: clarifying what is to be judged, defining related criteria, analyzing in terms of criteria, making the judgment, checking the judgment with others

GENERALIZATIONS

The basic value of human dignity underlies our way of life.

Free societies keep open the path of free inquiry for their own well-being.

Criteria should be defined in terms of values and used to decide what is good or ought to be.

Ideas and proposals must be subjected to critical examination if their value is to be determined.

INQUIRY-CONCEPTUAL QUESTIONS

What values should we use to judge the treatment of minority groups? [recalling, defining]

How does enlightened loyalty differ from blind patriotism? [defining, contrasting]

Who can explain the statement that human dignity underlies our way of life? [interpreting]

How can equality of opportunity be improved for this group? [evaluating]

INQUIRY COMPONENTS OF STRUCTURE

Values, models, modes, and methods of inquiry are dynamic aspects of the core disciplines used to investigate topics, questions, and problems. Values of inquiry indicate the attitudes held by those who truly search for the best new ideas and test old ideas about human relationships. Models of inquiry are helpful guides in the study of problems; they are also helpful in planning a balanced program. Specific methods of inquiry can be put to use in units of instruction at all levels.

Values of Inquiry

Free and open inquiry clearly underlies the work of anyone who wants to find the best possible explanations for cultural and natural phenomena. Individual opinion, tradition, pronouncements of authorities, and other ideas not based on critical study must be opened to review and investigation.

Several values of inquiry are stressed in social studies projects and may be found in teaching guides and units of instruction.[2] Especially important are curiosity about the causes and consequences of human behavior and ways of studying human relationships; definition of terms in precise language so that the meaning is clear to others as well as to the inquirer; awareness of the effects of one's own background, views, feelings, position, and values on the way problems are viewed, how they are studied, and how findings are interpreted; objectivity so that findings will be reliable and can be readily checked by others; and skepticism marked by thoughtful questioning and critical review of methods of study, findings, interpretations, and conclusions. Equally valuable are a thorough search for evidence to test hypotheses, answer questions, support conclusions, and weigh alternatives; respect for differing views based on evidence gathered through systematic study and critical analysis of causes and consequences; regard for logical thinking in defining problems, framing questions and hypotheses, making plans for study, classifying and interpreting data, and drawing conclusions; rigorous analysis of assumptions, premises, biases, possible errors, special meanings, ideas behind interpretations, and other subjective aspects of inquiry; and corroboration or double-checking of findings by repeating studies and making comparisons with the findings of others.

Although few individuals hold and practice these values fully, they can serve as ideals toward which to guide inquiry into human relationships. A beginning can be made early in the social studies program, for curiosity is characteristic of all children and can be kept alive by exploring a variety of problems. Such values as clear definition of terms, demand for evidence, and meaningful classification of ideas can

[2] See, for example, Roy A. Price, Warren Hickman, and Gerald Smith, *Major Concepts for Social Studies* (Syracuse: Social Studies Curriculum Center, 1965); and Edith West, *Project Social Studies* (Minneapolis: School of Education, University of Minnesota, 1968).

be developed as problems and topics are studied in different units of instruction. Objectivity, personal preferences and feelings, thoughtful skepticism, and respect for differing views can be nurtured by considering such questions as "Will we get the same result if we do it again?" "Are we consistent in the way we do it?" "Did we control our feelings about it?" "Is this a good idea because we like it or because it works?" "Is this a fair statement?" "What questions do we have about it?" "Where might mistakes have been made?" "What is good about that idea?" "How can we use that idea?" "Is that a sound argument?"

Models of Inquiry

Special note should be made of the need to use models flexibly and to adapt them to problems under study. The rigid following of predetermined steps irrespective of new insights gained as one studies a topic is the antithesis of sound thinking. Creative thinking is a key ingredient in inquiry and should be employed to the fullest to adapt models to differing situations.

Models of inquiry used in different disciplines have been adapted from the references at the end of this chapter and are presented in Chart 5-4. Notice that the general pattern or sequence begins with identification of problems and ends with conclusions or interpretations and suggestions for further studies. The importance of helping children grow in the ability to identify problems cannot be overemphasized. Also important is the need to be on the lookout for what to study next. These two elements of inquiry are directly related to the goal of developing competence in learning how to learn. Notice that the section at the top of the chart lists common phases of inquiry. Check these points with those for individual disciplines and note the similarities.

Careful analysis of the models in Chart 5-4 reveals that for most purposes in the social studies one can use a generalized model that incorporates basic features common to all. In fact, the general model for guiding group inquiry presented in the next chapter includes the common aspects of inquiry noted in this chart. Sometimes, however, study can be sharpened by relaying mainly on two other models. The example given for anthropology is especially useful when planning or conducting field trips (detailed information for field trips is presented in Chapter 13). The models for political and economic analysis have much in common and are useful in analyzing and managing value conflcts and in decision-making studies.

Methods and Materials of Inquiry

The underlying principle in drawing materials and methods from the social sciences is to use only those that are most helpful for obtaining the data needed to attain stated objectives. In historical studies extensive use is made of techniques involved in analyzing and synthesizing data from records and other remnants of the human past. In studies of con-

Chart 5–4

Common Phases of Inquiry

Define the problem and clarify objectives.
State questions or hypotheses to guide study.
Make a plan to gather data.
Appraise, organize, and interpret data.
Make and check conclusions.
Consider further needs for study.

Geography

Identify and define the topic or problem to be studied.
Consider all related factors.
State questions or hypotheses related to each factor.
Gather data related to each hypothesis or question.
Evaluate and organize data to test hypotheses or answer questions.
Interpret findings and draw conclusions.
Suggest other needed studies.

Anthropology

Define objectives for the field study.
Make a plan for each phrase.
Gather materials for recording data.
Make necessary arrangements.
Gather data by direct observation, interview, and participation (if feasible).
Organize and interpret data in light of objectives.
Summarize findings and draw conclusions.
Compare findings and conclusions with those of others.

History

Define the question or problem to be studied.
State hypotheses or questions to guide study.
Collect and evaluate sources of information.
Analyze and synthesize data in the sources.
Organize findings to answer questions and test hypotheses.
Interpret findings in relation to social, economic, and political developments.

Sociology

Define the problem and relate it to existing knowledge.
State hypotheses to guide study.
Select an adequate sample.
Use appropriate techniques to gather data.
Organize and analyze the data to test each hypothesis.
Interpret findings and draw conclusions.
Suggest other studies.

Political Analysis	Economic Analysis
Define the problem and clarify related values.	Define the problem. Where are we in terms of where we want to go?
Consider different choices or solutions.	Identify goals and place them in order of priority.
Evaluate each choice or solution in terms of values, facts, and historical background.	Consider the resources available to attain the goals.
Identify possible consequences of each choice or solution.	Consider alternative ways to attain goals with usable resources.
Evaluate the consequences in light of values.	Analyze consequences of each alternative.
Make judgments as to which choice or solution is best.	Choose the best alternative in light of objectives.

temporary problems, a variety of techniques and data sources may be used to obtain up-to-date information. The following examples are adapted from reports on various disciplines and from recent social studies materials.

COLLECTING DATA

Sources

Written materials: textbooks, references, letters, diaries, minutes, newspapers, magazines, government reports and documents, business records, biographical materials, case studies

Art objects: paintings, murals, tapestries, vases, plaques, medals, jewelry, wall paintings, portraits, ornaments, sculpture

Orally transmitted materials: folklore, legends, sagas, ballads, anecdotes, stories, eyewitness accounts

Recorded materials: photographs, slides, films, tapes, records, maps, diagrams, graphs, charts

Inscriptions: monuments, plaques, buildings, coins, clay tablets, walls, grave markers, bridges, art objects

Physical remains: buildings, monuments, implements, tools, utensils, weapons, pottery, baskets, clothing, textiles, costumes, furnishings, musical instruments

Techniques

Content analysis of printed materials, films, and other instructional media to gather data on meanings of terms, changes and trends, uses of resources, use of words to stir the emotions, underlying assumptions, and the frequency of occurrence of other items under study

Field trips to collect data on farming, business activities, conservation, transportation, communication, artifacts in exhibits, and other topics under study

Observation of activities of family members, construction workers, and other community workers; of the roles of police, firefighters, and other public officials; of changes in the weather and seasons; of meetings of the city council, school board, and other groups

Interviews, polls, and questionnaires to gather data from fellow students, parents, community officials, business people, health workers, experts on conservation, and other experts on issues and questions under study

Role playing and simulation of activities and decision making in families, markets, banks, and other situations in which identification with others and involvement in decision-making processes are important

Experiments to determine what happens when different procedures or treatments are used, such as selecting and testing hypotheses about division of labor or presenting objects of varying sizes or colors to find out how one's perception of them changes

RECORDING, ORGANIZING, AND PRESENTING DATA

Making notes on or recording data obtained through interviews and on field trips

Constructing maps to show the distribution of homes, businesses, population, resources, and other phenomena; how such distributions as transportation networks and cities are related; and the flow of people, goods, and services between places

Constructing models, diagrams, graphs, tables, and charts of objects and processes under study to demonstrate and explain how they work and how they are used

Preparing sketches, drawings, displays, and exhibits to illustrate processes, show the uses of objects, and highlight relationships between objects and human activities

Preparing reports, oral or written, to share findings and conclusions with others

EVALUATING INQUIRY AND MATERIALS

Keeping logs, diaries, or other records for use in evaluating both individual and group activities

Constructing and using rating scales, charts, and checklists to appraise reports, maps, films, other sources of information, and individual and group activities

Participating in discussions to appraise and improve the effectiveness of both individual and group inquiry

These various methods of inquiry should be referred to and used as guides when planning units of study. Students need opportunities to develop skill in using many different methods of gathering data. By embedding them in units of instruction, it is possible to make them an integral part of the problem-solving process.

QUESTIONS, ACTIVITIES, EVALUATION

1. Examine two or three social studies textbooks and note examples of the following:
   - **a.** Concepts, concept clusters, generalizations, and inquiry-conceptual questions
   - **b.** Models and methods of inquiry suggested in the related teacher's manual
   - **c.** Relative attention to material from core disciplines
2. Examine a course of study and do the same.
3. Examine a unit of instruction and do the same.
4. Which of the models of inquiry presented in this chapter do you prefer? Discuss and defend your choice with others.
5. Which of the methods of inquiry do you think will be most useful in a unit you plan to teach? Note examples of how they might be used.
6. Prepare six to eight inquiry-conceptual questions, using concepts presented in this chapter.

REFERENCES

BANKS, JAMES A., and AMBROSE A. CLEGG, JR., *Teaching Strategies for the Social Studies.* Reading, Mass.: Addison-Wesley, 1973. Social inquiry, separate chapters on disciplines, value inquiry model.

BEYER, BARRY K., and ANTHONY N. PENNA, eds., *Concepts in the Social Studies.* Washington, D.C.: National Council for the Social Studies, 1971. Readings on concepts and how to develop them.

BOUTWELL, CLINTON E., *Getting It All Together—The New Social Studies*. San Rafael, Calif.: Leswing Press, 1972. Inquiry model, concepts, and generalizations from disciplines.

GERLACH, RONALD A., and LYNNE W. LAMPRECHT, *Teaching About the Law*. Cincinnati: W. H. Anderson Company, 1975. Illustrative activities, lessons, resources, and evaluation techniques.

JAROLIMEK, JOHN, and HUBER M. WALSH, eds., *Readings for Social Studies in Elementary Education*. New York: Macmillan, 1974. Section on social sciences, humanities, and history.

JOYCE, BRUCE R., *New Strategies for Social Education* (2nd ed.). Chicago: Science Research Associates, 1972. Chapters on social science.

MICHAELIS, JOHN U., and A. MONTGOMERY JOHNSTON, eds., *The Social Sciences: Foundations of the Social Studies*. Boston: Allyn and Bacon, 1965. Chapters on eight core disciplines; major generalizations from the social sciences in appendix.

MORRISSETT, IRVING, and W. WILLIAMS STEVENS, JR., eds., *Social Science in the Schools: A Search for Rationale*. New York: Holt, Rinehart and Winston, 1971. Sections on the disciplines.

MUESSIG, RAYMOND H., and VINCENT R. ROGERS, *Social Science Seminar Series*. Columbus, O.: Merrill, 1965. Volumes on history, geography, economics, political science, anthropology, and sociology.

PRESTON, RALPH C., and WAYNE L. HERMAN, JR., *Teaching Social Studies in the Elementary School*. New York: Holt, Rinehart and Winston, 1974. Chapters on social sciences.

THOMAS, R. MURRAY, and DALE L. BRUBAKER, *Teaching Elementary Social Studies*. Belmont, Calif.: Wadsworth, 1972. Section on social sciences and humanities.

WESLEY, EDGAR B., and STANLEY P. WRONSKI, *Teaching Secondary Social Studies in a World Society*. Lexington, Mass.: Heath, 1973. Chapters on history and social sciences.

Focusing Questions

What guidelines can be used to develop thinking processes in the social studies program?

What strategies can be used to develop inquiry processes that are basic to effective thinking?

How can problem-solving procedures be used to bring thinking and inquiry processes together in social studies instruction?

Developing Thinking & Inquiry Processes

The need to develop student's thinking processes is emphasized in all areas of the curriculum, and intensive efforts have been made to identify processes and related teaching strategies that can be used to cultivate thinking ability. Although the results of the many psychological and educational studies of recent years have provided a number of guidelines, this chapter includes only those strategies and techniques believed to be most useful in classroom instruction. An overview of basic aspects of thinking is presented first, followed by a discussion of concept development. Detailed attention is given to strategies for developing inquiry or cognitive processes central to effective thinking. Model questions are presented for each process to serve as guidelines for planning units and lessons, and for guiding discussion. The final section is a discussion of how group problem solving may be used to bring together various aspects of thinking and inquiry in a unified manner.

BASIC THINKING AND INQUIRY PROCESSES

Chart 6–1 shows selected aspects of thinking that are important in instructional planning. Notice that the process of thinking involves symbols, signs, and signals that stand for objects and events. Thinking is initated by problems, questions, perplexities, needs, wants, or difficulties. To think in really profitable directions, the student must be able to identify, recognize, and clarify the

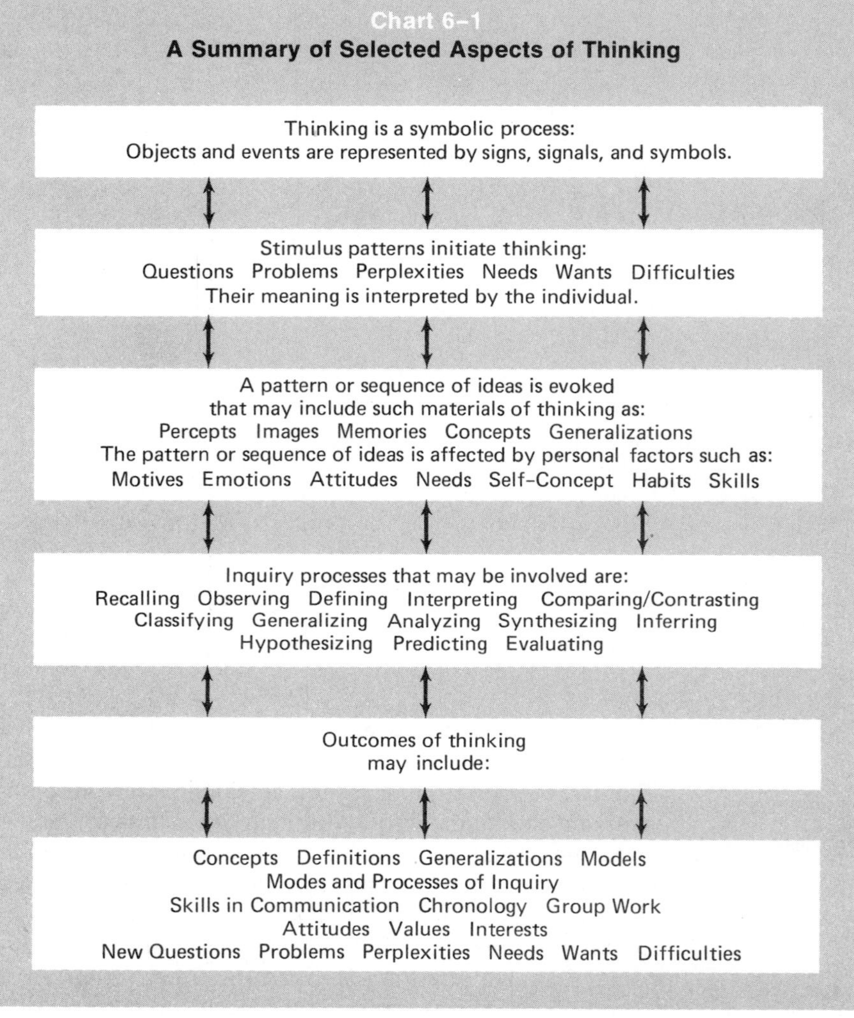

problems to be studied in various units of instruction. The materials of thinking—what a student uses to think—may include perceptions based on observation and memory, images, concepts, and generalizations gleaned from past experience. What students observe and recall, therefore, are key factors in determining the quality and level of their thinking.

Chart 6–1
A Summary of Selected Aspects of Thinking
Thinking is a symbolic process:
Objects and events are represented by signs, signals, and symbols.
Stimulus patterns initiate thinking:
Questions Problems Perplexities Needs Wants Difficulties
Their meaning is interpreted by the individual.
A pattern or sequence of ideas is evoked
that may include such materials of thinking as:
Percepts Images Memories Concepts Generalizations
The pattern or sequence of ideas is affected by personal factors such as:
Motives Emotions Attitudes Needs Self-Concept Habits Skills
Inquiry processes that may be involved are:
Recalling Observing Defining Interpreting Comparing/Contrasting
Classifying Generalizing Analyzing Synthesizing Inferring
Hypothesizing Predicting Evaluating
Outcomes of thinking
may include:
Concepts Definitions Generalizations Models
Modes and Processes of Inquiry
Skills in Communication Chronology Group Work
Attitudes Values Interests
New Questions Problems Perplexities Needs Wants Difficulties

The inquiry or cognitive processes listed in the center of Chart 6–1 are of critical importance. Observing, recalling, comparing/contrasting, classifying, defining, interpreting, and generalizing are central in concept development and prerequisite to the use of higher level processes. Inferring, hypothesizing, and predicting extend ideas beyond given data. Analyzing breaks a whole into parts, and synthesizing integrates parts into a whole. Evaluating involves critical thinking in which standards are used to make judgments of worth. The outcomes of thinking in social studies are as broad as the objectives—conceptual, inquiry, skill, and affective learning. Also important as outcomes are new questions and problems that can be used to begin new rounds of thinking in an ongoing sequence.

CRITICAL AND CREATIVE THINKING

Of special importance in all phases of the social studies program are critical and creative thinking. Ways they may be used and developed should be kept in mind as instruction is planned and as learning experiences are developed in the classroom.

Critical Thinking

In critical thinking, emphasis is given to making an evaluation in terms of standards or criteria. Concepts involved in the standards or criteria must be understood, a clear perception of what is being appraised is essential, judgment must be suspended until the evidence is weighed, and feelings must be controlled if a sound appraisal is to be made.

In social studies, critical examinations are often made of ideas, proposals, issues, points of view, discussion procedures, committee work, statements in reading materials, and ideas presented in audiovisual materials. For example, in evaluating discussion, the direction of thinking is set by standards embedded in such questions as "Did we stick to the topic?" "Did each individual participate?" "Were different points made?" Were important questions raised?" While thinking about each question, students attempt to recall pertinent points and to analyze their behavior and that of others.

Critical thinking processes also are used in the evaluation of ideas presented in instructional materials. For example, statements in textbooks and current materials, arguments presented on current issues, descriptions of cause-effect relationships, terms and phrases that stimulate emotions, treatment of women and ethnic groups, propaganda techniques, and exaggerated and incongruous points may be selected for critical review. Facts may be differentiated from opinions, relevant and irrelevant information may be noted, the evidence for various statements may be examined, and conclusions may be checked against the facts presented to support them (see Charts 6–2 and 6–3).

As children gain experience, critical thinking may be put to use in examining beliefs and values that are meaningful to them. For example, taking turns, fair play, equal opportunity, and rights of others may be considered in terms of why we value them, how they improve working relations, and how we can extend them to various situations. Beliefs or values that are just "taken on" because of association with others will not be firmly grounded in understanding. A person who takes on beliefs uncritically is trained, not educated. If learners reflect, reconstruct, and test

Chart 6–2
Thinking Critically As You Read

Select points that are related to questions and problems.
Check statements against facts.
Separate facts from opinions.
Figure out the writer's point of view on problems.
Find all sides to issues and problems.
Look out for words that stir feelings.
Consider all the evidence before making a judgment.

Chart 6–3
Thinking Critically As You See Films

Look for ideas related to questions and problems we are considering.
Check the facts against other sources.
Look for main ideas and supporting facts.
Watch for terms or scenes that have special meaning.
Look out for short parts that cover a long period of time or space.
Look for new and different ways of doing things.
Make comparisons between the ways you do things and the ways that are shown.

beliefs, they will be more likely to have evidential grounds and not just an emotional basis for holding them. Both the meaning and significance of treasured values and beliefs are thus enhanced. Additional examples and a teaching strategy are presented in the section on evaluating.

Creative Thinking The term *creative* implies something new or original. For a child it may be a new interpretation, a grasp of new relationships, an original synthesis and expression of ideas, a new proposal or hypothesis, or a new way of doing something. Originality rather than conformity, divergent thinking in which multiple responses are made rather than convergent thinking in which unifying responses are made, and production of new ideas rather than reproduction of old ideas are signs of creative thinking. Basic to creativity are such traits as sensitivity to problems, fluency of ideas and words, expressional fluency, semantic flexibility and elaboration, originality, perception of objects and activities in new ways, and redefinition of symbols.

In social studies, creative thinking is stimulated whenever children are encouraged to suggest new ideas or ways of doing things, express thoughts and feelings in original ways, and propose solutions to problems. Examples of experiences in which creative thinking may be developed are planning and arranging work centers and displays, framing hypotheses, organizing and summarizing information in new ways on maps and charts, constructing objects, dramatizing, expressing thoughts and feelings through art and music, expressing ideas through oral and written language activities, and planning activities to culminate a unit of instruction. But creative thinking is not limited to special activities; it is an approach to

Along the Trail
Slowly
Autoharp
F
C7
F
Gm
C7
The trail from dawn to sun-set was dust-y, hard, and long. The
Gaily
F
C7
F
C7
F
pi - o - neer at ev'ning re-laxed with dance and song.
Snowflakes
Down, down, down they came,
A few at first, and then so many
That when I looked up toward the sky,
All I could see was whirling, twirling,
Soft white flakes of snow.
Louise
Sand Storm
The trees rocked back and forth.
The wind howled around the eaves of the house.
It blew sand out of the gutters.
The screens and doors slammed and slammed.
Sailboats
There goes a sailboat out to sea.
Think of the colors the sails might be.
In the morning, yellow; at evening, brown.
But when it gets dark, they all come down.
Grade 4

Creativity takes many different forms and may be expressed by individuals or groups. What other modes of expression might be used in the social studies? (San Bernardino County, California)

problems or a way of viewing them that can open new horizons. For example, as different pictures, films, and other materials are used in units of instructions, questions such as the following will stimulate creative thinking:

> What do you see in this picture that is new? In what other ways could it have been shown? How could we express it?
>
> What do you think about that statement? Which words have special meaning? How could it be improved?
>
> How is this film related to an experience you have had? How is it different?
>
> How did this part make you feel? How would you tell it or write it to express your feelings?

Creative thinking processes are also put to use in reading. Creative reading takes the reader beyond literal interpretation to implied meanings, appreciative reactions, and evaluation. The reader visualizes what is read, identifies with characters, recalls experiences and compares them with experiences presented in the text, anticipates what is coming, notes biases, searches for new relationships, and tries to bring together ideas from several sources. Chart 6–4 and 6–5 illustrate specific points related to creative reading.

A first step in promoting the development of creative thinking is to build a rich background of experience. During this phase, attention is given to the perception of relationships, development of concepts, use of expressive terms and phrases, use of pictures and other materials that stimulate imagery, reading of materials that help to build word pictures, discussion of reactions, and consideration of the most significant aspects of the topic under study. A closely related phase of creativity is the organizing, reorganizing, and consolidating of new learnings. Some preliminary attempts at creative expression may be seen in the discussion, sharing, planning, and evaluation that take place as children clarify meanings, express reactions, and begin to explore possibilities. Fluency of thinking and flexibility in handling ideas develop along with increasing depth of understanding and the ability to reorganize ideas into new patterns. Then new insights and relationships, and possible ways of expressing them, are discovered. Some writers refer to this as the stage of illumination, or discovery, in which the individual says, "I've got it!" For children it is the discovery of a fresh and original way in which they can express the thoughts and feelings that have been building up within them.

Chart 6–4 **Creative Readers**	Chart 6–5 **Getting a Feeling for Others As You Read**	Chart 6–6 **Creative Thinkers**
Find special meanings of words and phrases. Grasp the main ideas and supporting details. Relate ideas to their own experiences. Discover hidden or implied meanings. Think of ways ideas and meanings can be related. Search for ways to apply ideas.	Try to picture how they live. Look for words and phrases that stir your feelings. Look for humor, exaggeration, and comparisons. Try to put yourself in their place. Try to figure out why they do things their way. Try to guess how they do things and then check to see if you are right.	Build up a background of ideas See objects and activities in new ways Organize ideas in new ways Search for original ways to express ideas Select the best from the old and new Are willing to try new ideas Put ideas to use in other activities

In the next phase, students proceed to try out, or verify, the creative idea they have discovered. In the process of creating something—whether it be a mural, model, dramatic portrayal, picture, hypothesis—a child may change it, redo it, alter a part of it, or start anew after evaluating the adequacy of expression of the original idea. Vital elements in this phase are the original conception of the idea, the perception of progress in expressing it, and the integration of various elements into a harmonious whole. The child's self-evaluation is important in determining how to proceed and what form the final product will take. Additional suggestions are presented later in the section on synthesizing; Chart 6–6 summarizes the steps.

How might you use activities such as these to develop concepts? (San Diego, California)

THE IMPORTANCE OF CONCEPT DEVELOPMENT

Concepts are basic tools of thinking and inquiry in social studies. Continuing attention must be given to their development, and both direct and vicarious kinds of experiences should be provided. For example, study trips, constructing and processing materials, and dramatic representation along with films, pictures, and models can provide the kinds of direct or sensory experiences that make concepts meaningful. But learning should not stop at this point. Vicarious experiences are needed to take students far beyond objects and events they can experience directly. Through reading, use of maps, discussion, individual research, and other vicarious experiences, thinking and learning can be extended as old concepts are enriched and new ones developed.

An effective approach to concept building is to consider the specific experiences in a unit of work and to determine the most significant concepts. Their value is shown by the need for their use that arises in class and by the misconceptions children reveal regarding them. Thus, concepts that are needed in reading materials, films, study trips, construction, dramatic play, discussion, and other experiences may be noted and developed in a manner similar to that used in the following examples.

In a unit on the farm, a group of lower-grade children developed and used concepts of such words as *silo, corral, feeding, milking, crush, bottle, calf, seeds, garden, barn, chute, hay,* and *fodder* by visiting a dairy farm to see a silo, corral, barn, and the feeding and milking of cows; by engaging in and discussing dramatic play related to chores on the farm; by constructing and using corrals and barns in dramatic play; by collecting seeds, planting them, and caring for a garden; by finding out how plants grow with different types of soil and varying amounts of sunshine and water; by reading and listening to stories related to life on the farm; by expressing group and individual experiences through art, rhythms, discussion, group chart making, and songs; and by seeing a film on farm life.

Teachers can develop various shades of meaning by using literature, art, and music. A reading of tales about Daniel Boone extends the meanings of *scout, defending the fort,* and *adventures of early explorers.* Recordings of songs sung by the pioneers as they went west and carefully selected pictures that depict the joys, sorrows, hopes, and aspirations of the pioneers as they established homes and towns give overtones of feeling to terms such as *husking bees, clearing, attack, homemaking, hardship, courageous,* and *fearless* that can be attained in no other way. Similarly, folk dances help children see how the pioneers enjoyed themselves. Such qualitative aspects of concept building must not be overlooked.

Group sharing of experiences through discussion, reporting, and storytelling aids in concept building; pictures, models, and objects should also be used to clarify specific meanings. Children and resource persons who have taken trips to places being studied can tell about them and show pictures and photographs to the class. Materials brought by children that relate to concepts in the unit can be discussed, demonstrated, and used to increase understanding. During a study of Mexico, for example, one child brought pottery, clothing, and jewelry. In a study of China, two children brought in and demonstrated the use of ehru, temple bells, and a gong. Another child brought pictures of Chinese boats and pointed out the differences between junks, sampans, and other kinds of Chinese boats.

Without discussion of objectives, clarification of problems, evaluation, and reflection on relationships to past experience and future action, activities have little value. One child illustrated this point very well during an activity involving construction designed to develop concepts of a Mexican bazaar. When asked what he was making, he said, "I'm just nailing boards to this box." He had not been in on the planning, discussion, and evaluation of the bazaar for use in the study of Mexico. In terms of his experiences, he was truly just nailing boards.

Both the number and the difficulty of the concepts must be considered; too many concepts at one time may lead to misconceptions, confusion, boredom, word-calling without meaning, and little or no comprehension. A long, tedious list of ideas to check on a study trip, during a film, or in a dictionary may result in superficial learning. In each unit, children need opportunities not only to develop new concepts, but to enrich and extend concepts they already have. For example, in a well-planned study of colonial and pioneer life, concepts such as these will be learned: *town* meeting, dame schools, church services, food, clothing, candlemaking, ways of travel, utensils, and weapons. At the same time, children should extend and enrich their understanding of how the early Americans met their needs for food, shelter, and clothing.

Types of Concepts One way of classifying concepts is as *concrete* and *defined.*[1] Concrete concepts such as round, red, and smooth call for identification of properties or attributes such as shape, color, and texture. Defined concepts are more abstract and include meanings that go beyond directly observable properties. Examples are resources, family, and justice, each of which calls for careful definition, use of many examples, and identification of key relationships—for instance, relationships among members of a family. Another way of classifying concepts is as *observed, inferred,* and *ideal.*[2] Observed concepts such as tree, hot, and loud are formed from sensory experience—seeing, touching, hearing, smelling, tasting. Inferred concepts such as anger, tolerance, and concern for others are formed by making inferences about actions. Ideal concepts such as nationalism, free enterprise, and democracy call for precise definition and comparative analysis of several examples. A third way of viewing concepts is as *conjunctive, disjunctive,* and *relational.*[3] Conjunctive concepts such as carpenter, doctor, and truck are based on observed characteristics; similarities are emphasized—for example, the role of doctors, the uses and features of trucks. Disjunctive concepts such as citizenship (by birth, or by passing examinations, or because one's parents were born here) have either-or characteristics or one of several attributes that must be recognized. Relational concepts such as population density, per capita income, and area are based on relationships (such as people per square mile).

Social studies planning may be carried out by using the categories concrete and defined and subsuming the other types of concepts under them. Concrete concepts include many observed concepts, are easiest to teach, and call for sensory experiences. Defined concepts include all the other types and call for a series of vicarious learning experiences that help develop the meaning of abstract concepts such as justice, population density, and culture. Even though defined concepts are stressed in the social studies, both types should be given attention and students should enrich and deepen their meaning as they are encountered in new situations.

Of special importance is instruction designed to help students recognize the specificity and generality of concepts used in social studies. Land, resources, family, community, and nation are generally applicable across cultures, time periods, and geographic areas, but concepts such as

[1] Robert M. Gagne and Leslie J. Briggs, *Principles of Instructional Design* (New York: Holt, Rinehart and Winston, 1974).

[2] Bruce R. Joyce, *New Strategies for Social Education* (Chicago: Science Research Associates, 1972).

[3] Jerome S. Bruner, Jacqueline J. Goodnow, and George A. Austin, *A Study of Thinking* (New York: Wiley, 1956).

muckrakers, caste system (in India), the Loop (in Chicago), and New England colonies are specifically applicable only in designated cultures, places, or time periods. Generally applicable concepts are used to formulate generalizations that may cut across topics or settings under study. Specifically applicable concepts are used to highlight features of particular cultures, places, and time periods. Students should recognize the culture-bound, place-bound, and time-bound characteristics of specifically applicable concepts and not, for example, confuse the caste system in India with the social class system in other places, or life in the New England colonies with life in the Southern colonies.

Concept Development Strategies

Two teaching strategies for developing concepts are widely used in current programs of instruction: direct instruction and the Taba plan.[4] Like most concept development strategies, they include attention to identification of common features, use of examples and nonexamples, classifying or grouping items, naming or labeling the group, and using the concept in ongoing activities. Learning should go beyond verbal definitions to include demonstration of understanding by pointing to or grouping examples, finding new examples, and using the name or label correctly in new situations.

Direct instruction includes the following steps:

1. State the concept to be learned, or pose a question: "Today we are to learn about peninsulas." Or, "What is a peninsula?"
2. Identify defining characteristics (critical attributes). "Notice this example on our map. Which parts are surrounded by water?"
3. Present several examples: "Look at the map on page 68. See the peninsula shown at the bottom. Find the one on the next page."
4. Present nonexamples: "Notice the island on page 68. Why is that *not* a peninsula? Find others that are *not* peninsulas."
5. Have students state or write a definition.

The Taba strategy, which emphasizes the classifying process, includes the following steps:

1. Have students observe and identify items to be grouped: "What items are shown in this picture?"
2. Identify features for use in grouping the items: "Which items seem to belong together? why?"
3. Name, label, or define each group: "What is a good name for each group?"

[4]Hilda Taba, et al., *Teacher's Handbook to Elementary Social Studies* (Reading, Mass.: Addison-Wesley, 1971).

Several of the processes that follow include elements of the above strategies, while others call for application of concepts that have been developed.

STRATEGIES FOR DEVELOPING INQUIRY PROCESSES

An effective way to improve children's thinking ability is to provide instruction on basic inquiry or cognitive processes that can be put to use in the instructional program. But what processes should be emphasized? One answer to this question lies in identifying the processes used in new instructional materials. This section is based on a content analysis conducted to identify basic processes and related teaching strategies.[5]

Attention is given first to the simpler processes: recalling and observing to generate data; defining and interpreting to clarify meaning; comparing/contrasting, classifying/ordering, and generalizing to organize data. The more complex processes—analyzing and synthesizing to reorganize data; inferring, hypothesizing, and predicting to apply and extend data; and evaluating to clarify values and used related standards to make judgments of worth—are then considered.

Before discussing the individual processes, several points need emphasis. First, the processes include those in Bloom's taxonomy of the cognitive domain discussed in Chapter 1 plus others that are essential to effective thinking and inquiry. Second, the set of processes may be used to formulate questions in units and lessons as suggested in the booklet by Sanders, which is based on Bloom's taxonomy, thus giving a more complete coverage of the cognitive operations used in thinking.[6] Third, no rigid order of the use of the processes is implied, although the order in which they are presented is frequently followed in instructional materials. Among the exceptions are inferring, which may follow interpreting as students "read between the lines," and hypothesizing, which may be done early to guide data collection. Fourth, some processes included in other lists are subsumed under those in this section. For example, translation is part of defining and interpreting. Communicating is a broad and inclusive activity that may be used to express observations, generalizations, and other thoughts and feelings gained by using processes. Application of data, concepts, and principles is involved in such processes as inferring, hypothesizing, and predicting; in fact, application may be involved in all processes in an inquiry-conceptual program because concepts are used as tools to guide observing, interpreting, and other processes.

In the pages that follow, each process is defined and key questions for initiating use of the process are noted. Teaching strategies are presented for several processes, including the three proposed by Taba. The

[5]John U. Michaelis. *Inquiry Processes in the Social Sciences* (Berkeley, Calif.: School of Education, University of California, 1973).

[6]See Sanders reference at end of chapter.

strategies and the sample questions and illustrations may be readily adapted for use in any unit of instruction. The accompanying charts contain ideas that may be used directly with students.

Recalling and Observing These two processes are basic to all others because they provide the data for inquiry. Students draw on their own backgrounds of experience and make observations to gather data as various topics and problems are studied. They need to use the knowledge they have plus new data obtained from observation to make comparisons, interpretations, or use other processes.

Recalling. To recall as a part of inquiry is to retrieve *selectively,* to recognize, or to remember items related to the topic under study. Both cognitive and affective elements may be recalled. A key outcome for the teacher is identification of a student's knowledge about a topic, degree of interest, and misconceptions or biases—all of which can be used to improve learning. Open-ended questions are used to guide recall during initiating and opening activities, and to initiate classifying, interpreting, and other processes. The examples that follow and the material in Charts 6–7 and 6–8 provide guidelines for instruction.

What do you know about ______? What can you recall about ______?
What have you learned before about ______? What does ______ make you think of?
Who remembers what ______ means? What feelings do you have about ______?
Who can recall activities that may be useful in studying ______? Can you think of materials that may be helpful?

Chart 6–7
Improving the Ability To Recall

Have a clear purpose for study.
Take notes, make an outline, put ideas in your own words and use them in discussion and other activities.
Try to get ideas the first time, but review as needed to clarify them.
Organize facts around key terms (concepts) and main ideas.
Think of how ideas may be used on other problems, how they may be applied to other situations.

Chart 6–8
Using Clues To Aid Recalling

Key dates, persons, places, events
Retrieval charts in which facts are grouped under people, problems, causes, effects, resources, or other items
Organizers such as production, goods, role, customs, region equality, and other concepts
Activities and materials used before on similar problems
Difficulties met on similar problems and how they were solved

Observing. To observe is to perceive, examine, or focus attention on an object or activity with a purpose in mind. Observation is an intake process used to collect data, and may be direct or indirect. Direct observation is firsthand perception of objects and activities by looking, listening, touching, smelling, tasting. Indirect observation includes reading and listening to secondary sources; examining pictures, maps, and other data sources; and the like. Some model questions that may be adapted for use in a variety of units to guide observing follow:

> What do we need to find out about ______? What should we look for?
> How can we find out? look? listen? ask someone? What other ways might be used?
> What can we find in this ______ (picture, map, reading)?

Effective observing requires the ability to (1) identify a focus or purpose, (2) identify appropriate data sources, (3) identify relevant data, (4) control feelings, (5) make necessary records, and (6) check observations for accuracy and completeness. Charts 6–9 and 6–10 illustrate the application of these abilities.

Chart 6–9
Good Observers

Know what they are looking for and keep a sharp focus
Use direct observation—look, listen, touch, smell, taste as appropriate
Use indirect observation—read, watch films, and use other data sources
Find it as it is, not as they think it ought to be
Check findings with others and against other sources

Chart 6–10
Observing

Know what you want to find and keep a focus.
Use a question, concept or hypothesis as a guide.
Identify major and minor items.
Make records as needed for future use.
Double-check findings to be sure they are accurate.

Defining and Interpreting

These two processes are essential to the clarification of meaning. They are basic to the use of reading materials, maps, and other media. At times they are used together to clarify and explain thoughts and feelings presented in various sources of data.

Defining. To define is to state or otherwise indicate the meaning of a word, map symbol, phrase, or problem. A good definition is precise, sets limits on what is included, is stated in terms different from the one being defined, and is useful in further inquiry. Defining problems or issues calls for several definitions as terms and phrases are clarified, emotive aspects of terms are considered, and elements to include are identified.

The most useful type of definition should be selected in any given situation. The following examples, stated by students, illustrate different types of definitions:

Demonstrating: "Watch while I show what candle dipping means."
Showing: "This picture shows what a tugboat is."
Using analogies: "A governor is like a president except he runs a state."
Using synonyms or antonyms: "Rapid means fast." "Rapid is the opposite of slow."
Using glossaries or dictionaries: "The glossary says that a vaquero is a cowboy."
Stating behavior (behavioral definitions): "A legislator campaigns for office, writes bills, serves on committees, things like that."
Stating operations (operational definitions): "You figure population density by dividing the population of an area by the square miles in the area."

These model questions and Charts 6–11 and 6–12 may be used to focus attention on different types of definition.

Chart 6–11
Questions To Guide Defining

What is to be defined? word? phrase? map symbol? behavior? operation? feelings?
How is it like and different from others we know?
What is included? not included?
What kind of definition will be most useful? example? analogy? picture? demonstration? behavioral? operational?
Have you checked the definition? Did you use terms different from the one being defined? Is the meaning clear? useful?

Chart 6–12
How Do Feelings Affect the Meaning of These Terms?

Fair play	Lobbyist
Justice	Dictator
Freedom	Majority
Rights	Minority
Demands	Democracy
Poverty	Communism
Police	Environment
President	Pollution
Politician	Ghetto

What do you mean by ______ (producer, goods, urban function)? Or, What does ______ mean?
What is the meaning of ______ (freedom, injustice, and the like)? What feelings do you have about it? How might feelings affect our definition?
What is a good way to clear up the meaning of this term? Using a picture or model? demonstrating the meaning? other?

Who can define ______ (carpenter, judge, scout) by telling what he does?
Who can define ______ (average income per family, population density) by stating how it is figured?
Which meaning(s) of ______ (bank, pollution, democracy) should we use? Which one best fits the context?

Interpreting. To interpret is to explain the meaning, to state the significance, to translate or illustrate the thoughts and feelings one has obtained from looking at and thinking about a map, graph, picture, or other data source. Interpreting can be defined more broadly than this to include inferring and other processes, but it is not done here because of the importance of accurate interpretation of the intended meaning that should be derived from a given source of data. After interpretations are made and checked for reasonableness and accuracy, students should proceed to generalizing, inferring, or other processes. The following model questions and the material in Charts 6–13, 6–14, and 6–15 may be used to guide the interpretation of data.

What main idea(s) and supporting evidence did you find in this ______ (film, reading, table, and so on)?
Can you explain the diagram that shows the main steps in ______ (processing mail, making clothes, passing a bill)?
What relationships did you find on the map between ______ and ______ (location of homes and schools, travel time and terrain)?
Can you explain this ______ (activity, behavior, and the like) in your own words?
How can we ______ (summarize, demonstrate, act out) the main points presented in this material?
What is your interpretation if you use ______ (specialization, interdependence, factors of production) to explain it?

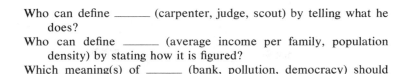

Chart 6–13
Using Concepts and Main Ideas To Interpret Findings

How can we use division of labor to explain family activities?
How can we use interdependence to interpret trade between them?
How can we use equality of opportunity to explain their position?
How can we use expectation of others to explain his role?

Chart 6–14
Interpreting Maps

Check the title to note content.
Check the key to define symbols, colors, and scale.
Identify directions by finding the north arrow, parallels, and meridians.
Use colors, flow of rivers, contour lines, and hachures to identify changes in elevation.
Identify relationships between items.

Chart 6–15

A Strategy for Interpreting

Procedure	Focusing Questions	Illustrative Application
Study the data source to get the intended meaning. →	What does this show? contain? tell? present? How can we use the data? →	What does this transportation route map show? How do the title and map key help to interpret it?
Identify and discuss basic data and main ideas. →	What did you see? find? note for use? Which ideas are most important? →	Who can describe the main transportation routes? What major cities are linked by them?
Identify and describe relationships, similarities, differences. →	Which items are related? What similarities and differences are important? →	How are transportation routes and city locations related? How are the main routes alike? different?
Summarize, explain, or conclude (be sure to stick to the data). →	How can we summarize the key ideas? What can we conclude? →	What can we conclude about main routes and location of cities? How might we explain the relationship?

Why is a farm like this in Hokkaido? How might the concept of cultural borrowing be used to make an interpretation? (International Society for the Study of Education, Tokyo)

Comparing/ Contrasting and Classifying/ Ordering

These two processes are used extensively in concept formation and organization of data for further use. Information that has been recalled or observed and interpreted may be compared and classified in retrieval charts, outlines, or other forms. Data may be ordered from largest to smallest, most important to least important, or in some other sequence. Then such processes as generalizing, analyzing, and predicting can be put to more effective use.

Comparing/contrasting. To compare is to identify similarities in objects and activities; to contrast is to identify differences. In everyday usage the term *comparing* is used to include the identification of both similarities and differences. Probably no questions are used more in the social studies than those that focus attention on comparing and contrasting:

How are they alike? How are they different?
How are ______ and ______ (work of mothers and fathers, goods and services, imports and exports) alike? How are they different?
How can ______ (jobs or community workers, these two cities) be compared? Or, on what points can we compare ______?
Who can summarize how they are alike? Who can state how they are different?

Charts 6–16 and 6–17 illustrate conceptual models that may be used to guide the systematic comparing and contrasting of selected topics.

Chart 6–16
A Model for Comparing Communities

Population	Major zones
Location	Government
History	Urban problems
Industry	Renewal plans
Transportation	Minority groups
Recreation	Special features

Chart 6–17
A Model for Comparing Populations

Number	Settlement patterns
Growth rate	Areas of concentration
Ethnic makeup	Central cities
Distribution	Other cities
Migrations	Predictions

Classifying/Ordering. To classify is to group, sort, or place items in categories according to identified characteristics or other criteria. To order is to arrange items according to amount, size, area, value, or other characteristics. Classifications may be single-stage—for example, based on one criterion such as goods made by mothers—or they may be based on two or more criteria, such as goods made by mothers that are worn by members of the family. Three widely used means of grouping in the social studies are by descriptive characteristics, function or use, and relationships. These model questions and Charts 6–18, 6–19, and 6–20 provide some guidelines.

> How can we group these ______ (fruits, houses, and the like, by descriptive characteristics)?
> Which ones are ______ (red, large, nearest, and other descriptive characteristics)?
> Which items are used for ______ (food, recreation, other)?
> Which ones are ______ (health, postal, and so on, by function or activity) workers?
> How can these ______ and ______ (resources and products, events and time periods, and other related items) be grouped?
> Which items are part of ______ (a dairy farm, steel production, etc., to show part–whole relationships)?

The ordering of items calls for straightforward use of such questions as these:

> How may we arrange these from ______ to ______ (largest to smallest, longest to shortest, most important to least important)?
> How can we rank these in order according to ______ (population, area, amount of production, distance from New York?
> In what order should we place these items (dates on a time line, pictures for a pictorial graph, columns in a bar graph)?

Chart 6–18 **Grouping Workers**	Chart 6–19 **Why Should We Classify Items?**	Chart 6–20 **Ways To Group**
Which ones produce goods? Which ones produce services? Which ones work at home? Which ones work in town?	To develop the meaning of a concept To clear up what is included in a definition To store ideas for later use To compare and contrast items more effectively To identify how items are related To help interpret, analyze, or evaluate To use for other purposes	By uses—tools, materials, other items By appearance—color, size, other features By relationships—parts of a whole, causes and effects, and the like

The teaching strategy for classifying in Chart 6–21 begins with clarifying what is to be grouped, moves to identification of common features as a basis for grouping, and ends by labeling the groups and considering

Chart 6–21
A Strategy for Classifying

Procedure	Focusing Questions	Illustrative Application
Observe and identify items to be grouped. →	What did you see? hear? find? read? note? →	What items (goods and services) are shown in these pictures?
Identify common features for use in grouping. →	Which ones may be grouped together? or, How might we group them? →	How are some items alike? How are others alike?
Decide on a basis for grouping. →	Why can they be grouped this way? or, How are these alike? →	Which ones are things someone makes? Which are not things, but are useful work?
Name, label, or define each group. →	What is a good name for each group? →	Who has a name for each group? Which can be called goods? Services?
Consider other possible groupings, if appropriate. →	What other groups might we make? How are they alike? →	Are there other ways we can group them? How about work of police? work of firefighters?

other possible groupings. Notice that observing, recalling, comparing, and defining are involved.

Generalizing Generalizing is central to the effective use of higher level processes such as hypothesizing, synthesizing, and evaluating. It is frequently linked with interpreting and inferring as students move beyond interpreted data and inferences drawn from data to formulate main ideas. It provides generalizations that serve as a basis for analyzing, synthesizing, predicting, and making other applications of learning.

To generalize is to derive a principle or main idea from data. Two or more concepts are included in a generalization—for example, "Many schools are located in the residential part of the community"; "All cities provide education, transportation, business, and other services"; "How people use their environment is influenced by their culture." To qualify as generalizations, statements such as the foregoing should be (1) based on evidence; (2) be shown widespread, prevalent, or usually the case; (3) based on two or more concepts; and (4) be applicable to most if not all members of a group. Charts 6–22 and 6–23 contain guidelines and questions that may be used to improve ability to generalize.

Chart 6–22
What Can We Say in General:

About the main problems cities are facing?
About the work of urban planners?
About the purposes of urban renewal plans?
About the main difficulties in renewal projects?

Chart 6–23
How To Generalize

Get data from pictures, reading materials, and other sources.
Find what is common or general in the data.
State a main idea that describes what is common or general.
Check to find out if the main idea fits data in other situations.

The following model questions may be used to focus attention on the formulation of different types of generalizations:

In general, what can we say about ______ (the uses of lumber, the role of mayors)?
What are the main ______ (causes of air pollution, functions of government, reasons for urban problems)?
According to the evidence, what are the relationships between ______ and ______ (scarcity and prices, supply and demand, travel routes and location of cities)?
What is the main difference between ______ and ______ (producers and consumers, the work of mayors and governors)?
What are the main ways that ______ (homes, cities, the New England states) have changed?
What general statement describes ______ (the advantages of dividing the work, the weaknesses in the Articles of Confederation, how specialization and interdependence are related)?

The teaching strategy in Chart 6–24 begins with identification of data on which the generalization is to be based, followed by identification of common elements and formulation of a tentative generalization. The tentative generalization is checked against the data and if necessary revised or made subject to conditions or other qualifications. Further checking of the generalization may be made against other data to find out if it applies in other situations. This last step is essential in formulating generalizations of broad applicability.

Analyzing and Synthesizing These two processes may be viewed as opposite sides of a coin. Analyzing focuses on breaking down a whole into parts, whereas synthesizing focuses on bringing together parts in a new way.

Analyzing. To analyze is to take apart, to divide, to identify elements, relationships, and principles. The focus of analysis may be on (1)

Chart 6–24

A Strategy for Generalizing

Procedure	Focusing Questions	Illustrative Application
Get the data (facts) clearly in mind and interpret them. →	What did you find? see? hear? read? note? →	What did you find to be major governmental activities at the local and state levels?
Identify common elements, relationships, or main ideas. →	What common elements did you find? Which items are related? →	What common activities did you find? (executive, legislative, judicial)
Make a tentative generalization. →	What can we say in general? →	What seems to be a sound conclusion about activities common at both levels?
Test the tentative generalization against other data. →	Does our generalization hold up as we check other data? →	What does this report (film, filmstrip, reading) show to be the main governmental activities at both levels? Is our generalization valid?

parts, kinds, types, groups, qualities, objectives, motives, assumptions; (2) common elements in several events or different elements in a single event; (3) time/space elements and relationships; or (4) causes, reasons, effects, consequences, organizing principles. The following model questions and Charts 6–25 and 6–26 can be used to guide the making of different types of analyses.

What are the main ______ (parts of this picture, mural, reading selection; regions of this country; time periods in the growth of our state)?
Why did the ______ (author, artist, speaker) break the problem or topic into these parts?
How are the steps in ______ (making bread, passing a bill, the leader's rise to power) related?
How are the parts of this ______ (story, report, mural) related?
How are ______ (problems, activities, regions, time periods, concepts, themes, values) used to organize this material?
What ______ (topics, themes, headings; pictures, objects, maps) can we use to organize and present our ideas?

Chart 6–25

Analyzing Stories

What are the main parts?
How does it begin? move ahead? end?
In what order are the main events presented?
How are your feelings about characters related to what they said or did?

Chart 6–26

Analyzing Pictures

What main things are shown?
What is the central idea? How are other items related to it?
How can we use the information to answer questions?
How do reactions or feelings aroused by it affect what we see in it?

The strategy in Chart 6–27 begins with clarification of the need to break the topic or problem into parts, then moves to ways in which it might be analyzed—causes, regions, and the like. The meaning of each part selected for analysis should be defined to guide the identification and organization of related data. After information is classified under each part and explored, a summary or conclusion should be made.

Chart 6–27

A Strategy for Analyzing

Procedure	Focusing Questions	Illustrative Application
Identify useful ways to break the problem into parts. →	How can we break the problem into parts? What main parts (types, reasons, causes) should be studied? →	How can we break down our question on urban land use? What are the main types of land use in cities?
Define each part clearly. →	What is the meaning of each part? What does each part include? →	How can we define each type? commercial? industrial? residential? recreational? other?
Identify and organize data related to each part. →	What information do we have on each part? How are these parts related? →	What data can we classify under each type of land use?
State summary, conclusion, or explanation, based on the analysis. →	What does our analysis show? What can we conclude? →	Who can summarize the types of land use in order from greatest to least? How might we explain the differences?

Synthesizing. To synthesize is to bring parts together into a meaningful whole, to integrate, to create a new product. Parts or elements are put together to form a unified structure around a key concept, theme,

Chart 6–28
Presenting Ideas on Community Life

What to present: early settlement and growth? main zones of the community? transportation networks? other items?

How to present them: pictures? charts? maps? booklet? reports? exhibit? other form of presentation?

Chart 6–29
How Can We Use These To Combine Ideas in New Ways?

Models	Flow charts	Rhythms
Murals	Diagrams	Dances
Maps	Time lines	Games
Reports	Stories	Simulations
Booklets	Poems	Dramatization
Scrapbooks	Exhibits	Role playing

question, principle, or other organizer as in Chart 6–28. The completed synthesis may take the form of an original oral or written report, exhibit, map, mural, dramatization, or other creative product, as shown in Chart 6–29.

Special attention should be given to creativity because a desired outcome of synthesizing is a new and original product created by the

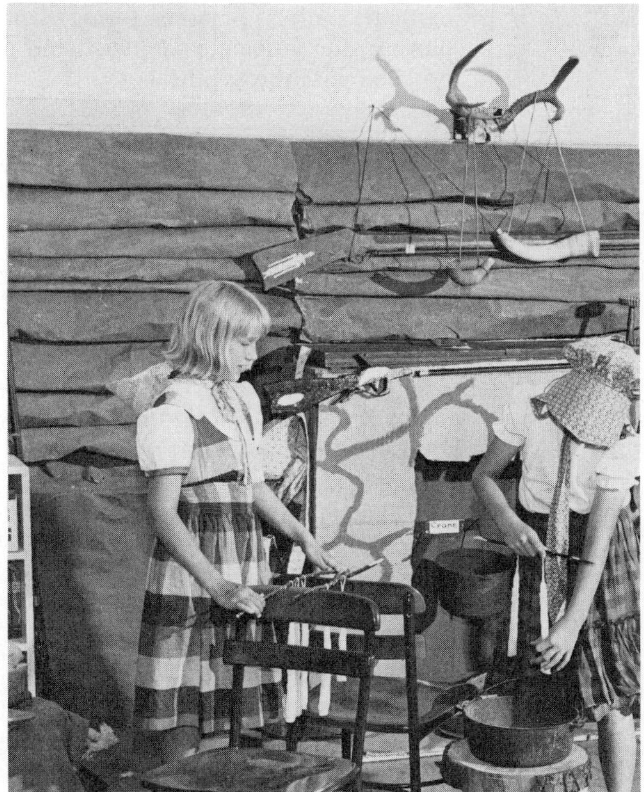

In what other ways might learnings about life in early America be synthesized? (Los Angeles, California)

students. If originality is not evident, the activity is better classified as generalizing, interpreting, or other process, depending upon the operations involved. The following questions are illustrative of those that may be used to spark creativity in synthesizing:

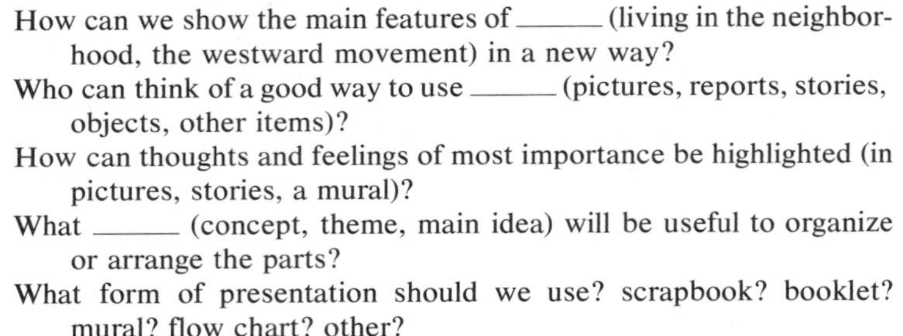

How can we show the main features of ______ (living in the neighborhood, the westward movement) in a new way?
Who can think of a good way to use ______ (pictures, reports, stories, objects, other items)?
How can thoughts and feelings of most importance be highlighted (in pictures, stories, a mural)?
What ______ (concept, theme, main idea) will be useful to organize or arrange the parts?
What form of presentation should we use? scrapbook? booklet? mural? flow chart? other?

The teaching strategy in Chart 6–30 begins with a focus on what is to be synthesized. The main parts or items to be combined are typically considered next, followed by organizing ideas and ways of combining the parts. It is essential that students be open to ideas when they are considering themes or other organizing ideas, pondering the use of exhibits, murals, or other forms of presentation, and the like. After exploring alternatives, students should make plans that will enable them to proceed with the synthesis.

Chart 6–30
A Strategy for Synthesizing

Procedure		Focusing Questions		Illustrative Application
Clarify the purpose, or what is to be produced (synthesized).	→	How can we bring together the main ideas of this topic in a new way?	→	What are some new ways we can show major aspects of frontier life?
Identify basic parts or items to include.	→	What are the most important items (ideas, activities) to include?	→	What should we include? shelter? clothing? recreation? food? protection?
Identify organizing idea(s) and form(s) of presentation.	→	How should the parts be organized (arranged, portrayed, shown)?	→	What theme(s) might we use? What form(s) of verbal and pictorial presentation should we use?
Decide on fruitful plan(s) and proceed with the synthesis.	→	What plan(s) do you prefer? why? What is needed to proceed?	→	What theme(s) do you prefer? why? What form of presentation? mural? scrapbook? report? dramatization?

Inferring, Hypothesizing, Predicting These three interrelated processes go beyond the data at hand. An inference is logical, reasonable, sensible, and applicable in a specific situation. A hypothesis is more general and should apply to all similar cases. It should also be testable. A prediction should be reasonable and supported by evidence, but one must usually wait to see if it is accurate—as, for example, a prediction about an election.

Inferring. To infer is to state a logical consequence, draw an implication, read between the lines, or derive other thoughts and feelings that are not explicit in a given data source. The following model questions illustrate those used in instructional materials to focus attention on inferring, and Charts 6–31 and 6–32 contain examples, questions, and guidelines that may be used in various units of study.

How do you think they must feel about ______ (moving into a new neighborhood, the new civic center, his election)?
How do you think they must have ______ (felt about it, learned to do that, done so much in such a short time)?
Why do you say that ______ (they felt happy, he did it to help others, the writer of the article is biased)? or, Why do you think that ______?
What might be ______ (the next step, her reason for doing it, the effect of that decision)?
What do you suppose someone would do if ______ (he were in that situation, some individuals violated the rules, she were appointed to the pollution control committee)?
Why do you suppose ______ (the behavior surprised them, they decided to take that action, these areas are more populated than others)? or, What are the possible reasons that ______?

Chart 6–31
What To Infer

How someone may feel in a given situation
What someone may think about a problem
What someone may say or do in a situation
What the motives or purposes of an individual may be
What behavior or action may follow from an incident
What the reasons may be for an event

Chart 6–32
Can You Infer

Why the population is greater in some areas than in others?
What may be produced from the resources they have?
What minority problems they may have from the information on population makeup?
What the climate may be from the data on location and elevation?
What their feelings about neighboring countries may be from the treaties they have signed?

Hypothesizing. To hypothesize is to state a tentative explanation, solution, generalization, or proposition that shows how two or more items are related. Hypotheses are useful in guiding the search for data. They may be generated during introductory activities, as study of a unit progresses, and at the end of one topic to lead into the study of another. Hypotheses confirmed by evidence become conclusions or generalizations. Hypotheses can be stated as questions, if–then propositions, or generalizations—for example, "What reasons did people have for moving westward?" "If people moved westward, did they move for different reasons?" "People moved westward for many reasons, not a single one." Hypotheses such as these indicate a condition (moving westward) and what is usually related to it (reasons).

The following model questions may be used to stimulate hypothesizing about different types of relationships, along with the material in Charts 6–33 through 6–36.

Chart 6–33
A Good Hypothesis

Is a question, statement, or if–then proposition that can be answered or tested.
Shows how two or more items are related.
Helps to explain the topic or problem under study.
Is a tentative generalization of data or inferences.
May be drawn from experience, evidence, inferences, principles.

Chart 6–34
Hypothesizing

Should we state it as a question, statement, or if–then idea?
What evidence, principle, or experience can we use as a basis?
What should be stated as given and what should we look for?
What cause–effect or other relationship is involved?
Does it apply to all or most cases, not just a particular one? Can it be tested?

Chart 6–35
How Can the Following Be Completed?

If workers specialize, then dependence on others ______.
If the supply of an item is greater than demand, the price ______.
If a place has a Mediterranean climate, then living conditions usually are ______.
When people migrate, the main reasons usually are ______.

Chart 6–36
Stating What Usually Happens

What usually happens when one part of an ecosystem is damaged?
What environmental problems usually arise in densely populated cities?
What usually happens when building construction exceeds the rate of forest renewal?
What benefits can be obtained from recycling of wastes?

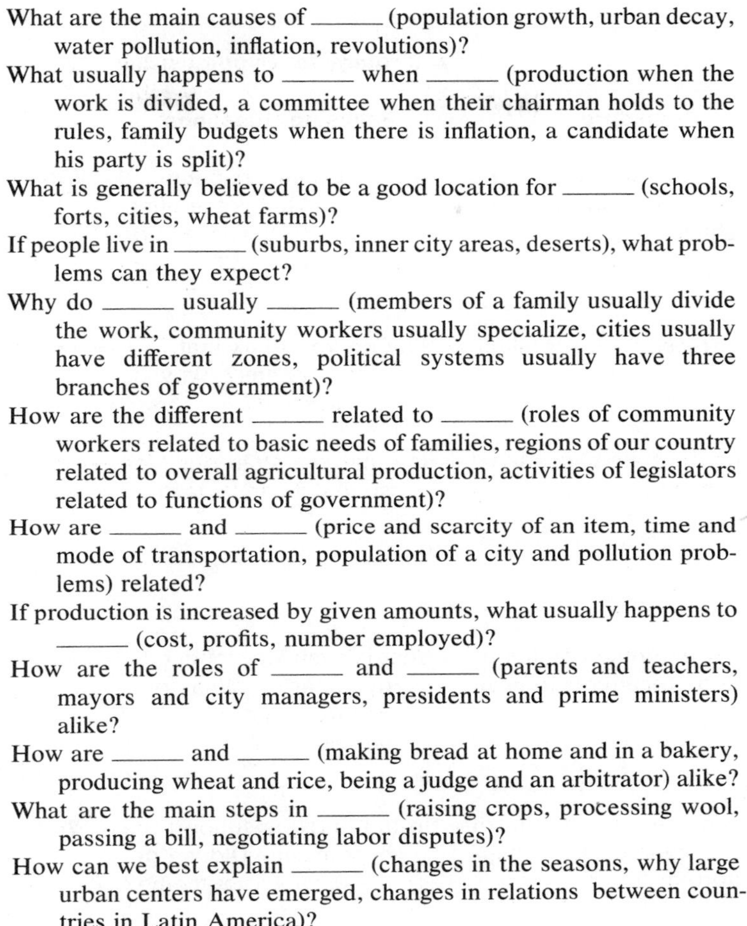

What are the main causes of ______ (population growth, urban decay, water pollution, inflation, revolutions)?
What usually happens to ______ when ______ (production when the work is divided, a committee when their chairman holds to the rules, family budgets when there is inflation, a candidate when his party is split)?
What is generally believed to be a good location for ______ (schools, forts, cities, wheat farms)?
If people live in ______ (suburbs, inner city areas, deserts), what problems can they expect?
Why do ______ usually ______ (members of a family usually divide the work, community workers usually specialize, cities usually have different zones, political systems usually have three branches of government)?
How are the different ______ related to ______ (roles of community workers related to basic needs of families, regions of our country related to overall agricultural production, activities of legislators related to functions of government)?
How are ______ and ______ (price and scarcity of an item, time and mode of transportation, population of a city and pollution problems) related?
If production is increased by given amounts, what usually happens to ______ (cost, profits, number employed)?
How are the roles of ______ and ______ (parents and teachers, mayors and city managers, presidents and prime ministers) alike?
How are ______ and ______ (making bread at home and in a bakery, producing wheat and rice, being a judge and an arbitrator) alike?
What are the main steps in ______ (raising crops, processing wool, passing a bill, negotiating labor disputes)?
How can we best explain ______ (changes in the seasons, why large urban centers have emerged, changes in relations between countries in Latin America)?

The strategy in Chart 6–37 begins with the stating of propositions that show how two or more items are related. The hypothesis should be more general than an inference, because a good hypothesis covers most or all cases or instances under study. By asking such questions as "What usually happens if . . . ?" or "How are these items related in most situations?" it is possible to get students to think in more general terms than when they are inferring. After students state tentative hypotheses and give reasons for them, they should try to refine their statements for testing. Next comes the testing, followed by discussion of the findings. Finally, a decision should be made whether additional evidence is needed. If it is, another test may be devised.

Chart 6–37
A Strategy for Hypothesizing

Procedure	Focusing Questions	Illustrative Application
State preliminary hypotheses that show relationships. →	What usually happens if ____? What is the effect of ____? How is ____ related to ____? →	What may happen if we divide the work in making party favors? Will more or fewer favors be produced?
State reasons for preliminary hypotheses. →	Why do you think that usually happens? Why do you say that? →	Why do you think more will be produced? What reasons can you give?
Refine the statement so that it can be tested. →	How can we state our idea so that it can be tested? →	How can we sharpen the statement? "If the work is divided, more favors will be produced than by individuals working alone"?
Identify essential conditions and procedures for testing. →	What is a fair way to test the hypothesis? What procedures and materials are needed? →	How can we test our idea? What tools and materials do both groups need? What other conditions are essential?
Analyze the data to find if the hypothesis is supported. →	Do the findings support the hypothesis? Did we get the expected outcome? →	Which group produced more? Who can summarize and explain the findings?
Decide if more evidence is needed. →	Do we need more data? If so, how may we gather it? →	Are we sure of our findings? Do we need to run another test?

Predicting. To predict is to forecast, prophesy, or anticipate what might happen. A prediction is based on relevant information but goes beyond it to identify what may happen in (1) a different time dimension (what future population may be), (2) a different sample (what one city may do to curb pollution because of what others have done or plan to do), and (3) a related activity or topic (an increase in steel production because of projected increase in car production). The following model questions and Charts 6–38 and 6–39 may be used to guide making different types of predictions.

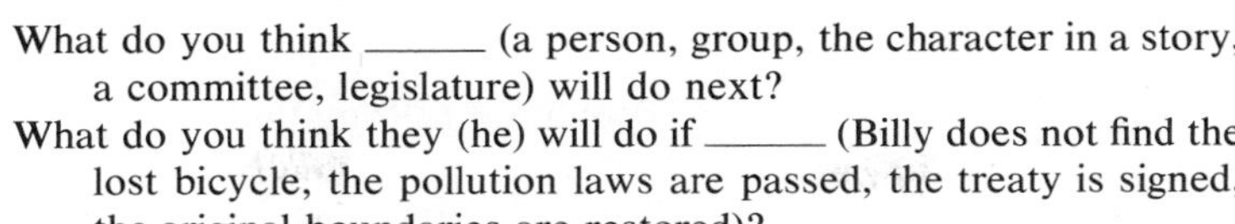

What do you think ______ (a person, group, the character in a story, a committee, legislature) will do next?
What do you think they (he) will do if ______ (Billy does not find the lost bicycle, the pollution laws are passed, the treaty is signed, the original boundaries are restored)?
What do you think will happen if ______ (the school bonds are not approved, new housing is located on the outskirts of town, aid to African countries is stopped)?
What do you think will be the main effects of ______ (the urban renewal project on business, their decision to move ahead with low-cost housing, their intervention in the Middle East)?
What do you estimate the ______ (school enrollment, population of our state, production of steel) will be in ten years?
Where do you think they will locate the ______ (new school, shopping center, factory, nuclear power station)?

Chart 6–38
What Do You Predict?

What new laws on water pollution may the legislature pass?
What may happen to agriculture after the new dam is finished?
What may happen to the environment after it is built?
What critical problems can we expect if the antipollution program is approved? if it is not approved?

Chart 6–39
Checking Predictions

Basis: What change or process is involved?
Conditions: Under what conditions will the change occur?
Probability: What is the likelihood of its occurrence?
Consequence: If it does occur, what might be the effect?

The teaching strategy in Chart 6–40 begins with defining what is to be predicted and then searching for a basis for making predictions. Various predictions and the reasons for them are considered next, followed by giving attention to any factors that may have been overlooked and final shaping of the predictions to fit the data and relevant factors.

Evaluating To evaluate is to make a judgment of merit, worth, or value in terms of defined criteria. Clarification of the standards or criteria to be used is essential, for otherwise students can only give opinions instead of forming considered judgments. Evaluation may be done along with other processes to test the effectiveness with which they are being used, or it may be a final step to appraise objects and events (see Charts 6–41 and 6–42).

Focusing questions are needed for two different types of evaluation. The first involves the use of internal evidence or standards for assessing the reports, documents, reading selections, and other materials. Typical standards are accuracy, consistency in use of terms, flow of ideas, sound-

Chart 6–40
A Strategy for Predicting

Procedure	Focusing Questions	Illustrative Application
Clarify what is to be predicted. →	What changes (trends, developments) are shown here? What might we predict from this evidence? →	What do these data indicate about population growth in our community? What changes can you find?
Analyze the data to find a basis for predicting. →	What is a good basis for making predictions? →	How much growth was there during each period?
Make tentative predictions. →	What predictions can we make? What do you think will happen? →	What do you think the growth will be during the next period?
Review reasons or bases for predictions. →	Why do you think that will happen? How can you support your prediction? →	What was your basis for the prediction? How many think the growth rate will be the same?
Consider related data or conditions that may have been overlooked. →	What else may be important to consider? Are other facts needed? →	What about the reports on decreased birth rate and lack of land for houses?
Modify predictions to fit new data or conditions. →	How should we change our predictions? How can we use new data to improve our predictions? →	How should we change our predictions because of the data on birth rate and lack of land?

ness of arguments, and relation of conclusions to evidence. Model questions:

How can ______ (our report, map; or this graph, plan) be improved? Is it accurate? well organized? meaningful? useful for our purpose?
How accurate (adequate, useful, consistent, biased) is this ______ (document, diagram, flow chart, report)?
To what extent are the ______ (conclusions, generalizations, inferences) supported?

The second type of evaluation involves the use of external standards related to the objectives to be achieved and the means of achieving them. The standards may be the objectives, commonly used criteria, or comparison with a recognized standard of excellence. Examples of each type of standard are: (1) using objectives for urban renewal as criteria to assess plans, (2) using defined standards of freedom of speech to judge the conduct of a meeting, and (3) comparing one conservation program with another acknowledged to be outstanding. Model questions are:

To what extent will this ______ (plan, program, type of action) lead to the stated goals?
Which of the alternatives is most desirable in terms of ______ (individual benefits, group benefits, objectives)?
To what extent were standards of ______ (justice, freedom, personal security) upheld during this period?
How does this ______ (report, antipollution proposal, airport, political system) compare with the model of an outstanding one?

Chart 6–41
Appraising Alternatives

What is the problem or purpose?
What are the different proposals or plans?
What standards should be used to assess them? Are they fair?
What will be the outcome or effects of each plan?
Which plan will have the most desirable outcomes in terms of the standards?

Chart 6–42
Evaluating Interpretations

Can you explain the intended meaning?
Did you stick to the data?
What relationships did you find?
Can you state the main idea and supporting details?
Can you summarize it in your own words and state what is most important or significant?

The strategy presented in Chart 6–43 begins with identifying and defining what is to be appraised, followed by attention to the standards or criteria that should be used. In actual practice these phases may be joined together, provided students understand the focus of the evaluation. Next, attention is given to gathering and interpreting evidence to show the extent to which the defined standards are met. The next step is necessary if alternatives—different plans, materials, or proposals—are being assessed. Direct attention should be given to consideration of possible outcomes or consequences of each alternative, with an attempt to identify the one that will have the most desirable uses or effects in light of the standards. Finally, a judgment or evaluation should be made of the quality or merit of the item(s) under appraisal, with suggestions for improvement as appropriate.

PROBLEM SOLVING AS A UNIFYING PROCEDURE

Problem solving may be used to bring together the various aspects of thinking and inquiry. The model that follows is especially useful in group work and provides a setting within which individual activities

Chart 6–43

A Strategy for Evaluating

Procedure	Focusing Questions	Illustrative Application
Identify and define the focus of evaluation. →	What is to be appraised? Why should ____ be assessed? →	Why should we evaluate the renewal plans? How can we judge them?
Identify and define standards of appraisal. →	What standards (values, criteria) should be used? →	What are the goals for urban renewal? Are they up to standards? What other standards might be used?
Collect data related to each standard. →	What is the evidence? What data can we find for each standard? →	What evidence do we have to show how the objectives will be achieved?
Identify possible outcomes (effects, consequences) of each proposal. →	What are likely outcomes of each proposal? Which one will have the most desirable outcomes? →	What may the effects of each proposal be on traffic? business? beautification? other objectives?
Make a judgment, including suggestions for improvement. →	Which ____ best meets the standards? How might it be improved? →	In general, which proposal is best? why? In what ways can it be improved?

may be generated. The different inquiry processes are used as needed. Like any model, this one should be used flexibly. Vary the steps or phases as appropriate to guide the creative study of selected topics and to avoid the pitfalls of a regimented, step-by-step procedure. The major phases are these:

1. Clarifying and defining questions and problems
2. Recalling information and hypothesizing
3. Group planning of next steps
4. Finding, interpreting, appraising, and classifying information
5. Generalizing and further processing of information as needed
6. Evaluating procedures and outcomes

Clarifying and Defining Questions and Problems

This is the first step as new units are introduced and as different problems arise in a unit that is under way. The objective is to get pupils to recognize and understand the problems or questions to be studied. During the initiation of a unit, selected materials may be used to stimulate thinking.

Pictures, maps, objects, and other resources may be arranged to highlight significant questions or problems. After the students have examined the materials, there should be a discussion of the questions or problems to be attacked first. After first problems are defined and clarified, they may be listed on the chalkboard or on charts, as illustrated in Charts 6–44, 6–45, and 6–46.

Chart 6–44
Work at Home

What does mother do?
What does father do?
What can children do?
What do others do?

Chart 6–45
Boonesboro

Why was it built?
Who built it?
Where was it?
When was it built?
How was it built?
How did people travel to it?

Chart 6–46
Early Times in Our Community

Who were the first settlers?
What were the first buildings like?
Where was the first school?
Where were the first streets?
When was the railroad begun?
What changes have taken place?

Recognition and clarification of problems should be emphasized throughout the unit of instruction; each unit should become a series of problem-solving experiences with a smooth transition from one problem to the next. For example, moving from the work of members of the family to how the family obtains food calls for a definition of new questions and problems. Similarly, in units on our community, our state, westward movement, and other lands, a series of specific questions and problems should be defined with one growing out of the other.

Recalling Information and Hypothesizing

This phase of problem solving should be both systematic and creative. Students may recall previous information plus information introduced during the initiation of the unit as the teacher asks: "What can you recall about this topic?" "What have you learned before that we might use?" "How is it like other topics we have studied?" This may be followed by questions designed to elicit hypotheses: "What ideas do you have on this topic?" "What do you think we will find?" "What answers might we find to the questions we have listed?" The objectives of these two sets of questions are to retrieve information related to questions posed by the group during definition of the problem, to get students to state hypotheses regarding what they may find, to identify misconceptions they may have, and to involve them more fully in investigative processes.

Teachers sometimes ask whether tentative answers or hypotheses should be proposed for every problem that arises. No! When students lack the background for hypothesizing, the best procedure is to begin study of the questions noted during definition of the problem. But if a unit flows out of a preceding one, students should be able to state hypotheses and set the stage for effective investigation. Opportunities to hypothesize also arise during a unit as relationships are explored and key concepts developed. Because this phase of problem solving is sometimes neglected, the following examples are given to indicate the nature of children's hypotheses.

> In a unit on the home, a procedural problem arose: How can we get furniture for our playhouse? The children's suggestions were
> If the custodian has some, maybe we can borrow it.
> If we can get some wood and tools, we can make some.
> I can bring some from home. Can others bring some?

> In a unit on the post office, the question was "What happens to letters that are put in mail boxes?" Children's comments were
> A mailman picks them up. Then they are taken to the right place.
> Wait! They have to be sorted by somebody. I think they are taken downtown. Maybe they are sorted by workers or a machine.
> There must be a plan or a system. Then a mailman can deliver them.

> In a unit entitled Living in Early America, the problem of obtaining clothing was being considered. The question was "How did the early settlers process flax?" Hypotheses were
> If you pounded it flat, then you could cut it into strips.
> Maybe they dried it and then pulled out stringy fibers.
> I think you would need to soak it and then press it flat. If you scraped off the outside, then the stringy fibers could be pulled apart.

> In a unit on the westward movement, this problem on travel routes was considered by the group: Check the relief map of the United States and plan a route to California from St. Joseph, Missouri. Then check to see if your proposed route is the same as one of those used by early settlers. The children made the following proposals and comments:
> Go straight across the plains and mountains to San Francisco. If you go this way, you would have to find mountain passes through the Rockies and Sierra.
> Go along the Missouri to the Platte River and on to the coast across Utah and Nevada. If you would keep close to rivers, you could get water and there would not be many steep grades. I heard that some railroads and highways are built along water level routes.
> Go along south to Santa Fe and on to Los Angeles across New Mexico and Arizona. This would be a good route in the winter.
> Why couldn't we start our trip in St. Louis? Then we could use boats all the way to San Francisco.

In all these examples, the teacher was drawing on previous learning in order to propose tentative solutions or hypotheses. Creative thinking was involved as the children tried to relate past experiences to new problems. Divergent thinking was involved as they made multiple suggestions and considered different proposals. Critical thinking was involved as they evaluated the proposals and the ideas suggested in support of them. Suspended judgment was emphasized and the need for additional information was established. The question or problem was further elaborated and clarified, and the stage was set for group planning of ways to solve the problem.

Group Planning of Next Steps

The group planning phase often provides clues to tentative solutions and hypotheses, and to the best ways to proceed. Ways to gather information, possible sources of information, and assignment of responsibilities are considered. Questions such as the following are raised: "How shall we proceed?" "What are the next steps?" "How can we obtain needed information?" "What sources of information should be used?" "Should any jobs be assigned to individuals or small groups?" "Does everyone know what he has to do?" Attention may be given to a wide range of sources and procedures, as noted in Charts 6–47 and 6–48. A careful selection is made of the best possibilities, and children are urged to be on the lookout for others.

Chart 6–47
Sources of Information

Textbooks	Pictures
Clippings	Films
Magazines	Filmstrips
Newspapers	Slides
Maps and globes	Study trips
Encyclopedias	Visitors
The library	Find others

Chart 6–48
Procedures To Use

Reading	Drawing
Note taking	Mapping
Observing	Constructing
Collecting	Writing for information
Demonstrating	Outlining
Experimenting	Find others
Interviewing	

Finding, Interpreting, Appraising, and Classifying Information

With plans in mind, students proceed to gather and interpret data related to the questions, problems, or hypotheses that have been listed. Observation and related study skills are used to collect data; the meaning of terms may be defined; pictures, maps, and other data sources are interpreted; comparisons and contrasts may be made; and information is evaluated in terms of accuracy and relevance. Different sources of information are used and cross-checked. Double-checking may be necessary if differences are noted in interpretations, or if there is doubt about the accuracy of data. At times it may be necessary to reshow a film, reread a section of a reference, check one reference against another, or interview an expert to resolve a difference in fact or in interpretation of data.

Classifying information, along with comparing and contrasting, may be done to help interpret, share, and use information in generalizing, analyzing, synthesizing, and evaluating. Such questions as these may be used: "How can we group our findings?" "Which items seem to go together?" "Should we make a chart?" "How about a table?" "What about a map?" "What is best for our purposes?" "Are there other suggestions?"

Evaluation is called into play as children consider different possibilities. If directions for making something or steps in a sequence of events are involved, they may be listed on a chart, the chalkboard, or worksheets. If relationships between physical and cultural features are to be summarized, then a map or chart may be used. If major activities during historical periods are to be shown, then a time line, sequence chart, or an arrangement of sets of pictures and drawings may be made. An outline, a summary of notes, or simply sharing and grouping ideas as they are discussed may be adequate for other purposes.

Generalizing and Further Processing of Information

Generalizing frequently follows the phases discussed above, but other processes also are put to use. In most units of instruction, students proceed to draw inferences, test hypotheses, formulate generalizations, make predictions, and synthesize findings in new forms. For example, after interpreting data related to population growth in their city, students may draw and check inferences about possible environmental effects, state generalizations about the main causes of growth, make predictions about future growth and future ecological problems, and synthesize findings in graphs or maps to highlight growth during selected periods or in defined zones of the city. The following examples are illustrative:

> In a unit on our changing community, one group moved beyond interpretations and made the following generalizations and predictions:
>
> Changes have been faster in recent years. Some changes were made to take care of population growth. Some changes were occasioned by inventions and new ways of doing things.
>
> We predict that school enrollment will be 23,000 in ten years. Population will probably be around 112,000.

> In a unit on environmental problems, students proceeded to infer, generalize, predict, and synthesize as follows:
>
> Feelings about flood control and environmental problems seem to be high enough to get some action. Some people seem to be changing their ideas about what is important.
>
> The proposed legislation on environmental problems will be passed. If it is passed, the dam will probably be constructed at point A on the map, because it is best for preserving wildlife.

How people use the land is important in flood control. Some of the things done to prevent floods cause ecological problems.

A map was made to show location of flooded areas, points at which damage occurred to wildlife and to people, and possible sites for a dam.

Evaluating Processes and Outcomes Evaluation is a continuing phase of group inquiry that begins with the definition of the problem and moves on to the forming of generalizations and final appraisal of the effectiveness of individual and group work. During each phase of problem solving, attention is given to evaluation. During the definition of problems, for example, the teacher may ask: "Is the problem clear?" "Have main parts of the problem been considered?" Or, during the planning phase: "Have good sources of information been noted?" "Does each individual know what to do?" Similarly, during the classifying, interpreting, and further processing of information: "Are facts related to main ideas?" "Are relationships shown?" "Have we selected the best means of summarizing information?" By getting clues through observation, the teacher raises questions and makes comments that help children to appraise and to improve the skills and processes used in the problem-solving approach.

In addition to the ongoing evaluation that is part of daily activities, there may be periodic and systematic appraisal of various aspects of thinking and learning. Teachers may use tests to check grasp of vocabulary, concepts, basic information, reading skills, and study skills. Charts, checklists, and other devices may be used to appraise work habits, use of materials, discussion techniques, committee work, outlines, reports, maps, and other activities and products. Charts 6–49, 6–50, and 6–51 are illustrative. Both self-evaluation and teacher appraisal are used to improve the attitudes, skills, and understandings that are

Chart 6–49 **Appraising Sources of Ideas**	Chart 6–50 **Judging Facts and Opinions**	Chart 6–51 **Appraising Talks and Reports**
Is it related to the topic? Is it recent enough for our purposes? Is it reliable? valid? Is it published by a special interest group? Does it contain enough information? Can it be checked against reliable sources?	Is it related to our questions? Is the source reliable? Is it consistent with related ideas? Is it supported by evidence? Is it too general to be useful? Is it advanced for a worthy cause?	Is the title descriptive of the topic? Does the introduction set the stage? Are the ideas in good order? Are main ideas supported by facts? Are opinions distinguished from facts? Do conclusions tie ideas together?

essential to effective thinking (a detailed discussion of principles and procedures of evaluation is presented in Chapter 15).

Teachers should be able to recognize certain common errors and difficulties in thinking as they evaluate and plan work. Among the more common errors in thinking are confusing the real and the fanciful, mixing facts and opinions, generalizing in terms of purely personal experience or from just a single instance, taking an "either-or" position when clear-cut alternatives do not exist, failing to check information, making errors in observation, organizing ideas to favor a point of view, and failing to consider consequences. The teacher should give such problems attention as they arise. Then, after students have identified errors and difficulties in their own thinking and problem-solving activities, they need experience in applying what they have learned to new situations. Charts 6–52 and 6–53 illustrate points that may be given direct attention in discussion and used in both self-evaluation and teacher appraisal.

Chart 6–52
Look Out For These Errors in Thinking

Mixing up the real and fanciful
Believing that there is only one way to do it
Thinking that one example "proves the rule"
Confusing facts and opinions
Believing that one thing caused another because they happened together
Letting our feelings hide some of the facts
Can you find others?

Chart 6–53
Did You Remember To Do Each of These?

Get facts on all sides of the question.
Check facts from different sources.
Summarize information so that it is clear and easy to use.
Check the meaning of terms and phrases that are not clear.
Compare your findings with others.
Make tentative conclusions that can be checked.

QUESTIONS, ACTIVITIES, EVALUATION

1. Identify four or five concepts that should be developed in a unit of your choice. Note two or three direct and vicarious experiences that might be used to develop them. Note how one of the concept development strategies might be used.
2. Indicate two or three examples of creative and critical thinking that you might include in a unit.
3. Examine a recently published social studies textbook to identify the types of questions that are included. Using the model questions in this chapter as a guide, classify them according to the process that

is the focus of each question. Which processes are used most? least? Revise several of the questions so that the focus is shifted to analyzing, synthesizing, or other higher-level processes.

4. Make a set of questions that you might use in a unit of your choice. Be sure to include two or three for each process, arranging them in a sequence that you think will be meaningful for students. Base the questions on a reading selection, map, filmstrip, or other resource.
5. Make an outline that shows how you can include each of the following in a unit of your choice:
   a. Recalling and observing
   b. Comparing/contrasting, classifying/ordering
   c. Defining, interpreting, generalizing
   d. Analyzing, synthesizing
   e. Inferring, hypothesizing, predicting
   f. Evaluating

   Which were most diffcult to put to use? why? Which processes do you think might be most diffcult for students to develop? why? How might the difficulties be overcome?
6. It is sometimes argued that only able children can learn to use inquiry processes. Others point out that all children need to learn how to use them. What is your position? How can instruction be individualized so that all children have an opportunity to develop them to the maximum of their ability? What suggestions in the chapter on individualized instruction might you use?

REFERENCES

BEYER, BARRY K., *Inquiry in the Social Studies Classroom.* Columbus, O.: Merrill, 1971. A model for inquiry and illustrative applications.

______, and ANTHONY N. PENNA, eds., *Concepts in the Social Studies.* Washington, D.C.: National Council for the Social Studies, 1971. Readings on concepts and how to develop them.

COLE, HENRY P., *Process Education.* Englewood Cliffs, N.J.: Educational Technology Publications, 1972. Guidelines for making processes a part of the curriculum.

FAIR, JEAN, and FANNIE R. SHAFTEL, eds., *Effective Thinking in the Social Studies* (37th Yearbook). Washington, D.C.: National Council for the Social Studies, 1967. Principles and procedures for developing thinking skills.

FRASER, DOROTHY MCCLURE, ed., *Social Studies Curriculum Development: Prospects and Problems* (39th Yearbook). Washington, D.C.: National Council for the Social Studies, 1969. Article by Tanck on concepts and generalizations.

HILLS, JAMES L., "Building and Using Inquiry Models in the Teaching of Geography," in *Focus on Geography* (40th Yearbook). Washington, D.C.: National Council for the Social Studies, 1970, pp. 305–35. Eleven processes identified and illustrated.

MARTORELLA, PETER H., *Concept Learning in the Social Studies.* Scranton, Pa.: International Textbook, 1971. Review of studies and models.

PHILLIPS, RICHARD C., *Teaching for Thinking in High School Social Studies.* Reading, Mass.: Addison-Wesley, 1974. Emphasis on processes.

RATHS, LOUIS E., SELMA WASSERMAN, ARTHUR JONES, and ARNOLD M. ROTHSTEIN, *Teaching for Thinking.* Columbus, O.: Merrill, 1967. Activities that may be used to develop processes.

RYAN, FRANK L., and ARTHUR K. ELLIS, *Instructional Implications of Inquiry.* Englewood Cliffs, N.J.: Prentice-Hall, 1974. Inquiry processes, selecting data sources, gathering and processing data, and examples of applications.

SANDERS, NORRIS M., *Classroom Questions.* New York: Harper & Row, 1966. Questions on seven cognitive levels.

TABA, HILDA, MARY DURKIN, JACK R. FRAENKEL, and ANTHONY MCNAUGHTON, *Teacher's Handbook for Elementary Social Studies* (2d ed.). Reading, Mass.: Addison-Wesley, 1971. Strategies for concept development, generalizing, and applying principles (predicting).

Focusing Questions

How can democratic values and behavior patterns be developed?
What strategies and techniques are used to develop attitudes?
What strategies can be used to develop, analyze, and clarify values?

Developing Values, Attitudes, & Valuing Processes

Even though the United States is the world's oldest democracy, the controversy and strife of recent years make it clear that we need to improve our methods of learning and teaching the democratic ideal and how to make it work. The challenge today has been sharpened by the disparity between ideal and reality, and by the discrimination that continues to deny equality of opportunity to so many Americans. But the magnitude of the problems that face us must not lead to discouragement and apathy or to a disapproval of the importance of equality, human dignity, and concern for others. Rather, the time is overdue to make the changes that will enable progressive generations to bring ideals and reality closer together.

Our choice of approach is critical. To focus on the bright side—on the promises and ideals of democracy, on our achievements, on the progress made over the years—risks disillusionment when students later discover that everything is not right, that much has not been done. To focus on the dark side—on the problems, issues, misdeeds, and failures—can generate bitterness, cynicism and then apathy. A far more acceptable approach is to take a reflective stance, to consider events in the light of such values as equality, justice, and concern for the individual. This approach opens opportunities to develop thinking and valuing processes, concepts, and skills that are essential to effective participation in a democratic society. And it allows for consideration of both positive and negative instances of action and behavior, of why both success and failure are found in human affairs, and of alternative ways of moving ahead to bring ideals and realities closer together.

VALUES, PROCESSES, GENERALIZATIONS

The idea of democracy is one of the most powerful ever conceived. The power and greatness of the idea stem from people's desire to govern themselves, the responsibilities each individual must assume, the emphasis on cooperation rather than on coercion, and faith in the use of intelligence to solve problems. The democratic values and processes that are so important in our lives today constitute one of the richest parts of our cultural heritage. From the first concepts of democracy in the distant past to the great power of the democratic idea in the present, there has been a continuing struggle to win and extend human freedom and equality. If present and future generations are to extend that freedom and equality, they must have a thorough understanding of democratic values and processes:

Consent of the governed, equality of justice and opportunity, due process of law, general welfare
Use of intelligence and cooperative action to solve problems
Freedom of speech, press, assembly, religion, and inquiry
Individual rights, responsibility, creativity, and self-direction
Respect for majority rule, minority rights, and property
Faith in people's ability to improve conditions and solve problems
Open-mindedness, fair play, and respect for the views of others irrespective of class, color, creed, or sex

Values such as these are part of units of instruction in the social studies program. Such units as family life, community living, our state, and the United States include much relevant material, and specific values are treated in depth in units on our American heritage; the Constitution; the Bill of Rights; and local, state, and national government. The conceptual foundations of values are developed by giving direct attention to the meaning of such concepts as consent of the governed, due process of law, and equality of opportunity. Both contemporary and historical events are used as case studies to highlight the strength and enduring quality of basic values. The outcome should be an appreciation of the power of the democratic idea in the past and in the present. Instruction is pointed toward the development of such generalizations as the following (outlined by a group of political scientists):[1]

Democracy implies a way of life as well as a form of government.
Democracy is based on certain fundamental assumptions. Among these are the integrity of man, the dignity of the individual, equality of opportunity, man's rationality, morality, practicality, and ability to govern himself and to solve his problems cooperatively.

[1]John U. Michaelis and A. Montgomery Johnston, *The Social Sciences: Foundations of the Social Studies* (Boston: Allyn and Bacon, 1965), pp. 317–18.

Man develops his fullest potential in a climate of freedom. Much of civilization's advance can be traced to man's search for a larger measure of freedom.

Civil liberties—freedom of thought, speech, press, worship, petition, and association—constitute the central citadel of human freedom.

Basic to democracy is belief in progress. A free society is hospitable to new ideas and to change and encourages the unfettered search for truth. Peaceful action rather than violence is one of its hallmarks.

Certain factors are necessary for democracy to succeed. These include: (1) an educated citizenry, (2) a common concern for human freedom, (3) communication and mobility, (4) a degree of economic security, (5) a spirit of compromise and mutual trust, (6) respect for the rights of minority groups and the loyal opposition, (7) moral and spiritual values, (8) participation by the citizen in government at all levels.

Strategies for Making Applications

In addition to developing generalizations that include key values, students should have opportunities to use democratic values and processes in daily activities. Participation and involvement give students a feeling for the self-discipline and individual and group responsibility that are part of democracy. The following examples illustrate how key values can be put to use.

Government of a group is most effective if there is government by the group. In classrooms where this value is applied, children have opportunities to develop group standards they can use in planning and working together. Individual and group work are evaluated in such a way that each child grows in responsibility, self-control, and self-direction. Rules and regulations are viewed in the light of group welfare and individual rights and privileges. Changes are proposed and evaluated as new needs arise. Valuing strategies are put to use in analyzing and evaluating problems of concern to the group, as suggested later in this chapter. When such units as our community, our state, and our nation are studied, the class develops specific concepts that relate to government by the group. As children mature, they have opportunities to develop more appreciation of their own contributions, as well as those of others, to the improvement of human affairs through government of, by, and for the people.

Each individual is respected and accorded equal justice and opportunity. Each child is respected as an individual who can make special contributions to group activities and who needs individualized learning experiences. Mutual respect among children is emphasized in an atmosphere that promotes individual and group effort, fair play, and concern for others. Children analyze contributions of men and women in their own and other ethnic groups, and changes that should be made in the treatment of minority groups and women. Case studies of court decisions and selected events bring home the significance of due process and other

The Bill of Rights
The Bill of Rights guarantees important freedoms:
of religion, speech, press
to assemble
from excessive bails or fines
from cruel punishment
from unreasonable search
The Bill of Rights
The Bill of Rights guarantees these rights:
to bear arms
to life, liberty, property,
to just compensation for property
to fair trial
The Writ of Habeas Corpus
BEFORE
He does not know why he is held.
AFTER
He can speak for himself.
Some Services of the State Government
Administration
Protection
Making Laws
Courts
Prisons
Police
Education
State Univ.
Conservation
Communication
Hospitals
Parks
Bridges
Highways

What value concepts are essential to an understanding of the main ideas summarized in these charts? What basic generalizations about government in a democracy might be formulated? (San Bernardino County, California)

rights. As the Constitution and its amendments are studied, students discover how it provides guidelines for extending equal justice and opportunity.

Freedom of inquiry and use of intelligence to solve problems are valued. Freedom of thought, speech, and belief are respected, and emphasis is given to accuracy in reporting information, responsibility in checking its validity, analysis of various sides of issues and problems, and formulation of conclusions after careful study of the facts. Critical thinking and decision-making processes are put to use as students define issues and problems, clarify related values, consider alternative proposals, weigh consequences in light of values, and make decisions or judgments on what should be done. Many units of study provide opportunities for students to discover that the efforts of individuals and groups to promote freedom of inquiry in the past must be maintained and extended. The school and community serve as laboratories for making learning relevant and meaningful, and provide opportunities for involvement and participation in activities that call for freedom of inquiry and use of intelligence to solve problems.

Democratic Behavior Patterns

Other concrete and meaningful applications can be made by giving attention to the development of democratic behavior patterns. The first step is to clarify inclusive categories of behavior consistent with the values and processes outlined above. The following concepts are frequently included in courses of study, instructional media, and units of study.

Responsibility. At the very center of the democratic idea is the concept that individuals can and will carry out responsibilities. Every right, privilege, decision, or plan of action carries related responsibilities. The success of democracy depends on the acceptance of responsibility by the people, both as individuals and as members of various groups.

Responsibility is developed in the social studies program as children plan, carry out, and evaluate learning activities. Beginning in the early grades with responsibilities such as those related to sharing and discussing ideas, using equipment and materials properly, and carrying out group work standards, the instructional program is extended in later grades to include a wide range of responsibilities related to gathering information, preparing reports, interviewing experts, participating in discussion, analyzing issues and problems, planning programs for parents, and evaluating critically the effectiveness of individual and group work. Concepts of responsibility are extended through direct study of the responsibilities carried out by members of the family, community workers, officials of government, great men and women of the past and present, and people in other lands. Behavior is rooted in values and concepts that add to the ability to accept and carry out responsibilities in a variety of situations.

Concern for others. Individual development and group welfare are nurtured when concern for others is evident in all facets of living. Various aspects of concern for others are reflected in such expressions as "give them a break," "look out for others," and "lend a helping hand." Mutual respect, sensitivity to the needs of others, and a willingness to help are evident in the behavior of those who show concern for others.

Those who are developing concern for others rely on orderly methods of achieving purposes and consider the rights and responsibilities of others as well as their own. Respect is accorded others when differences in race, religion, status and sex are considered, common needs and similarities recognized, and differences appreciated. There is recognition of the need for rules and duly constituted authority in the home, school, and community. As children mature, they begin to understand that in a democracy authority rests with the people, and that maximum concern for others is secured only when the people give adequate time and thought to the problems of government.

Open-mindedness. Clear thinking and problem solving, which are essential in a democracy, call for open-mindedness. Group action is most effective when all points of view are considered in planning and evaluation. Individual study and action can be improved when various ideas are considered and a critical selection is made of those that are most appropriate in a situation. Prejudice and superstition can be rooted out as differing points of view and authenticated facts are considered. As Jefferson put it: "Error of opinion may be tolerated where reason is left free to combat it."

Those who are developing open-mindedness consider and explore the value of the ideas of others as well as the value of their own. They are learning to be impartial, to report facts accurately, to analyze problems, and to appraise the validity of information. They consider facts and opinions in the light of the source from which they were obtained, their relationship to issues and problems, and their usefulness in solving problems. They seek better ways of doing things, establish reasons for making changes in ongoing activities, and support what they believe is right with evidence and reason. They are growing in the ability to recognize the impact of feelings on their thinking, and in the ability to curb emotions that lead to bias, prejudice, and erroneous conclusions. They are beginning to recognize the closed mind and the propaganda techniques used to instill distorted facts and ideas in the minds of susceptible individuals.

Units of work on the community, state, nation, and other settings reveal how open-mindedness has been a potent factor in clarifying issues and solving problems. The advantages of an open society in which problems are examined and discussed freely become even more evident when an analysis is made of the disadvantages of a closed society in which selected doctrines must be followed.

Creativity. Much of America's greatness has come from the creativity of her people. Through the years the people of America have found new ways of doing things as frontier after frontier has been reached and passed and new ones opened. The children of America need opportunities to develop creative ways of doing things so that democratic living will be continually improved by a constant flow of new ideas.

Creativeness in children is shown by new or original responses to solving problems, organizing and expressing ideas, using materials, carrying out plans, and making improvements in individual and group work. Those who are growing in creativeness search for and use new ideas to solve problems and to express thoughts and feelings. They are sensitive to originality in others and are growing in their appreciation of the creative contributions made by individuals in the past as well as in the present. They are growing in the ability to express ideas clearly in oral and written form, as well as through various art media, and are developing an appreciation of the ability of others to express ideas creatively. As they study various units, they are developing an understanding and appreciation of the value and importance of creativity in the lives of people at home and in other lands.

Cooperation. The ability to cooperate is very important in our society. The teamwork required in industry, education, science, government, and other significant activities illustrates this point. From the early days, when neighbors worked together to raise the walls of a log cabin or to have a town meeting, to the present time, when a crew of workers erects a skyscraper or a group participates in a meeting of the city council, our progress has virtually depended on our ability to cooperate; and now cooperation among nations has become necessary not only for progress but for survival itself.

Those who are developing cooperative behavior pool ideas, make plans, carry them through to completion, and evaluate the effectiveness of their work. When plans are changed on the basis of group decisions, they continue to work with others to achieve common goals. As they study various topics in social studies, they discover examples of cooperation in the home, school, community, state, and nation. As they mature and undertake more advanced studies, they gain insight into the need for teamwork in solving international problems, and they critically assess the actions of individuals and agencies working together to improve human welfare.

STRATEGIES FOR DEVELOPING DEMOCRATIC BEHAVIOR

Each social studies unit should help build the values that are at the base of democratic behavior; each unit should also help children to learn and practice the kind of behavior that demonstrates democratic values. Three interrelated strategies may be used. First, plans must be made for specific things that children can *do,* since democratic attitudes and behavior are best learned through active and reflective participation. Second, plans should be made for children to *observe* democratic behavior in action in the school and community. Third, plans must be made for children to *study* and *analyze* democratic behavior as portrayed in books, films, and other instructional resources. Notice the three levels of abstraction in the suggested planning: doing, observing, and studying. Although actual doing is essential, observing and studying should not be minimized, for they make it possible to extend and enrich the concept of democratic behavior. The two examples that follow illustrate the kind of planning that should be undertaken in each unit.

In a home and family living unit, cooperation may be developed to higher levels through experiences such as the following:

Doing: Planning and arranging a playhouse; sharing tools and materials, working together, and helping each other make furniture, home furnishings, dishes, table settings, dolls and doll clothes, pet cages, and scrapbooks; planning and participating in dramatic representation centered on home activities; making and carrying out standards to use on a study trip to see a home under construction; taking turns and sharing in a group discussion of unit activities

Observing: Members of the family working together at home; children cooperating at home and at school; monitors and committees at work; men working together to build a house in the neighborhood; ways in which the janitor, teachers, and children in school work together to make the school a happy, clean place in which to work and play

Studying: Pictures, filmstrips, and films showing members of a family gardening, cleaning the yard, shopping, and having fun together; picture and story books that portray cooperation among children, children and parents, and adults taking part in neighborhood activities; stories and poems that highlight teamwork in home and family living. (Responsibility, creativeness, concern for others, and open-mindedness may be outlined in a similar manner for this unit of instruction.)

To illustrate ways to develop democratic behavior in upper grades, a life in early America unit has been selected. Specific attention is given to ways in which creativity may be developed (the other categories of behavior may be analyzed in a similar manner).

Doing: Planning and using a variety of ways to organize information, that is, pictorial summaries, booklets, dioramas, and slides; creating songs and rhythms related to such activities as quilting, husking, hunting, weaving, and churning; making instruments to accompany songs and rhythms; drawing pictures and murals; making candles, dolls with authentic costumes, utensils, and other objects for use in creative dramatics, discussion, and reports

Observing: Individuals invited to school to demonstrate the use of spinning wheels, looms, and other objects; models, utensils, quilts, and other objects arranged in an exhibit or museum to highlight creative uses of materials in early times; authentic folk dances and songs performed by community or school groups; plays, pageants, and TV programs to celebrate holidays and events of historical interest; creative contributions made by members of the class as the unit of work develops

Studying: Pictures, films, books, and other instructional materials that portray creativeness in the use of resources for food, shelter, and clothing; art, music, and literature of early times; contributions of great men and women during the early days of our country; explorers and ways in which they blazed trails and opened up new territories.

These examples illustrate practical procedures that teachers have used to develop democratic behavior. The point should be emphasized that examples on the doing level can be found in nearly all activities in the social studies program that involve group work; they also can be found in daily living throughout the school program. On the observing level, children can be guided to notice examples in the classroom, elsewhere in the school, and in the community. As historical units or units on faraway places are developed, the children can see plays, festivals, pageants, programs developed by school and community groups, and demonstrations by individuals invited to school. On the third level—studying—books, films, filmstrips, and other resources offer many good examples of democratic behavior. Television and radio programs should not be overlooked, particularly those related to topics in social studies. Finally, current events are a good source of examples. Occasionally a bulletin board of pictures and clippings can be arranged to emphasize concern for others, open-mindedness, or one of the other categories of behavior. By giving systematic attention to the development of democratic behavior in all these ways, a practical and realistic contribution to citizenship can be made in the elementary school.

DEVELOPING ATTITUDES

Whether we pay attention to their development or not, attitudes are inevitable outcomes of instruction. Too often in social studies, little thought is given to them. Some teachers assume that constructive attitudes will develop "naturally" in the course of instruction. This may be true in *some* cases, but too much is at stake to leave it to chance.

A Dynamic Program

Multiple learnings are involved in any learning activity; concepts, appreciations, and attitudes do not emerge one by one. A student searching for necessary information in a study of pioneer life may be learning several things simultaneously: some new facts, how to locate information with greater skill, an appreciation of the hardships of the pioneers, how much easier it is to talk about needed information than it is to find it. Some outcomes may be more potent than those the teacher had planned. For example, the teacher's objective may be to improve study skills and the grasp of certain ideas, but the child *may* be developing poor attitudes toward the activity itself and even a dislike for the social studies program.

Because attitudes are rooted in feelings, activities in social studies should evoke positive emotional overtones for children. Positive attitudes and appreciations flourish in a dynamic learning situation. The two examples that follow highlight the importance of a dynamic program of instruction. First, let us consider a group that is studying the westward movement in a rather dull, stultifying manner. Very little is being done to arouse the children emotionally, challenge their intellectual capabilities, or create motivation from within the context of their study. The objective of the lesson, in the teacher's plan at least, is to have the class find out how the pioneers obtained their food.

> ***Teacher:*** Today we are to study ways in which the pioneers secured their food. Our textbook contains information on how they got their food. Read pages 68 to 75 and keep a list of all the ways of getting food that you find in your reading. Raise your hand if you have a question.

In the following situation, students and teacher are working together and attacking the same type of problem. Notice the difference in the approach being used.

> ***Teacher:*** Yesterday as you dramatized life in Boonesboro, several of you raised questions regarding the ways in which food was secured. What were your questions?
> ***Child A:*** Well, I was wondering how they got food outside of the stockade and how they brought it in.
> ***Child B:*** Didn't they raise it right inside?
> ***Child C:*** I was wondering how the women help to provide food.
> ***Child D:*** I read that they had a hard time getting food in winter.
> ***Child E:*** I think they ate nuts and berries and deer meat.
> ***Teacher:*** Those are good suggestions. How do you think we could find some more information on ways and means in which they secured food?

In the discussion that followed, the children themselves proposed many procedures for getting at this problem. The emotional response was especially gratifying. Real interest was evident as the group proceeded to solve problems that were significant to them.

Strategies for Developing Constructive Attitudes

The behavior of those who guide children must reflect positive attitudes. Teachers must be aware of their own attitudes; they must be careful about their remarks, facial grimaces, expressions of likes and dislikes, anecdotes and jokes, and any other evidences of negative attitudes, since children are quick to imitate and take on such behavior as their own. When children themselves exhibit negative attitudes toward others, they should be helped to find the reasons behind their behavior and to discover that their behavior is not consistent with such standards as fair play and respect for others. Acceptance by the teacher of a child's negative behavior toward others may lead other children to believe that such behavior is approved.

Knowledge and understanding properly learned and used, not just memorized, can lead to improvement in attitudes. All of us have heard someone say, "Had I known that, I would have acted differently." Or, "Is that so? Then we must do this." A common error, in using knowledge to improve attitudes, however, is assuming that telling is teaching, or that learning about something inevitably leads to a proper attitude toward it. This error can be avoided in part by centering the gathering of information on key problems as they arise, and by using information to interpret the behavior of others and to solve emotionally charged problems. In addition, children need guidance in interpreting facts in the light of fair play and other values. If any change in attitudes is to result, information must be put to use and interpreted in situations vital to children.

Community activities are part of the attitude-building program. Participation by children in community activities, cooperation of parents and other adults in developing positive attitudes, use of resource persons in the school program, and use of community resources by the school are illustrative of the many possibilities. Festivals, pageants, holidays, and special events in which individuals of many different backgrounds participate are helpful. The spirit in which these activities are carried on and the skill with which children are made a part of them determine their contribution to changes in attitudes.

Symbolism and ceremony have long been used to develop values and attitudes. When approached in a way that develops clear insight into their significance, the following have been found to be helpful: flag ceremonies, observance of holidays, pageants, assemblies, musical programs that emphasize patriotism, exhibits, special television and radio programs, trips to historical shrines, anniversaries, films and filmstrips, and recordings. These contribute to the development of attitudes and ideals to the extent that children recognize their significance in their own lives and in the lives of others. Adults must also realize that the way they approach and participate in such activities greatly conditions the way children will react and learn.

As children mature, they tend to accept attitudes that are the result of their own thinking; they need many opportunities to discover positive examples *on their own*. Discussion, group planning, group decision making, creative expression, actual participation in ceremonies and community activities, and other skillfully guided activities may be used to help them make their own discoveries. Teachers should provide follow-up activities in which their discoveries can be applied, evaluated, and used again.

Experiences that kindle the imagination, create upbuilding emotional responses, and arouse positive feelings are also useful. Poetry, stories, drama, films, folk games, art, and music can all be used to create a *feeling tone* that promotes warmth, vitality, and other positive emotional reactions. Unless such feelings are developed, there will be no learning of a permanent nature. This is one of the major reasons why related experiences in art, music, and literature are so important in the social studies program.

Individual and group guidance techniques need to be used in some instances to develop wholesome attitudes and to redirect behavior into more positive channels. Individual counseling and small-group discussion can be used as individual needs are discovered. Presentation of problem situations for group analysis and completion by the class of a story begun by the teacher are effective if related to problems that have arisen. Group standards and codes of behavior developed before study trips, interviews, and programs help to guide expression of attitudes in a positive way. Simple attitude inventories can be used as a basis for individual counseling and group discussion. Case conferences in which a particular child's difficulties are analyzed by the teacher and other school workers are helpful in unusual or extremely difficult cases. In some instances, specialists may be needed to assist in the development of a long-term program of therapy.

Dramatic play and role playing give children opportunities to improve attitudes, release tension, identify with others, and find a positive role in group activities. Children may be guided to try *new* attitudes toward others, and as roles are played, they may gradually be helped to take on more positive attitudes or reject negative ones. An incident involving a negative attitude may be "acted out," discussed, and reenacted in a positive way. After discussion of an incident, a positive portrayal of a solution may be tried. Through role playing, a problem situation may be dramatized creatively with a solution emerging as children portray what to them seems fair and reasonable. Children may act out roles in preparation for a situation they are about to face. Situations may be dramatized depending on the attitudes or problems needing emphasis. Meanwhile, the teacher tries to find clues to the children's feelings, needs, and values. These clues form the basis for discussion, planning, evaluation, and follow-up activities. A teaching strategy for role playing includes these steps:[2]

1. Warming up, in which the group clarifies the problem and interprets the problem story

[2]Fannie R. Shaftel and George Shaftel, *Role-Playing for Social Values* (Englewood Cliffs, N.J.: Prentice-Hall, 1967).

2. Selecting participants after describing or clarifying roles to play
3. Setting the stage by discussing use of space, order of action, and questions about roles
4. Preparing observers by assigning tasks and clarifying points to watch
5. Providing for role playing, with help as needed to begin and maintain it
6. Discussing and evaluating actions, ability to get inside the situation, and points made by observers followed by attention to proposed changes
7. Resumption of role playing, with emphasis on changes, next steps, and other points made by the group
8. Discussion and evaluation to make further changes
9. Sharing and generalizing, with attention to similarity to experiences of students and values for use in future conduct

Children should not play the same role every time, so that the feelings of others in given situations will become more real to them. A child with one background can play the role of another, a leader can be a follower, or a child in one situation can take the part of a child in another. In selecting roles, however, a child should not be given one for which he or she is unfitted or unwilling to try. Throughout, teachers should emphasize sincere expression of the roles being acted so that each child gets close to the feelings of the characters he or she portrays at different times. Once children grasp how others feel, they may begin to take on more positive attitudes toward them.

Certain procedures are helpful in dealing with examples of prejudice and negative incidents found in reading materials, films, or reports of experiences made by children. After the incident has been summarized and the main details noted, possible causes should be discussed and effects on the parties involved should be considered. Children should be encouraged to "get inside the other person's shoes." The proposed solution should be evaluated in terms of fairness, respect for the persons involved, and other pertinent values. Specific relationships to situations in the children's own lives should be clarified. Finally, immediate application of generalizations should be made by the group to situations that are vital to them.

Attitudes may be evaluated on several levels according to degrees of internalization.[3] The first level is characterized by an awareness of an object, activity, or person; the next level is one of response; and the third involves a deeper feeling that may be expressed as a commitment or conviction. At still higher levels are those attitudes and values so deeply internalized that they are an inherent part of a person's way of life. The

[3] David R. Krathwohl, Benjamin S. Bloom, and Bertram B. Masia, *Taxonomy of Educational Objectives: Affective Domain* (New York: McKay, 1964).

checklists and test items given in the final chapter are illustrative of methods that may be used to assess attitudinal change.

Examples in Units of Instruction Each unit offers opportunities to develop wholesome attitudes toward others. For example, units on the home and family can be developed so that children discover many likenesses and common needs and at the same time understand differences among families in size, composition, type of home, work of father and mother, religious affiliation, and the like. Children can be helped to understand that what is natural to them may be strange to others, and what is strange to them is natural to others. Each family wants to be respected and accepted by others, just as each child wants his or her own family to be accepted.

In such units as our community, emphasis can be given to such understandings and appreciations as these: Different types of work and services are essential. Rules must be made and followed so that all may have justice and equal opportunity. Communities vary and depend on each other for food, shelter, and clothing. There is really no one best kind of community, although we may prefer one kind. The many different kinds of communities (farming, fishing, manufacturing) enable us to share and live more effectively in our own.

Units on state, region, or nation provide children with opportunities to discover contributions of others, common needs, examples of sharing, the great range of differences, and so on, on a wider scale. Strength through diversity, power through teamwork, and unity through democratic values should be brought home realistically as reading materials, films, pictures, and other resources are used. A solid beginning can be made in developing appreciation of the contributions of individuals of different ethnic background, interdependence among regions, respect for the supreme worth of the individual, the need for people with different abilities, and the efforts of those who, from early days to the present, have tried to extend and preserve the rights of all people.

Appropriate attention should be given to ethnic and minority groups in units on community, state, or nation, with emphasis on misconceptions, stereotypes, and biases; how they develop; why they should be eliminated; and how they work against attainment of basic democratic values. All students need opportunities to discover and take pride in the contributions of black Americans, Mexican Americans, Puerto Ricans, Asian Americans, native Americans, and others to our society. The abundance and variety of new materials make it possible to provide instruction leading to positive attitudes and basic understandings of lasting value.

Units on Africa, Mexico, Asian countries, and other areas may be developed to highlight the rich cultural heritages that exist in different parts of the world. All students, whether members of minority groups or not, need opportunities to develop appreciations of the creative ways in which very different societies have met and solved problems, interacted with other societies, and contributed to the growth of civilization.

Why are religious values important in our culture and other cultures? (Social Studies Workshop, University of California, Berkeley)

STRATEGIES FOR DEVELOPING VALUES

Many strategies have been proposed and used to develop, clarify, analyze, and act on values. They range from direct instruction (inculcation) and moral development to value analysis, value clarification, and action learning, as noted by Superka and Johnson (see References at the end of the chapter). Those most useful in the social studies program have been selected and adapted from the sources listed in the References.

Direct Instruction

The main direct approaches are modeling to set good examples, reasoned persuasion, and behavior modification. The following paragraphs present illustrative strategies for these direct approaches.

Modeling to set examples. Models of valued behaviors are presented and discussed to provide good examples of honesty, fairness, cooperation, concern for others, and other values. The teacher, exemplary students, and others serve as models. Outstanding athletes, heroes and heroines in stories, film and TV stars, great men and women, individuals from ethnic and minority groups, and other admired persons may be used as examples. Students are asked to find and share good examples and to criticize poor ones. High commendation is given to students who follow good examples and who set examples for others. At times, the teacher or another individual may play the role of devil's advocate and present a negative example for criticism.

Reasoned persuasion. Sound reasons for accepting values and behaving in accord with them are presented to students in a variety of ways. Individual conferences may be used, especially when problems and difficulties arise. Small-group discussions may be held to consider the common needs, concerns, and problems of a selected group of students. Large-group discussions may be used to emphasize the importance of values and related behavior. Episodes in films, stories, and other materials may be used to convince students of the value of accepting and living by democratic ideals.

Behavior modification. A variety of forms of behavior modification may be used to elicit and reward behavior that is consistent with desired values. In general, procedures such as the following are used:

1. Specify behavioral objectives: To demonstrate concern for others in discussion by taking turns, listening to others, and raising questions.
2. State a criterion: Janice will demonstrate the desired behavior 80 percent of the time in discussions during the coming week.
3. Select a procedure: Positive reinforcement through praise is to be used.

4. Plan the environment: Janice is to be moved from the rear of the room to the center.
5. Carry out the procedure: After discussing the situation, a contract is made and Janice participates in discussion according to plan. Praise is used to reinforce desired behavior.
6. Evaluate and repeat the procedure if necessary: Provide for discussion with reinforcement and find out if the criterion is met. If not, repeat the procedure or try a new one.

Other direct approaches. Emphasis on adherence to rules and regulations and the consequences of not following them are highlighted in all programs. Limiting choices in terms of maturity is used to aid students in analyzing issues and problems and in making decisions. Appeals to conscience and to adherence to the Golden Rule are used to get students to think more deeply about what is right and wrong in a given situation.

Moral Reasoning

This strategy has been derived from the work of Kohlberg and others.[4] Students analyze moral dilemmas, take a position, and present reasons for their positions. Teachers determine the students' level of moral development, conduct discussion on that level, and endeavor to move reasoning to the next higher level. Emphasis is given to the eliciting of reasons from students, to analyzing and evaluating those reasons, to considering consequences, and to guiding discussion to consider various facets of the dilemma. Here are the main steps, with an example of each:

1. Present a moral dilemma: A boy's hat is caught in a tree. Carol has promised not to climb trees, but no one else is there to help.
2. Have students take a position and give reasons for it: Have groups of four discuss the dilemma. The teacher moves from group to group encouraging participation and identifying stage of development.
3. Analyze and evaluate positions and reasons: Obtain statements of positions and reasons, getting them out in the open. Discuss best and poorest reasons. Raise questions if others need to be considered. Consider consequences of positions.
4. Test reasons further, as appropriate: Provide for a debate in which a judge decides which team has the best reasons. Or have a jury decide after reasons for helping or not helping are presented.

Model for Rational Analysis

Models for rational value analysis are closely related to the problem-solving model discussed in the preceding chapter. The main difference is in

[4] *First Things: Values* (New York: Guidance Associates, 1971); and Galbraith and Jones reference at end of chapter.

the emphasis on arriving at a value decision and testing it, as shown in the following outline of steps of procedure:[5]

1. Clarify and define the value question or problem: What is the problem? What issue or issues are involved? What terms need to be defined? What is to be judged?
2. Gather purported facts: What facts are available? Are others needed? Which are facts and which are opinions?
3. Assess the facts: How can the facts be checked? Which are supported by evidence? What do experts say?
4. Clarify and select relevant facts: Which facts are related to the issue or problem? Which are needed to make a value judgment or decision?
5. Make a tentative judgment or decision: What seems to be a reasonable judgment or decision? What are the reasons for it?
6. Test the value principle inherent in the judgment or decision: Does it apply to other cases? Is it consistent with other key values? Does it apply to everyone, including ourselves? What would the consequences be if it were adopted universally?

Planned questioning strategies. Charts 7–1 through 7–3 present strategies for identifying and exploring feelings, alternative solutions to problems and conflicts, and values in behavior and events. The strategies have been adapted from those developed in the Taba Curriculum Project.[6] The first strategy, designed to help students explore feelings aroused by stories, films, incidents in their own lives, and current events, begins by recalling information related to the incident under discussion. Students are next asked to state how the people in the incident must have felt, how they would feel if they had been in it, or how they did feel if it was a personal experience. Reasons for their feelings are explored, and they are invited to identify other feelings that might have been involved.

The second strategy, which can be used with case studies, stories, current events, or problems presented by the teacher or students, moves from asking students what they think should be done and what the reaction of others might be to different types of behavior in the situation to a direct consideration of similar experiences students have had and to what they might do differently if a similar situation should arise. The third strategy can be used to identify values that underlie behavior and events. After describing the event selected for analysis, students are asked to offer reasons the people involved acted as they did, and then to explore the reasons to identify values of importance to the individuals in the situation. The students are next asked to project themselves into the situation, to state what they would probably do, and to identify the reasons and related values for their hypothetical behavior.

[5] See reference by Metcalf at end of chapter.

[6] See the Wallen reference at the end of this chapter.

Chart 7–1
A Strategy for Clarifying Feelings

Procedure	Focusing Questions	Illustrative Application
Recall and clarify the event. →	What is the problem? What happened? What did they do? →	What happened to Jim on the vacation trip?
Infer possible feelings. →	How do you think they (he, she) felt? Why might they feel that way? →	How must his parents have felt when he got lost? How do you think he felt? Why?
Infer other possible feelings. →	What other feelings might have been involved? Why? →	What other feelings might they have had? Why?
Infer the feelings of other persons. →	How did others feel about it? the same? different? Why? →	How did the ranger feel? the hikers? Why?
Relate to experiences of students. →	Has something like that ever happened to you? How did you feel? Why? →	Have you ever been lost? How would you feel in Jim's place? Why?

All these strategies call for an open atmosphere in which students are free to express feelings and values without any fear of reproach by the teacher. The teacher's role is to help students clarify the situation that is the focus of analysis, seek a variety of responses, be supportive, encourage students to identify all the feelings and values involved, and help students explore and understand alternative views and feelings. The focusing questions in each strategy may be varied as needed to fit the situation.

Value Clarification Strategies

Value clarification strategies in which the teacher's role is to help students clarify values should generate lively interest. An open atmosphere is provided in which everyone's response is accepted, students have the right to pass if they wish, honest and diverse responses are encouraged, and there are no questions or comments that inhibit thinking. A *value* is defined as something chosen, prized, and acted upon by the individual. The following processes are basic in the complete act of valuing: (1) Choosing: making choices freely, from alternatives, and after reflection; (2) prizing: cherishing the choice, being happy with it, and affirming it; and (3) acting: acting on the value and doing it repeatedly.

Chart 7–2

A Strategy for Analyzing Problems

Procedure	Focusing Questions	Illustrative Applications
Clarify the problem.	→ What is the problem? issue? difficulty?	→ Why is there so much litter around the school?
Identify alternative solutions and reasons for them.	→ What should be done? Why? What else might be done? Why?	→ What should be done about it? How can it be prevented? Are there other suggestions?
Identify strengths, weaknesses, and possible reactions.	→ Which is the best solution? What might the reaction be to each one?	→ Which proposals will work best? How might others react to them?
Relate to students' experiences.	Have you ever had a problem like this one? What did you do?	→ What has been done before? What did you do to help?
Identify reasons and related values.	→ As you look back, was that a reasonable thing to do? Why?	→ How did it work? Would you do it again?
Consider alternatives and reasons for them.	→ Is there anything you would do differently? Why?	→ What might be done differently this time? What might work better?

Many of the strategies proposed for clarification of personal values can be adapted for use in social studies units. The guiding principle is to use the strategies in connection with value-laden topics and issues. The following examples have been adapted by the writer and teachers in workshops on valuing in social studies from strategies proposed by Raths and Simon.[7]

Clarifying responses. The values that underlie students' statements may be clarified by asking open questions that stimulate students to think through the values they hold and why they hold them. The teacher responds to comments about people, places, and activities under study by raising such nonjudgmental questions as these:

Is this what you mean? [The teacher restates a student's comment]
Why do you feel (think, act) that way? How long have you felt that way?
Where did you get that idea? Are you glad you feel that way? Do others feel that way? Might some people feel differently about it?

[7] See Raths, Harmin, and Simon in References.

Chart 7–3
A Strategy for Identifying Values in Events

Procedure	Focusing Questions	Illustrative Applications
Clarify the facts. →	What is the situation? What happened? →	What did the story say was happening to the buffalo?
Identify main reasons. →	Why did it happen? What reasons can you think of? →	Why were they being killed? Are there other reasons?
Infer values from the reasons. →	What do the reasons indicate that is important to them? →	What was most important to the hunters? the companies? the Indians?
Identify possible student action and reasons. →	What would you do in the same situation? Why? →	What do you think should have been done?
Identify student values from reasons. →	How does this show what is important to you? →	How does your view show what is important to you?

Can you give an example of what you mean? Is that really what you feel (think, believe, value)?
What are some alternatives? Can you think of others?

Value sheets. A value sheet is used with groups to provoke thinking about such topics and issues as neighborhood and community problems; state, national and international issues; civil liberties; treatment of ethnic groups; activities of individuals under study; and historical events. Value sheets are also used to stimulate thinking about friendship, courage, fairness, concern for others, and other value concepts in social studies materials.

An effective value sheet contains a problem situation that is discussed in a paragraph or two, or even a single provocative statement. Sometimes pictures, cartoons, part of a film, or some other resource may be presented. As shown in the following examples, the presentation is followed by a few questions that focus on choosing, prizing, and acting.

HONESTY

Recall the story of the pioneer boy who found the knife on the trail. What should he do about it? What would you have done? What does honesty mean to you? to your friends? In what ways do you show honesty? your friends? How important do you think it is to be honest? If you plan to make any changes, what will they be?

THE FUTURE

"Change, change, change! People should expect even faster and greater changes in the next twenty-five years. Changes in homes, styles of living, friends, recreation, everything. And there will be changes in what we value." What do you think you will value most in twenty-five years? Which of the following will be most important? least important? Rate each one from 1 to 5, with 1 indicating the most important, 2 the next, and so on.

Personal Values: ______health ______wealth ______hard work ______liberty ______intellect
Group Values: ______serving others ______teamwork ______respect for others ______devotion to family ______being generous
Social Values: ______education ______welfare ______law and order ______patriotism ______national freedom
Environmental Values: ______clean air ______clean water ______open space ______use of energy ______beautification projects

MIGHT MAKES RIGHT!

What does this saying mean to you? What did it mean in the story we just read? In what situations should "might make right?" In what situations should it not? Why? How do you feel about using the idea in relations with others?

ON INDIANS

"They are savages who need to be civilized and kept on reservations." "When treated like human beings they prove to be helpful and responsible." Why might such statements have been made by early settlers? As we look back, why does one statement seem more reasonable? Can you think of any statements about groups today that are similar? What might you do when unreasonable statements are made? How important do you feel it is to do something?

Voting. This simple and quick procedure for exploring values may be used as a springboard to discussion or study of a topic. The teacher uses the root question "How many of you ____?" in such forms as "How many of you think the city council should pass the new bicycle safety law?" "How many believe the schools should be open all year?" "How many of you would like to be a carpenter? a teacher? a nurse? a politician? an owner of a business?" Students in favor of a position raise their hands, students who are undecided fold their arms, and students who are opposed keep their hands down.

Rank ordering. Students are presented with three or four alternatives and asked to place them in rank order. Illustrative questions and activities:

Which are your first, second, and third choices for a career? ______ health services ______education ______business ______other.

In what order of priority should these be placed? ______energy development ______ecology ______aid to the poor ______school improvement.

If you had been at the Alamo, how would you have ranked these? ______stay and fight ______leave to save lives ______leave but fight guerrilla warfare.

Number in order five places that you would like to visit: ______China ______England ______Germany ______Israel ______France ______Japan ______Russia.

Number in order five places that you would like to learn more about: ______China ______England ______Germany ______Israel ______France ______Japan ______Russia.

Number in order the field trips we should take: ______airport ______canning factory ______museum ______the old fort ______zoo.

Value surveys. Students are presented with a list of activities or values and are asked to check those they think are most important, or to rate them as to importance. Examples:

Make a check by the ones you think are important: ______being on time ______finishing each lesson ______putting things in place ______taking turns ______helping to keep the room clean.

Imagine you are a legislator and rate the following as to importance, with 1 for most important, 2 next in importance, and 3 least important. ______honesty ______fairness ______wisdom ______speaking ability ______cooperation ______health ______wealth ______courage ______responsibility ______equality for all.

Number the following in order of importance to you: ______happiness ______health ______wealth ______education ______friendship ______food ______clothes ______family.

Imagine you are an early settler in the West. Number the following in order of importance to settlers: _____happiness _____health _____wealth _____education _____friendship _____food _____clothes _____family.

Position on a continuum. Students identify where they stand on an issue or problem by marking their position on a line at or between two extremes. A variation is to mark a line on the classroom floor and have students stand on the point indicative of their position. Examples:

Where do you stand on these issues?

Full freedom .... FREEDOM IN SCHOOL .... Strict rules

Always do it .... DOING SCHOOL WORK .... Forget it

Full control .... GOVERNMENT CONTROL OF ENERGY SOURCES .... No control

Completing unfinished statements. Several different forms of open-ended or incomplete statements may be used, as shown in the following examples:

I WONDER

After reading the story, I wonder ________________
After seeing the film on China, I wonder ________________
I wonder about ________________
I wonder why ________________
I wonder what would have happened if ________________

FEELING BEST

I feel best in social studies when ________________
I feel best in discussion when ________________
A doctor must feel best when ________________
A child in colonial times must have felt best when ________________

FEELING PROUD

I am proud that I can ________________
I am proud of my schoolwork in ________________
A carpenter must feel proud when ________________
Teachers must feel proud when ________________

I LEARNED

In the unit on community workers, I learned that ________________
In the study of Martin Luther King, I learned that ________________

During the film on air pollution, I learned that ____________
From our guest speaker on energy, I learned that ____________
During the committee report on growth of our city, I learned that ____________

I WAS SURPRISED

While listening to the story about Helen Keller, I was surprised to find out that ____________
In the unit on black history, I was surprised to find out that ____________
I was surprised that the President ____________
I didn't know that ____________

IF I WERE, OR IF I HAD BEEN

If I were the mayor, I would ____________
If I were a union leader, I would ____________
If I were in charge of the schools, I would ____________
If I had been a city planner when our community was founded, I would have ____________
If I had been an Indian when the colonists arrived, I would have ____________

IF I HAD, OR IF HE OR SHE OR THEY HAD

If I had three wishes ____________
If I had a magic box, in it I would like to find ____________
If I had a lot of money, I would ____________
If the President had three wishes, he would ____________
If the leaders of equal rights for women had three wishes, they would ____________

If the city council had a lot of money, it would ____________

Special diaries. Special diaries are focused on a single topic and may be an extension of several of the strategies noted above. For example, students may keep a diary from the beginning to the end of a unit. A series of valued ideas may be recorded and shared and discussed from time to time.

Coat of arms. This strategy may be used to identify and record important traits, events, and contributions in the lives of individuals under study. Students are to find out and write the following on a shield divided into six spaces: (1) name of the individual, (2) field of work, (3) greatest contribution, (4) one quotation, (5) two wishes for today, and (6) a fitting motto.

Weighing alternatives. Students evaluate alternatives related to issues or problems under study by listing and checking them, as shown below.

	Check your position:		
List alternatives	Should try it	Should study it	Should not consider it
1. ____________	________	________	________
2. ____________	________	________	________
3. ____________	________	________	________

Either-or choices. Students are asked to choose between two alternatives. They may express their choices orally or in writing. Two students with opposing choices or views may pair off for discussion, or large-group discussion may be undertaken. Illustrative choices:

Is your favorite vacation place in the mountains or on the seashore?
Should the city council increase or decrease spending on recreation?
Should school attendance be required or not required?
Should ecology or energy be given top priority?
Was President Truman more of a statesman or a politician?
Should we increase or decrease contacts with China?

Action Learning

This approach provides opportunities for students to act on their values in the classroom and in the community. Action projects should be selected in terms of levels of cognitive and affective development, and controversial issues and problems should be screened in terms of criteria noted in the following chapter. The valuing strategies presented in the preceding sections of this chapter may be put to use as the following steps are taken:

1. Clarify the problem or issue: What, if anything, should we do about water pollution?
2. Consider data and expert judgment, and take a position: What are the facts? What do experts recommend? What is our position?
3. Decide whether or not to act: Should we get involved? What might we do? What are the actions we might take? What are the consequences?
4. Plan and carry out action steps: What steps should we take individually and as a group? Carry out the plan, making revisions as needed.
5. Evaluate actions taken and project future steps: Which actions were most effective? least effective? What should we do in the future?

QUESTIONS, ACTIVITIES, EVALUATION

1. Examine one or two social studies textbooks and note examples of each of the following: democratic values, democratic behavior, attitudes, value analysis, value clarification.
2. How are the above presented? How might you guide study and discussion of them? Which of the strategies presented in this chapter might you use? What modifications might you make in the strategies?
3. Examine a course of study and do the same as in 1 and 2 above.
4. Examine a unit of instruction and do the same as in 1 and 2 above.
5. Critically evaluate the ways in which values, behavior, feelings, and conflicts are treated in the above sources. What improvements can you make? Do the same for the suggestions contained in this chapter.
6. Prepare a list of specific ways in which democratic behavior might be developed in a unit you are planning to teach. Make a worksheet for each category of behavior—for example, responsibility:
   Doing: ______________________________
   ____
   Observing: ______________________________
   ____
   Studying: ______________________________
   ____
   Note specific examples in the appropriate spaces. Share and discuss your examples with others.
7. Select three or four of the value clarification strategies in the last section of this chapter and state how you might use them in a unit you are planning. Discuss your proposed use of them with others to find out how they might be improved.

REFERENCES

GALBRAITH, RONALD, and THOMAS M. JONES, "Teaching Strategies for Moral Dilemmas," *Social Education* 39 (January 1975): 16–39. Applications of Kohlberg's theory of moral development.

HARMIN, MERRILL, HOWARD KIRSCHENBAUM, and SIDNEY B. SIMON, *Clarifying Values Through Subject Matter*. Minneapolis: Winston Press, 1973. Illustrative uses of clarification strategies in subject areas.

HANNA, LAVONE A., GLADYS L. POTTER, and ROBERT W. REYNOLDS, *Dynamic Elementary Social Studies* (3rd ed.). New York: Holt, Rinehart, and Winston, 1973. Chapter on development of democratic values.

METCALF, LAWRENCE E., ed., *Values Education* (41st Yearbook). Washington, D.C.: National Council for the Social Studies, 1971. Rationale, strategies, procedures for valuing.

MICHAELIS, JOHN U., and EVERETT T. KEACH, JR., *Teaching Strategies for Elementary Social Studies*. Itasca, Ill.: Peacock Press, 1972. New trends in concept and valuing strategies.

RATHS, LOUIS E., MERRILL HARMIN, and SYDNEY B. SIMON, *Values and Teaching*. Columbus, O.: Merrill, 1966. Concrete suggestions for working with values in the classroom.

ROCKEFELLER PANEL REPORT ON AMERICAN DEMOCRACY, *The Power of the Democratic Idea,* VI Report. Garden City, N.Y.: Doubleday, 1960. A classic statement of democratic ideals and processes in human affairs.

SHAFTEL, FANNIE R., and GEORGE SHAFTEL, *Role-Playing for Social Values*. Englewood Cliffs, N.J.: Prentice-Hall, 1967. Strategies and episodes for role playing focused on key values.

SIMON, SIDNEY B., LELAND W. HOWE, and HOWARD KIRSCHENBAUM. *Values Clarification*. New York: Hart Publishing, 1972. Collection of practical strategies based on the Raths model.

"Special Issue on Moral Education." *Phi Delta Kappan,* 61 (June 1975): 638–670. Moral reasoning, value clarification, and other approaches with critiques of each approach.

SUPERKA, DOUGLAS, and PATRICIA JOHNSON, *Values Education: Approaches and Materials*. Boulder, Colo.: Social Science Education Consortium, 1975. Chapters on approaches, materials, and bibliography related to different approaches.

WALLEN, NORMAN E., et al., *Final Report: The Taba Curriculum Project in the Social Studies*. Menlo Park, Calif.: Addison-Wesley, 1969. Public domain version of report on social studies project.

Focusing Questions

What contributions are made to social studies objectives by the study of current affairs and special events?

What criteria should be used to select current affairs?

What approaches are used to the study of current affairs?

What guidelines and techniques should be used to handle controversial issues?

What guidelines should be used to provide instruction on holidays and special events?

Investigating Current Affairs & Special Events

Current affairs and special events receive attention throughout the social studies program. This chapter presents guidelines and teaching strategies for making these two recurring topics a dynamic phase of social studies instruction. Consideration is given first to contributions to social studies objectives, followed by criteria for selecting current affairs, approaches to instruction, activities and sources of information, and teaching strategies for special events, holidays, commemoration, special weeks.

CONTRIBUTIONS TO SOCIAL STUDIES OBJECTIVES

The study of current affairs and special events adds dimensions of relevance, reality, and immediacy to the social studies program. Meaningful bridges can be built between life in and out of school and between the past and present. Students' interests can be extended and deepened as they investigate events, issues, and holidays related to their own concerns, to long-term social trends, and to actions of individuals and groups. Material presented in textbooks, films, and other instructional media can be brought up to date. A beginning can be made in developing a continuing interest in the analysis of current affairs and the ability to evaluate the information that flows from the mass media.

Other contributions may be highlighted by considering conceptual, process, skill, and affective objectives. When these four central objectives of the program are kept in mind, planning is more effective, unity of purpose is maintained, and peripheral matters that sidetrack learning can be avoided. This does not mean that significant events will be overlooked; rather, it means that selected events will be related to one or more of the following objectives:

To extend the development of concepts and main ideas by identifying and describing roles of individuals, due process, interdependence and other concepts in current and special events

To apply processes of thinking, inquiring, and problem solving by distinguishing between significant and trivial events, consistent and inconsistent points of view, accurate and inaccurate statements, straight and slanted reports, incidents and trends, and sound and unsound decisions and actions

To strengthen reading, study, map and other skills as they are used to gather, organize, and report data related to events selected for study

To develop attitudes, values, and valuing processes by using equality, concern for others, and other values to describe, interpret, and evaluate actions and decisions in current and special events

Instruction in current affairs grows more important each year, as people move and travel more, communities change, environmental problems become more acute, and interdependence at home and abroad becomes greater. In addition, the demands of ethnic and minority groups for equality, the women's movement, the need to improve the political process, the impact of scientific and technological developments, the pervasiveness of television and other mass media, and the increased interest in local, national, and international affairs leave no doubt that the present and the future must be as much a part of the social studies program as the past.

SELECTING CURRENT AFFAIRS FOR STUDY

Because of the multiplicity of events, issues, and problems, the selection of those to be studied is no simple task. Although help can be obtained by relying on the use of children's weekly newspapers, problems still exist in selecting local and state events, adding events not included in the periodical, and screening out some that have been included. As with the selection of content for the overall social studies program, teachers should apply such criteria as the following:

1. Educational value: Will children learn something significant? Is the event or issue related to fundamental objectives? Will study of it contribute to conceptual, process, skill and affective objectives?
2. Appropriateness: Is it appropriate in terms of the maturity, experience, and competence of pupils? Is it appropriate in terms of community conditions, values, and feelings?
3. Relatedness: Is it related to past and future learning? Can it be related to basic units of study? Can it be tied in with other experiences?
4. Available information: If needed, can background information be obtained? Are suitable teaching materials available?
5. Available time: Is sufficient time available to obtain adequate depth of understanding?
6. Reliability: Is accurate information available? Can facts be differentiated from opinions? Can differing points of view be noted?
7. Timeliness: Is it current? Is up-to-date information available? Is it related to basic trends? Are significant consequences discernible?

Every effort should be made to select events that are *significant for the particular class in which they are to be used.* Children should be guided so that they will avoid sensational, lurid, and trivial events. In addition, specific attention must be given to the teaching of criteria, and direction must be provided in the selection of current events to be shared in class. In the following section, several techniques are suggested for this purpose.

One of the most effective procedures is to direct the students' search for current events related to a topic or unit they are studying. Problems and topics in such units as home and family, community workers, environmental problems, transportation, living in our state, regions of the United States, living in Canada, and living in Mexico make excellent focal points around which student-selected current events can be organized. When this is done, skills in critical and evaluative reading are enhanced, and the events are placed in a setting that gives them meaning.

Teachers can apply the same idea to current events bulletin boards, panel discussions, and other activities by setting a major theme or concept to guide the selection of events. Some teachers also make use of basic concepts such as cooperation, interdependence, creative contributions, and people's use of resources. When current events are gathered and discussed in terms of these basic concepts, growth in depth and breadth of understanding invariably takes place.

Scrapbooks or notebooks prepared individually, by small groups, or by the class can also be organized around specific concepts and themes. At times an entire scrapbook may be organized around a single concept or problem; at other times a scrapbook may include several related concepts or problems with clippings placed in each section. In all cases, pictures, charts, maps, and other illustrative materials should be included to enhance understanding. The point is to help children relate the selection of current affairs to main objectives and to the activities used to achieve them. Continuing guidance of selection is essential and can be improved by utilizing standards that children themselves have helped to formulate. Charts 8–1 and 8–2 illustrate some useful techniques.

Chart 8–1
Sharing the News

About parents' work
About our own work
About trips we take
About community activities
About changes in seasons

Chart 8–2
Finding Current Events

Is it important?
Do I understand it?
Can I report it well?
Will it be interesting to others?
Is it related to other topics?

APPROACHES TO THE STUDY OF CURRENT AFFAIRS

The several approaches to the study of current affairs described below each have strengths and weaknesses. Many teachers use a combination of approaches, depending on the objectives to be achieved, the significance of the events involved, the units under study, and the availability of materials.

Relating Current Affairs to Basic Units

A good general policy is to relate current affairs to basic units of instruction, for the problem of obtaining background material and giving perspective to current affairs then becomes less difficult. As regional units such as areas of our state, Midwestern United States, and regions of South America are studied, current events can be selected to highlight recent developments. As historical units such as early times in our state and colonial life are studied, current events can be selected to contrast "then and now." Charts 8–3 through 8–6 show topics in selected units that can be used as guides for finding related current affairs.

The great problem here is one of timing. As one teacher put it: "So many significant events occur either before or after I teach a unit." Many teachers meet this problem by using current events to launch units, by collecting clippings and having children collect clippings related to units that are to be developed; by timing the introduction of certain units to coincide with holidays, sessions of the state legislature and Congress, and other scheduled events; by keeping files of children's weekly newspapers related to future units; by relating events to past units; and by continuing certain strands from unit to unit, such as transportation, communication and conservation.

Chart 8–3
We Need News Items on Our Changing Community

Activities of people
Housing developments
Highways and traffic
Health and safety problems
Conservation problems
Recreation facilities
Water supply
New schools and libraries
Relations with other communities

Chart 8–4
We Need News Items on Our State

Population	Government
Industries	People
Agriculture	Cities
Education	Rural areas
Conservation	Health
Recreation	Safety
Transportation	Communication
Relations with other states	Exports to foreign places

Chart 8–5
Find Items on These Regions for Further Use

New England states
Southeastern states
North Central states
South Central states
Rocky Mountain states
Southwestern states
Far Western states

Chart 8–6
Look for News Items on Canada Related to These Topics

Cities	Transportation
Provinces	Communication
St. Lawrence Seaway	Government
Oil pipelines	Education
Mining	Conservation
Trade and industry	Relations with the United States
Value of the dollar	Relations with other countries

Weekly Study of Periodicals Many teachers provide for the study of children's periodicals during one period each week. It is convenient and relatively easy to assign the reading of articles, carry on discussion, and have students complete the activities and tests included in each weekly issue, but there are dangers in this approach. These include routine reading and answering of questions, superficial learning caused by an attempt to cover too many topics, and failure to relate current events to basic topics and units. The suggestions presented later in this chapter in the section on weekly periodicals for children are helpful in avoiding these dangers and in getting maximum benefit from the weekly study of current affairs. In addition, a sound procedure is to direct the study of weekly periodicals by stressing points noted in Chart 8–7.

Miscellaneous Reporting This approach may take the form of daily or weekly sharing of news, or it may be done at irregular intervals. Daily sharing is frequently used by

Travel agencies and transportation companies have pictures related to new developments. How might such materials be related to the study of current events? (Pan American World Airways, Inc.)

Chart 8–7
Studying Weekly Newspapers

Skim it first to get a general idea of the contents.
Study pictures, maps, charts, tables, and graphs.
Note articles related to topics we are studying.
Note articles on which background material is given.
Note articles on which background material is needed.
Look up the meaning of any words you do not understand.
Look for facts, opinions, and differing points of view.
Be ready to raise questions and make comments during discussion.
Check your understanding by completing the tests.

teachers in primary grades and in some middle grades. Some teachers like to have reporting on a weekly basis or at assigned times. Items are obtained from newspapers, radio and television newscasts, and children's periodicals. Five to ten minutes may be used in daily sharing, but a full period may be used if a weekly plan is followed. The weaknesses in this approach include the reporting of trivial events, superficial learning because of a lack of depth of study, isolation of events from past experiences and basic units of study, and the tendency for discussion to wander. These weaknesses can be overcome in part by directing the selection of current affairs, suggesting better sources of news items, systematically relating current affairs to basic topics and units, holding to discussion standards, and providing for deeper study of more important current affairs. What at first may appear to be isolated events can sometimes be related to significant topics. For example, a bicycle accident may lead to a discussion of safety rules with emphasis on showing concern for others; a news item on minority groups may lead to a discussion of rights and responsibilities, fair play, and other democratic values in community living.

Because of television and discussions with adults at home, children may raise questions that are beyond their level of maturity. Such questions should be dealt with on levels of experience and understanding appropriate for the group. After adequate comment or discussion, the teacher should direct the group's attention to other questions, reports, or topics. At times, particularly in the primary grades, children may report events about family life that are of a personal nature and not proper topics for group discussion. When this happens, a tactful and unobtrusive shift should be made to other topics. Sometimes a wise course is to suggest that a particular topic is one that the child may discuss later with the teacher.

Short Current Affairs Units

Current affairs of special significance cannot always be dealt with in the daily or weekly period or incorporated in units of work. An important community or state event or problem, a major election, activities related to our bicentennial, the coming of a nation to the forefront in international affairs, the study of an individual of current national and international importance—any of these may require an intensive short unit in which current materials and related background material are used. Sometimes special units featured in children's weekly periodicals need a more extended period of study. By noting related materials and suggestions contained in the teacher's edition of the weekly newspaper and by collecting pamphlets, books, films, and other resources, a teacher can achieve important objectives through study of special units.

Whichever approach or combination of approaches is used, every effort should be made to have students attain the highest possible levels of thinking and understanding. Three levels may be identified quickly as one visits classrooms. The *first level* is the routine reporting of events. Each child has seen, read, or heard about an event and shares it with the group with little or no discussion by the class or analysis of relationships to other experiences. The *second level* involves the reporting of an issue or event followed by discussion of the most interesting points. This level involves more thinking by the class, may prove to be entertaining for those who participate in discussion, and may stimulate interest on the part of others. Usually it does not penetrate far beneath the surface to basic concepts, trends, and relationships and does not involve any critical analysis of related issues and problems. The *third level* involves the use of problem-solving and critical thinking skills through attention to the significance of the event or issue, review of supporting facts, consideration of differing points of view, need for additional data, and other pertinent factors. To be sure, this third level cannot and should not be applied to all current affairs. However, when truly significant events are selected for study, there are usually many ways to guide children from level one to three and thus increase the value of the experience.

ACTIVITIES AND SOURCES OF INFORMATION

Many activities and sources of information are put to use in the current affairs program. In selecting them, teachers should consider those that can be used by individuals and small groups as well as by the entire class. In fact, good group discussion and analysis of current affairs depend on adequate individual preparation. Students too should be concerned about the selection of activities and sources of information appropriate for the event or issue under study. Charts 8–8, 8–9, and 8–10 suggest activities and sources of information that may be used. Charts 8–11 through 8–14 illustrate guidelines for preparing, checking, and reporting current affairs.

Weekly Periodicals for Children

Fortunately, well-prepared classroom periodicals are available for use in the elementary school. They are prepared by highly qualified writers, editors, and illustrators, and contain a variety of current affairs that meet the criteria discussed earlier. Properly used in the classroom, they are an excellent resource. The following are used in many schools throughout the country: *My Weekly Reader* (grades K-6, *Current Events* (grades 7–8), American Education Publications, Education Center, Columbus, Ohio 43216; *Let's Find Out, News Pilot, News Ranger, News Trails, News Explorer, News Citizen, Newstime* (grades K–6), *Junior Scholastic* (grades 6–8), Scholastic Magazines, 50 West 44th St., New York, N.Y. 10066.

These publications are designed to present the most significant national and international current affairs. A special effort is made to select events and issues appropriate for study in the elementary school. Various points of view are presented, related background information is frequently given, trends are highlighted, and related tests and exercises are included. Suggestions for teachers that accompany various issues are to the point and consistent with sound principles of teaching.

The following guidelines should be observed in the use of children's newspapers in order to get maximum value from them and to avoid misusing them:

1. Individual needs can be met by selecting editions that are appropriate to the reading levels in a class. Thus, one may find editions on three or four reading levels in the same class.

Chart 8–8
Which of These Should Be Used in Our Current Affairs Program?

Individual reports	School intercom	Pictures	News maps
Committee reports	Bulletin board	Charts	Globe
Panel or debate	Quiz games	Murals	Models
Classroom newscasts	News files	Scrapbooks	Exhibits
Tape recorder	Picture file	Cartoons	Dramatizations

Chart 8–9
Finding Current Events

Radio and television newscasts
Newspapers and magazines
Interviews of experts
School and neighborhood library
News file
Our weekly newspaper
Bulletin board

Chart 8–10
Periodicals in the Library

Weekly Reader	Newsweek
Newstime	Time
News Explorer	U.S. News & World Report
Young Citizen	The Times
Current Events	Evening Star
Junior Scholastic	Chronicle

Chart 8–11
Preparing News Reports

Note the main ideas.
Select the most important facts.
Have pictures or other items to show.
Be ready to locate it on a map
Be ready to answer questions.
If possible, relate it to a topic under study.

Chart 8–12
Checking Reports

Is it accurate?
Is it up to date?
Who reported it?
Can the facts be checked?
Are there opinions in it?
What do others say?

Chart 8–13
Reporting Current Events

Is it important to the group?
Do I know it well?
Can I give illustrations?
Can I give it in my share of the time?
Do I have the main ideas?
Can I relate it to other topics or events?

Chart 8–14
Listening to News Reports

Do I understand it?
Do I have questions to ask?
Is it related to my report?
Is it related to something we are studying.
Is other information needed?
Is it controversial? If so, are all sides given?

2. Effective teaching techniques should be used, with attention to developing readiness for reading, clarifying purposes, building vocabulary, anticipating difficulties, interpreting maps and graphs, and discussing and summarizing key ideas. As with textbooks, films, and other resources, children's periodicals do not take the place of good teaching.
3. An effort should be made to use each issue of the periodical at a time when it will be most effective. Although one period each week may be set aside for intensive study, many teachers provide for study and discussion when the related topics are being studied.
4. The whole-class approach to the study of selected sections of the weekly newspaper may be appropriate at times, but it should be supplemented by individual and small-group study in accord with individual needs.
5. Whenever possible, relationships between the current affairs presented in the newspaper and basic units of instruction should be made. Isolated items and incidents are soon forgotten, but events and issues related to basic studies become a part of the child's growing background of concepts and knowledge.
6. Both formal and informal evaluation should be made of learning resulting from the use of current periodicals. Tests provided in the periodicals, discussion, sharing, reporting, follow-up activities, and observation can be used to appraise basic outcomes.
7. A teacher should not expect a weekly periodical to constitute the entire program of current affairs study. There must still be careful selection of significant local and state news items as well as important national and international items that may not have been included in a particular issue.
8. By maintaining files of back issues, a teacher can provide reference material on topics and units in the basic program.
9. New maps that appear in periodicals can be used to improve competence in map reading and map making.

Controversial Issues

The statement is sometimes heard that "elementary school children have inadequate backgrounds to study controversial issues." Ordinarily the speaker has in mind the study of critical issues currently being debated by adults and the achievement of adult levels of understanding. Certainly, many current issues are beyond a child's understanding; but controversial issues do come up in social studies, and experienced teachers wisely select some of them for study. Such study is based on the assumption that some issues will be approached as unanswered questions toward which there are differing points of view that should be studied in a thoughtful manner. Some may be handled briefly, others may simply be introduced as continuing problems that will be reviewed in the future, and still others may be studied in detail because of their importance.

In the primary grades, attention is generally given to issues and problems close to the lives of children, issues and problems that come up in school, in the neighborhood, and in the community. Examples of these are differences of opinion on ways of carrying out classroom activities, ways of improving the conservation of resources, utilization of parks and playgrounds, fair play in the treatment of others, contributions of others, and conflicts between individuals and groups. At times, attention may be given to issues raised by children concerning elections, campaign issues, minority group demands, housing problems, ways of preventing discrimination against others, and other problems growing out of community living. These should not be ignored, nor should they be handled in a way that is beyond the ability of children to understand. A simple answer, an explanation of the problem, a clarification of the issue, or a brief discussion may suffice. The important thing is to keep the way open for such questions, to discuss them on an appropriate level, and to begin to lay a foundation for ongoing study of issues.

In the middle and upper grades, more involved issues and problems are encountered as children undertake such units as our state, living in the United States, Mexico, Canada, countries of Latin America, the Middle East, Africa, and growth of democracy. In addition, current events periodicals present issues that may be related to basic units of study. Other issues are presented on television and radio programs, discussed at home, and reported in newspapers.

The study of selected current issues and problems is usually governed by policies set by the board of education. The following statement is typical of the policies followed in many school systems:

1. Only significant issues and problems understandable to children, and on which children should begin to have an opinion, should be selected for study in the elementary school.
2. Instructional materials must present differing points of view, discussion should include all points of view, and respect for the views of others should be shown.
3. Teachers must guide learning so as to promote critical thinking and open-mindedness, and they must refrain from taking sides or propagandizing one point of view.
4. Special attention must be given to a consideration of background factors, possible consequences of various proposals, the need for additional information, and the detection of fallacies of thinking, logic, and argumentation.
5. The importance of keeping an open mind—that is, the willingness to change one's mind in the light of new information—should be stressed.

The criteria listed in the first part of this chapter must be applied rigorously in the selection of current issues and problems for study in the elementary school. Of special importance are those criteria related to educational value, significance, and appropriateness in terms of children's background of experience and community conditions. Generally, issues are not selected if they are offensive to individuals and groups in the community or will place the school in the center of a heated debate.

Checking with other teachers and with the principal is a good idea when there is any doubt about the appropriateness of a particular issue. In some instances, committees made up of school personnel and members of the community have worked together to define policies that should govern the teaching of controversial problems. This should be done when serious issues and problems that appear appropriate for study are also controversial issues in the community. Such issues generally concern morality and religion, sex, race relations, and ideological aspects of economics and politics.[1]

Serious problems arise when a teacher becomes a crusader for a cause and goes all out to get students to adopt the same point of view. Behavior of this type is a violation of professional ethics and a misapplication of the concept of freedom in teaching. Teachers at all levels of education are expected to guide the study of controversial issues in an impartial, unemotional, and unprejudiced manner. The teacher's prestige and position in the classroom must not be used to promote a partisan point of view. When the teacher is asked to express an opinion, it should be given and noted as an opinion, and not as the final answer.

The atmosphere in which current problems and issues are studied should be conducive to thoughtful discussion. Free expression is needed in order to examine differing viewpoints. Partisanship and bias should be detected. The quality of the evidence should be considered, with attention to inadequacy or unavailability of information, opinions based on limited experience, opinions of experts, purposes of proponents of various points of view, and consequences of various courses of action. At times, one must consider why different groups believe that a given point of view is reasonable to them, to see it from their standpoint. At all times, one should not be embarrassed to change one's point of view in view of new information. Charts 8–15 through 8–22 illustrate special points to be emphasized in middle and upper grades.

SPECIAL EVENTS

Special events—holidays, special weeks, and commemorations—are a vital part of every cultural heritage. They have been set aside as a time for celebration and the expression of treasured values, ideals, and beliefs. Through special days and weeks, attention is called to significant events, institutions, documents, great

[1] M. P. Hunt and L. E. Metcalf, *Teaching High School Social Studies,* rev. ed. (New York: Harper & Row, 1968).

Chart 8–15
Defining Issues and Problems

How shall we state it?
Do we understand each term?
What are the subproblems?
What parts are most important?
Do we have ideas about any part?
Which parts need most study?

Chart 8–16
Checking Materials

What is the author's background?
What group sponsors or publishes it?
What is the group's purpose?
Are there other points of view?
What materials present other points of view?

Chart 8–17
Discussing an Issue

Define it clearly so that all sides are known.
Consider each position.
Find facts related to all sides.
Verify and organize facts.
Make and change conclusions on the basis of facts.

Chart 8–18
Checking Points of View

What facts do I have?
How do I feel about it?
What do others believe?
How do they feel about it?
What would I believe and feel if I were in their place?

Chart 8–19
Working on Problems

Recall ideas related to it.
Think of possible ways to solve it.
Find information related to each possible solution.
Check and summarize information.
Try out the best solutions. Select the one that works best.

Chart 8–20
Forming Conclusions

Wait until facts are checked and organized.
Be sure facts are separated from opinions.
Consider outcomes and consequences.
Test tentative conclusions.
Make final conclusions.

Chart 8–21
Watch Out For

Name-calling and not giving the facts
Making general statements that sound nice but are vague
Using popular words so that the idea will be accepted
Saying that so-and-so believes it, therefore we should believe it
Saying that plain folks believe it, therefore we should
Giving only those facts that support one side
Stating that many people are accepting the ideas, so we should too

Chart 8–22
Feelings and Issues

Control your feelings and help others control theirs.
Try to put yourself in the other person's place.
Try to understand other points of view.
Give facts when stating your own position.
Search for deeper causes of the difficulties.
Try to find reasonable proposals and next steps.
Make tentative conclusions and be ready to change them when feelings calm down.

men and women, and customs that have been valued through the years. The manner in which special days and weeks are presented, the depth and quality of understandings and appreciations that are achieved, the historical perspective that is developed, and the attitudes that result determine in large measure their meaning and significance in the lives of children.

Contributions to Basic Objectives

The study of special days and weeks may contribute to the development of wholesome attitudes and deeper appreciations as children learn about the contributions of great men and women, discover the deeper meaning of Thanksgiving, find out how Christmas and New Year's Day are celebrated in different countries, express friendship and affection for others on Valentine's Day, and discover how they can show appreciation on Mother's Day and Father's Day. The responsibilities of citizenship take on deeper meaning as children are directed in their observance of Bill of Rights Day, Constitution Day, General Election Day, Veteran's Day, Washington's Birthday, Memorial Day, Flag Day, and Independence Day. Concepts such as interdependence, cross-cultural sharing, and cultural diversity are deepened and broadened as children discover similarities and differences in modes of celebrating holidays at home and in other lands. Intergroup understanding may be increased as children observe Brotherhood Week and join with others in observing Hanukkah as well as Christmas, a practice increasingly common in recent years. International understanding may be increased as Pan-American Day and United Nations Day are observed. Reading, study, discussion, and other

Chart 8–23

What Contributions Did These Women Make?

Jane Addams	Paulina Wright Davis	Mary Church Terrell
Susan B. Anthony	Lucretia C. Mott	Sojourner Truth
Marian Anderson	Florence R. Sabin	Harriet Tubman
Ida Wells-Barnett	Sacajewea	Mary E. Walker
Mary McCleod Bethune	Elizabeth Cady Stanton	Emma H. Willard
Marie S. Curie	Henrietta Szold	Frances E. C. Willard

What others can we find?

____________	____________	____________
____________	____________	____________
____________	____________	____________

skills are sharpened as children find and share information related to special days and weeks (see, for example, Chart 8–23).

Grade Placement Two policies are widely followed in the grade placement of special days and weeks. First, certain holidays are considered in all grades, beginning in kindergarten and the first grade. In succeeding grades opportunities are provided for more advanced learning through background studies, short units, relationships to basic social studies units, and varied activities. Second, certain special days and weeks are assigned to particular grades depending on the background and experience of children and the basic units in the program. An examination of grade placement charts usually reveals a pattern similar to this one:

Kindergarten and Grade 1: Halloween, Thanksgiving, Christmas, New Year's, Washington's Birthday, Lincoln's Birthday, Valentine's Day, Easter, Hanukkah, Mother's Day, Father's Day, Flag Day

Grades 2 and 3: Continue the above on higher levels and add Columbus Day, American Indian Day, Fire Prevention Day, Veteran's Day, Book Week, American Education Week, Arbor and Conservation Day, Memorial Day, Independence Day, and the day our community was founded.

Grades 4–6: Continue the above on higher levels and add Labor Day, United Nations Day, Constitution Week, Admission Day, Bill of Rights Day, Franklin's Birthday, Susan B. Anthony's Birthday, Brotherhood Week, Black History Week, Pan-American Day, Women's Equality Day, International Goodwill Day, Armed Forces Day, other special days and weeks of significance in the community or state, and special days of importance in other countries that are studied.

A Calendar of Selected Days and Weeks In some school systems a calendar or listing of special days and weeks is provided so that teachers may select and do preplanning for their classes. Because practices vary greatly among school systems and among states, the calendar must be developed to fit local and state policies. The calendar in Chart 8–24 was prepared by a group of teachers in a social studies workshop. Teachers should be alert to special days and events not shown in Chart 8—24 that are of importance to various ethnic groups. For example, German Day, Polish Bazaar, Mexican Independence Day, Cabrillo Day, and the Chinese Moon Festival in September; Madonna Del Lume (Italian), Irish Festival Week, Dia de la Raza, and Ohi Day (Greek) in October; Finnish Independence Day, Our Lady of Guadalupe, and Santa Lucia Day (Swedish) in December; Republic Day (India) and

Chinese New Year in January; Our Lady of San Juan de Los Lagos (Mexican), St. Patrick's Day, and Greek Independence Day in March; Russian Easter, Cinco de Mayo (Mexican), Polish Constitution Day, and Norwegian Constitution Day in May.

Chart 8–24
Calendar of Selected Days and Weeks

September	
Labor Day	first Monday
Citizenship Day	17
Constitution Week	includes 17
American Indian Day	fourth Monday

October	
Junior Red Cross Enrollment	date announced
Fire Prevention Day	9
Columbus Day	second Monday
United Nations Day	24
Veteran's Day	fourth Monday
Halloween	31

November	
Veteran's Day	11
Book Week	date announced
American Education Week	date announced
General Election Day	first Tuesday after first Monday
Thanksgiving	fourth Thursday

December	
United Nations Human Rights Day	10
Bill of Rights Day	15
Christmas	25
Hanukkah	date announced

January	
New Year's Day	1
Martin Luther King, Jr.'s Birthday	15
Franklin's Birthday	17
Inauguration Day	20
Franklin D. Roosevelt's Birthday, March of Dimes	30

February	
Lincoln's Birthday	12
Brotherhood Week, Black History Week	includes 12
Valentine's Day	14
Susan B. Anthony's Birthday	15
Washington's Birthday (observed third Monday)	22

March	
Luther Burbank's Birthday	7
Conservation Week	includes 7
Arbor Day	various dates
Easter Week	in March or April
Passover	date announced

April	
Pan-American Day	14
Kindness to Animals Week	date announced
National Youth Week	date announced
Earth Day	date announced

May	
May Day	1
Child Health Day	1
International Goodwill Day	18
Mother's Day	second Sunday
Armed Forces Day	third Saturday
Memorial Day	last Monday

June	
Flag Day	14
Father's Day	third Sunday

July	
Independence Day	4

August	
National Aviation Day	19
Women's Equality Day	26

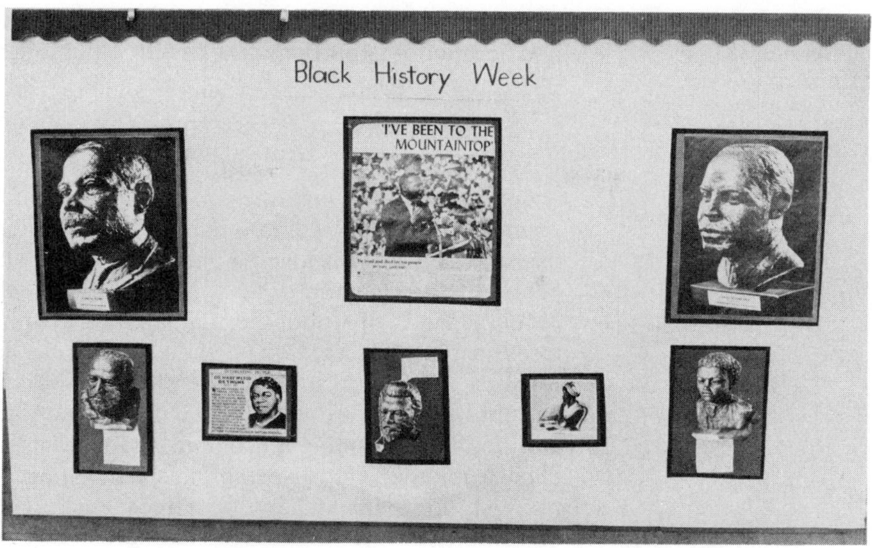

What contributions have these and other black Americans made? (Richmond, California)

DIFFERENTIATING EXPERIENCES FROM GRADE TO GRADE

Because many special days and weeks are given attention in each grade, overall planning is needed to make sure that children develop deeper appreciations and understandings as they progress through the grades. The following example on Arbor and Conservation Day includes activities that may be provided beginning in kindergarten and on through grade 6. Notice how many of them can be made a part of such units as the home, our community, living in our state, and conservation.

ACTIVITIES FOR ARBOR AND CONSERVATION DAY

Kindergarten–Grade 2

Taking a nature walk in the neighborhood; making collections of leaves; observing birds and listening to bird calls; observing the growth of certain trees and shrubs; caring for plants and pets; learning about the many uses of wood; reading and hearing stories and poems about trees; writing original poems and stories; making a display of leaves; seeing films on forest animals; drawing pictures of trees, flowers, and animals; taking a study trip to see a house under construction; learning about synthetic fibers, paper, and other things made from wood; making picture books and scrapbooks; participating in a tree-planting ceremony

Grades 3–4

Observing and identifying trees in the community; learning about commercial, recreational, and decorative values of trees; learning about logging and other aspects of the lumber industry; visiting a sawmill; making a collection of different kinds of wood; learning about the importance of trees in the conservation of water, soil, and animal life; learning about our state's watersheds and water supply; learning about new uses of wood in construction, industry, and hobbies; planning a program and sharing it with parents or another class; seeing films on logging, lumbering, reforestation, and water resources; making charts, a mural, or a movie roll box to summarize basic concepts

Grades 5–6

Establishing a nature trail and making signs to mark trees, plants, and other objects; establishing feeding and watering stations for birds; arranging an exhibit of flowers and leaves of common trees and shrubs; inviting conservation experts to discuss questions and problems raised by the class and to report on newer practices; learning about the consequences of poor conservation practices in ancient civilizations in China and the Middle East; learning about present-day problems in the United States; learning how resources are interrelated; discussing the balance in nature and how man must work in harmony with nature; finding out the steps that are being taken to improve conditions; reading and reporting on contributions to the conservation movement of men such as Theodore Roosevelt and Gifford Pinchot; studying and making maps of forest areas and state and national parks; making rules of camping; creating poems, pageants, and programs that highlight conservation needs, problems, and forward-looking practices; seeing documentary films or TV programs; planning and carrying out a tree-planting ceremony to which other classes will be invited; making scrapbooks containing pictures, clippings, and notes on conservation

Practices in Primary Grades

In the primary grades, major emphasis is given to the introduction of customs, traditions, ceremonies, rituals, special meaning of terms, and the significance of selected special days and weeks. Activities and materials are selected in terms of the children's maturity and background of experience in a given class. Beginning with storytelling, simple art activities, and participation in classroom and school activities, the program moves to reading stories, reporting and sharing ideas found by children, and more advanced activities.

Units of instruction in the social studies provide many opportunities for deeper study of special days and weeks. The home and family unit gives background to Mother's Day and Father's Day. The contributions of many different workers, a key learning related to Labor Day, takes on greater meaning as school and community workers are studied. Thanksgiving activities may be made a part of units on Indians or Pilgrims. Valentine's Day is made a part of the study of the post office in many classrooms. As communities in other lands are studied, attention may be given to ways in which New Year's, Christmas, and other holidays are celebrated. Arbor Day activities may be related to the study of conservation, which is a basic strand in many units from grade to grade.

Classroom parties may be held as activities related to such special days as Halloween, Thanksgiving, Christmas, Hanukkah, Valentine's Day, and Easter. Children plan and make room decorations, greeting cards, party favors, hats, masks, and other items and enjoy appropriate songs, games, rhythms, poems, and stories. Bulletin-board displays, flower arrangements, centers of interest, and exhibits may be arranged, and murals, movie box rolls, and programs may be planned and shared with others.

Gifts and greeting cards may be made in connection with such special days and weeks as Junior Red Cross Week, Veteran's Day, Christmas, Valentine's Day, Easter, Mother's Day, and Father's Day. Participation in ceremonies, assemblies, parades, and pageants is possible in connection with many special days. Films, television and other audio-visual resources, reading materials, interviewing individuals in the community, creative activities, and study trips to places in the community are also utilized.

More Advanced Learning in Later Grades

Instruction in middle and upper grades should be planned to increase children's depth and breadth of understanding. Both the teacher and the class should search for new stories, poems, pictures, articles, and activities related to special days and weeks. After discussing what children have learned in earlier grades about a given day or week, some teachers use leading questions to guide the search for new ideas and materials—for example, "How did this special day originate?" "How was it celebrated in early times?" "What early customs have we kept for our own?" "How is it celebrated in other lands?" "What individuals worked to make it a holiday in our country?" "What are some famous stories and poems about this holiday?"

Questions such as these can be applied to a large number of special days and weeks. In addition, other specific questions relate to particular holidays. These have to do with special meanings of terms, specific reference to individuals, and whether the holiday has civic, religious, or personal-social significance. The examples that follow illustrate questions that can be used to guide children's study of background material related to different types of special days.

Veteran's Day: When was Armistice Day first proclaimed? Why was Armistice Day changed to Veteran's Day? Why is the unknown soldier honored each year at the National Cemetery in Arlington? What is meant by "preservation of fundamental principles of freedom"? What obligations should each individual assume for the peace, welfare, and security of our country?

Thanksgiving: What were harvest festivals like in ancient times? Why did people have them? What was the first Thanksgiving like in our country? How was it different from earlier harvest festivals? Who was Sarah Joseph Hale, and what did she do to make Thanksgiving a national holiday? Which President issued the proclamation that made Thanksgiving a national holiday? What are your favorite stories and poems about Thanksgiving? Can you find some new ones?

Christmas: What is the origin of the word Christmas? Where did we get the customs of having holly, mistletoe, and the yule log? Where did the composers of our favorite Christmas carols live? How is Christmas celebrated in Mexico? In other lands?

Washington's Birthday: Where did Washington live as a boy? What was his home like? How was he educated? What are the main periods of his service to our country? What traits of leadership caused his countrymen to call on him to be the first President? Why is he honored as "the father of our country"? What is meant by "first in war and first in peace"?

Mother's Day: What country first had a special day for mothers? Who was Anna Jarvis, and how did she contribute to the establishment of Mother's Day in our country? Which state was the first to have Mother's Day as a state holiday? Which President signed the resolution of Congress establishing Mother's Day? How did the custom of wearing carnations originate?

Certain special days and weeks are studied in detail at a time when they may be made parts of units of work; this may be in addition to a short observance that is held as a part of classroom or school activities. For example, Constitution Day, Bill of Rights Day, United Nations Day, and the contributions of Franklin, Lincoln, Washington, and other historic

BIRTH OF A NATION

How can commemorations be made meaningful to students? What values should be identified? How can bicentennial activities be extended from the birth of our nation to adoption of the Constitution and beyond? (Social Studies Workshop, University of California, Berkeley)

leaders are included in units on the United States and the growth of democracy. Pan-American Day and International Goodwill Day take on deeper significance when tied in with such units as South America and other lands. Great men and women and special days of importance in the child's state should be included in the unit on our state.

Sometimes it is a good idea to provide for short-term units to give background to a special day or week. Examples are fire prevention, Red Cross activities, and the Parent-Teachers Association. Short units on topics such as these give children the background they need to understand the purposes and activities of organizations and agencies that render services that benefit both children and adults. Other short-term units may be developed on great men and women, special weeks, or days of special importance in the community or state.

More and more, individual study and preparation of reports on related background information are used to develop greater depth of understanding. The following are examples of reports written by children in the fifth grade.

HARVEST FESTIVALS BEFORE THE PILGRIMS HAD THEIR FIRST THANKSGIVING

Long ago, before the Pilgrims landed, people had celebrations at harvest time. They were happy to have a good harvest. Some would make offerings to the spirits and gods that they thought made seeds fertile and made the crops grow.

The oldest known harvest festival, Succoth, was in Israel. Thanks were given for finding a place to live and for the harvest.

In ancient Greece there was a celebration that lasted nine days. It was in honor of the goddess of the harvest called Demeter. Demeter was also the goddess of corn.

The festival of the harvest moon was held in old China long ago. The Chinese would bake moon cakes. They also thought that a rabbit lived in the moon.

Some of our early settlers had learned about harvest festivals in England. The English would have feasts and share what had been raised. People in the villages would get together and each family would buy something.

The peasants in Old Russia had feasts and dancing. One custom was to place a wreath of grain by the house. A new one was put there each year. They thought it would help make a good harvest.

The Iroquois Indians had feasts at different times. One was in the spring at maple syrup time. Another was at planting time. Still another was at harvest time. They also had a bean and a corn festival. All together they had about seven festivals a year.

WHAT SUSAN B. ANTHONY DID

Susan B. Anthony worked hard to get the right for women to vote. She also wanted equal rights for women in other things. She was a teacher once and only got paid $10 a month while men teachers were getting $40 a month. She said that this was not fair. She also said that women should choose their own jobs and take care of their own property. She also said that they should be able to go to college just the same as men.

I didn't know that women never used to have all these rights. It is a good thing that Susan B. Anthony came along. My mother says that some women take these rights for granted. They should remember what Susan B. Anthony did. I am going to remember her birthday on February 15.

Some teachers take time before the school year ends to consider special days that occur during summer vacation. For example, Independence Day and the events leading up to it can be studied as a part of units on the United States. Children can be asked to watch for special reports and activities as celebrations take place during the summer. National Aviation Day, August 19, should not be overlooked as an opportunity for children to collect clippings and other materials for use in transportation and aviation units when school starts in the fall. Similarly, Labor Day celebrations and activities in early September are sources of experience and information that can be put to use at the beginning of the school year. Checklist 8–1 is a summary of activities and materials for special days and weeks.

Checklist 8–1

ACTIVITIES AND MATERIALS CHECKLIST

Listening: Individual and group reports, material read by others, tapes, records, guest speakers, panel discussions, radio programs

Viewing: Films, filmstrips, slides, stereographs, photographs, painting, television programs, picture files, exhibits, demonstrations

Reading: Stories, articles, poems, essays, biographies, autobiographies, diaries, local documents and pamphlets, reference materials, clipping files, items on bulletin boards

Writing: Songs, poems, plays, skits, quiz games, reports, stories

Designing and Making: Room decorations, greeting cards, greeting card boxes, costumes, hats, masks, costume dolls, maps, puppets, gifts, gift wrappers, party favors, booklets, scrapbooks, shadow boxes, peep boxes, movie box rolls, dioramas, sandbox displays, time lines, murals, picture files, clipping files, charts, labels

Arranging: Bulletin boards, flowers for special occasions, room decorations, the classroom for parties and programs, special centers of interest, exhibits of book jackets, products, and other items related to special days

Visiting: Museums, special exhibits, historic places, homes of famous people, special agencies, and organizations

Interviewing: Old-timers, writers, scholars, experts on conservation, resource persons from special agencies, and organizations

Participating in or Witnessing: School assemblies, ceremonies, parades, pageants, plays

Investigating: Origins of holidays, contributions of great men and women, holidays in other lands, customs brought from other lands around the world

SOURCES OF INFORMATION

Children's weekly newspapers and monthly magazines include stories and articles on great men and women, holidays, and special weeks. At times they feature new stories and activities that may be used to provide fresh learning experiences. The teacher's guides that accompany weekly periodicals occasionally list related films, filmstrips, television programs, books, pamphlets, and other materials.

Children's encyclopedias are excellent sources of information. The background materials, stories, pictures, time lines, reading lists, dates of holidays, and other information they contain can be used for individual study and reference. *The World Almanac* lists the dates set for holidays each year and includes information on holidays observed in different states and public days in Canada.

The *Teacher* and *Instructor,* both magazines for teachers, include stories, articles, units, bulletin-board suggestions, construction activities, reading lists, bibliographies, and other material. Excellent sources for teachers, they are also useful to more able children who are pursuing individual studies or who wish to find directions for making things related to a particular holiday.

Television and radio programs should be checked in newspapers, weekly program guides, and program bulletins issued by broadcasting companies and school systems. Newspapers and magazines for adults feature special reports and articles that can be read and shared by many children. Specific suggestions on special days and weeks are included in courses of study, units of instruction, and bulletins on special days made available by state departments of education and many local school systems. For information on bicentennial activities and materials, write to: The Bicentennial Administration, 2401 E Street NW, Washington, D.C. 20276; and People's Bicentennial Commission, 1346 Connecticut Avenue NW, Washington, D.C. 20036.

QUESTIONS, ACTIVITIES, EVALUATION

1. Which of the objectives for studying current affairs do you believe most difficult to achieve? which the easiest? Which are most significant in early grades? later grades?
2. Apply the criteria for selecting current affairs to two or three items from the local newspaper. Which criteria are most difficult to apply? Which criteria do many articles *not* meet?
3. Next, check the articles in one or two of the children's periodicals listed in this chapter. Do all articles meet the criteria?
4. Which approach to the teaching of current affairs do you believe to be the best for general use? Might times occur when other approaches should be used? Give examples.
5. Which of the activities suggested for use in current affairs might you use in a unit of instruction you are planning?
6. Review several periodicals for children and identify articles, maps, charts, test items, and other material that you might use in a unit of instruction.
7. Examine a bulletin on special days and weeks issued by a local school system of the state department of education. Which days and weeks are included? What learning activities are suggested? Which activities might you use in a unit you are planning?
8. Make a calendar of special days and weeks that are appropriate in your community. Indicate the grades in which certain days and weeks might be emphasized.
9. Which of the charts presented in this chapter might you put to use in your teaching? What adaptations might be made to meet the needs of children in different grades?

REFERENCES

For specific suggestions on holiday observances, see current issues of *Instructor, Teacher, School Activities,* and *School Arts.*

"Bicentennial Multimedia Materials," *Instructor,* April 1975. Detailed list of materials from publishers and producers.

CHASE, W. LINWOOD, and MARTHA T. JOHN, *A Guide for the Elementary Social Studies Teacher* (2nd ed.). Boston: Allyn and Bacon, 1972. Section on current affairs in Chapter four.

Comprehensive Calendar of Bicentennial Events. Washington, D.C.: Superintendent of Documents, Government Printing Office, 1975. State, national, and international events.

FRANKSON, CARL E., and KENNETH R. BENSON, *Crafts Activities Featuring 65 Holiday Ideas.* West Nyack, N.Y.: Parker Publishing Co., 1970. Practical activities for special days.

FRASER, DOROTHY M., "Current Affairs, Special Events, and Civic Participation," in *Social Studies in Elementary Schools* (32nd Yearbook). Washington, D.C.: National Education Association, 1962. Principles and procedures for teaching current affairs, holidays, and civic participation.

HUNT, M. P., and L. E. METCALF, *Teaching High School Social Studies* (rev. ed.). New York: Harper & Row, 1968. Useful in upper grades on controversial issues.

JAROLIMEK, JOHN, *Social Studies in Elementary Education*. New York: Macmillan, 1971. Chapter on current affairs.

KRAVITZ, BERNARD, "Factors Related to Knowledge of Current Affairs in Grades 7 and 8," *Social Education,* XXVI (March 1962), 143–45. A report on the relationships between achievement in current affairs and reading achievement, social studies achievement, and mental ability.

LEE, JOHN R., *Teaching Social Studies in the Elementary School*. New York: Free Press, 1974. Chapters on American and international issues.

MUESSIG, RAYMOND H. (ed.). *Controversial Issues in the Social Studies: A Contemporary Perspective*. 45th Yearbook. Washington, D.C.: National Council for the Social Studies, 1975. Models for teaching followed by discussion of selected issues.

MYERS, ROBERT J., *Celebrations: The Complete Book of American Holidays*. Garden City, N.Y.: Doubleday, 1972. Helpful to middle- and upper-grade students as well as to teachers.

PRICE, CHRISTINE, *Happy Days*. New York: Dutton, 1969. A UNICEF book of special days in different countries.

SECHRIST, ELIZABETH H., *Red Letter Days* (rev. ed.). New York: Macrae Smith, 1965. Significance of holidays and celebrations in several countries.

Focusing Questions

What are the values and limitations of group work?

What whole-group and small-group activities are used? What group work skills need attention at various levels?

How should discussions be handled? How can they be improved by using planned questioning strategies?

What skills are needed for productive independent study?

Providing for Group & Independent Work

The quality of children's learning in social studies is closely related to the skill with which teachers guide group activities. The core of instruction is provided in groups, and many independent activities grow out of group planning, discussion, and evaluation. The focus of this chapter is on practical ways to plan for group and independent activities, organize whole- and small-group instruction, guide discussion, use questions to improve discussion, and make plans to develop outlining, reporting, and other independent study skills.

GROUP WORK

Values and Limitations

Organized groups may well be viewed as laboratories for firsthand learning about human interaction. Both individual and small-group inquiry can be stimulated and improved through interaction with others. Concepts can be clarified, hypotheses stated, generalizations formulated and assessed, and motivation sparked and directed toward worthwhile objectives. Feelings of belonging, security, acceptance, respect, and mutual trust can be developed. Study can be more productive as the best thinking of individuals in the class is tapped. A constructive and experimental approach to learning can be nurtured, and the excitement of discovering and sharing ideas with the group can increase the depth and breadth of learning. Democratic attitudes and behavior patterns such as open-mindedness, responsibility, creativity, concern for others, and cooperation can also be developed.

Teachers should know the limitations as well as the values of group work. First, group work should be limited to activities with some purpose that members of the group can share. Without a shared purpose, those in the group will waste time and derive little or no benefit from the activity. Second, group work should be limited to activities for which children possess or can be taught the needed skills. If children are to benefit from panel discussion and committee work, for example, they must possess certain skills, which are noted later. Third, group work should be limited to activities in which cooperative action is required to achieve stated purposes. If an activity can be completed by an individual, or by several individuals working independently, there is no need to organize a working group. Fourth, group work should be limited to activities in which effective working relationships can be maintained. If interpersonal conflicts and differences in points of view cannot be reconciled, progress cannot be made by forcing individuals to work in a group. Fifth, group work should be limited to situations in which diverse talents can be put to use. If each child is required to do the same thing and individual differences are ignored, the unique contributions that different members could make will be lost.

Whole-Group and Small-Group Activities

Two kinds of group work are needed, depending on the kind of activity. The whole group is involved in planning dramatizations, things to make, displays, use of materials, stories, simulation games, ways to obtain information, and how progress will be evaluated; and in observing demonstrations, films and other audiovisual resources, people and activities on field trips, role playing, committee reports, changes in the neighborhood and community, and resource visitors. The entire group discusses observations, interpretations, generalizations, classifications, inferences, hypotheses, predictions, analyses, syntheses, and evaluations based on data gathered from reading materials, community resources, and audiovisual materials; it also evaluates plans, projects, use of materials, displays, dramatic activities, discussion, demonstrations, group behavior, sources of data, role playing, interviewing, and other data-gathering techniques.

Small-group activities are needed to carry out work planned by the whole group and to meet special needs and interests of students. Small groups make maps, charts, graphs, labels, dioramas, murals, clay and papier mâché figures, instruments, objects needed in dramatizations, booklets, displays, and plans for reporting and sharing; they investigate topics, problems, questions, and hypotheses raised in whole-group discussion by means of interviews, library research, and use of materials in study centers, and collect pictures, stories, articles, postcards, objects, and other items related to questions under study.

Small-group activities are usually coordinated so that each group is making a contribution to the work of the whole group. For example, on

This group is gathering data to share with the class. How might you use small groups to investigate selected topics? (Hatboro-Horsham School District, Pennsylvania)

field trips four or five groups may be set up to obtain information on different questions. Several groups may be set up to interview different individuals. The construction of different objects for a supermarket, airport, dramatization, or other activity may be assigned to small working groups. Parts of murals, time lines, bulletin-board arrangements, scrapbooks, and other projects may also be handled by designated groups. Chart 9–1, a flow chart illustrating key aspects of small-group work, is arranged to show the development of work skills from a beginning to an advanced phase. Items in the beginning phases should be used in the early grades, and in later grades with students who are inexperienced in group work. Students should be moved to the intermediate and advanced phases as they develop the necessary skills. By the time children are in the middle and upper grades, they should be able to work at the advanced phase.

Selecting and Organizing Groups

One of the most effective ways to select and organize groups is to structure them *in terms* of compatibility, individual needs for the development of leader and follower skills, readiness for the activity, and the job to be done. Sociometric grouping, in which children make choices of those with whom they wish to work, may be used when special interest groups are formed and the considerations noted above are not of primary importance. Selection by children of working groups listed on the chalkboard is used when choice of activity is a basic consideration. When special topics are to be researched by using textbooks or library resources, it is wise to use reading groups.

Chart 9–1

Developing Group Work Skills: A Continuum of Skills*

	Beginning Phase		Intermediate Phase		Advanced Phase
Objectives	Brief, specific	⟶	Longer, yet directed	⟶	Long, more complex
Planning	Planned primarily by the teacher	⟶	Planned jointly by the teacher and pupils	⟶	Planned primarily by pupils
Duration	Short, one or two days	⟶	Longer, several days	⟶	Several days to several weeks
Materials and sources of data	Use of single source or few sources or materials	⟶	Varied sources and materials	⟶	Variety of media and materials
Organization, interaction	Informal, parallel activities; little interaction	⟶	Chairman selected, tasks varied and assigned, some interaction during work	⟶	Chairman or coordinator; much interaction in all phases
Reports	Parallel reports, or one student reporting with others filling in	⟶	Each member reports, or pupils share in reporting pooled information	⟶	Synthesis of information in one report; planned and given by the group
Evaluation	Informal; emphasis on sharing of best ideas	⟶	Attention to both content and procedures; self-evaluation encouraged	⟶	Emphasis on self-evaluation of activity in greater depth

* Grateful acknowledgment is made to Dr. Ruth Grossman, The City College of the City University of New York, for this chart.

Group work can be facilitated by making space arrangements to accommodate groups of varying size. Open space schools provide for an unlimited number of arrangements, and movable furniture provides a high degree of flexibility, as shown in Chart 9–2, which is taken from the Pasadena Schools Curriculum Guide.

Chart 9–2
Space Arrangements

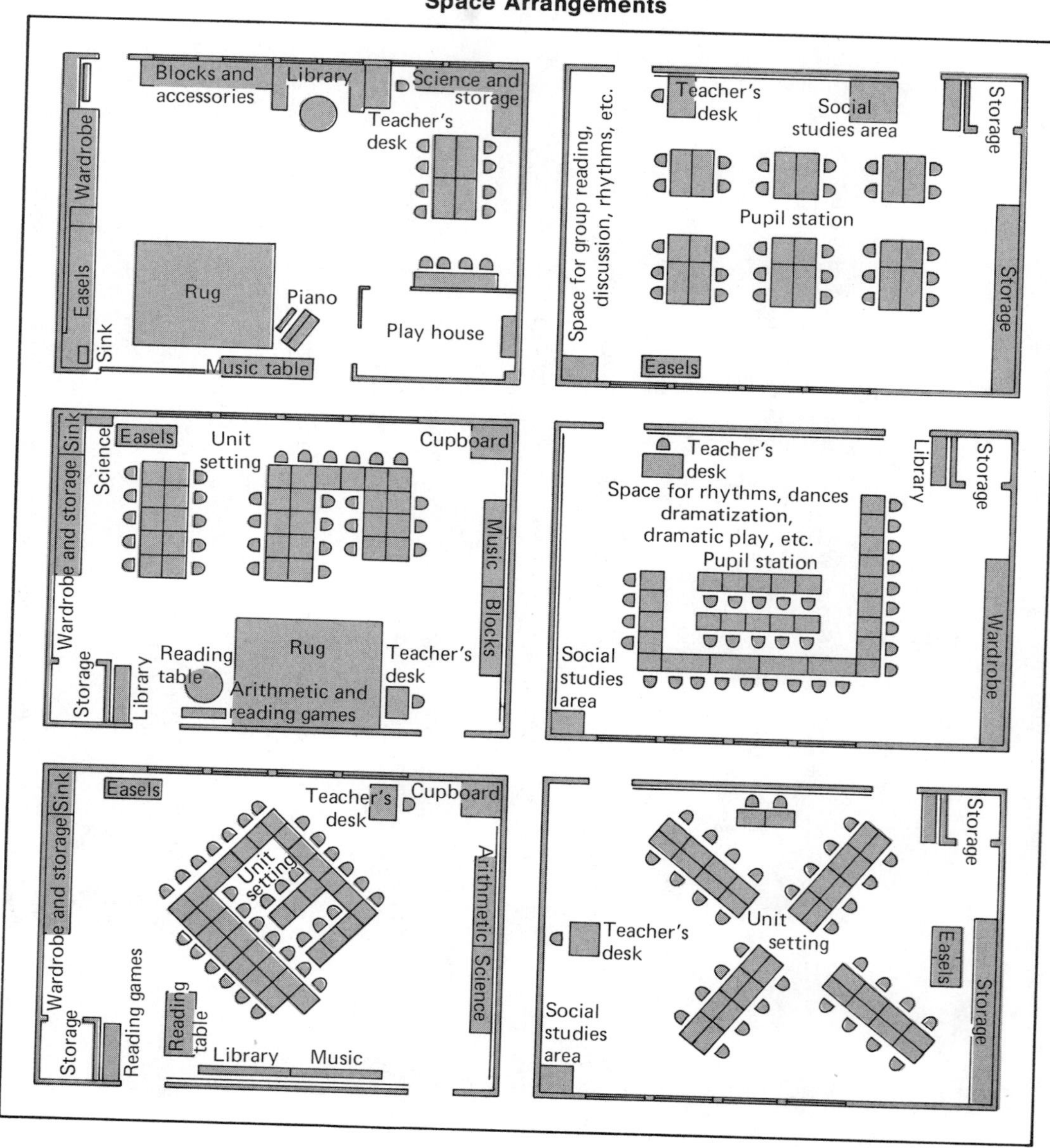

Planning Planning and replanning as problems arise are features of effective group work. Initial planning is carried out in group discussion, with special attention to questions, problems, and responsibilities. Replanning is necessary as new needs arise and as special problems are presented for consideration. Planning should be more than a search for sources of information. For example, attention should be given to formulating problems, devising ways to secure data, setting up work standards, deciding on things to construct, considering ways to secure and use materials, overcoming obstacles, helping others, extending interests, investigating proposals, submitting suggestions, asking for help, and finding out about others' opinions and ideas. Planning is also essential in getting ready for research activities, construction, dramatic play, processing of materials, field trips, and creative expression through art, music, literature, and rhythms.

In guiding group planning, teachers should keep the following principles in mind:

1. Problems and questions expressed by the children should receive major attention. Problems neglected by the children can be pointed out by the teacher.
2. Constructive suggestions should be secured from the group; negative comments should be redirected into positive suggestions.
3. Records should be made and kept as needed to further group action; examples are charts, directions, reading guides, work sheets, notes, and minutes.
4. Group decisions growing out of planning should lead to specific plans of action.
5. At the end of planning discussions, check to see that each child understands what to do, where to do it, how to proceed, materials to use, work standards to follow, and how to get help.

Initiating Small-Group Work Guidelines for starting committees and other small working groups are as follows:

1. Make plans to begin with one group. Give attention to the task to be completed, directions to guide work, and arrangement of needed materials and working space.
2. After the rest of the class is busy, take the small group to the work area, clarify what is to be done, and see that members are off to a good start. Provide supervision as needed during the work period.
3. After the task is completed, guide the sharing of the group's efforts with the class. Discuss procedures that were used as

well as outcomes, giving attention to any problems that arose and how to prevent them in the future. Summarize standards that similar groups can use.

4. Make plans for other working groups in a similar fashion. Move from one group to two or more as needs for group work become clear and children assume the necessary responsibilities. Have worthwhile independent activities ready for children who become overstimulated in small-group work and are not ready to assume the appropriate role in group activities.
5. Move from group to group as needed to supervise and direct. Note ideas for the follow-up evaluation that provide more effective ways of working together.
6. As class members develop group skills, provide them with more freedom to work on their own. Arrange groups so that children who are advanced in group skills can help others and keep the group moving in profitable directions. Give close supervision to those who continue to have difficulty working with others.

Many teachers give a demonstration of good committee work after real needs have arisen for guidance. This can be done by selecting a group to demonstrate for the class, or by using the class as a committee with the teacher as chairperson. The standards that develop should be placed on the chalkboard or on charts. Charts 9–3 through 9–5 are illustrative.

Chart 9–3
Committee Members

Know what to do
Divide the work
Do each job well
Discuss problems quietly
Plan the report carefully
Are ready to answer questions

Chart 9–4
Committee Reports

Stick to the questions
Use pictures, objects, and maps
Be ready to answer questions

Chart 9–5
Committee Chairpersons

Keep the main job in mind
Get ideas from all members
See that each member has a job
Are fair and do not talk all the time
Urge everyone to do his and her best
Say *our* committee, not *my* committee

Guiding Activities

As children engage in group activities, the teacher should observe carefully in order to get information for use in evaluation. Attention should be given to acceptance of responsibilities, cooperation, courtesy, and self-control. Attention should also be given to the various materials being used, techniques that need to be improved, and misconceptions or erroneous ideas that arise. The teacher has many opportunities to move about and give help as needed. A child may be having difficulty in locating material in a given reference, or some children may be having difficulty using tools and materials. Particular attention must be given to those few youngsters who appear to be at a loss as to just what they should do in an activity. By giving judicious assistance, the teacher can make sure that effective learning takes place. For example, in a unit on pioneer life, one teacher noticed that several youngsters were having difficulty using a table of contents. Others were not sure of the topics to locate in the index. Notes were made for use in a later discussion that centered on skills involved in locating materials.

How children use the work standards they have helped to set should be noted by the teacher. Commendation should be given to those who carry out group-made standards and who help others to do so. In some cases the teacher may have to ask a child to stop an activity for a few minutes and review the significance of group standards and related behavior. In a few instances, some children must be excluded from the group until they realize that they must accept all the responsibilities involved in the activity. Following the work period, there should be time for a careful reconsideration of group standards and ways in which they can be used by each member of the group.

This group is extending concepts of the environment. How might you extend concept development through group activities? (Bethlehem School District, Pennsylvania)

Evaluation Evaluation is an essential element in all phases of group action—from initial definition of problems to appraisal of the effectiveness of work. During evaluation, the group answers such questions as these: "Is each individual doing his part?" "Are the plans effective?" "Are leadership responsibilities being carried out?" "Are our objectives being achieved?" "Are additional resources needed?" "What next steps should be taken?" In making appraisals, the group may use discussions and charts or checklists, refer to a log or diary of activities, get assistance from the teacher, examine work materials, or use other evaluative devices. Emphasis should be given to self-evaluation and specific ways in which group activities can be improved.

Discussion Discussion is one of the most valuable techniques used in group work. Its use is essential to effective clarification of objectives, planning, and evaluation. Discussion provides a practical opportunity to set objectives, state hypotheses, raise questions, and appraise various experiences. Social skills are put to practical use, critical thinking is sharpened, and attention is focused on common problems. Ideas are shared, points of view expressed, leaders selected, responsibilities delegated, and respect is shown for the right of others to express themselves. Group discussion also provides opportunities for the teacher to note behavior, attitudes, and ability to express ideas. Creativeness of contributions, sharing of ideas, respect for the opinions of others, consideration of differing points of view, shyness, boldness, and the like can be observed and given attention as individual needs arise. Many teachers find discussion situations to be a valuable source of information regarding children's needs, potentialities, and backgrounds.

The role of the teacher (or discussion leader) in securing maximum participation of members of the group is a point that needs to be emphasized, because too often discussion is merely a conversation between the teacher and individuals in the group. For example, the teacher raises a question and gets a response; the teacher responds and another child contributes; and this rhythm of teacher to child to teacher to child goes on, with the teacher making 90 to 95 percent of the contributions. In sharp contrast is the situation in which the teacher or leader makes a contribution and several children make comments before the teacher intervenes. Charts 9–6 and 9–7 illustrate the difference. The lines indicate the flow of discussion from one individual to another. Chart 9–6 illustrates teacher (or leader) domination; Chart 9–7 illustrates group interaction. Sometimes children should lead the discussion, particularly in intermediate and upper grades. When this is done, attention must be given beforehand to the development of guidelines for leading the discussion. Chart 9–8 shows guidelines developed by a group in the fifth grade in order to meet problems that had arisen.

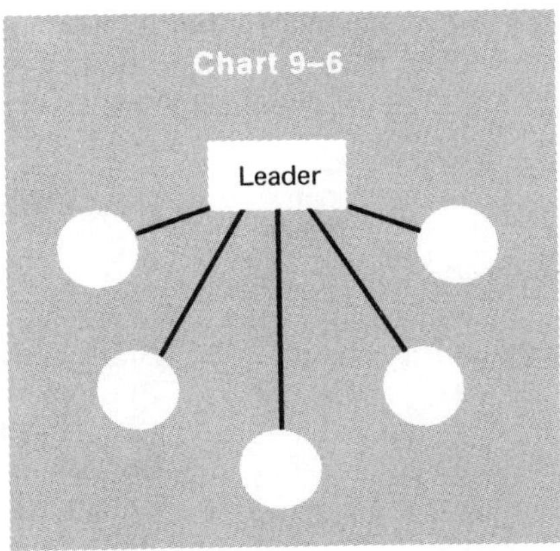

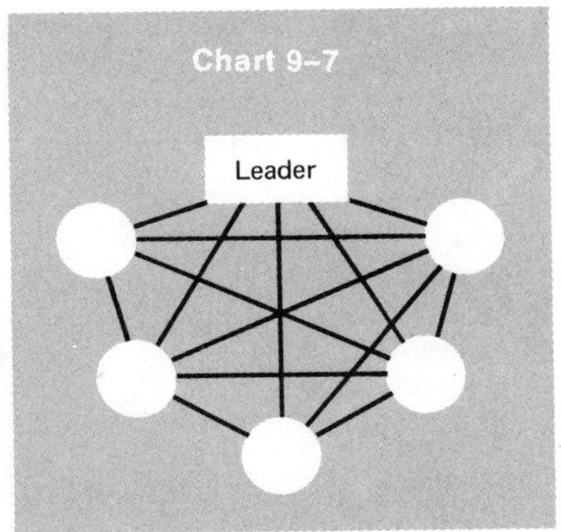

Discussion takes a variety of forms and may be improved through the use of special reports and small-group techniques. Group sharing of experiences and objects, group reports on special topics, and panel presentations are used in many units in social studies. Small discussion groups, sometimes called "buzz sessions," also may be used to summarize ideas on specific questions or topics. Charts 9–9 and 9–10 illustrate standards and guidelines that have been used successfully.

Chart 9–8
Discussion Leaders

Call the group to order
Clear up the problem
Get ideas from the group
Call on different children
Get answers to questions from the group
Summarize the discussion

Chart 9–9
Group Sharing

We share pictures, stories, and other items related to our unit.
We hold objects so that all can see them.
We speak clearly so all can hear.
We watch and listen courteously.
We take turns and use only our share of the time.

Chart 9–10
Small Groups

Each group has a topic or question to discuss.
Each group includes four to six pupils.
Seats are arranged so that each member of the group can see the others.
The chairperson opens the discussion.
The recorder keeps notes and reports back to the class.

Evaluation should be carried out by both teacher and group with specific attention to points and problems that have arisen. The teacher should keep in mind both the essential elements of effective discussion and the maturity of the children. The discussion itself can be appraised in terms of the items listed in Charts 9–11 through 9–13. The teacher must consider each child's role so that effective planning and guidance can be carried out. Checklist 9–1 suggests several points to keep in mind as each child's growth is considered. Others may be added or some may be deleted, depending on the maturity of the group and the specific needs requiring attention.

Chart 9–11
Primary Grades

Take turns.
Help make plans.
Listen to others.

Chart 9–12
Intermediate Grades

Help state your problem.
Give your ideas.
Consider other ideas.
Listen carefully.
Help to make a plan.

Chart 9–13
Upper Grades

State problems clearly.
Stick to the point.
Respect ideas of others.
Make a contribution.
Weigh the evidence.
Raise questions on issues.
Help in making decisions.
Help in summarizing.

Checklist 9–1

GROWTH IN DISCUSSION

Note: Check each child two or three times during the term to see if growth is taking place.

Behavior To Be Checked	**Names**		
Understands the problem			
Listens while others speak			
Is an interested and willing listener			
Interjects ideas at appropriate points			
Considers contrary ideas			
Sticks to the topic			
Does not repeat ideas given by others			
Gets to the point without delay			
Speaks clearly and distinctly			
Uses appropriate language			
Uses concepts accurately			
Is interested in comments of others			

Using Questions to Improve Discussion

It is helpful to plan specific kinds of questions related to various aspects of discussion—talking about content, responding to members' comments, and structuring the discussion.[1] Definitions and examples of questions keyed to these three basic steps are given below; other strategies that can be used to guide discussion are found in Chapters 6 and 7, which focus on developing thinking and valuing processes.

Content questions. Open-ended, specifying, clarifying, and extending questions are directly related to the content of discussion. Open-ended questions are frequently used to initiate discussion, elicit a variety of responses, and invite students to participate—for example, "What did you see on the field trip?" "What should we do to improve bicycle safety?" "What do you remember about the Gold Rush?" "How many different ways can you think of to solve this problem?" To get at details and data essential to understanding, specifying questions such as these are injected: "What steps in processing almonds did you see on the field trip?" "How can we improve bicycle safety around the school?" "How were claims established during the Gold Rush?" "What can we do right now to help solve this problem?"

Clarifying questions are used during discussion to get at the meaning of terms, phrases, and statements: "Can you give some examples to show what you mean?" "Can that be stated in another way?" "Are you saying that they wasted their resources?" "What do you mean by civil liberties?" Extending questions probe for additions, explanations, alternatives, and other elaborations of content: "Are there other suggestions or comments?" "What can be added to our list?" "Are there other ways to handle the problem?" "What other reasons can you give?"

Student comments. Effective discussions take place in a classroom climate marked by accepting, supporting, and encouraging behavior on the part of teacher and students. Students inevitably make irrelevant comments, interject unrelated ideas, and put forth erroneous statements. And some students hold back during discussion and need encouragement to participate. The following comments and questions are illustrative of the kind of teacher behavior students should be encouraged to emulate.

Accepting questions and comments are used by the teacher when a student gets off the point, repeats an idea, interjects irrelevant comments, or responds to a question raised earlier. For example, "That's interesting, Betty. Can we come back to it later?" "I see that you agree with what Paul said." "Have we already listed that? Let's check." Discussion can also be facilitated by teaching students to precede remarks that may be off the immediate topic with such explanatory comments as "I just thought of something related to an earlier question." "Getting back to what Jane

[1] Adapted from Helen McGinnis, *Retrieval, A Social Sciences Handbook for Teachers,* Social Science Project, Area III Superintendents (Sacramento, Calif.: County Office of Education, 1972).

said, . . ." "This isn't on the question, but may I say . . ." "An idea that may be useful later is . . ."

Supporting questions and comments are helpful when a child makes an error or needs help in making a point, or when an unpopular or shy child comments: "Can we look that up later?" "Who can help Alice make her point?" "Let's give Robert a chance to have his say." Encouraging questions and comments are used to bring students into the discussion: "Has anyone else something to say?" "Are there any items that should be changed?" "Does anyone want to raise a question about any points made so far?"

Questions to structure the discussion. When the emphasis is on classifying for concept formation, interpreting data, and generalizing, for example, preplanned questions are needed to structure the discussion. They are used to move from one step to the next and to higher levels at a pace the students can handle.

Focusing questions direct thinking step by step and shift discussion from one phase of a teaching strategy to the next. Notice in the following examples of classifying for concept formation how the questions shift discussion: "What did you find? see? hear? note?" (focus on data); "Which ones can be grouped together?" (focus on grouping); "Why can they be grouped together?" Or, "How are they alike?" (focus on reasons); "What is a good name for this group?" (focus on labeling). Refocusing questions bring students back to the point under discussion; they may be a repetition or rewording of focusing questions: "What does *this* chart show, rather than the one on air pollution?" "Can we wait on that and get more examples of waste pollution?" "Which activities in the home, not in parks, add to waste pollution?"

Lifting questions, a special type of focusing question, are used to move thinking to higher levels. They guide discussion from a consideration of data to processing of data and then to application of data, concepts, and generalizations. Notice how the last three questions in the examples that follow lift thinking beyond information: "What can you recall about ways to prevent air pollution?" "How can we group the different ways?" (lift to grouping); "What would happen if everyone helped to prevent air pollution?" (lift to predicting); "Why do you think that would happen?" (lift to analyzing reasons).

Varying the pattern of questioning. Three question patterns are generally used, depending on the situation. The teacher varies the pattern by considering ways in which to guide students to interpret data, to generalize, and to interpret feelings.

The first pattern is frequently used after completing a reading, seeing a film, interpreting a map, or using another resource. The objective is to discuss the meaning obtained from the resource and to use what has been learned to get at questions and problems under study. Questions may be used in this sequence: (1) What does this map (film, reading, picture) show? (2) How can we summarize the key ideas? (3) Which ideas can we use to answer questions on our chart?

The second pattern is used when students have spent considerable time in gathering and organizing information on retrieval charts or in some other form and know it well. Questioning may begin with a focus on generalizing, as in the following example: (1) Look at our chart on consumers and producers. (2) What is the main thing consumers do? (3) What is the main thing producers do? (4) What is the main difierence between them?

The third pattern is useful in inferring the feelings aroused by a current event, listening to a story, seeing a film, or some other experience. Here is an example: (1) What happened? What is the problem? What did they do? (2) How do you think they (she, he) felt? Why might they feel this way? (3) Has something like that ever happened to you? How did you feel? Why did you feel that way?

From Data to Data Processing to Application

In general, planned questioning strategies such as those noted above and in Chapters 6 and 7 move from consideration of data to processing of data and on to application of ideas gleaned from data processing. The teacher's role is to initiate the discussion, encourage and note responses, and respond to comments. The shift from level to level must not be pushed beyond students' capabilities because mastery of each level is a prerequisite for the next higher one. The following example illustrates the three levels of thinking and the teacher's role.

> ***Teacher:*** What can you recall about ways to save energy?
> ***Student:*** Turn out lights, use mass transit, etc.
> ***Teacher:*** Any others to add to our list?
>
> ***Teacher:*** How might we group the ways to save energy?
> ***Student:*** By ways to save at home, traveling, etc.
> ***Teacher:*** Can each way be grouped under these headings?
>
> ***Teacher:*** What might happen if everyone saved energy in these ways?
> ***Student:*** No more shortages, saving of money, etc.
> ***Teacher:*** Why do you think that would happen?

During the first sequence, consideration of data, the teacher emphasizes the recalling of needed data from observations made by students in films, books, and other resources. During the second sequence, processing of data, the emphasis is on comparing, contrasting, classifying, defining, interpreting, and generalizing. In the third sequence, application, students are encouraged to infer, hypothesize, predict, analyze, synthesize, and evaluate.

Interaction Analysis Ned Flanders has developed a method for checking the interaction between teacher and students.[2] Attention is given to the amount of teacher talk and pupil talk, as follows:

Teacher Talk

A. Indirect influence with much student freedom and interaction
   1. Teacher accepts feelings expressed by students.
   2. Teacher praises and encourages students.
   3. Teacher accepts or uses ideas of students.
   4. Teacher asks questions of students.

B. Direct influence with less student freedom and interaction
   1. Teacher lectures to students.
   2. Teacher gives directions.
   3. Teacher criticizes or justifies authority to improve student behavior.

Student Talk

A. Student responds to the teacher.

B. Student initiates the talk.

The teacher records and analyzes interaction with students in terms of the categories given above, and in a third category notes periods of silence or times of confusion during which communication cannot be understood. Some teachers have found it helpful to make and analyze a tape recording to determine if appropriate attention is being given to the involvement of students and if changes are needed in the pattern of interaction.

INDIVIDUAL WORK SKILLS

Many individual activities provided in the social studies program call for the use of independent study skills—note taking, outlining, using multiple sources of information, preparing reports, listening, and good study habits. These skills are important in carrying out tasks that emerge from group planning as well as in independent study activities selected by or assigned to individual students.

Note Taking The primary purpose of note taking is to jot down information for future use—information related to questions, problems, directions, reports, discussions, and special projects. Notes may be taken as children read textbooks and reference materials, see films, take a field trip, interview

[2] Ned Flanders, *Analyzing Teacher Behavior* (Boston: Addison-Wesley, 1970).

individuals, study a map, review a picture file, or gather information from other resources. The form of the notes may vary from a short list of items to a summary of main ideas related to a topic, depending on the purpose for making the notes, the source that is used, and the capabilities of the children. Charts 9–14 through 9–16 contain suggestions for note taking.

Chart 9–14
Take Notes

To answer questions
To prove points
To get directions for making things
To summarize ideas
To get ideas for reports, charts, discussions, murals, and scrapbooks

Chart 9–15
Notes from Interviews

List each question to be asked on a half-sheet of paper.
Arrange the papers in order.
Jot down main points as each question is answered.
Ask questions about points that are not clear.
Take notes on new ideas.

Chart 9–16
Notes from Films

Write the title of the film.
Note the main reasons given for seeing the film.
Get the main ideas as presented in the introductory part of the film.
Note main points as the film is shown.
Check to see if you have notes related to each reason for seeing the film.

Outlining Outlining skills are used in social studies for summarizing information from textbooks and references; organizing ideas from discussions, interviews, and study trips; planning reports; making booklets; listing items needed for projects; and organizing information for future use. Outlines are especially helpful for getting ideas in sequence, clarifying main ideas and supporting details, classifying information, organizing ideas related to a topic, and grasping relationships among main ideas and related subtopics.

The sequence of development of outlining skills begins with short lists of sentences or items dictated by the group and written by the teacher on the chalkboard or on charts. In the middle and upper grades, more complex outlines are made. They range from a short numerical or alphabetical listing of items to three-step outlines with main headings, subheadings, and support details. Charts 9–17 through 9–21 give examples of how to develop this skill.

Using Information from Several Sources The use of a number of textbooks, reference materials, and other resources calls for special skills in locating and pooling information. A first step at all levels of instruction is a sufficiently detailed discussion of the question or problem so that each child will know just what information

Chart 9–17
On Our Study Trip

1. We saw cows.
2. We saw horses.
3. We saw chickens.
4. We saw pigs.
5. We saw the farmer.
6. We saw buildings.

Chart 9–18
Fruits and Vegetables

Fruits	Vegetables
1. Apples	1. Beans
2. Bananas	2. Beets
3. Grapes	3. Carrots
4. Peaches	4. Lettuce
5. Pears	5. Peas

Chart 9–19
Community Workers

I. Builders
  A. Bricklayers
  B. Carpenters
  C. Painters
  D. Plumbers
II. Business people

Chart 9–20
Uses of Different Means of Transportation

I. Airplanes
  A. Transportation
    1. People
    2. Mail
    3. Goods
  B. Agriculture
    1. Crop sowing
    2. Crop dusting
  C. Defense
II. Trains
  A. Transportation

Chart 9–21
Outline Form

I. ____________
  A. ____________
    1. ____________
    2. ____________
  B. ____________
    1. ____________
    2. ____________
II. ____________
  A. ____________
    1. ____________
    2. ____________

is needed. After the question or problem is clear, several simple procedures are helpful in developing the necessary skills.

In primary grades, children can be asked to refer to two or three books in which colored slips of paper have been placed to indicate where information on certain topics can be found. For example, in a unit on the home, a red slip may be used to show the location of a page or two on the work of the mother, a blue slip the work of the father, and a yellow slip the work of the children at home. After children have developed an adequate vocabulary, labeled slips may be used in place of colored slips. After appropriate number concepts have been developed, page numbers may be listed on the board or on a chart.

Once material has been located in several sources, help is needed in pooling ideas obtained from them. One effective procedure is to have children study one source carefully, and then to summarize the three or four main ideas obtained from it in oral discussion. This is followed by studying a second source and discussing similarities and differences, and then checking a third source. The main ideas obtained from the references are summarized in oral discussion and listed on the board. The next step is to have children check two or three references on their own.

Preparing Reports Oral and written reports are an effective means of individualizing instruction because they provide opportunities for each child to gather and organize information on topics of special interest from reading materials and other sources of information. Reporting skills used in the social studies program are shown in Charts 9–22 through 9–25. The following examples show the abundance of topics for reports in various units.

The Home: Work of Mother, Work of Father, Work of Children, How Work Is Divided, Care of Pets, Taking Care of the Baby, Workers Who Come to the Home, How the Family Has Fun Together, How the Family Saves Energy

Our Community: Contributions of Leaders, Producers of Goods, Producers of Services, How Mail Is Handled, Our Water Supply, How to Prevent Pollution, Local Transportation Services, How Newspapers Are Printed, Our City Parks, Future Plans

Early Days in Our Community: Old Indian Villages, The First Settlers, What Early Homes Were Like, The First Stores, How People Traveled, The First Telephone, Early Mail Service, Our Trip to the Old Fort, How Our Community Got Its Name, The Early Fire House, The First School, The Story Behind City Park

Our State in Early Times: Where the Indians Lived, Early Explorers, The First Settlers, How the Missions Were Built, The Building of Forts, The First Town, Admission to the Union, Our First Governor, Travel Routes to Our State, How the Capital Was Chosen, How Our State Got Its Name, How Our State Got Its Nickname, The Story of Our State Flag

Our State Today: Urban Centers, Changing Population, Contributions of Ethnic Groups, Changing Industries, Why Agriculture Is Important, What We Send to Other States, What We Get from Other States, Air Transportation, How Rivers Are Used, Transportation Networks, Developing Our Water Resources, Conservation of Forests, Environmental Problems, Our State Parks, Future Developments

Regions of the United States: Major Industries, Resources, Kinds of Farming, Manufacturing Centers, Major Rivers, Central Cities, National Parks, How Steel Is Made, New Industries, Conservation of Land, Environmental Problems

Life In Early America: The Plymouth Colony, A Colonial Home, The Town Meeting, The First Thanksgiving, How Children Were Educated, Games Played by Children, The Erie Canal, The Tom Thumb Locomotive, Drake's Oil Well, The Saugus Ironworks, How Clothing Was Made, How the Colonists Lighted Their Homes, The Making of Candles, Contributions of Men and Women, Events to Remember During Bicentennial Observance

Living in Mexico: What the People Are Like, Famous Murals, The Piñata, The Posada, Activities at a Fiesta, Contributions of Leaders, Trade with the United States, Major Industries, Early People of Mexico, Why the Spanish Came, Early Explorers, How Mexico Gained Independence

Living in Other Lands: What the People Are Like, Home Life, Relations with Other Countries, Clothing, Airports and Seaports, Highways and Railways, Central Cities, Interesting Places to Visit, Village Life, Imports and Exports, Changes That Are Being Made, Use of Resources, Things We Get from Them, Things We Send to Them, Main Occupations, Weather and Climate, Customs, What Their Schools Are Like, Art and Music, Games, Future Prospects

Chart 9–22
Choosing a Topic

Is it an important topic?
Is it interesting to you and to others?
Are good sources of information available?
Is it small enough so that you can finish it on time?

Chart 9–23
Selecting Ideas

Think of the questions your report should answer.
List the main topics that should be included.
Select ideas related to each topic.
Include only important ideas.

Chart 9–24
Planning Reports

Have a good introduction.
Put the main ideas in order.
Put points under each main idea.
Have a short conclusion.
Think of a title that tells what the report is about.
Give the sources of information.

Chart 9–25
Reports on TV and Radio Programs

Select a program related to our unit.
Note title of program, time, and station.
Note ideas related to topics in our unit.
Select two or three ideas to share with the group.

Oral reports. Oral reports are used to share information on topics, questions, and problems of concern to the group. Informal reports based on information from textbooks, current periodicals, news reports, and other sources of information are frequently made a part of classroom discussion. Formal reports based on more detailed studies of topics are generally used as the group moves from one major topic in a unit to another, and as a part of concluding activities. Oral book reports may be used in relation to the topics under study. Individual reports are used on topics that can be handled by a child working alone; group reports are used on broad topics that are broken down into several related parts.

Written reports. Written reports may take a variety of forms, including individual papers, charts, scrapbooks, notebooks, booklets, newspapers, logs, and diaries. Individual papers and charts are helpful in organizing and sharing ideas on specific topics. Scrapbooks and notebooks are used to compile a series of reports as a unit progresses. Booklets are useful in organizing information on a topic in greater detail and depth. Class newspapers are sometimes used to organize ideas related to current events and issues and to portray historical incidents and events as if "you were there." Logs and diaries are helpful in recording information over a period of time. Pictures, drawings, maps, tables, and graphic charts are used in different types of reports to illustrate, highlight, and summarize key ideas.

Listening Vitally important in social studies, listening skills can be sharpened as children share reports; discuss topics and problems; note directions for activities; observe demonstrations; listen to recordings, radio, and television programs; enjoy stories and poems read by others; hear resource people report on places; and watch films on ways of living in other communities and lands. Objectives for listening in social studies are to gain ideas on a topic, to enjoy what is being read or reported, to follow steps in a sequence, to get directions, to understand an explanation, to visualize a description, to note related ideas, to learn new terms in context, to clarify concepts, to contribute to discussion, to appreciate mood, tone, and feeling, to appraise ideas, to react to statements, and to raise questions. These objectives vary in terms of the following somewhat overlapping levels of listening:

Level 1: Getting ideas during conversation and informal discussion
Level 2: Enjoying stories, poems, and other selections
Level 3: Getting directions, questions, and problems clearly in mind
Level 4: Noting main ideas and related details
Level 5: Evaluating statements of fact and opinion

Chart 9–26
Listening for Enjoyment

Is the mood set in the beginning?
What will the climax be?
Which parts can be visualized?
Which parts are most exciting?
Is the climax what you expected?

Chart 9–27
Listening for Information

Have a clear objective.
Get ideas in order.
Relate supporting details to main ideas.
Take notes on needed items.
Ask questions on parts that are not clear.

Chart 9–28
Critical Listening

What is to be appraised?
Which statements are facts?
Is related evidence given?
Which statements are opinions?
What conclusions can be drawn?

A helpful procedure is to use a tape recorder so that points of disagreement can be checked, especially after a critical listening activity. Other helpful procedures are discussing points of courtesy as problems arise, considering ways to improve listening in the light of questions and problems raised by children, providing directed listening activities with immediate follow-up evaluation, and preparing standards for self-evaluation and group evaluation, as shown in Charts 9–26 through 9–28.

Good Study Habits

Much can be done in the social studies program to improve study habits because of the many opportunities for individual work and reports on topics included in each unit of instruction. Study habits developed in social studies are put to use in the classroom, in the library, and in study at home. Building on the foundation established in the primary grades, specific attention should be given in later grades to the extension and refinement of study habits such as those listed in Charts 9–29 and 9–30.

Chart 9–29
Good Study Habits

Know what to do!
Stop—Stop other activities so that you can get the direction clear.
Look—Watch the teacher so that you get each point.
Listen—Get the exact details on what to do.
Ask—Raise questions if you do not understand any part.
Proceed to do it!
Organize—Arrange the needed materials and plan the steps to take.
Concentrate—Stick to your job and do not be distracted.
Finish—Complete the assignment before starting other activities.
Check—Review your work to be sure it is complete and well done.

Chart 9–30
Better Home Study

Know exactly what you are to study.
Be sure to take the necessary materials home.
Plan your study time so that you will not have to stay up late.
Study in a place where you will not be bothered.
Arrange the study materials so that they can be used effectively.
Stick to the job once you have started it.
Do your own work even though others may help you with difficult parts.
Review the main ideas after you have completed your work.
Be ready to ask questions the next day on any parts you do not understand.

QUESTIONS, ACTIVITIES, EVALUATION

1. Which of the values and limitations of group work skills do you believe to be most significant? why? What do you think are some

dangers in overemphasizing them at the expense of independent study skills?

2. Note four or five whole-group activities you might use in a unit of your choice. Do the same for small-group or committee activities.
3. Visit a classroom and use the following questions to observe and analyze the teacher's role in guiding discussion: Was the initiating question clear? How did it give a focus to discussion? Note how each of the following was used:
   a. Open-ended, specifying, clarifying, and extending questions related to content of the discussion.
   b. Accepting, supporting, and encouraging questions related to student comments.
   c. Focusing, refocusing, and lifting questions related to the structure and flow of discussion.
4. Make a plan for including questioning strategies in a discussion you might guide in a unit of your choice. Note different types of questions that you might use (refer to Chapters 6 and 7 for examples of strategies).
5. Indicate ways in which the following might be used in a unit of study: (1) note-taking skills, (2) outlining skills, (3) organizing data from several sources, (4) oral and written reports, (5) listening skills, (6) home study.
6. Which of the charts presented in this chapter might you use in a unit you plan to teach? What changes might you make to meet instructional needs in different units at various grade levels?

REFERENCES

CARPENTER, HELEN M., ed., *Skill Development in the Social Studies* (33rd Yearbook). Washington, D.C.: National Council for the Social Studies, 1963. Basic reference on social studies skills.

CHAPIN, JUNE R., and RICHARD E. GROSS, *Teaching Social Studies Skills*. Boston: Little, Brown, 1973. Practical suggestions for all social studies skills.

JAROLIMEK, JOHN, *Social Studies in Elementary Education*. New York: Macmillan, 1971. Sections on group work and skills.

——— and HUBER M. WALSH, eds., *Readings for Social Studies in Elementary Education* (3rd ed.). New York: Macmillan, 1974. Articles on skills.

MCKEE, PAUL, *Reading: A Program of Instruction in the Elementary School*. Boston: Houghton-Mifflin, 1966. Sections on study skills.

MICHAELIS, JOHN U., and EVERETT T. KEACH, eds., *Teaching Strategies for Elementary Social Studies*. Itasca, Ill.: Peacock Press, 1972. Articles on skills.

RUDDELL, ROBERT B., *Reading-Language Instruction: Innovative Practices.* Englewood Cliffs, N.J.: Prentice-Hall, 1974. Chapter on research and study skills.

THOMAS, R. MURRAY, and DALE L. BRUBAKER, *Decisions in Teaching Elementary Social Studies.* Belmont, Calif.: Wadsworth, 1971. Sections on formation of groups and group work.

10

Focusing Questions

Why should expressive experiences be included in units of instruction?

How can creative writing, dramatic representation, and simulation games be used to improve learning?

How can music, arts and crafts, construction activities, and processing of materials be made a meaningful part of units of instruction?

Providing for Expressive Experiences

Expressive experiences are included in the social studies program to involve children deeply and personally in learning activities. Six types of expressive experience are presented in this chapter: creative writing, dramatic representation, simulation games, music, arts and crafts, and selected industrial or practical arts. A common element in all six types is active and creative involvement in the expression of thoughts and feelings. These experiences are helpful in several ways. They provide opportunities for children to express their own thoughts and feelings and to develop the capacity to distinguish shades of meaning that is a basic part of inquiry into human relationships. Cognitive, affective, and psychomotor dimensions of learning may be brought together in a unified way. Key ideas and feelings may be synthesized in expression that brings the "doing" side of thinking into play. And children may develop insights into the hopes, values, and aspirations of others as they attempt to identify themselves with the people and activities under study.

Expressive experiences are also helpful in personalizing and individualizing instruction. Able, disadvantaged, average, and less able children have opportunities to express their own thoughts and feelings. When children create stories or poems, construct objects, play simulation games, paint pictures, or respond to music, they are individualizing their learning by expressing themselves in ways that fit their cognitive and affective styles.

In the social studies program, expressive experiences are included in two basic ways. The first is to include material on the art, music, industrial arts, dramatic activities, and rhythmic expression of the people under study. For example, in such units as Indians of the Southwest, living in Japan, and South America, the rich storehouse of materials dealing with the arts should be drawn on and used. The second way is to provide opportunities for children to express their own interpretation of thoughts and feelings gleaned from experiences in each unit. For example, children may create poems, stories, descriptions, pictures, murals, skits, plays, and songs to highlight ideas and feelings for others as they are developed in units.

CREATIVE WRITING

Children should have opportunities to create and share poems, stories, and descriptions. After backgrounds of understanding have been built up in a unit of instruction, the teacher should encourage the children to express their thoughts and feelings in written form. In the early grades, a sound procedure is to have the group dictate their ideas to the teacher for recording on the chalkboard and on charts. As children develop writing skills in later grades, they may express their thoughts and feelings in written form and share them with the group. Studying and writing the poetry of people in other lands is a rewarding experience—as, for example, when children discover the Japanese *haiku* pattern, with five syllables in the first and last lines and seven syllables in the middle line (Chart 10–1).

Chart 10–1
Haiku

When the evening sun
shoots deep red lights in the sky
nighttime is close by.

Golden leaves flutter
as cooler winds start blowing
summer into fall.

Howling winds bending
tall pine trees in the forest
as white clouds pass by.

Related art and music activities may be coordinated with creative writing. Over a period of time, collections may be made and kept in individual or class scrapbooks, posted on the bulletin boards, and used in culminating activities in units of instruction. Charts 10–2 and 10–3 illustrate items to consider in group planning, discussion, and the evaluation of creative written work.

Chart 10–2
Ideas for Creative Writing

Stories and poems—topics, events, travel, people, activities
Descriptions—persons, places, things, events, and activities
Dramatization—sketches, playlets, plays, and pantomimes
Booklets, scrapbooks, leaflets, charts
Quiz programs
Radio and TV programs
Movie box rolls

Chart 10–3
Finding Expressive Terms

Check the vocabulary chart.
Use the picture dictionary.
Listen as others discuss topics.
Look for them in our books.
Use the classroom dictionary.
Get ideas from pictures.
Get ideas from films.
Think of feelings as well as facts.

DRAMATIC REPRESENTATION

Dramatic representation is used in social studies to enable children to identify with persons, activities, and situations being studied. It is *simulated* activity, in which children are guided to portray and interpret human relationships in the home, community, and places far removed in time and space. At its best, dramatic representation is a sincere, authentic, and dynamic reconstruction of vital and significant experiences. It is also an excellent substitute for firsthand experience with people, events, and situations far removed from the classroom. For example, children cannot actually direct activities in a control tower at the airport, a railway classification yard, or a wagon train, but they can participate in dramatic representation to gain insight into these activities. They cannot be firefighters, post office workers, pilots, colonists, pioneers, scouts, or early settlers, but they can identify with others through dramatic activities. They cannot take study trips to distant lands or go back in history to early times, but they can realistically re-create and interpret distant events, activities, and situations.

In addition, dramatic representation is a mode of expression children have used before entering school, in make-believe and imaginary play—for example, "being" Mother, Father, a teacher, bus driver, or airplane pilot. On entering school, children are eager to "act out" activities they are studying and to portray their impressions of people, events, and situations. Their interest and skill in dramatic representation may be capitalized on and used to steer learning in worthwhile directions. One point to be kept in mind, however, is that dramatic representation in school is different from make-believe play at home. At home, children engage in dramatic play on their own; in school, they are guided and supervised so that significant outcomes may be achieved. At home, children base their dramatic play on ideas and impressions they have gathered in an incidental fashion; in school, background information is

How might this type of dramatic representation be used in a unit you are planning? (School District 281, Minneapolis, Minnesota; photo by Tom Tripet)

gathered and used as the basis for dramatic representation of social studies experiences. At home, make-believe play is a means of keeping children occupied; in school, dramatic representation is a means of developing definite concepts, skills, attitudes, and appreciations.

Dramatic representation offers excellent opportunities to evaluate children's learning. As teachers observe dramatic activities, they can appraise how children use concepts, grasp main ideas, express attitudes, identify with others, and express themselves creatively. Children spontaneously reveal the ideas, feelings, and impressions they have gained, and the alert teacher can detect and use misconceptions and erroneous ideas to plan and guide subsequent study.

Forms of Dramatic Representation

Dramatic representation takes a variety of forms in the social studies program: dramatic play, rhythms, skits, pageants, pantomime, dramatizations, marionette and puppet shows, mock meetings, unfinished stories, and role playing. Dramatic play is used frequently in the early grades to portray activities in units on the home, school, neighborhood, and community. It is an informal and creative portrayal of experiences without a set pattern, refined staging, costumes, or memorization of parts. Dramatic rhythms involve the interpretation of activities and events by means of rhythmic bodily movement. They differ from creative dance in that the child is interpreting something learned in social studies, although the children give their own interpretations, not that of another.

Dramatic skits are more formal than dramatic play; they involve the enactment of a selected event or activity in which assigned roles are taken and lines are learned to portray a significant incident, such as the signing of the Mayflower Compact or the landing at Plymouth Rock. Pageants are used to portray a sequence of incidents or activities related to such unit topics as the history of our community, the development of our state, the growth of America, and living in Mexico. Dramatic skits prepared by small groups within the class are easily arranged as a pageant.

Pantomime may be used to portray simply and briefly an activity such as a plane landing, the movement of a boat into the harbor, or a scout on the lookout for Indians. Dramatization may be employed to present a playlet or play in which a script, costumes, and stage setting are used. Marionettes and puppets may be used for both creative dramatics and formal dramatization. Children may construct them, plan for their use, use them to present skits and plays, and use them in new situations by preparing new lines, staging, and costumes. Some teachers use them to build confidence in shy children as well as to provide a different form of dramatic expression for all children.

Mock trials simulate courtroom activities and roles, and mock meetings may be planned and conducted in the upper grades to simulate New England town meetings, city council meetings, and legislative sessions.

Unfinished stories or reaction stories may be used to stimulate the enactment of situations in which children show what they would do if they were involved. After hearing a story about such problems as fair play, helping others, carrying out one's responsibilities, respecting property, or minority group relations, children act out a solution and evaluate the enactment. Role playing or sociodrama may be used to develop insight into human relations, problems of others, a main idea, or the feelings and values of individuals in a critical situation.[1] After the role is portrayed in different ways, such questions as these may be discussed: Which role did you prefer? why? Which role was least desirable? why? How did each role make you feel? How might individuals feel in the actual situation? What might be done to improve the situation?

Sometimes a teacher may decide that a play written for children—for example, a program for a special occasion or a dramatic activity related to the commemoration of a special event—is more appropriate than creative dramatics. If this is the case, the play should be selected, rehearsed, and presented with full attention to the development of backgrounds of understanding, pupil planning and evaluation, and the attainment of other educational values.

Examples of Dramatic Activities

The following examples of activities to dramatize have been taken from different types of units. As you read them, note those you might use in a unit you are planning.

[1] See Chapter 7 for a role-playing teaching strategy.

The Home: Cleaning, gardening, washing and ironing; taking care of the baby, taking care of pets; preparing and serving meals; enjoying leisure activities, telephoning friends

The Supermarket: Being the grocer, butcher, cashier, fruit and vegetable person, a customer; stocking shelves, making signs and price tags, weighing items, sweeping

Community Workers: Being a firefighter; working in the post office, receiving, sorting, and delivering mail; operating a filling station, cleaning trucks; broadcasting news; running the airport

The Farm: Pitching hay, feeding and watering animals, herding and milking cows; fixing the corral, plowing land, planting seeds, irrigating, harvesting; picking, washing, and bunching vegetables; loading, hauling, and distributing produce in trucks

Our State: Early ways of transporting goods and communicating with others; hunting, trading, other life activities; outstanding episodes and personalities in the growth of the state; modern ways of transporting goods, earning a living, and communicating with others

Colonial Life: Pilgrims leaving Holland, the trip in the *Mayflower,* the Mayflower Pact; landing at Plymouth Rock, the first Thanksgiving; starting the first community, meeting Indians, getting food, cutting logs, planning the houses, planting and hunting, spinning and carding wool, making soap and candles; playing games such as leap frog, wood tag, spinning tag; a town meeting, a day in the colonial home, a visit with Indians, a quilting bee

Dramatic Rhythms

Children are quick to respond to the rhythm in life around them. Grain swaying in the field, waves rolling in to shore, birds flying from tree to tree, people at work in the community, trains starting and stopping—all these will stimulate rhythmical expression that is natural and spontaneous. Similarly, rich experiences in social studies lead to dramatic rhythms that are meaningful demonstrations of the children's impressions:

"I'll show you how the liner comes in," said a boy demonstrating the slow, even movement of a large ocean liner.

"Out goes the pilot boat," said a girl moving gracefully and speedily as she gave her interpretation of the pilot boat she had seen on a trip to the harbor.

"Here comes a tug to help," said another child moving slowly but powerfully to assist the liner.

"Here comes another tug. Chug! Chug! Chug!" said a boy who had seen a tug work in the harbor nearby. With considerable realism, he moved over to help bring the liner in.

Dramatic rhythms may be used in many different situations in the social studies program. The following examples have been taken from selected units developed by successful elementary school teachers. As

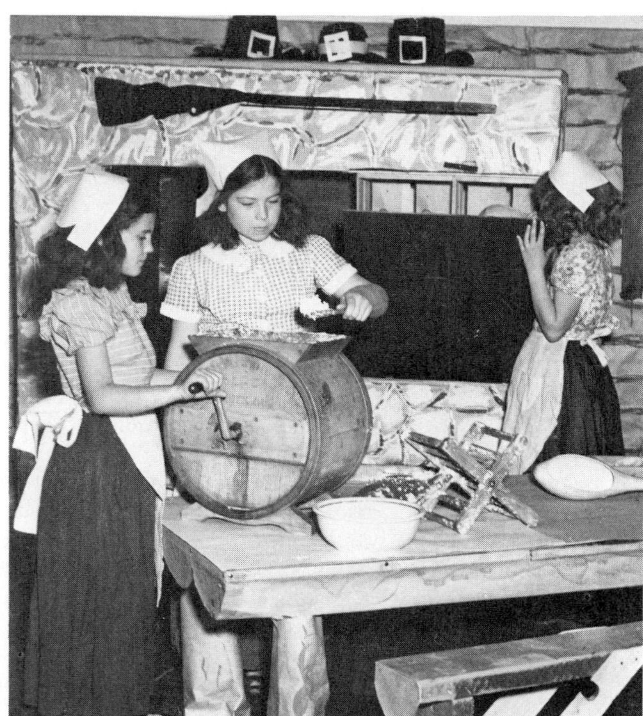

Notice the objects and costumes these children are using in their dramatization of life in early America. What research activities were necessary? What inquiry techniques might be used to check authenticity of costumes? (San Bernardino County Schools, California)

you read them, note ways you can use dramatic rhythms in a unit you may be planning.

The Home: Home activities such as washing and ironing clothes; digging, raking, and working in the garden; play activities such as swinging, sliding, climbing, seesawing; using fundamental rhythms, such as marching, skipping, running, galloping, hopping, and sliding to express thoughts and feelings; using rhythm instruments to accompany body movement

The Community: Rhythms related to growing things such as trees, flowers, and shrubs; community work activities such as loading and unloading trucks, building and painting houses; movement of trucks and trains; rain, snow, and wind; using fundamental rhythms and rhythm instruments creatively to express ideas grasped in social studies

The Farm: Activities such as working in the field, milking, riding horses, driving tractors, loading and unloading trucks; movements of farm animals; swaying wheat fields

Mexico: Carrying baskets to market, weaving; dancing at the fiesta; loading and unloading burros, hammering silver, working in the fields

Pioneers: Making candles, quilting, and weaving; building, cutting trees, digging, planting, hunting, making log canoes; movements of animals in the forest

In addition to interpretation through dramatic rhythms, there is a real place for folk games and folk dances in the social studies program. Many units would be incomplete if folk dances were omitted. For example, the "Fandango," "La Cucaracha," and "St. Michael's Wheel" in units on Mexico, and "Old Dan Tucker," "Virginia Reel," and "Captain Jenks" in units on pioneer life are most appropriate. Other examples can be found in the references listed at the end of this chapter.

Growth in dramatic rhythms progresses from simple interpretation of single episodes to more complete patterns of expression centered in a unifying theme. At first, children's responses to rhythm are short and simple. A single phase of an activity, such as the train starting, may be interpreted with real satisfaction. Other phases, such as gaining speed, slowing down, or going up a steep hill, may be added later. Still later, several phases are brought together in a pattern that is the child's portrayal of the complete activity. Finally, several children cooperate in rhythmic bodily expression of related activities, such as the train backing up to couple cars, starting up, traveling along, leaving cars at different places, and arriving at its destination. In this final stage, the group develops a unifying pattern that is more satisfying and meaningful than individual interpretations.

Mock Trials

Mock trials are useful in helping middle- and upper-grade students develop concepts of justice, learn key aspects of courtroom procedure, analyze issues, interpret facts, and evaluate decisions. In order to carry out a mock trial, students must learn the roles of judge, juror, attorney, and witness. They also need to know courtroom procedures and rules of evidence. Visits to courts, interviews of judges and attorneys, study of materials for students, TV programs, and films are useful sources of information.[2] An inexperienced group should begin with a simple mock trial that simulates a small claims court in which a judge hears the case and makes the decision with no attorneys present. After students have built up a background of knowledge and experience, a civil court mock trial may be simulated.

The main steps in a mock trial are briefing (preparation), conducting the trial (simulation), and debriefing (evaluation). Briefing should be thorough so that participants understand their roles, the issue, and the facts. The simulation should follow the steps outlined in Charts 10–4 and 10–5. Debriefing contributes much to learning as students evaluate

[2] See Gallagher, Lee, and Ratcliffe references at end of chapter.

how the roles were played, how they might be changed, the issue, which facts were relevant, how effectively they were presented, how sound the arguments were on each side, and how they might be improved. In addition, students should state whether or not they agree or disagree with the decision and whether or not they can think of sound reasons for an appeal.

Chart 10–4
Small Claims Court

The plaintiff and defendant appear before the judge.
The plaintiff states his case.
The defendant states his case.
The judge asks questions to clarify facts in the case.
The judge makes and explains a decision.

Chart 10–5
Civil Court

Open the court and swear in the jury.
Attorneys for the plaintiff and defendant make opening statements.
Examine and cross-examine witnesses.
Attorneys present closing statements.
The jury receives instructions, deliberates, and gives a verdict.

Guiding Dramatic Activities

An essential first step is to develop adequate backgrounds of understanding so that children will dramatize events and activities authentically and creatively. Much planning, discussion, and study are necessary, as shown in the following list of steps taken by a group of ten-year-olds who dramatized the journey of pioneer families into Kentucky.

1. Read and discuss stories about the journey and make a list of important points to incorporate in the play:
   a. Welcoming Daniel Boone home
   b. Talking things over with the settlers
   c. Preparation for the trip
   d. Problems of travel over the trail
   e. The departure for Russell Camp
   f. The Indians' attack, which was damaging to the settlers
   g. The returning home of many settlers
2. Find out what the settlers took with them.
3. Find out the ways the pioneers traveled. Decide which trail they took and find out about the dangers. Locate the trail and rivers on a map.
4. Read material about early settlers, hear stories read by the teacher, and write a creative story about them.
5. Find out how to mark trees, cut down obstacles, and stay on the trail.
6. Plan and incorporate these ideas in dramatic activities.
7. Carry out the plan and evaluate the effectiveness of individual and group activities.

After rich backgrounds of understanding have been developed, group planning may be employed effectively. Attention should be given to such questions as these: "What shall we dramatize?" "What space do we need?" "What materials do we need?" "What characters do we need?" "Who should take each part?" By beginning with *what* to do, the children can open up many possibilities without undue concern about *who* will take each part. Decisions on who will take each part may well be left until the last stage of planning, after what is to be included in the dramatic activity is clear. Once plans are made, the group should try out the different suggestions, discuss them, and make changes as needed. During dramatic activity, the teacher should look for needs, problems, and suggestions for improvement that may be used during follow-up discussion. Taking notes so that specific guidance can be given during evaluation is a good idea.

After a group has dramatized an episode, time should be taken to share and evaluate problems, questions, needs for materials, needs for additional information, and ways to make improvements. The teacher should guide the discussion so that appropriate points that have been noted during the activity will be considered. Group standards should be set up when needed to improve the value of the activity. For example, during a unit on the harbor, one group developed the standards in Chart 10–6 after a dramatic activity in which difficulties arose because of "wrong boat sounds," "boats clogging the harbor," and "fireboats tugging liners in." Following a skit involving life in Boonesboro, another group listed the standards in Chart 10–7 because several children had failed to dramatize their roles authentically. Continuous planning is needed to utilize dramatic activities effectively. Checklist 10–1 is a summary of specific factors that may be used for planning, guiding, and evaluating dramatic activities.

Chart 10–6
Running the Harbor

Share the boats with others.
Remember how each boat sounds.
Keep the harbor open for liners.
Let the tugs pull the liner in.
Listen to the captain's signals.

Chart 10–7
Protecting Boonesboro

Sentinels should keep a sharp lookout.
The gates should be closed on the signal.
Gun loaders should load guns and not shoot.
Scouts should sneak out through the little gate.
Get gunpower out of the powder horns.

SIMULATION GAMES

Simulation games are scaled-down models of real-life situations, problems, or activities. The players assume roles and make decisions according to specified rules. Such games can produce student involvement, develop and extend concepts, clarify key

Checklist 10–1

DRAMATIC ACTIVITIES CHECKLIST

Teacher Preplanning:

______ What needs have arisen for dramatic activities?
______ Are materials available?
______ Are space arrangements adequate?
______ Are new ideas and information needed? How should they be introduced?
______ Which children probably will wish to participate first? which should?
______ What will others do?

Group Planning:

______ Is attention given first to what to dramatize?
______ Do the children select important aspects of living to portray?
______ Are needs for materials considered?
______ Do individuals suggest roles that are essential?
______ Does each child who is to participate have a role and materials to use?
______ Are new ideas and materials introduced to enrich the activity?

During the Activity—Children:

______ Are the children identifying with the person and objects involved?
______ Are important aspects of living portrayed?
______ Are space and materials used effectively?
______ Are the suggestions made during planning carried out in the activity?
______ Are concepts being used accurately?

During the Activity—Teacher:

______ Are new needs emerging for:
a. clarification of ideas ______ c. group standards ______
b. authentic information ______ d. language expression ______
______ Are concepts being expressed accurately in language and in action?
______ Are any individuals confused or uncertain as to purpose, use of materials, or role?
______ Are changes needed in space arrangements or materials?

Group Evaluation:

______ Does the group appraise the activity in terms of the purposes set during planning?
______ Are newly discovered needs and problems considered?
______ Are inaccuracies and misconceptions clarified?
______ Have leads developed to other group and individual activities that will extend and broaden interests and keep the unit moving forward?

aspects of life situations, and develop abilities to weigh alternatives and make decisions. Simulations are more restricted and patterned than dramatic play, role playing, and sociodrama. Roles, rules, and materials are designed to portray the activity to be simulated realistically. Students compete with each other to win the game and must play within its rules and constraints.

Games for use in the social studies program have been constructed around urban, economic, political, and social problems and activities. Some of those suitable for use in the elementary school are Neighborhood, Dividing the Work, Market, The Barter Game, Making a Profit, Urban Planning, How Competition Works, and Caribou Hunting. The Charles and Stadsklev reference at the end of this chapter contains descriptions of a variety of games.

The Barter Game illustrates the main features of simulation games. Key instructional objectives are to demonstrate the nature of barter and the importance of using workers and resources wisely. There are three tribes with differing resources—food, tin, and copper. Each tribe must decide how to use workers, what to produce, and what to trade. The goal is to maintain an adequate food supply and to get as much tin and copper—the raw materials for bronze axes—as possible. The winning tribe is the one that has an adequate food supply and the most bronze axes. Students play the game by choosing leaders, assigning workers to various jobs, and making decisions as to what to trade. Each tribe gets cards indicating units of food, tin, and copper in relation to the number of workers assigned to different jobs. Each tribe decides what to trade and proceeds to barter with the other tribes. (For detailed directions, see the pamphlet by Younger and Aceti listed at the end of the chapter.)

Teachers have stated that some games take too much time and are too complex for elementary students, or that children overlook key objectives in their eagerness to play the game. Sometimes games become substitutes for important field studies, action projects, or other worthwhile activities. Arguments may arise over rules and roles, or the emphasis on winning may interfere with learning and attaining specific objectives. Problems such as these can be avoided by selecting games that are not too complex and that fit into available time limits, by planning for a balanced set of activities within each unit, by clarifying rules and roles in group planning, and by setting clear objectives before the game is started. Checklist 10–2 includes specific points to guide the use of simulations and to prevent problems from developing.

It is relatively easy to construct simulations that are directly related to problems and situations under study. After stating objectives, make a simplified model. Specify the role of each player; set the rules, conditions, and time limits; and prepare necessary cards and other materials. For example, a Gold Rush game could simulate the problems, hardships, and luck that prospectors experienced. A form board and Monopoly game procedures can be used as players endeavor to avoid such hardships as claim jumping, illness, running out of money, failing

Checklist 10–2

SIMULATIONS CHECKLIST

Preplanning:

_____ What problem or life situation should be simulated?
_____ How is it related to the unit under study?
_____ What concepts or principles are involved in its use?
_____ How can directions be made clear to students?
_____ What materials and space arrangements are needed?
_____ How many students will be involved, and what will their roles be?
_____ Which students should be assigned to different teams in order to provide for balance in abilities?

Group Planning:

_____ Are objectives clear to the participants?
_____ Does each participant understand his or her role?
_____ Are rules, use of materials, and time limits clear?
_____ What questions should be answered before beginning?

During the Simulation:

_____ Are roles being carried out in line with the rules?
_____ How can any confusion about objectives, concepts, and rules be overcome?
_____ What specific suggestions might be made to improve the activity?
_____ What items should be given attention during evaluation?

Group Evaluation and Debriefing:

_____ Which decisions and strategies were most useful? least useful? why?
_____ Which aspects were true to life? How can distortions be corrected?
_____ How can any problems or difficulties be overcome?
_____ What improvements might be made in directions, rules, and roles?
_____ How might the simulation be modified? Can a better one be created?
_____ What contributions were made to key objectives?

to get a grubstake, and the like, and at the same time to obtain mining claims of greatest value. Examples of other simulations that can be created to fit different units are Deciding on a Vacation, Saving at a Sale, Curbing Pollution, Lost and Found, Touring a Country, City Council, Getting a Bill Passed, Exports and Imports, and Stock Market.

Several guidelines should be followed in constructing simulations. Of key importance are the investigation and planning that precede actual game construction so that essential information is available. Students can benefit greatly from being involved in all phases, from initial research and planning to tryout of the simulation. Basic guidelines are as follows:

1. Select a problem that can be simulated in a way that helps to achieve objectives of the unit under study.
2. Note the concepts and principles from economics, geography, or other fields to be emphasized.
3. Make a simplified model that shows the elements to be simulated.
4. List the information and materials participants need to carry out the simulation.
5. Specify the groups needed and the roles in each group that individuals should play, noting goals for each participant.
6. Write the directions for starting, carrying out, and concluding the simulation, giving attention to rules, use of materials, time limits, and use of space.
7. Try out the simulation with a small group and make revisions as needed to clarify objectives, roles, and rules.

MUSIC ACTIVITIES

The world's musical heritage is a rich source of content and activities for use in gaining an understanding of people and their ways of living. People in cultures at home and around the world have expressed their customs, traditions, and values in music. Patriotic music has been written to stir feelings of loyalty, to highlight great events, and for festivals, ceremonies, and religious activities. Poems, stories, legends, and other literary works have been set to music. Folk songs and dances have evolved from everyday activities. Musical instruments have been invented to provide unique modes of expression. In addition, cultural interdependence has been increased as the music created in one part of the world has had an impact on people in other parts of the world.

The following six types of music activities are used in social studies units of instruction: singing, listening, rhythmic activities, instrumental activities, creative expression, and research. By directing participation in each type of activity, a teacher can guide children to make meaningful cross-cultural comparisons, one of the main reasons for giving attention to music in social studies. If the program is limited to singing and listening activities, as is the case in some classrooms, learning will be greatly limited. But if all six types are carefully planned and carried out, the study of music as a part of human activities will be broader and more fully grounded in its cultural setting.

Singing

Singing is the music activity most extensively used in social studies. Many songs related to topics in each unit of instruction may be found in children's music books. Children's identification with others is increased as they sing songs about human experiences and activities—for example, work at home, activities of community workers, working on the farm, living in a hogan, trekking westward across the plains, and living in other lands. In social studies, special attention is given to the development of backgrounds of understanding of the songs included in each unit. The questions in Chart 10–8 may be used to guide study and discussion.

Chart 10–8
Understand the Songs We Sing in Our Unit

What thoughts and feelings are expressed?
What is the mood, the rhythmic pattern, and the melody?
Is this a song of work, play, worship, adventure, nature, fantasy, or patriotism?
Is this song sung at home, at festivals, or at ceremonies?
What type of accompaniment is appropriate?
What instruments might be used to play the melody?

Listening Through directed listening experiences, children can learn much about the folk songs, dances, instruments, festivals, holidays, patriotic events, composers, and performing artists of greatest importance in each unit. Recordings of different types of music may be used to give learning realism and authenticity. In addition, use is made of radio and TV programs, community concerts and folk festivals, individuals invited to school, and children's own recordings. Courses of study, units of instruction, and music textbooks all have many suggestions on listening experiences to include in the social studies program. Examples of questions that may be used to guide listening experiences are given in Chart 10–9.

Chart 10–9
Listening to Music from Other Lands

How is it like ours? How is it different?
What rhythmic patterns are used?
What tonal patterns are used?
What instruments are used?
What types of songs do they enjoy?
What moods are portrayed?
How is their music related to customs and traditions?

Rhythms Four types of rhythmic activity that may be provided in the social studies program are *informal* rhythms, in which children express patterns without direction from the teacher; *formal* rhythms, in which the teacher directs children to move to the rhythm (skip, gallop, and the like) as music is played; *creative* rhythms, in which children express their responses in original ways; and *dramatic* rhythms, which were discussed in the preceding section. As these activities are used in social studies, special attention is given to patterns characteristic of the music, folk dances, and activities included in units of instruction (see Charts 10–10 through 10–12). Rhythm instruments, recordings, native instruments, the piano, and the autoharp are used to accompany rhythmic activities and to play rhythmic patterns.

Chart 10–10
Rhythms Around Us

People working
Horses trotting
Trees swaying
Motors humming
Hammers pounding
Bells ringing
Horns tooting

Chart 10–11
Rhythmic Patterns

Walk	March
Trot	Waltz
Hop	Polka
Skip	Gavotte
Gallop	Minuet
Slide	Schottische
Swing	Tango

Chart 10–12
Finding Rhythms

Songs and poems
Folk dances
Recordings
Radio and TV
Activities of people
Animals moving
Trains, planes

Instruments Musical instruments of various types may be used in social studies to extend children's learning. Rhythm instruments such as drums, sticks, blocks, bells, triangles, cymbals, gongs, rattles, and tambourines may be used to accompany rhythmic and singing activities, produce sound effects, and play rhythmic patterns. Chording instruments such as the autoharp and harmolin may be used to accompany various activities and to demonstrate harmonic and rhythmic patterns. Simple melody instruments such as melody bells, tuned bottles or glasses, song flutes, and recorders may be used to play tunes created by children as well as melodies discovered in the songs and recordings presented in units. Native instruments may be examined and played to give authenticity to music activities. Examples of these are the claves, guiro, maracas, cabaca, bongo, conga, antara or pipes of Pan, quena or flute, and chocalho in units on South America; and the bamboo xylophone, gong, temple block, and finger cymbals in units on Oriental countries. Chart 10–13 gives a summary.

Creative Expression Creative expression through music may be brought to high levels in the social studies program as children develop insight and appreciation through activities in units of instruction. Poems and verse created by children may be set to music as the children hum or play tunes on simple melody instruments while the teacher records them on the chalkboard, a chart, or a tape recorder.

Chart 10–13
How Can We Use These Instruments in Our Unit?

Percussion		
Drums	Woodblocks	Triangles
Shakers	Tambourines	Cymbals
Gong	Castanets	Scrapers
Sticks	Jangles	Maracas
Melody		
Bells	Recorder	Water glasses
Songflute	Psaltery	Harmolette
Tonette	Harmonica	Xylophone
Harmony		
Autoharp	Harmolin	Marimba

Accompaniments for songs, rhythmic movement, choral readings, and dramatic activities may be created by children as they catch the mood and rhythm of the thoughts and feelings to be expressed. Special sound effects may be created and background music selected for skits, plays, and pageants. Simple instruments may be made of gourds, bamboo, bottles, glasses, and other materials. Creative expression through art, writing, dramatics, and rhythmic movement may be stimulated as children listen to recordings. A range of creative processes may be brought into play as children plan and develop culminating activities that include a script, lyrics and melodies, costumes, staging, musical accompaniments, and their own special effects. Chart 10–14 gives some guidelines for composing songs.

Chart 10–14
Composing a Song for Our Unit

What moods or feelings shall we try to express?
What words and phrases shall we use?
Shall we hum, whistle, play, or sing to create the melody?
What rhythm shall we use?
Shall we record the lyric and the melody?
What key shall we use?

Research Individual and group research activities may be undertaken to find background information on the music emphasized in units of instruction. A trip may be taken to a nearby museum to examine instruments and to see costumes used in folk dances. Experts may be interviewed or invited to come to the classroom to give demonstrations. Encyclopedias, library resources, and supplementary music books may be reviewed. Notebooks and scrapbooks may be compiled to summarize information. Illustrative questions that may be used to guide research activities are listed in Chart 10–15.

Chart 10–15
Finding Out About Music in Other Lands

What are some of the best-known songs?
What folk dances do they have? How are they related to festivals?
What costumes do they wear?
What music do they play at ceremonies and other activities?
What folk instruments do they have? How are they made?
What composers and artists live there?
What influences have others had on their music? How has their music influenced ours?
What customs, traditions, and beliefs are expressed through music?
What events, deeds, and activities have been set to music?

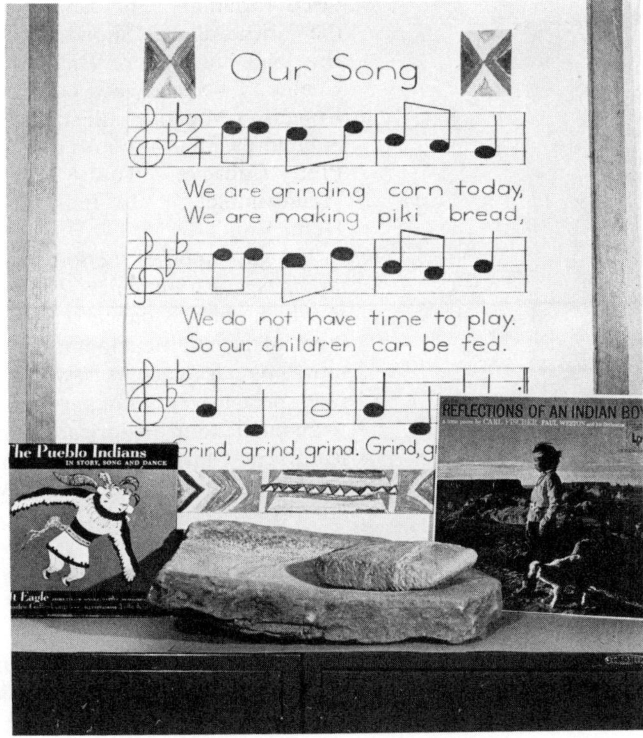

How can the composing of a song such as this one be related to the processing of materials? How might it be related to their experiences? (San Bernardino County, California)

The diversity of the musical heritage of people in different cultural settings should be explored by the class. For example, in units on South America, Africa, Europe, Canada, and the United States, many different types of music may be found and the influences of diverse cultural backgrounds discovered. Folk music, adaptations of music from other lands, music created by native composers, and famous performing artists may be made a part of units. The following examples drawn from units on countries in South America are illustrative:

Argentina: Influences of the Italians, Indians, and Spaniards are evident. "El Estilo," a melancholy, nostalgic song of the pampas, shows the Italian influence. The tango shows Spanish influence. The rich folk music shows the Indian influence. The compositions of Alberto Ginastera and Juan José Castro and the folk music recordings and publications of Carlos Vega show the richness of Argentina's musical heritage. Well-known songs that may be found in children's music books are "Sí Señor," "Palapala," "Adiós Te Digo," "Chacarera," "Song of the Pampas," "The Gaucho," "Vidalita," and "Ay, Zamba."

Brazil: Indian, Portuguese, and African influences are evident. Tender and sentimental ballads show the influence of the Portuguese, who sang the "Modinha" to drive away homesickness. The *chôros* is a rhythmically rich musical form that includes improvised variations. The samba, one of the most sophisticated of the carioca dances, shows African influence. Among the famous Brazilian singers are Bidú Sayão, Elsie Houston, and Olga Coelho. Two renowned composers are Heitor Villa-Lobos and Francisco Mignone. Illustrative of the Brazilian songs included in children's music books are "The Painter of Cannahay," "My Pretty Cabacla," "Tutu Maramba," "Cantilena," "Sambalele," "Bambamulele," "In Bahia Town," "O Gato," and "Come Here, Vitu."

Chile: The gay mood of the folk and popular music of Chile shows a strong Spanish influence. The scarf dances (*danzas de pañuelo*) in which couples dance separately have been brought to a high level of artistic development. The *cueca* or *zamacueca* is the most popular dance. A new *cueca* may be created to commemorate special events ranging from the winning of a football game to an outstanding historical event. Among the renowned musical figures in Chile are Claudio Arrau (pianist), Domingo Santa Cruz (composer), and Ramon Vinay (tenor). Illustrative songs are "San Severino," "The Lovely Chilean Maid," "Buy a Dozen," "El Marinero," "Pol Perica," "Dance Song," and "Bom Bom Bom."

Arranging a Classroom Music Center

A classroom music center may be arranged and changed as different units of instruction are developed. Song books, instruments, other music materials, and pictures showing musical activities may be placed in the music center. If headphones are available for listening to recordings, children may go to the center at different times for individual listening. Other items may be placed in the center from time to time. Current events materials about musicians in places being studied, announcements of related programs on TV and radio, a list of recordings for individual listening, charts containing information on songs, rhythms, dances, and instruments, and pictures showing native musical activities may be put on the bulletin board. Textbooks and references containing folk songs, rhythms, stories of musicians, descriptions of instruments, and accounts of musical activities may be placed in the center as necessary, along with a collection of instruments used by the people being studied. A listening post (phonograph and headphones) for individual and small-group listening, maps showing the locale of songs and musicians, an autoharp and rhythm instruments for musical accompaniment, and a flannel board for showing rhythm and tonal patterns may also be part of the music center.

ARTS AND CRAFTS From ancient times to the present, people have expressed their thoughts and feelings through various art forms. Artists and artisans of each generation have selected ideas and created forms that clarify, simplify, and interpret the times in which they lived. Line, form, color, texture, space, and other elements have been unified in ways that are expressive of the artist's intentions. Touches of beauty have been added to dwellings, clothing, utensils, festivals, ceremonies, and other objects and activities. Folk crafts have been developed to meet everyday needs and have provided opportunities for creative expression in homes and villages throughout the world. (See Charts 10–16 through 10–18).

Chart 10–16
How Are These Portrayed in Arts and Crafts?

Ideas	Aspirations
Ideals	Superstitions
Hopes	Traditions
Fears	Customs
Feelings	Nature
Beliefs	Religion
Values	Recreation

Chart 10–17
Which of These Items Do They Make?

Pottery	Baskets
Tiles	Rugs
Figurines	Blankets
Mosaics	Shawls
Copperware	Instruments
Silverware	Containers
Jewelry	Featherwork
Leatherwork	Beadwork

Chart 10–18
Can You Discover Creative Uses of the Following?

Line	Design
Form	Integration
Color	Movement
Texture	Variation
Space	Repetition
Balance	Perspective
Rhythm	Emphasis
Unity	Subordination

In many ways, the study of art contributes to learning in each unit of instruction. For example, deeper insights and appreciations are developed as children discover the impact of art on homes, furnishings, cars, trains, airplanes, buildings, bridges, and other man-made objects. Appreciation of the beauty in nature may be increased as children study such units as the community, state, nation, and other lands. Subtle shades of meaning may be developed as children consider the work of artists who have portrayed great events, heroes and heroines, landscapes, poems, songs, everyday activities, ceremonies, festivals, and holidays. Basic concepts may be enriched as children see and discuss pictures that simplify and clarify changes in the seasons, dense jungles, storms lashing a seacoast, a ship being tossed by the stormy sea, a lagoon by a tropical isle, earth-moving machines cutting a road through mountains, and workers toiling in the fields. A feeling for modes of expression enjoyed by others may be kindled as children discover the concepts of nature in the sand paintings of the Navajo, the simple beauty of the Puritan church, the delicate patterns in Japanese paintings, the search for harmony between people and nature in Chinese art, the recurring themes and patterns in Egyptian art, the grandeur of Roman architecture, and the desire for freedom boldly revealed in the Mexican artist Rivera's murals. Cultural interdependence may be highlighted as the thunderbird, the cross, geometric forms, and other designs are discovered in the art of people in different lands.

Creative and appreciative experiences may be intertwined as children engage in art activities. For example, the sand paintings of the Navajo may be considered in terms of the concepts of nature, human activities, myths, and ideas that they portray. Paralleling such study may be activities in which children engage in sand painting to portray their impressions of selected activities. In a study of Mexico, pictures of the murals of Diego Rivera may be explored to discover the ideas, hopes, and values expressed. This may be paralleled or followed by an activity in which children create a mural to portray their own impressions of life in

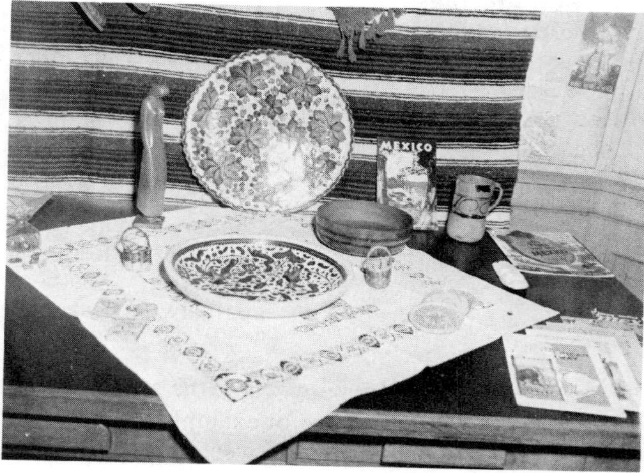

What elements of design might be discovered as children examine these items? What appreciation might be extended? (Berkeley, California)

Mexico. When such parallel activities are provided, care must be taken to be sure that children's expression is truly creative, truly their own, and not a copy of that of others. (Charts 10–19 through 10–22 give suggestions for using arts and crafts in the social studies program.)

Chart 10–19
Find Out How People Express Themselves Through Art

- Study pictures in our textbooks.
- Look at reproductions of pictures and art objects.
- See films, filmstrips, and slides.
- Visit a museum or art gallery.
- Examine textiles, pottery, jewelry, and other objects.
- Interview people who have visited other cultures or studied their art.
- Read art books, reference materials, and current periodicals.
- Collect pictures from magazines, newspapers, and travel folders.

Chart 10–20
Which of These Crafts Are Used in Other Cultures?

- Weaving mats, tapestries, cloth, rugs, wall hangings
- Basket making from reeds and raffia
- Creating designs on cloth, bark, woven raffia, parchment, skins, metal, stone, clay, wood
- Embroidering or appliquéing on clothing, costumes, and textiles
- Carving in wood, stone, ivory, and bone
- Modeling and constructing objects out of clay
- Making objects out of metal
- Dyeing cloth, leather, bark, and other materials
- Making masks, costumes, and objects for use in ceremonies and festivals

Chart 10–21
How Can We Use These to Show Main Ideas?

- Drawing, painting, sketching, illustrating
- Making items out of paper, cardboard, metal, wire, wood
- Weaving, sewing, stitching, embroidering, appliquéing
- Modeling, carving, sculpturing, whittling
- Making dioramas, panoramas, shadow boxes

Chart 10–22
Making a Mural

- What main ideas shall we show?
- What related ideas are needed?
- How shall the ideas be arranged?
- What materials shall we use?
- What colors will be most effective?
- What contributions can each person make?

As a general guideline, creativeness should be emphasized in both appreciative and creative activities. As the artwork of other people is studied, each individual will respond in unique ways. To be sure, children may have similar understandings of background ideas about the culture in which the piece of art was created and certain common understandings regarding the processes that were involved. But the individual's reaction, response, and feelings are always unique. Similarly, as children engage in art activities, every effort should be made to ensure creative expression on the part of each child. What is desired is individual interpretation and expression of thoughts and feelings. Some teachers ask, "But what if a child has misconceptions and erroneous ideas about the people or activities portrayed?" The way to correct misconceptions is to provide for additional study; simply telling or showing a child how to draw something is not a substitute for developing backgrounds of understanding of people and their ways of living. The ideas to be expressed and the media and pro-

Checklist 10–3

CHECKLIST OF ART ACTIVITIES

Drawing and Painting: ______ pictures ______ murals ______ friezes ______ posters ______ cartoons ______ illustrations ______ sketches ______ designs ______ backgrounds ______ landscapes ______ decorations ______ borders ______ greeting cards

Modeling, Sculpturing, and Carving: ______ animals ______ utensils: ______ dishes ______ bowls ______ pots ______ vases ______ jugs ______ jars ______ trays ______ tiles ______ candlesticks ______ jewelry ______ beads ______ figurines ______ plaques

Designing: ______ booklets ______ programs ______ announcements ______ greeting cards ______ fans ______ mats ______ markers ______ borders ______ wrappers ______ containers ______ stage scenery ______ prints ______ backgrounds for collages ______ mosaics

Arranging: ______ displays ______ exhibits ______ flowers ______ gourds ______ driftwood ______ fruits ______ cornucopias ______ textiles

Paper and Cardboard Construction: ______ mats ______ wall hangings ______ table covers ______ designs ______ puppets ______ marionettes ______ notebooks ______ scrapbooks ______ booklets ______ posters ______ montages ______ collages ______ mosaics ______ masks ______ mobiles ______ stabiles ______ buildings ______ ornaments ______ furniture ______ decorations ______ containers ______ dioramas ______ panoramas ______ shadow boxes

Weaving, Sewing and Stitching: ______ bags ______ mats ______ wall hangings ______ caps ______ head bands ______ belts ______ rugs ______ scarves ______ curtains ______ stuffed animals ______ costumes

Using Mixed Media: ______ paint and yarn ______ chalk and paper sculpture ______ cut paper and tempera ______ chalk, crayon, and paint ______ watercolor and chalk ______ paper, cork, and wire ______ combinations of discarded materials

Printing and Stenciling: ______ designs ______ borders ______ textiles ______ decorations ______ programs ______ announcements ______ greeting cards

cesses used in an art activity may be enriched through directed study. But when children proceed to express the ideas, they use their own techniques if the experience is to be called an art activity. Otherwise it is merely copying, illustrating, or reproducing the techniques of another person. It is not art.

Checklist 10–3 includes the main types of art activity used in the social studies program. Each major type is followed by examples of items that may be made, designed, or arranged by children.

The Classroom Art Center

A work center for the arrangement of art materials facilitates work and makes possible more effective utilization of art activities in social studies. Materials in the work center should be changed as new topics are studied in the unit of instruction. Related pictures may be displayed on the bulletin board, and selected art objects may be exhibited on nearby shelves, window sills, or tables. Space should be provided to display completed work and for storing unfinished work. Materials such as those noted in Checklist 10–4 may be selected and placed in the work center as needed.

What art forms were created in early America? What values did they reflect? How did they enrich life? (Social Studies Workshop, University of California, Berkeley)

Checklist 10–4

ART MATERIALS CHECKLIST

Paper: ______ newsprint ______ drawing ______ watercolor ______ construction ______ poster ______ bogus ______ wrapping ______ tagboard ______ posterboard ______ tissue ______ crepe

Paint: ______ powdered ______ finger ______ watercolor ______ textile ______ silk screen ______ poster

Brushes: ______ easel ______ enamel ______ watercolor ______ paste ______ wash brush

Crayons: ______ large primary size ______ large colored ______ standard size

Chalk: ______ white for sketching ______ large colored ______ standard size colored

Clay: ______ plastic modeling ______ wedged ______ dextrine ______ slip ______ glaze ______ underglaze paints ______ plastic to keep from drying ______ kiln ______ sponges ______ workboards ______ crocks ______ rollers ______ wire tools

Crafts: ______ soap ______ papier-mâché ______ raffia ______ reeds ______ carpet warp ______ cloth ______ wood ______ cardboard ______ tin ______ copper ______ tools ______ string ______ yarn ______ looms ______ beads ______ buttons ______ jute ______ needles ______ scrap materials

Printing and Stenciling: ______ pens ______ India ink ______ spray guns ______ brayers ______ cutting tools ______ sheet glass ______ water-base inks ______ sticks ______ carrots ______ potatoes ______ sponges ______ linoleum blocks ______ inner tubes ______ gum erasers ______ silk-screen materials

Other: ______ charcoal ______ scissors ______ knives ______ paste ______ rubber cement ______ fixative ______ tape ______ pins

INDUSTRIAL OR PRACTICAL ARTS

Two types of industrial or practical arts are included in this section. The first is construction of objects for use in various social studies activities; the second is the processing or changing of raw materials to usable forms. Both types of activity are provided to help children develop realistic and authentic concepts and understandings related to people's use of objects and resources to meet basic needs.

Construction

Construction as used in the social studies program may be defined as the use of tools and materials to make authentic objects needed to promote growth of social concepts and understanding of social processes. Construction involves the development of objectives, group planning, selec-

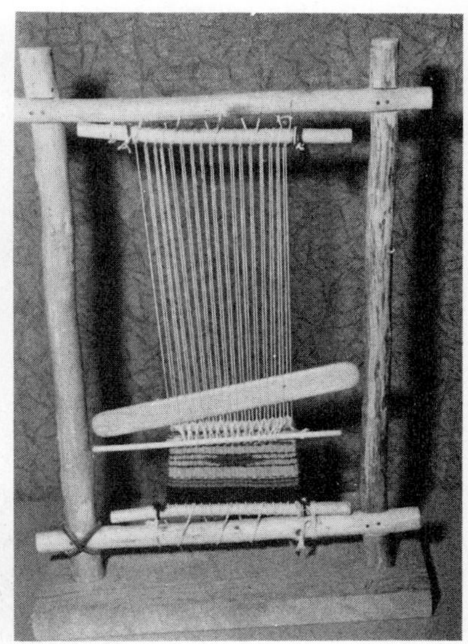

How might the construction and use of objects like these be used to further inquiry in a unit you are planning? (Education Workshop, University of California, Berkeley)

tion of materials, appropriate use of tools, manipulative skills, group evaluation, and planning for use in related social studies activities. Examples include making and using airplanes, trucks, boats, looms, furniture, weapons, utensils, and various models. The value of construction lies in its contribution to inquiry, not in the products that are made. Lasting values can be achieved only if construction serves significant objectives, involves careful planning, is authentic, and is used to motivate learning in the unit of instruction.

Construction may be closely related to dramatic activities in the social studies program. Dramatic representation of activities in units on the home, the farm, the harbor, the airport, colonial life, Mexico, and other lands creates needs for objects, models, props, and scenery. Children can plan and make essential items and thus relate making objects to stated objectives.

Precision and authenticity in construction grows steadily as children gain in maturity. In the primary grades, children are satisfied with blocks, boxes, boards, and simple items. A box may be used as a truck to haul things, two boards nailed crosswise can serve as an airplane, blocks may be arranged to serve as a corral, and a can fastened to a board is used as a tank car or oil truck. Older children desire more detail and precision in materials used in dramatic play. The freight car has sliding doors, the wagon can be pulled and is authentic in detail, the airplane is complete from prop to tail assembly, and the airport is a realistic representation of one that has been visited.

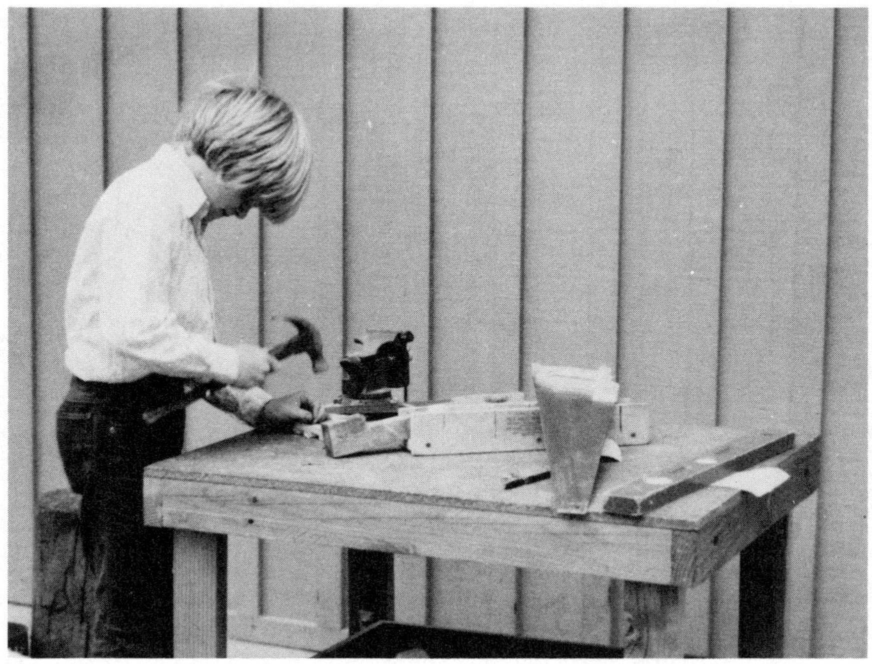

How might you arrange a work center like this one for a unit you are planning? (Walnut Creek, California)

Criteria. If the educational values are to be achieved, criteria such as the following must be used to select activities involving construction.

1. Does this activity contribute to the attainment of stated objecives?
2. Is it practical in terms of available time, tools, and materials?
3. Is it more effective than other experiences that can be provided?
4. Will it help to develop accurate concepts?
5. Does it bear a direct relationship to other experiences in the unit?
6. Do children have readiness for it in terms of backgrounds and skills?
7. Will it promote critical thinking and problem-solving skills?

Uses of construction. The following examples of objects that children may make are taken from units of instruction frequently taught in elementary school. As you read them, note specific activities that you might carry out in a unit for some group you have in mind.

The Home: Playhouse furnishings, including chairs, tables, cupboards, flowerboxes, rugs, curtains, wallpaper, and dishes

Community Life: Simply made houses, stores, schools, churches, and other community buildings; various types of trucks, such as oil, lumber, pick-up, milk, mail, and delivery; crates, boxes, bags, fruits and vegetables, hand trucks, and sheds for use in the market

The Farm: Farmhouse, barn, fences, chicken coops, pens, corrals, silo, trucks; milking and feed barns, nursery for the calves, bottling plant, stanchions, feeding troughs, grain sacks, and milk trucks for a dairy farm

Boats: Different types of boats—for example, an oil tanker, tug, liner, freighter, lumber boat, fireboat, speedboat, rowboat, fishing boat, and pilot boat; items for a harbor, such as piers, breakwater, buoys, drydock, and drawbridge

Colonial Life: kitchen, fireplace, bed, table, rag rugs, chair, benches, cupboard, lamps, candles; spoons, ladles, brooms; horn books, powder horns, bullet pouches, rifles; tape and box looms

Aviation: Model planes, gliders, wind sock, control tower, hangars, maintenance shops, runways, model airport

Tools and materials. Only simple tools are used in construction in the social studies program. Saws, C clamps, hammers, T squares, brace and bit, mallet, chisels, and a hand drill are adequate for most activities. Proper use of tools, safety measures, and care of tools are taught systematically so that accidents and injuries can be avoided. Portable tool racks permit many groups to use the same tools and also provide a good storage place for tools and materials.

Materials for construction may be obtained in the community. Soft pine is especially useful. Crates and boxes can be used for buildings such as houses, barns, stores, hangars, and depots. Boards of varying size are used to make boats, trucks, looms, airplanes, and the like. Doweling ranging in size from a quarter-inch to an inch can be used to make masts, steering shafts on trucks, derricks, funnels, smokestacks, and any other item that is cylindrical and of appropriate size. Wooden button molds ranging in size from one to two and a half inches in diameter should be used for wheels. Awning pole, two and a half inches in diameter, is excellent for making tank cars, tanks for milk and oil trucks, and locomotive boilers. Tin roofing caps make excellent headlights or hub caps on trucks. Tops of cans, scraps of tin, bottle tops, spools, screws, screweyes for hooking railroad cars and trailer trucks, sandpaper, nails, brads, brushes, and paints round out the list of supplies used most frequently. Once materials such as these are assembled, children under the guidance of a creative teacher will think of innumerable objects to construct; real ingenuity will be shown in using different combinations of materials.

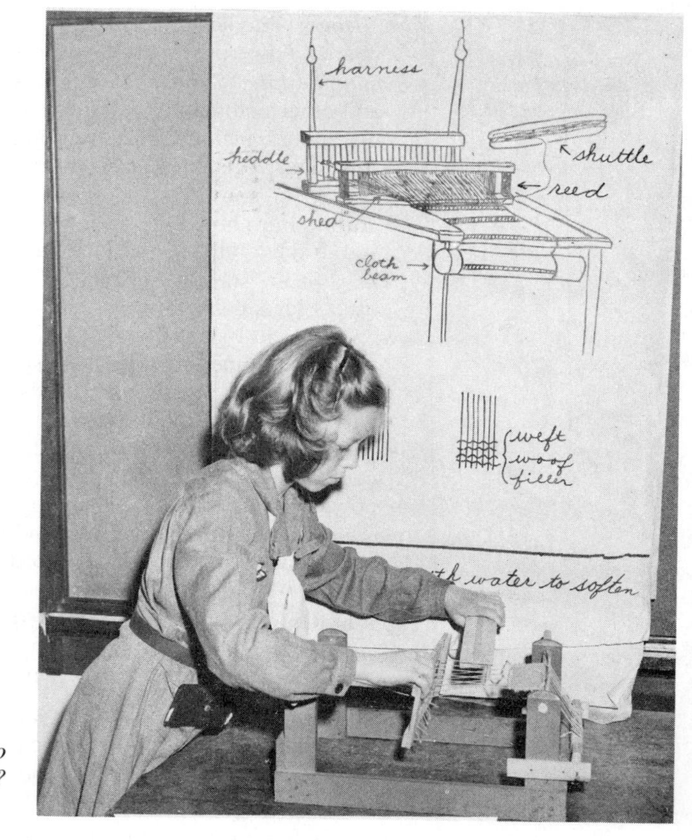

Can you think of a better way to inquire into processes of weaving? (Los Angeles, California)

Processing Materials

Processing materials is similar to construction in terms of values, planning, techniques, instructional procedures, and skills. In social studies, processing materials may be defined as changing raw or semiprocessed materials (yarn, for example) into products that can be used. Typical examples are making cottage cheese, processing wool and flax, dyeing fabrics, weaving, drying fruit, and making soap. As children engage in such processes, emphasis should be on the development of concepts and understandings regarding creative ways in which people have met their needs without benefit of sophisticated technology.

Years ago, children had many firsthand experiences with processes in everyday life in the home and community. They knew the planting, harvesting, and grinding of wheat into flour; and baking bread was an everyday activity. Shearing sheep, and washing, carding, spinning, and weaving wool; catching, cleaning, and salting fish; processing meat; felling and sawing trees and using the lumber for buildings; cleaning and tanning hides to make shoes and clothing; collecting berries and dyeing clothes; and using tallow to make candles were familiar activities. They watched the blacksmith as he forged implements from iron and saw flour ground at the mill. Today, children see finished, packaged products in the store and have little opportunity to learn about how they were made.

Outlined below are a few examples of processes that have been used successfully in units at various grade levels. Steps to take to carry out several processing activities are shown in Charts 10–23 through 10–28,

Chart 10–23
Making Butter

Materials: ½ pint of whipping cream, ¼ teaspoon salt, a pint jar.
Pour cream into jar and seal it.
Shake until butter appears.
Pour off bluish milk.
Place butter in a bowl and add salt.
Add a few ice cubes and water; work with spoon to remove milk.
Pour off water and mold butter into a block.

Chart 10–24
Washing, Carding, And Spinning Wool

Materials: wool sheared from a sheep, soap, pair of cards for carding.
Wash wool in soapy lukewarm water, rinse it, and dry it.
Place a small amount of wool on one card and draw other card over it.
Continue carding until fibers are separated into slivers.
Shape slivers into a fluffy roll by rolling them between back of cards.
Stretch and twist the roll into yarn for weaving.

Chart 10–25
Dipping Candles

Materials: three lbs. tallow, candle wick cut into 7-inch lengths, two tall cans
Chop tallow into small pieces and try out grease.
Pour grease into one can and keep it hot.
Pour water into other can.
Dip wicking into grease and then into water.
Repeat dipping until the candle is the desired size.

Chart 10–26
Making Apple Leather

Peel some apples and cook them in water.
After apples are cooked to a mush, spread them on a cloth to dry.
Let them stand for a day or two.

Chart 10–27
Making Pumpkin Rings

Cut a pumpkin crosswise into halves.
Remove seeds and cut rings ½ inch thick.
Place rings on a pole to dry.
Put small ends and pieces on a string to dry.

Chart 10–28
Making Pumpkin Leather

Peel small pieces from the pumpkin.
Cook the pieces in water.
Stir until water is cooked out and mixture is thick.
Spread the cooked peelings on a board to dry.

and additional suggestions may be found in the references at the end of this chapter.

The Home: Making popcorn, applesauce, and cornstarch pudding; decorations and clay dishes
The Dairy Farm: Churning butter and making cottage cheese
Mexico: Drying corn and peppers, grinding corn with a metate; making candles, carding and spinning wool, making pottery, weaving, preparing and using natural dyes; cooking food; making adobe bricks; making sombreros, serapes, and rebozos
Colonial and Pioneer Life: Weaving and quilting; dipping and molding candles; tanning hides; making soap; rippling, retting, curing, breaking, scutching, heckling, and spinning flax; carding and spinning wool, knitting, making a quilt; making dyes; drying apples, making salt; making brooms and brushes; making clothing
China: Cooking rice, Chinese cabbage, and bean curd; making tea; raising silkworms, reeling silk from cocoons; making paper, ink, and block prints

The planning and guiding of construction and processing activities are similar in many ways to the planning and guiding of study trips, dramatic activities, and other "doing" activities in the social studies program. Four basic steps are involved: (1) preplanning by the teacher, (2) planning with the class, (3) providing guidance during the activity, and (4) evaluating progress after the activity, as shown in preceding checklists.

QUESTIONS, ACTIVITIES, EVALUATION

1. Locate and list poems, stories, and other literary selections you might use in a unit you are planning. Note two or three creative activities.
2. Which forms of dramatic representation discussed in this chapter do you believe most useful in social studies? Indicate specific ways in which you might use each form.
3. Review two or three music books for children and note songs, rhythms, listening activities, and instrumental activities you might use in a unit. Make a brief plan to show how you might provide for creative expression and for investigative activities in a unit.
4. Review the checklist of art activities and indicate specific ways in which you might use each major type in a unit. Note the materials that should be provided for each activity.
5. Select one construction and one processing activity and note how you might use them in a unit.
6. Select three or four charts presented in this chapter and modify them for use in a unit you are planning.

REFERENCES

BROWN, JAMES W., RICHARD B. LEWIS, and FRED F. HARCLEROAD, *A-V Instruction* (3rd ed.). New York: McGraw-Hill, 1973. Sections on constructing and dramatizing.

CHARLES, CHERYL L., and RONALD STADSKLEV, eds., *Learning With Games*. Boulder, Colo.: Social Science Education Consortium, 1973. Descriptions of 70 games and guide to sources.

DIMONDSTEIN, GERALDINE, *Exploring the Arts with Children*. New York: Macmillan, 1974. Teaching procedures for various art forms.

GALLAGHER, ARLENE F., ed., "Special Issue: Children," *Law in American Society* 2 (May 1972): 1–51. Special issue on teaching law to children; small claims court simulation.

HANNA, LAVONE A., GLADYS L. POTTER, and ROBERT W. REYNOLDS, *Dynamic Elementary Social Studies* (3rd ed.). New York: Holt, Rinehart and Winston, 1973. Chapter on dramatic play, role playing, simulations, and games.

HEINIG, RUTH B., and LYDA STILLWELL, *Creative Dramatics for the Classroom Teacher*. Englewood Cliffs, N.J.: Prentice-Hall, 1974. Practical suggestions.

LEE, JOHN R., *Teaching Social Studies in Elementary Schools*. New York: Free Press, 1974. Chapters on games and role playing.

MCCASLIN, NELLIE, *Creative Dramatics in the Classroom*. New York: McKay, 1974. Practical procedures.

MAIDMENT, ROBERT, *Simulation Games: Design and Execution*. Columbus, O.: Merrill, 1973. Procedures for using and creating simulation games.

MICHAELIS, JOHN U., ed., *Social Studies in Elementary Schools* (32nd Yearbook). Washington, D.C.: National Council for the Social Studies, 1962. See articles by Brown, Sagle, and Shaftel.

——— and EVERETT T. KEACH, JR., eds., *Teaching Strategies for Elementary School Social Studies*. Itasca, Ill.: Peacock Press, 1972. Articles in Chapters six and nine on literature, folklore, poetry, and simulation games.

NESBITT, WILLIAM A., *Simulation Games in the Social Studies Classroom*. New York: Foreign Policy Association, 1971. Guidelines for using and making games.

NYE, ROBERT, and VERNINE NYE, *Essentials of Teaching Music*. Englewood Cliffs, N.J.: Prentice-Hall, 1974. Practical guide to development of concepts and skills.

RATCLIFFE, ROBERT H., *Teacher's Guide to Law in a New Land*. Boston: Houghton-Mifflin, 1972. Section on presenting a mock trial.

RUDDELL, ROBERT B., *Reading-Language Instruction: Innovative Practices*. Englewood Cliffs, N.J.: Prentice-Hall, 1974. Chapter on literature.

SHAFTEL, FANNIE R., and GEORGE SHAFTEL, *Role-Playing for Social*

Values. Englewood Cliffs, N.J.: Prentice-Hall, 1967. Guidelines for expressing values through role playing.

THOMAS, R. MURRAY, and DALE L. BRUBAKER, eds., *Teaching Elementary Social Studies: Readings*. Belmont, Calif.: Wadsworth, 1972. Articles on simulations and role playing.

YOUNGER, JOHN C., and JOHN F. ACETI, *Simulation Games and Activities for Social Studies*. Danville, N.Y.: Instructor Publications, 1969. Pamphlet containing directions for several simulation games.

11

Focusing Questions

What guidelines for utilization can be applied to all instructional media?

How are instructional media used in each phase of problem solving?

What criteria are used to select instructional media?

What sources of information can be used to locate instructional media?

Instructional Media: Guidelines, Criteria, Sources of Information

Advancements and refinements continue to be made in instructional technology; and systems that include books, films, slides, and other media are available for a variety of units and courses. Educational television and videotapes of selected programs, films produced by TV networks, and TV equipment for use in the classroom are very useful in many units of instruction. Film loops, transparencies, multimedia kits, cassettes, and sound filmstrips are available on a variety of topics. Computerized programs have been tried in many classrooms, and instructional media centers now provide a variety of services ranging from collection and distribution of materials to the actual handling of classroom projects by remote control.

The point for instruction is to provide the richest possible learning environment by including any medium that helps to attain a specified objective. Instructional media are integral parts of a teaching system, not aids to use if time permits. An instructional system may include any of the following that are useful in improving inquiry in a unit of instruction: reading materials, audiovisual materials, and community resources. Basic guidelines for using instructional media, criteria for selection, and sources of information are presented in this chapter. The following chapters deal with specific media in detail.

BASIC GUIDELINES

1. *Look upon instructional media of all types as sources of data.* Use reading materials, audiovisual materials, and community resources as data sources for testing hypotheses, answering questions, developing concepts, formulating main ideas, and solving problems that arise in individual and group inquiry.

2. *Instructional media, like teaching strategies, should be used to achieve specific objectives.* Only those media that help to solve problems or to achieve the objectives of a group are appropriate for that group. When considering an instructional resource, teachers should ask themselves these questions:

> What specific objectives can be achieved by using this resource?
> What concepts and main ideas can children develop through its use?
> Which inquiry processes and skills can be strengthened?
> What attitudes, values, and interests may be modified?

The principle that instructional media should be used to achieve specific objectives may be illustrated by considering ways in which films may contribute to the improvement of critical thinking processes. Children should be guided to discover how questions and problems are elaborated, opened up, and clarified in the film. How are the ideas presented, organized, and summarized? Do the conclusions, suggestions, or content square with other sources of information? Propaganda effects, use of props, use of music to produce various effects, and related emotion-stimulating devices should be considered in the light of such questions as these: "Do they affect our judgment and stimulate an emotional reaction?" "Are our judgments and conclusions distorted?" (The teacher may need to show the film again in order to answer questions like these.)

3. *The varying levels of concreteness should be recognized.* The following hierarchy of materials in terms of levels of abstractness, from direct experience to experiences with verbal symbols, is helpful in considering instructional resources:[1]

1. Direct, purposeful experience: gardening, making something, weaving
2. Contrived experience: operating a working model
3. Dramatic participation: identification of self with others by participating in a play, tableau, or pageant (observing a play is on the next level)

[1] Edgar Dale, *Audio-Visual Methods of Teaching*, 3rd ed. (New York: Dryden Press, 1969).

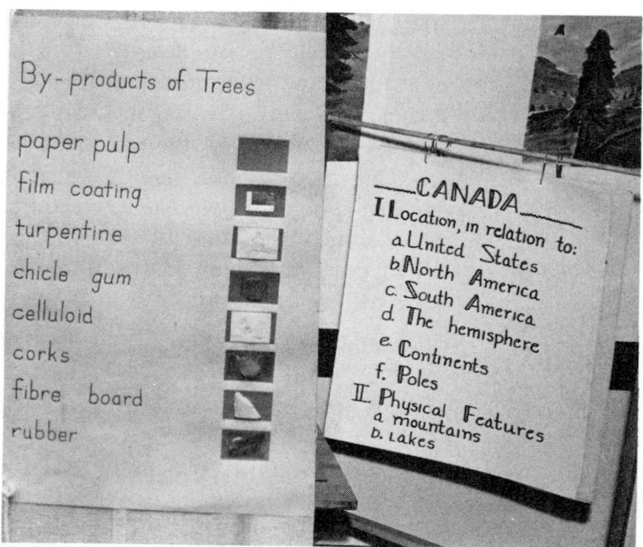

Teacher-made charts can be used to define problems, summarize key ideas, present information, and guide evaluation. Try to anticipate ways in which you can use charts in a unit. (Los Angeles, California)

4. Demonstration: observing as someone demonstrates a process or activity (a more direct type of experience if followed by doing)
5. Field trip: observing people at work or processes in a natural setting (more direct if interviewing is included)
6. Exhibits: seeing planned arrangements of materials (more direct if working models are used)
7. Films and television: watching a planned series of pictures with action and movement involved
8. Photographs, pictures, radio, recordings: seeing or hearing (these are one-dimensional aids)
9. Visual symbols: charts, graphs, and maps
10. Verbal symbols: reading, writing, speaking, listening

This list does not give the best type of experience to provide; it simply suggests an order of concreteness. A teacher must determine the best for a given class on the basis of the children's maturity, available time, availability of materials, and other criteria discussed below.

4. *The classroom should be viewed as a laboratory—a planned environment—to stimulate learning.* Materials should be arranged in such a way as to focus attention on key problems and questions. Different types of materials should be selected and used so that the classroom environment will help to move thinking and planning in profitable directions. The overall arrangement of the room, as well as learning centers, receive attention.

5. *Materials should be used to improve each phase of problem solving.* The following examples are illustrative:

Recognizing and defining problems: Use pictures, maps, realia, charts, films, exhibits, and displays to stimulate questions and to direct thinking toward problems and main ideas to be considered first.

Recalling ideas and posing questions and hypotheses: Have students recall related ideas, using pictures, maps, and other items as clues. List questions and hypotheses on charts or the chalkboard.

Group planning: Use pictures, models, charts, maps, suggestions in textbooks, and ideas from other sources to give direction to planning. Have the group assist in identifying data sources and in planning study guides, reading lists, picture files, and other aids to inquiry.

Finding, interpreting, appraising, and classifying information: Use study guides, contents, indexes, the card catalog, and guides to data. Use books, maps, films, filmstrips, and other media. Appraise information by comparing ideas from different sources, rereading or reshowing films to "prove" points at issue, and interviewing experts on conflicting data. Classify data under concepts, questions, problems, or other appropriate headings. Make charts, graphs, tables, diagrams, and other items for further use as needed.

Generalizing and further processing of information: Proceed to use information in formulating generalizations, testing hypotheses, making analyses, making predictions, and drawing inferences. Key ideas may be synthesized in murals, exhibits, dramatic activities, and models.

How can open-space learning centers such as these be used for individual and group study? Why are preplanning and guidance essential to effective use of the media available in such centers? (Phoenix, Arizona; Raleigh, North Carolina)

Evaluating processes and outcomes: Use charts, checklists, and tests for individual and group evaluation. Guide the group to appraise and consider ways of improving maps, reports, booklets, and other items they have made. Use techniques of evaluation suggested in teacher's manuals, units of instruction, and textbooks.

6. *Maximum learning can be secured only if the use of materials is carefully planned.* First, a teacher should plan a unit in which major topics or problems with related experiences and materials are sketched. This sets the use of materials in proper perspective and enables the teacher to think through the selection, timing, and appropriateness of materials for different needs and problems. Second, attention must be given to the specific details involved in the use of different materials. The teacher must make sure that needed equipment is available, distracting elements are eliminated, purposes are clear, and necessary arrangements are made. For example, a study trip may be of little educational value if the guide has no knowledge of the objectives and level of understanding of the class.

7. *Equipment and materials should not draw attention away from the main ideas to be developed.* This has occurred in units on Indians and pioneers, in which realia such as tomahawks, knives, and muskets have been used for simulated battles during a major part of the study. It has occurred in studies of Mexico in which recordings and films related to fiestas and folk dances were overemphasized. This is not a plea for the elimination of materials; it is a plea for clear objectives to guide the use of materials.

8. *Rules of procedure cannot be followed arbitrarily in the utilization of materials.* In one situation, for example, a teacher was unable to make specific plans before a TV program related to a unit on the growth of democracy was shown. In spite of this, the teacher used the program effectively because notes were made during the program. Although this kind of deviation from recommended procedure should be avoided, in this instance it was the thing to do.

9. *Materials should be organized and arranged in a systematic manner.* One of the most effective ways to organize materials in social studies is to place those related to a unit in a kit in the sequence in which they will most likely be used. For example, in planning a unit on Mexico, the related pictures, pamphlets, reference lists, construction plans, names of films and recordings, possible field trips, and plans for their use can easily be filed in a kit under appropriate headings. If certain items such as large realia and films cannot be included, they should be noted in the unit plan with procedures for securing them. Each kit should be accompanied by a unit plan in which learning experiences and related materials are listed.

10. *A multimedia approach to the use of instructional materials promotes learning and meets individual needs.* The use of several different instructional materials—pictures, films, books, and the like—

to achieve objectives is an extension of the multitextbook approach to include other instructional resources. For example, in developing an appreciation of the difficulties experienced by the pioneers, use should be made of textbooks, supplementary references, stories, films, recordings, maps, and pictures.

11. *Materials should be evaluated before, during, and after use.* Appraisal is an essential aspect of selection and use. Once materials are selected, their contribution to the program should be appraised to determine whether further use is justified. The teacher should note pupil reactions, giving attention to interest, level of difficulty, vocabulary, provision for individual differences, and appropriateness to the maturity level of the group. After the materials have been used, attention should be given to the types of activity stimulated by the material, and to significant outcomes such as concepts, appreciations, or changes in attitude.

12. *Opportunities should be provided for students to create materials.* The creation of materials by students is an excellent synthesizing activity. Motivation is high and the need for planning and research quickly becomes evident. The concepts, skills, and processes involved in creating materials take on real significance. The products may range from picture sets, paper movie rolls, and short booklets to slide sets, closed-circuit TV programs, films, and comprehensive scrapbooks. Production contributes to the unit of study underway and, most important, to better appreciation, utilization, and evaluation of commercially prepared materials.

SELECTION OF MATERIALS

Teachers are involved in the selection of materials in three basic ways. The first and most frequent is the ongoing selection of materials from those available in school, instructional media center, and the community. The second is the selection of free and inexpensive materials. The third is the less frequent but important involvement of selected teachers in evaluating new materials being considered for adoption.

From Available Resources

The following criteria are helpful in selecting materials available in the instructional media center, the community, and the school.

Appropriateness. The level of difficulty of instructional materials must be appropriate to the maturity of the children who are going to use them. A range of materials wide enough to stimulate gifted, average, and less able children should be chosen.

Objectives. Clarification of the objectives for which a film, filmstrip, or other item is to be used is essential. Both the objectives for which it has been produced and the objectives for which it is to be used should be

Notice the many materials in this display that can be used to develop accurate and authentic concepts. How might they be used to enrich meaning as textbooks, films, and other resources are used? (Oakland City Schools, California)

checked. The latter may vary because different teachers may use an item for different objectives. For example, one teacher used a film on Mexico to initiate a unit; another teacher used the same film as a part of concluding activities to summarize key ideas. Both knew, however, that the film was designed to portray basic aspects of life in Mexico.

Content. The nature of the content of a resource in large measure determines its usefulness. Double-check authenticity, clarity of presentation, bias, stereotypes, difficulty of concepts, and specific contributions to topics under study. Note the treatment of women and ethnic and minority groups, and any biases or other distortions. Then students can be guided to develop an awareness of bias, prejudice, and other distortions in the materials they use.

Variety. Variation is needed to meet objectives, promote interest, stimulate thinking, develop the skills involved in using different resources in problem solving, and meet individual needs. In addition, various media serve different objectives. For example, if the objective is to show how something works, a working model is useful. If the way an activity is carried out by a group—weaving by Indians, for example—needs clarification, a film will portray the action and movement. Such objectives as learning about types of dwellings or homes may be met by using pictures. Sound films are helpful in giving realistic conceptions of activities in which both sound and motion are important elements. Film loops are helpful in developing single concepts, such as preparing meals in a Japanese family. Colored slides are helpful in studying types and colors of clothing and costumes, landscapes, and the arts and crafts of various peoples. Where sound alone is important, recordings or the radio may be used. If the objective is to analyze an activity in its natural setting, a study trip may be essential.

Time, effort, expense. The time, effort, and expense involved in using instructional resources are important considerations. Some study trips that require traveling a great distance from school are highly desirable, but they may be unnecessary if other available resources are adequate. On the other hand, a study trip may be more economical than other resources in terms of time, effort, and expense, because of the educational value it possesses.

Physical qualities. Maps, films, and charts are valuable only if their format, printing, sound, photography, and organization are satisfactory. Attractiveness, clearness of presentation, and continuity or sequence of ideas are significant determinants of educational value.

Manuals. The teaching manuals that accompany many maps, films, filmstrips, slides, recordings, radio programs, and books should be reviewed critically to identify objectives and helpful suggestions.

Free or Inexpensive Materials

Special care must be exercised in the selection of free or inexpensive materials—for example, maps, charts, diagrams, pamphlets, leaflets, booklets, and pictures. Many school districts have policies for the selection and use of materials distributed by companies, consular offices, travel agencies, state and local groups, national organizations, and government agencies. In general, high standards are set for the free or inexpensive materials distributed by reputable agencies and groups, but to select and use such resources indiscriminately and without strict adherence to established policies is unprofessional and contrary to the best interests of children. Criteria such as the following should be applied:

1. Is the material produced by a reputable group?
2. If controversial issues are included, are they presented fairly and on a level that is meaningful to children?

3. Are concepts, style of presentation, symbols, and language appropriate to the capabilities of the children who will use them?
4. Is the content related to units of instruction?
5. Are sources of information given?
6. Is the material free of bias and prejudice?
7. Is the material up to date and available from standard sources?
8. Are type size, spacing format, and other technical qualities satisfactory?
9. Is material free of objectionable or obtrusive advertising?
10. Will the school be obligated if it uses the material?

New Materials Teachers are called upon to assist in the selection of materials submitted for adoption. Standard procedure is to evaluate materials in terms of criteria such as those shown in Checklist 11–1.

Checklist 11–1[2]

CRITERIA FOR SELECTING MATERIALS

A. Basic social studies goals should be reflected in both learner and teacher materials.
B. Materials shall include attention to statewide requirements regarding history, government, and other mandated areas of study.
C. Materials for students must meet the following legal requirements:
   1. Accurately portray the cultural diversity of our society, including
      a. Contributions of men and women in all types of roles—professional, vocational, executive.
      b. Role and contributions of native Americans, black Americans, Asian Americans, Mexican Americans, and other ethnic and cultural groups.
      c. Role and contributions of entrepreneur and labor.
   2. Accurately portray, whenever appropriate, the place of people in the ecological system and the need to protect the environment, and the effects of drugs and other dangerous substances.
   3. When appropriate to comprehension of students, textbooks shall contain the Declaration of Independence and The Constitution.
   4. No material shall reflect adversely upon persons because of their race, color, creed, national origin, ancestry, sex, or occupation.
   5. Materials shall be suited to needs and comprehension of students at each grade level, and be accurate, objective, and current.
   6. Supplementary materials shall provide resources that reflect cultural pluralism.
D. The following criteria apply in addition to the above requirements:
   1. Materials shall be presented in many forms: expository, adversary, statistical, maps, graphs, case studies, stories, drama,

[2] Adapted and condensed from *Criteria for Selection of Instructional Materials in Social Studies, K–8* (Sacramento, Calif.: State Department of Education, 1974).

music, art, recordings, film, film loops, videotapes, transparencies, simulated games, artifacts, globes.
2. Materials shall motivate critical thinking and problem solving, provide for differences in learning styles, interest, and achievement, and include suggestions for independent study and research.
3. Materials shall present varying points of view on issues, include primary and secondary sources, and (where appropriate) use metric measures.
4. Materials shall include the significance of religion in shaping moral and ethical precepts and the contributions of religion to literature, art, music, law, and morality. No single belief system should be imposed or ridiculed.
5. Methods of analyzing controversial issues shall be provided.
6. Materials shall provide for application of learning and opportunity for decision making and defense of a decision.
7. Materials of an inspirational nature shall be included, to commemorate the bicentennial.
8. Materials should be included that are parallel in other languages to material in English.
9. Illustrations shall be adequate, esthetic, appropriate, authentic, current, and related to content.
10. Materials shall be durable, esthetic, and appropriate for intended use.

E. Teacher materials shall include:
1. Supplementary data and background information.
2. An outline of learning experiences for each level and relationships to concept development and social science disciplines.
3. Meaningful student activities to increase interest and participation.
4. Suggestions for various teaching strategies.
5. Suggestions for evaluating student progress.

When appraising books and other materials on foreign cultures, teachers should consider these points: Is the author qualified? Has the author visited or lived there? Are facts presented accurately? Has a native reviewed the work favorably? How are values of the people treated? How are hopes and aspirations portrayed? Are stereotypes avoided? Are costumes, art, dances, and special customs portrayed in perspective along with current ways of living?

A common practice is to include criteria in rating forms so that points can be assigned to each criterion, as shown in Checklist 11–2. Other examples of rating forms may be found in school district offices and in the references at the end of this chapter.

At times, data on the actual use of materials with students should be considered in making adoptions. The most useful information is that obtained by actual tryout of materials under classroom conditions. Tryouts are needed when there are serious questions about usefulness of

Checklist 11–2

CHECKLIST FOR EVALUATING TEXTBOOKS

Directions: Rate each book on the specific points as follows: 5, superior; 4, good; 3, fair; 2, poor; 1, unsatisfactory.

Criteria for Rating Each Textbook	*A*	*B*	*C*	*D*	*E*	*F*
As an instructional resource:						
Is it related to the content of the program?						
Is it accurate and up to date?						
Can the children who will use it grasp the concepts and understandings?						
Is the level of reading difficulty—vocabulary, style of presentation, sentence structure—appropriate for children who will use it?						
Will it contribute to problem-solving skills?						
Do illustrative materials—maps, pictures, drawings—contribute to the meaningfulness of the content?						
Are study aids, suggested activities, and related references adequate?						
Physical features:						
Is it attractive and appealing to children?						
Are margins and page arrangements adequate?						
Are size, spacing, and type size adequate?						
Major emphases:						
Are men and women shown in a variety of roles?						
Are roles and contributions of ethnic groups presented adequately and fairly?						
Are there no adverse reflections related to color, race, creed, national origin, sex, ancestry, and occupation?						
Are controversial issues handled fairly and objectively?						
Does the book emphasize movements and trends rather than isolated events?						
Does it stimulate interests that lead to further study?						
Total						

(Column group heading: *Textbook*)

materials in terms of student capabilities and teacher qualifications. In most instances, however, criteria such as those noted above are adequate for making the selection.

Guiding Students to Discover Unfairness in Materials

In addition to evaluation of instructional media in terms of the treatment of women and ethnic groups, teachers should guide students to discover unfair treatment and suggest improvements. The fact is that students will encounter misconceptions, prejudice, and stereotypes. They should learn to detect unfair treatment, demonstrate how it may be avoided, and learn how to avoid it in their own behavior. Charts 11–1 and 11–2 include several points students should check; additional points may arise depending on the materials being used.

Chart 11–1
Discovering and Improving the Treatment of Women

In a variety of activities and jobs?
Variety of contributions reported?
Girls portrayed as passive, fearful, and changing their minds?
Boys portrayed as active, more mature, and larger?
Boys shown making things and earning money; girls, sewing, cooking, or playing with dolls?
Needed changes you can make?

Chart 11–2
Discovery and Improving the Treatment of Ethnic Groups

Variety of contributions presented?
Shown in a variety of roles and jobs?
Portrayal of any groups as problems? primitive? lazy? savage? dull? slow?
Values of cultural diversity presented?
Treatment of evils of discrimination? prejudice? stereotypes?
Equality, justice, and concern for others clarified?
Improvements you can make?

The Metric System

As noted in the criteria for selecting materials cited earlier, attention is being given to use of the metric system in the social studies program. Use of metric measures must be paced with instruction provided in the mathematics and science programs. Helpful activities include the use of rulers with both metric and English measures, conversion of scales on maps, and conversion of square miles, acres, and other quantities encountered in textbooks and other materials. Children should use metric measures in weighing and measuring themselves, operating the classroom "supermarket," making maps, making and recording weather observations, and other activities. Charts 11–3 to 11–6 may be used to make approximate conversions; all figures are for U.S. measures. Tables in mathematics books, encyclopedias, and other references should be used to make exact conversions.

Chart 11–3
Conversion to Metric

inches	X 25 =	millimeters
feet	X 30 =	centimeters
yards	X .9 =	meters
miles	X 1.6 =	kilometers
ounces	X 28 =	grams
pounds	X .45 =	kilograms
tons	X .9 =	tonnes
pints	X .47 =	milliliters
quarts	X .95 =	liters
gallons	X 3.8 =	liters
bushels	X 2.8 =	hectoliters
sq. in.	X 6.5 =	sq. centimeters
sq. ft.	X .09 =	sq. meters
sq. yd.	X .83 =	sq. meters
acres	X .4 =	hectares
sq. miles	X 2.6 =	sq. kilometers

Chart 11–4
Conversion from Metric

millimeters	X .04 =	inches
centimeters	X .4 =	inches
meters	X 1.1 =	yards
kilometers	X .6 =	miles
grams	X .035 =	ounces
kilograms	X 2.2 =	pounds
tonnes	X 1.1 =	tons
liters	X 2.1 =	pints
liters	X 1.06 =	quarts
liters	X .26 =	gallons
hectoliters	X .35 =	bushels
sq. centimeters	X .16 =	sq. in.
sq. meters	X 1.2 =	sq. yd.
sq. kilometers	X .4 =	sq. miles
hectares	X 2.5 =	acres

Chart 11–5
Metric Prefixes

giga	1,000,000,000
mega	1,000,000
kilo	1,000
hecto	100
deka	10
deci	0.1
centi	0.01
milli	0.001
micro	0.000001
nano	0.000000001

Chart 11–6
Temperature

Celsius = 5/9 (F — 32)
Fahrenheit = 9/5 (C + 32)

Effective use of Materials Principles that teachers can use in guiding utilization, follow-up, and evaluation of materials are summarized in Checklist 11–3, which is helpful in preparing to use all types of media presented in the following chapters.

Checklist 11–3

CHECKLIST FOR USING INSTRUCTIONAL MEDIA

Objectives:

_____ What objectives are suggested in the manual?

_____ To which core objectives is it related? _____ conceptual _____ process _____ skill _____ affective
_____ What questions in the ongoing unit can be answered?
_____ How does it fit into individual and group inquiry with other media?

Readiness:
_____ What suggestions for introducing it are in the manual?
_____ How should objectives be clarified for students?
_____ What terms and concepts need development in advance?
_____ How can it be related to questions in the unit?
_____ What experiences of students should be recalled and related to it?

During Use:
_____ What suggestions are presented in the manual?
_____ Should students observe? _____ take notes? _____ raise questions?
_____ What supplementary materials or comments are needed to enrich learning?
_____ Should a break be given during use for questions and comments?
_____ Should the resource be used a second time to emphasize points, clarify questions, or make explanations?

Follow-Up:
_____ What follow-up activities are suggested in the manual?
_____ What points should be stressed in group discussion and evaluation?
_____ How might other resources be used to check any points at issue?
_____ What related activities flow from it _____ map-making _____ chart making _____ reading _____ research _____ role playing _____ construction _____ other?
_____ How might group planning be used to project further inquiry?
_____ What hypotheses or generalizations might be made?
_____ Which objectives were and were not achieved?

Teacher Evaluation:
_____ Was the resource satisfactory for the group involved?
_____ How can its use be improved?
_____ Should supplementary resources be available before or after its use?
_____ Any special difficulties that should be noted for future reference?
_____ Does the manual suggest points for evaluation?

SOURCES OF INFORMATION

The first step in identifying sources of information for instructional materials is to review those available in the local school system. Although practices vary considerably among systems, information on materials may usually be found in units of instruction, teaching guides, catalogs of materials available in the instructional materials center, supplementary lists of recently acquired materials, and special lists related to basic units of instruction. Teachers should check the policies and procedures for requesting materials from the materials center and from various lending agencies outside the school system. In addition to school system catalogs and guides to instructional materials, the guides listed below should be checked. Most are available in college or university libraries as well as in instructional materials centers.

1. Detailed guides to commercially prepared materials: *Educator's Purchasing Guide* (Philadelphia, Pa.: North American Publishing Company); *Learning Directory* (New York: Westinghouse Learning Corporation); NICEM (National Information Center for Educational Media) (Los Angeles: University of Southern California).
2. Detailed analyses of materials: *Curriculum Materials Analysis System* (Boulder, Colo.: Social Science Education Consortium); *Educational Product Report* (New York: EPIE Institute).
3. Catalogs and lists of resources available from the county schools office, the state department of education, state university, colleges, and other agencies from which your school district obtains materials.
4. Periodicals: *Booklist, Bulletin of the Center for Children's Books, Teacher, Instructor, Library Journal, Scholastic Teacher, Social Education, Audiovisual Instruction, Educational Screen, Education Product Report, Preview: News and Review of Nonprint Media.*
5. Detailed source lists in professional textbooks on audiovisual materials (see the list of references at the end of this chapter).
6. Guides to free or inexpensive materials (also check special sections in the magazines listed above): Aubrey, Ruth A., *Selected Free Materials for Classroom Teachers* (Belmont, Calif.: Fearon Publishers); *Educator's Guide to Free Social Studies Materials, Elementary Teachers' Guide to Free Curriculum Materials,* and *Educator's Guide to Free Films* (Randolph, Wis.: Educator's Progress Service); *Free and Inexpensive Learning Materials* (Nashville, Tenn.: George Peabody College, Division of Field Services); *Vertical File Index* (Bronx, N.Y.: H. W. Wilson); *Economic Education* (New York: Joint Council on Economic Education); and

Selected United States Government Publications, Superintendent of Documents, Government Printing Offce, Washington, D.C. 20402 (ask to be put on the mailing list).

7. Guides to social studies reading materials: *Basic Book Collection for Elementary Grades, Subject Index to Books for Primary Grades,* and *Subject Index to Books for Intermediate Grades* (Chicago: American Library Association), check latest edition; *Best Books for Children and Children's Books in Print* (New York: Bowker), check latest editions; *Bibliography of Books for Children* (Washington, D.C.: Association for Childhood Education), check latest edition; Dallman, Martha, Roger L. Rouch, Lynette Y. C. Chang, and John J. DeBoer, *The Teaching of Reading,* 4th ed. (New York: Holt, Rinehart, and Winston, 1974), detailed list of sources, guides to materials, and publishers; Huus, Helen, *Children's Books to Enrich the Social Studies for the Elementary Grades* (Washington, D.C.: National Council for the Social Studies), check latest edition.
8. Information on materials related to ethnic groups: African-American Institute, 866 United Nations Plaza, New York, N.Y. 10017, publications and guides to materials; Anti-Defamation League of B'nai B'rith, 315 Lexington Ave., New York, N.Y. 10016; Association for the Study of Negro Life and History, 1538 9 St. N.W., Washington, D.C. 20001; Banks, James A., ed., *Teaching Ethnic Studies,* 43rd Yearbook (Washington, D.C.: National Council for the Social Studies, 1973).

QUESTIONS, ACTIVITIES, EVALUATION

1. Recall vivid learning experiences that you had in school. Can you remember the instructional materials that were part of them? What other factors were involved?
2. The level of concreteness of materials is one factor to consider in selecting resources for a group. What are some other factors? How might learning in social studies be affected if only direct experiences were provided?
3. Visit an instructional materials center and examine the types of resources available. Note those that might be useful in a unit you are planning to teach.
4. Examine one or more of the guides to free and inexpensive materials listed at the end of this chapter. Get some by writing to the pub-

lisher of each item and appraise them in terms of the criteria presented in this chapter.

5. Note ways in which the instructional resources discussed in this chapter can be used under each phase of inquiry in a unit of instruction of your choice.

REFERENCES

BROWN, JAMES W., RICHARD B. LEWIS, and FRED F. HARCLEROAD, *A-V Instruction: Materials and Methods* (4th ed.). New York: McGraw-Hill, 1973. Principles and procedures for using all types of instructional materials, and a listing of source materials; criteria for rating materials.

Checklist for Selecting and Evaluating U.S. History Textbooks. Washington, D.C.: National Education Association, 1973. Detailed checklist that may be adapted for checking other materials.

DALE, EDGAR, *Audio-Visual Methods of Teaching* (3rd ed.). New York: Dryden Press, 1969. A comprehensive treatment of instructional materials; criteria for rating materials.

HANNA, LAVONE A., GLADYS L. POTTER, and ROBERT W. REYNOLDS, *Dynamic Elementary Social Studies* (3rd ed.). New York: Holt, Rinehart, and Winston, 1973. Chapter on use of multimedia.

How to Do It Series. Washington, D.C.: National Council for the Social Studies. Leaflets on how to use various media.

LAYBOURNE, KAY, ed., *Doing the Media*. New York: Center for Understanding Media, 1972. Section on storyboarding.

MICHAELIS, JOHN U., and EVERETT T. KEACH, JR., eds., *Teaching Strategies for Elementary School Social Studies.* Itasca, Ill.: Peacock, 1972. Readings in Chapter X on instructional media; rating form for evaluating materials, pp. 411–16.

MINOR, ED, and HARVEY R. FRYE, *Techniques for Producing Visual Instructional Media* (2nd ed.). New York: McGraw-Hill, 1970. Techniques for making materials.

WITTICH, WALTER A., and CHARLES F. SCHULER, *Instructional Technology: Its Nature and Use.* New York: Harper & Row, 1973. Treatment of all media; section on visual literacy.

12

Focusing Questions

What procedures should be used to improve the use of textbooks?

What should be included in instruction on the use of encyclopedias, other reference material, and the library?

How can literature be used to extend and enrich learning in the social studies?

How can different types of charts be used to aid learning?

What practice materials can be used to improve the reading of social studies material?

How can basic reading skills be applied and further developed in the social studies program?

Using Reading Materials & Developing Reading Skills

Reading materials open gateways to a multitude of new discoveries in social studies. Family and community living, people and places near and far, ways of living at home and in other lands, contributions of ethnic groups, activities of great men and women, events of historic significance, places in the news, holidays and special events, life in early and modern America, changes stemming from scientific developments, emergence of new nations, human progress through the ages, and a host of other topics are included in social studies reading materials. As a result of reading experiences, children can identify themselves with others, develop richer appreciations of their ways of living, and gain new concepts and understandings. Their reading and study skills are strengthened as they engage in critical reading to solve problems and gather information on questions that have come up in units of instruction. Recreational and independent reading are motivated as stories, novels, poems, and biographies are introduced in connection with units. For most children, no materials contribute more to learning in social studies than do reading materials.

Two basic objectives should be achieved as reading materials are used in social studies. First, children should get an abundance of ideas for use in problem solving. Second, reading ability should be improved as children apply reading skills to materials that range from textbooks and references to charts and practice materials. In order to attain these outcomes it is necessary to give attention to effective utilization of different types of material and to developing basic skills as materials are being used.

USING A VARIETY OF READING MATERIAL

Textbooks

Textbooks are used in several different ways in the social studies program. In some schools, a series of textbooks is used as the basis for the instructional program. Children in each grade are helped to learn as much as they can from the text, related audiovisual materials are used to enrich the text, the reading of supplementary materials is encouraged, and special help is given individually or in small groups to less able children.

Some teachers use a basic textbook as a general guide and provide for other materials in conjunction with various chapters of the text. This approach, a step beyond reliance on a single textbook, gives children planned opportunities to use materials on different readability levels, provides different points of view, and develops the skills involved in pooling information from various sources. Many teachers use this approach when they undertake new areas of study, when they are trying to build up backgrounds of understanding, and when they want students to become acquainted with the large number of appropriate reading materials. The basic textbook provides for a core of learning for the group, and related materials are used to meet individual differences in reading ability.

In schools in which units of instruction are used, reading or study guides that include references to several textbooks and other reading materials are helpful. For example, one or more questions or problems followed by related readings may be duplicated or listed on the chalkboard. Certain readings may be assigned to the entire group, and others included for children with high and low reading ability. Each child proceeds to gather information from the listed references, which include textbooks and materials on varying levels of reading difficulty. Teacher guidance is given as needed in the selection of references appropriate for individual children, for groups within the class, and for the entire class. No matter which approach is used, social studies textbooks may be used for a variety of objectives:

1. To provide an introduction to, or an overview of, a unit as children check appropriate sections of the contents, consider headings and subheadings as main topics for further study, read and discuss introductory paragraphs, discuss pictures, recall previous experiences related to ideas presented in the text, discuss possible use of maps in the text, and get a feeling for main points to be stressed in the unit
2. To develop new terms and concepts related to the unit as children use picture clues, context clues, structural analysis, phonetic analysis, other word recognition techniques, and the glossary

3. To provide descriptions of homes, clothing, food, modes of transportation, and other ways of living as children read selected sections, discuss them, make comparisons, and attempt to identify themselves with others
4. To provide an initial background of ideas that children can use as a springboard in making comparisons, and to gain further information as they read other materials and use audiovisual materials that present different ideas, descriptions, and points of view
5. To find specific facts and ideas as children seek answers to such questions as these: What food do we get from truck farms? What different kinds of material are used to make clothing? How was lighting provided in colonial homes?
6. To provide for critical listening to selected sections read by the teacher or a superior reader
7. To "prove" specific points as children skim to note details or main ideas related to disagreements that have arisen
8. To find main ideas related to a topic, question, or problem as children locate the key idea in each of several related paragraphs
9. To provide instruction in basic study skills as children use the contents, headings and subheadings, index, glossary, and end-of-chapter study aids
10. To provide experience in reading and interpreting maps, charts, diagrams, graphs, tables, and pictures as children use them to answer questions and find key ideas
11. To summarize and bring together key ideas and basic concepts at certain points during the unit and at the end of the unit as children read summaries, note and discuss generalizations and conclusions, carry out selected end-of-chapter activities, and answer test items taken from the text, related workbooks, or the teacher's manual

Learning the Parts of Social Studies Books

Instruction should be provided on the main parts of social studies books. For example, when a textbook is introduced to the group, the title page may be discussed, the year of publication noted, and the contents reviewed. Features of many social studies books to discuss with students are lists of maps, map sections that can be used as an atlas, reference tables on population and other items, data banks or resource centers and how to use them, the glossary of terms, and special items in the appendix. Particular attention needs to be given to the use of the index, with directed practice in using it guided by such questions as "In what order are topics listed?" "When are last names placed first for a topic?" "What names are always capitalized?" This should be followed by actually using the index to find data on topics under study.

USING REFERENCE BOOKS

Encyclopedias

Encyclopedias may be used as children search for information, pictures, diagrams, tables, charts, maps, and graphs related to questions and problems in units they are studying. In primary grades, the pictures are most helpful, although more able children can benefit from reading selected sections related to topics under study. Beginning in the fourth grade, systematic instruction is usually provided in the use of encyclopedias, with review and additional instruction in later grades as needed. Guidelines for using the particular encyclopedias available to students should be developed as shown in Chart 12–1.

Chart 12–1
Using Our Encyclopedias

Articles beginning with *A* are in Volume 1, *B* in Volume 2, and so forth.
Articles are arranged in alphabetical order like words in the dictionary.
Guide words at the top of the pages tell what is reported on each page.
Places, such as New Guinea and New York, are found under the first name.
The names of people are found under the last name.
The index gives main articles and related articles. It also gives some facts not included in articles.
The index lists maps, charts, tables, pictures, and graphs.

Dictionaries

In addition to finding the spelling, pronunciation, and meaning of terms in dictionaries, children should use them to find illustrations of terms and concepts used in social studies. Picture dictionaries contain excellent illustrations, and standard classroom dictionaries include a large number of spot maps, drawings, and sketches. Because the drawings and sketches are made simply and are uncluttered with detail, they are easy for children to interpret. See Charts 12–2 and 12–3 for suggestions on how to use the dictionary.

Chart 12–2
Using the Dictionary

Know the alphabet.
Use the guide words.
Note the spelling.
Check the accent mark.
Check the diacritical marks.
Check the pronunciation key.
Note how plurals are formed.
Choose the appropriate meaning.

Chart 12–3
The Dictionary As a Data Source

Definitions	Abbreviations
Spelling	Pronunciation
Synonyms	Antonyms
Diagrams	Pictures
Tables	Charts
Weights	Measures
Foreign terms	Country maps

What else can we find on social studies topics?

Other References A variety of other reference materials may be used in social studies, particularly in the upper grades and by more able children in grades 3 through 5. Yearbooks and almanacs contain much information on many topics and should be used when latest facts and statistics are needed.

The *World Almanac,* for example, is a book of facts about large cities, capitals, states, countries, business, trade, exports, imports, production, transportation, sports, conservation, education, communication, organizations, political parties, population, lakes, mountains, rivers, United Nations, special days and dates for the current year, major events of the past year, and so on. Other information books are *Information Please Almanac* (similar to the *World Almanac*); the *Economic Almanac,* which contains facts about business, labor, and government; and the *Statesman's Yearbook,* which includes facts on countries throughout the world.

Library Resources The resources of school libraries are especially helpful in social studies. In some areas, traveling libraries or bookmobiles are operated for the convenience of schools and communities. Of great help are the materials in public libraries and in central school library facilities. Many teachers make a practice of checking out a varied collection of reading materials, prints, and pictures related to the unit they are planning. In some school systems, teachers may order a kit of materials related to the unit from the central school library; in others, catalogs may be provided so that specific materials may be ordered as needed.

Classroom libraries facilitate the use of references and supplementary reading materials. As different units are studied, the reading materials should be changed. Materials from the school library, public libraries, and the central school library should be drawn upon freely for placement in the room library.

Children should be given planned experiences in library use so that they can make full use of library resources. Teachers should take their groups to the library to learn the location of materials, how to check out materials, rules and procedures, and the use of the card catalog. Librarians are eager to help and should be consulted before the visit so that detailed plans, appropriate to the maturity of the group, can be made.

Specific attention must also be given to skills involved in using reference materials. The following resources are used in connection with many different units in upper grades.

- Card catalogs
- City directories
- Dictionaries
- Encyclopedias
- School atlases
- Government directories
- Guides, timetables, and folders
- Periodicals
- *Readers' Guide*
- Telephone directories
- *The Junior Book of Authors*
- *Who's Who in America*
- *World Almanac*
- *Statesman's Yearbook*

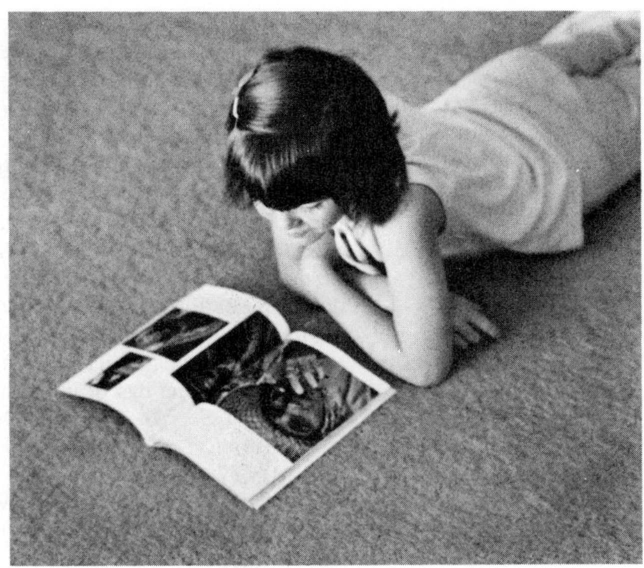

Time to read and time to choose. How can materials selected by children themselves enrich learning in the social studies? (Fremont, California)

LITERATURE

Literature makes rich contributions to social learning in the elementary school. As Ernest Horn said many years ago: "Of all the subjects not traditionally included under the social studies, none is more intimately affiliated with them than literature."[1] Literary selections are used in the social studies program to heighten interest, deepen understanding, create mood and atmosphere, portray the diversity of ways of living and thinking among people in various cultures, stimulate imagination, give colorful backgrounds, promote more complete identification with others, give a warm feeling for the problems of others, improve attitudes toward others, build appreciations for the contributions of others, provoke creativity, and give vivid impressions of ways of living being studied in various units. A feeling for the joys, sorrows, and problems of others can rarely be kindled through the use of factual material alone; hence the importance of poetry, stories, biography, fiction, letters, legends, and travel literature to take children beyond facts to the spiritual and esthetic qualities and values involved in human relationships. The following examples of the uses of literary selections in various units may serve to clarify the specific contributions that can be made to the enrichment of the social studies program.

In studying pets as a part of a unit on the home, one group was thrilled by the teacher's reading of Hill and Maxwell's *Charlie and His Puppy Bingo,* and Gemmill's *Joan Wanted a Kitty;* selected poems were also enjoyed from *Sung Under the Silver Umbrella* (Association for Childhood Education).

[1] Ernest Horn, Methods of Instruction in the Social Studies (New York: Scribner's, 1937), p. 265.

A primary group learning about the community enjoyed Field's *General Store,* Clymer's *The Big Pile of Dirt,* and Chute's *Rhymes About the City;* another group studying the farm liked Chute's *Farmers* and Nast's *A Farm Story;* a group studying trains enjoyed Tippett's poem "Trains," and Lenski's *The Little Train.*

In a study of life in the United States, several children read Gate's *Blue Willow* and expressed keenly felt sympathy for the problems of the itinerant worker's child. Others read Buffler's *Rodrigo and Rosalita,* Lenski's *Blue Ridge Sally, Bayou Suzette,* and *Strawberry Girl,* which enriched their understanding of life in different sections of the country, and Kurelek's *A Prairie Boy's Winter,* which portrays the end of autumn, the long cold winter, and finally the beginning of spring. Several were sensitized to the thoughts and feelings of individuals in ethnic groups by reading Jackson's *Call Me Charley,* De Angeli's *Bright April,* Davis' *Americans Everyone,* Eberle's *Very Good Neighbors,* Sommerfelt's *My Name Is Pablo,* and Beim's *Two Is a Team.* These books were also helpful in showing how individuals and groups can work and play together even though differences exist.

A study of the growth of democracy was greatly enriched for upper-grade children who read D'Aulaires' *George Washington,* Daugherty's *Abraham Lincoln,* Forbes' *Johnny Tremain* and *America's Paul Revere,* and Barksdale's *The First Thanksgiving,* and who listened to recordings such as "Ballad for Americans," "The Lonesome Train," and "Mine Eyes Have See the Glory." A greater appreciation of the contributions of famous Americans was developed by those who read Franklin's *Autobiography,* Petry's *Harriet Tubman,* Pace's *Clara Barton,* Gray's *William Penn,* and Holt's *George Washington Carver.*

In using literary selections, the teacher should check for authenticity of material, explanations of deviations from reality, comparisons between factual and fictional materials, distortions because of author's point of view, setting, and inaccuracies in content. The attitude of the group should be one of delight and enjoyment. In general, when using a literary selection the teacher should keep the following points in mind:

1. Enjoy it, do not dissect it; analyze it only if analysis increases enjoyment.
2. Share it, do not ask questions; do not give tests on it or evaluate it, as is done with factual materials.
3. Approach it to have fun, not to study, as is done in work-type materials.
4. Be aware of fiction and fantasy; do not teach them as facts.
5. Let the children discover values, moods, and meanings; do not moralize or struggle to develop certain points of real interest to yourself.
6. Let children memorize their favorites.

7. Use varied techniques and activities to share and enjoy literary selections in social studies—book reports, card files of favorite poems and stories, choral reading, creative writing, dramatization, filmstrips, independent reading, films, oral reading by children, oral reading by the teacher, programs and pageants, puppets and marionettes, radio and TV programs, recordings, and storytelling.

MAKING AND USING CHARTS

Charts are among the most practical reading materials used in the social studies program. They can be used in units of instruction at all levels, in all phases of problem solving, and in a variety of learning activities. Charts are also helpful in promoting the development of reading ability. As concepts and related terms are developed and used in making charts, children develop the backgrounds of meaning needed to read them. Thus the language experience approach to reading can be put to use in the social studies program. The most widely used types of charts are as follows:

Question charts guide individual and group study during units of instruction. Experience charts are used for reading and discussion based on study trips, construction and art projects, and other firsthand experiences; creative expression charts record songs, poems, and stories; vocabulary charts are used for listing frequently used terms or special terms needed in various units. Sequential charts show a series of events, time lines, records of activities, the sequence in producing various items, steps in making something, and calendars of events. Classification charts record such information as types of pollution problems, dwellings, food, clothing, utensils, crafts, and modes of transportation. Retrieval charts summarize information about cities, states, countries, leaders, resources, and other items. Organization charts show committee memberships, structure of government, economic systems, and organization of other institutions or groups. Group standards charts are useful in work periods, discussion, dramatic activities, reports, simulation games, and committees. Direction charts guide field trips, map making, the use of tools and materials, and other activities. Then progress charts record the completion of individual and group activities.

The content of charts should be based on the experiences of the class and directly related to activities in the unit. Vocabulary and sentence patterns should be appropriate to the level of maturity of the group. The language in the chart should be simple, and use should be made of descriptive phrases and sentences dictated by the group. Illustrations should be attractive and add to the meaningfulness of charts. Correct punctuation, capitalization, spelling, and meticulous sentence structure and language usage are essential.

The format and composition of charts should be similar to those presented on page 360. Lettering should be legible and easy to read.

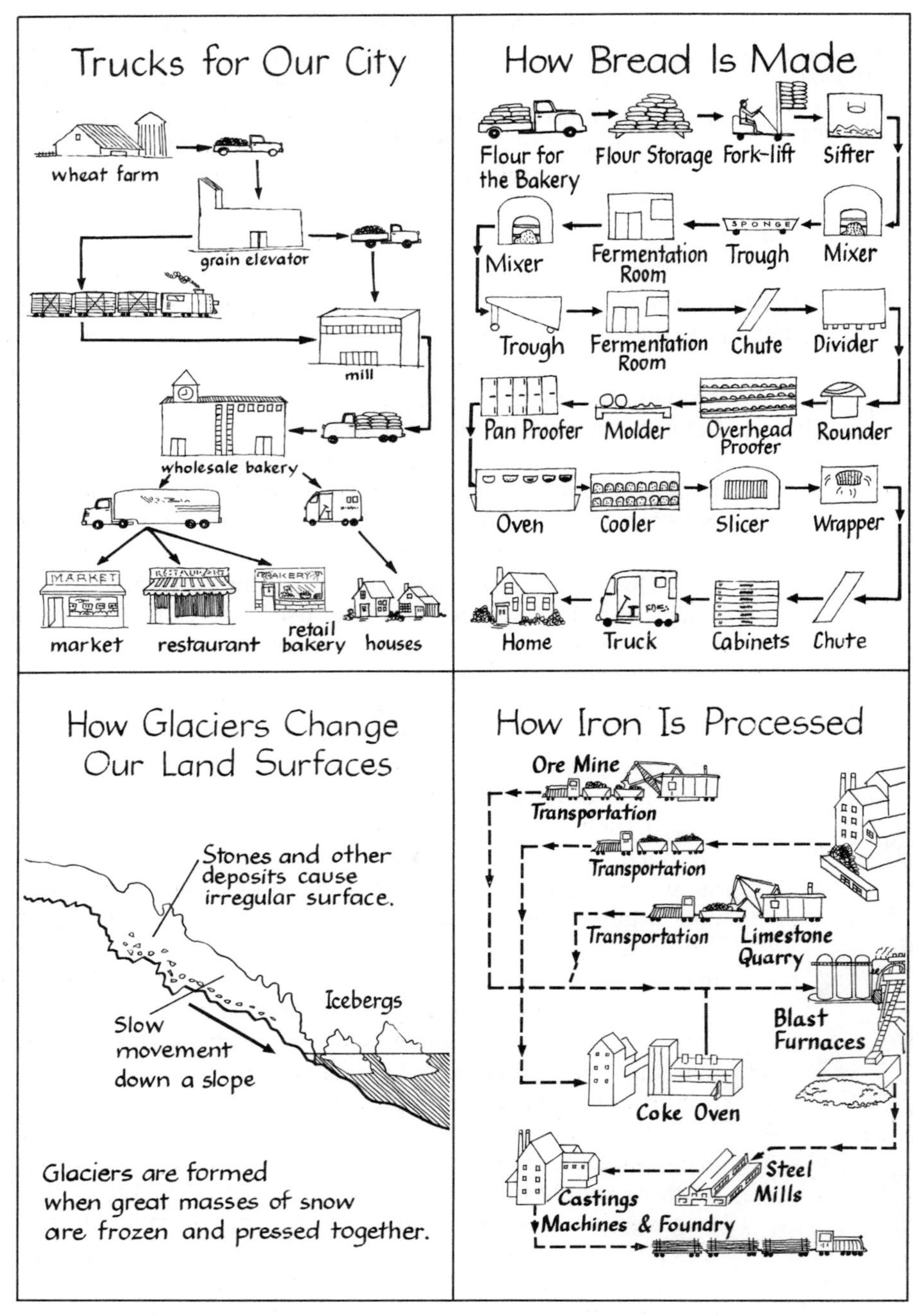

Why will such flow charts increase children's understanding of the processes depicted? (San Bernardino County Schools, California)

Sharp contrast between lettering and paper, standard paragraph form, balanced placement of illustrations, adequate spacing of words and lines, consistent use of standard letter forms, and margins similar to those on picture mats are other essential considerations.

PRACTICE MATERIALS FOR IMPROVING SKILLS Practice materials for use in developing reading and other skills in the social studies program should be selected and used in accordance with sound principles of reading instruction. A widely accepted principle is to provide practice materials for individuals and small groups in the light of specific difficulties that have arisen. A second principle is to provide practice when it can be used to strengthen skills that will be put to use in the ongoing program of instruction. A third principle is to provide multilevel practice materials that match reading levels of children in the group. A fourth principle is to relate practice closely to the reading materials, maps, and other resources that children use most frequently. A fifth principle is to provide for immediate feedback on progress and needs for further improvement. In short, the same care should be taken to provide for individualized practice in social studies as is taken in reading, arithmetic, and other areas of the curriculum.

Many different materials are available for use in the social studies program. The major problem for teachers is to make a critical selection. The following list gives some of the practice materials available on social studies reading skills, independent study skills, map-reading skills, and the interpretation of tables, graphs, charts, pictures, diagrams, and cartoons.

1. The teacher's manual that accompanies social studies textbooks. Individual activities for pupils, questions to guide the organization of information, test items, vocabulary-building techniques, and other activities that are based on the text are provided. In addition, helpful suggestions for teachers to use in meeting the needs of more able, average, and less able children are usually included.
2. End-of-chapter activities in children's textbooks. Summarizing activities, map-making activities, vocabulary extension activities, study skill suggestions, and other suggested activities are directly related to the text and are worded in children's language.
3. Children's weekly news periodicals for all grades. Practice materials and tests are provided on reading and study skills, interpreting graphs, tables, diagrams, pictures, and cartoons, and map-reading concepts and skills. Editions on different readings levels are available. (See Chapter 8 for a complete list.)

4. Supplementary practice materials on different skills and concepts.
   a. Booklets on study and map skills from publishers of children's periodicals—for example, Weekly Reader, Education Center, 1250 Fairwood Ave., Columbus, Ohio 43206, and Scholastic Magazines, 50 West 40th St., New York, N.Y. 10018.
   b. SRA Basic Skills Series, Science Research Associates, 259 East Erie St., Chicago, Ill., 60611. Multilevel kits on (1) Graph and Picture Study Skills, (2) Organizing and Reporting Skills, (3) Map and Globe Skills.
   c. *Teacher* and *Instructor*, magazines for teachers. A variety of practice materials are included on different skills; suggestions are given for all grades in the elementary school.
5. Social studies units of instruction. Resource units contain many specific examples of ways in which basic skills may be developed as an inherent part of learning activities.
6. Social studies workbooks that accompany children's textbooks. Some teachers select practice materials from workbooks for different grades, cut them apart, mount them on tagboard, use them for individualized practice, have children write the responses on sheets of paper, and thus use them over and over again.

DEVELOPING BASIC SKILLS

Building Vocabulary

To read social studies materials, children must be able to identify and grasp the meaning of the words that are used, and use the meaning to interpret what is written. Each unit of instruction calls for the development of new terms and concepts, and the teacher must identify the specific terms and concepts that should be developed and make plans for developing them at appropriate times as the unit progresses.

Identifying concepts. There are a number of procedures for finding terms and concepts to be developed in each unit. (1) Check the word lists in units. New terms are often listed in the introductory section or in different sections of the unit in which they will be used. (2) Check the vocabulary list in the back of the teacher's edition of textbooks for primary grades. Many basic textbooks list the pages on which new terms are introduced. (3) Check the teacher's manual that accompanies textbooks. Specific terms to be taught before the reading of different chapters are presented along with techniques to use to develop them. (4) Skim new materials to note words that have not been used in class. By skimming materials ahead of time, a teacher can note new terms and concepts and plan to develop them. (5) Keep a list of words that are difficult for children. As different materials are used, note difficult terms and have children do the same.

Vocabulary-building techniques. In social studies, the teacher utilizes the full range of vocabulary-building techniques. Those developed in the reading program are supplemented by techniques and procedures suggested in units and in teacher's manuals. Some of the most helpful are given below.

Independent decoding or word-recognition skills developed in the reading program can be used. Context clues are perhaps the most helpful aids to word recognition in social studies because the meaning of many terms is determined by their use. For example, the specific meaning of such terms as *bank, range, lock, set, run,* and *strike,* and the basic meaning of such terms as *humid, prevailing, swampland, fertile, soil robber, growing season, yield,* and *crop rotation* are developed in context in newer textbooks.

Structural analysis is helpful in unlocking the meaning of words made up of common roots, prefixes, suffixes, and inflectional endings. Examples are *play, playmate, player, replay, playground; way, byway, expressway, highway, superhighway; large, larger, largest; impossible, improbable, impolite; disarm, disband, disclose, displace, disqualify, dissolve; colony, colonial, colonist, colonization, precolonial;* and *depend, dependent, independent, dependence, interdependence.* Phonetic analysis may be used to derive the pronunciation of certain common terms such as *run, sun, fun, hat, hut, home, parade, provide, travel,* and *transportation,* but it should not be used when such names as *Belem, Chile,* and *Spokane* are encountered. Fortunately, many textbooks contain pronunciation guides and glossaries that show how to pronounce such names.

Picture clues are another helpful device. Social studies materials contain pictures, sketches, maps, and drawings that illustrate a variety of terms and concepts. Children's attention should be directed to them through questions and comments so that they develop the habit of using picture clues to unlock the meaning of words. The many illustrations in dictionaries and encyclopedias should also be used to clarify word meanings.

Certain concepts can be developed through firsthand experiences—study trips, demonstrations, construction, processing of materials, and dramatic play. For example, a study trip to a dairy farm can be used to clarify such terms as *silo, corral, milking parlor, stanchion,* and *milking machine.* The processing of wool can be used to develop the meanings of *washing, carding, spinning,* and *weaving.* Related audiovisual materials—films, filmstrips, slides, and pictures—may be used to enrich concepts presented in reading materials. For example, *broad grassy plains, towering redwoods, tundra, steppes, jungle, plateau,* and *glacier* may be visualized as films and other pictorial materials are shown.

Group discussion may be used to define terms, give explanations, correct misconceptions, list difficult words, consider descriptive phrases, point out changes in word meanings, use roots to build new terms, and consider specific questions raised by children. Directed listening, such as oral reading and story-telling by the teacher, may be used to introduce or enrich selected terms and concepts. Materials on an advanced reading level may be used with special explanation of selected words and phrases.

Vocabulary aids—card files of new words, word lists kept in notebooks, picture dictionaries made by the class, scrapbooks arranged in alphabetical order, illustrated cards classified under such headings as transportation, communication, housing, and so forth, and pictures collected to illustrate terms and concepts—may be used in connection with each unit of instruction. Glossaries and dictionaries are two of the most valuable aids in social studies. Each child should develop skill in using them to select the meaning that fits the context in which a word is used.

Because of the heavy vocabulary load in social studies, considerable attention must be given to the direct study of terms and concepts. Practice materials, charts, phrase cards, workbook exercises, synonyms and antonyms, classification of related terms, word parts, use of new words in oral and written expression, and vocabulary testing are frequently used word study materials and activities. There is no substitute, however, for wide reading of supplementary materials in connection with each unit. Concepts are deepened and broadened, new terms are learned in context, independent word-recognition skills are put to use, and familiar terms are encountered in new and novel situations.

Reading to Interpret Meaning

Comprehension and interpretation of the author's intended meaning call for a variety of basic reading skills *plus* an understanding of special concepts, aids to reading, and patterns of organization used in social studies materials.

Preparation for reading a selection. The first step is to be sure that the group is ready for the selection, whether it is a pamphlet, section of a chapter, story, or some other material. When literary or descriptive materials are used, children should be sensitized to the mood or setting through teacher-guided recall of related experiences, viewing of a related film, discussion of pictures, or similar activities. Specific questions can focus children's attention on aspects of their own experiences that are related to the selection; both similarities and differences may be brought out. New terms and background concepts to be encountered in the reading material should be presented so that they will be interpreted meaningfully. Whenever possible, the reading selection should be related to questions under study. These questions may be supplemented by others that fit the selection so that each child has a clear purpose for reading.

Using clues to meaning. Through direct instruction and discussion of examples in social studies materials, students should be taught to use a variety of clues to meaning. Shifts in word meaning and definition of terms may be determined in context and by use of pictures and drawings as students encounter *bank* used in different ways, *capital* and *capitol,* pictures of *steppes,* and the like. Students should be on the lookout for com-

How can reading materials be used to develop understanding of the contributions of ethnic groups? What specific objectives might be achieved? (Richmond, California)

parisons with things familiar to them in such statements as "The *canal* was like a huge *ditch*." Common prefixes, roots, and suffixes encountered in social studies should be taught so that students can unlock such terms as *nondiscrimination, irresponsible, hemisphere, antipollution,* and *transportable*. Awareness of synonyms and antonyms helps to clarify the meaning of a term like *govern,* which is used synonymously with command, manage, and rule, or *justice,* which has such antonyms as favoritism, partiality, and injustice.

Using pictorial, graphic, and other aids. The many headings, pictures, graphs, charts, and other graphic devices used in social studies materials have a definite contribution to make to the comprehension and interpretation of the text. The tendency of some children to skip over them can only lead to problems and difficulties in getting a clear understanding of the ideas presented. A helpful practice is to direct attention to headings and graphic aids and to raise questions about them during discussion.

Understanding the organization. The organization of reading materials in social studies should be explored carefully as selected materials are used. With children in the middle and upper grades, for example, the group should discuss the major headings, subheadings, and minor headings in a text, giving attention to ways they can be used by the class, the way the ideas are arranged, why the material has been organized in this particular way, and the relationship of headings to topics and problems in the unit.

If clear objectives for reading are developed, children may be guided to discover that topical headings are especially helpful in locating key ideas and information related to stated purposes. Furthermore, the problem of reorganizing the material to meet various needs becomes easier if objectives are clear and meaningful to the class. Other items related to organization of materials are format; use of pictures, charts, and diagrams; chronological presentation; logical development of topics; cross references, references to maps and charts on distant pages; sequence of topics; and use of italics. These should be considered in connection with the specific materials a group is using, with attention to their helpfulness in locating key ideas, explaining selected sections, and summarizing basic data. See Chart 12–4 for some suggestions.

Chart 12–4
How Is It Organized?

Is the organization explained in the first paragraphs?
Do the headings give clues to the organization?
Are steps given for a sequence of activities?
Is the order of major events given?
Is a time line or a series of pictures included to show the order?
Do other clues reveal the way ideas are organized?

Skimming and Scanning

Skimming is used in the social studies program to preview and select material, get an overview, review material, decide if material is pertinent, get a general idea of content, find main ideas, and select material for detailed study. Scanning is used to check titles of references on a bookshelf; find a chapter title in a table of contents; find a topic in an index; answer a specific question; find a date, name, or a number; find a definition; check the location of a place; find a reference; or find a particular map, chart, table, or diagram. Their use can be improved by guiding children to use chapter titles, headings, subheadings, introductory paragraphs, topical sentences, and captions as clues to the location of particular items in reading materials. Sometimes the needed information may be on a map, diagram, chart; in a table; or in pictures, illustrations, and sketches. Points to emphasize with students are included in Charts 12–5 and 12–6.

Reading to Form Sensory Impressions

Much reading in social studies involves forming sensory impressions as various terms, phrases, and sentences are encountered: "The swirling snowflakes covered the city with a soft blanket"; "They listened to the tooting of the boats in the harbor." Descriptive terms, phrases, sentences,

Chart 12–5
Skimming

Does the title tell what is and what is not in it?
Do headings and subheadings give clues to main points?
Do first and last paragraphs contain essential ideas?
Do questions raised at the beginning reveal main points?
Do beginning sentences in each paragraph reveal main points?

Chart 12–6
Scanning

What specific question do you wish to answer?
What are you trying to find? a date? fact? name? number?
Do titles of chapters give clues to its location?
Do headings and subheadings give clues?
Does the table of contents or index give clues?

and paragraphs are used to create a host of impressions and feelings—for example, *the room cluttered with paper, the noisy traffic, the color of the leaves in autumn, the cold barren landscape, the grassy plains, the rolling hills, the roaring river, the steaming jungle, the dense tropical foliage, the jagged shoreline, the gay fiesta, the busy vendors at the bazaar*. The child who does not form accurate sensory impressions fails to grasp the meaning or appreciate the full flavor of the author's ideas.

Some procedures, activities, and resources that may be used to help a child form clear sensory impressions follow.

1. Raising questions such as these: Have you ever seen a roaring river? What was it like? Where was it? How large was the river? Was it like the one we are reading about?
2. Discussing the feelings, images, sounds, and other impressions stimulated by the text
3. Recalling the children's past experiences and comparing them with those in the text
4. Comparing words or phrases such as *a gushing spring* and *a trickling spring, a windswept plateau* and *a tree-covered mesa, the grassy plains* and *the golden wheat fields*
5. Drawing pictures and making murals to illustrate descriptions
6. Comparing descriptions of mountains, rivers, historical events, and other items as presented in different materials
7. Comparing children's descriptions of various items with descriptions of the same items as given in textbooks, films, and other materials
8. Using films, pictures, slides, filmstrips, and other visual materials to illustrate verbal descriptions given in the text
9. Discussing the feelings evoked by statements such as "The cunning Indian chief sent the fiercest braves to fight the poor settlers." "The wise Indian chief knew that his brave warriors

could not withstand the hordes of gold-seekers." "The brave Indian chief sent his best warriors to stop the Spanish conquerors."

10. Using the strategies presented in Chapter 7 to identify feelings and values.

Reading to Discover Relationships Specific attention to the discovery and understanding of relationships enhances the development of basic concepts and understandings and at the same time contributes to growth in reading ability. For example, analogous relationships may be found in materials that highlight similarities in activities such as steps in baking bread at home and in a bakery, modes of travel used by early settlers and Indians, and means of transporting goods in different countries. Guiding questions are "How are they alike?" "What similarities can you find?" "What is common in both activities?"

Quantitative relationships in social studies materials include relative time and distance to various places, size and population of states and nations, population density, and value of resources and products. Guiding questions are "Which is larger?" "How do they compare in size?" "Which resource is most valuable?" "How long does it take by train? by airplane?" "Which area is most densely populated?" Questions to use to guide the discovery of cause and effect, sequential, part-whole, and place relationships are presented in Charts 12–7 through 12–10.

Skills for Learning How to Learn One promising current practice is to teach students reading skills that contribute to knowledge of how to learn. These skills are summarized in Charts 12–11 to 12–17. Notice that Chart 12–11, Reading on Our Own, includes basic points that are elaborated in the subsequent charts. Ef-

Chart 12–7
Can You Find Causes and Effects?

What caused them to do what they did?
What were the effects of their action?
Why did that happen? What reasons can you find or infer?
What were the effects of the invention discussed in the story?
Were there several causes and effects related to that event?
Why are there usually several causes of human behavior? Several effects?

Chart 12–8
What Is the Sequence?

In what order did the events occur? How are they related?
What are the main steps in making ______? (bread, steel)
What were the main periods in the growth of our ______? (community, state)
What steps are taken to ______? (build a cabin, pass a bill in the legislature)
Why was that event called a turning point?
What happened before? after?

Chart 12–9

Finding Part-Whole Relationships

What is needed for a complete _____?
(dairy farm, transit system)
How do different parts of _____ depend on each other? (community, state)
How are the main regions of our _____ interrelated? (state, country)
Why is that part of _____ important to all of us? (our state, country)
How do the parts work together?

Chart 12–10

How Are Places Related?

Why was the school located there?
Why are so many large cities near waterways?
Why did _____ develop in that region? (farming, industry)
Where is it in relation to _____? (our community, New York)
How are elevation and distance from the equator related to climate?

fective study habits for students are in Chart 12–12, Concentrating as You Read. Chart 12–13, Finding Word Meaning, includes techniques that are used extensively in social studies. Finding Purposes for Reading, Chart 12–14, includes points each student should master to improve independent reading skill. Chart 12–15, Speed of Reading, is designed to guide students to discover when they should vary reading speed in terms of purpose and type of material. Reviewing What You Have Read (Chart 12–16) suggests ways to clinch key ideas and to engage in self-evaluation after completing a selection; Using Reading Aids in Books (Chart 12–17) contains points on how to extend meaning by using headings, graphs, and other aids.

Critical, Creative, and Appreciative Reading

When a reader goes beyond word identification, casual reading, and reading to get the author's intended meaning, he or she enters what may be referred to as creative reading—reading for implied or inferred meanings, reading for appreciative reactions, and reading for critical evaluations. The three overlapping types of reading may be put to extensive use in the social studies program. For example, as children read about the hot, moist summer climate of Iowa, they may make inferences about the kind of crops that will grow there. Or, as children read about people in other lands and identify with them, they may respond with new feelings to their hopes, aspirations, and problems. Or, as children distinguish between fact and opinion, relevant and irrelevant information, and right and wrong, they use standards to evaluate statements in reading materials. Thus, each of the three types of reading is a step beyond literal interpretation of the material.

The following illustrations of critical reading skills suggest activities to employ in social studies to develop critical reading abilities:

Making inferences, judgments, and decisions in the light of facts, ideas, and values

Chart 12–11
Reading on Our Own

Concentrate on what you are reading.
Have a clear purpose or specific questions in mind.
Fit your speed of reading to your purpose and the material.
Get ideas from headings, pictures, maps, charts, tables, and graphs.
Figure out the meaning of each word.
Review the points related to your purpose or questions.

Chart 12–12
Concentrating as You Read

Focus your thinking on what you are reading.
Have note-taking and other needed materials ready for use.
Keep the purpose or question in mind and search for related ideas.
Use headings for clues as to what is coming next.
Do not let noise or activity of others distract you.

Chart 12–13
Finding Word Meaning

Look for:
- Definitions
- Context clues
- Picture clues

Use:
- The word box
- The glossary
- The dictionary

Ask:
- When you have tried but cannot find the meaning

Chart 12–14
Finding Purposes for Reading

Does the title suggest a purpose?
Do main headings suggest questions to be answered?
Do you have questions of your own?
Are questions to guide reading given in the first part of the selection you are reading?
Can questions listed during group discussions be answered?
Can you find purposes by skimming the material?

Chart 12–15
Speed of Reading

How does speed vary when reading:
- Main ideas?
- Specific details?
- Directions?
- Familiar ideas?
- Graphs? tables?
- Flow charts?
- Definitions?
- Time lines?
- Maps? diagrams?
- Stories

Chart 12–16
Reviewing What You Have Read

Can you recall ideas related to your purpose for reading?
Can you recall ideas related to headings in the chapter?
Can you answer questions at the end of the chapter?
Can you answer questions listed during group discussion?
Can you think of questions about main ideas to ask others?

Chart 12–17
Using Reading Aids in Books

Do you check headings to get an overview?
Do you use pictures to clarify words and ideas in the text?
Do you get the main ideas from graphs and tables?
Do you follow the steps in charts and diagrams?
Do you use the contents and the index to locate material?

Evaluating the author's purpose, organization of ideas, clarity of expression, appropriateness of ideas, relevance of information, relation of content to generalizations

Describing relationships, comparisons, contrasts, cause and effect, sequence of ideas, and order and structure of content

Classifying terms, facts, ideas, concepts, principles, generalizations, motives, moods, feelings, dates, places, events, people, objects, products, resources, surface features, cities, states, regions, countries

Distinguishing fact and fancy, fact and opinion, relevant and irrelevant, implied and stated ideas, evidence and hearsay, warranted and unwarranted assertions

Predicting or anticipating outcomes, next steps, order of events, future trends

Selecting main ideas and related details to make generalizations, proving statements, preparing directions, constructing objects, processing materials, making charts, preparing reports, planning programs, making maps

Reorganizing information in outlines, summaries, reports, charts, graphs, diagrams, tables, maps, murals, drawings

Forming conclusions, sensory impressions, associations, concepts, generalizations, reasoned opinions

Identifying elements of style, issues, problems, differences of opinion, purpose of the author, character traits, values, cultural factors

Interpreting figurative and idiomatic expressions, mood, tone, elements of style, humor, motives, emotional reactions

Judging ideas and outcomes in terms of author's purpose, standards, evidence, reasonableness of arguments, relevance of facts

Valuing contributions of members of the family, community workers, current leaders, famous men and women, resources provided by nature, use of resources in improving ways of living, conservation of resources, creative ways of meeting problems, factors that contribute to change, growth of democracy, increasing interdependence

Critical evaluation. Critical evaluation of ideas obtained through reading is essential. Controversial issues, prejudices, biases, opinion vs. fact, varied interpretations, irrelevant ideas, generalizations, inaccuracies, mood and interest of the author, usefulness of ideas, and the like should be noted and discussed thoroughly by the group. Ideas should be checked against other references and sources of data as needs arise. Misconceptions and biases on the part of the reader should also be considered. In addition, children should be helped to detect the difference between information and fiction.

In evaluating ideas obtained through reading, several key questions may be considered by the group. The choice of questions for consideration will depend on their appropriateness and on the maturity of the class with which they will be used. The following are illustrative: Is the writer's purpose clear? Are facts presented clearly and differentiated from opinion? What type of proof is given? Does the author appeal to emotion? Are generalizations supported by ample evidence? Do the ideas square with other sources of information? How are figures of speech used? analogies? similes? metaphors? Are differing views presented on controversial issues? Are cause and effect relationships clear? Are conclusions clearly established? Charts 12–18 and 12–19 illustrate points to stress in the critical evaluation of reading materials. Such charts also can be used in situations other than reading, and thus have double value because they are clearly related to the problem-solving process.

Chart 12–18
Critical Readers

Check the facts
Compare ideas
Raise questions
Find out about the author
Notice general statements
Look for proof
Check conclusions

Chart 12–19
Critical Thinkers

State problems
Find facts
Filter facts
Organize facts
Base conclusions on facts
Act on conclusions
Change conclusions on basis of new facts

QUESTIONS, ACTIVITIES, EVALUATION

1. Examine a textbook and make notes on how you might use it in a unit. Examine the table of contents and index. How might you provide instruction on using them?
2. Visit a library and examine a set of encyclopedias and other reference materials. Make notes on how you might use them in a unit. What instruction might you provide to develop the skills involved in using them effectively?
3. Make a sketch of a chart you might use in a unit. Indicate what type it is and how it would be used.
4. Make a list of poems, stories, and other literary selections for use in a unit. Note different ways in which they can be shared and enjoyed by the group.
5. Visit a class and observe children during a reading period. Note techniques the teacher uses to develop vocabulary, set purposes,

and improve reading skills. Which of the skills mentioned in this chapter are given attention? Note ways to use and improve reading skills in a unit of your choice.

6. How might you provide for creative and critical reading in a unit? Indicate actual materials that might be used and the procedures you would employ.

REFERENCES

ARNSDORF, VAL, "Selecting and Using Collateral Materials in Social Studies," *Reading Teacher,* 20 (April 1967), 621–25. Concrete suggestion on supplementary materials.

BURRON, ARNOLD, and AMOS L. CLAYBAUGH, *Using Reading to Teach Subject Matter.* Columbus, O.: Merrill, 1974. Techniques for improving reading in content subjects.

DALLMAN, MARTHA, ROGER L. ROUCH, LYNETTE Y. C. CHANG, JOHN J. DEBOER, *The Teaching of Reading* (4th ed.). New York: Holt, Rinehart, and Winston, 1974. Practical techniques for use in improving reading skills.

KARLIN, ROBERT, *Teaching Elementary Reading* (2nd ed.). New York: Harcourt, Brace, Jovanovich, 1975. Chapters on content fields and literature.

MCCULLOUGH, CONSTANCE, and MILES A. TINKER, *Teaching Elementary Reading* (4th ed.). Englewood Cliffs, N.J.: Prentice-Hall, 1975. Chapters on study skills and content fields.

MCKEE, PAUL, *Reading: A Program of Instruction for the Elementary School.* Boston: Houghton-Mifflin, 1966. Illustrative lessons on critical reading and other skills; list of guides to children's books.

PRESTON, RALPH C., and WAYNE L. HERMAN, JR., *Teaching Social Studies in the Elementary School.* New York: Holt, Rinehart, and Winston, 1974. Chapter on reading in social studies.

ROBINSON, ALAN H., *Teaching Reading and Study Strategies: The Content Areas.* Boston: Allyn and Bacon, 1975. Chapters on readiness, vocabulary, and social studies.

RUDDELL, ROBERT B., *Reading-Language Instruction: Innovative Practices.* Englewood Cliffs, N.J.: Prentice-Hall, 1974. Chapter on reading in content areas.

SPACHE, GEORGE D., *Good Reading for Poor Readers.* Champaign, Ill.: Garrard, 1974. Materials on easy reading levels.

13

Focusing Questions

How are community resources and audiovisual materials used in the social studies program?

What guidelines should be followed in using daily experiences, study trips, and resource visitors?

How can realia, exhibits, dioramas, panoramas, and demonstrations be used to improve learning?

What guidelines are helpful in using films, TV and radio programs, and recordings?

What guidelines are recommended for the use of pictures, projected materials, and bulletin, flannel, and magnetic boards?

What techniques should be used to improve learning from posters, cartoons, time lines, tables, and the chalkboard?

Using Community Resources, Audiovisual, & Graphic Materials

Community resources, audiovisual materials, and graphic materials are essential to a well-rounded program that includes a variety of data sources. They contribute directly to concept development, processes of thinking, skills, clarification of values, and other objectives. These instructional media are especially helpful in another way; they contribute to the development of visual literacy. Visual literacy includes such skills as identifying and naming what is seen on field trips, in pictures, and in other visual resources, as well as distinguishing likenesses and differences, comparing and contrasting items, detecting relationships between items, and inferring feelings. As students develop competence in visual literacy, they are able to evaluate what is presented and the effectiveness of the mode of presentation.

IDENTIFYING COMMUNITY RESOURCES

The community is a laboratory for firsthand inquiry into human activities. Geographic, historical, economic, and other concepts can be developed in a realistic setting. Changing conditions and the factors that produce them can be studied as changes take place. Holidays, special events, and commemorations can be experienced with others. Field trips, interviews of experts, local publications, and historical sites can be used to enrich instruction. Processes of interaction can be studied directly as students observe various groups and participate in them. Indeed, if we are to have "schools without walls," extensive and critical use must be made of community resources. Teachers should first make a brief survey in order to become well acquainted with the nature and history of the community. The following model is suggestive of items to include in a survey; the items are also useful in depth studies of our community and other communities:

Population	Landmarks	Health services
History	Transportation	Welfare services
Geography	Communication	The arts
Government	Conservation	Safety conditions
Resources	Education	Pollution problems
Industry	Religions	Special problems
Business	Ethnic groups	The future

An effective strategy is to involve students in the community survey if depth study of the community is included at their grade level. Observation skills may be sharpened as students check safety hazards, type and location of residences, housing conditions, the business and industrial sections, and parks and playgrounds. Interviewing techniques can be improved as they talk with old-timers, business people, school administrators, public officials, and other community workers. Skill in content analysis can be developed as they examine pictures, letters, newspapers, chamber of commerce reports, and other local documents.

One of the most useful parts of the community survey is the identification of resources that can be used to further children's learning. Some school systems provide reports that include data on the most useful resources, such as study trips, resource visitors, persons to interview, TV and radio programs, service projects, field studies, and sources of materials.

Once gathered, information and materials should be organized so as to promote classroom use. This may be done by: (1) making a handbook of community materials and resources, (2) incorporating the material and selected references into units, (3) including materials and references in the courses of study, (4) preparing a special series of community life bulletins, (5) developing a reference volume on community information for school use, and (6) preparing kits containing materials for use in the classroom. In general, the material will be used most effectively if it is organized in a manner that clearly indicates its use; for example, in units, in courses of study, or in teaching kits.

USING COMMUNITY RESOURCES

To achieve greatest efficiency, the teacher should specifically consider each type of resource and the problems incident to its use. In this section, daily ex-

Daily Experiences

periences, study trips, resource persons, and interviewing are considered. The everyday experiences of children in the community constitute one of the teacher's most valuable resources. As children see buildings under construction, watch changes in the season, see workers in action, observe holidays and celebrations, enjoy radio and television, hear and discuss current events, buy articles in stores, use the transportation system, attend churches, and engage in a host of other activities, they discover many things and are stimulated to raise questions. Alert teachers capitalize on these experiences and use them in the social studies program.

Study Trips

Many different types of study trips are taken in dynamic social studies programs. They may be completed in a class period, a full day, or a period of several days. At times they may be taken over the weekend, with the children's parents coming along. The following list suggests some of the many opportunities for the use of study trips in social studies.

Aquarium	Farms	Petroleum company
Airport	Firehouse	Police station
Art gallery	Forest service	Post office
Bakery	Greenhouse	Radio station
Bank	Historic homes	Railroad station
Botanical Garden	Housing construction	River
Bottling works	Lake	Road construction
Cannery	Library	Sawmill
City Hall	Lumbermill	Shipyard
Construction sites	Mission	Stores
Courtroom	Museum	Telephone exchange
Dairy	Newspaper	Television station
Docks	Observatory	Weather station
Factories	Park	Zoo

Some of the most valuable study trips are informal walks that can be taken in the immediate neighborhood. Examples include short walks to see a house being built, changes in the season, operation of a ditch-digging machine, a special garden, soil erosion, a collection of pictures and objects, or a modern bakery. Children may take short walking trips to gather specimens, see an old building, study architectural changes in the neighborhood, visit an expert to get answers to questions, study safety problems, and the like. Walking trips such as these are informal and easy to plan, require a minimum of organization, save time, and make children more critical observers of their immediate environment.

Planning Study Trips. The one great difference between a study trip and just going somewhere is that educational objectives exist for the study trip. Careful planning is essential in order to achieve learnings of greatest value to the children (see Checklist 13–1).

Group planning is one of the most effective techniques to use. Attention should be given to questions to be raised, ways to record information, and procedures to follow during the visit. Health and safety precautions should be given thorough consideration. Each child should know what to do in case of an emergency on the bus or at the place to be visited.

Standards of courtesy and protection of property should be discussed. Each child has a responsibility to be courteous to the bus driver, people at the place being visited, and the guide. Respect for property both on the bus and at the location of the visit should be kept in mind. Any parents who accompany the group on the trip should be given specific instructions regarding ways they can help. If, for example, they are responsible for a group of eight children, they should learn the names of the children in their group and carry out specific directions regarding standards and regulations that have been set up. The parents should be introduced to the children for whom they are responsible, and the children should understand their role on the trip. A teacher's role at the place of the visit is that of general supervisor. Explanations should be made as needed; questions should be raised when something is not clear to the group; difficult terms should be explained; behavior problems should be met as they arise; and contact should be kept with all children.

It is sound procedure to summarize specific plans on charts, on the chalkboard, or on duplicated sheets of paper so that important points are

What can we learn from recordings? What can we learn from old-timers who live in the area? What other ways to gather data can we use on field trips? (Sacramento and Colma, California)

Checklist 13–1

GUIDE FOR THE PLANNING OF STUDY TRIPS

First Considerations

______ Have adequate backgrounds, ideas, and objectives been developed?
______ Are related materials—films, books, pictures—available?
______ Are there profitable follow-up activities?
______ Will it strengthen the school-community relations?
______ Other: ______________________

Preliminary Arrangements

______ Has administrative approval been given?
______ Has the approval of parents been secured?
______ Are eating and toilet arrangements satisfactory?
______ Has the time schedule been prepared?
______ Has the guide been advised on problems, needs, and maturity of the group?
______ Have travel arrangements and expenses been arranged?
______ Are assistants needed to help supervise the group?
______ Has a list been made of the names, telephone numbers, and addresses of those children who are going?
______ Other: ______________________

Group Planning

______ Are questions prepared and understood?
______ Are recording procedures and assignments clear?
______ Have behavior standards been developed?
______ Have safety precautions been considered?
______ Have the time schedule, travel arrangements, and expenses been clarified?
______ Have significant side interests been noted?
______ Has attention been given to appropriateness of dress?
______ Are monitorial assignments clear?
______ Other: ______________________

Follow-up Plans

______ Do next experiences contribute to objectives?
______ What findings are to be reported?
______ What summaries and records should be made?
______ Is attention given to the development of charts, maps, diagrams, displays, murals, models, scrapbooks, construction, dramatic activities, and floor layouts?
______ Are procedures in mind to discover and clarify misconceptions?
______ Are letters of appreciation and samples of follow-up work to be sent?
______ How is learning to be evaluated?
______ Other: ______________________

clear to each member of the group. Charts 13–1 and 13–2 show the planning done by a first-grade group that took a short walk to the food section of a supermarket. After their walk to the store, the children engaged in dramatic play and developed the needs for materials shown in Chart 13–3, thus putting to use the information gained from the study trip.

An advanced type of planning for a study trip to an airport is illustrated in Chart 13–4, which was developed by a sixth-grade group. The class was divided into four committees, each responsible for five questions.

Chart 13–1
Let's Find Out

1. Where are vegetables kept?
2. How is meat kept fresh?
3. What is in the storeroom?
4. Who keeps the shelves full?

Chart 13–2
Our Walk to the Store

1. Stay together.
2. Watch where you walk.
3. Ask questions in turn.
4. Listen to the answers.

Chart 13–3
We Need for Our Play

A grocery store	Counters
Tables	Delivery trucks
Cash register	Shopping bags
Vegetable stand	Refrigerator

Resource Visitors

Community studies are enriched when firefighters, police, journalists, and other workers meet with the class to discuss problems and questions that have arisen. In such units as living in South America or Japan, much help can be gained from individuals who are natives or who have made visits there. Questions that arise in units on industrial America, aviation, transportation, lumbering, and marketing may be answered by individuals who are well acquainted with them. The showing of realia, pictures, and slides along with the discussion enhances the contributions of resource visitors.

A sound procedure is to organize a file of resource persons who can make valuable contributions to the social studies program. A simple card system can be used by noting the following information on 3x5 index cards:

Contribution ______________________________
Name ____________________ Telephone __________
Hours available ____________________________

At the airport
we can see
Hangars Airplanes
Runways Beacon lights
Windsocks
Office Building
A control tower

What concepts and main idea might be developed as a result of a study trip to the airport? (San Bernardino, California)

Will come to school? ______________________________
Children may visit at home or office? ________________
Comments ______________________________________
____

Who is available of course depends on the kind of community, but one group of teachers in a social studies workshop compiled the following list of resource visitors:

Airport employees	Foreign students	Old-time residents
Authors	Forest rangers	Police
Business people	Gardeners	School administrators
City officials	House builders	Ship workers
Consuls of foreign nations	Industrial workers	Social workers
	Lawyers	Soil conservationists
Dairy workers	Librarians	Store clerks
Dentists	Merchants	Traffic safety specialists
Doctors	Ministers	
Farmers	Musicians	Travelers
Fellow teachers	Newspaper workers	Urban planners
Firefighters		Utilities workers

Chart 13–4

Questions We Want to Answer

Committee 1

1. How many passengers does a 747 carry? an L–1011? a DC–10?
2. What airlines use the airport?
3. How many planes come into the airport each day?
4. How high off the ground is the cockpit where the pilots sit?
5. How long are the runways?

Committee 2

6. How many runways are there?
7. At what altitude does a westbound plane travel? eastbound? northbound? southbound?
8. What kinds of cargo are the planes carrying?
9. From where do the planes come?
10. How many men work in the control tower?

Committee 3

11. What do members of the flight crew do?
12. What is a flight log? How is it made up?
13. How many instruments does the plane have on the control board?
14. What do these instruments tell the pilot?
15. How many pounds of baggage is one passenger allowed?

Committee 4

16. Where does the ground crew put the fuel in the airplane?
17. What are runways made of? How long are they?
18. How long does it take a pilot to get his license?
19. What does one have to study in order to become a pilot?
20. Where is the baggage stored? How cold does it get?

What resource visitors in your community can share authentic costumes or other materials and discuss their uses? (Cheltenham Township Schools, Pennsylvania)

Interviewing Resource Persons. An interview is a desirable procedure to use when a resource person cannot come to school, essential materials must be kept on the job, or when seeing the person in a working situation is more beneficial. Interviews may be conducted by an individual pupil or by a small group. The same kind of planning as that for the use of resource visitors is needed. In addition, attention must be given to good interviewing techniques. Charts 13–5 to 13–13 are illustrative of questions and topics to include in interviews during study trips or with resource persons. See the end-of-chapter reference by Wurman for other examples. The points in Chart 13–14 illustrate the standards that can be set up through group planning.

USING AUDIOVISUAL MATERIALS: REALIA

The term *realia* means real things or artifacts. Here it refers to objects, models, specimens, and items in museums, exhibits, dioramas, and panoramas. Specific materials used in the social studies program that may be classified as

Chart 13–5
The Bakery

How do production workers load and unload machines?
How is dough mixed? What makes the dough rise?
How do workers divide the dough?
How is the bread kneaded? Why is it kneaded?
How is bread moved to ovens? How hot are the ovens?
How is the bread wrapped and sliced?

Chart 13–6
City Hall

What does each of these departments do?

Streets	Transportation
Water	Public Affairs
Planning	Redevelopment
Records	Personnel
Finance	Public Health
Police	Recreation
Fire	Procurement
Licenses	Public Welfare

Chart 13–7
City Planning

Ask about each of these:
Planning Commission
Technical staff
Aerial photographs
Maps of the future
Census predictions
Short- and long-range plans
Metropolitan planning
Mass transit planning

Chart 13–8
The Courtroom

What is the role of each of these?

Judge
Jury, Prosecutor
Defense attorney
Witness
Defendant
Recorder clerk

What rules are followed:

To show the judge respect?
To make an objection?
To cross-examine witnesses?
To refuse to answer questions?
To be found in contempt?
To declare a mistrial?

Chart 13–9
The Library

What is the role of these workers?

Administrators
Clerks
Accountants
Catalogers
Bindery repair artists

What machines are used?

Photographic book charging
Microfilm
Pneumatic tubes
Conveyors
Binders
Computers

What special services are there for the blind?

Chart 13–10
The Newspaper

What is the role of these workers?

Editor
Reporter
Writer
Photographer
Artist
Accountant
Secretary

What equipment is used?

Teletype
Linotype
Presses
Photographic Delivery
Recycling

Why is the morgue needed?
What is the editorial policy?

Chart 13–11
Social Workers

What is the role of these social workers?

- Family service
- Child welfare
- School
- Psychiatric
- Medical
- Public assistance
- Group
- Correctional
- Rehabilitation
- Community organization
- Probation and Parole
- Others

What kind of education is required?

Chart 13–12
Television Station

What is the role of these workers?

- Producer
- Show director
- Script director
- Announcer
- Technical director
- Writer
- Camera person
- Prop people
- Boom person
- Stage manager
- Engineers
- Clerk
- Others

How are network programs handled?

Chart 13–13
Public Health Department

What services are provided?
What is the role of various workers?
How are health records kept?
How are inspections made?
How are air and water checked?
What hospitals are run by the city?

Chart 13–14
How To Interview

Introduce yourself.
State questions clearly.
Listen attentively.
Let the other person talk.
Ask questions on special points.
Take notes on hard points.
Do not waste time.
Express thanks when finished.

realia include jewelry, ornaments, money, clothing, authentically dressed dolls, utensils, tools, dishes, tableware, products, manuscripts, documents, facsimiles, seals, letters, timepieces, communications devices, models of transportation equipment, musical instruments, art objects, sample foods, models of shelter, and weapons.

Children cannot go back in time and space to early times and to the many other eras and places considered in social studies, but they can have experiences with real things, or replicas of them, related to the unit. For example, in a study of colonial living, one group made extensive use of candle molds, muskets, powder horns, cooking utensils, tableware, a

How can realia such as these be used to develop concepts and main ideas? What appreciations of changes in ways of living might be developed? (Albany, California)

spinning wheel, and clothing of the period. In a study of Mexico, another group ate tortillas, frijoles, chili, and enchiladas. In addition, they had access to sombreros, serapes, rebozos, huaraches, and models of furniture and utensils. In a study of communication, one class used a simple crystal radio set, a telegraph key, drums, hollow logs, whistle, bone horn, bells, telephone, and flag signals. In using realia and models, increased learning is possible if the following guidelines are observed:

1. Use realia to initiate a unit, to enrich concepts encountered in the unit, and to share experiences during concluding activities.
2. Allow children to handle them and see how they work. If they are fragile, have their use demonstrated to the class.
3. Be alert to children's questions and comments as they handle them; they may be vital clues to interests and misconceptions.
4. Encourage their use in dramatic activities and in construction.
5. Relate their use to pictures, reading materials, films, and experiences children have had on trips.
6. Have children see them in realistic settings—museums, restoration, displays, exhibits, dioramas, and panoramas.
7. Use them in connection with real problems that arise in the unit, not as gadgets.

Realia and models may be seen or obtained in many places. They are available in the instructional materials center in many city and county school systems and, in some elementary schools, they are available in the school museum or the materials center. At times they can be obtained from individuals in the community; this is especially true of Indian and colonial realia and materials gathered on trips to various countries. Children themselves may collect and construct many different items. Other sources used by teachers include public museums, commercial and industrial organizations, and theatrical supply houses. Once individuals in a community have learned that the materials will be put to effective educational use, they are eager and willing to share them, and in some instances they will give them to the school.

Exhibits

Exhibits are used to display a variety of materials in social studies. In one study of transportation, models and pictures of boats, aircraft, trains, wagons, carts, and other items were arranged in a chronological sequence. The background used for the exhibit was in a time line with explanatory material and related pictures. In a study of China, another group made an exhibit of the processing of silk, starting with the cocoon and ending with a piece of cloth. In a study of industrial America, another class made several exhibits showing the processing of iron, petroleum, and soybeans from raw material to finished product. Other examples of exhibits used successfully in the social studies program are art in the community, growth of democratic institutions, basic documents in American democracy, changes in transportation, the development of communication, ethnic group contributions, uses of energy, and environmental changes. To be most effective, the following guidelines should be used in planning exhibits:

1. Select a theme, concept, or main idea for the exhibit.
2. Work out space arrangements using tables, bulletin boards, and other objects to display materials.
3. Select items that fit the theme, but avoid the cluttered effect that results from too much detail.
4. Plan the color scheme, background, labeling, and lettering to fit the theme and to appeal to the group.
5. Place the most important objects in strategic positions so that the eyes will naturally move to them.
6. Give attention to eye level in arranging materials; provide for effective lighting.
7. Arrange for demonstrations, discussions, and reports in order to make the exhibit more effective.
8. Use movement and sound if they add to the value of the exhibit.
9. Make plans to share the exhibit with other classes, parents, the library, or museum.

Materials for exhibits can be obtained from several sources. Parents, pupils, and individuals in the community are often happy to share hobbies and collections when they are to be put to educational use. Materials may also be obtained from governmental agencies, chambers of commerce, and industrial plants. Some instructional materials centers provide exhibits to accompany social studies units.

Dioramas and Panoramas

A diorama is a scene in perspective, using three-dimensional models to depict the activity. They may be used to present scenes such as life in Boonesboro, living in a log cabin in pioneer times, neighborhood helpers at work, and activities at the airport. Careful attention must be given to the setting in which the diorama is placed. Panoramas are broad scenes in which models are used to depict a topic; they are not necessarily in perspective. Panoramas are used to show industries, activities of the United Nations, branches of the federal government, recreational opportunities, activities in a lumber camp, and the like. Many teachers have found that children will do a great amount of research to make their dioramas and panoramas realistic.

Dioramas made by individual children have been stacked to make this exhibit depicting life in Mexico. Why must children do intensive planning and research to make such dioramas? (Richmond, California)

Demonstrations The social studies program offers many possibilities for the use of demonstrations. In a unit on the home and family, appropriate demonstrations include ways of growing plants and flowers, making things for the playhouse, and arranging the playhouse for different uses. In a study of pioneers, demonstrations may be given of carding wool, candle making, operating the spinning wheel, making soap, and processing flax. Other illustrative demonstrations that can be given at many different levels include proper use of tools, materials, utensils, musical instruments, art media, maps, globes, and models. Objects brought from home can be demonstrated by children as they relate to questions and topics in the unit.

The procedures involved in effective demonstrations may be illustrated by considering a demonstration of candle making carried out during a study of colonial life. The objectives were to identify the processes the colonists used to make candles, to show early methods of providing illumination in the home, and to develop readiness for candle making by the children. Need for the demonstration had arisen in a discussion of how the colonists provided light and heat in their homes. The class decided to invite a local resident (a resource visitor) who had a collection of colonial candles and candle-making equipment. The resource visitor and the teacher planned the sequence of steps in the process, giving attention to timing, space arrangements, and materials the children should use following the demonstration. During the demonstration, the children were seated so that all could see and hear, and the teacher guided questions. Afterward, the steps in candle making were summarized on a chart. This was followed by a candle-dipping activity; the class made several candles with the assistance of the resource visitor and the teacher.

USING AUDIOVISUAL MATERIALS: SOUND AND FILM RESOURCES

Films Films are used extensively in the social studies program because of their effectiveness in portraying action. A broad sweep of events may be seen with various relationships highlighted, as in films showing the development of inventions, the growth of institutions, or the contributions of great men and women. Time and speed can be controlled by slow-motion and time-lapse photography to show activities that are better understood when seen at varying rates of speed. Film loops can be used in individual and small-group study to develop specific concepts. In addition, films are interesting to watch, hold attention, and can exert a great impact on attitudes. Guidelines for their use follow.

1. Note concepts, main ideas, and other learnings appropriate to the group. Increased understanding of role, use of resources, change, culture, and other concepts should be achieved. All films touch on one or more fundamental aspects of human living. No one can remember hundreds of

facts, but one can organize thinking around basic concepts and generalizations.

2. Note aspects of human behavior, such as cooperativeness, acceptance of responsibility, creativeness, and concern for others. Human behavior in many different situations is brought to children in films; examples may well be considered by the class. All too frequently significant aspects of behavior are pushed aside and attention is centered on "the number of bananas loaded on the boat," "the products raised," or a similar set of facts. Although these are important, they must not rule out attention to effective human relations and group processes.

3. Use films to improve observing, analyzing, and other inquiry processes. Observing can be sharpened as students focus attention on portrayed events to gather ideas related to questions and problems. Classifying, analyzing, and inferring can be put to use as information is organized, broken down into parts, and extended to include implications. Synthesizing and generalizing can be brought into play as ideas are brought together and main ideas are formulated. On occasion, run a film without sound and ask students to supply the commentary.

4. Detect size, space, and time distortions, and any parts which give wrong impressions. Time, space, and cultural concepts are telescoped in many motion pictures. Highlights given to selected activities of a cultural group may lead to stereotyped thinking. Showing the development of a nation in a thirty-minute film may lead to inaccuracies in historical perspective. Moving from border to border in a few minutes may give inadequate conceptions of size. Through discussion, reading, and the use of maps and other related materials—a multi-media approach—realistic conceptions can be developed and erroneous impressions corrected.

5. Explore values, attitudes, and feelings that may be reflected in behavior portrayed in films. This may be done by raising such questions as "Why do you think that happened?" "Why did they do that?" "What does this show to be important to them?" "How do you think they must have felt?" "How would you have felt?" Such questions help to bring out shades of feeling and meaning, and help to develop the process of inferring.

6. Note difficult ideas and concepts that require further development. Difficult concepts and terms are used in many films—for example, *steppe, latitude, prevailing westerlies,* and *conservation.* Film-makers cannot develop all the concepts completely in one or two reels, and teachers must use such related procedures as discussion, pictures, study trips, and research activities to clarify them.

7. Relate ideas in the film to ongoing activities in the unit. A film should be viewed as another input of data to be used in problem solving. A good question is "How can we use these ideas?" The answer will be found as students relate ideas to those presented in other sources and use them to answer questions, state inferences, raise additional questions, or engage in other follow-up activities.

8. Enjoy films with the group. Too often teachers lose group interest during follow-up discussions of a film because of an overly zealous attempt to analyze the facts involved and a failure to enjoy the film's interesting parts. This may occur when formally imposed and poorly understood written assignments or artificial checkup tests follow each and every film. This pitfall can be avoided by relating follow-up activities to the objectives established for the use of the film, and by guiding the group to enjoy and share its interesting features.

9. Provide opportunities for students to create a motion picture. In early grades the "production" may be a simple one that portrays roles of community workers, a dramatization of events in growth of the community, contributions of individuals and groups to community life, or other topics of interest and concern to children. In later grades production may be more involved with much planning and research to portray dramatic aspects of the westward movement, present a documentary on environmental problems, depict selected events and activities in other cultures, or dramatize the contributions of ethnic and minority groups. Portable TV taperecorder-camera systems, widely available in local school systems, are especially useful because of immediate replay capability and reuse of tapes. Scenes can be revised and shot again if needed. If there is need for a permanent copy, the tape may be kept or the final production may be shot on film with a motion-picture camera. Production should be preceded by making a storyboard as described later in this chapter.

Nearly all these points also apply to television programs, because many programs are in reality films or tapes shown on a definite schedule. However, programs that are "live" have added realism and interest because we are able to witness an event as it occurs. Yet difficulties arise in selecting and scheduling radio and television programs. The teacher should keep in mind the points made about films when planning to utilize television and radio resources.

Television and Radio

Educational TV programs are designed to contribute directly to the attainment of instructional objectives. Some commercial programs can also be related to social studies instruction. Documentaries, plays, selected movies, forums, round-table discussions, interviews, news reports, editorals, and other programs may be used to enrich and extend learning in authentic and interesting ways. Special feature programs on holidays, commemorations, campaigns, and festivals can be used to help students gain insight into their significance. Often, programs are taped for future use. With a library of videotapes available, it is possible to use programs when they fit into ongoing instruction.

Some of the best programs are presented in the evening and on weekends. Children should be encouraged to watch them so that the programs can be shared and discussed in class. Some teachers successfully employ a simple forum technique, in which four or five children are asked to report on a particular program. Other members of the class are urged to be ready to ask questions and make additional points about it, and are thus encouraged to watch the same program. By rotating membership in the "forum group," the teacher can get the entire class to participate in a direct and challenging manner. As the reports and discussion are carried out in class, relationships to units of instruction and other classroom experiences can be emphasized.

Listening and viewing skills. Children develop and use several skills in connection with radio and television programs. Although radio programs require listening without the aid of related visual imagery, both types of program require a clear purpose as a basis for use: to learn the story behind a person or event, to get new ideas on a topic, or to note points related to a question. Critical listening and viewing, as outlined in Chart 13–15, is the outcome that many middle- and upper-grade children can achieve.

Chart 13–15
Critical Listeners and Viewers

Be alert from start to finish.
Remember the most important points.
Be ready to ask questions at the end.
Be ready to agree or disagree.
Note ideas we can use in our unit.
Note ideas we need to learn more about.

Recordings

Recordings are made and used for many different purposes in social studies. They provide excellent background and sound effects for dramatization, pageants, creative work, and choral and individual readings. Recordings may be made of children's work, speeches of famous people, school visitors, travelogs, and radio programs. Growth in planning, discussion, reporting, and group evaluation may be appraised if recordings are made at various times during the year. Stories, rhythms, comments for use with slides or filmstrips, and music for folk dances and accompaniment may be recorded and used as needed.

USING AUDIOVISUAL MATERIALS: PICTURES AND PICTORIAL REPRESENTATIONS

Still Pictures

Still pictures are the most widely used of all audiovisual materials. The photographs and illustrations in textbooks, encyclopedias, and other reading materials add interest to reading and help to clarify difficult terms and understandings. Use of the opaque projector to show pictures on the screen enables the group to focus attention on specific details that have been enlarged. Slides and filmstrips are used to present a series of related pictures in sequence. Postcards, cutouts from magazines and newspapers, and children's pictures are used in displays, bulletin board arrangements, and exhibits. Stereographs are viewed individually or projected for group viewing to give a realistic three-dimensional effect.

Carefully selected pictures can serve many objectives. Units can be introduced in such a way as to emphasize major topics and problems. Key questions can be raised and interest stimulated. Reports and scrapbooks made by children can be made more meaningful. Erroneous ideas and misunderstandings can be corrected. Symbols on maps can be visualized. Emotions can be stirred. Critical thinking can be sharpened as children use pictures to prove points at issue—for example, how tools such as the adz were used, how a serape should be adorned, or how iron ore is processed.

A child's growth in ability to get ideas from pictures proceeds from enumeration (telling about, or counting objects—"I see a cow, a barn, a farmer.") to description (describing colors, activities, or objects—"See the red barn. The cows are eating hay."), to inferences and interpretations (saying what may happen next, or noting relationships—"The farmer is going to milk the cows. The cows are milked in the barn."). Pictures are especially helpful in developing visual literacy, such as recognizing and naming objects, interpreting what is seen, analyzing what is portrayed, and inferring feelings, relationships, and other possibilities about the people, objects, or events being observed. When several pictures are seen, students may compare and contrast items, identify a sequence of processes or actions, and evaluate what is shown and how well it is portrayed.

Chart 13–16
Interpreting Pictures of Land Scenes

Where is the scene located?
What items stand out? hills? valleys? rivers? other?
How high, large, or small are they?
Are crops or gardens shown? If so, what is being raised?
Are there indications of the weather? temperature? amount of rainfall? wind? snow?
Are there roads? canals? railroads? buildings?
Other man-made items?
Can you estimate the area included in the picture?

Chart 13–17
Interpreting Pictures of Human Activities

Where is the activity located?
What are the people doing?
Is individual or group work emphasized?
What tools and materials are being used?
Are their ways of working modern or traditional?
What kind of clothing are they wearing?
Are homes or other buildings shown?
Are animals, roads, means of transportation, and other items shown?
Can you estimate the area included in the picture?

In order to promote maximum learning, pictures should be used in accordance with sound guidelines:

1. Select and arrange pictures carefully to initiate each unit so that significant questions are raised as children examine them. Use a few pictures at a time, holding back pictures related to topics that will arise later. This is a good way to move children from one part of the unit to another.
2. Use labels and captions, colored paper for mounting, colored paper arrows and strips to highlight important items in pictures, related maps and charts, and attractive arrangements that will add to the instructional value of pictures through eye appeal.
3. In directed picture study, guide the discussion from simple counting of objects and brief descriptions of what is portrayed to interpreting and noting relationships (see Charts 13–16 and 13–17). For example, in a picture showing men building a home, children may be guided to interpret uses of materials such as lumber and cement, and people working together cooperatively.
4. Provide for individual and small-group use of pictures such as making scrapbooks, arranging displays and bulletin boards, making reports, planning picture-and-label matching games, proving a point in discussion, illustrating steps in construction or processing of material, and answering questions about food, clothing, shelter, transportation, and other topics in a unit. Teach children to use pictures for various objectives, as shown in Charts 13–18 and 13–19.
5. Organize picture collections around main ideas or problems in the unit and place them in a kit or file for easy handling and utilization. Mount them to add to their attractiveness and durability. Place them in labeled folders or large envelopes and make an index for easy reference. Keep the collection up to date by adding new pictures and replacing old ones. Obtain pictures from magazines, newspapers, old textbooks, travel agencies, business concerns, chambers of commerce, information offices of governments, libraries, and commercial publishers and distributors.

Opaque Projections

Opaque projections used in the social studies program include a variety of nontransparent materials—pictures, drawings, diagrams, pages in books and encyclopedias, maps, charts, coins and paper money, songs, illustrations from newspapers and magazines, postcards, textiles, and other items that are magnified for class discussion. Since the pictures are projected by means of reflected light, a dark room is essential. Opaque projections are valuable for several reasons. Up-to-date materials can be

Chart 13–18
How We Use Pictures

To explain new words
To prove points
To make reports more interesting
To show difficult ideas
To show places on maps
To arrange bulletin boards

Chart 13–19
Helping with the Bulletin Board

Bring pictures that fit the topics.
Use postcards, photographs, and cutout pictures.
Select the very best ones.
Arrange them so that everybody *wants* to see them.
Use colored paper background.

used in units; maps and graphs can be enlarged easily; picture interpretation can be improved; attention can be focused on significant details in illustrations; children's work can be shared; reports can be made more interesting; and the entire class can examine an item at once instead of having it passed around the room. By hinging several drawings together or pasting them on a strip, children can make simulated motion pictures to illustrate stories and reports.

Stereographs

Stereographic pictures have a realistic three-dimensional effect that ordinary photographs do not possess, and many are available for units commonly used in social studies. Because of their realistic effect, they are a most practical aid for individual use. Inexpensive stereoscopic reels (colored slides in a circular mounting for use in a plastic viewer) are available on places throughout the world. A helpful practice is to select reels related to topics under study and to place them and a viewer in the reading center for individual use.

Filmstrips and Slides

Filmstrips and slides are among the most popular audiovisual materials used in social studies. They are easy to project; they are accompanied by helpful manuals; they cover a variety of topics; they are available in both color and black and white; they are relatively inexpensive; and their use enables a teacher to show selected materials when they are needed, and to discuss them as long as the situation demands. Some filmstrips are accompanied by recordings and thus require little or no commentary as they are being shown. Slides are easy to make and can be shown in any order, but cost more than filmstrips and must be handled carefully to avoid damage. Where order of showing is not a fundamental problem or the sequence of pictures in the filmstrips is satisfactory, the filmstrip is probably more desirable because of lower cost and ease of use and storage.

Overhead Projections Teachers may use overhead projectors to project material while facing the class. A teacher can write on transparent plastic or point to diagrams, sketches, or maps and guide discussion while they are being projected. An effective technique is the preparation of overlays (laying one drawing over another) to show relationships. For example, one drawing may show the topography of the United States; on this is placed a second one showing forests or some other item. By showing the sketch of topography and then laying the sketch of forests over it, pupils can grasp relationships quickly. By taping one drawing to another along one edge to achieve a hingelike effect, the second drawing can be folded over the first so that borders line up correctly. By choosing colors carefully, the teacher can obtain dramatic and realistic effects. The technique of making overlays is similar to that of placing sketches made on clear plastic over a relief map to show relationships.

The Storyboard A storyboard is used to guide the making of a film, filmstrip, videotape, or photo essay; it consists of sketches or pictures arranged in a sequence to portray a story, theme, or topic. The main steps in making one are these: (1) select a topic related to the unit under study; (2) make sketches or select pictures to tell the story; (3) place the sketches or pictures in sequence; (4) add notes for making the photo essay, film, or tape; (5) make the resource; and (6) evaluate. Some teachers find that just making a storyboard is a rewarding experience because of the contribution it makes to the development of visual literacy.

The Bulletin Board The bulletin board is useful for initiating units, stimulating new interests, clarifying problems, posting children's work, and displaying materials. In initiating units, display materials that will evoke interest and stimulate questions related to those topics that come first in the unit. By changing and rearranging materials to stimulate new interests, the development of the unit can be guided in sound directions. Related materials, such as posters, drawings, charts, maps, or graphs, should be posted as they are needed to solve problems that arise. Children's work may be displayed for purposes of sharing and summarizing the various learning experiences. Charts 13–20 and 13–21 give some guidelines.

Flannel Board and Magnetic Board Although the flannel (or felt) board is not used so extensively in social studies as in other subjects, it does have certain uses that should not be overlooked. It is especially helpful in presenting events or ideas in sequence as a story unfolds, a report is given, a demonstration is performed, steps in a process are given, or basic concepts are presented in a definite order. It can also be used to show the layout of a farm, to experiment with different arrangements of items for a display or floor layout, to show—by

Chart 13–20
Bulletin Board Planning

Color	Space	Circles
Lines	Blocks	Models
Pictures	Objects	Symbols
Letters	Signs	Symmetry
Rhythm	Cloth	Textiles
Paper	Posters	Clippings
Charts	Graphs	Diagrams
Maps	Yarn	Strips
Tape	Contrast	Border

Chart 13–21
Trying Different Arrangements

Arrange materials on a table or on the floor.
Try different arrangements.
Try different background material.
Try different ways of placing the title and lettering.
Try lines, circles, arrows, and colors to accent ideas.
Try different mountings for pictures.

placing cutouts that represent areas on a map that has been sketched on the flannel board—how territory was added, to assemble jigsaw maps, to show how a bill becomes a law, and to make circle and bar graphs. One of the main advantages of flannel boards is their flexibility, which permits various arrangements to be tried experimentally.

The magnetic board is similar to the flannel board in its uses. Small magnets are attached to objects, pictures, maps, cutouts, and other items so that they will be drawn to the thin iron sheeting used to make the board. The magnetic board is used primarily to demonstrate key concepts, although it may occasionally be used as a bulletin board. Some schools have installed magnetic chalkboards, which serve the same purpose.

The Chalkboard

The chalkboard serves many purposes in social studies. It may be used for listing suggestions during group planning, sketching illustrations, listing reading materials, noting assignments, copying suggestions for charts, noting facts under main ideas, summarizing a discussion, recording group-dictated stories or letters, and so on. Many teachers increase the effectiveness of chalkboard use by adding simple stick figures to illustrate points, using colored chalk to emphasize key ideas, and using rulers, compasses, and stencils to obtain neat, artistic effects. Care must be given to the selection of materials to place on the chalkboard, since slides, charts, and duplicated materials are more effective when large amounts of information or detailed data are to be presented.

Several points in chalkboard use should be kept in mind in order to achieve maximum effectiveness: (1) write legibly and organize material neatly; (2) keep the chalkboard clean and uncluttered; (3) adjust room lighting to prevent glare and eyestrain; (4) write high enough so that all can see; (5) keep the amount of writing small (distribute duplicated materials if a large amount of information is to be presented); and (6) stand to one side so that each child can read what is placed on the chalkboard. Careful planning before writing on the chalkboard, practice in writing legibly, and systematic evaluation of one's use of the chalkboard are important considerations. Many teachers check material on the chalkboard from the back of the room or from a child's seat in order to see it from the child's point of view.

USING AUDIOVISUAL MATERIALS: SYMBOLIC AND GRAPHIC MATERIALS

Graphic materials are designed to present information or main ideas clearly, concisely, and convincingly. Some are created to stir feelings, others are designed to present facts and show relationships in an objective manner. As with other instructional resources, teachers must be alert to symbols, meanings, background factors, distortions, inaccuracies, and erroneous interpretations.

Posters

Posters are designed to convey an idea that can be grasped at a glance. They are used to sway people to a course of action in such areas as conservation, safety, politics, health, sports, recreation, welfare, citizenship, travel, and business. The primary purpose in using posters is to give a quick and lasting impression of an idea, topic, or activity. Effective posters, whether they are made by children or adults, possess the following characteristics.

1. A single idea or purpose is presented dramatically, clearly, and forcefully.
2. The use of space, color, lines, and pictures is planned to focus attention on the key idea; cluttering detail is avoided.
3. The poster is large enough to ensure quick and easy viewing in the place where it is to be located.
4. Those who will see the poster are familiar with the idea it portrays.

The making of posters by children may be a profitable learning activity in social studies. Experimentation with different materials and arrangements should be encouraged. Photographs, pictures from magazines, and children's sketches and drawings should be considered. Large show cards, heavy wrapping paper, pieces cut from old windowshades, the backs of old posters, and tagboard can be used. Three-dimensional posters can be made by using a cardboard base and attaching textiles, models, specimens, and other objects. Titles, labels, or captions can be prepared to highlight the key idea. Commercially prepared posters may be obtained from business firms, airlines, railways, bus companies, shipping companies, embassies or consular offices, travel bureaus, government agencies, and national associations. When commerical posters are used, care must be taken to (1) clarify the purpose, (2) discuss the title, (3) note special appeals and points of view, (4) rewrite the title if needed to relate the poster to current activities, and (5) edit or delete obtrusive or objectionable advertising.

Cartoons

Cartoons are designed to convey an idea by means of caricature, humor, oversimplification, emotional appeal, symbols, exaggeration, satire, or stereotype. The cartoonist's purpose is to present a person, event, or activity by emphasizing a feature that will quickly convey the meaning. Use is made of such well-known symbols as Uncle Sam, John Bull, the English bulldog, the golden eagle, the dove of peace, the vulture of disease or death, the hobnailed boot of the oppressor, the cigar-smoking lobbyist, the Republicans' elephant, and the Democrats' donkey.

To get the meaning of a cartoon, a reader must know the meaning of the symbol and understand something about the situation in which it is used. This is why so many political cartoons that amuse adults have little or no effect on children. Each symbol must be clarified, and an understanding of the issues, conditions, events, or problems must be developed. An effective approach is to make use of cartoons related to current affairs and units of instruction being studied by the group. Here are some guidelines for using cartoons:

1. Relate them to historical and current events and issues. Be sure to include cartoons that present different points of view on selected issues.
2. Encourage children to bring in cartoons that are related to topics under study. Again cartoons that present different points of view are needed.
3. Take time to analyze selected cartoons in detail with attention to the symbols used, the purpose of the cartoonist, and the points that are exaggerated. Raise such questions as "What is the title?" "Why was it chosen?" "What is the cartoonist's purpose?" (to explain something? to make a joke of a situation? to arouse people? to reveal an injustice? to influence voters?) "Why was this symbol used?" "What is the cartoonist's point of view?" "What are other points of view?" "What ideas are distorted?" "In what other ways might ideas be expressed?"
4. Have children make cartoons related to current affairs and to topics in units of instruction. Have them use stick figures, simple sketches, and drawings that depict situations, problems, and events under study.

Time Charts and Time Lines Time charts and time lines are used to clarify time relationships, to relate events to major time periods, and to relate events in one country to those in another. In the early grades, charts may be made to show events of the day, major events during the week, events related to the growth of the community, changes in transportation, changes in farming, and changing ways of providing food, shelter, and clothing. In later grades, charts and time lines may be used to show events during major periods of the history of the state, nation, other lands, transportation, communication, and the like. Throughout all grades, emphasis is given to the use of units of time that children comprehend and that can be used as a basis for making comparisons.

Children should be guided to develop a time base or frame of reference for interpreting time periods and time relationships. Many teachers have children use their own age for this purpose. For example, the following were noted by a group of ten-year-olds:

> Decade—10 years, equal to my age, about one third my parent's age
> Generation—33 years, a little more than three times my age, about the same as my parents' age
> Century—100 years, ten times my age, about three times my parents' age

In all grades, emphasis is given to use of units of time students understand, a meaningful theme for selecting events, and use of an appropriate and accurate scale.

Time charts and time lines take many different forms, as shown in Charts 13–22 through 13–25. A commonly used form is simply a list of events in order with space provided between the events to show elapsed time. Another is to string a wire across the room and to space dated

Chart 13–22
Main Events in Our Community

1940	1950	1960	1970

Chart 13–23
Main Events in Early America

1760	1770	1780	1790

events written on cards at proper intervals. A third is to place large envelopes under time periods so that children can place pictures or names of events in them. A fourth is to place events in two or more regions or countries in parallel form, one under or beside the other, to show what occurred in different places at the same time.

Chart 13–24
Time Line of Discoveries, Explorations, and Other Main Events

1400—	1500—	1600—	1700—	1800—	1900—
1.	1.	1.	1.	1.	1.
2.	2.	2.	2.	2.	2.
3.	3.	3.	3.	3.	3.
4.	4.	4.	4.	4.	4.
5.	5.	5.	5.	5.	5.

List events on the card under the correct time period.

Chart 13–25
Major Events in the Western Hemisphere

	1700	1750	1800	1850	1900	1950	1960	1970
United States								
Canada								
South America								

Tables

In the social studies program, tables are used to present comparative information on products, crops, value of commodities, exports, imports, elections, population, distances, time to various places, length of rivers, height of mountains, elevations, sea depths, area, and many other items. Tables may be presented along with related graphs and thus provide children with opportunities to compare two different ways of presenting information. Tables are also used as the basis for making graphs, so children should understand how to make them as well as how to interpret them.

The first tables made or interpreted by children may simply be a short list of figures headed by a title—for example, daily classroom attendance for a week, temperature readings over a period of time, distances to nearby places, travel time to various places, value of state products, and the like. The next step is to make and interpret tables that contain two or more columns, thus moving from single-topic to multiple-topic tables. Charts 13–26 and 13–27 are illustrative. Charts 13–28 through 13–31 summarize questions and pointers that can be used to direct attention to the construction and interpretation of tables.

Chart 13–26
Animals on Paul's Farm

Animal	Number
Cows	14
Pigs	31
Sheep	6
Horses	4

How many cows are there?
How many pigs are there?
How many more sheep are there than horses?

Chart 13–27
Weather and Temperature During the Week

Day	Weather	Temperature
Monday	Fog	57
Tuesday	Rain	52
Wednesday	Rain	54
Thursday	Cloudy	66
Friday	Sunshine	72

How many days of rain did we have?
How many days of sunshine?
On how many days was it cloudy?
On what days was it coldest?
On what day was it warmest?
What was the temperature on the foggy day?
What was the temperature on the sunny day?

Graphs The major types of graphs are pictorial, bar, circle or pie, and line. In general, pictorial and one-dimensional bar graphs are the easiest to make and to interpret, and line graphs, which are two-dimensional, are the most difficult. Circle graphs are usually the best for showing relationships of parts to the whole.

In the early grades, use of graphs is limited to simple pictorial and bar graphs to show such information as daily temperature; collection of money; enrollment; books read; products and animals on farms; and simple time, distance, and speed relationships. In the middle and upper grades, graphs may be used to show such information as population growth; production of goods; extent of resources; comparison of exports and imports; relative sizes of cities, states, countries, and continents; relative distances between places; relative speeds of travel by different modes of transportation; increase in number of cars, telephones, and other items; sources of revenue; and expenditure of funds. In all grades, the interpretation and construction of graphs must be paced with the children's grasp of the related mathematical terms, concepts, and skills. The suggestions presented in arithmetic textbooks for interpreting and making graphs are excellent for use in the social studies program. Chart 13–32 illustrates ways in which distortion and varying impressions may be identified in graphs. Charts 13–33 through 13–36 illustrate points to

Chart 13–28
Understanding Tables

Is one topic presented?
Are two or more topics presented?
Is the title clear?
Are column headings clear?
What do the numerals mean? units? hundreds? thousands? millions? other?
What measures are used? pounds? kilograms? miles? kilometers? other?

Chart 13–29
Getting Ideas from Tables

What questions can be answered by using information from the table?
What does the title indicate?
What comparisons can be made?
Are changes or trends shown?
Can you find the greatest, average, and least amount shown?
Can any conclusions be made?
Can you think of a similar table you might make?

Chart 13–30
Making a Table

What information is to be given?
How many columns are needed?
What heading is needed for each column?
Place the information in each column.
Plan a complete title.

Chart 13–31
Ideas for Tables

Growth of school enrollment
Yearly construction of new homes
Growth of population
Agricultural products
Manufactured products
Can you think of others?

emphasize as students make graphs. Specific instruction is needed on the following items when graphs are used in social studies:

1. Read the title or heading carefully to determine exactly what is presented and note key terms such as *growth, decline, change, size, trends, average, area, value, predicted,* and the like.
2. Note what each picture or symbol represents on picture graphs, and the size of scales on bar and line graphs.
3. Note the source of information and check the original source if questions arise.
4. Look out for distortions, breaks in the scale, changes in size of symbols, and graphs drawn in perspectives that may give false impressions.
5. Develop the terms and concepts needed to discuss graphs: *key, symbol, bar, grid, grid lines, scale, horizontal, vertical, row, column, portion,* and *sector*.
6. Avoid erroneous interpretations, such as inferring that one thing causes another because the two are presented together on a graph.

Chart 13–32

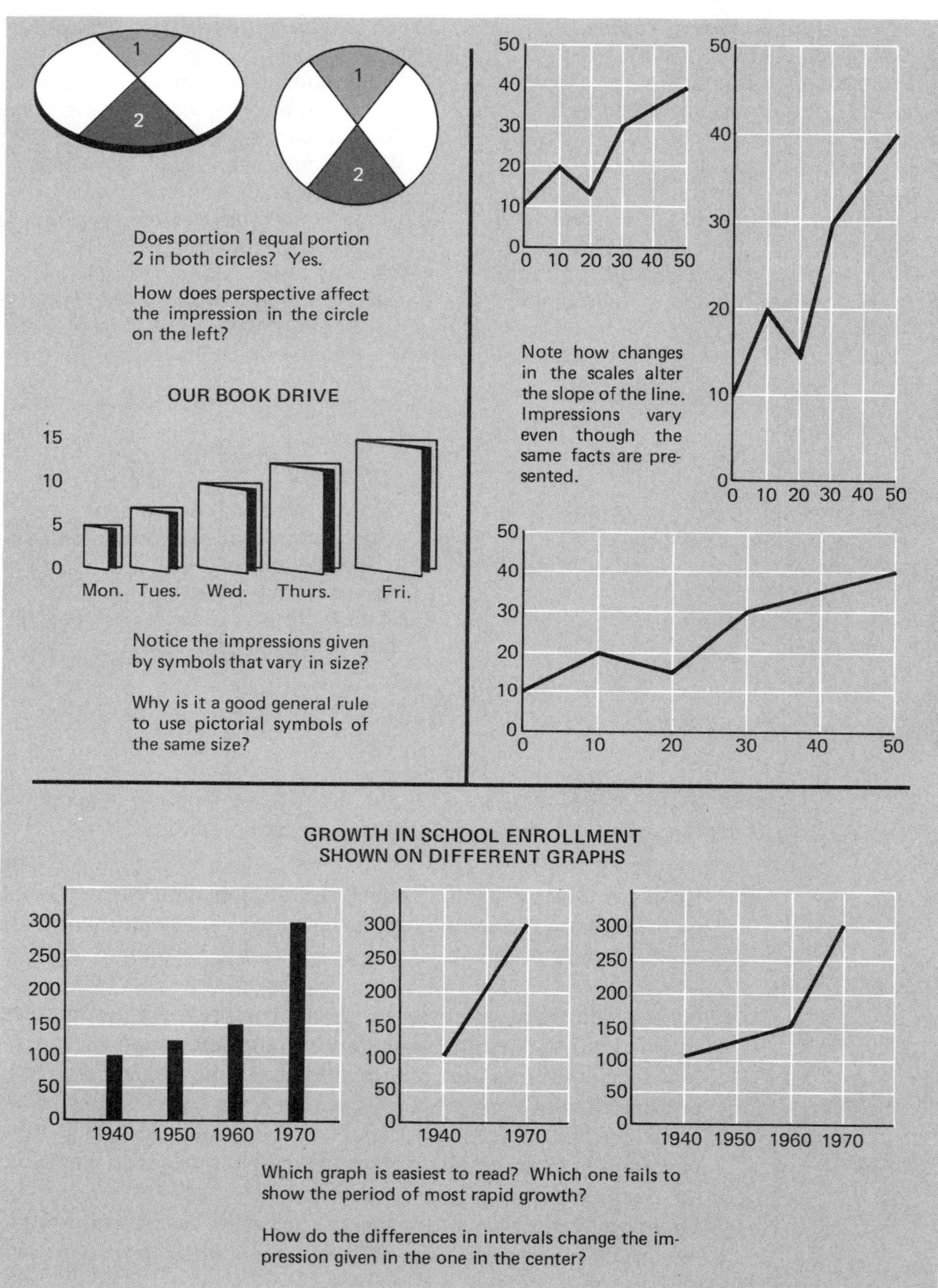

1
2
1
2
Does portion 1 equal portion 2 in both circles? Yes.
How does perspective affect the impression in the circle on the left?
OUR BOOK DRIVE
15
10
5
0
Mon. Tues. Wed. Thurs. Fri.
Notice the impressions given by symbols that vary in size?
Why is it a good general rule to use pictorial symbols of the same size?
50
40
30
20
10
0
0 10 20 30 40 50
Note how changes in the scales alter the slope of the line. Impressions vary even though the same facts are presented.
50
40
30
20
10
0
0 10 20 30 40 50
50
40
30
20
10
0
0 10 20 30 40 50
GROWTH IN SCHOOL ENROLLMENT
SHOWN ON DIFFERENT GRAPHS
300
250
200
150
100
50
0
1940 1950 1960 1970
300
250
200
150
100
50
0
1940 1970
300
250
200
150
100
50
0
1940 1950 1960 1970
Which graph is easiest to read? Which one fails to show the period of most rapid growth?
How do the differences in intervals change the impression given in the one in the center?

Chart 13–33
Making Circle Graphs

List the facts to be shown and find the total.
Figure the amount that each part is of the total.
Measure each part or sector on the circle.
Draw lines for different portions and label them.
Select a title and put it on the graph.
Put the source of information on the graph.

Chart 13–34
Making Bar Graphs

Identify the facts to be shown.
Cut strips of paper or use tape for each bar.
Decide if bars should be vertical or horizontal. Try both ways to find out which is better.
Be sure the title fits what is presented.
Give the source of data at the bottom.

Chart 13–35
Making Line Graphs

Identify the data to be shown.
Figure out the vertical and horizontal scales. Check the arithmetic book for ideas.
Try out different scales to get the best one.
Plot the points on graph paper. Double-check before drawing the lines.
Select a good title and put the source of data on the graph.

Chart 13–36
Checking Bar Graphs

Is it of proper size to show the facts clearly?
Is the title complete and easy to read?
Is each bar labeled and drawn correctly?
Are the bars the same width and evenly spaced?
Is the lettering clear and easy to read?
Is the source of information given?

QUESTIONS, ACTIVITIES, EVALUATION

1. Select one of the following and make a plan for using it in a unit: a study trip, resource person to visit the class, or individual for a committee to interview.
2. Discuss the checklist on planning study trips. Is each point clear? What points might be added because of conditions or regulations in your area?
3. Obtain some magazines, pamphlets, and bulletins that contain pictures related to a unit you plan to teach. Cut out and mount the best pictures and organize a picture file. Select pictures that can be used to improve defining, classifying, analyzing, and other inquiry processes.

4. Preview a filmstrip or film. Make a plan showing how it might be used in a unit.
5. Reread the section on realia. Can you construct any for use in a unit? Which ones can be obtained locally? How might they be used in a unit you plan to teach?
6. Which of the following might be made by students in a unit you are planning: cartoons, posters, time charts, time lines, tables, graphs? Sketch examples that you think would be appropriate.

REFERENCES

See also references at the end of Chapter 11.

ARNSDORF, VAL E., "An Investigation of the Teaching of Chronology in the Sixth Grade," *Journal of Experimental Education,* 29 (March 1961), 307–13. Report on how instruction improves understanding of time relationships and chronology.

DEBES, JOHN L., and CLARENCE M. WILLIAMS, eds., *Visual Literacy.* New York: Pitman, 1970. Background readings on visual literacy.

JAROLIMEK, JOHN, *Social Studies in Elementary Education.* New York: Macmillan, 1971. Sections on graphs, cartoons, charts.

LORD, CLIFFORD L., *Teaching History with Community Resources.* New York: Teachers College Press, Columbia University, 1964. Practical techniques for using local resources.

LOWENSTEIN, DYNO, *Graphs and Surveys: How to Prepare and Interpret Them.* Columbus, O.: Xerox Publications, Education Center, 1973. A how-to unit booklet.

MCCUNE, GEORGE H., and NEVILLE PEARSON, "Interpreting Material Presented in Graphic Form." In *Skill Development in the Social Studies* (33rd Yearbook). Washington, D.C.: National Council for the Social Studies, 1963. Techniques and illustrative activities.

MCKEE, PAUL, *Reading: A Program of Instruction for the Elementary School.* Boston: Houghton-Miffln, 1966. Sample lessons on graphs.

WURMAN, RICHARD S., ed., *Yellow Pages of Learning Resources.* Cambridge, Mass.: MIT Press, 1972. Questions and study guides for using community resources.

14

Focusing Questions

How can maps and globes be used to improve learning in social studies?

What strategies and techniques can be used to develop map and globe concepts and skills?

What kinds of charts are helpful in guiding instruction?

What techniques are helpful in map making?

Using Maps, Globes, & Map-Making Activities

This chapter focuses on the use of maps and globes in the social studies program and the development of skills and concepts essential to their utilization. Both commercial maps and maps made by students and teachers have a place in individual and group inquiry. In social studies, maps and globes are used to locate places in the community, state, nation, and other lands, such as parks, resources, products, ports, water bodies, historical sites, cities, transportation routes, mountain ranges, and population distribution, and to find distance and time between places, along travel routes, and across areas. They are also used to determine direction from one place to another, of travel routes, of the flow of rivers, of migrations, and to compare selected regions with reference to area, population, resources, water bodies, landforms, products, occupations, and urban centers.

In addition, maps and globes are used to interpret data needed to answer questions and test hypotheses, and to discover relationships and draw inferences regarding climate and living conditions, industries and resources, terrain and travel routes, and location of cities in relation to topography. Map making is used to synthesize data related to topics under study, distribution of items in selected areas, associations between items, and interconnections within and between regions. Charts 14–1 and 14–2 give some suggested uses for maps and globes in the classroom.

Chart 14–1
Get Information from Maps

Locate places	Find major cities
Find distances	Note waterways
Find elevation	Find air routes
Note directions	Note highways
Find water bodies	Note railways
Note rainfall	Compare areas
Note products	Note products

Chart 14–2
Using the Globe and Maps to Answer Questions

Where is it?
How far is it?
In what direction is it?
How large is it?
What is the climate?
What is produced?
Where do people live?

THE GLOBE

The globe is the most accurate representation of the earth's surface; it should be referred to whenever questions arise about relative location, size, distance, direction, and shape of land masses and water bodies. Because the globe is a sphere like the earth, it has properties that cannot all be found on any one flat map: (1)

How might students use a markable globe in a unit you are planning? (College Elementary School, Chico, California)

distance between places in correct proportion, (2) correct shape of land masses and water bodies, (3) areas in correct proportions, and (4) true directions. When a sphere is transferred to a flat surface, some distortion is inevitable; in many flat maps it is greatest at the outer edges.

The globe should be used in conjunction with maps whenever there are problems of distortion, and when misconceptions need to be corrected. Such misconceptions as the belief that Greenland is larger than South America (it is about one-eighth as large), or that the shortest distance from San Francisco to Moscow is across the Pacific (a polar route is shorter), can be avoided by referring to the globe. The relative position of continents, the shapes of land masses, and the size of various regions should be checked in a similar manner.

The globe should also be used to develop fundamental concepts about the earth and its surface features. In the early grades, the globe is used to develop concepts of the roundness of the earth, directions, the extent to which water covers the earth's surface (about three-fourths), differences in surface features from place to place, and size differences among major land masses and water bodies. In later grades, the globe is used to develop concepts related to night and day, time zones, changes in seasons, rotation and revolution, and high, middle, and low latitudes. Concept development of this kind is essential to the development of map-reading skills and is closely related to the development of major geographic concepts (see Charts 14–3 through 14–8).

Chart 14–3
Show These on the Project Globe

- Main land masses and water bodies
- Names of the oceans, the continents, and islands
- North Pole, South Pole, equator
- Tropic of Cancer, Tropic of Capricorn
- Arctic Circle and Antarctic Circle
- Prime Meridian and International Date Line

Chart 14–4
Find These on the Globe

- Northern hemisphere
- Southern hemisphere
- Western hemisphere
- Eastern hemisphere
- Land hemisphere
- Water hemisphere
- Daylight hemisphere
- Darkness hemisphere

Chart 14–5
Show Directions on the Globe

- North toward the North Pole
- South toward the South Pole
- North along the meridians
- South along the meridians
- East along the parallels
- West along the parallels

Because the globe is such a useful teaching device, there should be at least one in each classroom. In the primary grades, a raised relief globe that clearly shows land and water features is helpful in giving children the "feel" of the earth's surface. Raised relief globes are available in light-

Chart 14-6
Rotation and Time on the Globe

Demonstrate the cause of day and night.
Show how to find time in different places.
Locate the hour circles or meridians and compare them with time zones.
Show noon and midnight by finding opposite meridians.
Show how the calendar is adjusted when crossing the International Date Line.

Chart 14-7
Great Circles on the Globe

Show that a great circle divides the earth into two equal parts.
Show that the equator is a great circle.
Show that the meridians are great circles.
Show that parallels north and south of the equator are not great circles.
Show a great circle route from New York to Bangkok.

Chart 14-8
Revolution and Seasons

Show how the earth's axis is tilted.
Show the orbit of the earth as it goes around the sun.
Show the sun's rays during the summer and winter solstices.
Show the sun's rays during the spring and fall equinoxes.
Show the northern limit of the sun's vertical rays.
Show the southern limit of the sun's vertical rays.

weight plastic that can be marked with crayon or chalk. These globes, which children can handle easily, can be used to develop initial concepts of the roundness of the earth, main land and water areas, and general nature of surface features. A good globe for the next stage of instruction is the simplified merged-color beginner's globe. By comparing it with the raised-relief globe, children quickly grasp the meaning of the colors used to show relief. Also helpful is the markable project globe that simply shows major features in outline form with land clearly differentiated from water. This globe can be used in different grades to develop concepts of direction, to mark the location of places and special features, and to outline countries, regions, travel routes, and other items. For middle and upper grades, a physical-political globe that clearly shows main surface features, yet is not cluttered with detailed printing, should be available in each classroom. A physical-political globe with a horizontal mounting that can be used to develop concepts of motion, time, distance, seasonal sun position, and the like is helpful in the seventh and eighth grades, and for advanced children in the fifth and sixth grades. Small desk globes (8 inches in diameter) for individual projects can be used to develop concepts and skills in all grades.

MAPS

Maps are needed to show areas in large perspective. The globe is too small to show distributions of items so that they can be studied in detail. The wide range of content shown on maps enables one to see at a glance many surface conditions and relationships that cannot otherwise be portrayed as clearly and as efficiently.

Content Maps may be classified according to content into such types as political, physical, physical-political, economic, historical, and special feature. The following list illustrates the diversity of the information shown on maps:

Political—boundaries, cities, states, countries, blocs of countries
Physical—mountains, lowlands, rivers, lakes, oceans
Climate—rainfall, temperature, winds
Population—density, relation to surface features
Economic—resources, crops, occupations, products
Physical-political—combinations of the above
Historical—explorations, events, territorial changes
Travel—trade routes, roads, railroads, air routes
Community—streets, buildings, agencies, harbors
Special—parks, monuments, literary works, religions

Guiding Principles Because maps are symbolic representations, attention must be given to the gradual development of map language. First of all, simple maps with very little detail should be selected for use in the primary grades. In later grades, more detailed maps may be used to meet the various problems that arise. The symbols, colors, and terms on the maps should be identified, learned, and used in reading and making maps. In general, a new symbol should be taught when needed for functional use. The legend should be analyzed and the symbols and colors contained in it located on the map and interpreted. Important terms should be learned and located on the map. Children should have opportunities to use the terms as they write on slated globes and maps and complete desk and wall outline maps. Compass directions should be pointed out and reviewed as children change rooms, as new maps are introduced, and as questions arise. The scale of miles should be learned and used in measuring distances between places being studied in the unit. The different colors relating to elevation should be considered and related to places of varying elevation visited by children in the class. Sizes of cities, distances between places, and types of climate should be associated with cities children already know, places they have visited, and places in which they have lived. And experiences in making maps or models of familiar areas (classroom, school, neighborhood) should be provided to build concepts of distance, direction, scale, use of symbols, and functions of maps. Charts 14–9 and 14–10 illustrate the kinds of maps in atlases and encyclopedias.

Chart 14–9
Using Our World Atlas

Basic Maps:	
World maps	Asia
North America	Africa
South America	Australia
Europe	Polar regions
Other Maps:	
Climate	Population
Temperature	Resources
Vegetation	Products
Tables:	
Rivers	Population
Mountains	Sea depths
Glossary:	
Places	Map terms

Chart 14–10
Using Maps in Our Encyclopedias

Location of cities, states, countries, continents, and water bodies
Maps of major cities that show famous landmarks
Physical relief maps that show surface features
Political maps showing cities, states, provinces, and countries
Regional maps of the United States, Central America, and other places
Historical maps of notable events
Interesting places such as parks, monuments
Comparison maps that show relative size of states and countries
Pictorial maps that show plants, animals, products, and resources

The Grid Maps and globes are made on grids that include reference lines—for example, east-west lines or parallels, and north-south lines or meridians. The importance of these grid lines can be brought home to children in several ways. One widely used technique is to use a large ball in place of a globe and ask children to show the location of their community or another well-known place on it. Immediately the question of reference points and lines will arise: Where should we mark the North Pole, the South Pole, and the equator? Do we need other lines? After checking the classroom globe, they should proceed to mark reference lines on the ball with chalk and to locate the given place on it.

A similar procedure can be used to locate surface features on a piece of paper. For example, when children are asked to locate places in the neighborhood, they must mark lines to show the different streets and then proceed to locate homes, the school, and other important places. In later grades, the same procedure can be used for locating states, countries, and other places by first drawing squares on the paper to serve as a grid and then sketching the places to be shown. Other helpful procedures are to review the grid lines on road maps, state maps, maps of the nation, wall maps of various continents, and the globe.

Preparation for Map Reading Before children can use maps constructively, certain skills and understandings should be taught. Most important among these are directions, surface features, and concepts of the earth.

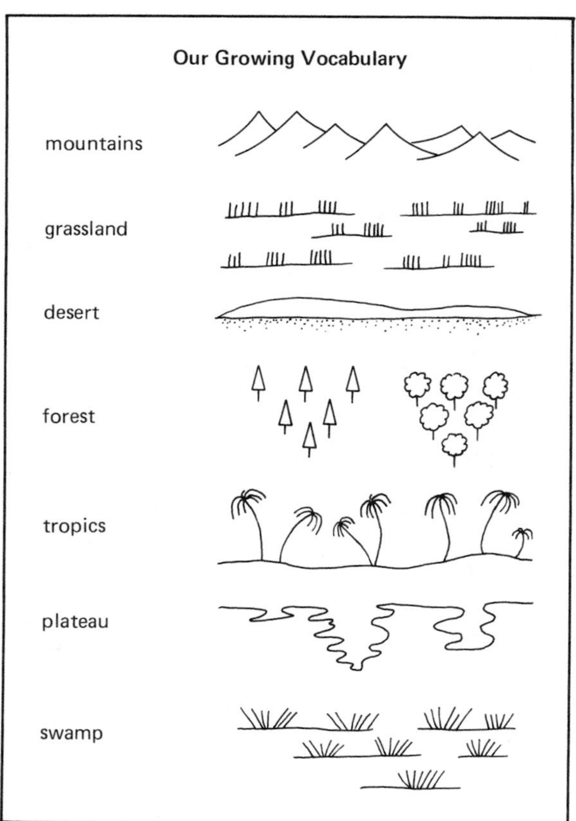

Map reading requires systematic attention to concepts and symbols. (Education Workshop, University of California, Berkeley)

Cardinal directions. The directions—north, south, east, and west—can be taught in terms of the specific locations known to the child. For example, in what direction does his house face? the school? What is the direction from home to school? to the grocery store? to other familiar places? What buildings are north? south? east? west?

Another technique is to have a group of children stand with their backs to the sun at noon. Expain that they are facing north, that south is in back of them, that east is to their right, and that west is to their left. Have them locate the same directions in the classroom. Cards with the directions written on them can be shown later with the suggestion that individual children point in the direction shown. Some teachers place labels showing directions on the appropriate walls of the classroom. Many teachers find it helpful to summarize key learnings about directions on the chalkboard or on charts, as shown in Charts 14–11 and 14–12.

Surface features. Children need specific experiences to develop an understanding of surface features shown on maps and the terms used to

Chart 14–11
Finding Directions at Noon

Stand with your back to the sun.
You are facing north.
East is to your right.
South is in back of you.
West is to your left.

Chart 14–12
The Sun and Directions

The sun rises in the east.
The sun sets in the west.
At noon the sun is south.
Our shadows are toward the north at noon.

express them. Both natural features (landforms, water bodies, and other concept clusters listed in Chapter 5) and man-made features (highways, canals, dams, and the like) should be given attention. The objective should be to develop a clear concept of the landscape features represented by symbols used on maps (see Chart 14–13). Then children can bring meaning to map reading, as they should bring meaning to other kinds of reading.

Chart 14–13
Can You Find Examples of These Concept Clusters on Maps?

Natural Resources	Major Landforms	Bodies of Water
Soil	Plains	Rivers
Water	Hills	Lakes
Minerals	Plateaus	Gulfs
Wildlife	Mountains	Oceans

On short walks and study trips, point out and discuss different surface features. Children's ability to observe should be sharpened; they should be encouraged to ask questions about what they see. Films, pictures, terrain models, and charts showing map terms should be discussed to clarify specific concepts such as *plateau, bay, gulf, harbor*. Commercial or teacher-made charts and pictures of surface features with appropriate labels attached to them are especially helpful.

Children should report on trips they have taken to mountains, beaches, lakes, valleys, canyons, parks, dams, and other places where various surface features could be seen; they should share and discuss postcards and photographs that show the features they are studying. Maps with raised relief should be used to help them visualize mountains, valleys, winding rivers, and other surface features. Sketches and drawings made by children as well as those in textbooks also should be used in discussion. When textbooks are used, teachers should be sure to clarify new concepts through discussion, pictures, or films and filmstrips. Another helpful technique, illustrated in Chart 14–14, is to have children in intermediate grades locate pictures or sketches that illustrate specific features. The next step is to have them locate the same features on a map.

Chart 14–14
Find Pictures to Show Each of These Features

The rugged coastline of a fiord
Mountain land
A broad plateau
The hub of the highways
A long, winding river
A network of railways
Area of dense population
Desert as far as the eye can see

Concepts of the earth. Specific concepts of the earth can be developed through showing and discussing a simplified globe. Begin by discussing the fact that the globe is a good representation (not a picture) of the earth. The surface is land and water, and where we live is one small part of the earth. Explain that the earth is shaped like a ball and that the globe shows the main land and water features. Introduce the term *sphere* and have children tell about objects they know that are shaped like a sphere or ball. Explain that the earth is a sphere, too. Teach the meaning of the term *hemisphere* by cutting an orange or ball of clay in half; point out that hemisphere means half of a ball. Hold the globe so that they can see the hemisphere on which they live.

The North Pole should be located; explain that this is the farthest point north. Next locate the South Pole and point out that we are farther from the South Pole than we are from the North Pole. Explain the term *equator;* locate it and point out that it is midway between the poles. Show the northern and southern hemispheres and have the group tell in which hemisphere we live.

Directions on the globe should be clarified. North is toward the North Pole; south is toward the South Pole. Never use the terms *up* and *down* to indicate north and south. Explain that *up* is away from the earth, and that *down* is toward the center of the earth (see Charts 14–15 and 14–16). The diagrams in geography texts are helpful in this connection. Point east and west and have students identify known places to the east and west of their state.

The major land and water bodies should be discussed. Begin with North America, explaining that this is the continent on which we live. Have students locate the Atlantic and Pacific Oceans. Which states are

Chart 14–15
Do You Use These Terms Correctly?

North—toward the North Pole, not up
South—toward the South Pole, not down
Up—away from the earth, higher
Down—toward the center of the earth, lower

Chart 14–16
Directions on the Globe

North—along meridians, toward the North Pole
South—along meridians, toward the South Pole
East—along parallels, toward the rising sun
West—along parallels, toward the setting sun

between them? Which one is not? What countries to the north and south are between them? Show other continents, beginning with those that have been discussed in class. Point to one or two places on each continent that are familiar to children. Show the Indian Ocean, and point out that it is south of the equator and between the Atlantic and Pacific Oceans. Have students compare the sizes of the continents and the oceans (see Charts 14–17 and 14–18).

Chart 14–17
The Continents

How many major continents are there?
On which continent is the United States?
In what direction is each continent from our continent?
Which continent is largest?

Chart 14–18
Use the Globe

To find distance
To find directions
To find location
To note distortion in flat maps
To compare places
To find shortest travel routes

Symbols Clear perception and meaningful association are involved in learning map symbols. Children should be helped to visualize the feature for which the symbol stands, using the following procedures:

1. Each map symbol should be visualized, and pictorial and semipictorial symbols should be introduced before nonpictorial symbols.
2. After a symbol has been taught, provide for review without any label so that children will learn the symbol and not rely on the label.
3. Be sure each child checks the legend before using a map. Discuss any new symbols or new uses of color. Review any symbols about which there is a question. Do this for textbook maps

as well as for wall maps. Points to consider at different times are shown in Charts 14–19 through 14–23.

Chart 14–19
Check the Legend

What is the scale of miles?
What do the colors mean?
What do the symbols mean?
Are other facts given?

Chart 14–20
Check the Key to the Map

What do the colors mean?
What do shadings mean?
Can you figure elevation?

Chart 14–21
Can You Find These on Our Maps?

Plain	Hill	Island
Desert	Mountain	Isthmus
Tundra	Valley	Peninsula
Forest	Volcano	Continent

Chart 14–22
How Are These Shown on Our Maps?

Capitals	Lowlands
Cities	Plains
Seaports	Plateaus
Roads	Mountains
Boundaries	Products
Railways	Rainfall
Airways	Population
Rivers	Resources

Chart 14–23
Symbols on Maps in Our Books

1. Straight lines show roads on level land.
2. Curved lines show roads on hilly land.
3. Black squares show houses.
4. A cluster of squares shows a town.
5. Lines winding between hills show rivers.
6. The winding line by the ocean is the coastline.

4. Compare the symbols on a new map with those used on a familiar map; be alert to changes in symbols.
5. Give specific attention to symbols for cities of different size, rivers, coastline, boundaries, canals, dams, and the like (see Chart 14–24).
6. Explain and illustrate the uses of color to show elevation, countries or states and vegetation (see Chart 14–25). Point out that various shadings of black and white, lines, or dots may be used to show some of the same features (see Chart 14–26).

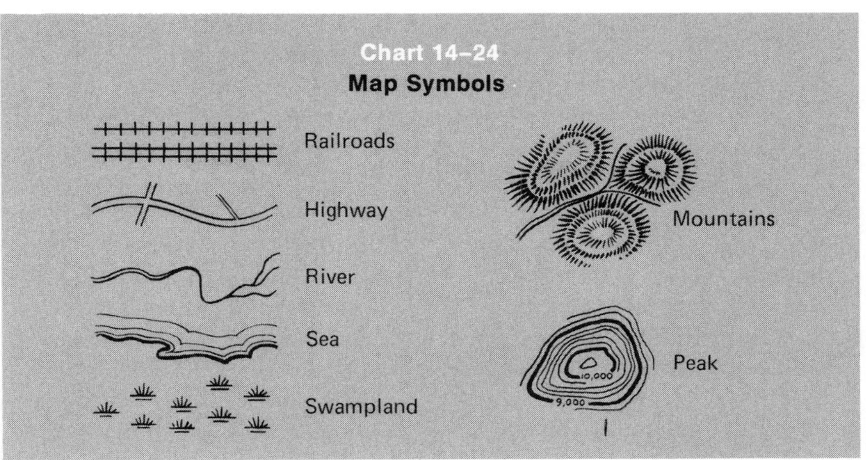

Chart 14–24
Map Symbols

Chart 14–25
Which Are Shown by Colors on Our Maps?

Elevation of lands?

States and countries?

Distribution of resources?

Density of population?

Other information?

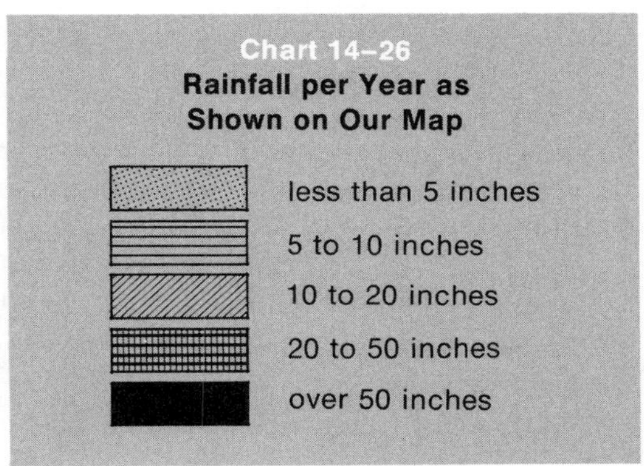

Chart 14–26
Rainfall per Year as Shown on Our Map

Have the group summarize what the colors and shadings represent.

7. Discuss the key on a map showing elevation. Explain that elevation is measured from sea level and that the colors show the elevation. Discuss profiles of mountains as illustrated in textbooks, and have the class make profiles showing elevation. Relate these to color maps showing elevation, explaining that the colors enable us to determine elevation; summarize the colors and elevation represented by them, as shown in Charts 14–27 and 14–28.

Teachers can add to the meaningfulness of maps by using them in conjunction with related study trips, pictures, filmstrips, motion pictures, the globe, reading, and discussion. For example, pictures of vegetation, landscapes, products, and types of shelter create in a child's mind impressions of the actual conditions in the area being studied. Aerial photographs

Chart 14–27
What Heights or Depths Do These Colors Show?

Shades of red
Shades of brown
Shades of yellow
Shades of green
Shades of blue

Chart 14–28
Elevation on Our Wall Maps

Red	10,000 and up
Dark brown	5,000–10,000
Light brown	2,000–5,000
Yellow	1,000–2,000
Light green	500–1,000
Dark green	0–500
Grayish green	Below sea level

should be compared with related sections of the map. Symbols used for canals and other cultural features become more understandable after a child sees them in picture form.

Locating Places on the Map First experiences in the locating of places should be carried out on floor layouts and maps of the community. The school, children's homes, and main buildings in the neighborhood should be given first attention. As the broader environment is studied, other places can be located, such as the airport, railroad yards, nearby farms and dairies, and other places visited on study trips (see Charts 14–29 and 14–30).

Chart 14–29
Where Is It?

1. What direction is it?
2. How many miles away?
3. How many hours by air?
4. What is the latitude?
5. Check the globe and atlas.

Chart 14–30
How Big Is It?

1. Compare it to our state.
2. Compare it to our country.
3. See it on the globe.
4. Check equal-area maps.
5. Use maps with same scale.

In state and regional studies, experiences may be provided in locating significant places on road maps. The grid on road maps—numbers and letters to designate east-west and north-south lines—is fairly easy to use. Call children's attention to the index of places and guide them to find the point on the map where the given numbered and lettered lines meet. For practice use several places that are familiar to children; for example, Chart 14–31 shows places in Wisconsin as listed in the index of a road map. Incidentally, the map inserts that show major cities can be projected easily by means of an opaque projector in order to make simple maps of the community. This is an excellent procedure if the desired community is shown, because one can eliminate unnecessary detail and thereby secure a large map than can be used for many different purposes.

Chart 14–31
Find These Places on Road Maps

Green Bay	3-O
La Crosse	3-S
Madison	4-E
Milwaukee	4-G
Superior	2-B

When maps of the children's state or the United States are introduced, they should be placed on the floor or on a table, so that they can be oriented properly and directions can be noted realistically. Have the children find where they live, and then point out neighboring cities and states. This may be followed by locating places they have visited or read about. Discuss places being studied in the unit with attention to direction and distance (time as well as miles) from where they live.

The problem of relative location—location of a place in relation to other places or surface features—should include attention to such factors as accessibility, transportation facilities, and terrain. Some places may be nearby "as the crow flies," but difficult to reach because of some barrier such as a mountain range, or because of the absence of transportation facilities such as an airport or natural waterways.

Specific attention should be given to the effect of mountain ranges, rivers, lakes, oceans, deserts, swamps, and jungles on accessibility to given places. Ways in which people change the environment and overcome barriers—roads, canals, railways, airports—should be discussed too. Relative distance and location change as improvements are made in transportation facilities. Modern air routes that follow great circles can be considered to bring home the importance of the area around the North Pole as related to travel among our country, Japan, and Europe. The location of many cities near natural waterways and the availability of markets and resources to industrial centers also should be discussed.

A clear understanding of direction on maps and globes will help children grow in their ability to find and describe the location of places. Most fifth graders and many fourth graders can grasp the idea that lines of latitude are true east-west lines, and that meridians are true north-south lines. At first the terms *east-west lines* and *north-south lines* may be used; later the terms *latitude, parallels, meridians,* and *longitude* can be introduced. *Degrees* as a concept of measure should be taught in relation to latitude and longitude, and the location of main places. Guide children in their use of lines of latitude to note places north or south of their city or state, and places nearer to or farther from the equator. Also show them that places on the same line of latitude, or parallel, are east or west of each other because parallels are true east-west lines.

By checking meridians, children can be guided to note places to the east or west of their city or state. For example, Los Angeles is east of San Francisco (even east of Reno), and South America is located east of most of the United States. They also should be shown that places on the same meridian are directly north or south of each other because meridians are true north-south lines.

Great-circle routes, longitude, and an acquaintance with a few of the commonly used map projections can be learned and used by many students in the upper grades. A great circle around the globe forms two hemispheres, and the shortest distance between any two points is along a great circle. The meridians and the equator are great circles; others can be shown by stretching a tape measure or string tightly along the surface of the globe. A simple global ruler can be made for measuring great-circle distances as follows: measure the circumference of the globe, divide 25,000 by the circumference, and you then know the number of miles per inch. Have students use a global ruler to find great-circle distances between places.

Consideration of time zones should begin with those in the United States, followed by a consideration of time in Europe, beginning with time at the Prime Meridian and moving toward the United States and then on across Eurasia. A globe should be available for the discussion, and students should discover that meridians (on most globes) are spaced 15° apart, showing one hour of time (360° ÷ 24 = 15°). They should also check time zones in the United States to find deviations from meridians.

Scale of Miles

Several points should be kept in mind in teaching the scale of miles. The scale of miles on maps may be expressed graphically (0 200 400), as a statement (one inch equals 500 miles), or as a ratio (1:1,000,000). The graphic scale is relatively easy to use to compute distances between places. Use of the inch-to-mile scale requires a child to measure accurately in inches and then to convert to miles. Both the graphic and inch-to-mile scale should be taught in the intermediate grades and reviewed in the upper grades. The ratio scale is the most difficult to understand because its use requires an understanding of fractions and ratio, and conversion to miles requires the use of simple algebra. However, since the scale on most maps and globes is expressed graphically or in terms of inches to miles, the ratio scale need not cause undue difficulty in the elementary school.

Several practical techniques can be used to help children understand distance as expressed by a scale. First, specific concepts of distance should be built up by considering familiar distances such as home to school, school to downtown, and to neighboring towns and cities. This should be followed by noting the same places on community maps and road maps. In this connection, community maps used in the primary grades should be drawn to scale by the teacher, or use should be made of simple community maps furnished by business concerns. Road maps can be used effectively by many third and fourth graders if emphasis is given to distance between known places.

Many intermediate-grade teachers have found the following activities helpful in teaching scale: drawing a sketch of the classroom to scale; making neighborhood or community maps; comparing two places shown on maps of different scale; discussing distance and travel time between places the children have visited; making maps of their state or region to scales of varying size; discussing the use of small-scale maps to show a large area; comparing outline maps (used by the children) with wall maps and noting the difference in scale; discussing the scale used on textbook maps; comparing distances between places being studied and familiar places (such as between New York and Chicago) and noting the scale; and comparing cities, states, and countries with respect to size. Of vital importance is the actual use of the scale on maps to answer questions that come up in daily classwork.

Discovering Associations and Making Inferences

The discovery of associations is a major objective of units in which geographic understandings are emphasized. Proper use of maps and the globe will contribute to this end. However, their use should be combined with reading, viewing materials, and plenty of guided discussion so that any stated association has a basis in fact. Caution also must be exercised in discussing cause-and-effect relationships; have children double-check their inferences by consulting other sources of information.

Among the important associations that children can be guided to infer are the following: (1) elevation and growing season, (2) elevation and density of population, (3) highlands and grazing, (4) lowlands and farming, (5) soil and farming, (6) mountains and rainfall, (7) growing season in relation to altitude and latitude, (8) natural vegetation in relation to rainfall, soil, and growing season, and (9) industry and natural resources.

Systematic use should be made of globes and maps to help children discover associations such as those listed above. One technique is to have children compare two maps showing different facts about the same area. For example, after comparing a map showing population of the United States with one showing topography, children can discover that few people live in high mountainous areas; they can later find out if this relationship exists in other places. Or, by comparing a physical relief map and a map showing crops, children may discover that much farming is done in lowlands. Another technique is to have children study a map and make inferences about conditions there on the basis of information they already have. For example, if a desert is shown, have them infer living conditions they might expect to find. Or, if a rainfall map is being used, can they make inferences regarding areas where crops may be grown and areas that are too arid to support crops? (In this connection, they also may discover something about soil in relation to rain and crops.) Or, if a place of relatively low elevation is near the equator, what inferences can they make about climate? Or, as shown in Chart 14–32, can they make inferences about the effect of the ocean currents, winds, the Gulf Stream, and other factors on climate in various areas? Still other inferences can be made after a careful study of symbols representing resources, industries, and similar items (guiding questions are shown in Charts 14–32 and 14–33).

Chart 14–32
How Do These Influence Climate?

Gulf Stream
California Current
Japan Current
Prevailing winds
Mountain ranges
Elevation
Distance from equator

Chart 14–33
How Are These Resources Used?

Coal	Titanium
Iron	Petroleum
Lead	Forests
Tin	Water
Silver	Soil
Gold	Animals
Uranium	Fish

In discussing people-land relationships and making inferences about ways of living, teachers should avoid the erroneous idea that "human behavior is caused by the environment," or that people must always do what they are doing at the present time. Rather, they should make it clear that custom, tradition, education, and the values of the people living in a particular area are also involved in the choices they make. As ideas and values change, changes take place in ways of living and resources may be used differently.

SUMMARY OF MAP AND GLOBE CONCEPTS AND SKILLS

The summary that follows is based on recently published courses of study, manuals that accompany social studies textbooks, handbooks on map and globe use, professional books for teachers, and recent studies of children's map-reading ability.[1] The grade designations are illustrative of the levels at which the concepts and skills are introduced and put to use in units of instruction. Grade placement should be flexible, with children moving ahead in terms of their abilities and backgrounds of experience.

[1] Grateful acknowledgement is made to Dr. Val Arnsdorf, University of Delaware, and to Dr. Haig Rushdoony, Stanislaus State College, for their comments and suggestions on this section.

Kindergarten to Grade 2 In the beginning grades, concepts and skills are developed concretely in daily experiences of students. The following are introduced by the end of the second grade.

Directions: Left, right; up, down; north, south, east, west; how to find directions by using a shadow stick, compass, the sun

Orientation: Within the classroom, on the playground, and in the neighborhood

Distance: Blocks from school to the home, to the store and other places; relative distance to places on neighborhood and community maps; using distance between two well-known places as a basis for comparison

Time: In relation to distance from home to school and to main places in the community

Symbols: Pictorial and semipictorial symbols; lines to show streets, roads, and boundaries; use of color for land and water

Physical features are clearly shown on raised relief maps. How might this map be used to develop concepts of major landforms? (Social Studies Workshop, University of California, Berkeley)

Legends: Used on simple maps to represent items meaningful to children—for example, houses, school, stores in neighborhood

Globe: A model of the earth—it is round to represent the earth; how land and water are shown; how the earth makes one complete turn every day (cause of day and night); measuring the distance around the globe to show that it is the same in every direction

Comparisons: Distance and time between familiar places; map symbols with what they actually represent and with pictures; large-scale maps with what they represent—classroom, school, neighborhood, community

Locations: Principal's office, nurse's office, library, and other places in the school; lakes, parks, main streets, and other features on simple maps; land, water, community, state, nation, and continent on a globe

Map making: Floor layouts and floor maps; sand table maps; pictorial symbols to show places on neighborhood community maps; simple maps related to study trips; a floor plan of the classroom; legends for own maps

Inferences: Time and distance to places in the community; directions to places; check inferences

Definitions: Terms related to uses of maps and globe—for example, land, highway, road, steet, freeway, hill, river, lake, ocean, mountain, county, city, town, bridge, tunnel, north, south, east, and west

Grades 3 and 4 In these grades, concepts and skills are developed in community and regional studies at home and around the world. The following are introduced by the end of Grade 4.

Review: Concepts and skills introduced in earlier grades

Directions: Relation to poles and equator; intermediate directions—northeast, northwest, southeast, southwest; grid lines on the globe and on maps as direction lines; direction of flow of rivers; upstream, downstream; use of compass

Orientation: Of textbook, outline, highway, wall and other maps; identification and use of north arrow on maps

Distance: Blocks in miles and kilometers; miles and kilometers to places studied and to places discussed in current events

Time: In relation to distance to places; time of rotation and time of revolution of the earth

Symbols: Identifying towns, cities, capitals; color; coastline; roads; boundaries; relating pictures and symbols; recognizing relief shown by shading; using the map symbols chart; noting how symbols may vary on different maps

Legends: Checking before and while using maps

Scale: Used in making maps—for example, one inch to a foot, one inch to a block, one inch to a mile; measuring distance to places studied; checking scale on textbook and classroom maps

Globe: A sphere that represents the earth; axis of the earth; poles; equator; Arctic and Antarctic circles; orbits of the moon and people-made satellites

Comparisons: Distances to places studied; relative sizes of oceans, lakes, rivers, cities, counties, states, countries, continents; lengths of rivers

Locations: Resources; travel routes; rivers, canals; airports; cities, states, countries, continents; places on outline maps, and the globe

Map making: Pictorial maps; relief model maps; special maps on desk, outline maps, outline wall maps, and slated maps; legends for own maps

A chart of geographical terms should be available for frequent reference use. How might this chart be used to improve map-reading skills? (George F. Cram Company)

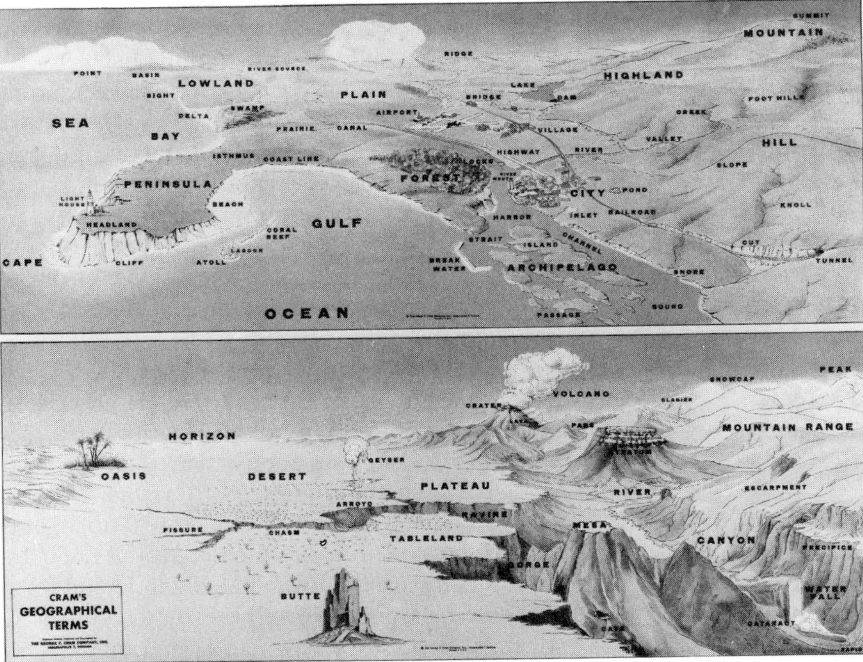

Inferences: General type of climate in relation to location and elevation; centers of population; major products

Definitions: Sea, island, bay, delta, tributary, desert, plateau; climate, irrigation; harbor; continent, country, state, province, city, town, village; capital, capitol; hemisphere, region, poles, equator; coast, fiord

Grades 5 and 6 Building on concepts and skills developed earlier in the program is extended to include the following:

Review: Concepts and skills presented in earlier grades

Directions: Using lines of latitude and longitude to determine directions; east-west lines as lines of latitude or parallels; north-south lines as lines of longitude or meridians

Orientation: Orienting the globe to show position of the earth in relation to the sun at different seasons of the year

Distance: Using great circles to find distances between places on the globe; measuring distances north or south of the equator in degrees, miles, and kilometers

Time: Time needed to travel by various means to places studied; time zones; time in relation to rotation of the earth; time in relation to longitude; Prime Meridian and International Date Line

Area: Comparison of area of home state and other places; comparison of area of the United States and other places; distortion on different projections used in class; conversion of square miles to square kilometers and acres to hectares

Symbols: Reading charts of map symbols; interpreting relief as shown by colors; visualizing steepness of slope from change in colors; interpreting contour lines

Legends: Habit of checking before and while using maps

Scale: Comparing maps of differing scales; using the scale to compare and to determine distances between places and to places by different routes

Globe: Tropic of Cancer as a line of latitude 23.5° north of the equator (the sun is directly over it about June 21); the Tropic of Capricorn as a line of latitude 23.5° south of the equator (the sun is directly over it about December 22); area between them referred to as the low latitudes. The Arctic Circle as a line of latitude 66.5° north of the equator, the Antarctic Circle as a line of latitude 66.5° south of the equator; the area between each circle and its corresponding pole as a polar region, these areas referred to as high latitudes. Lines of longitude, or meridians, as great circles that pass through the poles; the prime meridian (zero degrees) at Greenwich near London, longitude measured from 0° to 180° east or west of the Prime Meridian; longitude used to determine time, 15° equal one hour (360° ÷ 24), twenty-four time zones of 15° each; setting the clock ahead when traveling eastward through time zones; setting it back when traveling westward.

Comparisons: Size, elevation, surface features, products, climate, and other characteristics of places studied; distances; early and modern maps; size of other places in relation to home state and the United States; surface features in areas studied—mountain ranges such as the Appalachians, Rockies, and Sierras; lakes, oceans, rivers; shipping routes to Europe

Locations: Places studied by noting direction and distance from the United States; by using latitude and longitude; states, regions, and countries in relation to others; changes in boundaries—for example, expansion of the United States, formation of new nations

Map making: Special feature maps on desk outline maps, outline wall maps, and slated wall maps; overlays on clear plastic for placement on physical, climatic, and other maps to show relationships to travel routes, population, products, and other features

Inferences: Temperature at places near the equator and at high and low elevations; location of population centers and travel routes; types of industry in relation to resources and level of technology; climate in relation to location, elevation, ocean currents, and other factors; checking inferences by gathering and organizing related data

Definitions: Mesa, peninsula, isthmus; reef, ocean currents, prevailing winds, wind currents; canal, strait, cape, gulf; upland, lowland, rapids, swamps, watershed, timber line; rotation, revolution, latitude, longitude, altitude, elevation, degrees

Grades 7 and 8 Considerable review and additional instruction are provided in these grades. By the end of the eighth grade, attention is given to the following:

Review: Concepts and skills introduced in earlier grades

Directions: Reading directions on different map projections; noting changes in direction on great circle routes

Orientation: Systematic orientation of maps as they are used

Distance: Using statute and nautical miles, and kilometers; changing degrees of latitude and longitude to miles and kilometers

Time: International Date Line: Showing where calendar time is changed and the new calendar day begins; associating longitude and time; determining time in major cities around the world

Area: Square miles and kilometers; acres and hectares; distortion on maps; use of ratio in comparing relative size of states, countries, and other areas

Symbols: Contour lines to show relief and elevation; hachures to show elevation and slope; International Color Scheme; isobars and isotherms

Legends: Independence in determining the meaning of symbols by checking the legend

Scale: Understanding of ratio scale and graduate scales

Globe: Using the analemma to find the latitude at which the sun's rays are vertical at noon at a given time; using the ecliptic to find where the vertical rays of the sun strike the earth on any day during the year; understanding the equinoxes

Comparisons: Changing frontiers; travel routes westward; early and modern routes; mountain ranges, great river valleys, and other surface features; metropolitan areas; map projections; old and modern world trade routes; ocean currents and their effects on countries

Locations: Countries and continents in high, middle, and low latitudes; places by latitude and longitude; historical and current events; natural and cultural surface features

Map making: Desk outline, slated, relief, and special-purpose maps

Inferences: Climate; type of vegetation; products; population centers; travel routes; farming areas; industrial centers

Definitions: Analemma, ecliptic, contour line, isobar, isotherm, continental shelf, equinox, solstice

MAP MAKING

In addition to using maps, children should have many opportunities to make them. Careful attention should be given to accuracy so that correct impressions rather than erroneous ideas of geographic conditions in places being studied will be learned. Have children check their maps against comparable commercial and textbook maps as well as against information secured from reading and from audiovisual materials. A good supply of outline maps should be available for use in both individual and group map-making activities. Where possible, standard practices should be observed in the use of colors and map symbols. The following list includes types of maps children can make:

Floor maps using blocks, boxes, and models, or chalk, tempera, and crayon on linoleum, paper, or oilcloth; simple line maps in the schoolyard

Pictorial maps of community buildings, harbors, products, types of housing, food, clothing, plant and animal life, minerals and other resources, birthplaces of famous people, arts and crafts, modes of travel, methods of communication, raw materials

Specimen maps using real items such as wheat, corn, cotton, and rocks

Relief maps of papier-mâché, salt and flour, plaster of paris, clay, or moistened sand; large relief maps on a section of the schoolyard

Mural maps with strips of paper for streets, pictures or silhouettes for buildings, and so forth

Wall outline maps made by using an opaque projector or a pantograph

Jigsaw puzzle maps of states and countries

Slated maps and globes, or individual and wall outline maps to show air routes, famous flights, early explorations, trade routes, physical features, boundaries, rivers, and so forth

Political and physical maps using symbols and colors to show various features

Transportation maps using various line and dot patterns to show railroad lines, airplane routes, steamship lines, and major highways

Progressive or developmental maps of a region or topic such as the westward movement, colonization, or industrial America

Communication maps using symbols to show telephone lines, cable crossings, radio networks and television networks

Special interest maps such as national parks, state parks, major imports, major cities, seaports, and river systems

Historical maps of the colonies, early travel routes, and early settlements

Transparent maps of resources, transportation networks, and other distributions to project and to place over other maps in order to show relationships

Certain techniques can be used to improve map making. Teachers should select, from the suggestions that follow, those most appropriate for children in their classrooms in terms of maturity, available materials, and needs for map making.

First Experiences First map-making experiences should be realistic and concrete; they must be related to the children's immediate environment and based on concepts they understand. The following experiences are illustrative of those used by primary-grade teachers.

Use blocks or boxes to make a simple floor layout of the neighborhood around the school. Begin with the school and the main street in front of the school; add other items known to the children. Do not get involved in a long, drawn-out, detailed modeling project; keep to a few areas and structures.

Make a simple drawing of the school and nearby places on a large strip of wrapping paper placed on the floor. A good time for such a project is after a study trip. Begin with the school, trace the route, put in key places seen, and mark the main streets clearly. Use colored paper cutouts or crayon drawings to show important places. A floor map of a farm can be made by using objects made by children—barn, fences, trees, animals,

Black tape can be used to show streets on the community maps. If a change is needed, the tape can be lifted and moved. (Washington School, Oakland, California)

trucks, silo, other buildings. Similarly, a layout can be made of the airport or the harbor.

On a map of the school district on which the school and streets are shown, have children locate the school, their homes, and the more important buildings. Small pieces of colored paper can be used to show the children's homes. Use larger pieces of paper to show the school, stores, and other buildings.

Sand table maps can be made to show different features: farm layout, airport or harbor layout, a well-known park, a section of the community, the child's community, and neighboring towns. Line up the table so that it parallels a major street or road. Discuss the direction the road runs and where the sun rises and sets in relation to the table. Consider space between places, and locate major features accurately. Streets and roads should be laid out after a discussion of distances between places, thus providing readiness for later use of the scale. Use blocks, cutouts, or miniature buildings to locate places. Color hills, valleys, and bodies of water.

A flannel board can be used effectively to show different space arrangements. The layout of the school grounds, neighborhood, or a farm are examples of possible use.

Airplane-view maps can be made of a farm, airport, or the community. They may be made on a large piece of paper on the floor. One group, for example, after seeing an airport from the control tower, laid out the runways, hangars, beacons, nearby roads, and buildings as seen from above. Another group made a map of a section of their city after viewing it from a tall building. They also compared their map with aerial photos of the same section of the city.

Freehand drawing or sketching of maps is done in many classrooms after a trip, film, or discussion in which the purpose is to make a map of a small area, and when a map of the area is not available. If time permits, a helpful method is to lay out the area first with blocks or in sand, so that the children get a realistic impression of the surface features.

Making Map Outlines

Use the opaque projector to make map enlargements; project maps from textbooks, newspapers, magazines, or references. Another method is to use slides; these may be made by tracing on a frosted glass placed over the desired map, or they may be purchased. A third technique is to project and trace maps contained in filmstrips or slides that present geographic content.

Use proportional squares to make enlargements. Draw small squares over the map to be enlarged, or trace a copy on tissue and then draw the squares. Draw the same number of large squares on butcher roll or tagboard. Mark the outline shown in each square on the matching large square.

Make chalkboard map stencils by punching small holes one inch apart on a large map outline. Hold this against the chalkboard and pat

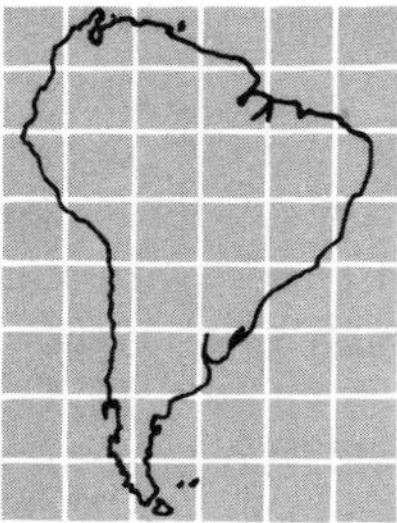

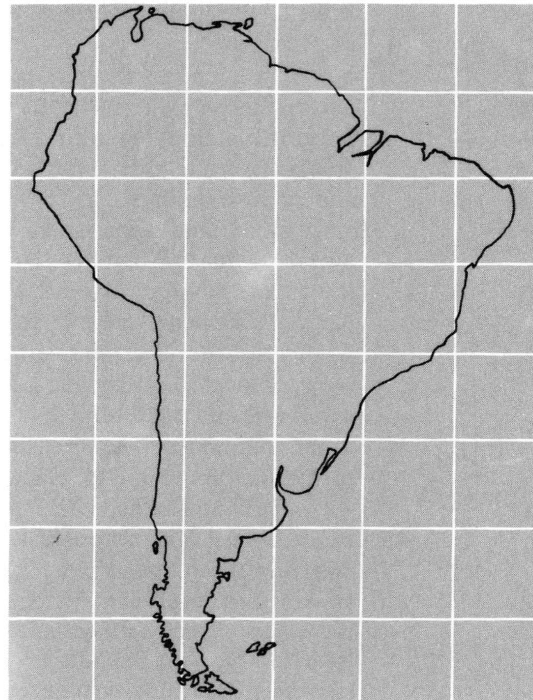

Proportional squares may be used to make enlargements of maps.

over the holes with an eraser containing chalk dust. Mark a heavy line over the dots to show the outline clearly. Another procedure used by some teachers is tracing maps on the chalkboard using cardboard outlines as a pattern.

Small outline maps can be prepared on stencils for reproduction on duplicating machines; in some school systems, audiovisual departments furnish such outline maps on request. Printed desk maps can be secured inexpensively from commercial publishers.

Tracing paper or onionskin can be used to make maps if no projectors are available. If a large map is to be traced, use Scotch tape to fasten individual sheets of tracing paper together. Place the tracing paper over the map to be copied and outline the desired features. Place carbon paper on the sheet to which the map is to be transferred, lay the tracing paper on it, use weights (books or blocks) to prevent slipping, and go over the map outline. Remove the tracing paper and carbons carefully to prevent smearing. (See Charts 14–34 and 14–35 for a summary of guidelines.)

Chart 14–34
Making Maps

What is to be shown?
What facts are needed?
What size should the grid lines be?
What symbols should be used?
What colors should be used?
What would be a good title?
What should be in the legend?

Chart 14–35
Making Outline Maps

Project the slide on the mapping material.
Trace the boundaries and main features.
Locate other important items.
Mark basic symbols on it.
Label important places.
Color the parts according to plan.
Make a complete legend.
Print a clear title.

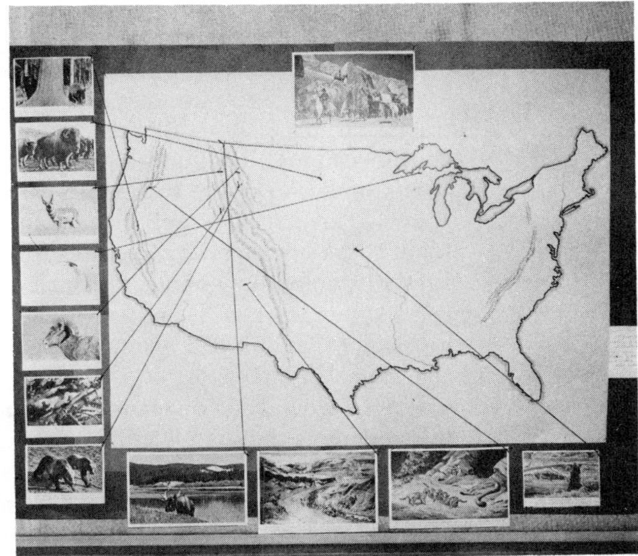

How might you plan for the use of a large outline map in combination with pictures to show specific locations? (Social Studies Workshop, University of California, Berkeley)

Completing Outline Maps Materials for use in making flat maps should be selected with care. If tagboard or other slick-surfaced materials are used, India ink and pens for printing and sketching are better than wax crayons or calcimine paint. Colored drawing pencils also may be used. On softer papers such as bogus, newsprint, construction, mimeograph, manila, chipboard, and certain types of wrapping paper, wax crayons and tempera paint can be used successfully. Crayons and tempera also can be used on windowshades, muslin and percale.

In using colors for making physical maps, the standard international color plan should be used—blue for water, green for lowlands, and yellow, orange, and brown for higher altitudes. In using colors to show other features—states, countries, historical changes such as the frontiers during different periods—be sure to use colors that contrast well and that do not decrease visibility of lettering. The end product should be a map that is clear, sharp in color contrast, and easy to read.

If lines, dots, or shaded areas are used, be sure to plan for contrast and clear lettering. Some teachers have pupils print the lettering on white strips that can be placed over shaded areas and thus stand out. Lettering should be tried out ahead of time.

All lettering on maps should be done clearly and neatly. Have children print difficult terms first on a piece of practice paper. Give attention to spacing, spelling, and proper use of abbreviations. Wherever possible, have all words printed parallel to each other. Guide children in close examination of wall and textbook maps in order to discover ways to line up lettering effectively on their maps.

Encourage the use of pictures and specimens to highlight ideas portrayed on maps. Use ribbon, yarn, or tape running from the picture (or specimen) to its location on the map.

Guide the group to select symbols that effectively portray what is shown. Have them check other maps and identify symbols that seem to them to be appropriate. Consider the use of paper cutouts, hand-drawn symbols, colored symbols, pins and colored bead heads, symbols carved in pencil eraser heads, or stick-prints, which can be reproduced easily by pressing on an ink pad and stamping on the map. Movable symbols may also be used.

The legend can be planned for placement in a corner of the map. The title, symbols, colors, shading, scale, and other pertinent data should be shown clearly. A neat border around the legend will set if off clearly and add to its appearance. Make the legend on a separate piece of paper so that the map will not be ruined if a change must be made.

Give attention to directions on the map. Use arrows where necessary to show the flow of a river, wind currents, or ocean currents. Orientation of the map may be shown by using arrows in one corner to show the cardinal directions.

Puzzle maps (jigsaw maps) can be made from plywood, beaverwood, or heavy chipboard. Outline the map, trace in major features to be shown (states, regions, produce areas), and color in rivers, lakes, and other significant features. Saw into reasonable and logical sections by means of a jigsaw or coping saw. Fasten the border that remains to a whole piece of plywood; this can be used as a holder into which the cutout pieces can be placed. If it is a map of the United States, the border can be labeled to show relative location of the Atlantic and Pacific Oceans, and Canada and

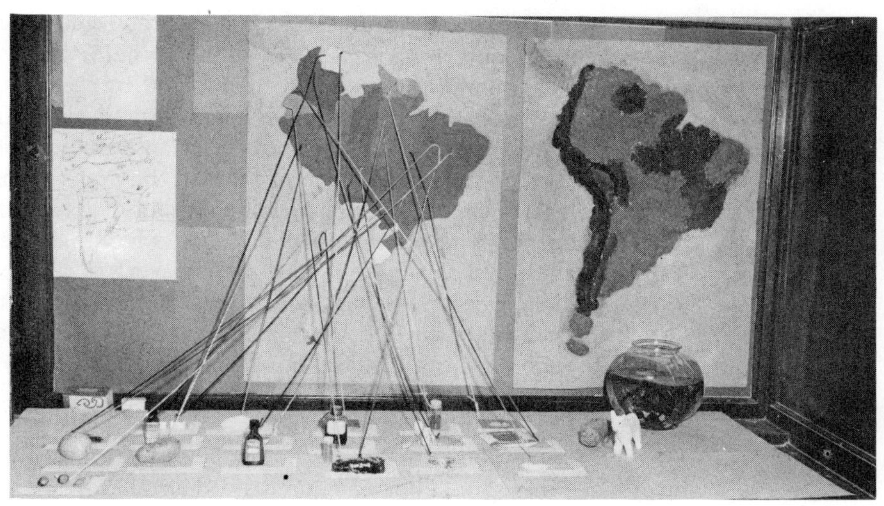

How might you use this device to show the distribution of products in a unit you are planning? (Richmond, California)

Mexico. Encourage children to make puzzle maps of their own out of chipboard.

Another type of puzzle map can be made of felt. Secure a large piece of green felt for the base and several smaller pieces of colored felt to use as sections. Make a paper pattern of the desired region—for example, the United States. Lay the pattern on the large piece of green felt and cut around the edges. Glue the whole map to a piece of plywood, cardboard, or chipboard; this is the base map on which the smaller sections can be placed. Next, mark sections on the paper pattern (New England states, Pacific states, and so forth); cut the pattern into marked sections; place each section on a colored piece of felt and cut around the edges of the section. The cutouts will adhere to the base map when placed on it. Make other cutouts to represent different regions and thus vary the use of the puzzle map.

Transparent maps for projection can be made by using special pencils and inks on plastic, by placing colored plastic cutouts on a plastic base map, and by making copies of maps in copying machines.

Hooked-rug maps are decorative and not difficult to make. Outline the map on a piece of burlap with chalk and tack it to a box or wooden frame. Use a hooked-rug needle to sew in heavy yarn. Select colors to show boundaries, states, provinces, or other features. Have children practice using the needle before they work on the map.

MODELED RELIEF MAPS Modeled relief maps can be used in discussing such problems as why people settle in certain places, why highways are built in certain places, where mountain passes are located, how mountain ranges cause certain areas to be dry and other areas to receive much rainfall, how climate is affected by terrain, how areas are drained by rivers, and a host of other questions related to distance, travel, evaluation, and topography. The use of relief maps enables children to visualize surface features and conditions in the areas being studied.

Remember that the vertical scale on relief maps is different from the horizontal scale. For example, Pike's Peak, which may be prominent on a relief map, is only a tiny pinpoint on the earth's surface when its elevation (under three miles or 4.8 kilometers) is considered in relation to the circumference of the earth (25,000 miles or 40,225 kilometers). However, one child who has seen it said, "It was no pinpoint from where I saw it," thus indicating that relief on smaller areas stands out dramatically and realistically. By mapping a smaller area, less distortion is introduced. However, when large areas are mapped, considerable distortion will be introduced and should be considered as children grow in their understanding of map scale. One technique is to draw a long line on the chalkboard to represent the distance across the area being mapped. Then draw vertical lines to show the relative height of mountains, plateaus, and other features to be shown. Thus, if a mountain approximately 3 miles high is located in an area 300 miles long, the vertical line would be 3 inches while the base line would be 300 inches.[1] After such a demonstration, one fifth grader said, "That mountain isn't so high when you think of how long the ground is." When distortion exists, the teacher should explain that features are relatively higher than they should be to show them more clearly.

The outline on which the relief map is made should be prepared carefully. A wise procedure is to make two outline maps and to use the second one as a working guide while the modeling material is being placed on the relief map. Then, when one area is covered or one layer is on, the second outline map is available for easy reference. Make a list of the features that are to be shown; show pictures illustrating them (the jagged Rockies, long flat prairies, great valleys) and guide children to find them on physical maps, either wall maps or maps in atlases.

Make the map outline by means of a projector or one of the other methods discussed above. Sketch in rivers, mountains, other features, and contour lines. After the outline is mounted on a base board, drive brads and small nails to show relative height and position of peaks, mountain ranges, and hills; these serve as guides during the modeling process. Anticipate and discuss common errors, such as gross distortion of features (hills and mountains too large), omission of significant features (lakes, valleys, dams), inaccuracy of slope (rivers running uphill), errors in relative location of features (Appalachians and Rockies same height). Plan for gradual upslopes from plains to hills to mountains where appro-

[1]Corresponding metric measurements; mountain, 4.83 kilometers high; length of area, 483 kilometers; vertical line, 7.6 centimeters; and base line, 760 centimeters.

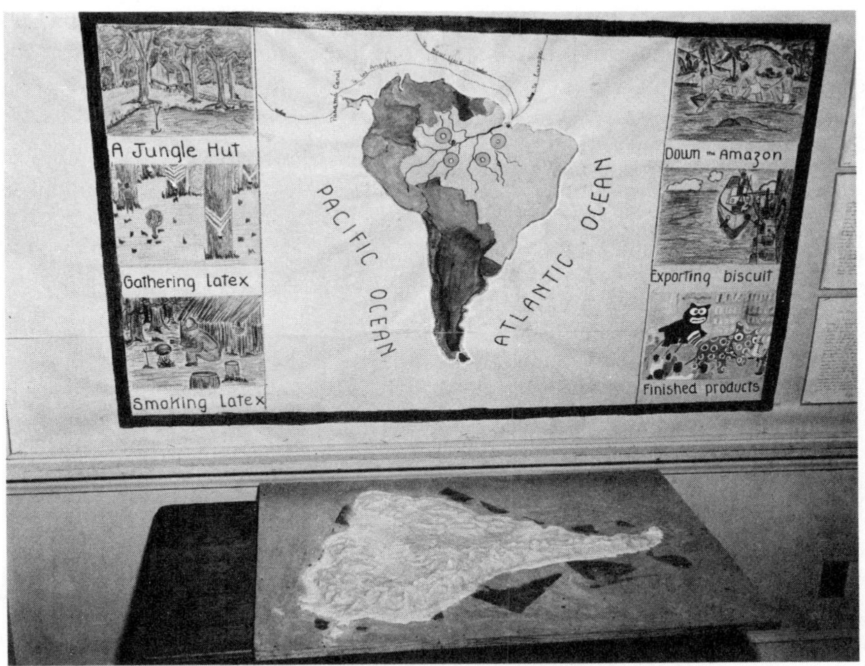

Arrange flat maps and modeled relief maps so that children can make comparisons. (Los Angeles, California)

priate. Some teachers also find it helpful to show and discuss relief maps made by classes of preceding years.

Many relief maps can be made and used without coloring them in any way. The features will stand out clearly and the surface will speak for itself as children use the map. In other instances, the surface can be painted to highlight features and to show contrasts. Tempera water paint works very well; the surface can be protected by shellacking after it has dried. Enamel also can be used if the surface is shellacked first. Another effective technique is to place sawdust in a can or jar of powdered paint and to shake thoroughly. After coating the areas to be colored with glue, sprinkle the sawdust on and allow the glue to dry. Brush off any loose particles. Clean sand can be used in a similar manner. Be sure to plan carefully for the use of different colors on appropriate sections of the map so that they will be clear in contrast and consistent with standard uses of color on maps. See Charts 14–36 and 14–37 for guidelines.

Recipes for Modeling Material

Several different materials can be used to model relief maps. If the maps are to be used for a short period of time, simple and inexpensive recipes should be followed, and finishing the surface with paint and shellac will be unnecessary. If the maps are to be used often, they should be well made and shellacked to protect the surface.

Paste and paper. Tear paper towels or newspapers into 1 1/2-inch pieces. Put paste on one piece at a time, wad it or shape it with your

Chart 14–36
Clay Relief Maps

Have a map to guide modeling.
Mix clay or use ready-mixed clay.
Spread the clay over an outline map.
Build up mountains, hills, and valleys.
Trace rivers with a pencil.
Use tiny sticks to show trees and other items.

Chart 14–37
Papier-mâché maps

Have a map to guide modeling.
Put one layer of papier-mâché on outline map.
Add other layers as needed for hills and mountains.
Form valleys and river channels.
Allow the map to dry.
Paint with enamel or water paints.

Relief and outline maps may be used together to highlight relationships. (Oakland and Fresno City Schools, California)

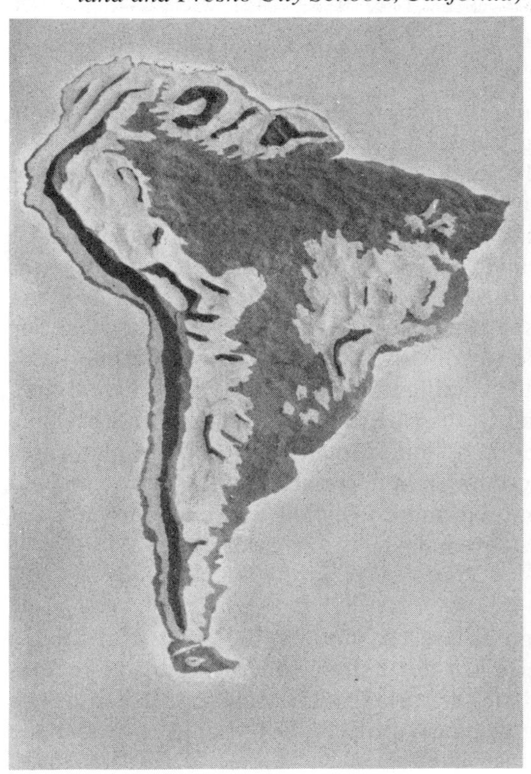

fingers, and stick it on the map outline. Build up hills and mountains as desired. Paint with tempera paint after the paste has dried.

Paper strips and paste. Use crumpled paper to build up terrain; use string or masking tape to hold paper in place. Dip half-inch strips of toweling into wheat paste and place them on the crumpled paper form. After two layers have been placed on the map, coat the entire surface with paste and allow it to dry; secure the base of the map so that it cannot buckle. After the map is dry, paint with calcimine paint.

Sawdust and paste. Mix any sawdust, except redwood or cedar, with wheat paste (from wallpaper store); spoon paste into sawdust until it is well moistened and of good modeling consistency. Good proportions are five cups of sawdust to one cup of wheat paste. The mixture may be applied directly to wood or cardboard. Paint it after it is dry.

Papier-mâché. This is one of the most popular modeling materials. Tear twenty to twenty-five newspaper sheets (or paper towels) into fine shreds and soak them for twenty-four hours. Pulverize the soaked paper by rubbing it over a washboard, or by kneading it. Add wheat paste (or 4 cups of flour and 2 cups of salt) until mixture is of the same consistency as modeling clay. Build up mountains, plateaus, and hills by applying papier-mâché mixture to the surface. After three to six days of drying, paint elevations, water, and other features.

Salt and flour. Mix equal parts of salt and flour, using only enough water to hold the ingredients together. Apply to map outline, modeling the terrain according to plan. (Keep out of humid places because salt attracts moisture.)

Burlap and patching plaster. Finished results can be obtained by immersing burlap in patching plaster. Build terrain on outline by using crumpled paper and masking tape. Lay a piece of burlap (or towel) over the outline and cut along edges to get a good fit. Remove burlap and soak it thoroughly in Spackle or some other patching plaster mix that has been mixed to the consistency of pancake batter; knead the plaster mix in so that the burlap is well soaked. Lay the soaked burlap over the outline, fitting it into hills, valleys, and other features. After about thirty minutes and before the plaster is completely dry, paint with calcimine paint. If it is completely dry, the paint may flake and crack.

Plaster. Because maps made of plaster are heavy, many teachers use this material only for small maps. Mix five pounds of plaster with two handfuls of wheat paste. Add water to get consistency of modeling clay. Build up layers, let dry for three to six days, and paint.

Plaster and sawdust. Mix one pint of plaster, one pint of sawdust, and a quarter pint of paste that has been dissolved in water. Knead and apply to map outline. Paint after the mixture has set for fifteen to thirty minutes.

Plaster and papier-mâché. Add two pints of plaster, a quarter tablespoon of LePage's glue, and a half pint of water to prepared papier-mâché. Be sure that the mixture is of modeling consistency. Paint after mixture has set for thirty to forty-five minutes.

Plastic starch and detergent. Mix one part plastic starch with four parts detergent. Beat mixture until it is fluffy and apply to map outline. Be careful of the surface because it crumbles easily.

QUESTIONS, ACTIVITIES, EVALUATION

1. Which of the examples of map and globe use presented in this chapter might you incorporate in a unit you are planning? Can you think of additional uses of maps and globes in the social studies program?
2. Study a recently published map and check the legend, the use of colors, and the information presented. Can you find related pictures for use in illustrating items on the map?
3. Prepare a list of questions you can use with children to direct their attention to items on the map. Review the summary of map and globe concepts and skills to identify specific points to include in your questions.
4. Study the charts presented in this chapter and note ways you can adapt them for use in a unit.
5. Examine two or three social studies textbooks that contain maps and notice how they are discussed in the text. Note questions that can be answered by children as they use the maps. Refer to the accompanying teacher's manual for suggestions.
6. Select one of the map-making activities and indicate how you might use it in a unit.
7. Make a plan for using one of modeling recipes to construct a relief map.

REFERENCES

BROWN, JAMES W., RICHARD B. LEWIS, and FRED F. HARCLEROAD, *A-V Instruction: Materials and Methods* (4th ed.). New York: McGraw-Hill, 1973. Section on maps and globes; list of sources.

GABLER, ROBERT E., ed., *A Handbook for Geography Teachers.* Normal, Ill.: National Council for Geographic Education, 1966. Section on equipment, materials, and sources.

HANNA, PAUL R., ROSE E. SABAROFF, GORDON F. DAVIES, and CHARLES R. FARRAR, *Geography in the Teaching of the Social Studies.* Boston: Houghton-Mifflin, 1966. Basic concepts and skills; list of sources of materials in Appendix A; map and globe symbols in Appendix B.

HARRIS, RUBY M., *Map and Globe Usage.* Chicago: Rand McNally, 1967. A handbook of teaching suggestions for all grades.

KENNAMER, LORRIN, "Developing a Sense of Place and Space." In *Skill Development in the Social Studies* (33rd Yearbook). Washington, D.C.: National Council for the Social Studies, 1963, pp. 148–70. Concepts and skills involved in using maps and globes.

PRESTON, RALPH C., and WAYNE L. HERMAN, JR., *Teaching Social Studies in the Elementary School.* New York: Holt, Rinehart, & Winston, 1974. Chapter on maps and globes.

RUSHDOONY, HAIG A., "Children's Ability to Read Maps: Summary of Research," *Journal of Geography,* LXVII (April 1968), 24–28. Review of studies.

WHIPPLE, GERTRUDE, *How To Introduce Maps and Globes: Grades One Through Six.* Washington, D.C.: National Council for the Social Studies, 1969. A how-to leaflet.

15

Focusing Questions

What guidelines can be used to evaluate children's learning?

What devices and procedures are most helpful?

How can self-evaluation by students be provided?

How can charts, checklists, and other devices be used in ongoing evaluation?

How can test items be constructed to fit instruction?

What types of standardized tests are available for use in the social studies program?

Evaluating Children's Learning

Evaluation is the process of determining the extent to which objectives have been achieved. It includes all the procedures used by the teacher, children, principal, and other school personnel to appraise outcomes of instruction. Evaluation involves such steps as (1) formulating objectives, (2) securing evidence on the achievement of objectives in selected situations, (3) summarizing and recording evidence, (4) interpreting evidence, and (5) using interpretations to improve instruction and report pupil progress.

Evaluation has many functions in the social studies program. Objectives can be clarified and redefined as a result of the appraisal of children's learning. Through evaluation, teachers gain insights into children's progress, problems, strengths, and weaknesses. Evaluative evidence is helpful in planning units, guiding learning activities, selecting materials of instruction, appraising methods of teaching, and revising the instructional program. Feelings of security for both the teacher and children can be enhanced if results are used constructively to strengthen the program. Finally, evaluation is essential in gathering evidence needed to interpret and report student progress and to carry out an accountability program.

Assessment may be done at the local, state, and national levels. Local assessment is stressed in this chapter because it is most useful in improving instruction. Statewide assessment tends to emphasize achievement in reading and arithmetic. The National Assessment of Educational Progress, a project of the Education Commission of the States, includes the testing of nine-, thirteen-, and seventeen-year-olds in social studies/citizenship, and other areas. Available reports include data on male-female differences, regional differences, type of community, performance of blacks, and educational level of parents. The program's purpose is to provide baseline data on achievement and on progress in meeting objectives believed to be of nationwide importance.[1]

GUIDELINES TO EFFECTIVE EVALUATION

Evaluation should be based on several guiding principles that serve as a framework for effective development and use of evaluative devices in all aspects of appraisal. They may be used in guiding self-evaluation, in teacher appraisal of classroom experiences, and in appraising the overall effectiveness of the program.

Point of view. Teachers occupy a key position in evaluation, since their point of view, methods of teaching, knowledge of children's growth characteristics, selection of materials, and ability to make intelligent value judgments determine the quality of evaluation.

Teachers must be aware of the point of view they use in evaluation, since values determine the emphasis given to appraisal of learning experiences. Consider the case of two teachers attempting to foster self-evaluation in children. Both used charts, examples of which follow, to guide the evaluation of discussion.

One teacher developed Chart 15–2 cooperatively with the class on the basis of needs that had arisen; the other imposed Chart 15–1 on the class, using it as an admonition to work harder. One teacher conceived evaluation as part of the instructional program; the other saw it as a tool to secure obedience. One viewed it as being cooperative, the other as teacher-dominated. Thus, each teacher's point of view brought about a vastly different type of evaluation.

Chart 15–1
Good Workers

Answer all questions
Check work for errors
Hand in work on time

Chart 15–2
Working Together

Help in group planning
Carry out group plans
Use many sources of ideas

Integration with instruction. Appraisal cannot be separated from instruction in the classroom. The alert teacher observes and notes chil-

[1] National Assessment of Educational Progress, 700 Lincoln Tower, 1860 Lincoln, Denver, Colorado. *NAEP Newsletter* and list of reports available on request.

dren's needs and makes changes to improve the program as it is being developed. Some of the most valuable evaluative procedures, such as group discussion, observation by the teacher, making charts on group standards, and using checklists, are part of instructional procedures.

Ongoing process. This principle flows from the one immediately preceding and suggests that effective evaluation is always going on in the classroom. This means simply that throughout the day, from day to day, and from week to week throughout the year, appraisals must be made both by the children and the teacher. This guideline clearly implies that evaluation is not something that is done just before the report cards are given out.

Diagnostic, formative, and summative evaluation are part of the ongoing process of assessment. Diagnostic appraisal is done to determine individual and group needs. Formative evaluation provides evidence on learning and on how instruction should proceed. Summative evaluation at the end of a unit or course is done to get evidence on the attainment of stated objectives. All three should be blended together and made a part of the instructional process.

Cooperative process. Evaluation must be cooperatively done with other teachers, the children, parents, supervisors, and administrators. All have a stake in the program. The teacher and the children share in the clarification of objectives and in the use of various techniques of evaluation. Group evaluation and many types of self-evaluation are based on group-made standards and goals. Parents should be involved in the discussion of goals, the clarification of goals in terms of the hopes they have for their children, and the interpretation of information gleaned through the use of evaluative instruments. Supervisors and administrative officers cooperate in the program in order to give it balance, direction, and systematic consideration.

Clear link with objectives. The central function of evaluation is to determine the extent to which objectives are achieved. In appraisal by the teacher and in self-evaluation by children, objectives should be clear. Clarity may be achieved by stating objectives in performance terms, as indicated in Chapter 1. To give an example, responsibility may be appraised specifically and concretely when defined in terms of the student's ability to (1) state ways to carry out the tasks agreed upon in group planning, (2) state rules to follow in individual and group activities when little or no teacher supervision is provided, (3) describe and use a variety of data sources without help from others, and (4) describe improvements that can be made in group and individual work.

Such a statement enables a teacher to do down-to-earth appraisals in getting at such points as the experiences most effective in developing this type of behavior, which children need help, and the situations that should be provided.

Variety of settings. Children's growth in attitudes, interests, concepts, and group-action skill can be appraised in group planning, discussion, sharing, reporting, and evaluation. Behavior in dramatic activities, construction, rhythms, and role playing reveals many evidences of growth. The ways in which children use materials, share materials with others, take and give suggestions, accept newcomers, and work together are of special importance. These and other situations should be used to determine whether key learnings are carrying through into a variety of situations.

Creative efforts also reveal evidence of learning. A teacher should be alert to new ideas, new ways of doing things, originality in construction, dramatic play, and artistic expression, and suggestions that arise in group discussion. These are excellent clues to cognitive and affective development.

Variety of devices. If all outcomes are to be appraised, then many different instruments and techniques are needed. For example, checklists can be designed to appraise cooperation, discussion, and use of materials. Tests are available for measuring concepts, information, and study skills. Anecdotal records, charts, rating scales, and other devices can be used as special needs arise. The following list contains the devices now in use in many school systems:

Directed observation	Logs	Case studies
Informal observation	Diaries	Activity records
Group discussion	Autobiographies	Tape recordings
Small-group interview	Scrapbooks	Cumulative records
Individual interview	Collections	Pupil graphs
Case conference	Samples of work	Profiles
Checklists	Teacher-made tests	Sociograms
Rating scales	Group-made tests	Flow-of-discussion charts
Inventories	Standardized tests	
Questionnaires	Sociometric tests	Behavior journals
Charts	Anecdotal records	Evaluative criteria

The selection of evaluative devices depends on the objectives being evaluated, the conditions under which children are working, and the type of behavior involved. If a teacher desires insight into the *use* of concepts, attitudes, or group processes, the children should be observed in discussion, dramatic play, construction, or similar situations. The ways in which children use concepts and attitudes may be recorded in anecdotal records, a behavior journal, or a specially prepared recording form. If, on the other hand, a teacher must determine the *accuracy* of concepts or the attitudes of children toward certain objects or persons, tests or attitude questionnaires should be used.

Of course, the teacher should not use only one device to evaluate a given objective. Observation may be used continuously even though checklists, ratings, or tests are employed. A combination of devices is generally better than a single device. The important point is to decide on the kind of evidence needed, and then to select and use those devices that will secure it. For example, in a social studies workshop, one group proposed the following methods for evaluating various outcomes:

Concepts and Main Ideas: Observation, group discussion, tests, samples of work, individual and small-group interviews

Modes and Processes of Inquiry: Observation, group discussion, charts, checklists, interviews, samples of work

Basic Skills: Observation, tests, charts, checklists, group discussion, worksheets, rating devices

Attitudes, Values, Interests: Observation, questionnaires, checklists, rating devices, anecdotal records, recordings, discussion, interviews, drawings

As far as possible, evaluative instruments selected for use in social studies should meet the criteria of validity, reliability, objectivity, practicality, applicability (curricular validity), usefulness, appropriateness, and descriptiveness. The instruments should measure what they purport to measure, measure consistently and accurately; give similar results for different persons; be easy to administer, relatively inexpensive, and not too time-consuming; be related to the social studies program; contribute evidence that can be put to use; be related to the level of development of the group with which they will be used and fit into the overall program of evaluation; and give evidence that describes the behavior of children.

Self-evaluation. Self-evaluation that promotes increasing self-direction is an essential aspect of evaluation in social studies. It is a mode of appraisal used throughout life. Through self-evaluation, children gain the ability to analyze their own skills, attitudes, behavior, strengths, needs, and success in achieving objectives. They develop feelings of personal responsibility as they appraise the effectiveness of individual and group efforts. They learn how to face squarely the competencies needed in various tasks and to assess their own potential and contributions. Their role in group processes can be clarified as they check themselves on cooperatively made criteria. Social learning is sharpened and enriched through self-evaluation because the child is participating more extensively in the learning process.

If children are to be capable of self-evaluation, they must learn how to develop objectives to guide their evaluative efforts. This may be done through group discussion. Attention also must be given to the preparation of checklists, charts, and rating devices that children can use. The following devices are commonly used to promote self-evaluation:

Group discussions and interviews
Samples of the child's work gathered through the term
Standards developed by the group and placed on charts
Checklists made by the individual or group
Scrapbooks made by each child
Diaries or logs containing examples of ways the child has been cooperative, shown concern for others, and so forth
Recordings of discussion, reporting, singing, and so forth
Graphs kept by each child

Organization for interpretation. Information should be summarized in a form that can be easily interpreted. If a picture of the status of children in a class is needed, a list may be prepared giving each pupil's name with related data summarized in tabular form. If information on a child's attitudes or interests is needed, a simple profile may be developed. In other instances, graphs, charts, summaries of anecdotes, sociograms, or a complete case study may be used.

In addition, a cumulative record should be kept for each child in order to develop a composite picture of growth. The cumulative record should include space to record information about units of instruction the child has completed, growth in problem-solving ability, social attitudes, democratic behavior, skill in group work, interest in social studies and strengths and weakness in various types of activities. When such information is included, subsequent teachers can make more effective plans for the child's continuous growth.

Interpretation in terms of individual development. Each child has a unique rate of growth and development, personality, background, level of achievement, interests, problems, and needs. A child's growth to increasingly higher levels of behavior (not merely the child's status in the group or position with reference to national norms) should be the concern of each teacher. Arbitrary standards for all children are unrealistic and impractical.

Norms are helpful, however, as a frame of reference for considering the relative achievement of an individual or of a group. If a bright child falls far below the average, the reason for the deviation should be studied. If a group "deviates from the norm," the reasons for the deviation should be investigated. In all instances, the first question is why deviations exist, not what to do to get them up to the norm. After the reasons for the deviations are determined and needs of the child or group are established, steps can be taken to provide significant learning experiences.

Application. Data gathered by the teacher or by the children through self-evaluation should be used to improve learning experiences.

Group evaluation in the classroom should reveal next steps, needs for materials, new sources of ideas, and improved standards of work. Overall evaluation of the effectiveness of the program should lead to clarification of objectives and better use of activities, materials, and evaluative techniques. Conferences with parents and interpretation of the program are other illustrative uses of evaluative data. Evaluation that does not lead to improvement is just another form of busywork.

The accountability system. One major use of evaluation data and procedures is in the accountability systems that have mushroomed in school districts throughout the country in recent years. Evaluation data on the social studies program are fed into the accountability system along with data from other subjects. The attainment of objectives set by teachers is appraised and the findings used to make improvements in the instructional program. The findings are also used as feedback to make changes in various components of the accountability system, as shown in Chart 15–3.

Accountability systems include procedures for evaluation of the performance of teachers and other school personnel. Pupil progress toward the attainment of specified objectives is used in many systems as the basis for appraising the work of teachers. The teacher and evaluator should cooperatively determine the objectives to be assessed by completing initial planning sheets, in which terminal instructional objectives are identified and related instructional objectives are specified. Pre- and postassessment measures are used to determine pupil progress. The teacher and evaluator cooperatively determine the means of assessment, which may include observation, checklists, test items and other methods. The following examples illustrate this procedure at three different grade levels.[2]

GRADE 1

Terminal Objective: To demonstrate the occurrence of day and night
Instructional Objective: Given a flashlight and a globe, the child will show how day and night occur
Preassessment: Teacher observation
Postassessment: Teacher observation

GRADE 3

Terminal Objective: To distinguish between rules and laws in the community

[2]Adapted from *Suggested Terminal Objectives* (Los Angeles: Instructional Planning Division, City Schools, 1972).

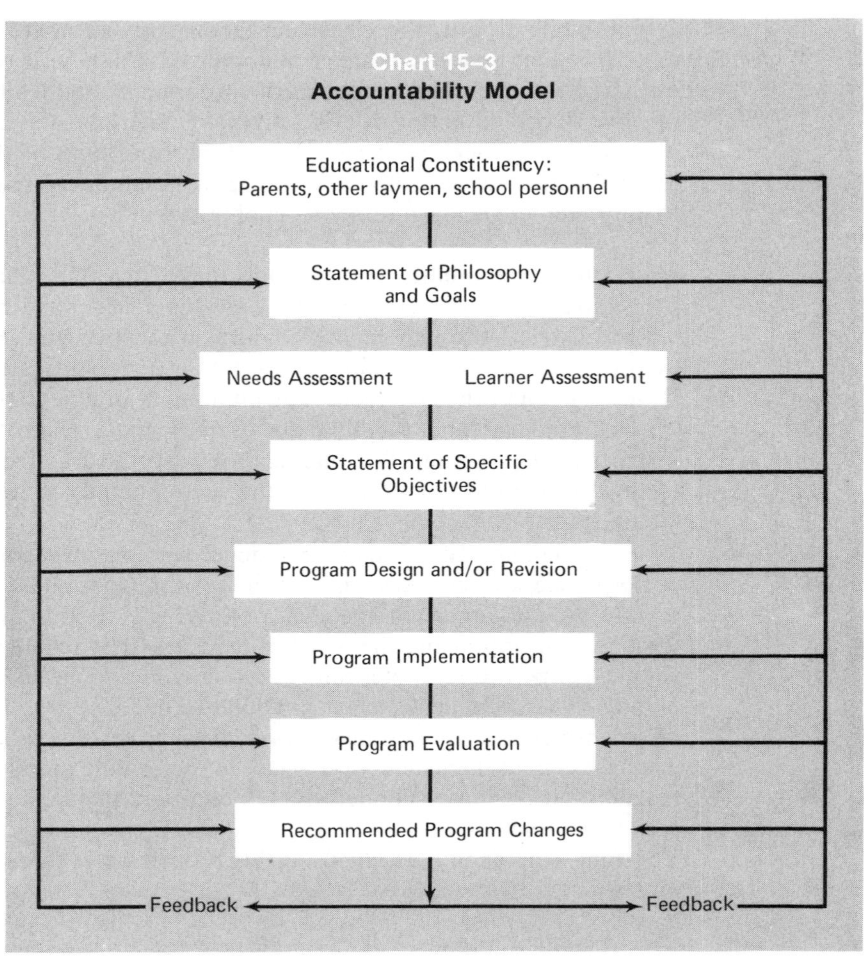

Instructional Objective: Given several examples, the student will state which are rules and which are laws

Preassessment: Write an *R* by each item below that is a rule; write an *L* by each item that is a law.

_____ Crossing streets at a signal
_____ Taking turns in a game
_____ Not running in the halls

Postassessment: Write an *R* by each item below that is a rule; write an *L* by each item that is a law.

_____ Not throwing rocks at passing cars
_____ Asking permission to leave the classroom
_____ Not taking things belonging to others

GRADE 5

Terminal Objective: To identify contributions of Americans of different ethnic backgrounds to our culture
Instructional Objective: Given a list of individuals, the student will write at least one contribution each has made
Preassessment: Write one contribution of each person listed below:
W. E. B. Du Bois ______________________
Susan B. Anthony ______________________
Edward R. Roybal ______________________
Postassessment: Write one contribution of each person listed below:
George Washington Carver ______________________
Harriet Tubman ______________________
Cesar Chavez ______________________

In the operation of the accountability system, avoid such pitfalls as specifying easily attainable objectives, overemphasizing skill objectives at the expense of other objectives, making unwarranted comparisons between classes and schools, failing to interpret data in terms of background factors, scapegoating of teachers, and failing to give highest priority to instruction geared to individual differences. In short, the guiding principles noted above should operate throughout the program, and accountability systems should contribute to the improvement of children's learning and the professional integrity of school personnel, not detract from them.

EVALUATION TECHNIQUES

Observation by the Teacher

Day-to-day observation of children gives a developmental picture of growth that cannot be obtained in any other way. It is especially effective in social studies because of the variety of experiences the program provides. Children themselves create new and different situations (such as forming groups, meeting new problems, and locating new sources of information) in which learning may be observed. A teacher may create other situations in which specific concepts, attitudes, and skills may be observed; their carryover to out-of-school enterprises also may be noted. The actual behavior of children in new situations—the goal of the experienced evaluator—thus becomes the focal point of evaluation.

The uses of observation for evaluative purposes are as varied and numerous as the types of experiences provided in the social studies program. A teacher may obtain evaluative data by listening to discussions, oral reading, dramatic play, comments about objects or persons, questions, and spontaneous expression during construction or on study trips.

By watching children at work and at play, data may be obtained regarding interests, attitudes, concern for others, group processes, use of time and materials, use of skills, physical ability, emotional adjustment, attentiveness, persistence, ability to carry out directions, and acceptance of responsibility.

In using observation as an evaluative device, teachers must recognize that similar types of behavior may reveal different kinds of learning. Different purposes, needs, and backgrounds produce different responses. Some children offer to help others because they are growing in cooperative skills; others offer help because they want to "move in on" another's activity. Some children may accept one responsibility eagerly to avoid another more important one, whereas some accept it because it is in line with objectives. A teacher can gain competence in meeting these problems by knowing each child's background and by becoming a skillful observer.

Checklists are helpful guides to observation. They should be specific, descriptive of desirable behavior, and easy to use. They may be used as overall guides in many situations, or they may be applied specifically to the child's behavior in planning, discussion, research, or construction. Checklists 15–1 and 15–2 are illustrative; others are presented in later sections of this chapter.

Checklist 15–1

APPRAISAL OF STUDY HABITS AND ATTITUDES DURING RESEARCH PERIOD

Behavior To Be Observed	Names of Children								
Locates sources of information									
Uses the contents									
Uses the index									
Gets information from study aids—charts, tables, maps									
Uses encyclopedias effectively									
Uses dictionaries effectively									
Uses library facilities									
Takes notes related to topics under study									

Uses correct form in outlines									
Organizes information from several sources									
Arranges ideas in good order									
Selects illustrative material for reports									

Checklist 15–2

CONCERN FOR OTHERS

Note: Check each child two or three times during the term to determine if growth has taken place.

School ____________

Date ____________

Behavior To Be Observed	Names of Children								
Is sensitive to needs and problems of others									
Helps others meet needs and solve problems									
Willingly shares ideas and materials									
Accepts suggestions and help									
Makes constructive suggestions									
Sticks to group plans and decisions									
Works courteously and happily with others									
Gives encouragement to others									
Respects the property of others									
Enjoys group work									
Thanks others for help									
Commends others for contributions									

The kinds of charts, rating devices, and other evaluative instruments that children can use in self-evaluation may be discovered through teacher observation. For example, after noting specific needs and problems in a discussion, one teacher guided the class in the development of a chart that listed these points: (1) Stick to the topic; (2) be brief so that others may have a turn; (3) speak so all can hear; (4) give turns to others; and (5) listen to others.

The effectiveness of observation as an evaluative device may be improved by the use of the following guidelines:

1. Notice little things that may have great value in understanding the child's behavior.
2. Be alert to the uniqueness of each child and to creative contributions.
3. Look for constructive, improved behavior; avoid fault-finding.
4. Do not assume that similar expressions of behavior indicate the same learning for all children.
5. Be aware of your own feelings and prejudices.
6. Be sensitive to the halo effect, since some characteristics may not be related to others.
7. Develop and use specific observational guides to appraise specific aspects of behavior.
8. Make necessary records while the data are fresh in mind.
9. Record what actually happened, not your reaction to it.
10. Use observation to secure evidence on many different types of learning, not on conduct alone.

Group Discussion

In social studies programs, extensive use is made of group discussions in which children evaluate work periods, study skills, research activities, and specific problems as they arise. Each member of the group can participate, charts and checklists can be developed, attention can be given to problems as they arise, specific instances of behavior can be considered, and cooperative and continuous appraisal can be carried on. The essence of group evaluative discussion is constructive consideration of the needs and problems of the group. Emphasis should be given to contributions of individuals and committees. Negative comments should be tactfully redirected toward constructive suggestions for improvement. Attention should be focused on the job to be done, ways to help each other, and next steps that should be taken to achieve stated objectives.

Many teachers raise specific questions during discussion when various learnings are being evaluated. Clues to the types of questions to raise may be noted as children engage in research activities, use the library, work in committees, use audiovisual resources, engage in dramatic play and construction, or participate in other activities. *How* and *why* questions, which bring children's thinking to bear on causes, effects, and reasons involved in various situations, should be used as well as *what, when,* and *where* questions.

Questions should be directly related to the objectives of the unit currently underway. In the primary grades, for example, questions related to home, school, and community might include the following: How do we share at home? What jobs (responsibilities) do children, parents, and community workers have? Who helps us get library books? In later grades, when the teacher is appraising skills in problem solving, these questions might be used: Where can we find out about this? How shall we share what we find out? Why must all ideas be considered? How shall we put our ideas to use? Questions such as these reveal quickly and easily which children are grasping key ideas; they also indicate points of emphasis for the teacher. They make evaluation a part of the instructional program—*as it should be.*

Also helpful, particularly in small-group discussions, are questions involving what comes next and what is missing. Questions of this type may be used to assess a child's ability to grasp the whole of a situation, to predict outcomes, to use ideas to solve problems, and to identify with others. For example:

1. Cover part of a mural, map, picture, exhibit, chart, diagram, or collection and ask, "What is covered?" or "What is missing?"
2. Remove an object from an exhibit, a part of a jigsaw map, or a part of a model and ask, "What is missing?"
3. Give incomplete directions for making something, going somewhere, using something, conducting a meeting, or introducing someone, and ask, "What is missing?"
4. Cover part of a time line, or do part of a demonstration and ask, "What comes next?"
5. Tell part of an incident or a story and ask, "What comes next?"
6. Show several pictures in sequence and ask, "What comes next?"

Another technique that may be used as part of discussion, or at least introduced during discussion, involves arranging objects or ideas in sequence or in proper order. For example, consider the following activities:

1. Show a set of pictures or cards with phrases or sentences, and have children arrange them in order.
2. Show pictures that belong in a scene (for example, airport, farm) and have children arrange them in relative position.
3. Have children put together, in proper position, parts of maps or large pictures that have been cut to show key ideas, such as relative location, relative size, and distance.
4. Have children arrange a floor layout of the community, a farm, or an airport.

The discussion that follows such activities is often as revealing of what children have learned as the manner in which they carry out the activities.

Good sources of evaluative data are unstructured discussions in which children talk over problems and questions of individual and group concern that come up spontaneously or with a minimum of teacher guidance. In such discussions, children usually reveal attitudes toward others, concepts, erroneous ideas, reasoning ability, individual needs, and ability to participate in group work.

Charts and Checklists

Charts are especially helpful in individual and group self-evaluation. They should be cooperatively developed by the group so that each member of the class will understand their meaning. Charts can be referred to by individuals in the group or used in group discussions in which specific items are being evaluated. Charts 15–4 to 15–16 can be used to assess the development of inquiry processes discussed in Chapter 6. Other charts presented in preceding chapters may also be used to evaluate learning.

Checklists are very helpful in evaluating many aspects of social learning. Specific behavior, interests, skills, and concepts have been appraised by means of checklists. Some are designed for use by teachers; others are used by the children themselves for self-evaluation. Some are

Chart 15–4
Recalling

Is the problem clear?
What can you think of that is related to it?
How can you check what you recall?
Can you tell how it is related to the problem?

Chart 15–5
Observing

What did you observe?
How do your findings check with others?
How can you explain any differences?
Do we need to check our findings?
Was everyone looking for the same thing?

Chart 15–6
Comparing/Contrasting

Have comparable features been identified?
Has each feature been defined?
Can you state how they are alike? different?
Do we agree? If not, why?

Chart 15–7
Defining

Is the meaning clear? If not, how can you find it?
Can you state the meaning?
Do others agree? If not, how should the definition be changed?
Does it check with the glossary or dictionary?
Is it useful in communicating with others?

Chart 15–8
Classifying

What is the objective for grouping?
What characteristics did you use to group the items?
Are the groups mutually exclusive?
Does each item fit into a group?
What other groups might be made? On what basis?

Chart 15–9
Interpreting

Can you explain the findings in your own words?
Can you state how some items are related?
Have you interpreted it as it is, not as you want it to be?
How does your interpretation compare with other interpretations?

Chart 15–10
Generalizing

Did you identify the facts?
Did you find what is common in them?
Have you stated the central idea?
Have you checked your statement against the evidence?
Can you state the main idea and supporting details?

Chart 15–11
Inferring

Can you state the evidence or reason for your inference?
Does it make sense? Is it reasonable?
Does it follow from what is given or from the reason you used?
Does it make sense to others?

Chart 15–12
Predicting

Can you state the factors or reasons you used?
What evidence did you use?
Have you double-checked to be sure you considered all factors or conditions?

Chart 15–13
Hypothesizing

Can you state how it helps to explain the topic or problem?
Is it consistent with other ideas related to the topic?
Can it be tested by finding evidence?

Chart 15–14
Analyzing

Have you identified the main parts?
Can you describe each part? Tell why it is important?
Can you state how the parts are related?

Chart 15–15
Synthesizing

Did you bring together the most important items?
In what way is it a new or original presentation of ideas?
Can you state the organizing idea(s) that you used?
Are you satisfied with the form of presentation?

Chart 15–16
Evaluating

Was the focus of evaluation clearly defined?
Were standards of appraisal clearly defined?
Was related evidence gathered?
Can the judgment be supported by evidence or reasons?

used in group work; others are used by individuals. The teacher makes many checklists to meet specific group needs, and other checklists are planned cooperatively by the class. Checklists 15–3 through 15–5 illustrate practical devices that can be developed in social studies classes.

Checklist 15–3
WORKING WELL WITH OTHERS

Name: ______________________ Date: ______________________
School: ______________________ City: ______________________

How do you work with other students in making plans, discussing problems, making things, looking up ideas, and using materials? All of us need to check ourselves to see if we are doing those things that improve the work of the group. By checking ourselves, we can learn things to do to improve group work. We need to know our good points and shortcomings and to consider things to do to improve. Read the statements below and place a check in the square that tells how often you do each item in the list.

How Often Do You Do Each Item Listed Below?	**Always**	**Usually**	**Sometimes**	**Never**	**?**
1. I stick to the job until it is finished.					
2. I take part in many different activities.					
3. I work with everyone in the class.					

4. I am eager to try out new ideas and to work on new problems.					
5. I share materials with others.					
6. I help set up plans and directions and follow them.					
7. I work happily without grumbling or losing my temper.					
8. I give in if my ideas conflict with the best interests of the group.					
9. I consider the rights of others.					
10. I am courteous and use good manners.					

Checklist 15–4
HOW DO I WORK?

1. Do my own job	Yes	No
2. Finish each job	Yes	No
3. Follow directions	Yes	No
4. Listen attentively	Yes	No
5. Return materials	Yes	No
6. Clean up properly	Yes	No

Checklist 15–5
AM I COURTEOUS?

1. Listen to others	Yes	No
2. Take turns	Yes	No
3. Share materials	Yes	No
4. Express thanks	Yes	No
5. Return materials	Yes	No
6. Work quietly	Yes	No

Interviews Both formal and informal interviews are helpful in appraising learning. Informal interviews are helpful in talking over immediate problems, determining difficulties, and clarifying group standards and procedures. Formal interviews ordinarily involve checklists, lists of questions, or rating scales carefully planned ahead of time. In either type of interview, the teacher should aim to achieve and maintain rapport, be a good listener, guide the interview so that the purpose is achieved, and maintain a sympathetic attitude so that tensions are not created. Written records of interviews are helpful because they can be added to the child's cumulative record and thus give a more descriptive picture of growth.

Logs and Diaries Both individual and group diaries or logs are useful for evaluation of learning. The group-made log contains material dictated by the class, much of it growing out of group planning and evaluation. The individual log is a record of such activities as cooperation, acceptance of responsibility, work completed, or books read. Many teachers have group discussions regarding the items to be kept in individual logs and to share ideas as the logs are being written. Pictorial logs are usually made in primary grades because the skills necessary for written self-expression have not been developed.

Questionnaires and Inventories Questionnaires and inventories are helpful in determining interests, hobbies, attitudes, home background, and other items about individual children. Many teachers make and use informal inventories and questionnaires to meet specific needs as they arise in class. Checklists 15–6 and 15–7 illustrate those teachers themselves can make.

A variety of attitudes, values, feelings, and appreciations may be assessed by questionnaires or inventories based on five possible responses to an item. The responses range from strongly agree (or like, approve) to strongly disagree (or dislike, disapprove), as shown in the examples below. Students may respond directly on a rating scale or record their responses on a separate answer sheet.

1. We should try to understand the people of Russia better.

   Strongly agree | Agree | Uncertain | Disagree | Strongly disagree

2. I like things that are made by the Japanese.

   Definitely like | Like | Uncertain | Dislike | Definitely dislike

3. How do you feel about the decision to employ women on the police force?

   Very happy | Happy | Uncertain | Unhappy | Very unhappy

4. What do you think about increasing trade with China?

   Strongly favor | Favor | Uncertain | Oppose | Strongly oppose

5. We should have more units on black Americans, Chicanos, and native Americans.

   Strongly approve | Approve | Uncertain | Disapprove | Strongly disapprove

6. How well did you like the city council's decision on bicycle safety?

   Really liked | Liked | Uncertain | Disliked | Really disliked

The semantic differential is useful in measuring a generalized attitude toward almost any person, group, object, place, or event included

Checklist 15–6 **PEOPLE FROM MEXICO**			
Check Each of the Following:	**Agree**	**Disagree**	**Not Sure**
1. People from Mexico are hard workers.			
2. It is fun to listen to Mexican music.			
3. Drawings and paintings from Mexico are beautiful.			
4. Many intelligent people live in Mexico.			

Checklist 15–7 **INTEREST IN TRANSPORTATION**			
Do You Like to Do the Following?	**Like**	**Do Not Like**	**Not Sure**
1. Make model planes?			
2. Play with planes?			
3. Talk about planes with friends?			
4. Read stories about pilots?			
5. Visit the airport?			
6. Ride on planes?			
7. Make boats?			
8. Read stories about seamen?			
9. Visit the railroad yards?			

in the social studies program.[3] Students check their position on a seven-point scale with bipolar objectives at each end, as shown in the following example.

[3] See Bloom, Hastings, and Madaus reference, end of chapter.

The People of China

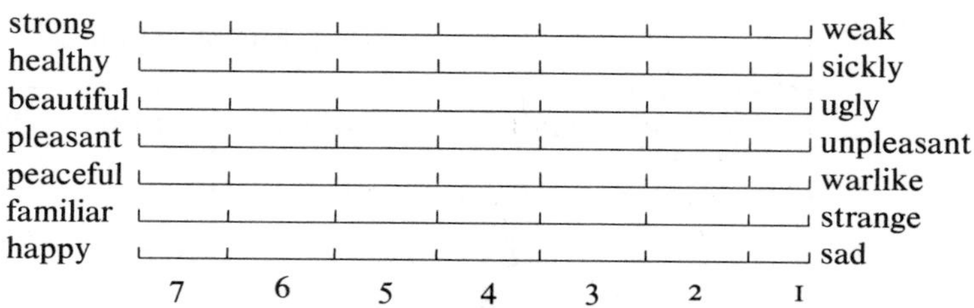

Many of the value clarification strategies discussed in Chapter 7 may be used to assess values and attitudes. For example, the value-sheet strategy may be used as suggested for situational tests. The rank-order strategy, value survey, completion of unfinished sentences, position on a continuum, weighing alternatives, and either-or choices are good examples of devices that may be used to assess values. These and the other strategies should be reviewed at this point.

Anecdotal Records Anecdotal records are brief sketches of specific instances of behavior. Checklist 15–8, an excerpt from a behavioral journal, concerns a child who was receiving help in working with others.

Checklist 15–8

BEHAVIOR JOURNAL

Name: Walter Doe Class: Miss Smith Grade: IV

Date	Incidents	Comments
9–21	Did not share the picture with others.	Needs help in carrying out standards.
10–2	Helped to make rules for using materials; shared only a few tools.	Group chart may help.
10–19	Discussed need for sharing with others.	Seems to understand reason for sharing; needs to work with one or two children.
11–2	Worked with David in preparing a report.	Growth in evidence; must place in a group of three or four as a next step.

Because anecdotal records are time-consuming, every effort should be made to simplify the procedures involved in making them. Some teachers simply keep a page headed by each child's name and make entries during the day or after school. Others make brief notes as incidents arise and drop them in a folder prepared for each child. Records should be limited to three or four aspects of behavior for which evidence of growth is needed, evidence that cannot be recorded in other ways. Anecdotes are most valuable when specific instances, such as those listed above, are recorded. General comments such as "Paul cooperated with Mary" or "Peter was unkind in his manner" are of little value.

Case Studies and Case Conferences

Some teachers make a case study of one or two children each year. Pertinent information on such items as home background and previous school experience, health records, anecdotal records, and data from tests are brought together and analyzed. Such a procedure gives a more complete understanding of a child's growth and has great value for guidance and teaching.

Case conferences are helpful in analyzing and interpreting the information regarding a child's development. In a case conference, all available evidence is considered by the child's teacher, former teacher or teachers, the principal, and guidance workers. The pooled judgment of several individuals is thereby brought to bear on specific questions and problems.

MAKING AND USING TESTS

Three kinds of tests are used in social studies programs: teacher-made tests, teacher/pupil-made tests, and standardized tests. All have a place in a complete program of evaluation, provided that they are selected or constructed in accordance with the needs of the children and the objectives of the program.

Tests may be criterion-referenced or norm-referenced. Criterion-referenced tests are directly related to stated objectives and show whether or not a student has achieved them. Norm-referenced tests provide information on the relative achievement of an individual or group in the form of grade-equivalent, percentile or other scores. Criterion-referenced tests are being used with increasing frequency as part of accountability systems and to give feedback for individualizing and improving instruction.

Teacher-made Tests

Effective teacher-made tests are an integral part of instruction. They reveal individual needs, facilitate grouping, and give teachers and students clues to progress, problems, strengths, and weaknesses. Conceptual, process, skill, and affective objectives may be evaluated. Situational or problem items should be included along with standard items. Pictures and graphics in textbooks and other media should be used to design some items. And items should be designed for assessing affective as well as cognitive objectives. The following paragraphs illustrate these points with examples.

Situational items. A valuable type of test for appraising students' ability to evaluate ideas, infer feelings, and handle problems is the situational, interpretive, or problem-solving test. A situation or problem is presented in a sentence, paragraph, or short selection and followed by appropriate items, as shown in the following examples.

1. A class was having a discussion on the duties of a committee chairperson. Listed below are suggestions as made by different children. Make a + mark beside the suggestions that you think are *good ones* for the chairperson to follow:

   ___ Get ideas from all members. ___ Urge everyone to do his best.
   ___ Tell each person what to do. ___ Ask members to stick to the topic.
   ___ Ask others to accept the plan. ___ Do most of the talking.

   (Objective: To identify desirable actions of a chairperson)

2. After reading the following paragraph, make a list of the feelings Bob must have had.

   Bob had saved his allowance for six weeks. He was saving to buy a birthday present for his father. The day before his father's birthday he put the money in his back pocket, got on his bike, and went to the store. He locked his bike and went into the store to buy a present. When he reached into his back pocket to get the money, it wasn't there. He must have lost it somewhere between his home and the store.

   Make a list of as many feelings as you can think of that Bob must have had.

   ______________ ______________
   ______________ ______________
   ______________ ______________

   (Objective: To identify feelings in an incident or personal experience)

3. A boy who is liked by his classmates is walking home from school. As he turns a corner, he sees three students teasing Jose about the way he speaks English. The boy can go for help, make them stop, or turn around and go the other way.

   What should the boy do?
   ___ Go for help ___ Make them stop ___ Go the other way
   What would you do?
   ___ Go for help ___ Make them stop ___ Go the other way
   (Objective: To demonstrate concern for others by choosing a helpful course of action)

When making situational or interpretive tests, teachers should be careful to present problems that are realistic and challenging to the group. The kind of situation that could be used as a topic for discussion is usually satisfactory. In fact, some teachers base situational tests on topics the group has discussed. By making notes on comments during discussion, the teacher can obtain leads to plausible answers or responses to include in the test.

Items based on pictures and graphic materials. Special attention should be given to the construction of items based on pictures, maps, charts, tables, and diagrams in textbooks and other instructional media. Here are some examples:

1. Look at the pictures on pages 38–39 that show the steps in baking bread. List the steps in order.
   A.____________________ B.____________________
   C.____________________ D.____________________
   (Objective: To interpret pictures by listing the steps shown in sequence)
2. Look at the picture of the school on page 33.
   How is it like our school? State two ways it is similar.
   How is it different from our school? State two differences.
   (Objective: To compare and contrast by stating two similarities and two differences)
3. Look at the picture map of the community on page 25. Point to the building that is City Hall.
   Which building is closer to City Hall, the hospital or the railroad station?
   How many blocks is it from the hospital to the railroad station?
   (Objective: To interpret maps by identifying items shown, finding relative distance between places, and determining distance between two places)

What regions are identified by the numerals? Write the numerals in the spaces to identify each region: __Far Western __Midwestern __Northeastern __Southeastern __Southwestern. (Social Studies Workshop, University of California, Berkeley)

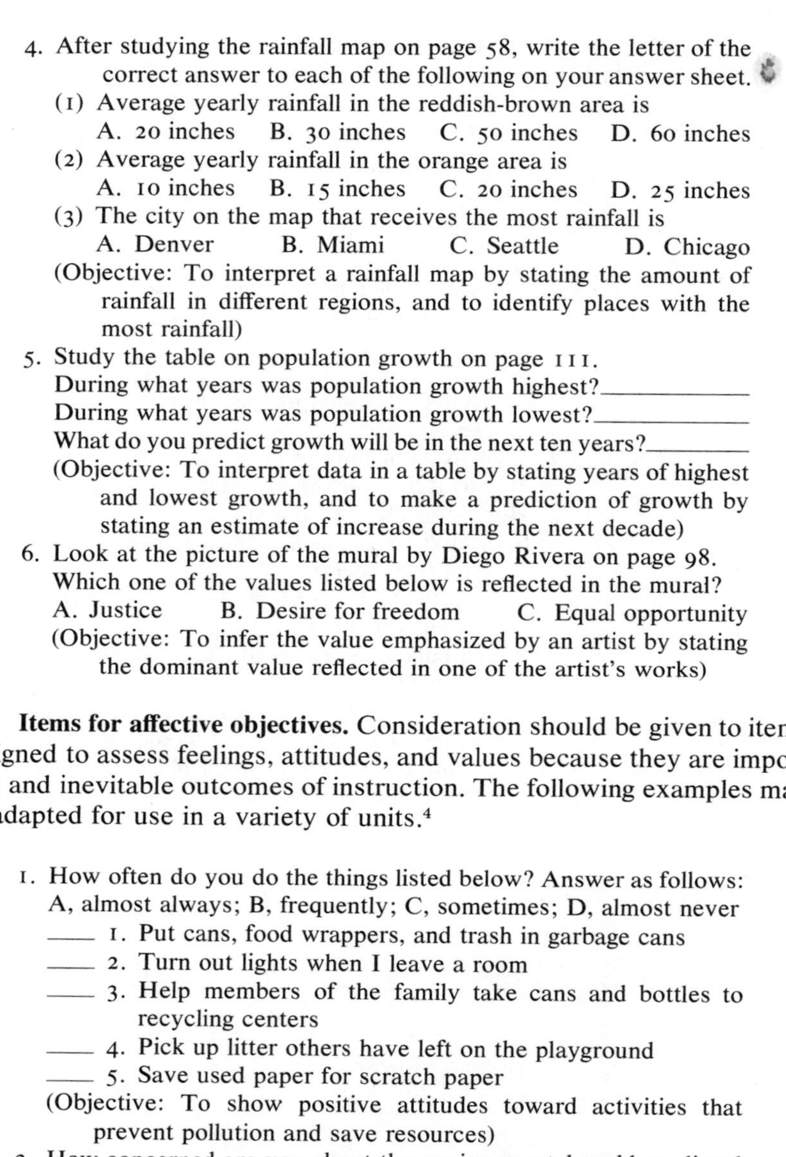

4. After studying the rainfall map on page 58, write the letter of the correct answer to each of the following on your answer sheet.
   (1) Average yearly rainfall in the reddish-brown area is
   A. 20 inches B. 30 inches C. 50 inches D. 60 inches
   (2) Average yearly rainfall in the orange area is
   A. 10 inches B. 15 inches C. 20 inches D. 25 inches
   (3) The city on the map that receives the most rainfall is
   A. Denver B. Miami C. Seattle D. Chicago
   (Objective: To interpret a rainfall map by stating the amount of rainfall in different regions, and to identify places with the most rainfall)
5. Study the table on population growth on page 111.
   During what years was population growth highest?__________
   During what years was population growth lowest?__________
   What do you predict growth will be in the next ten years?________
   (Objective: To interpret data in a table by stating years of highest and lowest growth, and to make a prediction of growth by stating an estimate of increase during the next decade)
6. Look at the picture of the mural by Diego Rivera on page 98. Which one of the values listed below is reflected in the mural?
   A. Justice B. Desire for freedom C. Equal opportunity
   (Objective: To infer the value emphasized by an artist by stating the dominant value reflected in one of the artist's works)

Items for affective objectives. Consideration should be given to items designed to assess feelings, attitudes, and values because they are important and inevitable outcomes of instruction. The following examples may be adapted for use in a variety of units.[4]

1. How often do you do the things listed below? Answer as follows: A, almost always; B, frequently; C, sometimes; D, almost never
   ____ 1. Put cans, food wrappers, and trash in garbage cans
   ____ 2. Turn out lights when I leave a room
   ____ 3. Help members of the family take cans and bottles to recycling centers
   ____ 4. Pick up litter others have left on the playground
   ____ 5. Save used paper for scratch paper
   (Objective: To show positive attitudes toward activities that prevent pollution and save resources)
2. How concerned are you about the environmental problems listed below? Answer as follows: A, very concerned; B, concerned; C, undecided; D, unconcerned; E, very unconcerned
   ____ 1. Air pollution
   ____ 2. Water pollution
   ____ 3. Waste pollution
   ____ 4. Noise pollution
   ____ 5. Esthetic pollution

[4]Adapted from Nancy Dyar, *Environmental Education* 4–9 (Los Angeles: Instructional Objectives Exchange, 1974).

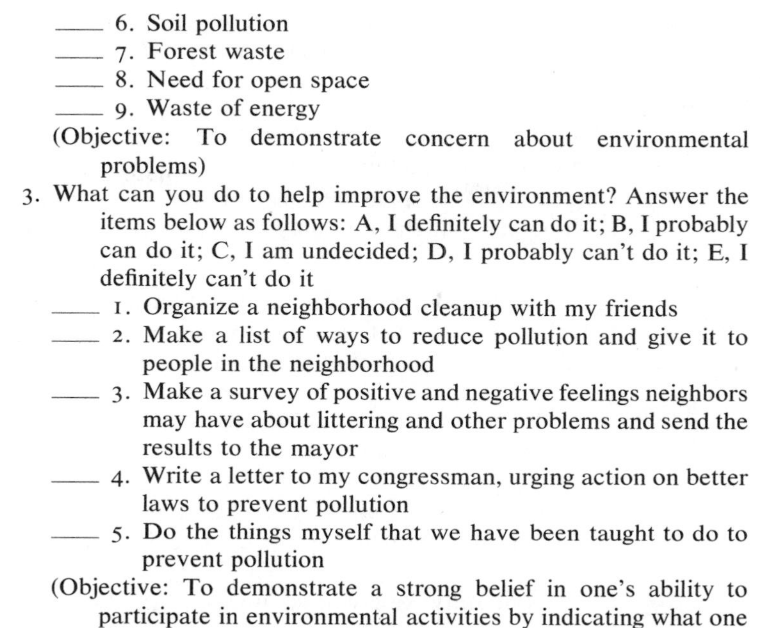

____ 6. Soil pollution
____ 7. Forest waste
____ 8. Need for open space
____ 9. Waste of energy

(Objective: To demonstrate concern about environmental problems)

3. What can you do to help improve the environment? Answer the items below as follows: A, I definitely can do it; B, I probably can do it; C, I am undecided; D, I probably can't do it; E, I definitely can't do it

____ 1. Organize a neighborhood cleanup with my friends
____ 2. Make a list of ways to reduce pollution and give it to people in the neighborhood
____ 3. Make a survey of positive and negative feelings neighbors may have about littering and other problems and send the results to the mayor
____ 4. Write a letter to my congressman, urging action on better laws to prevent pollution
____ 5. Do the things myself that we have been taught to do to prevent pollution

(Objective: To demonstrate a strong belief in one's ability to participate in environmental activities by indicating what one can and cannot do)

Writing Test Items

Teachers should keep several basic guidelines in mind when they prepare multiple-choice, matching, simple recall, completion, and alternative-response test items. Each item should be clearly worded and written on a level of difficulty appropriate to the group. Textbook wording should be avoided; otherwise children will engage in rote memorization and will not learn to apply ideas and principles. Items that provide answers to other items should not be included. Also avoid tricky questions and items that do not have definite answers. No clues or suggestions that can be used to figure out the correct answer to an item should be given. Directions should be clear, and space for responses should be arranged to facilitate answers and scoring. Items of the same type should be grouped together in separate sections (completion, true-false, and the like).

In addition, specific points must be kept in mind for each type of item most frequently used in the social studies program.

Simple recall items. Simple recall items should measure a child's ability to recall an important name, place, concept, or date. A child must recall the appropriate response rather than identify it from a list of possible answers. Questions or statements involving *who, when, where, what, how many,* and *how much* can be presented in oral or written form to measure a variety of specific learnings, as shown in the following examples:

What should we say when someone helps us? ____________________
Who helps us check out library books? ____________________

Which airport worker tells planes when to land? ______________
What are the four major land forms? __________, __________, __________, __________

Simple recall items should be short. Questions are usually easier to prepare than statements and are more meaningful to a child. Adequate space should be provided for answers. The items should be written in such a way that there is only one correct response.

Completion tests. The completion test is another form of recall; it may be either a sentence or a paragraph with blanks to fill with words, numbers, or phrases that complete the meaning. For example:

The president during the War of 1812 was (1) 1. ______________
from the state of (2). 2. ______________

Several points must be kept in mind if this type of item is to be used effectively in appraising learning in social studies:

1. Omit only key words, phrases, or dates, not minor details, common words, or everyday expressions. For example, "The pioneers ate much ______." Many different common words could be used here—food, meat, berries, and the like.
2. Use blanks of uniform size for all responses, since children use variations in size as clues to answers.
3. Avoid textbook phrases and sentences. Use definite statements with omissions that call for only one correct response; but if another response turns out to be acceptable, give credit for it.
4. Avoid the use of *a* and *an* before a blank so that no clues will be given, for example, "Bill took an __________ from the fruit basket." *Apple* or *orange* are possibilities, but *banana, pears, plum,* or other fruit beginning with a consonant can be eliminated.
5. Do not omit several words in any one statement; if too many words are omitted, one cannot get the meaning. For example, "Jamestown was __________ in the year __________ by __________." If used at all, this item should be written: "Jamestown was settled in the year __________."
6. Arrange the test so that answers can be written in spaces at the right as shown in the example at the beginning of this section.

Multiple-choice tests. This type of item is used more frequently than any other by professional test makers. It consists of a question or incomplete statement (called the stem) followed by two or more responses.

(The correct or best one is the answer; the others are distractors.) The usual procedure is to have children select the correct response from among three to five choices. Variations on this procedure are (1) select the best answer, (2) select the incorrect answer, and (3) select two or more correct answers. In the primary grades, children should be asked to underline the correct or best answer so that no difficulty will arise in marking letters or numbers which designate answers.

> *Directions:* Look at all four words and draw a line under the one word that makes the sentence true. (A variation: Draw a line through the incorrect words.)
>
> 1. Workers in sawmills make
>   nails bricks plaster lumber

In later grades, numerals or letters may be marked, or machine-scorable answer sheets may be used successfully with most children.

> *Directions:* After each question there are four words that might be used to answer the question. Only one of the words is correct or better than any of the others. Make a circle around the letter in front of the word you think is best.
>
> 1. From which country did the United States purchase the Louisiana Territory?
>   A. England B. Russia C. Spain D. France

If an answer column is provided, the directions should indicate the marking procedure:

> *Directions:* One of the four numbered answers is best for each exercise. Choose the one you think is best and write its number in the space at the left.
>
> ______ Which reference would you use to find the number of people in Illinois last year?
>
> (1) An atlas (3) An almanac
> (2) An encyclopedia (4) A geography

The following suggestions are helpful in making multiple-choice items:

1. Use them to check recognition and discrimination. Use the simple recall form if the children should be expected to remember a given fact. Use the alternative-response form if there are only two possible answers.
2. Place the major portion of the statement in the introduction or stem, not in the possible answers. Make the stem clear and complete so that the nature of the answer will be known to the pupil. Avoid negative statements in the stem whenever possible; they tend to be confusing.

3. Be sure all possible answers are plausible; children quickly eliminate absurd options. Word the incorrect responses as carefully as the correct ones; make some of them about the same length as the correct response if more than one word is involved.
4. Avoid clues such as words or phrases in the introduction that also appear in the correct answer, or placing *a* or *an* at the end of the introduction when the options do not all begin with a vowel or consonant. For example, "A pictogram is an A. illustration B. narrative C. tool D. mural" can easily be answered by associating *an* with the option that begins with a vowel.
5. Phrase all choices so that they are grammatically correct when joined to the introduction; avoid choices that overlap or include each other—for example: "Last year air travel increased. A. less than 10 percent, B. less than 20 percent, C. more than 30 percent, D. more than 50 percent." Place choices at the end of the item; distribute them evenly among answer positions; include at least four choices whenever possible; and keep all choices in the same category—that is, do not mix persons, places, or things.
6. Arrange the items in groups of five with a double space between groups. Group together items with the same number of choices—that is, do not mix three-choice and four-choice items.

Matching. Matching items are used to measure the ability to associate events and dates, events and persons, terms and definitions, principles and applications, tools and their uses, pictures and concepts, causes and effects, and the like. They should be used only when several pairs of items are sufficiently homogeneous to require a child to think critically in order to make proper associations.

Fairly simple matchings are used in the primary grades. For example, pictures of household objects such as a refrigerator, stove, or sweeper may be matched with words or phrases that describe each picture. Or, parts of sentences or pairs of words may be matched, as shown in the two following examples:

1. Draw a line between the two parts in each sentence that belong together.

The farmer keeps baby chickens	in the corral.
The farmer keeps horses	in a pen.
The farmer keeps pigs	in a brooder.

2. Draw a line from each worker to the word that tells what he uses.

carpenter	cement
electrician	lumber
mason	pipe
plumber	wire

Two basic varieties of matching used in later grades involve simple matching, as shown in the first example below, and classification into categories, as shown in the second example:

1. In the space before each of the duties, write the letter of the official responsible for it.

Duty	Official
____1. Collects taxes	A. Assessor
____2. Determines the value of property	B. Clerk
____3. Keep records	C. Judge
	D. Sheriff
	E. Treasurer

2. In the space before each of the responsibilities, write the letter of the branch of government that carries it out.

Responsibility	Branch
____1. Makes laws	A. Executive
____2. Interprets laws	B. Judicial
____3. Enforces laws	C. Legislative
____4. Appropriates money	
____5. Prepares the budget	

Guessing is minimized in the first example because of the number of names in the second column; it is minimized in the second example because some responses must be used more than once.

Another form of matching involves the use of maps, diagrams, or pictures lettered to show significant features. For example, a map of the United States may be marked with large letters to show regions in which different types of production are carried on. The map is placed in the front of the room and children are asked to study it and then write the letters in the spaces before matching questions such as the following:

____1. Which area is noted for steel production?
____2. Which area is noted for cotton production?

The following suggestions should be used when matching items are prepared:

1. Place related material in each matching exercise; do not mix people and events with other associations such as causes and effects.
2. Keep the number of items small (three to five); provide extra responses (two to three) in the second column, or permit certain responses to be used more than once in order to minimize guessing.
3. Arrange the items in the first column in random order; arrange those in the second column in alphabetical, chronological, or some other reasonable order.

4. Keep the columns close together and on the same page so that children will not become confused looking back and forth or turning the page to check matching pairs.
5. Use consistent form so that items in each column can be associated without difficulty. If parts of sentences are to be matched, be sure no grammatical clues are introduced.

Alternative-response tests. Items in this category may be written in several forms: true-false, yes-no, right-wrong, correct-incorrect, and two-option multiple choice. They may be dictated or presented in written form. Carefully constructed alternative-response items can be used to appraise interests, attitudes, misconceptions, superstitions, and understanding of principles and generalizations. They should be used when only two logical responses are possible, such as north or south, right or left, larger or smaller, and the like. Examples of several different forms follow.

1. (The true-false variety is simply a statement.) The area of Brazil is greater than the area of the United States. T F
2. (The yes-no variety consists of a question.) Do you have the right to break a rule made by your class if you you did not vote for it? Y N
3. (The cluster variety is a statement with several completions.) Agriculture is profitable in the South because:
   1. many workers are available. T F
   2. the land is mountainous. T F
   3. there are many forests. T F
   4. there is a long growing season. T F

Avoid items for which more than two plausible responses may be made, such as "The pioneers came to Sutter's Fort on the Wilderness Trail." The multiple-choice form should be used in this instance because the Oregon Trial, Mohawk Trail, and California Trail could be used as other choices.

Alternative-response items may be used in a variety of ways. Places on a map can be marked by letters or numbers and children can be asked to write T or F in response to statements regarding what is grown, what conditions exist, and the like. Comprehension of a topic can be appraised in a similar way after children have read a selection, heard a report, or seen a film. More than mere knowledge can be tested with items that require application of concepts:

If Iowa were in a mountainous region, its corn crop would be larger. T F

The ability to make comparisons can be tested by an item such as this one:

Make a + beside each of the items found in Mexico and California:

______ oil	______ forests
______ gold	______ coal

The ability to read and interpret maps can be measured by preparing items based on textbook or wall maps.

New York is farther from San Francisco than from Shannon. T F

The ability to describe conditions or activities can be measured by an item like this one:

Make a + beside each of the objects listed below that pioneers took on hunting trips:

______ blankets	______ canned foods
______ kettles	______ hatchets

The following suggestions are recommended for use in making alternative-response items:

1. Include an equal number of true and false statements; be sure the true statements are not consistently longer than the false statements; arrange true and false items in random order.
2. Avoid specific determiners—for example, items containing *alone, all, no, none, never, always,* and the like are usually false, whereas items containing *generally, should, may,* and the like are usually true.
3. Be sure each statement is definitely true or false; avoid ambiguous terms such as *few, many,* and *important.* Place the crucial element of the statement in the main part of the sentence, not in a phrase or subordinate clause. Avoid double negatives.
4. Make each item short and specific. Avoid unfamiliar or figurative language.
5. Simplify the marking of correct responses (and scoring) by placing T and F (or Y and N for *yes-no*) in a column at the right, as shown in the examples above. For scoring, make a stencil (with holes punched in the position for correct responses) to place over the answer column. If the items are dictated or no answer column has been provided, instruct the children to write + for true and 0 for false, which are easier to score than T and F or + and −.

Essay tests. Although not widely used in the elementary school, essay tests are helpful in the upper grades when students are mature enough to express themselves by writing answers to selected items. Essay items are useful in obtaining evidence on attitudes, problems, and issues, and such processes as synthesizing ideas, analyzing causes and other elements, evaluating decisions, and interpreting data. They are also used to assess skill in organizing and summarizing information, applying principles, and describing significant events, persons, and places. The element of free response frequently gives clues not secured by objective devices. They should not be too broad in scope or used to test information alone. Each question should be phrased so that children will know exactly what is expected of them. For example, the question "How did the pioneers in Boonesboro live?" is too general. A better question is "How did the pioneers in Boonesboro obtain food?" In general, essay questions should be used only when children will not experience undue difficulty in handling the writing, spelling, and composition skills involved in answering them; otherwise they should be used in small-group discussion or broken down into small units and objective test items prepared.

Teacher-Pupil Tests

Tests made by students under the guidance of the teacher are valuable evaluative devices. Children gain increased appreciation of the reasons for testing, gain insight into the selection of key ideas, get practice in analyzing material, and grow in the ability to express themselves with precision. By helping to make tests, children also clarify objectives and see some of the relationships between instruction and testing.

Tests designed by children should focus on specific problems in the unit. Each item should be accompanied by the answer and its source. Although the same rules of test construction that the teacher uses should be applied, reasonable standards must be set for each group. Children can be guided to see the importance of not copying items from the book, not using "giveaway" terms, and sticking to the topic. Major outcomes should be improved precision in expression, self-evaluation, and understanding of the topics being studied.

Preparing Items on Various Levels

Questions and test items should be formulated on various levels of cognitive and affective response.[5] The examples that follow give the kinds of questions and items that can be used with beginning students.

LEVELS OF COGNITION

Knowledge: Which of these pictures shows goods produced at home? (Have children select or point to pictures you have selected.) Make a line under each picture that shows goods. (Provide duplicated test that contains pictures of goods and services.)

[5] See Bloom and Krathwohl references.

Comprehension: Can you tell us the difference between goods and services? Make a red line under each picture that shows goods and a blue line under each picture that shows services.

Application: How can we find out about goods and services in other families? Make a line under the pictures that show goods produced by the Eskimo family.

Analysis: How is the work divided at home to produce goods and services? Make a line under the pictures that show father producing services.

Synthesis: What shall we include in our picture chart to show goods and services? Select pictures of goods and services from the table and arrange them on the chart.

Evaluation: How can we change our picture chart to show goods and services produced at home? Point to each picture on the chart that shows something made or done at home.

LEVELS OF AFFECTIVE RESPONSE

Receiving (Attending): What did you notice that was interesting when we visited the dairy farm? Draw something that you liked at the dairy farm.

Responding: What was most interesting on the farm? Draw a picture of what you would like to do on a farm.

Valuing: Can you tell why you would like to live on a farm? Make a line under the pictures that show things you would like to do.

Standardized Tests

Standardized tests are available for the evaluation of concepts, information, word-study skills, and critical thinking. They are helpful in determining growth over a given period of time, in planning curriculum revision, in giving group and individual guidance, in appraising methods and materials, in conducting surveys, and for research purposes. They should *not* be used as the basis for marking, promotion, rating of teachers, child-to-child or school-to-school comparisons, or for rating a school system in terms of national norms; these matters require a wider range of data.

Standardized achievement tests are only one part of the total program of evaluation. Reasonable expectations should be employed for each child and each group on the basis of mental ability, growth rate, past achievement, and pertinent background factors. If tests are given early in the year, they may be used to indicate both individual and group needs, and thereby improve planning.

In selecting standardized tests in social studies, several criteria should be considered in addition to reliability, validity, objectivity, expense, and ease of administration.

Is this test related to the social studies topics being considered?
Does this test cover the key learnings of importance to the children for whom it is intended?
Is the level of difficulty appropriate for the children?
Is this the best available test for the purpose?
If norms are to be used, are they suitable in terms of local needs and conditions?
Can the test results be used with other information to assess children's progress?
Does this test fit into the total pattern of evaluation?

One recent trend in standardized tests has been to include items that assess children's ability to apply understandings and to use work-study skills, as well as items that measure basic concepts, information, and generalizations. Chart 15–17 shows items from the Stanford test.

Sources of Information on Standardized Tests Many standardized tests are available for the social studies program. Some of them are included in general achievement tests, and others are available as separate tests. The following are social studies tests illustrative of those used in elementary schools:[6] Iowa Tests of Basic Skills, Houghton-Mifflin Company (for grades 3 through 9; work-study skills including map reading); Metropolitan Achievement Battery and Stanford Achievement Tests, Harcourt, Brace, Jovanovich (for grades 5 through 9; information and skills); Sequential Tests of Educational Progress, Educational Testing Service (for grades 4 through 6 and 7 through 9; understanding and skills.

QUESTIONS, ACTIVITIES, EVALUATION

1. Consider practical ways to use each of the basic guidelines to effective evaluation presented in the first section of this chapter in the social studies program. Which do you believe to be the most difficult to apply? Which do you believe now need greater emphasis?
2. In what ways can you provide for student self-evaluation in a unit you are planning?
3. Examine a cumulative record currently being used in a school system in your area. What provision is there for recording progress in social studies? What additional provisions, if any, are needed?

[6] See Buros references for descriptions of these and other tests.

Chart 15–17
Achievement Testing

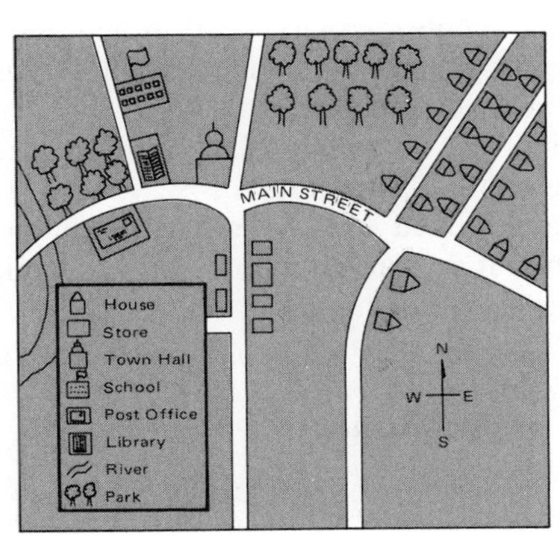

The school is closest to which of these?

⑤ houses ⑦ library
⑥ post office ⑧ stores

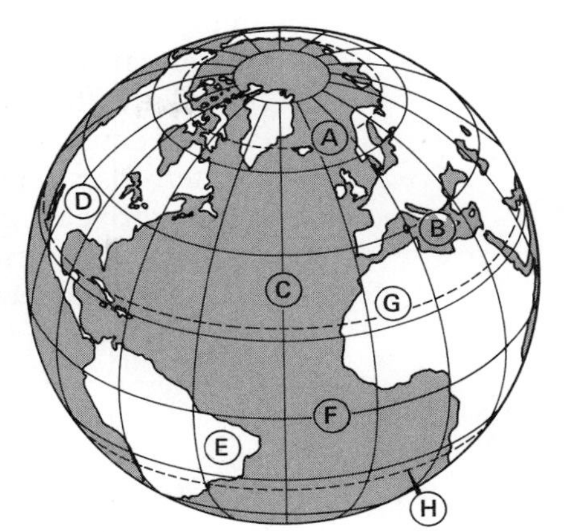

Area E is in —

1 Africa 3 South America
2 India 4 Canada

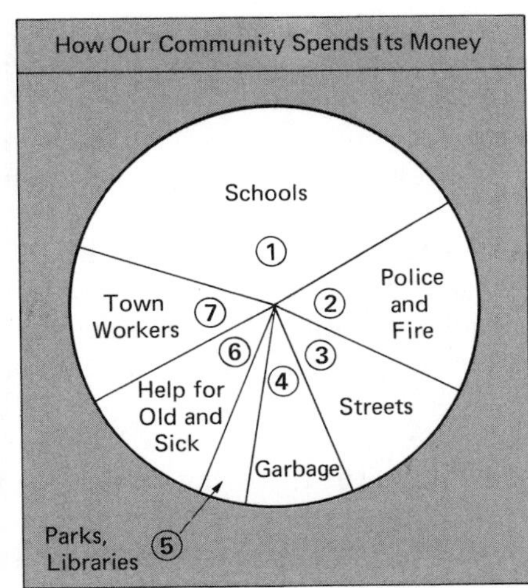

This community spends the largest part of its money for —

5 streets 7 schools
6 garbage 8 police

Before there were schools, children were taught by —

1 the government
2 the family
3 watching television
4 reading newspapers

Magellan and his crew were the first to —

1 conquer Mexico
2 discover the West Indies
3 sail around the world
4 explore Brazil

The use of tools and language shows that people have a —

1 culture
2 government
3 family
4 village

Source: The Stanford Achievement Test, copyright © 1973, by Harcourt, Brace, Jovanovich, Inc. Reproduced by permission of the publisher.

4. How can you use observation as a technique of evaluation in a unit you are planning? discussion? anecdotal records? interviews? logs and diaries? case studies?
5. Prepare a sample chart, a sample checklist, and a brief questionnaire that you might use in a unit you are planning to teach. Discuss them critically with fellow students or teachers.
6. Prepare several objective test items in each form discussed in this chapter. Plan items you can use in a unit.
7. Examine one of the standardized tests listed in this chapter. What outcomes of instruction is it designed to appraise? How might it be used in a complete program of evaluation?

REFERENCES

ANDERSON, SCARVIA, SAMUEL BALL, and RICHARD T. MURPHY et al., *Encyclopedia of Educational Evaluation.* San Francisco: Jossey-Bass, 1974. Articles on all phases of evaluation.

BEATTY, WALCOTT, ed., *Improving Educational Assessment: An Inventory of Measures of Affective Behavior.* Washington, D.C.: Association of Supervision and Curriculum Development, 1969. Guidelines and instruments for evaluating affective outcomes.

BERG, HARRY D., ed., *Evaluation in the Social Studies* (35th Yearbook). Washington, D.C.: National Council for the Social Studies, 1965. Practical suggestions for different aspects of evaluation.

BLOOM, BENJAMIN S., ed., *Taxonomy of Educational Objectives: Cognitive Domain.* New York: McKay, 1956. Sample items on various levels.

BLOOM, BENJAMIN S., J. THOMAS HASTINGS, and GEORGE F. MADAUS, *Handbook on Formative and Summative Evaluation of Student Learning.* New York: McGraw-Hill, 1971. Guidelines, sample items, and specifications for measures in the cognitive and affective domains.

BUROS, OSCAR K., *The Seventh Mental Measurements Yearbook.* Highland Park, N.J.: Gryphon Press, 1972. Review of tests in this and earlier yearbooks.

———, *Tests in Print II.* Highland Park, N.J.: Gryphon Press, 1974. Index and review tests of all types.

FAIR, JEAN, ed., *National Assessment and Social Studies Education.* Washington, D.C.: National Council for the Social Studies, 1975. Critical review of strengths, weaknesses, and needed changes.

FRASER, DOROTHY M., ed., *Social Studies Curriculum Development: Prospects and Problems* (39th Yearbook). Washington, D.C.: National Council for the Social Studies, 1969. Chapter on new dimensions in evaluation.

KRATHWOHL, DAVID R., BENJAMIN S. BLOOM, and BERTRAM B. MESIA,

Taxonomy of Educational Objectives: Affective Domain. New York: McKay, 1964. Sample items on various levels.

KURFMAN, DANA G., and ROBERT J. SOLOMON, "Measurement of Growth in Skills." In *Skill Development in the Social Studies* (33rd Yearbook). Washington, D.C.: National Council for the Social Studies, 1963, pp. 274–95. Techniques and sample test items.

MORRISSETT, IRVING, "Accountability in the Social Studies," *Keeping Up* (January 1974). An accountability model for the social studies program, newsletter, social studies ERIC center, Boulder, Colorado.

TENBRINK, TERRY D., *Evaluation: A Practical Guide for Teachers.* New York: McGraw-Hill, 1974. Chapters on test items, checklists, rating devices.

THOMAS, R. MURRAY, and DALE L. BRUBAKER, *Teaching Elementary Social Studies.* Belmont, Calif.: Wadsworth, 1972. Section on evaluation and marking.

WESLEY, EDGAR B., and STANLEY P. WRONSKI, *Teaching Secondary Social Studies in a World Society.* Lexington, Mass.: D. C. Heath, 1973. Chapters on evaluation.

APPENDIX
Unit on Environmental Problems

The material in this appendix illustrates ways in which current problems of primary importance may be incorporated in the social studies program and how conceptual and inquiry components drawn from supporting disciplines may be used to make plans for instruction. It may also be used as a resource for planning teaching units for a particular group of middle- and upper-grade students.

INVESTIGATING ENVIRONMENTAL PROBLEMS

Goals and Objectives

Environmental education contributes directly to the attainment of conceptual, process, skill, and affective objectives. A central goal is to develop an understanding of environmental problems, their causes and effects, and ways of solving them. Inquiry processes and basic skills should be sharpened as students tackle controversial issues, sift fact from propaganda, analyze predictions, and evaluate proposals for improving the environment. Values and attitudes that reflect a concern for the quality of life should be coupled with positive action. Major understandings to be developed and specific instructional objectives are identified in the unit plans presented below.

Conceptual Structure

Of key importance in environmental education are the following concepts, concept clusters, themes, and generalizations, which have been drawn from Chapter 5, from materials for students, and from references for teachers.

CONCEPTS

Environment, ecology, ecosystem, balance of nature, food chain, resources, interdependence, interaction, population, urbanization, land use, conservation, pollution, pollutants, quality of life

THEMES

Interaction and interdependence, variety and pattern, survival and adaptation, continuity and change

CONCEPT CLUSTERS

Environment: All surroundings; rural, urban; natural, cultural; living, nonliving; human and natural resources; land forms, water bodies; atmosphere, weather, climate

Population: Change; growth; distribution; density; census; urban, rural; migration, shift

Natural Resources: Air, water, soil, plants, animals, minerals

Land Use: Rural, urban, agricultural, industrial, conservation, transportation, open space, residential, commercial, public agencies; wildlife preservation, research; planning, zoning, subdividing; uses of major landforms

Rural Areas; Farms, ranches, forests, mines, power plants, recreational areas; conservation; pollution problems, quality of life

Urban Areas: Population; suburbs, neighborhoods, inner city, metropolitan area, megalopolis; decay, blight, sprawl, pollution problems; planning, renewal, beautification; new towns, model cities; quality of life

Conservation: Human, water, soil, forest, wildlife, grazing lands, minerals, recreational areas; wise use, restricted use, substitution, recycling, education of consumers and producers

Types of Pollution: Air, water, thermal, soil, food, wildlife, plant life, solid waste, esthetic, noise; causes, effects; corrective and preventive measures; needed action

Action: Individual, group; local, state, national, international; public, private; political, legal, legislative; enforcement, demonstration, pressure

Action Groups: Families, schools, clubs, associations, private organizations, public agencies

Quality of Life: Personal, social, economic; physical, mental, emotional; rural, suburban, inner city, urban, regional, national

GENERALIZATIONS

Descriptive

The earth is a self-contained life-support system with innumerable ecosystems that depend on solar energy and the environment that surrounds them.

All living things affect the environment and are affected by conditions, interactions, and changes in the environment.

Cultural development has led to human domination of the environment, the creation of serious environmental problems, waste of energy, and the deterioration of natural resources.

Current problems of critical importance include overpopulation, waste of energy, limited food supply in many parts of the world, and widespread pollution of the environment by highly industrialized nations.

Prescriptive

Ecological, rural/urban, economic, and other types of planning are needed to identify corrective and preventive measures that will conserve energy and maintain a wholesome environment.

Programs involving personal, social, economic, political, and technological change are needed to solve environmental problems.

Immediate and long-term action should be taken by individuals and groups, associations and agencies, and public and private interests.

Assessment of proposals, action programs, and technological developments should be made in terms of values related to quality of life now and in the future.

Clarifying Current Concerns

The current concern about the environment is more intense than the two preceding waves of concern, because people themselves are now threatened. The first wave of concern, during the early 1900s, led by such great conservationists as Gifford Pinchot and supported vigorously by President Theodore Roosevelt, had as its primary goal to save and expand our great public domain. The second wave, during the 1930s, emphasized wise use and management of natural resources, with public works projects and government-supported conservation activities.

Of special concern in our country and in countries around the world are problems stemming from energy shortages and pollution of the environment. Warnings have been sounded that an ecocatastrophe is possible if present practices continue. Industrialized countries in particular must find ways to conserve energy and curb pollution of the air, water, soil, wildlife, forests, cities, and other aspects of the total environment. Current concerns should be faced squarely in the classroom. Charts A–1 to A–6 show ways to examine prospects for the future and responsibility for past and present conditions.

Chart A–1
How About the Future?

How long will concern about energy use and pollution last?
Will the desire for energy halt action to stop pollution?
Can pollution problems be kept in mind as other problems arise?
Will funds be found to do the job right?
Will the conflicts among personal, economic, and social interest be resolved?

Chart A–2
Whose Responsibility Is It?

Should our forefathers have planned better?
Should the government have passed more laws?
Should science and technology have been controlled more effectively?
Should population growth have been controlled?
Should all of us accept responsibility?

Chart A–3
What Will Be Needed by 2000?

Twice as much land for homes, schools, and other urban uses?
Twice as much land for recreation?
Twice as much food for people?
Twice as much timber and water?
Eight million acres for reservoirs?
Four million acres for transportation?
One-half million acres for wildlife refuges?
Over twice as much energy?

Chart A–4
What Will It Be Like in 2000?

Where will the 70 million more people live in our country?
How clean will the air and water be?
How will energy be provided?
What will cities be like with nine out of ten people living in them?
How will the transportation of people and goods be handled?
Will countries around the world be cooperating to improve the quality of life?

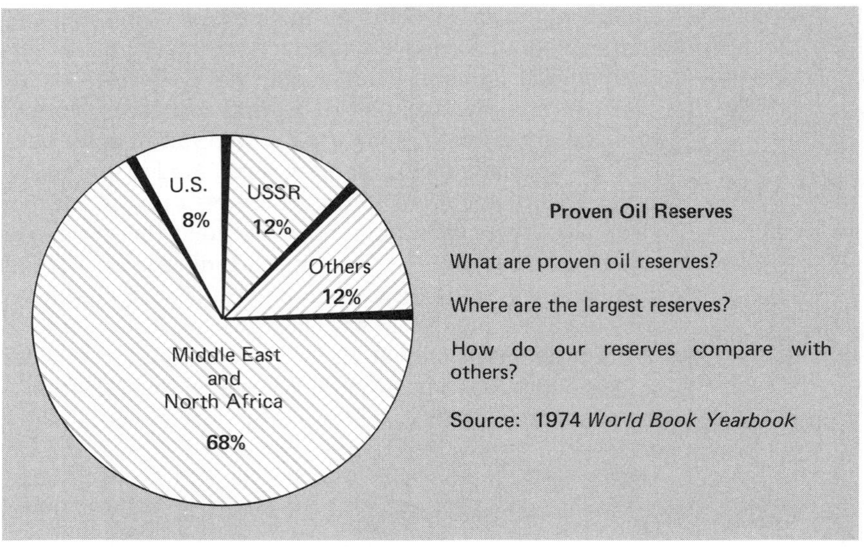

How long will oil resources last? Will derricks for windmills replace oil derricks in the future? What are the pros and cons of windmills as a source of power? (Social Studies Workshop, University of California, Berkeley)

Chart A–5
Must It Happen?

More electricity ⟶ more smoke
More sewage ⟶ fewer beaches
More cars ⟶ more smog
More freeways ⟶ fewer parks
More population ⟶ more slums

Chart A–6
What Can We Do?

As individuals at home and in the community
As members of groups and by supporting other groups
Through drives and campaigns
Through our elected representatives

Illustrative Unit Plans The plans in the following sections are based on units of study and materials currently used in the classroom. They are organized to show major understandings, specific instructional objectives, inquiry questions, and learning activities that can be used in daily instruction. Notice how major understandings and instructional objectives are related. The objectives describe in behavioral terms what students should be able to do as they acquire understandings. The inquiry questions provide specific means for attaining the objectives. Learning activities are suggested as ways of developing answers to the inquiry questions. A particular question may be developed in more than one activity and a particular activity may contribute to more than one question.

Inquiry processes that should be emphasized are noted in brackets in the section of each plan entitled Inquiry Questions to indicate ways in which the inquiry-conceptual approach should be implemented in environmental studies as well as in other units. Films, filmstrips, and other instructional materials available at the local level should be keyed into each plan as it is adapted for use in the classroom.

INTRODUCTION TO CONSERVATION AND POLLUTION PROBLEMS

Major Understandings Various agencies and individuals have worked to conserve our rich bounty of resources, but serious problems have arisen. Some resources have been misused and action is needed to handle pollution problems.

Objectives To make a chart of conservation problems, individuals and groups who have worked to solve them, and steps that are needed now and in the future; to describe pollution problems and causes and effects of different types of pollution.

Inquiry Questions What are some of the current threats to our environment that stem from a lack of sound conservation practices? How about conservation of water? energy? soil? forests and other plant life? animal life? minerals? [recalling]

What questions about conservation do you have? What hypotheses can we state about sound practices of water conservation? other types of conservation? [recalling, interpreting, hypothesizing]

What data do we need? What sources should we use? What can we find in classroom materials? libraries? in the community? [recalling]

What serious threats result from pollution of the environment? What are the main types of pollution? What are the causes and effects of each type? [recalling, classifying]

What questions about pollution should we investigate? What hypotheses can we state about causes? effects? preventive measures? [recalling, interpreting, hypothesizing]

What evidence do we need? What sources should we use? [inferring, recalling]

Which questions and hypotheses should be investigated by individuals? small groups? the whole class? On which ones can we get help from experts? What study trips will be needed to gather data? [inferring]

Illustrative Activities Have students investigate changes in the local environment and evaluate them in terms of risks, benefits, and other criteria, as shown in Charts A–7 to A–12.

Chart A–7
Investigating Changes

Why were they made?
When were they made?
What were the main effects?
What else might have been done?
Can wiser choices be made in the future?

Chart A–8
Effects of Changes

What have been positive and negative effects of

Growth of cities	Population growth
Mechanized farming	Flood control
Use of fertilizers	Other changes

Chart A–9
Are These Changes Helpful?

Forests: clear cutting, selective logging
Water supply: dams, reservoirs
Mining: strip mining, hydraulic mining, machine mining
Air pollution: smog-control devices, incinerators
Solid wastes: recycling, landfills
What other changes should we investigate?

Chart A–10
Which Urban Changes Are Desirable?

Housing: high-rise apartments, subdivisions, trailer parks
Transportation: rapid transit systems, freeways
Power supply: hydroelectric plants, nuclear plants, coal-burning plants
Industry: more to provide employment, recycling of water
What other urban changes should we investigate?

Chart A–11

Risk vs. Benefit

What are the risks and benefits of these?
Pesticides and herbicides
Nuclear generation of power
Supersonic air travel
Offshore oil drilling
Large oil tankers

Chart A–12

Making Judgments

What values should be used to judge environmental problems?
Economic need
Personal and social values
Concerns of the majority
Concerns about wildlife
Concerns about the future
Other needs and concerns

Gather data on changes in the environment, conservation programs, and pollution problems by taking field trips to housing developments, historic sites, lakes and reservoirs, lumber mills, power plants, and factories.

Interview individuals in urban planning centers, industries, colleges and universities, government agencies, and the local school system who are experts on conservation and pollution problems.

Investigate different natural resources to determine major uses and byproducts. Summarize findings as shown in Chart A–13.

What are the risks and benefits of the use of insecticides? (International Society for the Study of Education, Tokyo)

Chart A–13
Major Uses and Byproducts of Minerals

Minerals	Major Uses and Byproducts
Petroleum	Energy for vehicles, fuel, lubricants, medicines
Iron	
Copper	
Other	

Have students investigate how energy can be saved. Include conservation of energy in the home, school, and community. Have students collect and post advertisements that present ways to save energy.

Have students investigate changes and ways to prevent problems in the environment. Use Charts A–14 and A–15 to guide inquiry and organize findings.

Chart A–14
Environmental Changes Made in the Past, Currently Underway, and Predicted for the Future

Past	Present	Future

Chart A–15
Preventing and Solving Problems

Problems	Prevention	Solution
Flood Erosion Smog Forest fire Other		

Have children use physical and land-use maps of the United States and their own area to locate rural areas, forest areas, mineral areas, and bodies of water and to identify the approximate proportion of the nation's area that they occupy. Have them do the same to maps of other areas of the world.

To clarify such concepts as forest, shoreline, and estuary, have children collect and mount magazine illustrations and related data on concept or retrieval charts or as special bulletin-board arrangements.

Have students investigate the contributions of great conservationists such as George P. Marsh, J. Sterling Morton, Gifford Pinchot, President Theodore Roosevelt, John Muir, Charles R. Van Hise, Jay N. Sterling, Fairfield Osborn, and Paul B. Sears. They should also investigate individuals and groups in their own community and state who have made contributions to conservation, along with agencies at the national level that are working on pollution and conservation problems.

Form committees of five students each and have them plan and do a demonstration of how they might proceed to investigate different types of pollution. Each committee should choose a different type of pollution. Use this model: What questions or hypotheses will guide study? What data sources (classroom materials, interviews, field trips) will be used? How will data be checked, organized, and reported?

A helpful summarizing and synthesizing activity is to develop a chart like Chart A–16, which includes information on different types of pollution. Students can add to the chart as they collect data, share current events, and get ideas from resource visitors and study trips.

Chart A–16
Types of Pollution: Pollutants, Effects, Prevention

Types	Pollutants	Effects	Prevention
Air			
Water			
Soil			
Food			
Solid wastes			
Thermal			
Esthetic			
Noise			

FOREST CONSERVATION

Major Understandings

About one-third of our country's land is covered by forests that contain many vacation areas, trails, scenic rivers and mountains, and recreation facilities. Conservation of forests is related to conservation of wildlife, water, soil, and wilderness areas. Improvements have been made in forest conservation, but continued

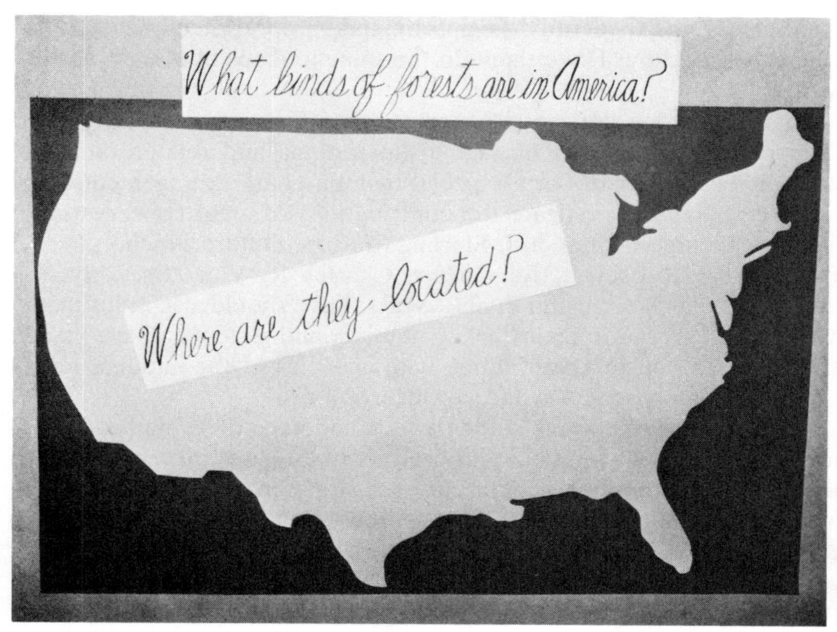

What kinds of forests are in America?
Where are they located?

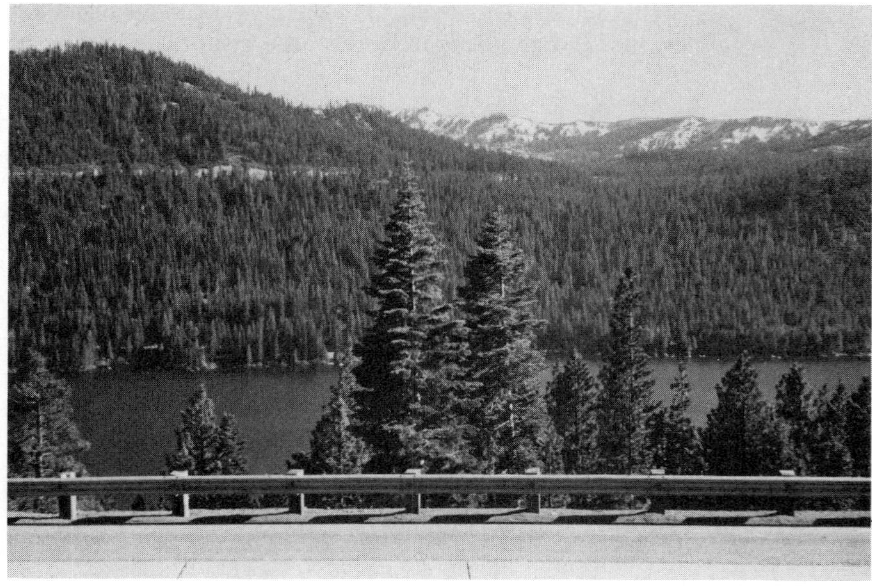

Where are our main forest lands? (San Diego, California)

action is needed to meet increased demands for products made of wood, recreational facilities, and resource conservation.

Instructional Objectives To describe the relationships between population growth and the use of timber; to identify steps being taken to prevent ecological damage in forests and to increase lumber supply; to identify needed additional steps and ways in which individuals and groups can help.

Inquiry Questions What has been the effect of population growth on the use of timber? for housing? for paper? for other products? [observing, interpreting]

What is being done to prevent damage to forests? to improve the supply of timber? What additional steps should be taken? [observing, interpreting, evaluating]

What are tree farms? What is reforestation? Why are both necessary? [defining, evaluating]

What is selective logging? What is clear cutting? What effects do they have on conservation of forests? [defining, analyzing]

How can waste of lumber be reduced? What byproducts are made of wastes? How does prevention of waste of paper and paper products help to save forests? How can recycling of paper help to save forests? [observing, interpreting, evaluating]

What substitutes for wood are being used in the construction of homes and other buildings? What substitutes are being used for paper? What are the advantages and disadvantages of substitutes? [observing, interpreting, analyzing]

What can individuals and groups do to conserve forests? What tactics can be used to bring about immediate and long-range improvement? [observing, interpreting, evaluating]

How is conservation of forests related to preservation of wildlife? watersheds? wilderness areas and trails? recreational areas? soil? other resources? [observing, analyzing]

Illustrative Activities Investigate latest developments by inviting a forest ranger or other expert to discuss measures used to conserve forests, improve logging practices, provide camp sites, and prevent forest fires.

Investigate conservation activities of private interests by obtaining films, filmstrips, and other materials from lumber and paper producers. Have students analyze them to identify practices designed to conserve forests, measures to prevent waste, and plans to provide adequate supplies of timber. Follow up by having students write letters that include specific questions about burning wastes, discharging mercury and other wastes in producing paper, and other concerns.

Make a pictorial and graphic synthesis of conservation practices by collecting pictures, maps, graphs, newspaper and magazine clippings, and other materials related to forest conservation. Have students use them in booklets, scrapbooks, reports, and bulletin-board arrangements.

Find out about national problems and activities by writing to the National Forest Service to obtain maps, folders, reports, and other materials. Have students use them as data sources to answer questions, in oral and written reports, and in displays.

Acquaint students with production processes and problems by taking a study trip to a nearby lumber mill, paper producer, or other forest-related agency or company. Have students make up questions to ask during the visit. Obtain free materials for further study.

Have the students write a haiku poem related to some aspect of forests. Use words with a total of five syllables in line one. Use words with a total of seven syllables in line two. Use words with a total of five syllables in line three.

URBAN–SUBURBAN PROBLEMS

Major Understandings

Population growth is greatest in urban areas of America and other countries, and contributes to pollution problems that have lowered the quality of life. Primary effects of rapid urban growth include air pollution, urban sprawl, inner-city decay, increase in ghettos, health and safety problems, energy shortages, and a heavy burden on basic services. It is predicted that by 2000 there will be three megalopolises in our country: the present one from Boston to Norfolk, a second one from Chicago along the Great Lakes into New York State, and a third from northern California to Mexico.

Instructional Objectives

To recognize the interrelationships of urban-suburban problems and population problems; to identify and describe urban problems, urban renewal, and various aspects of the quality of life in urban areas; to identify steps intended to improve the quality of life in urban areas; to identify ways in which individuals and groups can assist in improving the quality of urban life.

Inquiry Questions

How has the population of our community changed during the past decade? By what rate has the population of urban centers increased in the United States during the past decade? What are the predictions for 2000? [observing, interpreting]

What urban problems are most serious in our area? in other areas? How are they related to population growth? How are they related to other factors? [analyzing]

Which pollution problems are most serious? Air? water? noise? esthetic? other? [evaluating]

What steps are being taken to curb air pollution? water pollution? noise pollution? esthetic pollution? other pollution? [observing, interpreting]

How can individuals and groups help? What tactics will be most effective? [interpreting, evaluating]

What are the main causes of slums? What is being done to provide better housing? What additional steps are needed? [observing, interpreting, analyzing]

What is urban renewal? What urban renewal activities are underway in our area? [defining, observing]

What is urban sprawl? Is it evident in our area? What is being done to prevent it? [defining, observing, interpreting]

What are the advantages and disadvantages of freeways? rapid transit systems? What effects do they have on the environment? [evaluating, analyzing]

How might we rate the quality of life in city neighborhoods? in downtown areas? Which ideas in Charts A-17 through A-20 can we use? Are other standards needed? [interpreting, evaluating]

How have new towns been planned to meet current problems? to prevent pollution? to improve the quality of urban life? What problems do they still face? How might these be solved? [observing, interpreting, analyzing]

Illustrative Activities

Investigate growth of the school and community population over the past three decades. Interview school officials to find predictions for future growth or decline. Make graphs to show past and predicted changes. This

What historic places have been preserved? How can they be used to improve learning? (Boston, Massachusetts)

Chart A–17
Quality of Life in City Neighborhoods

What has been done to provide parks and open spaces?
Are rooftops used for recreation and relaxation?
Are some streets used as open space for recreation?
Are historic places being restored?
What unused buildings and vacant lots might be put to use?
What steps are being taken to curb air, noise, and esthetic pollution?

Chart A–18
Quality of Life in Downtown Areas

What has been done about parks and open spaces?
Are there malls and plazas for people only?
What steps have been taken to preserve historic sites?
Have points of special interest been identified?
Are air, noise, and esthetic pollution being curbed?
How adequate are transportation services into and within downtown areas?

Chart A–19
Urban Sprawl

What recommendations have been made by a regional planning group?
What attention has been given to zoning and building code improvements?
What attention has been given to planned land use, including urban, rural, agricultural, and conservation?
Are new towns being planned?
Is there ecological planning as well as urban/rural planning? Are both public and private interests represented?

Chart A–20
Metropolitan Areas

How is air pollution being curbed? Motor vehicles? Planes? Industries? Other?
How is water pollution being curbed? Sewage treatment? Factory effluents? Detergents? Oil? Thermal? Other?
How is solid waste disposal being improved? Recycling? Planned landfills? Special incinerators? Other?
Are noise abatement efforts adequate?
Is there a coordinating council? Are local units cooperating?

activity may be extended to include the state, the country, and other nations as appropriate.

Have students interpret and analyze data on our country and other countries. Use the *World Almanac, Ecology Fact Book,* encyclopedias, articles, children's periodicals, and newspapers as data sources. Illustrative questions to guide inquiry are these: What has been the population growth of our country over the past thirty years? What has it been in Latin America? in India? in Japan? In what areas has the rate of increase been greatest? What are the predictions for the year 2000? Why are some areas increasing so much faster than others? What measures have been proposed to curb growth or to meet problems caused by overpopulation?

Use techniques designed to clarify the meaning of population figures. For example, take the class outside and have them estimate the space needed for one hundred people after thirty-three of them stand close together. This may be followed by projecting the estimates for one thousand, ten thousand, and so on. Another technique is to use the population of the school as a base. For example, if there are five hundred in school, how many times larger is a school of twenty thousand? Similarly, the population of the community, the state, the United States can be used to make comparisons.

Study population distribution and density in different units. For example, in community studies give attention to high-rise apartments, subdivisions, trailer parks, and other areas of varying densities. Major population centers in the state, nation, and other countries can be observed on maps and located on maps made by students. The four great population areas of the world (China, India, Western Europe, and eastern United States) may be found on maps in textbooks and atlases. Where do most of the people live? is an important question in state and regional studies as well as in units on the United States and other lands.

Develop the meaning of the term *rapid growth* as follows: Provide students with half sheets of paper on which six 2-inch squares have been dittoed. Have them start with two beans and try doubling the number of

How can esthetic pollution be curbed? What regulations are needed? What steps should be taken to establish and enforce them? (Richmond, California)

beans in each square. Continue until each square is filled. Relate the rapid growth to population growth and predictions in selected areas. What are the implications for food? housing? health care? schools? environmental problems?

Have students collect and arrange pictures, charts, graphs, maps, and clippings that highlight population growth and related problems. Possible organizing themes: our community (our state or our nation) in 1940, 1970, 2000; population growth and related problems; planning to meet population growth.

Individual, small-group, and class inquiry activities can be carried out by having students investigate questions such as those in Charts A–21 to A–26.

Chart A–21
Urban Renewal

What buildings and historic sites are being restored?
What are the plans for malls, plazas, and green spaces?
What are the plans for walkways, landscaping, fountains, lighting, and attractive pavement?
Are urban specialists, architects, ordinary people, and others involved in planning?
What opportunities are there for public review of plans?

Chart A–22
Esthetic Pollution

What steps are being taken to design signs that add to the attractiveness of buildings?
What steps are being taken to place utility lines underground?
What improvements are needed in regulations for signs and billboards?
Are street benches being redesigned to fit into the surroundings?
What is the evidence that people are concerned about esthetic pollution?

Chart A–23
Noise Pollution

How can the noise abatement program be improved?
What changes are needed to improve regulations on jackhammers, honking of horns, and other noise makers?
What steps are being taken to require noise insulation in buildings?
What kind of action program will be most effective in getting widespread participation in noise abatement?

Chart A–24
Waste Pollution

What steps can be taken to improve enforcement of laws and ordinances?
Are trash and litter baskets available and being used?
What provisions are being made for the recycling of cans, paper, and other wastes?
How can all of us help to keep a year-round clean-up campaign going?

Chart A–25
How Adequate Are Regulations

To protect open space
To regulate housing density
To preserve historic places
To improve street lighting
To curb noise, esthetic, and other pollution

Chart A–26
What Changes Are Needed

In housing and building codes
In zoning regulations
In subdivision regulations
In other laws and regulations
In enforcement procedures and tax incentives

Have students identify sources and causes of pollution by tracing the production and uses of different products such as bread, plastics, clothing, or something made of steel. Individual students select a product and share and discuss findings as in the following example.

Name of product: ____________
Raw materials used: ____________
  How are raw materials produced? ____________
  Good effects: ____________
  Bad effects: ____________
Steps in production: ____________
  Good effects of each step: ____________
  Bad effects of each step: ____________
Uses of finished product: ____________
  Good effects: ____________
  Bad effects: ____________
Steps in disposing of waste: ____________
  Good effects: ____________
  Bad effects: ____________

Have students identify common wastes and trace the steps in disposing of them by completing items like the following ones.

1. What waste is collected after a meal? ____________
   List three steps in disposing of this waste.
   (1) ____________
   (2) ____________
   (3) ____________
2. What waste is a part of gardening? ____________
   List three steps in disposing of this waste.
   (1) ____________
   (2) ____________
   (3) ____________
3. What waste results from mail? ____________
   List three steps in disposing of this waste.
   (1) ____________
   (2) ____________
   (3) ____________

Discuss and list ways in which recreational activities may contribute to pollution of the environment:

	Type of Pollution			
Activity	Air	Water	Soil	Noise
Camping	______	______	______	______
Picnicking	______	______	______	______
Hiking	______	______	______	______
Boating	______	______	______	______

Make a map of litter in one of the following areas: schoolyard, parking lot, vacant lot, playground in a park, picnic area, or construction site. Guide the group to develop symbols for paper, glass, wood, metal, cans, bottles, other litter. Mark location of trash cans, walks, and entrances to nearby buildings. Consider relocation of trash cans and relationships between amount of litter and walks and entrances.

Make a survey of student attitudes toward litter by having them check their position on items like these:

Litter prevention is	____very important	____important	____not important

What steps can be taken to curb pollution from waste? What other action projects might be undertaken? (Berkeley, California)

Playground litter is	____a major problem	____a minor problem	____no problem
Litter at home is	____a major problem	____a minor problem	____no problem
I litter when	____no one is looking	____no trash can is handy	____in the country
People who litter	____are just careless	____are OK	____are law-breakers

Have students check available materials to find the activities and buildings in the major zones of a city. Their findings may be summarized under the following headings: Residential Area, Business Area, Industrial Area, Open Space.

List the following on the chalkboard and ask students to name as many places in the community as they can that provide them: food, shelter, clothing, recreation, education. Write the names of places suggested by students under the appropriate heading. Request students to be on the lookout for places to add to the list. After the list is completed, discuss differences in the length of each list and possible reasons for the differences.

Have students check available materials to find the ways in which space is used to provide for different forms of transportation. Findings may be organized as follows:

Mode of Transportation	Ways in Which Space Is Used
Mass transit	________________
	________________
	________________
Train	________________
	________________
	________________
Airplane	________________
	________________
	________________
Automobile	________________
	________________
	________________

Make and compare traffic counts on a selected corner at three different times: morning rush hour, midday, and afternoon rush hour. Count the number of the following during a half-hour period: cars, buses, trucks, bicycles. Make and use charts or graphs to compare the number of different vehicles during each time period and between time periods. Have students estimate the number of cars that would not be needed if buses were used. Another related activity is to have students predict the traffic count for another corner and follow up with a count.

Make a table-top or floor layout map of the neighborhood that shows use of space for the following:

Housing: single dwelling, condominium, apartment, other
Food: grocery store, supermarket, restaurant, bakery, other
Business: bank, department store, shopping center, other
Education: public school, private school, college
Transportation: street, parking area, service station, other
Recreation: park, playground, vacant lot, bowling alley, other
Miscellaneous: school, library, church, telephone exchange, other

Design an ideal city of the future, using boxes, blocks, construction paper, and other readily available materials. Use such questions as the following to stimulate group discussion, committee work, and individual research:

What major zones should we have: residential, business, industry, other? How should they be arranged? How should open space be used within them and between them?
What should the city population be? How much area will be needed to provide for the stated population?
How can traffic, housing, pollution, and other urban problems of today be avoided? How will transportation be provided? What kinds of dwellings will be needed? How will wastes be handled?
How will services be provided? education? health care? recreation? fire and police protection? welfare? other?
What other provisions should be made?

Role-play the interviewing of applicants for a position as ecologist in the community. Divide the class into committees with five members each to plan questions to use in the interview, prepare a job description, consider attitudes toward environmental problems, and how to evaluate performance.

AIR POLLUTION

Major Understandings

Air pollution is greatest in metropolitan areas of industrialized countries, where it has serious effects on the health of people, on animals, and on plant life, as well as on buildings, machinery, and other objects. Progress is being made in combating air pollution, but continued efforts are needed.

Instructional Objectives

To describe the necessity of air for life, causes of air pollution, and steps to prevent pollution; to identify the effects of air pollution on people, plants, animals, and various objects; to demonstrate the use of observing, interpreting, analyzing, predicting, evaluating, and other processes in studying air pollution and related problems; to describe values, attitudes, and feelings needed to obtain effective action; to state the advantages and disadvantages of proposals and the need for additional data on certain problems.

Inquiry Questions

What is smog? How many of you have been in smog? How did it make your eyes feel? Your throat? [recalling, interpreting]

What are the main causes of smog? Would the same causes be found in all parts of a city? Why? [recalling, inferring]

What is air pollution? What does Chart A–27 show as the main causes? What does the article report as the main causes? Is there agreement? [defining, interpreting, evaluating] In general, what are the main causes? [generalizing]

Let's watch this film on the effects of air pollution. What diseases may be caused? How have trees in some areas been affected? What are the effects on plants? What other effects are shown? [observing, interpreting]

How can we find out about air pollution standards for cars? factories? power plants? other sources? Who might be interviewed? What resource visitors might be invited to meet with us? What references can we use? [recalling]

What proposals have been made to stop air pollution? What can be done at home? in the neighborhood? in the city? in the metropolitan area? [recalling, observing, interpreting]

Where are the main sources of air pollution in our community? What steps are being taken to curb them? What else needs to be done? What can we do to help get it stopped? What approach will be most effective? [observing, interpreting, evaluating]

What about the future? What will life be like if air pollution continues? [predicting]

What national plans are being made to curb it? What state and city cooperation will be needed? How can individuals help? [observing, interpreting, inferring]

Illustrative Activities

Have students investigate the immediate area to identify causes of air pollution—motor vehicles, factories, burning dumps, power plants, others.

Invite an expert on air pollution to discuss effects of different pollutants and preventive measures that should be used.

Investigate the effects of air pollution on people and other living things by interviewing doctors, analyzing reports and articles, and viewing films and filmstrips. Have students compare their findings with those reported in Lavaroni and O'Donnell, *Air Pollution,* pp. 2–12.

Make a summary chart of effects of air pollution, including emphysema, bronchitis, lung cancer, other diseases, damage to agriculture, damage to trees and plants, and so on.

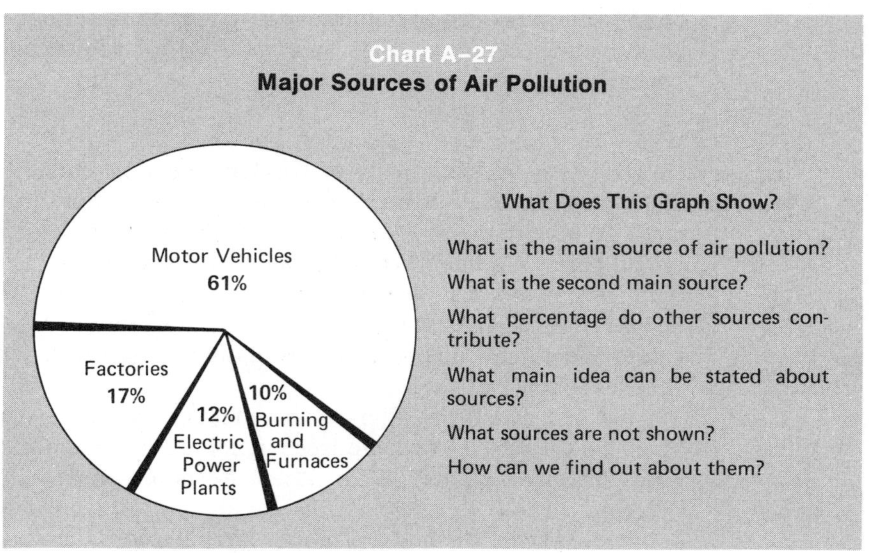

Chart A–27
Major Sources of Air Pollution
Motor Vehicles
61%
Factories
17%
12%
Electric
Power
Plants
10%
Burning
and
Furnaces
What Does This Graph Show?
What is the main source of air pollution?
What is the second main source?
What percentage do other sources contribute?
What main idea can be stated about sources?
What sources are not shown?
How can we find out about them?

Have a group of students interview a worker at the local weather station, air monitoring station, or smog control center. How is smog level determined? How is the amount of pollution determined? When is pollution usually greatest?

Investigate ways of removing waste gases from industrial emissions and municipal incinerators. Find out if these practices are being used in the local area.

Investigate control devices for motor vehicles, antipollution devices for jet planes, devices for use in industries to catch particulates and harmful gases, devices to improve municipal incinerators, and efforts at regional cooperation. Consider the ways that individuals can contribute along with what the government, factories, and other groups can do.

Evaluate the things individuals at home and in the neighborhood do to contribute to air pollution. Students may begin by listing such common polluting activities as smoking; burning trash, grass, and clippings; driving cars; using sprays on lawns and gardens; cooking outdoors; burning oil and coal in furnaces; and burning candles. Follow-up discussion should center on such questions as "Which activities are necessary?" "Which are not?" "What substitutes might be used?" "What habits should be changed? why?" "Which habits probably will be changed? why?"

Thinking may be extended by posing this question: "Why don't some people make the changes needed to prevent pollution and improve the environment?" Have students think of as many reasons as they can. Follow up by collecting more reasons through interviews and individual and group research activities.

Provide for simulation of an air pollution problem created by a large factory that emits smoke: There have been many complaints, but the company says their profit margin is too small to permit the expensive changes that would be needed to correct the situation. The company is supported by workers who will lose their jobs if the company is forced to shut down. The city council has called a meeting and must make a decision. The following persons are to make presentations to the council: the president of the company, the chairperson of Citizens for Clean Air, the chairperson of the Economic Development Commission, and the chairperson of the Resident's Committee.

WATER POLLUTION

Major Understandings

Water pollution is a problem of long standing that has become critical because of industrialization and urbanization. Primary water pollutants include sewage, factory wastes, agricultural chemicals, silt, feed-lot runoff, mining wastes, and oil spills. Strict standards are needed and pressure must be kept on municipal, state, and federal installations as well as factories and farms that contribute to water pollution. Families have a special responsibility to conserve water, prevent pollution, and support antipollution programs.

Instructional Objectives

To state the necessity of water for life, agriculture, industry, transportation, and recreation; to list the main causes of water pollution, the steps taken to curb it, and steps still needed; to state the effects of water pollution on people, plants, and animals; to describe effective proposals for curbing water pollution; to identify tactics that may be used to speed up the application of preventive measures.

Inquiry Questions

Why is water essential to life? How long can a person survive without water? What happens to crops during a long drought? [recalling]

How many of you have seen a polluted river or lake, or pictures of one? Who can think of another example? What was it like? How did it make you feel? What happened to fish in it? What was the shore like? [recalling]

What are the main causes of water pollution? What causes can we find in this film on Lake Erie? in other materials? [recalling observing, interpreting]

What are the specific causes of water pollution in our area? How can we find out? What sources of information might we use? [recalling]

How can we group the causes? What headings should we use? [classifying] What are the main effects of water pollution on people? animals? plants? beaches? water recreation areas? [recalling, observing, interpreting] In general, what are the main causes and effects? [generalizing]

What proposals for preventing water pollution can we find? Which ones appear to be most effective? most likely to be carried out? What would happen if they were to be carried out? [observing, interpreting, predicting]

What steps are being taken to prevent water pollution in our area? How adequate are they? What is a good way to present the facts to others? What action might we and others take? [observing, evaluating, synthesizing]

What is thermal pollution? What causes it? How does it damage ecosystems? How can it be prevented? [defining, interpreting] Is there thermal pollution in our area? What is being done to prevent it? [observing, interpreting]

Why are oceans important to us? to others? to people in other lands? [recalling] How are some oceans being polluted? What are the main causes? What do scientists predict the effects of ocean pollution may be? [recalling, observing, interpreting]

What steps should be taken to prevent ocean pollution? Why must different countries cooperate? What are the UN and other international agencies doing? [observing, interpreting]

What about the future? What do you think water bodies will be like in our area? why? What will major rivers and lakes be like in our country? why? What will the oceans be like? why? [predicting]

What can we do as individuals to prevent water pollution? What action can we and others take to get effective preventive measures established? [synthesizing]

Illustrative Activities

Make booklets, scrapbooks, or displays that show the causes and effects of water pollution. Include pictures, maps, children's work, clippings, and other media. Plan sections on water pollution at home, in the neighborhood, in the community, in nearby areas, and throughout the state and country. Give attention to ways in which individuals, groups, government agencies, industries, power companies, farmers, and others can help to prevent pollution (see Chart A–28).

Make an investigation of sources of water pollution in the community and the surrounding area (see Chart A–29). Have students make maps that show the locations of major sources of pollution. Interview public health officials and other available experts to find out what is being done and additional steps that need to be taken. Interview individuals at power companies, paper mills, and other industries to find out what they are doing to help prevent pollution. Identify critical needs and plan ways to pressure offenders.

Role-play the following people who are discussing the effects of dumping dirt from a mine several miles upstream from fishing grounds used by families on weekends: the mine owner, a miner, a secretary who works at the mine, a trucker who hauls ore, the mayor, a father of one fishing family, a boy and a girl from a fishing family.

Investigate the treatment of water for local consumption (coagulation and settling, filtration, disinfection, and other processes). Identify

Chart A–28
Helping To Prevent Water Pollution

Avoid dumping wastes in rivers and lakes.
Avoid using DDT, Aldrin, Dieldrin, Endrin, and other persisting pesticides.
Avoid adding organic wastes to water through sink disposals.
Don't waste water or electricity.
Don't put oil or other pollutants down the drain.
What else can be done?

Chart A–29
Investigating Water Pollution

What are our main sources of water pollution?
What specific pollutants come from each source?
What are the effects of water pollution on people, plants, animals, food?
What is being done to stop pollution in our area?
What further action is needed? What can individuals do? What can groups do?

the main sources of local water supply. What methods are used to provide clean water? What improvements do experts recommend? Is any untreated sewage entering the water system? Are industrial and agricultural wastes a problem? Is the community discharging untreated sewage that pollutes water for other people? What action can be taken to get improvements? Interview experts to gather data and to obtain ideas on possible action to take.

Investigate steps planned and already undertaken to provide for the future water needs of the community and surrounding area. Find out about the advantages and disadvantages of desalination of water. What other sources are possible? Why must ecological planning be a part of the planning for new sources of water? What damaging side effects might result from dams, desalination, and other means of obtaining water if balanced plans are not made?

Have students investigate and compile a report on all the ways in which water and electricity might be conserved. Consider individual as well as group conservation practices at home, in school, in the community, and on vacations. Arrange for selected students to interview power company officials, water company officials, and other experts to learn additional ways of conserving water and electricity.

Investigate ways in which water is being recycled. Find out how industries and power companies are recycling water by writing letters or interviewing officials. Check articles in encyclopedias and other sources.

NOISE POLLUTION

Major Understandings

Noise in urban areas has increased to such a point that it reduces the quality of life and creates health problems. Strict standards should be enforced. Cooperative action involving private and public agencies is needed at the local level, with support at the state and federal levels.

Instructional Objectives To describe the causes and effects of noise pollution, the difference between pleasant and unpleasant sounds, and ways of reducing noise; to demonstrate how inquiry processes can be used to improve the study of noise pollution; to describe differences in attitudes and feelings about noise, selecting those needed to obtain effective action against noise pollution.

Inquiry Questions What is the loudest noise you ever heard? How did it make you feel? Where did it happen? Why did it happen? Could it have been prevented? [recalling, inferring]

What sounds do you like? why? Which ones make you happy? sad? why? Do others agree? Why are there differences? [recalling, comparing] What sounds bother some people? why? Are there differences among us? Are there differences between us and others? why? [recalling, comparing]

What sounds do we hear downtown? Which ones are pleasant? why? Unpleasant? why? [recalling, interpreting, classifying]

What sounds can be heard out in the country? on farms? in the mountains? Which ones are pleasant? why? Unpleasant? why? [recalling, interpreting]

Let's make two groups of sounds: pleasant and unpleasant. Which sounds in the country should be put in each group? Which sounds in downtown areas should be put in each group? In general, where are more pleasant sounds heard? [classifying, comparing, generalizing]

What are the main causes of noise in our school? neighborhood? city? [recalling, observing] What does the booklet on noise pollution give as the main causes? Did we identify all of them? [observing, comparing]

Which of the proposals for preventing noise pollution might be useful in our area? why? What additional steps might be taken? [interpreting, evaluating]

If we were asked to make a plan to curb noise pollution, what should we include? Where might we find additional ideas? How should we organize and present our ideas? [synthesizing]

What are these items (ear muffs, ear plugs, and special helmets used to muffle sounds) used for? Why do some workers wear them? What happens when a person is subjected to loud noise over a period of time? [observing, interpreting, inferring]

What regulations does our city have to prevent noise pollution? Where can we find out? Whom might we interview? [recalling, inferring]

What about the future? What will happen if noise pollution standards are not raised? not enforced? [predicting]

Illustrative Activities Have students use a tape recorder to collect sounds in school, neighborhood, and community. Classify them in several ways: natural, people-made; pleasant, unpleasant; loud, soft; necessary, unnecessary; painful, not painful. Discuss differences in students' feelings about sounds. Why do some find certain noises pleasant while others feel they are unpleasant? Why are some sounds painful?

Discuss ways to reduce noise at home, in school, in the neighborhood, and in the community. Which noises are necessary? Which ones are not? How can they be reduced or eliminated? How about noises that don't bother students but might bother others? Discuss why noise is called *unwanted sound.*

Show and discuss ear muffs, ear plugs, and specially designed helmets worn by individuals who work at airports or other noisy places. Discuss the damage that results from being exposed to loud noise over a period of time. Ask students to recall any times that it was hard to hear after they were exposed to loud noise.

Discuss ways in which walls, partitions, doors, and sound-absorptive material control noise. Have students examine soundproofing material and observe soundproofing in cars. Have students investigate how airplanes, apartments, and rooms are soundproofed.

Obtain an instrument for measuring sound levels and demonstrate its use. Plan and carry out a study of sound levels in school and on the playground. Compare the decibels at different points. Have students find out how many decibels are reached by a person speaking (around 60), a car horn (around 90), and a jet plane when an individual is 100 feet away (around 140). If possible, have individuals or a small group obtain decibel readings in different places downtown. Map the noisiest areas, and discuss what might be done to curb noise pollution.

SOURCES OF MATERIALS

Local

Courses of study, units of instruction, bibliographies, catalogs of instructional materials in the local school system, community resource guides, school and community libraries, the county agricultural agent, local offices of state and federal agencies.

State

State departments dealing with natural resources, conservation, pollution problems, agriculture, water and waterways.

National

American Camping Association, Martinsville, Indiana 46151

American Forestry Association, 919 17 Street N.W., Washington, D.C. 20036

American Forest Products Industries, 1816 N Street N.W., Washington, D.C. 20036

American Nature Association, 1214 16 Street N.W., Washington, D.C. 20036

American Petroleum Institute, 1271 Avenue of the Americas, New York, New York 10020

Atomic Energy Commission, Education Services, Oak Ridge, Tennessee 37830

Bituminous Coal Institute, 1425 H Street N.W., Washington, D.C. 20036

Conservation Foundation, 1250 Connecticut Avenue, Washington, D.C. 20036

Environmental Science Center, 5400 Glenwood Avenue, Minneapolis, Minnesota 55422

Garden Club of America, 15 East 58 Street, New York, New York 10022

Izaak Walton League of America, 31 North State Street, Chicago, Illinois 60610

Keep America Beautiful, 99 Park Avenue, New York, New York 10016

League of Women Voters, 1200 17 Street, Washington, D.C. 20036

Manufacturing Chemists Association, 1826 Connecticut Avenue, Washington, D.C. 20009

National Audubon Society, 1130 Fifth Avenue, New York, New York 10016

National Coal Association, Southern Building, 15 and H Streets, Washington, D.C. 20036

National Education Association (Project Man's Environment, American Association of Health, Physical Education, and Recreation), 1201 16 Street N.W., Washington, D.C. 20036

National Wildlife Federation, 232 Carol Street N.W., Washington, D.C. 20036

Public Affairs Committee, 381 Park Avenue South, New York, New York 10016

Scientists' Institute for Public Information, 30 East 68 Street, New York, New York 10021

Sierra Club, 1050 Mills Tower, San Francisco, California 94104

Society of American Foresters, 1010 16 Street N.W., Washington, D.C. 20036

Superintendent of Documents, Government Printing Office, Washington, D.C. 20402

U.S. Department of Agriculture, Conservation Service and Forest Service, Washington, D.C. 20025

U.S. Department of Health, Education, and Welfare, Office of Education, Washington, D.C. 20025

U.S. Department of the Interior, Bureau of Reclamation, Fish and Wildlife Service, National Park Service, Water Pollution Control Administration, Washington, D.C. 20025

Wild Flower Preservation Society, 3740 Oliver Street N.W., Washington, D.C. 20015

REFERENCES

CARSON, RACHEL L., *Silent Spring*. Boston: Houghton Mifflin, 1962. The volume that stirred many to action.

CLARK, WILSON, and DAVID HOWELL, *Energy for Survival*. Garden City, N.Y.: Doubleday Anchor, 1974. Uses of energy and alternative energy sources.

DE BELL, GARRETT, ed., *The Environmental Handbook*. New York: Ballantine, 1970. Paperback of readings on ecology and ecotactics; bibliography of books and films.

DYAR, NANCY, *Environmental Education 4–9*. Los Angeles: Instructional Objectives Exchange, 1974. Objectives and test items.

EHRLICH, PAUL, *The Population Bomb*. New York: Ballantine, 1968. Controversial discussion of population problems.

Energy Choices for NOW: Saving, Using, Renewing. Washington, D.C.: National Education Association, 1974. Student's booklet and teacher's manual.

Environmental Education. Magazine devoted to environmental studies.

Environmental Education. Washington, D.C.: National Park Service, Department of the Interior, 1974. List of federal, state, and private sources of information.

Environmental Education: An Annotated Bibliography of Materials and Resources. Washington, D.C.: National Education Association, 1974. Detailed list.

EQ Index. Washington, D.C.: National Wildlife Federation. Annual report on conservation and pollution problems, colorfully illustrated.

HARRISON, C. WILLIAM, *Conservation: The Challenge of Reclaiming Our Plundered Land*. New York: Messner, 1973. Role of conservation in restoring the environment.

MICHAELIS, JOHN U., and EVERETT T. KEACH, JR., *Teaching Strategies for Elementary School Social Studies*. Itasca, Ill.: Peacock, 1972. Sources of information in Appendix B.

MILES, BETTY, *Save the Earth*. New York: Knopf, 1974. A handbook for children; includes community action projects.

Minneapolis Public Library, *Ecol Book Catalog*. Chicago: American Library Association, 1974. Over 2,800 titles indexed by author, title, main entry, and subject.

OWEN, D. F., *What Is Ecology?* New York: Oxford University Press, 1974. Discussion of people in an ecological framework.

SALE, LARRY L., GARDNER WEBB, and ERNEST W. LEE, *Environmental Education in the Elementary School*. New York: Holt, Rinehart, & Winston, 1972. Objectives, activities, sources of information.

Science Year: The World Book Science Annual. Chicago: Field Enterprises Educational Corporation. See ecology, environment, and related articles each year.

SQUIRE, C. B., *Heroes of Conservation*. New York: Fleet, 1974. Illustrated stories of seventeen conservationists.

WAGNER, RICHARD, *Environment and Man*. New York: Norton, 1974. Pollution, energy, population, wildlife, and other problems.

WATSON, JANE WERNER, *Our World Tomorrow: Toward a Better Environment*. New York, Golden Press, 1974. Approaches to solutions to problems.

WOLF, GARWOOD R., ed., *Environmental Information Sources Handbook*. New York: Simon and Schuster, 1974. Guide to civic, conservation, government, and other agencies, and to periodicals, libraries, and study centers.

Index